Encyclopedia of Governance

Encyclopedia of
Governance

II

Mark Bevir *Editor*
University of California, Berkeley

A SAGE Reference Publication

SAGE Publications
Thousand Oaks ■ London ■ New Delhi

For information:

 SAGE Publications, Inc.
2455 Teller Road
Thousand Oaks, California 91320
E-mail: order@sagepub.com

SAGE Publications Ltd.
1 Oliver's Yard
55 City Road
London EC1Y 1SP
United Kingdom

SAGE Publications India Pvt. Ltd.
B-42 Panchsheel, Enclave
Post Box 4109
New Delhi 110 017 India

Printed in the United States of America.

Library of Congress Cataloging-in-Publication Data

Bevir, Mark.
Encyclopedia of governance / Mark Bevir.
  p. cm.
2 vols. planned.
Includes bibliographical references and index.
ISBN 1-4129-0579-6 or 978-1-4129-0579-4 (cloth)
  1. State, The—Encyclopedias. 2. Public administration—Encyclopedias. I. Title.

JC11.B475 2007
351.03—dc22

          2006015219

This book is printed on acid-free paper.

06 07 08 09 10 10 9 8 7 6 5 4 3 2 1

Publisher:	Rolf Janke
Acquisitions Editor:	Lucy Robinson
Developmental Editor:	Paul Reis
Reference Systems Coordinator:	Leticia Gutierrez
Project Editor:	Tracy Alpern
Copy Editors:	Amy Freitag, Robin Gold
	Four Lakes Colorgraphics
Typesetter:	C&M Digitals (P) Ltd.
Indexer:	David Luljak
Cover Designer:	Michelle Kenny

Contents

List of Entries

Reader's Guide

The Reader's Guide provides a way to locate related entries in the encyclopedia. For example, if you look under Information Governance, you will find a list of the main entries on that topic, including Cyberspace, Data Protection, Internet Governance, and Public Information. Alternatively, if you are interested in global warming, you will find the entry under the heading Environmental Governance, where you also will find other related entries, including Climate Change, Kyoto Protocol, and Sustainability. The Reader's Guide also provides an overview of all the entries in the encyclopedia. You can look through all the headings, including Information Governance or Environmental Governance, pick one of particular interest to you, and then choose entries you might want to read.

Capitalism

Antiglobalization
Capitalism
Clientelism
Coordinated Market Economy
Fiscal Crisis
Fordism and Post-Fordism
Globalization
Glocalization
Human Capital
Human Capital Mobility
Industrialization
Investment
Liberal Market Economy
Liberalization
Monopoly
Oil Crisis
Physical Capital
Political Economy
Production Chain
Production Network
Public Investment
Regulation Theory
Social Capital
Triadization
Varieties of Capitalism Thesis

Citizenship

Citizen-Centric Government
Citizenship
Civic Capacity
Civic Engagement
Civic Republicanism
Civic Virtue
Civil Service
Civil Society
Common Good
Community Organizing
Consumption
Empowerment
Ethical Consumerism
Ethnic Groups
Ethnonationalism
Everyday Maker
Guest Workers
Immigration
Migration

Multiculturalism
Nation
Nationalism
Self-Government
Social Inclusion
Stakeholder

Cultures

Confucian Governance
Culture Governance
Ethnonationalism
Hindu Governance
Interpretive Theory
Islamic Governance
Multiculturalism
Nationalism
Neotraditionalism
Organizational Culture
Policy Style
Religion
Social Constructivism
Sociology of Governance
Taoist Governance
Tradition
Translation
United Nations Educational, Scientific
    and Cultural Organization

Decision Making

Bounded Rationality
Bureaucratic Politics Approach
Communicative Rationality
Cost-Benefit Analysis
Decision Making
Forecasting
Frame Analysis
Game Theory
Group Think
Hedging
Incrementalism
Local Reasoning
Majority Cycle
Negotiation
Optimal Decision Making
Pareto Optimality

Planning
Policy Learning
Prisoner's Dilemma
Problem Structure
Public Choice Theory
Rational Choice Theory
Rationality
Revealed Preference
Risk
Satisficing Behavior
Sensemaking
Social Choice
Social Learning
Strategic Planning

Democratic Theory

Accountability
Civic Republicanism
Common Good
Consensus Democracy
Consent
Deliberative Democracy
Democratic Deficit
Democratic Theory
Democratization
E-Democracy
Elections
Governance
Legislature
Legitimacy
Legitimacy Crisis
Liberalism
Participation
Participatory Democracy
Pluralism
Pluralist Democracy
Polyarchy
Representation
Representative Democracy
Self-Government
Social Democracy

Development

African Governance
Bretton Woods

Research and Development
Science
Technology
Technology Transfer
Virtual Agency
Virtual Community

Institutionalism

Association
Authority
Capacity Building
Common Pool Resource
Deinstitutionalization
Epistemic Community
Governance
Hybridity
Institution
Institutional Performance
Institutionalism
Institutionalization
Institutionalized Environment
Legitimacy
Logic of Appropriateness
Neotraditionalism
Network
New Institutionalism
Norms
Organization Theory
Path Dependence
Policy Network
Principal-Agent Model
Professionalism
Rule
Transaction Cost
Weak Institution

International Organization

Functionalism
Global Compact
Group of 7
Group of 77
International Courts
International Labour Organization
International Law and Treaties
International Monetary Fund
International Organization

International Regime
Kyoto Protocol
Regime
Regime Theory
United Nations
United Nations Conference on Trade and
    Development
United Nations Educational, Scientific and
    Cultural Organization
United Nations Security Council
World Bank
World Economic Forum
World Health Organization
World Trade Organization

Interpretive Theory

Action Research
Bottom-Up Approach
Decentered Theory
Dilemma
Discourse
Everyday Maker
Governance
Governmentality
Interpretive Policy Analysis
Interpretive Theory
Local Knowledge
Local Reasoning
Micropolitics
Narrative Theory
Sensemaking
Situated Agency
Social Constructivism
Social Practice
Tradition
Translation

Local Governance

Center-Local Relations
City-Region
Decentralization
Devolution
Fiscal Federalism
Intergovernmental Relations
Local Governance
Localization

Military Occupation
Oversight
Policy Implementation
Political Exchange
Polyarchy
Regime
Stakeholder
Transnational Governance
Welfare Reform

Policy Analysis

Bureaucratic-Politics Approach
Collaborative Governance
Collaborative Planning
Decision Making
Dialogic Public Policy
Evaluation Research
Evidenced-Based Policy
Frame Analysis
Governability
Governance
Incrementalism
Interest Group
Interest Intermediation
Interpretive Policy Analysis
Path Dependence
Planning
Policy Analysis
Policy Cycle
Policy Development
Policy Implementation
Policy Learning
Policy Network
Policy Predictability
Policy Style
Policy Transfer
Program Evaluation
Strategic Planning
Urban and Regional Planning

Public Administration

Accountability
Advocacy Networks
Agency
Bureaucracy
Citizen-Centric Government

Civil Service
Councils of Governments
Governance
Indigenous Governance
Multilevel Governance
Neighborhood Association
Ombudsman
Policy Network
Politics-Administration Dichotomy
Pooled Sovereignty
Public Administration
Public Sector
Quango
Regulation
Regulatory Enforcement
Regulatory State
Special District
State
Street-Level Bureaucrat
Virtual Agency

Public-Sector Management

Audit
Benchmarking
Budgetary Autonomy
Compliance Cost
Contracting Out
Cost-Benefit Analysis
Forecasting
Good Governance
Governance
Government by Proxy
Internal Market
Joint Venture
Liberalization
Marketization
New Public Management
Overload
Performance Measurement
Privatization
Program Evaluation
Public Administration
Public-Private Partnership
Public Sector
Purchaser-Provider Split
Quasi-Market
Service Delivery

Security

Arms Control
Confidence-Building Measure
Conflict Mediation
Crisis Management
Deterrence
Emergency Powers
Human Security
Humanitarian Intervention
Military Necessity
Military Occupation
Multilateralism
North Atlantic Treaty
    Organization
Organization for Security and
    Cooperation in Europe
Peace Process
Post-9/11
Private Military Companies
Sanctions
Second-Track Diplomacy
Security
Security Community
Terrorism
War on Terrorism

Society

Anarchy
Citizenship
Civic Virtue
Civil Society
Clientelism
Consent
Ethnic Groups
Global Civil Society
Individualism
Multiculturalism
Nation
Nationalism
Neighborhood Association
Neotraditionalism
Network Society
Nongovernmental Organization
Nonprofit Organization

Participation
Pluralism
Political Communication
Public Opinion
Public Sphere
Risk Society
Social Capital
Social Market
Social Movement Theory
Social Practice
Third Sector
Tradition
Transnational Social Movement
Virtual Community

Sociology of Governance

Authority
Autopoesis
Civil Society
Communication
Communicative Action
Cooperation
Economic Sociology
Embeddedness
Generalized Exchange
Governmentality
Legitimacy
Network
Norms
Organization Theory
Patrimonialism
Power
Rationalization
Reciprocity
Reflexivity
Social Capital
Social Constructivism
Social Movement Theory
Social Network Theory
Sociocybernetics
Sociology of Governance
Space
State
State Building
State-Society Relations

KEYNESIANISM

Keynesianism is an economic theory based on the works of the Cambridge economist John Maynard Keynes (1883–1946) that argues state intervention in a market economy is both desirable and necessary to avoid destabilizing levels of social unrest and high unemployment. Constructed in response to the economic and political difficulties of the 1920s and 1930s, Keynesianism reached the height of its influence during the post–World War II period, accompanying the emergence of social democracy in many Western capitalist nations. During the 1970s, however, Keynesian economic theory was largely discredited following its apparent inability to account for rising levels of unemployment, inflation, and economic stagnation. Since the 1980s, Keynesianism has been superseded by neoliberalism as the dominant economic policy framework for the capitalist West.

The "Keynesian Revolution"

The main body of Keynes's economic thought was developed during the interwar period in response to the perceived shortcomings of the classical economic theory that had held sway in Britain throughout the nineteenth century. This advocated a *laissez faire* style of economic management on the grounds that an unregulated free market would automatically tend toward an equilibrium state providing an optimal allocation of resources. As such, classical economics maintained that any rise in unemployment or decline in economic activity would ultimately prove to be self-rectifying through a corresponding reduction in wages.

Although Keynes accepted many of the tenets of classical economics, his central departure was to argue that economic theory needed to move beyond abstract propositions, and needed to account for the social forces and conditions in which a market economy operated. On this basis, Keynes argued that the mechanism of the free market would not of itself produce a state of full employment because the social factors determining the level of wages (primarily believed to be the increased organization of the trade union movement) would ensure that the price of labor did not adjust in a smooth, rapid, and automatic fashion. Instead, wage rigidity in a period of recession would exacerbate unemployment, compound the decline in consumption, and create industrial strife. As a result, an unregulated free market economy would tend toward an equilibrium state with an unnecessarily high level of unemployment and would therefore produce conditions that were incompatible with the goals of social harmony and political stability.

For Keynes, the central task was to discover a form of economic management that would preserve the centrality of the market while saving it from its own unpalatable consequences. In 1936, Keynes published his *General Theory on Employment, Interest and Money,* set within the context of a deep depression and the persistence of mass unemployment. Keynes believed the key cause of this was an insufficient level of "aggregate demand" for goods and services. Because the only means by which an unregulated free market economy could recover from a recession was through a process of falling wages, and because this offered no prior means of raising the level of aggregate demand, Keynes argued that active government intervention was now required to secure this objective.

The primary means by which Keynes envisaged that this would be achieved was through the use of a countercyclical fiscal policy. In the event of a recession, governments would be expected to use cuts in taxation and higher levels of public expenditure (including public works programs if necessary) to boost the level of aggregate demand and to thereby stimulate economic activity. In a contrary fashion, these policies were to be reversed should the economy start to expand too rapidly, with the use of higher taxation and cuts in public spending to constrain any inflationary tendencies.

Keynesianism in Practice

Keynesianism thus advocated a system of active macroeconomic management to regulate the market economy. The underlying aim was to manipulate the level of aggregate demand to raise or lower the rate of economic activity with a view to maintaining social and political stability. In practice, Keynesian ideas gained initial credence during the 1930s as many governments turned to increasing levels of state intervention in an attempt to surmount the difficulties of the depression. The full impact of Keynesianism, however, was only felt after World War II. By 1945, classical economics had fallen into disrepute as a result of the prewar slump, and huge social changes had raised public expectations of greater state intervention. Although the precise interpretation of Keynesian theory varied from country to country, these conditions nonetheless conferred a theoretical legitimacy on a range of social democratic practices, including a mixed economy, fiscal deficits, and economic planning.

The postwar dominance of Keynesian economics was further enhanced during the 1950s by the emergence of the greatest economic boom in the history of global capitalism. As the boom collapsed during the 1970s, however, the mantle of Keynesianism began to disintegrate. Most notably, critics argued that Keynesian demand management was now responsible for simultaneously high levels of unemployment and inflation accompanied with economic stagnation, a phenomenon known as stagflation.

These difficulties were effectively presented by emerging New Right theorists in the United States and Britain as being the inevitable consequence of excessive state intervention. This was believed to have unjustifiably raised public expectations about what the state could reasonably be thought to achieve, to have undermined the ability of the government to rule effectively, and to have impeded the efficient operation of the free market. By the 1980s, Keynesian ideas had been superseded as the dominant economic discourse in Western capitalist societies by the revival of neoclassical principles for economic management. Accompanying this, Western governments now turned to monetarism and to an increasingly *laissez faire* style of economic management in an attempt to address their growing economic difficulties. Although the effects of monetarism have been mixed in practice, and although the most recent variant of neoliberal economic management based on inflation targeting by an independent central bank allows for more active policy measures to help regulate the economy, Keynesian ideas have yet to rediscover the resonance they once enjoyed.

—*Steven Kettell*

See also Business Cycle; Functionalism; Monetarism; Political Business Cycle; Regulatory State; Social Democracy; Unemployment

Further Readings and References

Hall, P. (Ed.). (1989). *The political power of economic ideas: Keynesianism across nations.* Princeton, NJ: Princeton University Press.

Keynes, J. M. (1936). *The general theory of employment, interest, and money.* London: Macmillan.

Kindleberger, C. P. (1985). *Keynesianism vs. monetarism and other essays on financial history.* London: Allen and Unwin.

Skidelsky, R. J. (1996). *Keynes.* Oxford, UK: Oxford University Press.

KNOWLEDGE MANAGEMENT

Knowledge management is concerned with how organizations manage what they know and "need to know." It focuses on the mobilization, dissemination, use, and storage of knowledge for the realization of organizational ambitions. Much of the literature about knowledge management is oriented to private organizations, but there is increasing attention to it within the public sector. Two main areas of use for knowledge management can be identified in the public realm. The first deals with knowledge for (interactive or governance) policy processes, to realize rational and supported policy decisions. The second deals with the management of knowledge within public organizations, to build competent and learning public organizations. In both domains, different types of knowledge and management strategies are important. Both aspects are strongly interrelated, but for analytical reasons we deal with them separately.

Knowledge for Policy Processes

Policy decisions consist of a constellation of normative, empirical, and practical judgments. Knowledge management facilitates the decision-making process by generating the normative and empirical bases from which policy decisions can be made. There are two reasons for doing so: reducing uncertainty (a shortage of information) and reducing ambiguity (disagreement about the interpretation of information). For example, to convince political principals and the public, stakeholders and officials involved in a policy process usually want to know the possible effects of a proposal through studies such as cost-benefit analyses and impact assessments. Important aspects of knowledge management are

- formulating the research questions and selecting the knowledge producer;
- guaranteeing the quality and the timeliness of the research process, the independence of the researchers and the applicability of the results;
- managing the utilization of knowledge in the policy process.

In today's risk society, the rational underpinning of policy has never been so important and so difficult. Adequate knowledge is often not available, arrives too late, or is not authoritative enough to convince involved actors. C. P. Snow noted in 1964 that the different cultures and logics of the world of science and the world of politics cause major problems. There is the danger of what Liora Salter termed mandated science and science-driven policy or technocracy. Sheila Jasanoff noted that boundary work to define and guard the mutual rights of the domains of science and politics is necessary to safeguard a healthy distinction between these domains.

Ambiguity is the result of the different frames of reference that actors employ when participating in the policy process. Especially in controversial policy processes, actors do have widely different perceptions about the problem and the desired solutions. More information can politicize discussions because of the different interpretations actors give to it and because actors mobilize contra-expertise. Through the organization of processes of interaction and deliberation between actors with diverging frames, knowledge managers try to reach a process of joint fact-finding or social learning in which stakeholders are stimulated to develop shared images about the problem situation and desirable solutions.

This task of knowledge management focuses on a softer, more subjective, and constructivist interpretation of knowledge. Knowledge is seen as a constantly changing flow of interpretations that is constructed through social interaction and reflection. The main problem for reaching a process of frame reflection is the realization of a safe arena in which actors with highly diverging interests and perceptions are willing to discuss their own frames. Another problem has to do with the result of such a process. This is because the search for support and consensus can result in gray compromises, or what can be termed negotiated nonsense.

Knowledge for Public Organizations

Public organizations try to realize their organizational ambitions as well as possible and with minimum resources. Therefore, they need an effective and efficient way of dealing with their knowledge needs. There are two aspects of particular importance:

1. The organization of information and communication processes

2. The mobilization and development of competencies and expertise

The organization of information processes refers to the way in which an organization keeps an eye on its environment, develops knowledge about it, and organizes its knowledge store so that it can be used when necessary. Through regular monitors, surveys, trend studies, policy evaluations, and so forth, public organizations scan their environment. Scientific programs, think tanks, and advice councils deliver huge amounts of knowledge to government. Through information and knowledge management, especially through developing Information and Communications Technologies (ICTs) and other systems of knowledge storage, public organizations try to keep their knowledge up-to-date, available, and accessible.

The mobilization and development of competencies and expertise has to do with *human knowledge,* the tacit or implicit component of knowledge, strongly embedded in people. Competences are the abilities that are necessary to fulfill a job effectively. They are developed by learning, training, and experience. Public organizations have to invest in their human capital to realize their ambitions in an effective and efficient way. Problems for realizing ambitions include the high mobility of employees, the frequent use of external advisers who leave the organization after finalizing their projects, and the highly dynamic political and societal context of public organizations. Peter Senge wrote in 1990 that all these factors impel a frequent update of competences and thus the development of a learning organization.

—*Arwin van Buuren*

See also Capacity Building; Cost-Benefit Analysis; Evaluation Research; Evidence-Based Policy; Human Capital; Human Capital Mobility; Local Knowledge; Organizational Learning; Policy Learning; Social Learning; Technical-Rational Expertise

Further Readings and References

Beck, U. (1992). *Risk society: Towards a new modernity.* London: Sage Ltd.

Collingridge, D., & Reeve, C. (1986). *Science speaks to power: The role of experts in policymaking.* London: Frances Pinter.

Fischer, F. (2003). *Reframing public policy: Discursive politics and deliberative practices.* Oxford, UK: Oxford University Press.

Jasanoff, S. (1990). *The fifth branch: Advisers as policy makers.* Cambridge, MA: Harvard University Press.

Salter, L. (1988). *Mandated science: Science and scientists in the making of standards.* Dordrecht, Netherlands: Kluwer Academic.

Senge, P. (1990). *The fifth discipline: The art and practice of the learning organization.* New York: Doubleday.

Snow, C. P. (1964). *The two cultures and a second look: An expanded version of the two cultures and the scientific revolution* (2nd ed.). Cambridge, UK: Cambridge University Press.

KYOTO PROTOCOL

The Kyoto Information and Communications Technologies Protocol was adopted in 1997 by the member countries of the United Nations Framework Convention on Climate Change. The Protocol commits the signatory countries to mandatory targets for emissions of greenhouse gases. Although there are six main greenhouse gases—carbon dioxide, methane, nitrous oxide, hydrofluorocarbons, perfluorocarbons, and sulfur hexafluoride—one is by far the most significant: carbon dioxide. Before the Protocol could be valid, it had to be ratified by at least fifty-five nations, and these nations had to be responsible for at least fifty-five percent of all greenhouse gas emissions. These conditions were met when Russia ratified the treaty. The Protocol thus came into force on February 16, 2005.

The Protocol includes an overall target for developed nations to reduce their 1990 emission levels by at least five percent by 2012. Actual emission targets vary from nation to nation. The fifteen European Union countries, Switzerland, and most central and eastern European states must make an eight percent reduction. Canada, Hungary, Japan, and Poland must make a six percent reduction. New Zealand, Russia, and the

Ukraine are to maintain their current levels. Other countries can actually increase their emissions—Norway by one percent and Iceland by ten percent. And some developed countries have refused to sign the Kyoto Protocol, notably Australia and the United States.

The Marrakech Accords, adopted in 2001, are the rules for implementing the Kyoto Protocol. These rules allow the signatory nations some flexibility in how they meet their targets. A country can offset its target with "sinks," areas of forest that absorb carbon dioxide. Countries that have spare emission units can sell them to other countries that have exceeded their emissions thus creating a "carbon market." The Clean Development Mechanism allows countries to pay for projects that reduce emissions in developing countries; developed countries thereby can earn credits toward their own emission targets. Similarly, under Joint Implementation, a member country can implement a project in another member country and thereby earn credit. It is expected that these projects will be paid for by Western nations and built in transition economies, such as Eastern Europe and the former Soviet Union.

—*Mark Bevir*

See also Climate Change; Environmental Governance; Functionalism; Sustainable Development

Further Readings and References

Sari, A. (2005). *Developing country participation: The Kyoto-Marrakech politics.* HWWA Discussion Paper 333, November 2005. Retrieved from http://www.hwwa.de/Publikationen/Discussion_Paper/2005/333.pdf

Victor, D. G. (2001). *The collapse of the Kyoto Protocol and the struggle to slow global warming.* Princeton, NJ: Princeton University Press.

LEADERSHIP

Leadership is a multidisciplinary concept. The foremost academic journal on the topic, *The Leadership Quarterly,* asserts that it is an international journal of the political, social, and behavioral sciences, indicating the breadth of the disciplinary subjects where the concept is discussed. Within this range of subjects, much of the cutting-edge leadership research is focused on leadership in the business world and, more specifically, leadership in organizations. As with any topic, this literature has its own competing perspectives and initially bewildering terminology—LMX theory, MLQ tests, and so on. However, during the last couple of decades, the dominant paradigm in this area has been the charismatic or transformational approach. More recently, there has been a shift toward a "postheroic" model of leadership that emphasizes relational, dynamic leadership more than individualism.

Although the study of leadership in certain areas is marked by a coherent body of literature with its own history and terminology, the study of leadership from a governance perspective, meaning leadership from the perspective of political science, public administration, international relations, political psychology, and related disciplines and subdisciplines, remains underdeveloped. Barbara Kellerman and Scott Webster argued in 2001 that scholarly work in public-sector leadership is sorely lacking. This is perhaps surprising in the sense that the transformational approach

to leadership was initially formulated by James MacGregor Burns, a former president of the American Political Science Association, in a 1979 book that focused solely on political leaders. The task for students of leadership from a governance perspective is to try to formulate the concept more systematically and operationalize it more rigorously.

There was a considerable interest in the concept of leadership from a governance perspective in the 1970s and 1980s. However, this literature failed to establish a subdiscipline of leadership studies and no paradigmatic approach to political leadership emerged. Since then, the systematic study of political leadership has gone into abeyance. As a result, leadership from a governance perspective remains profoundly undertheorized. For example, there is no agreed-upon definition of political leadership. Kellerman and Webster state that a leader either creates changes or strives to do so. By contrast, Jean-Pascal Daloz wrote that the leadership relation involves two-way interaction, from top to bottom and vice versa. Burns provided a general definition when he wrote that leadership is a mixture of motives and purposes, mobilization, competition, and conflict; it involves institutions, politics, and psychology and seeks to arouse, engage, and satisfy followers. More often than not, though, writers fail to provide a definition of leadership and simply take the concept for granted. In any case, in the literature on political leadership there is no equivalent of the literature on power. It is not so much the case that, like the concept of power, the concept of political leadership remains essentially contested. It is more that in recent times the concept of political leadership has scarcely been contested at all. In short, the concept of leadership has remained almost completely untouched by political theorists for a couple of decades.

The undertheorization of political leadership means that only a few elements of the concept are generally recognized. There is a common recognition that leadership is not an individual process. Leadership must occur within a group context and constitutes a relationship between one or more people—the leader(s)—and the remainder of the group—the followers. Leadership must involve some form of activity by the leader, or aspiring leader. This activity may take many different forms, be it the articulation of an abstract vision or a set of specific proposals for policy change, but a leader is someone who is trying to change the status quo or who is knowingly trying to prevent the status quo from being changed where change would otherwise occur. Leaders must win support for their activities within the group context and they must do so by using essentially noncoercive means. Finally, political leadership may occur in both a constituted and nonconstituted context. That is to say, it may be exercised by people who hold formal positions of power as well as by people who hold no such position.

These elements may provide some basis for understanding the concept of leadership from a governance perspective, but in so doing they merely raise further questions. For example, it is not necessarily realistic to expect a leader to mobilize everyone within the group behind a particular vision, but what degree of support—or followership—is required for leadership to occur? Is there a minimum threshold of followership over which it can be said that leadership has occurred? Equally, what is meant by "essentially noncoercive means"? Does a three-line whip (an order for all party members to follow the leadership on a vote even if it is against their own beliefs) count as an essentially noncoercive act? Similarly, should there be a normative element to a definition of leadership? For instance, was Hitler a leader? Burns, for one, called him a power-wielder and not a leader. However, it might be argued that Hitler was both a leader and a power-wielder. After all, arguably he gained the followership of a particular group of people, perhaps even a large group of

people, by articulating a vision and by using essentially noncoercive means, even if his vision was unequivocally wrong and even given that he used state-sponsored coercion and murderous force to ensure the compliance of other groups. In one sense, there is no answer to these questions and others like them. This is true for many concepts in the social sciences. The difference between the concept of leadership and equivalent concepts is that the latter are usually the subject of intense theoretical and philosophical debate. This point does not apply to the concept of leadership.

Although the concept of political leadership remains undertheorized, the empirical study of leadership has a rich heritage. Perhaps more accurately, a large and distinguished body of work is concerned with the study of individual political leaders and the formal aspects of the leadership process. In other words, most of the empirical studies of leadership are only indirectly concerned with the concept of political leadership discussed previously. Thus, there is a disconnect between the empirical work and what theoretical work there is on the topic.

The empirical work on leadership includes biographies and autobiographies of political leaders. Most are narrative accounts of leaders and the events that they lived through. There are few examples of such work that explicitly try to link the narrative in question to the formal study of leadership, although Alistair Cole's 1997 biography of François Mitterrand is one instance. There is also a vast literature on particular leadership offices. There are empirical studies of presidents, prime ministers, cabinets, and so on, both comparatively and in specific countries. Again, though, few address the leadership literature directly. There is a wider debate about the merits of different types of leadership structures, specifically whether a parliamentary form of government is better than presidentialism. There is a growing literature on women in positions of political leadership. There is increasing attention paid to the selection of political leaders, particularly party leaders, and there is also a literature that focuses on the discourse of political leaders. Overall, although all this literature is relevant to the study of political leadership, only a small fraction of it is directly related to the concept of leadership itself.

One area where there has been a systematic approach to the study of leadership is in the area of personality and politics. There have been a number of influential studies in this area. For example, Alexander George and Juliette George's 1964 classic study of Woodrow Wilson argues that the president's behavior in office was shaped by events during his childhood, particularly the relationship with his severe and demanding father. Another example is James David Barber's 1977 study of U.S. presidents. He argued that presidents have different leadership styles that were a function of each president's character. Using psychological theory, Barber argued that presidential character was determined in childhood. Therefore, by examining the early life of presidential candidates, it would be possible to predict how they will behave in the White House. Barber came to fame when he predicted that Richard Nixon would not be a good choice as president. To the extent that his prediction seemed to be accurate, his work was the subject of some attention. However, the study of personality and politics has not lived up to its early promise. There is now a thriving subdiscipline of political psychology that, arguably, these studies and others like them helped to create. However, little of this work has fed back into the more general study of leadership from a governance perspective, although Juliet Kaarbo and Margaret Hermann showed in 1998 the potential for work in this area with their study of how the leadership style of British and German prime ministers affected foreign policy making.

The uncomfortable conclusion is that the study of leadership from a governance perspective is not in a good place, at least as a discrete and focused area of inquiry. Two developments are required. First, the concept of leadership needs to be more coherently conceptualized. What do we mean by the concept of leadership? How do we distinguish it from related concepts, such as power and authority? Work in this area would not lead to definitive answers to these questions, but the study of leadership would greatly benefit from contending approaches to the topic and from the development of opposing schools of thought that could debate systematically with each other and drive the study of the concept forward. Second, and arguably more importantly, the concept of leadership

needs to be operationalized more rigorously. How can we observe leadership? Few people would argue that leadership does not matter. Even people who prefer to explain political outcomes by reference to institutional theory or cultural theory usually acknowledge that agency, and hence leadership, can still play a role. If so, then how do we operationalize the concept of leadership empirically? Whether leadership is operationalized as an explanatory variable or a dependent variable, what proxies can be used to measure it? In more qualitative, narrative accounts, how is it possible to separate the leadership variable from other variables as determining factors in political outcomes? In a 2004 study, Michelle Bligh, Jeffrey Kohles, and James Meindl point the way with a rigorous study of charismatic leadership by George W. Bush after the September 11, 2001, terrorist attacks. To sum up, the study of leadership from a governance perspective requires two seemingly paradoxical developments: the development of political leadership as an academic subfield with its own paradigms or, better still, competing paradigms, and the mainstreaming of political leadership as a variable in academic inquiry. Both of these developments are still a long way off.

—Robert Elgie

See also Crisis Management; Governance; Hegemony; Organizational Culture; Patrimonialism

Further Readings and References

Barber, J. D. (1977). *The presidential character: Predicting performance in the White House.* Englewood Cliffs, NJ: Prentice Hall.

Bligh, M. C., Kohles, J. C., & Meindl, J. R. (2004). Charisma under crisis: Presidential leadership, rhetoric, and media responses before and after the September 11th terrorist attacks. *Leadership Quarterly, 15,* 195–210.

Burns, J. M. (1979). *Leadership.* New York: Harper & Row.

Cole, A. (1997). *François Mitterrand: A study in political leadership* (2nd ed.). London: Routledge.

Daloz, J.-P. (2003). Reflections on the comparative study of political leadership. In H. Baldersheim & J.-P. Daloz (Eds.), *Political leadership in a global age* (pp. 17–33). Aldershot, UK: Ashgate.

Elgie, R. (1995). *Political leadership in liberal democracies.* London: Macmillan.

Fletcher, J. K. (2004). The paradox of postheroic leadership: An essay on gender, power, and transformational change. *Leadership Quarterly, 15*(5), 647–661.

George, A. L., & George, J. L. (1964). *Woodrow Wilson and Colonel House: A personality study.* Mineola, NY: Dover.

Hunt, J. G. (1999). Transformational/charismatic leadership's transformation of the field: An historical essay. *Leadership Quarterly, 10*(2), 129–144.

Kaarbo, J., & Hermann, M. G. (1998). Leadership styles of prime ministers: How individual differences affect the foreign policymaking process. *Leadership Quarterly, 9*(3), 243–263.

Kellerman, B., & Webster, S. W. (2001). The recent literature on public leadership. Reviewed and considered. *Leadership Quarterly, 12*(4), 485–514.

LEGISLATURE

Legislatures are elected assemblies in charge of the approval of draft legislation. From the powerful U.S. Congress to the less influential national parliaments in Europe, legislatures occupy a central position in every political system. Thus, even if the notion of governance refers more directly to changes in public administration, legislatures have been affected by this dynamic.

Governance Versus Parliamentary Representation

As an attempt to modify the classic way of producing public policies, the concept of governance can first be perceived as a challenge for legislatures. Political assemblies and parliaments symbolize the vertical and partisan dimension of politics, whereas governance refers to the promotion of horizontal forms of coordination and an opening-up to representatives from civil society. The concept of governance supposes that the community of actors involved in the making of a given public policy is seriously interested in the outputs: The community of actors aims to improve the quality of public policy. More or less explicitly, doubts have been expressed that members of legislatures could efficiently play such a role because some of them are mainly motivated by electoral considerations and because others act under the control of party leaders.

For instance, the distributive approach of parliamentary committees considers that such committees are composed of high-demand representatives who bargain to distribute potential benefits from public policies ("pork-barrel politics").

The institutionalization of conflict, the pressure of electoral competition, and the significance of formalism and procedural rules constitute three features of legislatures that can be regarded as antagonistic to the principles of governance. Moreover, the promotion of governance partly results from a failure of legislatures to achieve some of those principles. The insistence on deliberation by the "good governance" agenda can be understood as a severe judgment on parliamentary debates routinely organized on the floor of the assemblies. The priority to make public decision making more open and accountable implies that the traditional legislative assemblies do not fill that role efficiently. The approval of the law by elected representatives does not guarantee that a transparent decision-making process actually includes a large variety of stakeholders. Thus, governance as an agenda eventually challenges the legislature's historical pretension to exercise a monopoly over legitimate popular representation. Instead, opening government to civil society partly results from the crisis of legitimacy of traditional parliamentary elites.

Concrete consequences for legislatures of effective prerogatives derive from this conceptual shift, particularly in Europe. For instance, the development of contracting procedures between central and local governments also contributes to limiting the ability of legislatures to influence the decision-making process. These contracts involve so many partners that once an agreement is achieved, local assemblies and the national legislatures can only rubber-stamp the document because reopening the bargaining process would be too costly.

Legislators as Actors of Governance Among Others

As political organizations, legislatures are logically in conflict with the conception of power behind the dynamics of governance. However, it is still necessary to investigate the actual contribution of legislators to the transformation of both public administration and state-society relations that governance encompasses. Indeed, there are four reasons why legislators can and must be regarded as actors of governance.

First, legislatures contribute to intersectoral coordination within public administration. Even if they are specialized in specific topics, legislators maintain a global rather than expert relationship to public affairs. In their constituencies, they can be questioned on any subject and they can also question the administration on any and everything. In so doing, legislators may contribute to putting some intersectoral issues on the agenda that the executive had not wanted or been able to do.

Second, legislators contribute to interterritorial coordination between organizations implicated in multilevel systems of governance. Legislatures can be regarded as organizations providing an institutionalization of territorial coordination because they force representatives of various parts of the territory to make collective decisions. Legislators thus occupy an intermediary position in multilevel systems.

Third, legislatures may paradoxically help nonpolitical actors become involved in the making of public policies. The parliamentary etymology of the word lobbying signals that houses of parliament have traditionally constituted privileged forums of coordination between political authorities and nonpublic actors. In addition, for some deputies and senators, their professional background is so pronounced that they can associate sectoral and private interests with the policy-making process.

Finally, if governance is defined as a normative agenda rather than a narrative, one can investigate whether legislatures are contributing to the reform of deliberation and management over public policies. It is arguable whether parliaments in their modern form serve as collective bodies where the authority of political power is questioned, controlled, and eventually limited. Assemblies can foster the transparency of consultations operated by the government when formulating public policies. The British term of scrutiny, used in the houses of Westminster, actually consists of controlling the activities of the cabinet pressing ministers to explain, justify, and take responsibility for

their decisions. Given that improved informational processes lie at the heart of the governance agenda, some authors have argued that legislatures could strengthen the transparency, openness, and imputability of public decisions through parliamentary reports, committee hearings, question time, written questions, enquiry committees, to name a few.

To conclude, legislatures refer both to the vertical traditional dimension of politics and to a place devoted to public and contradictory discussion more open to nonpolitical actors than to the administration. Legislatures can therefore be regarded simultaneously as conceptually divergent from the governance dynamic and as possible tools for changing the way public authorities interact with society. The problematic issue that remains is what roles legislators themselves are willing to play. From this perspective, and based on the informational theory of the Congress developed by Kenneth Krehbiel, certain commentators argue that (some) legislators do care about the substantive outputs of public policies. Even if there are some doubts that this theory is always relevant, notably in Europe, it does emphasize that legislators care about more than electoral short-term benefits, party loyalty, and day-to-day politics. Above all, informational approaches indicate that the capacity of a given legislature to take public policies seriously depends on the internal rules governing this legislature. This issue is crucial throughout the world because legislatures are still central institutions within political systems and because these assemblies constitute pedagogic arenas where future top decisionmakers learn their roles.

—*Olivier Rozenberg*

See also Accountability; Consent; Democratic Theory; Public Administration; Representative Democracy

Further Readings and References

Döring, H., & Hallerberg, M. (Eds.). (2004). *Patterns of parliamentary behaviour: Passage of legislation across Western Europe.* Aldershot, UK: Ashgate.

Krehbiel, K. (1991). *Information and legislative organization.* Ann Arbor: University of Michigan Press.

Pierre, J. (Ed.). (2000). *Debating governance: Authority, steering, democracy.* Oxford, UK: Oxford University Press.

LEGITIMACY

Legitimacy is the popular acceptance of a governing regime or system of governance. The word legitimacy can be interpreted in either a normative or a positive way. The first meaning refers to political philosophy and deals with questions such as, What are the right sources of legitimacy? Is a specific political order or regime worthy of recognition? Empirical approaches try to measure the degree of popular acceptance of existing regimes or try to test causal explanations for low or high degrees of legitimacy.

Legitimacy is a classic topic of political philosophy. In the current context of transformations from government to governance, the issue of democratic legitimacy has once again come to the forefront of political discussions because classic modes of gaining legitimacy that have been established during the last few hundred years are eroding. Vigorous debate is taking place about how to restore democratic legitimacy for sociopolitical systems that are characterized by processes of horizontal and vertical differentiation.

Classic Definitions and Discussions

Gaining legitimacy is a need not restricted to liberal democratic regimes, but considered a basic condition of rule because without at least a minimal amount of legitimacy, governing regimes would face deadlock or collapse. Therefore, every regime seeks to justify its reign, and this justification can be based on various concepts. In history, we have seen competition and changes between different concepts of legitimacy. Traditionally, the reign of monarchs was justified on the grounds of their divine origin. The Enlightenment and democratic revolutions challenged this religious source of legitimate rule and declared the will of the people to be the basic source of legitimacy. In this context of modernization, Max Weber developed a typology of forms of legitimacy that is still one of the most important points of reference. He differentiated a traditional, a charismatic, and a legal-rational type of legitimacy. He basically diagnosed a historical transformation from traditional to legal-rational types of legitimacy, in which legitimacy based on the charisma of a (revolutionary) leader formed a transitory phenomenon.

Weber's description of the modern type of legitimacy as legal-rational points to an orientation among modern conceptions of legitimacy that is strongest in the German-speaking world. A constitutionalist conception of legitimacy puts most emphasis on regular procedures employed to formulate the will of the people and also on normative limitations and judiciary controls of governing majorities to secure equal treatment and individual liberty. In contrast, conceptions of democratic legitimacy in the Anglo-Saxon world focus more on the aspects of popular participation and regime accountability secured by free and fair elections combined with a system of political checks and balances (in contrast to the legalistic approach of inter-institutional control in the constitutionalist perspective). Another line of thinking about democratic legitimacy, which has mainly French origins, has a different, more collectivist understanding of "the will of the people." Not so much the rules and the opportunities to participate but the affective commitment to the community and to its administrative representations lays the basis for democratic legitimacy. In consequence, patriotism and civic nationalism secure loyalty to the system of governance.

Collectivist approaches to democratic legitimacy based on a materialist worldview see the legitimacy of the governing regime primarily based on securing economic prosperity and equality. In communist states, this line of thinking led to the subordination of all social subsystems under the political system because only full control especially over the economic system enables the political system to implement the will of the people. After World War II, thinking about democratic legitimacy concentrated in the Western countries more on the output or performance of democratic regimes. The relationship between legitimacy and effectiveness of a political system was cast mainly in such a form that legitimacy was seen as a substitute for effectiveness. In such a perspective, legitimacy creates a reservoir of goodwill (diffuse support) and increases the willingness of the people to tolerate shortcomings of effectiveness (which reduces specific support).

Whereas in the Anglo-Saxon world the relationship between legitimacy and effectiveness has been at the center of debates, the discourse on legitimacy in Germany traditionally has had another focal point—the relationship between form (legality) and substance (morality) of legitimate rule. The differentiation of form/procedures and norm/substance of legitimate rule has been the basis for the establishment of a secular and liberal state and the distinction of "positive" law from theology and philosophy. Nevertheless, the German experiences with an inhumane Nazi regime, which based its rule officially on popular consent and on bureaucratic mechanisms for policy implementation, reinvigorated the constitutionalist tradition of complementing and restricting formally legitimate rule by substantive values.

Empirical Approaches to Measuring Democratic Legitimacy

Empirical approaches emphasize the subjective aspect of democratic legitimacy. If people believe that existing political orders or laws are appropriate and worthy of obedience, then those orders and laws are legitimate. By using polls and other empirical methods, researchers try to reveal these subjectively held beliefs on democratic legitimacy. Nevertheless, it is not easy to measure this phenomenon accurately because legitimacy is an abstract concept. Therefore, it is mostly measured indirectly by asking about political trust or confidence. Empirical studies in Western countries reveal that there is a loss of confidence in almost all advanced democracies. But there are significant differences with respect to what this gap of confidence refers to. Ruling parties and leaders face a high degree of mistrust, and many institutions that have central functions for classic liberal democracies such as parliament, parties, and public bureaucracies have to deal with low confidence. Nevertheless, only small minorities are dissatisfied or not at all satisfied with the way

democracy functions in their country, and even fewer people declare themselves in favor of radical change. Vast majorities still adhere to their democratic systems.

Current Challenges for Democratic Legitimacy

Current socioeconomic and political transformations pose serious challenges to the legitimacy of Western democracies. Supranational integration and decentralization characterize fundamental processes of rescaling governance. Both tendencies create vertically differentiated polities that are reintegrated mainly through intergovernmental negotiations. The proliferation of autonomous regulatory agencies, contracting out, public-private partnerships, and policy networks has led to a horizontally differentiated polity and blurred the line between the public and the private sector. All these processes create a situation where there is no clear and single locus of decision making and responsibility. Furthermore, the classic and clear line of representation and accountability, which connected the people first to the parliament, then to the government, and finally to the public administration, does not capture the real processes of interest aggregation, delegation, decision making, and control. In consequence, the democratic legitimacy of rule making in such a system seems to be in question.

Innovative thinking about democratic legitimacy started from criticism against the dominant form of democracy in Western countries: representative democracy. Since the 1960s, there has been a growing demand for complementing regular voting and party politics in parliaments by other means of public participation. Various strands and mechanisms of participatory democracy have been proposed and in many places implemented. There is a spread of elements of direct democracy such as referendums and recalls, and we find even more elements of associational and deliberative democracy. Concepts of associational democracy stress the contributions by organized groups to effective and adequate policy making. These concepts go beyond the pluralist conception of associations as pressure groups in state-centered processes of interest aggregation. Associations contribute to the democratic legitimacy of a political system because they open up new venues of civic participation but also possibilities for autonomy and self-governance. Furthermore, they provide meaningful voices in the public discourse and mechanisms for a smooth and effective implementation of those decisions in which they participated. The overlapping concept of deliberative democracy entails a recognition of an expanded social pluralism and cultural diversity, and even more, an awareness of that information and communication is fundamentally shaping the current world. The deliberative model of democracy is—in accordance with earlier republican lines of democratic theory—based on the conviction that "aggregate" conceptions of democracy with their central reliance on the mechanism of voting are inadequate because they neglect the fundamental processes that shape individual preferences and the will of the people. In consequence, this model stresses discussions on an equal and inclusive basis, which deepen participants' knowledge of issues and the awareness of the interests and identities of others. Discourse forms the core of legitimate political decision making and provides the basis for tolerating group autonomy and self-government. A quite different alternative to classic representative democracy is proposed by scholars of the public choice school. For them, fragmentation of the political system and privatization of public services open more opportunities for institutional competition and individual choice. Such a market approach to democracy envisions citizens as sovereign consumers who can choose between jurisdictions that offer divergent tax-service bundles. Freedom of exit and entry ensures the efficiency of such political orders and their legitimacy.

Critics of these new forms of democracy point out that not all social interests are equally represented in civic associations and highlight the dangers of populism that go along with direct forms of democracy. Furthermore, political communication takes place in a public sphere that is shaped by mass media and is less characterized by the exchange of arguments and mutual learning than by dramaturgical actions that feature rhetoric, strategic framing, infotainment, and the imperatives of gaining awareness. Finally, founding a

governance system primarily on the mechanisms of exit and entry leads to massive forms of segregation and undermines a sense of interdependency that is still necessary even for pluralist and diversified societies.

Because all forms of democracy have their specific advantages and risks, it seems reasonable to combine their diverse mechanisms in a "complex democracy" with checks and balances to enhance the overall legitimacy of the political order. Nevertheless, two problems remain: First, it is not yet clear whether such a combination is a positive-sum-game and which combination of these democratic mechanisms is productive. Second, a combination clearly leads to more complexity and maybe the biggest challenge will be how to satisfy the popular wish (maybe even the anthropological need) for transparency and orientation within a political system that cannot go back to simplicity.

The currently most vigorous debate about new ways for gaining democratic legitimacy has emerged where territorial boundaries between societies and polities have been blurred by processes of continental and global integration. The rapid growth of institutions of governance on supranational levels makes it evident that Weber's classic demarcation between the domestic (where legitimate authority resides) and the international (which lacks it) does not hold anymore.

Especially regarding the European Union (EU), which has acquired many rule-making competencies from its member states, it has been claimed that a "democratic deficit" or a lack of democratic legitimacy exists because the role of the European Parliament is much more limited in comparison with national parliaments. In this context, Fritz Scharpf has reintroduced the differentiation between input-oriented and output-oriented strategies for gaining legitimacy, hereby referring to Abraham Lincoln's famous definition of democracy as governing "of, by, and for the people." Input-oriented legitimization equals "government by the people." Political decisions are legitimate if and because they reflect the will of the people. Because there exists no European demos with a "thick" collective identity, decision making beyond intergovernmental negations will not enhance the legitimacy of the European Union. In consequence, Scharpf argues for output-focused strategies for gaining legitimacy (Lincoln's "government for the people"). In this perspective, political decisions are legitimate if and because they effectively promote the common welfare of the constituency in question. Such a strategy only requires a "thin" identity because all that is required is the perception of a range of common interests. According to Scharpf, the European Union must foster its output-legitimacy by complementing market-making policies with strengthening market-regulating policies, especially by accepting and fostering national social welfare policies, by agreeing on minimal standards for national welfare spending, and by permitting differentiated assimilation. Critics have pointed to his "social democratic" definition of a "common interest," but in general, the direction he scrutinizes for institutional reform has been accepted. There is widespread agreement that the efficiency and legitimacy of supranational governance can only be secured if it is complemented by elements of decentralization that take governance back closer to the people. In consequence, legitimate governance beyond the nation-state must be designed as a multilevel system based on the principle of subsidiarity. Another element of output-oriented legitimization, the positive valuation of independent expertise, has also found wider acceptance. The most important example for this is the trend toward central banks that are independent from central government.

Much more controversial is the "no demos thesis," and there has been a wave of research on identity formation that reveals both hurdles and existent and potential mechanisms for forming a European demos without neglecting the persistence of national demoi. One specific mechanism for identity-formation has again recently come to the forefront. This is the dialectic between external threat and internal cohesion. But it seems that Islamic terror does not serve as a catalyst for a European identity because Europe does not perceive itself as the main target. Furthermore, as long as some EU members perceive American imperialism and others Russian imperialism as the more pressing threat, no common political identity can emerge.

Given the much narrower scope and the lesser authority of international rule making in other regions of the world and on the global level, the discourse on legitimate governance there has had other focal points. The debate circles not so much around legitimate decision-making mechanisms as around legitimate actors. Traditionally, sovereign states have been the only legitimate actors in the modern international system. Therefore, other actors such as international organizations (IOs) and nongovernmental organizations (NGOs) are in a constant struggle to gain and maintain acceptance. Whereas IOs formally receive their legitimacy by state delegation, NGOs rely purely on their public reputation. The focus on actors shifted the debate toward the problem of accountability of these actors. Two forms of accountability can be distinguished: Internal accountability refers to authorization and control of agents by principals who are institutionally linked to one another as democratic governments are linked to their citizens by regular elections. External accountability refers to actors outside the acting entity who are nevertheless affected by it. It has become especially obvious that U.S. foreign policy affects people across the globe who have no institutionalized means to control the U.S. government. Not only the most powerful actor but almost all actors in international governance lack external accountability. Maybe neither input nor output but the boundary problem of "in" and "out" (inclusion or exclusion) that refers to the third element of Lincoln's definition of democracy—government of the people—will become the central issue of democratic legitimacy in a world where boundaries have lost their naturalness and therefore need justification.

—*Joachim K. Blatter*

See also Authoritarianism; Authority; Consensus Democracy; Crisis Management; Deliberative Democracy; Democratic Deficit; Democratic Theory; Embeddedness; Equity; Legitimacy Crisis; Participation; Political Exchange; Public Opinion; Satisfaction

Further Readings and References

Pharr, S. J., & Putnam, R. D. (Eds.). (2000). *Disaffected democracies: What's troubling the trilateral countries?* Princeton; NJ: Princeton University Press.
Roth, G., & Wittich, C. (1978). *Max Weber: Economy and society* (Vol. I). Berkeley: University of California Press.
Scharpf, F. (1999). *Governing in Europe: Effective and democratic?* Oxford, UK: Oxford University Press.

LEGITIMACY CRISIS

In a political system with widespread features of governance, a legitimacy crisis occurs if there is a loss of faith in the way governance processes operate. Some actions of the state may not be perceived as justified, and if such lack of faith becomes widespread, the whole system of government may lose its credibility in the population.

Under traditional liberal democracy, a crisis of legitimacy typically occurs because the holders of public office are seen as not following their election program, or breaking rules of democratic procedure, or showing indications of corruption. They are then perceived as serving themselves for purposes of power or personal material benefits rather than serving the public purpose. Under governance, the same may occur, but furthermore, loss of legitimacy might happen as a consequence of establishing nodes or points of decision that are not squarely located within the formal, democratic decision-making system. When powers are decentralized, contracted out, or deliberated in detail with third parties, some citizens may perceive the ways the political system makes its decisions as illegitimate because the rightfully elected politicians and their appointed bureaucracies are no longer appreciated as ruling in a sovereign capacity.

One example could be public-private partnerships that through steering groups and similar forums create influence channels for people associated with private firms, often in collaboration with local politicians and even more with staff from local public administration. Another example could be influence channels created after a process of decentralizing powers from a local government council to service institutions, furnished with a board of directors elected among the users. A third example might be decisions made by a firm to which certain public services have been contracted out, particularly if citizens perceive it as cutting back on the quality of those services. In these cases, the citizen who is neither involved in governing a partnership nor a user of schools, nor in a position to complain about the quality of outsourced services, may perceive a loss of possibilities for influence in matters that earlier were vested with some branch of public administration and the politicians who reside over that administration. As a voter, the citizen may exert some influence at elections, and he or she may express opinions in the media or become a member of a political party. These are the traditional and legitimate channels. Channels established by governance may be perceived by many voters as a weakening of their powers.

Across the world, there is a call for more citizen involvement in democratic governance. Paradoxically, this may also lead to a crisis of legitimacy insofar as the traditional democrats see governance as illegitimate. A tension will then arise between those who are active in governance and those who mainly act as traditional voters. Some call such a process a dispute between citizens on the one hand and stakeholders and users on the other hand.

—*Peter Bogason*

See also Contract Enforcement; Crisis Management; Failed State; Legitimacy

Further Readings and References

Bogason, P., Kensen, S., & Miller, H. T. (Eds.). (2004). *Tampering with tradition: The unrealized authority of democratic agency.* Lanham, MD: Lexington.

LIBERAL INTERNATIONALISM

Liberal internationalism is the name given to a cluster of ideas about how best to organize and reform the international system. The core of liberal internationalism lies in the belief that international progress is possible, where progress is defined as movement toward increasing levels of harmonious cooperation between political communities. In general, liberal internationalists regard violence as the policy of last resort, advocate diplomacy and multilateralism as the most appropriate strategies for states to pursue, and tend to champion supranational political structures (such as the European Union) and international organizations (especially the United Nations).

Liberal internationalism is typically contrasted with realism, and the recent history of the academic field of international relations is often characterized as a clash between variants of these two traditions. Realists accuse internationalists of being naïve, and even dangerously utopian; internationalists accuse realists of being overly fatalistic. Liberal internationalists have stressed a variety of agents of and strategies for reform. For some, transformation will come about mainly through a shift in international morality; for others, it requires the construction of international institutions. Most current internationalists focus principally on the role of institutions.

Origins and Evolution

Although it can trace its history to eighteenth-century precursors, liberal internationalism emerged as a powerful ideology during the nineteenth century, primarily (though not exclusively) in Britain. Among its main proponents were politicians including John Bright and Richard Cobden, and philosophers including John Stuart Mill and Herbert Spencer. Critical of the violence and hypocrisy of the international system, these proponents proposed a variety of ways to transform the system. They started by challenging what they identified as the root of the problem: the interests and actions of the ruling aristocracies. The transition from mercantalism to free trade and the domestic move toward democracy presented an opportunity to overthrow this feudal legacy. Liberal internationalism has always been conjoined with a domestic reform agenda.

The relationship between liberal internationalism and imperialism is complex. Some internationalists (including Mill) supported the idea that enlightenment could be exported to "backward" countries. However, many of the most prominent liberal internationalists (including Spencer) were ardent critics of imperialism. Today, a common criticism of liberal internationalism is that it is a veiled form of Western imperialism.

Internationalists were split between those who believed that reform would come about mainly or solely through a shift in norms (international morality) and those who thought that the only feasible route was through significant institutional construction at the international level. The former (including Cobden) focused on transforming the values of society, and in particular they promoted democracy. The latter proposed the creation of a variety of institutional structures, including regional and global federations, and transnational organizations, including international arbitration bodies. World War I dashed the hopes of many internationalists. In the interwar period, internationalists focused on defending and then reforming the League of Nations and developing international law. World War II dealt a further blow to their ambitions, although the postwar fortunes of internationalism are mixed. For much of the Cold War, internationalism was surpassed by realism, but many new internationalist institutions, such as the United Nations, played a major role in global politics.

Engines of Progress: Commerce and Law

Liberal internationalists have proposed two key engines of transformation: international commerce and international law. These are usually combined in liberal internationalist ideology, though the emphasis placed on each differs between thinkers. The economic argument claims that free trade leads to increasing levels of interdependence between states, thus decreasing the chances of war. Because free trade is not a zero-sum game, one of the key traditional sources of conflict is removed. Political cooperation follows from economic engagement. However, these arguments have been challenged. For example, free trade has been accused of increasing inequality and conflict. Moreover, the claim that economic interdependence automatically ameliorates the chances of conflict is disputable.

For realists, and many positivist lawyers, international law is either a misnomer because there is no sovereign to enforce it, or it is irrelevant because powerful states can ignore it. Liberal internationalists disagree, arguing that although far from perfect it is essential in regulating international behavior and in strengthening liberal norms. As states habitually comply with these rules, so cooperation across the system will increase. Furthermore, liberal internationalists argue, international law should be embedded in institutional structures, such as the UN, and in supranational judicial bodies, such as the International Criminal Court (ICC).

Modern Manifestations

Historically, liberal internationalism has been a prescriptive ideology. Its empirical claims were fairly minimal, consisting of extrapolations based on selective readings of systemic trends. Since the 1970s, a prominent social scientific strand of liberal internationalism has emerged. This used to be labeled complex interdependence; today it is frequently termed *globalization.* Numerous scholars have argued that the intensity of transactions (social, cultural, and economic) across national borders has increased enormously and that consequently the world is becoming interdependent. This has led (or will soon) to a qualitative shift in the nature of the international system. This is a conception of liberal internationalism as a historical process rather than as an ideal.

Following the fall of the Berlin Wall, liberal internationalism underwent a renaissance. The norm of inviolable state sovereignty was challenged widely, leading to numerous humanitarian interventions conducted in the name of universal human rights. The United Nations was (briefly) re-invigorated. Bodies such as the European Union presented a model for future supranational political structures. In the wake of 9/11, much of this optimism evaporated. Nevertheless, liberal internationalism is today a thriving area of academic study and political advocacy, both in academia (especially in international law and normative political theory) and in think tanks and international organizations throughout the world. Its impact on state behavior is, however, more contestable.

—*Duncan Bell*

See also Cosmopolitanism; Humanitarian Intervention; International Law and Treaties; International Organization; Mercantilism; Multilateralism; Post-9/11; Realism and Neorealism

Further Readings and References

Bartelson, J. (1995). The trial of judgment: A note on Kant and the paradoxes of internationalism. *International Studies Quarterly, 39,* 255–279.

Koskenniemi, M. (2001). *The gentle civilizer of nations: The rise and fall of international law, 1870–1960.* Cambridge, UK: Cambridge University Press.

Slaughter, A.-M. (2004). *A new world order.* Princeton, NJ: Princeton University Press.

Sylvest, C. (2005). Continuity and change in British liberal internationalism, c. 1900–1930. *Review of International Studies, 31*(2), 263–283.

LIBERALISM

Liberalism is the name for a diverse family of views about government and society that emerged in Europe following the Protestant Reformation and that now dominates political discourse throughout much of the world. The branches of this family are loosely united by shared commitments to toleration of a range of views about the meaning and ends of life, to the ideas of limited government and the rule of law, to the institution of private property as a means of limiting the reach of governmental authority, and perhaps above all, to the protection of personal liberty by whatever means are most likely to be efficacious. These branches have often been divided by feuds over just how far toleration should extend and whether governments should seek to bring about a more robust form of equality than that entailed by equality under law as well as by tensions over the idea of free markets and over the implications for the rule of law of the twentieth-century regulatory state. Some of these differences grow out of a major divide between two main trunks of the liberal tradition, one of which holds that liberty can best be protected by the adoption of limited aims focused on avoidance of tyranny whereas the other sets its sights on more ambitious social objectives.

The term *liberal* acquired its modern, political meaning gradually throughout Europe during the first few decades of the nineteenth century, beginning with Napoleon Bonaparte's use of the phrase *idées libérales* in his Proclamation of the 18th Brumaire in

1799. In 1810, a faction in the Spanish Cortes that opposed royal absolutism adopted the label as its own, and within a decade, liberalism had entered the English lexicon to signify the holding of liberal opinions in politics or theology. In the early years of the century, English writers often adopted the Spanish form *liberales* to give the label a pejorative connotation—ironically because the Spanish advocates of liberalism had from the beginning invoked John Locke and other British authorities in support of their cause. Only in the 1860s did the radical wing of the Whigs in British politics begin to call themselves the Liberal Party, about the same time as the Liberal Republicans began to use the label in the United States and a half-century before it was deployed consistently in American political discourse. Thus, the liberal tradition of political thought was originally constructed retrospectively by writers who discovered affinities between their own values and those of earlier thinkers who sought to limit the reach of political authority.

Liberalism emerged as a product of changes in values in early modern Europe and of the development of the modern state. To retrospective observers, the most conspicuous early signs of a transformation of values can be found in the writings of the Protestant reformers, especially Martin Luther. In contrast to the prevailing teachings of the Catholic Church, Luther insisted that Christianity is primarily a matter of faith, which involves a direct relationship between the individual and God. Luther's thinking led to the notion that nothing could be more important to a person than freedom of conscience and, by extension, the freedom to shape his or her life in accordance with his or her beliefs.

Luther appears to have believed that the meaning of the Scriptures on which Christianity rests is transparent, so that Christians freed of the encumbrances and distortions of church traditions would soon find themselves interpreting Christian doctrine in a uniform way. Actually, the Reformation led to a rapid proliferation of doctrinal differences, to the formation of a large variety of rival churches and sects, and ultimately to protracted violent conflict among protagonists with deep religious and other differences. To avoid the resulting destruction and expense, rulers began to practice toleration, often grudgingly. Their willingness to refrain from violent conflict with religious rivals reflected a shift in values no less important than that embodied in the Reformation, from a value system that at least ostensibly placed highest priority on salvation and the world to come to one that, as a practical matter, treated the lives, liberty, and well-being of individuals as the most eminent priority. This stance together with the notion that the freedom to shape one's life in accordance with one's most deeply held beliefs is of utmost importance to all people constitute the fundamental values on which liberalism rests.

Along with this transformation of values, the emergence of liberalism is intertwined with the development of the modern state, which began to emerge in the sixteenth and seventeenth centuries. In contrast to other political formations, including the manorial and feudal systems that prevailed in much of medieval Europe as well as earlier and contemporaneous empires, the state is characterized by authority that is centralized, extensive, and intensive to an unprecedented degree. Although the feudal system, which was based on a network of reciprocal relations in which superiors provided protection in return for obedience and service from those below them in a hierarchy, was arguably rather intensive by virtue of the obligations it imposed on vassals and villeins, it was highly decentralized. And although imperial authority was extensive, it was not at all intensive because regions or provinces normally retained considerable autonomy. The state, then, was a highly distinctive formation that deployed concentrated power and adopted standardized techniques to maintain order and extract revenues.

The development of the state contributed to the formation of liberalism in two major ways. First, the standardized techniques characteristic of modern states included the adoption of uniform codes and rules. For the state's newly extensive and elaborate structure of authority to operate efficiently, a clearly defined and universally applied system of rights and obligations of individuals was required. The development of these systems—which began to come to fruition fully only with the French Revolution and the collapse of the *ancient régime* toward the end of the eighteenth century—gave inspiration and support to claims about the rights of individuals, often regarded as natural rights and including rights against the state.

Second, the unprecedented concentration of power that is characteristic of modern states, which underpinned claims of absolute royal authority in the seventeenth century, gave rise to abuses against which subjects sought to defend themselves. Thomas Hobbes, the preeminent theorist of the early modern state, argued in 1651 that no state can be viable over the long term unless it includes some person or body of persons who possess total, random sovereign power, adding the deliberately provocative claim that there is no real difference between tyranny and sovereignty. Liberals from Hobbes's time onward have found this claim both preposterous and dangerous, and they have sought to refute it with claims about the inherent rights and liberties of individuals against the state.

The theory of liberal constitutionalism was developed in response to the threat of absolutism, with John Locke, who is sometimes regarded as the founder of the liberal tradition, one of its principal authors, along with Montesquieu and others in the following (eighteenth) century. Four points, including accretions to the theory after Locke's time, constitute the framework of this theory. First, the power of rulers should be limited by clear definitions of the scope of their authority as well as by a division of governing authority into discrete functions performed by separate persons or bodies of persons (separation of powers). Second, rulers should be constrained by the rule of law. In other words, they should rule by promulgating laws that are knowable to all as well as general in form and universal in application, so that they apply to the rulers as well as to all other citizens. Third, the state must respect certain rights of individuals, including a right to religious freedom and a right to own and to transfer private property. Fourth and finally, the authority of rulers rests ultimately on the consent of the ruled—a claim that underpinned liberals' move to embrace democratic political procedures in the nineteenth century.

The theory of liberal constitutionalism was the first and is the most basic model of a liberal regime. This theory is the product of a strategy for the reform of institutions that seeks to realize fundamental liberal values by arranging institutions so that they disperse power as far as possible while preserving sufficient concentration of power to maintain the security of individuals, to enforce the rule of law, and, for some liberals, to pursue additional objectives.

The Enlightenment produced a new trunk of liberal thinking that soon came to compete with and sometimes overshadow its original growth. Although Locke and other early liberals often made bold claims, their objectives were limited, partly because they remained wedded to the assumption that the capacity of human beings to reshape their social world is quite modest. A century after Locke, many thinkers, inspired by the apparently complete success of Newtonian mechanics to comprehend the phenomena of matter in motion, had cast this assumption aside. These thinkers believed that human beings are capable in principle of comprehending the social world, discerning the laws of nature that determine the ways in which it works, and, with this knowledge, designing institutions that would lead to the elimination of a host of miseries and imperfections.

This epistemically and politically ambitious outlook led to the growth of two extraordinarily influential ideas, one of which was nurtured by liberal thinkers from its inception while the other, initially developed by illiberal thinkers, came to play an important role in the later liberal tradition. The first idea is what Adam Smith called the system of natural liberty and later thinkers often call the market system. Smith argued that the primary engine for the generation of wealth, the division of labor, works most efficiently when it is based on a decentralized system of decision making by private individuals and businesses. He also argued that in this kind of economic system, human relations are based on equality and reciprocity instead of entrenched difference of status and privilege. In this vision, human relationships are thoroughly voluntaristic. The connection between this set of ideas and liberal values is transparent. The idea of a system of natural liberty seemed to represent the perfection of the early liberals' commitment to the freedom of individuals to shape their lives in accordance with their own values as well as promising to maximize the generation of wealth to bring human well-being to the highest possible level. This idea is the principal branch supporting a version of liberal theory that is often thought to have been dominant in the nineteenth century and is commonly called "classical" liberalism.

Two centuries after its formulation, many people still seem to regard the idea of a pure market system as a kind of utopia. However, the idea of such a system has two deeply disabling flaws. First, a pure market system would place no limits on the accumulation of private power by economic actors (firms), which can wield great power over employees. This potential for accumulation of power is at odds with the liberal strategy to develop institutions that disperse power as far as possible consistently with maintaining security and the rule of law. Second, in a pure market system, how well individuals do is entirely a function of how well they are able to compete in a market. Those who do well are those who can bring to the market something others want and are willing to pay for. People who have little to offer, for example for reasons of disability, would receive little in return. In a genuinely pure market system, some of those people would die, a consequence that is clearly incompatible with the liberal commitment to the lives, liberty, and well-being of individuals.

By the late nineteenth century, the manifest shortcomings of actual (if highly impure) market systems began to lead liberals to embrace the second influential social idea growing out of the Enlightenment, that of a bureaucratically regulated state. Originally developed by nonliberal thinkers such as Henri de Saint-Simon, the idea of a regulatory state came to seem attractive to liberals in proportion to the degree of their disaffection from the utopia of the market system. On the one hand, a regulatory state provided a means to control the accumulation of private power. On the other hand, it supplied a mechanism through which a political association could guarantee to all its members at least a minimal level of welfare. These features have appealed to many people who identify themselves as liberals from T. H. Green in the late nineteenth century to L. T. Hobhouse a few years later and John Rawls in recent years.

The primary drawback of the regulatory state is that it concentrates power in the hands of politicians and administrators. The tendency toward concentration is mitigated by democratic institutions and procedures, which force politicians to act with some degree of responsiveness to an electorate. Drawing upon the view of Locke and others that the authority of rulers ultimately rests on the consent of the ruled, many liberals in the nineteenth century, led by James Mill toward the beginning and John Stuart Mill at mid-century, began to support some degree of democratic control of political leaders, and in the twentieth century, most liberals have consistently endorsed democratic political institutions in some form. But democratic institutions cut both ways, in some respects supporting but in others undermining liberal values. For even though democratic institutions return some power to the people that would otherwise be wielded by political leaders responsible to no one except themselves, they return that power to the people as a collectivity, not as individuals. Liberals who believe that individuals should be as free as possible to shape their lives in accordance with their own values have reason to be troubled by the kind of concentrated power that is characteristic of modern regulatory states, even when their leaders are subject to democratic controls.

Liberalism is riven, then, by internal tensions between those who would like market systems to flourish as fully and freely as possible and those who favor a robust regulatory state. It is also divided by a tension between these schools of thought, both of which grew out of the optimistic rationalism of the Enlightenment, and the liberalism of limited aims focused on avoiding or combating tyranny. And liberals at the outset of the twenty-first century face challenges that go well beyond these longstanding internal tensions. For it is not clear how extensive the liberal tradition's resources are for facing some of the major problems on the horizon, including the problems posed by an international system that remains relatively anarchical and comprises states spanning a broad spectrum from the strong to those that have failed altogether; the difficulties created by a rapidly evolving world economic system in which crucial decisions are made by leaders whose lines of responsibility to those whose interests they serve are tenuous at best; and the dilemmas posed by powerful forces of nationalism and knotty questions about how and where to draw boundaries between political communities.

—*David C. Johnston*

See also Civic Republicanism; Civic Virtue; Cosmopolitanism; Development Theory; Liberal Market Economy; Participation; Pluralism; Property Rights; Religion; Rule of Law; Social Democracy

Further Readings and References

Johnston, D. (1994). *The idea of a liberal theory.* Princeton, NJ: Princeton University Press.

Laski, H. J. (1936/1962). *The rise of European liberalism.* London: Allen and Unwin.

Leonhard, J. (2001). *Liberalismus: Zur historischen Semantik eines europäischen Deutungsmusters* [The semantics of Liberalism in European comparison]. Munich, Germany: Oldenbourg Verlag.

Rosenblum, N. (1989). *Another liberalism.* Cambridge, MA: Harvard University Press.

Ruggiero, G. de. (1927/1981). *The history of European liberalism* (R. G. Collingwood, Trans.). Gloucester, MA: Peter Smith.

Spitz, D. (1982). *The real world of liberalism.* Chicago: University of Chicago Press.

Tuck, R. (1979). *Natural rights theories: Their origin and development.* Cambridge, UK: Cambridge University Press.

Waldron, J. (1987). Theoretical foundations of liberalism. *Philosophical Quarterly, 37,* 127–150.

LIBERALIZATION

Liberalization, which literally is the act of making less strict, refers to the loosening of government controls. Although sometimes associated with the relaxation of laws relating to social matters such as abortion and divorce, it is most often used as an economic term. In particular, liberalization refers to reductions in restrictions on international trade and capital. Liberalization is often treated as synonymous with deregulation: that is, the removal of state restrictions on business. Although the two are, in principle, distinct (in that liberalized markets can still be subject to government

regulations, for example to protect consumers), in practice both terms are generally used to refer to the freeing of markets from state intervention.

Recent decades have seen a significant shift toward both liberalization and deregulation. The liberalization of trade has progressed through the signing of a succession of free trade agreements such as the General Agreement on Tariffs and Trade (GATT) in 1947, the Single European Market (SEM) in 1986, and the North American Free Trade Agreement (NAFTA) in 1994. By the 1970s, free trade had extended to most Organisation for Economic Co-operation and Development (OECD) countries, with many developing countries following suit from the 1980s on (including the post-communist regimes of Central and Eastern Europe and, more recently, the People's Republic of China). Recent years have also seen a shift toward the removal of foreign investment regulations: According to United Nations Conference on Trade and Development (UNCTAD) figures, between 1991 and 1996, ninety-five percent of the 599 national foreign direct investment (FDI) regulations across the world were in the direction of further liberalization. Financial markets, too, have been freed from state interference, with the foreign exchange market the first financial market to liberalize in the mid-1970s, followed by the deregulation of domestic stock markets in the 1980s (for the advanced industrial nations) and the 1990s (for the newly industrializing countries).

Liberalization and deregulation have played a central role in stimulating the massive rise in international trade (which grew at an average rate of six percent per annum between 1948 and 1997), foreign direct investment (for which stocks and inflows have exceeded the rise in world trade), and foreign exchange and portfolio capital (with the average daily turnover of foreign exchange markets now in the trillions of dollars). Liberalization and deregulation are thus both seen to have contributed to the globalization of the world economy in recent decades.

There is significant controversy about the benefits of liberalization and deregulation. Both are central tenets of the "Washington consensus"—a set of market-oriented policy prescriptions advocated by neoliberal economists for developing countries to achieve economic growth. Yet critics of the Washington consensus have argued that, in practice, such policies are being used by corporations from wealthier nations such as the United States to exploit workers from the poorer countries. This is not least because—as activists and scholars alike have noted—markets are, in reality, neither free nor fair. Rather, as one political commentator has noted, the West's attitude to the rest is "you liberalize, we subsidize." For example, generous subsidies paid to cotton producers in the United States and the European Union artificially drive down prices, threatening the livelihoods of African cotton farmers. For many critics, the problem is therefore not so much the freeing of markets per se but, rather, that the wealthier countries are effectively cheating at the game they are exporting to the rest of the world.

—*Nicola Smith*

See also Liberal Internationalism; Liberal Market Economy; Market; Neoliberalism; Regulation; World Trade Organization

Further Readings and References

Cornia, G. A. (Ed.). (2004). *Inequality, growth and poverty in an era of liberalization and globalization.* New York: Oxford University Press.

Jomo, K. S., & Fine, B. (Ed.). (2005). *The new development economics: Post Washington consensus neoliberal thinking.* London: Zed Books.

Klein, N. (1999). *No logo.* London: Flamingo.

LIBERAL MARKET ECONOMY

According to the approach laid out by Peter Hall and David Soskice in their research on the "varieties of capitalism," liberal market economies (LMEs) are national economies that display a high share of competitive market arrangements in the governance of company relations. LMEs feature institutional arrangements that allow actors to pursue individual unconstrained strategies, often by matching demand and supply through relative prices. These mechanisms of company governance tend to differ from those in countries that the authors describe as coordinated market economies (CMEs), that is, systems in which nonmarket institutions are much more prevalent.

In each type of economy, strong complementarities exist between institutions from such realms as industrial relations, vocational training and education, corporate governance, interfirm links, and internal company relations. Conceived as tightly coupled institutional systems within which the presence of one institution increases the returns from another, both LMEs and CMEs endow their constitutive firms with a comparative institutional advantage for particular production strategies. Although CME institutions provide an edge to companies in mature industrial sectors, CME institutions have proven particularly adept at supporting service-sector companies and the establishment of new industries. LME structures are most prevalent in the Anglo-Saxon countries, that is, the United States, United Kingdom, Australia, Canada, New Zealand, and Ireland. In contrast to the successes of CMEs in "incremental" innovation, LMEs tend to be better in "radical" innovation sustained by the wide availability of venture capital financing, human capital investment in transferable skills, and financial reward for risk-taking behavior.

The distinction between liberal and coordinated market economies is the most recent embodiment of a long-standing research tradition that has attempted to account for the distinctiveness of national models of capitalism among the advanced industrialized countries. Hall and Soskice's focus on the firm as a strategic actor contrasts with earlier literatures that sought to explain national differences in economic structures and performance through national cultures, relative state strength, and the degree of corporatism in state-society relations. Hall and Soskice succeed at providing microfoundations for macro-divergences across economies by embracing the assumptions of the new institutional economics. Most importantly, they conceive of the national institutional matrices they describe as constituting equilibrium. The institutional equilibrium of the LME optimizes principle-agent relationships.

The United States is often invoked as the ideal-typical case of liberal market economies. The institutional structures of the U.S. economy do not allow the type of nonmarket coordination associated with

Europe's corporatist networks, or with the close state-society links, the *keiretsus* and enterprise unionism in Japan. Although the CME institutions in continental European countries or Japan promote labor productivity, LME institutions optimize the productivity of capital. As evidenced by a high number of mergers and acquisitions, an active market for corporate control exists. Individual investment decisions are motivated by the potential direct payoffs, less by systemic considerations. Rather than relying on established relationships, transactions between and within companies tend to be open, transparent, and have a focus on the short term.

—*Tobias Schulze-Cleven*

See also Embeddedness; Liberalism; Monetarism; Neoliberalism; Political Economy

Further Readings and References

Hall, P., & Soskice, D. (2001). *Varieties of capitalism: The institutional foundations of comparative advantage.* Oxford, UK: Oxford University Press.
Hall, P., & Soskice, D. (2003). Varieties of capitalism and institutional change: A response to three critics. *Comparative European Politics, 1,* 241–250.

LINE-STAFF ORGANIZATION

Classical theories of organization associated with Henri Fayol, Frederick W. Taylor, and others define formal organizations as collective enterprises identified by a clear division of labor and authority. These theories view decision-making power as flowing from a unified command structure. Relationships between individuals, groups, and divisions are based on lines of authority that are predetermined. Typically, work is carried out in accordance with specialized functions, and authority is exercised in a hierarchical manner. In a highly centralized structure, decisions are made by a few and flow downward through the enterprise. However, as organizations grow in scope and complexity, they need to be flexible in the extent to which coordination and control are centrally applied. The principle of line-staff organization introduces flexibility into hierarchical lines of authority, while trying to preserve a unified command structure.

Line groups are engaged in tasks that constitute the technical core of the firm or the subunit of a larger enterprise. They are directly involved in accomplishing the primary objective of the enterprise. In manufacturing, line groups engage in work related to production. In the service sector, the line group is responsible for its customers. Line groups have final decision-making authority regarding technical organizational purposes.

Staff groups are engaged in tasks that provide support for line groups. They consist of advisory (legal), service (human resources), or control (accounting) groups. Staff groups support those engaged in the central productive activity of the enterprise. Thus, staff groups create the infrastructure of the organization. Human resources, information technologies, and finance are infrastructural functions. Staff groups provide analysis, research, counsel, monitoring, evaluation, and other activities that would otherwise reduce organizational efficiency if carried out by personnel in line groups. Staff groups are therefore responsible to their appropriate line units. Although line and staff may operate at different levels of an organization, all positions are defined relative to their line or staff function. Differentiating line and staff functions is straightforward in that it involves identifying the beneficiaries of the activity, product, or service. If the beneficiaries are employees, then it is a staff function. Otherwise, the activity is related to the line organization.

By modifying organizational hierarchies to include staff functions, organizational capacity for processing information is increased without sacrificing lines of authority. However, studies indicate that although line-staff innovations may preserve the appearance of formal line authority, staff groups, particularly specialized staff, often assume de facto decision-making responsibilities because their lines of communication to upper management are shorter. This is the case for staff specialists who monitor and report on line performance. The authority of staff specialists may consist of pure advice-giving or specialists may have the right to pass along directives from upper management to those they do not formally supervise. This naturally leads to power struggles between line and staff. Communication failures, poorly defined responsibilities, and divergent interests create unclear lines of authority that lead to intra-organizational conflict and reduce organizational performance. Clarifying supervisory relationships reduces organizational dysfunction and increases effectiveness.

—*Matthew E. Archibald*

See also Formal Organization; Hierarchy; Organization Theory; Science; Technical-Rational Expertise

Further Readings and References

Fayol, H. (1949). *General and industrial management.* London: Pittman.
Scott, W. R. (2003). *Organizations: rational, natural and open systems* (5th ed.). Thousand Oaks, CA: Sage.

LOCAL GOVERNANCE

Local governance mirrors the general development in Western democratic societies of decentering governments as policy-making and service-delivering institutions. Governments increasingly depend on other organizations in society for reaching their goals. Governments and their agencies no longer are the sole decisionmakers on the distribution of public goods. Governance, and local governance in particular, is characterized by cooperation between governmental and private organizations, joint policy making, shared service delivery, and so on. Local governance is to be juxtaposed to local government.

Local governance can be defined as Peter John did: a flexible pattern of public decision making based on loose networks of individuals. The concept conveys the idea that public decisions rest less within hierarchically organized bureaucracies, but take place more in long-term relationships between key individuals located in a diverse set of organizations located at various territorial levels. The concept of local governance can easily be linked to that of regime, often used in U.S. literature. The difference, however, seems to be that a "regime"

is a nongovernmental coordination mechanism that compensates for the weakness of political authority, whereas governance includes political actors or is even led by them. One can, nevertheless, state that regimes are at the pinnacle of the process of governance; they are an extension of the processes of networking, trust building, and problem solving.

Governance advocates a specific approach to policy making. A rationalist approach does not apply to governance. According to Peter Bogason, policy making is not a rational process, but is characterized by cooperation, deliberation, and reasoning from parochial points of view. Even in the implementation of national policies, local governments have to adapt those policies to the wishes and potentialities of the local communities. They have to face fragmentation and new demands and are bound to organize contradictory demands. Paradoxically, the role of individual leaders increases. They may become more powerful, especially when they possess abilities to stimulate and persuade people and when they show a strong personality and charisma.

Causes for the Shift Toward Local Governance

A shift has taken place from government toward governance. John has formulated many causes. First, economies have become increasingly international. Local governments, when seeking to improve the local economy, therefore, have to attract private companies from all around the world and build alliances with private businesses. Second, in various policy fields, involvement of the private sector is demanded. Without cooperation of businesses, problems of pollution, traffic, economy, and labor market, to name only a few examples, can hardly be solved. Third, especially in Europe, public policies have an increasingly European character. Local governments develop channels of influence apart from those of national governments, and they become aware of the necessity of cross-border cooperation. Fourth, new policy challenges have been put on the agenda. Issues such as environmental protection and AIDS are by their nature too complex to be solved by governmental policies alone. Cooperation of individual citizens and private companies is much needed. Fifth, political participation has changed quite fundamentally. Many citizens no longer are satisfied with a rather passive role as voters and clients of government, but want to become involved in policy making and decision making themselves. All these developments point in one direction: the necessity of cooperation.

Local Government and Governance

Local governance is to be distinguished from local government. Both can be considered theoretical approaches to the study of how policies and decisions are being made at the local level.

The traditional government model, then, considers public administration as a unity, as if it were a bureaucracy, to be governed as such. Government is perceived as one system, basically founded on Max Weber's bureaucracy model. Between the various levels of government, clear distinctions are to be made, in a hierarchical and consolidated structure and combined with direct central government control. Those distinctions are, at least, of a legal nature, at best constitutional. A clear division of tasks between governmental levels is supposed to be essential. It will increase the transparency of government and will enable politicians as well as administrators to work within a set structure and clear responsibilities. Legal powers should be as exclusive as possible, the division is fixed, networks are closed ones, and policy making is routinized. This traditional government model is clearly linked to the representative democracy model (though some tensions between this one-to-one coupling can be formulated). Leadership has a collegial or clientelist character.

When applied to the study of local public administration, problems in how a system of subnational government functions are mainly the result of overlapping authorities, unclear distinctions of responsibilities, too much centralization, and a lack of autonomy for local governments. The solutions are greater clarity of responsibilities, decentralization, and, last but certainly not least, increasing problem-solving capacity of local government by facilitating amalgamation of local authorities. Intermunicipal cooperation is a

rejected solution because it is supposed to obscure the separate responsibilities of each autonomous municipality. If the geographic scale of local authorities is too small compared with the scale of the societal problems at stake, then amalgamation or even the creation of a new layer of government is preferred.

The governance model, on the other hand, focuses on cooperation between government actors and between government and nongovernmental actors. This approach is derived from insights coming from policy network studies. If this approach is being used, the focus no longer is on providing legal clarity or establishing a new layer of government, but on making things work. First, this approach emphasizes the relevance of checks and balances. The governance model starts from pluralism; the pluralistic society is the starting point. In that society, checks and balances are essential features for preserving freedom and preventing power monopolies. In addition to this normative consideration, actual decisions in the real world of local authorities are supposed to be made in a context of interdependencies in extensive networks. Many actors are involved, governmental as well as nongovernmental ones. Government responsibilities may be specific ones, but government agencies do not escape interdependencies, they often do need cooperation of nongovernmental actors. To put it differently, governments are supposed to lack control. Legal powers cannot displace actual interdependencies. In addition, policy processes are characterized by trial and error; it is quite common to experiment. Structures are decentered and fragmented, they are to ensure flexibility and innovation of government performance, and control is decentralized. The democracy model linked to the governance model of public administration is a mixed one. Representation is essential, as is participation. Democracy also is supposed to be experimental. Leadership, finally, is increasingly important and often mayoral or charismatic in nature.

The governance model recognizes that problems are centered around the difficulty of municipalities cooperating with each other, the possible inflexibility of the present division of tasks, the existence of veto power of some actors, and the existence of somewhat closed frames of reference. The solutions are facilitation of cooperation by creating overlapping authorities and making it more efficient. In this approach, it becomes clear that an efficient structure (at face value) often becomes penny-wise and pound-foolish. Intermunicipal cooperation is supposedly essential for all governmental entities because it can prevent power concentration. Autonomy of local government is impossible but also unwise.

To conclude, in the study of local authorities, one has the choice between the government model and the governance model. In the first, the focus will be on structures and procedures of government; in the latter, the focus will be on policy making in networks of governmental and nongovernmental actors. Or, as W. L. Miller and colleagues put it: local governance can be understood as the commissioning, organization, and control of services such as health, education, policing, infrastructure, and economic development within communities.

Features of Local Governance

Government and governance cannot only be considered analytical models for the study of (local) public administration. They can also be concrete pictures of what is actually going on at the local level, that is, models of reality.

John has formulated elements of the shift from government to governance. First, he points at trends of institutional reform, consisting of both institutional multiplication and institutional restructuring. New layers of government have been created, whether all-purpose ones or special-purpose ones. New public management ideas have been adopted. Second, there is a trend of governing in new networks. Local government institutions and the private sector create horizontal networks (or regimes). Especially in those parts of the world where nations are increasingly working together and boundaries seem to fade away, as is the case in the European Union,

municipalities tend to enter or create international networks. Third, new policy initiatives can be observed. Local governments and local networks seem somehow to compensate for the retreat of the state, in an innovative way. Thus, they are building capacity and trust to deal with issues in their communities. At the same time, a revival of central initiatives can be distinguished—new policies, new bureaucracies. Fourth and finally, there are responses to dilemmas of coordination and accountability. Policies being made in public-private networks necessarily lead to a search for new mechanisms of control and accountability, as well as to more prominent forms of executive leadership.

As a result, government and governance are different realities indeed (see Table 1).

It has to be kept in mind that government and governance are formulated as ideal types. In reality, elements of both models will be found. Despite trends toward local governance, the institutional framework of local government will still be important.

Dealing With Local Governance

Important parts of day-to-day political and administrative life consist of the delivery of local services, their production, and provision. One of the results of governance ideas (as contrasted to government) is the insight that the decisions about the provision of services and

Table 1 Local Government and Governance Contrasted

Element	Government	Governance
Number of institutions	Few	Many
Bureaucratic structure	Hierarchical	Decentered
	Consolidated	Fragmented
Horizontal networks	Closed	Extensive
International networks	Minimal	Extensive
Democratic linkage	Representative	Representative + new initiatives
Policies	Routinized	Innovative Learning
Central government	Direct control	Decentralized + micro intervention
Leadership	Collegial/clientelist	Mayoral/charismatic

Source: John, P. (2001). Local Governance, p. 17. London: Sage Ltd.

the quality level can be distinguished from the actual production. As Bogason put it: the body responsible—the municipality, the county, and so on—for the service must make the decisions about provision, but it does not necessarily have to produce the service. Service production can be provided by private and public organization (governance borrowed this insight from the new public management literature).

Further models of local governance can be distinguished. In further models, several elements play a key role. Differences can be observed regarding key goals of governance, attitude to local autonomy, attitude to public participation, key service delivery mechanisms, and key political mechanisms.

One of the main problems to be solved is the kind of democratic legitimacy each of the local governance models will have. Traditionally, democratic legitimacy is supposed to be guaranteed insofar as elected officials (local councils, in particular) are the main policymakers. In most governance models, elected politicians tend to lose that position, and the primacy of representative democracy erodes. Different ways of achieving legitimacy have to be found because the centrality of the representative democratic institutions has faded away. This means that other channels have to be created for effective citizens' input in collective decision making and legitimate outputs.

The local governance models discussed earlier each have their own way of safeguarding democratic legitimacy. The localist model tries to keep as close as possible to the representative democracy; it addresses citizens first as voters. As a result, it almost overlaps the local government model. Democratic legitimacy is guaranteed by elections and responsiveness of local politics. The second, or individualist, model perceives citizens as consumers and customers of local services. Consumer consultation and the formulation of consumers' rights (getting "value for money") are supposed to stimulate democratic legitimacy. Citizens can formulate their needs for services by ways of consultation. Dissatisfaction on the actual service delivery can be expressed as consumers' rights.

The third, or mobilization, model of local governance seems to get its legitimacy by dealing with the needs of disadvantaged and excluded citizens and

from their participation. It is unclear whether the opinions of other citizens are considered as well. Finally, the centralist model of local governance maintains national representative decision making as the main source for its legitimacy.

—Linze Schaap

See also Collaborative Governance; Government; Interorganizational Coordination; Participatory Democracy; Regime Theory; Urban and Regional Planning

Further Readings and References

Bogason, P. (2000). *Public policy and local governance: Institutions in the postmodern society.* Cheltenham, UK: Edward Elgar.

Goss, S. (2001). *Making local governance work: Networks, relationships and the management of change.* Houndmills, UK: Palgrave.

John, P. (2001). *Local governance.* London: Sage Ltd.

Kickert, W. J. M., Klijn, E. H., & Koppenjan, J. F. M. (Eds.). (1997). *Managing complex policy networks.* London: Sage Ltd.

Miller, W. L., Dickson, M., & Stoker, G. (2000). *Models of local governance, public opinion and political theory in Britain.* Houndmills, UK: Palgrave.

Rhodes, R. A. W. (1997). *Understanding governance.* Buckingham, UK: Open University Press.

LOCALIZATION

The term *localization* appears frequently in policy analysis within two contexts. The first we might call the organizational context, where localization fits with what have come to be termed new public management prescriptions for achieving greater responsiveness and customer-centeredness in the public sector by attempting to tailor services to local settings as much as possible. Localization is often used in tandem with decentralization as a governance strategy to attempt to achieve this greater responsiveness, but may have a different meaning than decentralization, which may or may not result in localization, depending on where the center is located in terms of geography or power at the beginning of the reform process,

Localization, in the managerialist sense of the term, is perhaps best thought of in the context of center-local relations, with decentralization as a strategy for achieving greater localization of governance. Localization can also be used to attempt to achieve greater participation in political decision making from communities or even individuals through their greater participation in public services, and so is often associated with notions such as citizenship and choice.

The second context of localization occurs on a larger scale—if the opposite of decentralization is centralization, the opposite of localization is globalization. Localization is often held in a dialectic relationship with globalization—as the latter occurs across time and space, often as a force for homogenization, the former appears as a form of resistance to it. Here localization is perhaps even more politicized than in the case of center-local relations, often being used as a term favored by antiglobalization writers as denoting a resistance to the branding of consumer goods and public services. In the context of governance, we might therefore expect attempts at pursuing uniform "global" programs to be encountered by resistance at a local level where "difference" is demanded instead. This clearly has strong links with the first context in which localization is used, but here it appears to be used in a different sense, being a source of activism, holding more dynamic meanings than is often the case in the rather top-down assumptions held in the organizational notion of localism.

—Ian Greener

See also Center-Local Relations; Citizenship; Decentralization; Globalization; Glocalization; New Public Management

Further Readings and References

Ferlie, E., Pettigrew, A., Ashburner, L., & Fitzgerald, L. (1996). *The new public management in action.* Oxford, UK: Oxford University Press.

Giddens, A. (1991). *The consequences of modernity.* Cambridge, UK: Polity Press.

Hudson, B., & Hardy, M. (2001). Localization and partnership in the "New National Health Service": England and Scotland compared. *Public Administration, 79,* 315–335.

LOCAL KNOWLEDGE

Local knowledge refers to people's knowledge of their own circumstances and lived experiences, whether those be community residents for whom public policies are being legislated or the legislators' staff members or the implementors of public policies (or any other setting). Local knowledge is the mundane, yet expert understanding of and practical reasoning about local conditions derived from lived experience. In this sense, it is often juxtaposed with "expert" knowledge—the phrase commonly used in reference to technical or professional expertise that derives from academic training. This latter form of knowledge is what is commonly understood to be possessed by policy and other experts—whether legislative staff, advisors to legislators and their staffs, or expert witnesses giving testimony in legislative hearings (in the U.S. context).

Local Knowledge and Phenomenological Situatedness

Local knowledge is primarily a phenomenological concept, or one that enacts phenomenological ideas, although it has been developed and used in various disciplinary settings, with especially strong roots in cultural or symbolic anthropology and ethnographic methods. Local knowledge manifests its phenomenological underpinnings in its insistence on the context-specific character of knowledge—the knowledge that people develop among themselves in interaction with the programs, operations, or objects (physical artifacts) that are specific to their local context, such as a work practice in an organizational setting or a lived experience with electromagnetic frequency (EMF) emissions.

Local knowledge develops from experience with the situation in question. Much of it is tacitly known in the sense that Michael Polanyi used the term in referring to the sort of knowledge one develops over time, typically from repeated actions in the course of everyday living or the practice of a craft, trade, profession, art, or hobby, as distinct from book learning. Such knowing is highly context-specific, and it is the kind of knowledge that is rarely made explicit. In some cases, as Polanyi noted, it is not possible to make such knowledge explicit or to do so without great difficulty.

Applied to a public policy or public administration setting, "local" workers (such as in a governmental agency implementing public policies) or residents affected by such policies and programs are seen as far more knowledgeable about the situation at hand than those without such experience or point of view. This means that there is a conceptual shift in the meaning of "expertise"—those possessing local knowledge are understood to have a form of expertise, although that expertise is not based on, for example, university training. Local knowledge has its own characteristics. The expertise embedded in local knowledge resides in intimate familiarity with and understanding of the particulars of the local situation. This is "everyday knowledge," as distinct from the more "scholarly" knowledge based in scientific training. This everyday knowledge derives from practical reasoning about context-specific events. For example, although scholarly knowledge is theory-based, abstract or general, scientific in construction, academy-based, and technical-professional, local knowledge is practice-based, context-specific, interactively derived, lived experience–based, and tacit and involves practical reasoning.

Although local knowledge is situational, that does not necessarily mean that it is lacking in specialized expertise. The character of the expertise is different: Local knowledge legitimates the experiential and the contextual as types of specialization equal in value (under certain circumstances) to the scholarly academic. Each has its place. Depending on the situation, local knowledge may well include technical or professional training because that is the source of knowing in that context. Perception and valuation of knowledge as local, rather than expert, seems to hinge, in some cases, less on its non-academic source than on its sociocultural character, the status of the perceiver(s) and of the person(s) "doing" the knowing, and structural features of the relationship between the two.

Local knowledge is sometimes associated with practical reasoning or political judgment, terms associated with the Aristotelian notion of *phronesis.*

Local knowledge is also widely associated with the work of anthropologist Clifford Geertz, after an essay included in an edited collection by the same name. He does not define there what he means by local knowledge, but it is possible to infer his meaning from how he uses the term. In the final chapter of his book, which is the title essay, Geertz compares four legal systems, addressing the question of whether law is a universal set of ideas or whether it is more closely tied to local practices. He sees a legal system as comprising knowledge that is place-specific, rather than placeless and general or universal, which means that its laws are part of what constructs and shapes social life. This relationship between what is particular and what is universal is closely related to Geertz's earlier arguments concerning the methodological requirement that interpretive methods provide a layering of detail in building a representation of their subject matter. Linking the two ideas together, we can see that writing thickly descriptive research reports requires intimate familiarity by researchers with the local knowledge of those they are describing. Indeed, researchers are building their own local knowledge as they observe, interview, and study policy- or agency-relevant documents. Interpretive research, then, is grounded in local knowledge, both substantively and methodologically.

Local Knowledge in Policy Analysis

The term *local knowledge* has often come into play in policy analyses in reference to circumstances in which policies designed at some distance from their point of implementation contain programmatic features that impede their enactment on-site. The newly (re)designed policy or program does not work because it does not fit the lived realities (or *Lebenswelt,* in the phenomenological term) of those for whom it was intended (the policy "targets," in the language of noninterpretive policy analytic writings). Not uncommonly, these features would not have been included by those with first-hand knowledge of the setting or actors in question and their entailments. "Locals," in other words, with their particular local knowledge, would have anticipated policy or program failure with the inclusion of these features. Locals need not be residents only, and their expertise can also be other than nontechnical everyday knowledge. In the field of technology policy and the assessment of risk, for example, analysis might focus on the technical expertise held by local workers that is not considered in designing policy. Mary Schmidt, for example, wrote about grouters pouring cement for the construction of a dam designed by policymakers at some remove from the site. The dam collapsed after site-based grouters' "intimate knowledge" of local rock conditions for cement preparation was ignored by project engineers on site and design engineers in the state capital, with a consequent tragic loss of life.

Interpretive policy analysts (and others), in arguing for more participatory policy design and implementation processes, often base their arguments on the need for local knowledge in anticipating developments such as these, in the understanding that according legitimacy to local knowledge might have yielded more effective policies and programs. Some of the arenas in which this has been an issue include development policy. One of the stories told about such problems describes efforts to remedy drought in a specific region, which had nomadic tribespeople dig more wells. Had planners accessed the local knowledge held by herders, they might have understood that adding wells was likely to encourage a tribesman to increase his herd size because of what owning livestock meant for his reputation. Such increases exacerbated the problem situation the policy was intended to resolve. In the context of science and technology policies, Brian Wynne relates the story of shepherds in northern England whose local, implicit knowledge of wind directions and sheep grazing patterns was ignored by scientist-experts advising policymakers concerned with fallout from the nuclear explosion at Chernobyl, far to the east, with detrimental economic results. In education policy, had policymakers in Boston and elsewhere understood what busing meant to White parents, they might have pursued differently the policy that led to "White flight," which undermined the policy's purpose. Contemporary arguments for evidence-based policies in various fields concern, in some respects, the debate about whether local knowledge may be considered a sufficient basis for evidentiary claims.

Local knowledge has also had a long-standing place in the context of planning—urban, regional, and international (development-related)—dating back to the late 1960s and 1970s. Many scholars argued against the model of planner-as-technical-expert making decisions for neighborhood residents, as if the latter had no knowledge of or agency regarding their own situations. The debates were joined in the work of Paolo Freire in development education, who sought to teach Mexican farmers and peasants to read by starting with words grounded in their own work and life situations. In many respects, the argument echoed a much earlier concern of John Dewey, Clarence Perry, and others for the neighborhood unit as the central element of both planning and education.

Accessing local knowledge has strong methodological associations with interpretive methods, such as ethnographic and participant observer research, as is done in interpretive policy analysis.

—*Dvora Yanow*

See also Evidence-Based Policy; Interpretive Policy Analysis; Interpretive Theory; Knowledge Management; Local Reasoning

Further Readings and References

Freire, P. (1970). *Pedagogy of the oppressed.* New York: Seabury.

Geertz, C. (1983). *Local knowledge.* New York: Basic Books.

Perry, C. A. (1929/1974). *The neighborhood unit.* Monograph reprinted in *Neighborhood and Community Planning* (Orig. v. 7 of *Regional Survey, Regional Plan of New York and Its Environs*). New York: Arno Press.

Polanyi, M. (1966). *The tacit dimension.* New York: Doubleday.

Schmidt, M. R. (1993). Grout: Alternative kinds of knowledge and why they are ignored. *Public Administration Review, 53,* 525–530.

Wynne, B. (1992). Sheep farming after Chernobyl. In B. Lewenstein (Ed.), *When science meets the public.* Washington, DC: American Association for the Advancement of Science.

Yanow, D. (2004, March). Translating local knowledge at organizational peripheries [Special issue]. *British Journal of Management, 15,* S15–S25.

Local Reasoning

Local reasoning refers to the creative capacity of individuals to change their beliefs. The concept of local reasoning maintains that individuals, by making decisions or reacting to experiences, may adopt, reject, or modify their beliefs in novel ways. This reasoning process is localized because it always takes place within the context of an individual's set of held beliefs. These inherited or already held beliefs situate an individual within a particular tradition.

Local reasoning denies that an individual's beliefs are merely functions of social structures, norms, or rules. Although traditions and prior theories influence the reasoning process, they do not necessarily determine the content of an individual's beliefs. Moreover, beliefs are not simple products of completely autonomous reasoning. Local reasoning claims that individuals adopt, reject, or modify beliefs as a reaction to a decision or experience and always as an agent situated within a particular tradition.

An interpretive, bottom-up study of governance will examine the local reasoning of individuals because explaining the changing beliefs of individuals affects the norms, practices, and systems of governance within a community. Analyzing the local reasoning of individuals highlights the interplay between inherited traditions, dilemmas, and the resultant beliefs and practices.

Local reasoning differs from other forms of reasoning. Local reasoning contends that beliefs arise out of a process where situated agents reason, make decisions, or react to experiences and then decide whether to adopt new beliefs or reject or modify already-held beliefs. Rational choice theory rejects situated agency and local reasoning by preferring to grant individuals complete rational autonomy. Individuals hold or change beliefs, according to this theory, by reasoning through a process of utility maximization. Thus, an individual can hold any belief whatsoever as long as it satisfies some variant of utility. Another school of thought, institutionalism, asserts that social norms or roles can best explain individual beliefs and practices. This denies the creative capacity of individuals to modify their beliefs. Changes in belief are constrained by objectified social norms or roles. Changes in practices and governance, then, are explained at the level of norms, rules, and external social forces rather than on the level of the individual.

Even within an interpretivist approach to governance, the concept of local reasoning distinguishes between a more strongly decentered approach and a quasi-structuralist perspective that sees beliefs as creatures of reified ideologies, discourses, or epistemes. Much like institutionalism, this approach appears to constrain the agency of individuals to change their beliefs by explaining beliefs and actions as an ideology or discourse. Local reasoning, then, distinguishes itself from these other views of rationality by rejecting the pure autonomy of the rational choice school while explaining changes in beliefs locally, within an individual's web of beliefs.

—*Ben Krupicka*

See also Decentered Theory; Local Knowledge; Situated Agency

Further Readings and References

Bevir, M. (2005). *New Labour: A critique.* New York: Routledge.
Bevir, M., & Rhodes, R. (2006). *Governance stories.* London: Routledge.

Logic of Appropriateness

The logic of appropriateness refers to a view of action that involves the matching of situations, roles, and rules. It defines a basis for decision making biased toward what social norms deem right, rather than what cost-benefit calculations consider best. Behavior in a specific situation is said to follow from the rules that govern the appropriate course of action for a given role or identity. The rules that determine appropriateness are institutionalized in social practices and sustained over time through learning. The logic of appropriateness furnishes governance with institutional order, stability, and predictability. At the same time, it may run counter to democratic principles by implying the substitution of tacit understanding for collective deliberation. The term was coined by organization theorists James G. March and Johan P. Olsen, but the concept has long been an important theme in social theory.

The logic of appropriateness is commonly distinguished from the logic of consequences. The latter evokes self-interested, rational actors with fixed preferences and identities, whose behavior is determined by the calculation of expected returns from alternative choices. Although the two logics are usually presented in mutually exclusive terms, they can also be understood as opposite poles of a single continuum. In the face of uncertainty and complexity, the analysis of a specific situation on the basis of experience, expert knowledge, or intuition, and using criteria of similarity, difference, analogy, and metaphor, may yield a variety of appropriate alternatives. Yet the choice among these may involve an assessment of the likelihood of different consequences and the costs and benefits of expected outcomes. Even in such situations, however, prevailing norms, beliefs, routines, procedures, roles, organizational forms, or technologies are assumed to force cognitive shortcuts. The reason is that the capabilities of attention, interpretation, evidence validation, and memory management are seen as imperfect.

The two perspectives of action have different implications for governance. The logic of appropriateness presumes that members of a polity follow rules because they are perceived as natural, valid, and legitimate. Rules may be replaced or modified over time through processes of selection and adaptation. This outlook emphasizes the notion of political community, its definition of accepted social relations, as well as acknowledged roles such as citizen, bureaucrat, elected politician, or court official. In contrast, the consequentialist logic stresses individual self-interest and views political order as an aggregation of rational actor preferences through processes of bargaining, negotiation, and coalition formation.

Even though the logic of appropriateness is an important factor for the effective functioning of large organizations and political orders, it is associated with inefficiency, rigidity, and incrementalism. In contemporary democracies, rules provide procedural and substantive fairness and protect individuals from the power of authorities and resource-rich actors. In an increasingly complicated institutionalized environment, however, the scope of action based on tacit understanding increases, as do the political opportunities of individuals with economic or intellectual resources.

—*Jörg Balsiger*

See also Bureaucracy; Communicative Action; Communicative Rationality; Decision Making; Institutionalization; Rational Choice Theory

Further Readings and References

March, J. G., & Olsen, J. P. (1989). *Rediscovering institutions: The organizational basis of politics*. New York: Free Press.
March, J. G., & Olsen, J. P. (1995). *Democratic governance*. New York: Free Press.

Majority Cycle

A majority cycle is a majority voting system's bias leading to a circular result, namely, every alternative loses to at least one other alternative. From both rational and ethical perspectives, majority cycles are undesirable because they undermine the principle of transitivity and are unsuitable for reaching consistent decisions.

The discovery of this phenomenon lies in the works of M. J. Condorcet, illustrated by his famous voting paradox. Drawing on the works of J. C. Borda, who exposed in 1781 that the result of an election largely depended on the voting rules—majority voting or individual ranking of candidates by voters—Condorcet demonstrated in 1785 that the method of simple majority voting may yield a majority cycle. In the simplest case of a poll composed by three voters and three candidates:

1. A (two votes) defeats B (one vote)

2. B (two votes) defeats C (one vote)

3. C (two votes) defeats A (one vote)

This election outcome is not stable. In this case, there is no Condorcet winner—a candidate who is undefeated by any other feasible alternative—because a majority cycle occurs (A>B>C>A). This result is paradoxical because it violates rationality to maintain the moral principle of majority.

The heuristic potential of majority cycles was rediscovered in 1951 by K. J. Arrow through his investigations on collective decision-making systems. In 1963, Arrow acknowledged that, from a formal viewpoint, a decision-making system based on the aggregation of individual preferences must ensure their transitivity (if A>B and B>C, then A>C) and completeness (if A and B are candidates, the only alternatives are A>B and B>A). Such ideal systems also should comply with four moral axioms. First, whatever the individual preference orderings are, there should be defined a collective preference ordering. Second, if an individual prefers A to B and the other individuals' preferences remain the same, the social welfare function should ensure that society still prefers A to B. Third, collective preferences made from any set of available candidates should depend only on individual preferences with respect to those candidates. Fourth, collective preferences should not depend on one individual whose preferences overcome the preferences of the other individuals.

As Arrow pointed out, these rational and moral conditions are mutually incompatible. As a consequence, no voting system is able to avoid the formation of majority cycles and also be legitimate. This theorem has inspired an important literature on various solutions to this impossibility by reducing, multiplying, or reformulating Arrow's postulates.

—*Jean-Baptiste Harguindéguy*

See also Election; Impossibility Theorem; Positive Political Theory; Rational Choice Theory

Further Readings and References

Arrow, K. J. (1951). *Social choice and individual values.* New Haven, CT: Yale University Press.

Arrow, K. J., Sen, A., & Suzumura, K. (Eds.). (2002). *Handbook of social choice and welfare* (Vol. I). Amsterdam: Elsevier.

Borda, J. C. (1781). Mémoire sur les Élections au Scrutin. *Histoire de l'académie.* Paris: Royale des Sciences.

Condorcet, M. J. (1785). *Essai sur l'application de l'analyse à la probabilité des décisions rendues à la pluralité des voix* [Essay on the application of the analysis to the probability of majority decisions]. Paris: Imprimerie Royale.

MARKET

In the standard conception, markets are spaces in which buyers and sellers (collectively, market agents) decide consumption and production based on price signals. Production, consumption, and price levels are often referred to as market outcomes.

Governance by markets and market governance connote two different conceptual and institutional devices. Governance by markets means that markets are employed to allocate resources instead of other mechanisms. Market governance is about the set of organizations and rules that governs how a market operates.

Theoretical Approaches to Markets and Governance

The relationship between markets and governance has been envisioned variously by neoclassical economists, new institutional economists, and political economists.

Neoclassical economists begin with the standard market perspective. Ideal markets are Pareto optimal mechanisms for allocating resources toward production and consumption. A number of assumptions define ideal markets. These assumptions can be violated in practice. Violations lead to inefficiency. Identifying violations and what to do to restore efficiency constitutes the neoclassical discourse.

In this discourse, liberal economists often emphasize that problems in markets stem from outside interference (or interventions) that distort the signals received by market agents. The appropriate policy response is to structure governance to allow market agents to receive the correct signals and to decide for themselves based on these signals. In cases where production and consumption decisions are not made in markets, the appropriate policy response is to introduce markets so that efficiency can be increased.

Opposed to the liberals, welfare economists emphasize that markets seldom do well on their own. The appropriate response is to make markets efficient with help from nonmarket agents such as government regulators. When they deem nonmarket agents incapable of correcting markets, welfare economists can argue for altogether abandoning markets in favor of alternative modes of production and consumption decision making such as government or other hierarchical mediation.

Outside the neoclassical discourse, new institutional economists emphasize that particular rules and regulatory organizations are critical to how markets operate. Property rights and their enforcement are particularly important. In addition, institutional economics emphasizes that costs associated with transacting in markets decide whether markets or alternatives are the efficient mechanisms for organizing how resources are used. Important alternatives include hierarchies and networks.

Political economists emphasize the political underpinnings and consequences of markets rather than free market assumptions. In this perspective, markets are primarily about distributing resources among groups or classes in society. The ways markets are governed enshrine particular bargains among dominant social actors and perpetuate the power of these actors. Political economists show that political bargains also lead to alternatives to market-based resource distribution such as the state or corporatist institutions.

Governance by Markets

Markets are one approach to allocating resources in society. This meaning is captured in the notion of a market economy. In a market economy, markets are the prevailing mode for distributing resources to production and consumption. An important historical alternative to market economies was the planned economies of the Soviet sphere of influence. In these economies, states dominated decisions about production and consumption.

Market economies come in different varieties. Differentiating factors include how actively the state works and how much social organizations work together to shape market outcomes. Market economies in which states play active roles are variously referred to as statist, dirigiste, or developmental. Market economies in which social organizations work together closely are often referred to as corporatist or coordinated. Market economies in which the state is less active and social organizations work together less are often referred to as liberal.

In public administration, the market has gained currency as a mechanism for economic decisions within the public sector. This corresponds to the emergence of the reform movement generally referred to as new public management, or NPM. A significant component of NPM is to shift resource allocations out of hierarchical bureaucracies into market type mechanisms, or MTMs. These types of reforms began in the 1980s in countries like Britain, New Zealand, and the United States. Many other countries have since used MTMs to reform their systems of public administration.

MTMs do not have to implement markets in full. Some take market features and introduce them into the public sector. For instance, many health care systems, including those in Sweden and Britain, have split sellers from buyers and have mostly retained public responsibility and ownership on both sides. Several government organizations, including many in New Zealand and the Netherlands, have been handed managerial autonomy on the model of private firms in a market.

Some MTMs introduce markets more completely. For instance, many services that governments once produced themselves have been contracted out (outsourced) to private firms or nonprofit organizations. This includes many technical support functions, but it also includes creating charter schools in the United States or contracting with specialty surgery units for elective treatments in public systems of health care. More recently, governments have also begun to allow private financing of public infrastructure and buildings. These projects are commonly known as public-private partnerships, or PPPs.

Market Governance

Where they exist, markets are embedded in regulations. Contracts define the relationship between buyers and sellers. Legislation supports and defines the content of contracts. But contracts are usually incomplete, calling for dispute resolution mechanisms. Courts and arbitrators help to resolve disputes.

Often organizations of the government are tasked with the regulation and enforcement of markets. An example is antitrust regulatory agencies. These agencies exist to ensure that competition is maintained in markets throughout an economy. Another example is securities market regulators. These exist to ensure compliance with the regulations of securities markets. This structure of contracts, legislation, dispute resolution mechanisms, and regulatory authority defines how markets are governed.

—*Erik Baekkeskov*

See also Capitalism; Competitiveness; Consumption; Coordination; Corporatism; Efficiency; Global Market; Hierarchy; Internal Market; Market Failure; Marketization; Network; New Institutionalism; New Public Management; Political Economy; Professionalism; Property Rights; Regulation; Varieties of Capitalism

Further Readings and References

North, D. C. (1990). *Institutions, institutional change and economic performance.* Cambridge, UK: Cambridge University Press.

Pindyck, R. S., & Rubinfeld, D. L. (2005). *Microeconomics.* Upper Saddle River, NJ: Prentice Hall.

Pollitt, C., & Bouckaert, G. (2004). *Public management reform: A comparative analysis.* Oxford, UK: Oxford University Press.

Williamson, O. (1975). *Markets and hierarchies, analysis and antitrust implications.* New York: Free Press.

MARKET FAILURE

Markets are said to fail when they deliver an outcome that falls short of the socially optimal or Pareto optimal result. In particular, the economic theory of market failure seeks to account for inefficient outcomes in markets that otherwise conform to the assumptions about markets held by neoclassical economics (i.e., markets that feature perfect competition, symmetrical information, and completeness). When failure happens, less welfare is created than could be created given the available resources. The social task then becomes to correct the failure.

The theory of market failure is at the heart of several economic analyses that support government action (intervention) in markets for goods and services or that justify outright government production. Many social welfare programs find their theoretical justification in market failure or in other violations of the standard market assumptions.

Criticism of the market failure notion and of using government to remedy its effects has been articulated in the public choice school of economics. Public choice scholarship has had great impact on contemporary reforms of the public sector, replacing the Keynesian and welfare economics logics that drove much public service expansion. Recent reforms that replace governments with markets to challenge or remedy market failure have been the practical consequence of these critiques.

The Theory

The descriptions of market failure were developed in the middle of the twentieth century as part of a larger school of Keynesian welfare and macroeconomics. Important contributors include Arthur C. Pigou, Francis Bator, William Baumol, and Paul A. Samuelson.

The theorists were concerned with the correspondence between free market outcomes and social welfare optimization. In standard economics, the invisible hand or duality theorem holds that *laissez-faire* market performance and Pareto optimality go hand in hand. When consumers and producers respond to price signals, they make their own decisions about whether to buy or sell and how to produce the good. The aggregate of these choices is the same as the Pareto optimal or socially optimal distribution. Welfare economists were concerned with conditions under which this correspondence failed and sought to describe such conditions.

The interest in exceptions to the invisible hand theorem led to the study of violations of the standard market assumptions. These assumptions include perfect competition, perfect information, complete markets, and the absence of market failures. Markets fail under any of three conditions: production has increasing economies of scale; goods in the market are public; or production or consumption has externalities.

Increasing Economies of Scale

When producing one more of a good leads to a lower average cost of producing each good, production of the good has increasing economies of scale. Economists have found that when economies of scale increase regardless of how much is produced, few or no firms can survive as producers in the market. The standard concern with increasing economies of scale is that market forces will lead to monopoly production. Monopolies are sole providers of goods in a market, so they can charge any price they find suits their needs. Economists find that this leads to a suboptimal level of production and consumption. In addition, increasing scales may push all producers out of a market if none can charge enough to cover costs. In this case, production ceases even if it benefits society. Hence, markets fail under increasing economies of scale.

Historically, several services necessary to running a modern economy were considered to have increasing economies of scale. Such services were often thought of as natural monopolies because free markets would create monopolies from them. These included telephone and other telecommunications, postal services, and electrical and water utilities. Since the early 1980s, however, the increasing economies of scale proposition has been challenged for these types of services.

Public Goods

Public goods are socially beneficial but are almost never produced by free markets. Three attributes of a good render it public. One is that no person can be excluded from using the good (nonexcludability).

Another is that one person using it does not prevent another from using it (nonrivalry). The final one is that no person can reject using the good (non-rejectability). When a good has these attributes, no single individual will pay for the good unless the individual gains so much utility from it that he or she can pay for the entire cost of producing it. This is because individuals can enjoy the good without paying for it—they can "free ride" on those who pay for it and "shirk their duty" to pay without losing the good. So in all but exceptional cases, public goods will not be produced by the private market, even though substantial parts of society benefit from having them.

Classical examples of public goods are streets, parks, national defense, broadcasts, and lighthouses. To use national defense as an illustration, whether or not citizens pay for it, the national armed forces will provide defense for them. Foreign invasions are denied, providing a benefit to each individual. But because individuals benefit regardless of whether they pay, few are likely to pay if they have a choice. If defense were a good in the market, it would earn no revenue because no one has to pay to enjoy it. But providing defense is costly, so no producers would undertake the task because they cannot make money doing so. The market has then failed because there would be no national defense, even though such defense is arguably socially optimal because it deters armed invasion.

Externalities

When goods are produced, they may create consequences that no one pays for. Such unaccounted-for consequences are called externalities. Because externalities are not accounted for in the costs and prices of the free market, market agents will receive the wrong signals and allocate resources toward bad externalities and away from good externalities.

Good externalities are consequences that benefit society. However, because these benefits are not accounted for in the price of the good, the price is higher than it should be, and too little of the good is consumed and produced. Bad externalities harm

society. However, because the costs of these externalities are not accounted for in the price of the good, the price is lower than it should be, and too much of the good is consumed and produced. In both cases, the market has failed to reach efficiency because it has allocated resources and production without considering the externalities.

Classical examples of bad externalities include industrial pollution and traffic congestion. Industrial pollution has harmful effects on people and the environment. Yet, the cost of producing goods does not include the cost of dealing with the effects of pollution. This means that in the free market, producers are responding to costs that are too low, and consumers are facing prices that are too low. More goods are produced and sold in the free market than should be, given the negative social effects of pollution.

An example of good externalities is private home renovation. Renovation has a beneficial effect beyond the renovated home because it increases property values in the neighborhood. But these benefits are not included in the home owners' calculations in a free market because their neighbors do not pay them to renovate. As a result, fewer home owners renovate in the free market than the beneficial social effects would justify.

Historical Remedies for Market Failure

In practice, the discovery of market failure helped arguments for sustaining government production, expanding social welfare programs, and market regulatory action in the 1960s and 1970s. If the goal is to achieve social efficiency, and if markets cannot provide it alone, the next step is to find a supplement to help the market or even to replace it as the means of distributing resources. The common thread in many polities was to remedy market failure with government-based initiatives.

Government has significant capacities that have been applied to counter market failure. Public goods can be produced by the government for the benefit of all citizens. Government can impose and collect taxes to pay for the goods so that no free riders or duty shirkers can sustain their behavior. The government can impose costs for negative externalities through taxes or fees on individual producers and consumers and encourage positive externalities through tax breaks or subsidies for the market agents. Monopolies can be regulated to limit price excesses or production encouraged through subsidies when a product has increasing economies of scale.

Welfare services, including education, child care, elderly care, and health care, are considered by many welfare theorists as sectors where markets fail. Suboptimal distribution of access to these services in free markets is most often at the heart of these arguments. Here, the suboptimal outcomes include that some citizens cannot access welfare services or that the welfare service levels available are not the same for all citizens. In place of markets, government can mandate or directly provide access for all citizens, and it can regulate or directly produce the desired level of service.

The post–World War II era saw dramatic expansions of government-based welfare service programs in most industrialized countries. The extent and character of programs vary considerably. But common to them is that they have constituted a major part of government activity, including spending and public employment, since the late 1960s in even the least expansionary countries such as the United States. This scale and scope has made welfare programs a prime target for government reformers, fiscal conservatives, and critics of welfare economic theory.

Contemporary Reforms and Market Failure

The practical critique of welfare economics challenges the reliance on governments to remedy market shortcomings. This critique is often associated with public choice theorists and the Austrian school of economics. If markets can fail to deliver socially optimal outcomes, so can governments. Bureaucrats are not altruistic but, rather, act from self-interest. Traditional civil service processes are opaque and make bureaucrats unaccountable for their actions. Incentives in the civil service promote decisions that are incompatible

with efficient production. These attributes of civil services lead to more inefficient production than open market conditions would yield. Markets may fail, but governments fail more. So if we are to solve market failures, government is not the answer.

Reforms of the public sector, in particular the variety developed in Britain and New Zealand in the 1980s, have relied on public choice scholarship for inspiration and guidance. Privatization, contracting out, and rationalization of public administration have changed how governments act to deal with market failure. The general trend in these reforms has been to introduce markets to alleviate the shortcomings of government controls while questioning or eliminating the conditions for market failure.

The most significant changes have probably been in how governments understand increasing economies of scale production. Whether or not telecommunications, utilities, and postal services are increasing returns to scale across all levels of output was challenged in the early 1980s. Before this, the consensus throughout the industrialized world was that they were. Hence, leaving production to the free market was inefficient because it would result in monopolies or no production at all. This logic could justify that governments either owned these producers or tightly regulated their pricing and structure. But beginning in the early 1980s, this consensus ended, and governments throughout the industrialized world have sold their stakes in these operations in whole or in part, or have broken up regulated, private monopolies. Evidence also indicates that governments have significantly increased their roles in market regulation in place of exercising ownership control. In general, governments now focus on setting the terms for property rights and competition. Pricing and production levels are left to individual firm and consumer decisions in the markets.

There are also initiatives that seek to introduce markets in place of government to deal with externalities. One is to make markets in air pollution rights in place of limits, taxes, and fines on individual producers. The 1990 amendment to the U.S. Clean Air Act introduced sulfur emissions rights, a market for trading them, and a total allowable level of sulfur emissions. The amendment set limits on the total allowable levels of sulfur in the air. It distributed Tradable Discharge Permits (TDPs) for sulfur among existing polluters. The act also implemented the Allowance Trading System, which lets polluters sell or buy rights from one another. In the period up to the year 2000, the U.S. government gradually decreased the total allowable level of sulfur emissions, but left the negotiation and distribution of the impact to market decisions by polluters. This reform attempts to transform sulfur pollution from an externality to a part of the cost structure of individual sulfur emitters.

Finally, goods traditionally considered public have been reconsidered. A prominent example is inner-city road pricing in London, England. Here, technology has affected the nonexcludability of public streets. Access to city streets is physically unrestricted. But by registering the cars that use the streets electronically and charging their owners, London is now able to charge users for the privilege. This effectively excludes drivers who are unwilling to pay. London streets are no longer strictly a public good.

—Erik Baekkeskov

See also Competition Policy; Efficiency; Externalities; Functionalism; Market; Monopoly; New Public Management; Public Choice Theory; Public Goods; Regulation; Unemployment; Welfare Reform

Further Readings and References

Barr, N. (2004). *Economics of the welfare state.* Oxford, UK: Oxford University Press.

Bator, F. (1958). The anatomy of market failure. *Quarterly Journal of Economics, 72,* 351–379.

Donahue, J. D. (1988). *The privatization decision.* New York: Basic Books.

Esping-Andersen, G. (1990). *Three worlds of welfare capitalism.* Princeton, NJ: Princeton University Press.

Samuelson, P. A. (1954). The pure theory of public expenditures. *Review of Economics and Statistics, 36,* 387–389.

Savas, E. S. (1987). *Privatization: The key to better government.* Chatham, NJ: Chatham House.

Steele, G. R. (1993). *The economics of Friedrich Hayek.* New York: St. Martin's.

Vif, N., & Kraft, M. (Eds.). (1997). *Environmental policy in the 1990s.* Washington, DC: CQ Press.

MARKETIZATION

Marketization involves introducing competition into the public sector in areas previously governed through direct public control. In its broadest usage, marketization refers to the process of transforming an entire economy away from a planned economic system and toward greater market-based organization. This process might include the liberalization of economic activity (e.g., removing price controls), reducing regulation, and opening the system for market-based allocation of resources. In more narrow terms, marketization refers to changes within the public sector, where market mechanisms and incentives are introduced within public or publicly regulated organizations. Marketization, in this sense, might include reforms that introduce contracting out or outsourcing components of public provision, client vouchers, stimulating competition among the providers of goods and services for public funding, or creating incentives for entrepreneurial responsibility in the delivery of goods and services. Marketization, then, can occur in varying degrees, from liberalizing an entire economy or economic sector to introducing more limited competition within a sector where the government continues to control entry and exit and pricing. What is common to these different approaches is that each, to some extent, shifts toward guiding the production and allocation of goods and services through market incentives rather than direct governance through command and control or network forms of organization.

Although marketization is often complementary to the move toward privatization, it is conceptually distinct. Privatization involves moving toward more private financing or private ownership of goods or services and can occur both with and without increased incentives for market competition. Equally, some forms of marketization can occur without a change in ownership. For instance, a number of governments have introduced market incentives within the public sector, creating an "internal market" where public organizations compete with each other.

The core motivating rationale for marketization is that increased competition within a sector will stimulate efficiency gains. Work on reforms to public or regulated utilities suggests that the threat of competitor entry may be enough to stimulate significant efficiency gains in markets for goods and services, even without direct privatization of ownership. This logic is central to most economic theory that advocates the gains associated with market-based organizations. In more restricted form, these arguments have also been advanced in the literature on public administration reform. In particular, scholars in the new public management school argue the introduction of competition or market incentives in the public sector, in lieu of public monopoly provision, will stimulate greater efficiency, innovation, and overall performance.

The process of marketization raises two related issues for public governance. The first involves the changing nature of public accountability. John Donahue and Joseph Nye argued in 2002 that the move toward marketization in the public sector substitutes "extensive" for "intensive" accountability. Put differently, marketization takes one away from a broad-based accountability on multiple fronts to multiple actors and toward more narrowly defined accountability based on market transactions. What this means is the government and service providers move toward being accountable for particular results in the delivery of the service rather than all aspects of the good or service. This movement raises a second question about how more intensive accountability can be introduced and maintained. Marketization can require a considerable extension and use of government power. Moving toward greater market forces in the economy or in the provision of public services often involves considerable regulatory capacity to ensure the rules of the market are adhered to and may involve transaction costs in defining outcomes and monitoring the activity of providers of services. Marketization, then, often requires a restructuring of public governance rather than a reduction of it.

A number of countries have introduced significant marketizing reforms during the past two decades with particularly dramatic effects in countries transitioning out of socialist economies. The reform of these non-market economies was most pronounced during the so-called big-bang period during the early 1990s in the post-Soviet states. These reforms moved quickly away from economic planning to a market-based economy and often combined wholesale privatization of the state-owned economy with a movement toward marketization in price liberalization and reduced regulation. Some commentators have argued that the marketization of the previously socialist economies occurred too rapidly and was conducted in too piecemeal a fashion to support the accompanying mass privatizations, thus leading to low levels of actual competition.

Marketization has also been a common strategy in the reform of the public sector in market-based economies. A number of countries began to marketize utilities and other public services beginning in the early 1980s. For instance, in the area of utilities such as electricity and telecommunication, some countries like the United Kingdom moved toward both marketizing and privatizing these sectors, whereas in Norway and Sweden, marketization occurred primarily within the public sector. In both cases, the energy and communication markets were opened to greater competition, and incumbent providers were transformed into corporate entities and given responsibility to respond to market incentives. Although marketization has been used less extensively in public social services such as health, education, and social care, a number of countries have introduced market elements in these areas as well. These reforms include, for instance, the introduction of school vouchers in public education systems, purchaser-provider splits in health care systems, and contracting out for services in care for the elderly.

—*Jane Gingrich*

See also Agency; Consumption; Internal Market; Market; New Public Management; Purchaser-Provider Split

Further Readings and References

Baumol, W., Panzar, J., & Willig, R. (1988). *Contestable markets and the theory of industry structure* (rev. ed.). San Diego, CA: Harcourt, Brace.

Donahue, J. D., & Nye, J. S. (Eds.). (2002). *Market-based governance: Supply side, demand side, upside, and downside (Visions of governance in the 21st century).* Washington, DC: Brookings Institution.

MARXISM

Marxism was born amid nineteenth-century social and political struggles, based on the writings of Karl Marx, and the close relationship between Marxist scholarship and revolutionary politics persisted well into the twentieth century. After the revolutions in the Soviet Union and China, Marxism became the official state ideology. Elsewhere, however, Marxism followed a different trajectory. In post–World War II Western Europe, socialist and "Eurocommunist" parties enjoyed great prestige. Marxist scholarship made significant advances and gradually broke free from the prevailing "official" Marxism. In the United States, where the socialist tradition was weaker, however, Marxist scholarship was sharply constrained as a result of the Cold War and McCarthyism, named for U.S. Senator Joseph McCarthy. During the 1960s, Marxism enjoyed a worldwide renaissance. Energized by the New Left as well as the global movement against colonialism and imperialism, a vibrant academic Marxism flourished in the West and became influential throughout the humanities and social sciences. However, the collapse of the post–World War II social settlement, disillusionment with "real existing socialism," and neoliberal "triumphalism" have greatly diminished the impact of Marxism. Revolutionary socialist parties and movements have been eclipsed by more narrowly focused social and antiglobalization movements as well as the preoccupation with identity and ethnicity. In many regions of the world, Marxism has been displaced by religious fundamentalism, and in the former Soviet Bloc, it has become virtually extinct. Finally, profound changes in the nature of production and work have led to a more fragmented and heterogeneous working class, thereby challenging key Marxist assumptions about the nature of class consciousness and working-class solidarity. Hence, Marxist politics have fallen into disarray, although Marxism could revive and resume its historical mission in future generations. Nevertheless, Marxist scholarship remains influential in Europe and, to a lesser extent, in the United States.

Concepts and Theories

Marxism is both a philosophy of science (dialectical materialism) and a theory of history (historical materialism). Marxism seeks to explain human social evolution by identifying a causal process that is internal to history and is focused on the transformational changes occurring in the most advanced and dynamic societies within a given mode of production. The mode of production refers to the set of property relations (e.g., feudalism or capitalism) within a given historical period that ultimately shape the legal and political superstructure as well as individual and collective consciousness. Put schematically, history can be understood as a progression from slave societies to feudalism, capitalism, socialism, and finally to communism.

All pre-communist modes of production are characterized by distinctive forms of exploitation and resultant class struggle. Within each, internal contradictions arise and intensify as the forces of production—technology, social organization, and class consciousness—develop and eventually conflict with social relations of production. The maturation of these forces in tandem with sharpening class consciousness and political leadership establish the conditions for a social revolution that gives birth to a more advanced stage of history.

The concept of proletarian revolution distinguishes Marxism from alternative interpretations of socialism and social democracy. Capitalism generates vast wealth in the form of profits (surplus value), but the ability of capitalists to distribute these profits to the working class is circumscribed by the need to maximize capital accumulation to compete favorably with rival capitalists. Capitalist economies routinely produce mass poverty and suffering and generate progressively more serious and more generalized global crises that cannot be resolved as a result of government intervention. The conditions of collective or social labor under capitalism provide the basis for the working class to become conscious of itself as a class and to recognize the necessity of socialist revolution. The "dictatorship of the proletariat" is a transitional stage that paves the way for the eventual abolition of classes and private property, culminating in a new phase of human history—communism. Because the concept of revolution is clearly at the center of Marxist thought, the resilience of global capitalism and the experiences of the Soviet Union and China present a serious challenge to Marxism. Nevertheless, Marxist scholarship with respect to history and contemporary capitalism retains considerable moral and analytical force.

Class and State

The Marxist conception of the state throws a spotlight on the fundamental basis of social power, an issue that is seldom addressed explicitly in the mainstream literature. With respect to scholarship on the state, Marxism provides a clear contrast to its mainstream competitors. Marxism provides a distinctive theory of the state in capitalist society and one that can be tested empirically and in rivalry with competing theories.

Mainstream approaches to political science and sociology view the capitalist state as either a neutral actor that is connected to society in theoretically unspecified ways (pluralism and social constructivism) or as an autonomous entity that has its own interests and preferences that are distinct from society and is capable of acting independently of social forces (state autonomy). Despite their many differences, these mainstream schools of thought share important similarities insofar as they adopt an essentially open-ended view of the possibilities for state action, which is assumed to result variously from public opinion, the preferences of various interest groups or factions, no one of which is assumed to be preponderant, shared norms and values, the beliefs and preferences of government officials, or the imperatives of geopolitics. Marxism, by contrast, proposes an organic connection between the state and the capitalist class that sharply circumscribes the limits of the possible in both domestic and foreign policy. The state is not neutral in its relation to society but, rather, serves as the agent of the ruling class in its struggle with the proletariat as well as with rival capitalist classes. The state must simultaneously undertake a set of potentially contradictory tasks: maintain the coherence of the ruling

class, contain the demands of the working class, and facilitate capital accumulation. Instrumentalist Marxist scholars have focused on the personal connections between leading state officials and members of the ruling class. Top government officials and politicians are generally drawn from elite social and cultural networks and develop a special sympathy for the problems of big business. These networks are especially well defined and exclusive in the area of foreign policy. Structuralist Marxists, by contrast, have emphasized the ways in which state actions are circumscribed by systemic factors. Regardless of their social and financial status, elected officials and civil servants are "structurally" linked to capital by virtue of the need to establish economic and political conditions favorable to capital accumulation as well as by their dependence on the approval of an essentially corporate media for electoral or policy success. Structuralists have expanded the definition of the state to the "ideology apparatus," including schools, churches, political parties, and the media. The need to promote acquiescence and stability in domestic politics and (to a much lesser extent) in the international sphere through granting concessions to subordinate classes and countries gives the state an outward appearance of neutrality, but the special bias toward capital and the need to promote capital accumulation is a distinctive and permanent feature. Social democratic critics of Marx have argued that political revolution is unnecessary because the link between the capitalist class and the state can be broken as a result of gradual reforms within the framework of the existing liberal democratic state. However, if the experience of "real existing socialism" casts grave doubt on Marx's revolutionary theory, the inability to sustain the social democratic project in the face of the neoliberal offensive has also challenged the logic of "parliamentary socialism."

The capitalist state is inevitably drawn into the international sphere—and consequently imperialist rivalry—as a result of the concentration and centralization of capital and the need to accumulate capital on a global scale. Marx recognized that colonialism played a key role in the early phase of capitalism or what he called "primitive accumulation." It was left to his successors to interpret variously the specific causes and consequences of a new phase of imperialism around the turn of the twentieth century. Whereas reformists such as the German socialist Karl Kautsky contended on the eve of World War I that the interdependence of global capital had given rise to a new stage of imperialism that rendered war obsolete, the Russian Marxist V. I. Lenin argued that the development of large-scale firms only intensified great power rivalry over access to raw materials and markets.

As capitalism evolved through the twentieth century, and especially after World War II, the leading imperialist powers became more actively involved in securing the social and political conditions for the reproduction of the labor force and the maintenance of market discipline. The concept of hegemony refers to the systematic supervisory functions that leading states, such as the United States in the post–World War II era, have undertaken. Although there is no "higher authority," imperialist rivalry can be moderated through the actions of a hegemonic power willing and able to maintain global order.

Marxist Scholarship in the Social Sciences

Since the 1960s, Marxists have made important contributions to scholarship in the social sciences. Within the field of history, revisionists rejected the prevailing Western Cold War narrative of Soviet aggression by reinterpreting American foreign policy to highlight the relationship between twentieth-century expansion and the requirements of American capitalism. These accounts resonated especially in the context of the Vietnam War and anticolonial struggles. Historical sociologists sought to explain various paths to European absolutist and bourgeois state formation in terms of the balance of power among peasantry, gentry, and industrial bourgeoisie. Marxists criticized mainstream economics for its narrow focus on prices at the expense of power relations. Marxists sought to elucidate the political bases of the national and international marketplace and applied crisis theories to understand the limits of Keynesian and neoclassical economists in the context of stagflation and uneven

development. The critique of Soviet orthodoxy led to rediscovery of the work of the Italian Marxist, Antonio Gramsci, whose concept of hegemony pointed to the role of ideas and agency in the mediation of social and political struggles.

Marxism was especially influential in the development of the subdiscipline of international political economy. Whereas liberal theories proposed a "diffusionist" or "stages of growth" model in which third-world countries developed through integration with the world market, dependency theorists adapted Marxist theories of imperialism to highlight the power relationship between the center and the periphery. Integration within the metropolitan division of labor had produced not generalized development but, rather, "the development of underdevelopment." Multinational corporations were envisioned as agents of monopoly power and exploitation. During the late 1960s and early 1970s, debates centered on the various strategies by which third-world countries could break their ties of dependency.

If the late 1960s and early 1970s represented the heyday of post–World War II academic Marxism, the late 1970s saw efforts to reassert concepts and theories that explicitly or implicitly challenged Marxist scholarship. Whereas during Marxism's renaissance the fields of political science and historical sociology were greatly influenced by society-centric approaches in which class conflict played a crucial role, beginning in the mid-1970s, there was a concerted effort to introduce theories and concepts designed to "bring the state back in" and thereby to challenge the causal role of social forces, including classes, in historical and contemporary developments. In proposing the "potential autonomy" of political institutions, state-centric models recalled more traditional approaches in political science deriving from institutionalism and public administration.

During the 1980s, dependency theory also experienced a withering attack. Realist critics argued that dependency theorists underestimated the latitude enjoyed by many third-world countries in their negotiations with Western banks and multinational corporations over the terms of trade and investment, while liberals cited the absence of alternatives to market integration. The critique of dependency theory clearly resonated in the context of 1970s commodity cartels, when third-world countries did gain political leverage. However, it was less clear by the 1980s that the debt crisis and the resulting International Monetary Fund (IMF)–imposed structural adjustment programs supported assumptions of mainstream development economists, even if dependency theorists could provide no convincing alternative to reliance on the world market.

A third counterattack emerged in the context of growing interest in democratic transitions as many Latin American countries emerged from authoritarian rule and the Soviet Bloc collapsed. Whereas pluralists traditionally argued that democracy resides in the clash of competing interest groups operating independently of the state, Marxists have asserted that the emphasis on interest groups overlooks the state's role in maintaining capitalism and the resulting limitations of liberal democracy. The widespread use of the concept of "civil society" reintroduced pluralist assumptions into the debate over democratic transitions. The concept reflected liberal suspicions of concentrated power but also de-emphasized the continuing role of national and international capitalism as factors that would limit the scope of democracy.

The turn to social constructivism constituted yet another challenge to Marxism. Against historical materialism, which seeks to understand the social and economic foundations of ideas, the constructivist emphasis on intersubjectivity and ideas represented a return to Talcott Parsons's structural-functionalism, which asserted the primacy of ideas as causal factors. Constructivism also accorded with the postmodern *zeitgeist,* which expressed skepticism about the veracity of historical narratives, the possibility of human progress, and indeed, the existence of objective knowledge.

Marxism and Global Governance

Although driven to the margins in many of the social sciences, Marxism has remained influential in the subfield of international political economy, and Marxist scholars have developed novel and influential interpretations concerning the causes and consequences of globalization and its implications for global governance.

Whereas mainstream political scientists and international relations scholars have tended to understand globalization through economic and technological change, Marxist scholars have sought to explain globalization as a new type of accumulation or regulatory regime. During the Bretton Woods period, a Fordist regime of regulation based on mass consumption and full employment emerged. This regulatory regime was grounded in the post–World War II social settlement between capital and labor and included a strong supervisory role for the state. However, the contradictions in this type of regulation intensified over time, eventually leading to the collapse of the regime and the emergence of a new neoliberal regulatory regime based on market discipline and a diminished welfare state. The causes of the collapse of Fordism have been variously attributed to the internal logic of capital accumulation leading to the falling rate of profit, or to a profit squeeze generated by militant labor empowered by a generation of full employment. Further debate has centered on the extent to which nation-states or regions such as the European Union (EU) can retain elements of the welfare state under conditions of capital mobility, and whether neoliberalism will eventually precipitate a generalized crisis of legitimacy.

Marxist scholars have also stressed the centrality of U.S. power in the transition to globalization and the tentative movement toward new forms of global governance. The United States has used its massive political and economic leverage to construct a transnational financial and monetary order that displaces economic and social contradictions from the United States to other parts of the world. Global governance and doctrines of humanitarian intervention with the implicit diminution of sovereignty have advanced American political and economic power, as evidenced by the trend toward unilateral intervention and the invasion and occupation of Iraq and the growing power of U.S.–led international economic institutions such as the IMF and World Trade Organization.

The unilateral deployment of American economic and military power under conditions of globalization raises a number of important questions concerning the future of global governance. A first question concerns the possibility that an alternative source of power such as the EU can emerge. A second set of questions concerns the potential instabilities deriving from an increasingly unstable American imperium, which despite its military and financial power is experiencing massive trade and budget deficits as well as significant deindustrialization. There is also debate concerning the nature of inter-imperialist rivalry under conditions of globalization. Marxist theories of imperialism have traditionally assumed an organic and more or less permanent relationship between national ruling classes and states. In recent years, however, "transnational historical materialists" have hypothesized that national states, and by implication national capitalist classes, are giving way to global or regional transnational ruling classes. According to this interpretation, inter-imperialist rivalry is dissolving into imminent global or regional class formations. This debate, which revisits the aforementioned debate between Kautsky and Lenin, thus brings Marxist theories of globalization and governance full circle.

—*Alan Cafruny*

See also Antiglobalization; Business Cycle; Capitalism; Communism; Economic Sociology; Fordism and Post-Fordism; Gramscian Theory; Hegemony; Neo-Marxism; Pluralism; Pluralist Democracy; Polyarchy; Regulation Theory; State; State-Society Relations; Varieties of Capitalism

Further Readings and References

Amin, S. (2004). *Obsolescent capitalism: Contemporary politics and global disorder*. London: Zed Books.

Cafruny, A., & Ryner, M. (Eds.). (2003). *A ruined fortress? Neoliberal hegemony and transformation in Europe*. Boulder, CO: Rowman & Littlefield.

Dumenil, G., & Levy, D. (2004). *Capital resurgent: Roots of the neoliberal resurgence*. Cambridge, MA: Harvard University Press.

Gowan, P. (1999). *The global gamble: Washington's Faustian bid for global dominance*. London: Verso Books.

Jessop, B. (2002). *The future of the capitalist state*. London: Polity Press.

Levine, A. (2003). *A future for Marxism? Althusser, the analytical turn, and the revival of socialist theory*. London: Pluto Press.

Rosenberg, J. (1994). *The empire of civil society: A critique of the realist theory of international relations*. London: Verso Books.

Rupert, M., & Smith, H. (Eds.). (2002). *Historical materialism and globalization*. London: Routledge.

van der Pijl, K. (1984). *The making of an Atlantic ruling class*. London: Verso Books.

Wood, E. M. (2003). *Empire of capital*. London: Verso Books.

MATRIX ORGANIZATION

Matrix organization describes a system characterized by a form of management with multiple chains of command. Unlike a traditional hierarchy in which each worker has one boss, a matrix system requires employees to report to two or more managers, each responsible for a different aspect of the organization's overall product or service (see Table 1).

For example, a video producer working at an advertising firm might report to the head of the media department (functional chain of command) as well as to the project manager for a given client product (project chain of command). The project manager is accountable for the overall performance of the product team, whereas the functional manager is responsible for the technical performance of the particular

Table 1 Matrix System

		Functional Areas			
		Function 1	Function 2	Function 3	Function 4
Project Areas	Project A				
	Project B				
	Project C				

employee task—in this case, video production. The benefits of a matrix organization approach can include improved communication flows, more efficient use of resources, increased flexibility, and better performance resulting from complementary expertise among managers. The drawbacks of a matrix system might include morale problems and conflicting priorities arising from multiple lines of authority, as well as higher overhead costs associated with increased system complexity and redundancy. Because of these challenges, the move from a traditional hierarchy to a matrix system typically requires the adoption of new information and communication technologies, as well as a concentrated effort to reform the organizational culture and expectations of members.

Although it is difficult to trace the exact origins of the matrix organization concept, the term first emerged from the aerospace industry in the 1960s. Aerospace firms that wanted to contract with the government were required to develop charts showing the structure of the project management team that would be executing the contract and how this team was related to the overall management structure of the organization. Rather than completely reconfigure their management systems to meet these requirements, companies chose to create horizontal project units to overlie their existing vertical hierarchies. This helped fulfill both the goal of the consumer—a transparent set of resources fronted by a clear group manager—and the producer's desire for continuity and accountability within the larger organization.

The development of the matrix approach reflects the need for organizations in a number of public and private spheres to adapt to increasing task and environmental complexity. Thus, matrix organizations are most likely to be found among firms and agencies that exhibit high levels of interdependence with environmental actors, high demands for information processing, and high levels of task diversity and complexity.

—*Brent Durbin*

See also Hierarchy; Hybrid Organization

Further Readings and References

Cleland, D. I. (Ed.). (1984). *Matrix management systems handbook.* New York: Van Nostrand Reinhold.

Davis, S. M., & Lawrence, P. R. (1977). *Matrix.* Reading, MA: Addison-Wesley.

Knight, K. (Ed.). (1977). *Matrix management.* New York: PBI-Petrocelli Books.

MEASUREMENT OF GOVERNANCE

Conceptualization must always precede measurement, so before we begin to think about measuring governance we will need to be sure of the meaning of the concept itself. This sequence of intellectual activity is especially important for a complex concept such as governance, which involves multiple actors and multiple activities and has been subject to considerable intellectual debate. In its most fundamental conceptual sense, governance means steering the economy and society toward some collective goals. This function traditionally has been allocated to the formal institutions of government, and although contemporary conceptions of governing tend to emphasize the importance of nongovernmental actors in governance, the public sector must remain a central focus for steering. This central role for the formal institutions of government is especially important when the measurement of success and failure in governance is a central concern. Unless there is a clear set of goals against which to compare outcomes and achievements, there can be no means of assessing governance. In this way, the governance literature in the social sciences is similar to the implementation literature; without a clear target for implementation, it is almost impossible to assess the success or failure of implementation.

Any conception of governance must, however, also have some sense of the dominance of the political and must recognize the role that governing plays in building and maintaining legitimacy for the political system as a whole. Thus, scholars (and practitioners) may want to measure the formal achievement of policy goals through the processes that have been developed for governing (involving private-sector actors to varying degrees) and the political consequences of those policy outcomes. In transitional regimes, building governance capacity may be especially important for legitimating the political system and will need to be at the center of any measurement of governance. Even for more completely institutionalized systems of governing, the effectiveness of the political systems is important for maintaining the confidence of citizens, and hence, becomes a central concern for governance.

Although it is relatively easy to define governance at a conceptual level, moving from the level of ideas to the level of operationalization and measurement is substantially more difficult. Even if the goals being pursued in governance were unambiguous, it might still be difficult to determine whether governance was successful or not. How close to the stated goals must programs approach to say that governance has been successful? Likewise, if there are unintended consequences of policies used to reach goals, how are they to be weighed against the achievement of the stated goals? And given the political nature of governance, how open and democratic does the process need to be, or how much does corruption need to be reduced, to claim that "good governance" has actually occurred, or has been successful?

Even if we could develop the nominal classifications—governance, nongovernance—moving to ordinal or interval levels of measurement would be even more problematic. Thinking in those terms, however, is important for making the governance literature more compatible with most contemporary social sciences that emphasize quantitative methodologies and rigorous measurement of the key concepts. As long as discussions of governance remain almost entirely at the verbal level, they are not likely to become central to the social sciences, although certainly the capacity of a society to govern itself is a key concern for both the social sciences and for real societies.

Types of Governance and Measurement

Measuring governance also becomes at once easier and more complex when we apply adjectives to the term and seek to identify important aspects of the more general concept. For example, the World Bank and other international organizations have been concerned with developing "good governance" in developing and transitional governments. By this term, they have meant primarily the reduction of corruption, and to some extent the improvement of administrative efficiency. There are some reasonable measures of corruption available that provide a picture of differences among systems and changes across time. Likewise, other scholars have been concerned with democratic governance and have sought to measure democracy. Another example of this tendency to qualify the term *governance* is the research on "informal governance," implying that governance is conducted through actors and processes outside formal government.

The more important question, however, is whether those terms measure "good governance" or whether they better measure less grandiose concepts such as reducing corruption. Both conceptually and operationally, it is also important to distinguish governance from other related concepts. For example, much of the discussion around this concept has implied that governance has numerous similarities with the usual conceptualizations of the policy process. Governance certainly does use policy as the principal mechanism for steering, but governance is a substantially broader concept and involves a wider range of action and actors. Likewise, advocates of "good governance" sometimes employ conceptualizations and measures that focus on political and administrative corruption. Minimizing corruption is certainly an important value, but it should be considered as a conceptual and measurement exercise in its own right, rather than as governance.

Dimensions of Governance and Measurement

As we move from the conceptual level to more operational levels, several dimensions of governance can be used to understand this general concept better. These dimensions represent moving from relatively simple process questions to more complex questions of actually delivering governance and being capable of steering the society. Although examining the processes are important and do tell us a great deal about how governance occurs, in the end the real question is, How well are those actors involved in governance—both public and private in most contemporary settings—capable of providing direction?

Processes

The easiest parts of governance to identify and perhaps to measure are the processes that are associated with governing. The measurement here involves the success and failure of the process as well as identifying who the participants are and what difference the involvement of different actors may make. It has been argued that one of the most important aspects of governing is establishing goals for the society. Further, there is a sense that governing requires goals that are reasonably compatible and coherent so that there is an integrated vision of governing and some common direction. In the 1970s, Richard Rose described government by consensus but without direction, but the problem often is government by nonconsensual directions and a failure to develop goals that cut across individual programs or organizations. Thus, one indicator of governance is how readily identifiable the goals of the political system are. It may be easy to find political statements of goals that are intended largely for public consumption, but it may be substantially more difficult to find clear statements of intentions and goals for a government. One of the more useful sources of information on this are the coalition agreements reached when governments are formed in the majority of the democratic countries of the world that have coalition governments. Thus, we can ask to what extent are processes in place that can produce clear statements of goals.

As well as identifying goals, governance requires bringing information and expertise to bear on the problems that are being considered. Although the public bureaucracy is often a major source of this expertise, nongovernmental actors may have a major role to play in providing alternative sources of evidence, and perhaps especially evidence that is less attainable for official actors, such as the reactions of the clients of programs.

Then, as a next stage of a process of governance, we must ask to what extent the multiple goals that exist in the political system are harmonized and integrated. Governments have any number of policy areas in which they must attempt to make policy, but it can be argued that to govern requires some attempt to create coherence across such areas.

Given all this, measuring governance processes means identifying the existence of the internal mechanisms within government, and between government and the private sector, that can translate demands on the system into effective outcomes. In this process, implementation or the translation of the programs of the public sector, along with their private-sector partners, into action becomes crucial. There is already a substantial literature on implementation that does not require repeating here. Implementation is important, however, not only for its obvious impact on the success or failure of public governance but also because this is the stage of the process in which the social partners tend to be involved most legitimately.

Outputs

At a second stage, we will want to ask the extent to which the processes mentioned previously produced the capacity to govern, or a set of intermediate outputs that could then be related to actual governance. One of these outputs may be the institutionalization of revenue collection and other intermediate capacities required for governance. Some political systems encounter significant difficulties in raising revenue from personal or corporate taxation, and therefore must rely on indirect taxes or fees for services.

In addition to the capacity to raise revenue, governance also requires building a substantial legal and regulatory capacity. If the actors responsible for governing have legal instruments at their disposal, they will be able to govern with greater ease than if they have to invest in other instruments that use money or organization to deliver. The importance of legal instruments, however, also points to the dynamic elements in governance. The capacity to govern with legal instruments largely reflects the legitimacy of the governing arrangements within the society, but that legitimacy depends partly on how well and how efficiently governance has been conducted in the past.

Outcomes

At the final level, we will want to measure the outcomes of the governance process. What has happened in society because of the interventions of government and the social actors involved with the efforts to govern? Have the goals of the processes been achieved, or do social and economic forces dominate the attempts of the nominal political authorities to create a collective vision on the society? These and related questions about the consequences of the formal and informal arrangements that exist for governance are central to the measurement of governance. The basic measurement question for governance, therefore, is whether governance has been successful, and indeed, whether governance, in terms of steering, has actually occurred.

Intellectually, we might begin with entropy or anarchy as the antithesis of governance. The incapacity of a political system to govern would be associated with the type of chaos observed in some less-developed countries, or periods following war, such as described by some in Iraq in 2004. Even though such absolute levels of chaos may not be observed often in real life, that is a standard against which to compare the levels of guidance for the society observed. At the other end of this dimension, we might envisage some form of totalitarian society in which there is little or no autonomous choice, whether for individuals or for social groups, and a dominant state attempts to control all aspects of life.

Some elements of the contemporary governance literature argue that governance of this standard is less and less possible, given the increasing mobilization and influence of social actors. Further, it also argued that the top-down version of governance discussed here is also not desirable on normative grounds, given the (presumed) capacity of more open forms of governance to involve social actors and enhance the democratic nature of governance.

If we refer back to the process ideas about governance, we can begin to develop measures of outcomes based on those indicators of the processes through which governance occurs. One can then, for example, assess at the end of the mandate of a coalition government the extent to which the goals that were articulated by the coalition were achieved. Likewise, if achieving policy coherence is an important component of an adequate policy process, then some attempts at measuring coherence are important.

The potential danger in relying on measures of governance that are based on the process stages, however, is that reaching any decision may be considered to be sufficient to say that governance has occurred. It is worth considering that governance has not occurred unless the decisions taken are clearly moving toward targets and have some real chance of reaching those targets. Alternatively, we might want to establish several levels of governance, with decision making that largely reflects and maintains existing relationships being ascribed a somewhat lower level in a hierarchy than governance decisions that do move the society toward articulated social goals.

As well as the achievement of substantive goals such as fulfilling a coalition mandate, there are also other, more transcendent outcomes in governance. Perhaps the most important is the creation and maintenance of legitimacy for the existing governance system. Legitimacy is usually discussed in reference to the government per se, but for governance, the legitimacy question must also refer to the total arrangements designed to steer. Thus, although academic analysts and many of the participants in these arrangements may consider them appropriate and desirable, if they are not legitimate among the public as a whole, then it is difficult to argue that governance has been successful.

Normative Criteria

Finally, in addition to the empirical questions about governance, we should advance some questions about normative criteria for assessing governance. In particular, although there is a normative element to governance, it is important to distinguish between the empirical and the normative in the analysis. It has already been mentioned that the notion of good governance has been advanced by international organizations. This has an empirical element—countries that have minimal corruption should be able to achieve their ends more efficiently than can those that pay the social costs of corruption. There is, however, also a strong normative element in the use of corruption as a negative indicator of governance. The use of democracy as a crucial attribute for governance also has a pronounced normative basis. Democracy is a crucial value for the analysis of politics and government, but unfortunately may not be central to a concept of governance per se.

—*B. Guy Peters*

See also Governance; Governance Indicator

Further Readings and References

Bovens, M., t'Hart, P., & Peters, B. G. (2001). *Success and failure in public governance: A comparative analysis.* Cheltenham, UK: Edward Elgar.

Christensen, T., & Piatonni, S. (2003). *Informal governance in the European Union.* Cheltenham, UK: Edward Elgar.

Jones, C. O. (1984). *An introduction to the study of public policy.* Monterey, CA: Brooks/Cole.

Kaufman, D. (1999). *Governance matters.* Washington, DC: World Bank.

Rose, R. (1974). *The problem of party government.* London: Macmillan.

Winter, S. (2003). The implementation perspective. In B. G. Peters & J. Pierre (Eds.), *Handbook of public administration.* London: Sage Ltd.

MEDIA FREEDOM

Media freedom designates the freedom of various kinds of media and sources of communication to operate in political and civil society. This term extends the traditional idea of the freedom of the press to electronic media, such as radio, television broadcasting, and the Internet. The term *media freedom* acknowledges that the media in modern societies consist of more than print sources. Media freedom is generally held to be necessary for democratic societies. Individuals generally cannot get

sufficient information on their own to make informed decisions on public matters, so they rely on media to provide information. In addition, the media are an outlet for public discussion and opinion. The media generally fulfill the functions of seeking truth, educating the public, and serving as a watchdog over government.

Free media help ensure that the democratic principle of publicity is satisfied. Publicity refers to making information about the operations of government public and provides the opportunity for public debate and scrutiny of matters of public concern. Many think that this function of the media prevents and corrects abuses of power. Conversely, the media provide information about citizen opinion and concerns to political leaders and others in power. Media freedom, and its protection of the principles of publicity, can be curtailed both by excessive government control and regulation and by market forces and practices. Other influences that can reduce the effectiveness of media are increases in elite or private modes of communication that evade public scrutiny, the reduced literacy of consumers of media, and lack of access to media for use by the public.

Media freedom implies media responsibility and accountability. If free media are going to fulfill their vital functions, then the public needs assurance that media are seeking the truth and acting to guard the public interest. Government regulations on media seek to ensure that media act within the parameters of public interest. However, many argue that all or many government regulations interfere with media freedom and violate the public's right to choose and own media sources. On the other hand, government regulations may be necessary to control corporate media outlets that dominate the public's access to information.

New forms of media, such as the Internet, blogs, and alternative magazines, create more issues in media freedom. Many think that these new, unregulated outlets for public discussion are democratizing public access to media and increasing participation in public debate. Others worry that unregulated channels of communication not subject to editorial review will increase false information, and potentially skew public opinion. Further, many new media are international in character and beyond the control of any one political society.

—*Jennifer L. Eagan*

See also Freedom of Information; Participatory Democracy; Political Communication

Further Readings and References

Dennis, E. E., Gillmor, D. M., & Glasser, T. L. (Eds.). (1989). *Media freedom and accountability.* Westport, CT: Greenwood.
Jenkins, H., & Thorburn, D. (Eds.). (2003). *Democracy and the new media.* Cambridge: MIT Press.
Lichtenberg, J. (Ed.). (1990). *Democracy and the mass media.* Cambridge, UK: Cambridge University Press.

MERCANTILISM

Mercantilism refers to the political and economic policies adopted by the European powers in the sixteenth to eighteenth centuries. However, no coherent theory was developed in this period that encapsulates mercantilist ideas, either by a single writer or by a group of largely like-minded individuals. It is therefore a somewhat hazy term that is used to refer to different things by different scholars. Nonetheless, certain key characteristics can be discerned. Mercantilists were concerned with increasing the military power of the state. They believed that a primary goal of the state should be to have a trade surplus (i.e., a situation in which the country exports more than it imports) because this led to a net inflow of bullion. Stocks of bullion, mercantilists believed, increased the wealth of the country and were the most important resource in the event of war. Mercantilists therefore advocated the extensive use of tariffs in an effort to prevent imports, coupled with an aggressive export strategy and other policies to improve economic self-sufficiency. In a wider definition, mercantilism has been characterized as the subordination of markets and the economics of efficiency to political considerations.

The Origins of Mercantilism

The sixteenth century saw the growth in influence and importance of merchants in the European states, who were engaged in long-distance trade with newly acquired colonies. Simultaneously, there was the consolidation of power in the nation-state, replacing the more fractured feudal system, and the introduction of large-scale professional armies both to protect the state from external attack and to aid expansion abroad. To fund these professional armies, governments required an inflow of gold and silver, which increasingly came from taxes levied on the activities of merchants. The merchant classes, in return for these taxes, induced the government to pursue policies that were beneficial to their activities, protecting their markets in the domestic economy from foreign competition through tariffs, providing subsidies to industries, banning the emigration of skilled workers, using the army and navy to protect investments abroad and to open up new colonies, and so on. Mercantilist policies are, therefore, as its name suggests, those favored by the merchant classes of the time.

The Liberal and Economic Nationalist Responses

Adam Smith's seminal 1776 treatise *The Wealth of Nations* aimed at repudiating mercantilist principles. He argued that trade in general is not the zero-sum game envisaged by mercantilists in which a gain for one country is necessarily a loss for another, but can be a positive-sum game by which both parties gain. He also criticized the capture of government policy by merchants, arguing that this did not benefit the general population as a whole who would generally benefit from the availability of cheaper imported goods.

Adam Smith's liberal economics in turn came under criticism from the school of economic nationalism, particularly associated with the German Friedrich List and Alexander Hamilton of the United States, who were concerned with the need for nations to industrialize, both to improve their standard of living and to ensure that they were militarily secure. To this end, List and Hamilton advocated the use of tariffs and subsidies to nurture infant industries until they were able to compete with foreign produced goods.

The school of economic nationalism therefore espoused some of the same policies as contained in mercantilism, most notably the use of tariffs in commercial policy and the importance of pursuing policies that strengthened state military capability. Consequently, the two bodies of thought are frequently treated as being the same. Although this is reasonable in the sense that there is a degree of haziness in the concept of mercantilism, it is unfortunate in that it masks important differences between the two. The economic nationalists, although they were writing in reaction to Smith's work, drew extensively from liberal thought. They considered free trade to be generally the best policy and emphasized (although it is frequently overlooked today) that tariffs introduced to protect infant industries should be abandoned when those industries were able to compete on world markets. Economic nationalists accepted Smith's argument that imports should not be seen as inherently damaging but did not accept that free trade was necessarily the best policy for economically weak nations. There are therefore important differences between the two schools of thought and the justifications for trade protection that they put forward, which are masked by conflating the two into a single classification.

Neomercantilism

Many writers nonetheless adopt a wide definition of mercantilism to encompass any articulation of the importance of politics and the nation-state with respect to economics and free markets. This is prevalent in the neomercantilist literature. Seeing economic systems as necessarily requiring a regulatory political framework, neomercantilists advocate the segmentation of the world economy into largely self-sufficient regions. Globalization, they believe, has rendered the nation-state unable to regulate the world economy, and consequently, bringing politics back to the economic sphere must occur at the regional level (hence neomercantilism) because only regions have the

capacity to bring market forces under some kind of political control.

Neomercantilism has two variations—benign and malevolent. The benign version sees the move to a regional segmentation of the economy as motivated by a need for political stability and the provision of social welfare through the control of market forces, which a fully open global economy is unable to provide. Malevolent neomercantilism places a greater emphasis on the desire of powerful states to increase their power and sees the shift to regionalism as the consequence of strong states seeking to increase their sphere of influence over neighboring states. As such, neomercantilism shares many of the assumptions underlying realist international relations theory.

—*James Scott*

See also Liberal Internationalism; Realism and Neorealism; Reciprocity; Regionalism

Further Readings and References

Buck, P. W. (1974). *The politics of mercantilism.* New York: Octagon.

Gilpin, R. (2001). *Global political economy.* Princeton, NJ: Princeton University Press.

Harlen, C. M. (1999). A reappraisal of classical economic nationalism and economic liberalism. *International Studies Quarterly, 43*(4), 733–744.

Hettne, B. (1993). Neo-mercantilism: The pursuit of regionness. *Cooperation and Conflict, 28*(3), 211–232.

List, F. (1885). *The national system of political economy* (Vol. 2, Chapters 14–15). London: Longmans, Green.

MERCOSUR

The Common Market of the Southern Cone (*Mercosur* in Spanish, *Mercosul* in Portuguese) was established in the 1991 Treaty of Asunción, signed by the governments of Argentina, Brazil, Paraguay, and Uruguay. Implemented on December 31, 1994, the Mercosur permits the free movement of goods, services, and factors of production between these economies; it establishes a common external tariff and a common trade policy; and commits the member countries to the coordination of macroeconomic and sectoral policies in a variety of areas such as agriculture, industry, and foreign trade. Chile and Bolivia became associate members of the Mercosur in 1996 and 1997, respectively.

Earlier attempts at integration in the region had resulted in the short-lived Latin American Free Trade Association (LAFTA) initiative of the 1960s, as well as the Argentine-Brazilian Economic Integration Program (ABEIP), which was signed in 1986 but stalled in the context of economic difficulties in both countries. With the election of Carlos Menem in Argentina and Fernando Collor de Mello in Brazil at the end of the decade, more concerted efforts were made to pursue integration as part of a broader market-led reform agenda and the negotiations were extended to include the governments of Paraguay and Uruguay. The Treaty of Asunción was followed by a series of summits between the four contracting states, which hastened the integration process and led to the implementation of the Mercosur.

From the outset, the Mercosur was intended to increase the competitiveness of the Southern Cone economies and to facilitate increased inflows of foreign direct investment. Commentators have also noted the utility of the Mercosur as a means of "locking in" politically sensitive market reforms in the four member states. However, a key problem since its inception has concerned the relative gains of integration enjoyed by the member states and the question of whether Brazil, in particular, would reap the greater reward as the largest economy. Economic and political divergences between the member states have contributed to the slow pace of integration in the late 1990s, with little progress in areas such as trade in services, exchange rate coordination, and intellectual property rights. The further "deepening" of the Mercosur has also been hampered by the devaluation of the Brazilian *real* in 1999 and the 2001 economic crisis in Argentina. These developments have prompted speculation about the future of the Mercosur, as the member states have tried to protect their economies from the threat of contagion.

Furthermore, it has been suggested that should the proposed Free Trade Area of the Americas materialize,

then the rationale for subregional initiatives such as the Mercosur might disappear.

—*Greig Charnock*

See also Economic Integration; Free Trade Area of the Americas; Hemispheric Integration; Interregional Relations; Mesoregionalism; North American Free Trade Agreement

Further Readings and References

Phillips, N. (2001). Regionalist governance in the new political economy of development: "Relaunching" the Mercosur. *Third World Quarterly, 4*(2), 565–583.

Roett, R. (Ed.). (1998). *Mercosur: Regional integration, world markets.* Boulder, CO: Lynne Rienner.

MESOREGIONALISM

The prefix *meso* is used to describe the middle or intermediate part of a structure or phenomenon. Applied to regionalism, the idea and classification of mesoregionalism and mesoregions cannot be properly understood outside a broader discussion of the emergence of regional economies and regionalist projects as key components of contemporary world order. Perhaps the simplest definition is to treat mesoregions as "regions within regions." Mesoregionalism, therefore, suggests deliberate projects to inaugurate, consolidate, and develop mesoregions. As with the broader debate about regionalism in the global political economy, a key question must be the extent to which mesoregions emerge through the deliberate collective decisions of authoritative actors versus the degree to which they reflect the *de facto* growth of transnational economic spaces.

Mesoregionalism is often understood to be one way in which economic space is being reconstituted in the post–Cold War world. If this world order is thought to be "regionalized," then mesoregionalism might be thought of as an intermediate level between the growth of macro regions, such as the European Union (EU), and smaller cross-border micro regions. Some mesoregions are supranational, but do not encompass entire regional spaces. Thus, formal projects such as Association of Southeast Asian Nations (ASEAN), Caribbean Community (CARICOM), and Mercosur have been identified as mesoregions because they constitute subparts of Asia or the Americas. These regions might be thought of as potential stepping-stones to wider Asian/Asia-Pacific or hemispheric integration in the same way that all regional blocs are considered by some to act as stimuli for globalization. But equally, mesoregions might form a node for resistance to wider macro-regional integration schemes. ASEAN, for example, could be read as an attempt to consolidate a tighter notion of Asia than is implicit within a body such as the Asia-Pacific Economic Cooperation (APEC).

This suggests that mesoregions tend to be formed by collections of states. Two qualifiers need to be added. The first is that some self-defined mesoregions include spaces that embrace only parts of states. For example, the Puebla Panamá Plan—which seeks to facilitate commercial exchange and develop common infrastructures—uses the concept of "Meso America" to describe a space defined by Belize, Costa Rica, El Salvador, Guatemala, Honduras, Nicaragua, Panama, and the southeastern states of Mexico. The second qualifier is that the term *meso* has long been applied to an emergent level of authority below national government, but above local governance structures. It follows that mesoregions may exist within existing states and as collaborative ventures between subregions of geographically adjacent states.

The formation and growth of mesoregions may follow economic or political rationales. They are often held to be interest driven insofar as they can be traced to networking and negotiations among elites. At the same time, most discussions of mesoregions hold that certain preconditions need to hold before they come into existence. Communication links, a transport infrastructure, and a mutually comprehensible industrial and economic culture may be key background conditions, but shared historical experiences and common values are equally held to facilitate the successful imagination of the mesoregion. The Baltic Sea region comes close to this model, where a commercial-economic project is underwritten by rhetorical appeal to a shared organic-historical rationale. The extent to which a mesoregion

flourishes may depend on these variables, but such projects are usually functional and thinly institutionalized. Mesoregionalist projects tend to lack the inherently expansive logics of entities such as the EU.

Mesoregions may also be created and promoted "from above." The EU delineation of its multiple and often overlapping regional territories is a good example. For the most part, this has involved the creation of subnational territorial units of analysis to allow the evaluation of regional disparity and to provide a statistical basis for the distribution of its structural funds. However, through programs such as INTERREG (an EU-funded program that helps Europe's regions form partnerships to work on common projects), the EU has also been responsible for quite deliberately delineating cross-border mesoregions such as the Baltic Sea, the western Mediterranean, and the Alpine Space. These may be long-standing areas of growth and transnational exchange and in many cases include territories that remain formally outside of the EU. There may be a common developmental rationale, or their formation may be provoked by perceived security imperatives in the EU "near abroad."

—Ben Rosamond

See also Asia-Pacific Economic Cooperation; Association of Southeast Asian Nations; Baltic State Cooperation; Caribbean Community; Economic Integration; European Union; Mercosur; New Regionalism; Regional Governance; Regionalism; Substate Regionalism

Further Readings and References

Bull, B. (2005) Between Bush and Bolivar: Change and continuity in the making of Meso America. In M. Bøås, M. Marchand, & T. Shaw (Eds.), *The political economy of regions and regionalisms* (pp. 13–32). Basingstoke, UK: Palgrave Macmillan.

Cappellin, R., & Batey, P. W. J. (Eds.). (1993). *Regional networks, border regions and European integration.* London: Pion.

Low, L. (2003). Multilateralism, regionalism, bilateral and cross regional free trade arrangements: All paved with good intentions for ASEAN? *Asian Economic Journal, 17,* 65–86.

Sharpe, L. J. (Ed.). (1993). *The rise of meso government in Europe.* London: Sage Ltd.

METROPOLITAN GOVERNANCE

See LOCAL GOVERNANCE

MICROPOLITICS

Micropolitics refers to small-scale interventions that are used for governing the behavior of large populations of people. Recent definitions of micropolitics, given by thinkers such as Michel Foucault and Gilles Deleuze and Félix Guattari, argue that micropolitics is a type of political regulation involved in shaping the preferences, attitudes, and perceptions of individual subjects. Micropolitics contributes to the formation of desire, belief, inclination, and judgment in political subjects. Its regulations take place at local and individual levels in locations such as prisons, hospitals, and schools, but also in movie theaters, churches, and family gatherings. When employed as a form of governance, micropolitical techniques include the discipline, surveillance, and examination of political subjects and are supported by specialized knowledge in the social sciences such as criminology, psychiatry, and sociology.

The study of micropolitical techniques began when early modern political thinkers turned their focus from legal sovereignty to the administration of complex economic and social systems. Early in the nineteenth century, Pierre-Joseph Proudhon observed that being governed was to be observed and controlled in all aspects of life. This observation points directly to the micropolitical techniques of governance in which behavior is coordinated through small, daily forms of regulation, measurement, and control rather than through legal statute.

Micropolitical power can be usefully distinguished from legal power. Law depends on the prohibition, interdiction, and restriction of behavior. In contrast, micropolitical techniques depend on instilling the attitudes, dispositions, skills, and capacities to shape behavior. Because they do not depend on legal power, micropolitical techniques allow the state to devolve functions of governance to other networks of administration.

The study of micropolitics requires social scientists to shift the focus of their inquiries away from the arena of high-level decisionmakers. Throughout much of the twentieth century, it had been assumed that political power lay primarily in the hands of the leaders of national institutions and that the appropriate method of study proceeded from the top down. The study of micropolitics, however, suggests that power is exercised at the minute level of individual subjects. Working from the bottom up, the study of micropolitics is concerned with everyday techniques that form the perceptions, desires, and judgments of individuals as they are embedded in their worlds.

—*Matthew Scherer*

See also Bottom-Up Approach; Decentered Theory; Governmentality; Interpretive Theory

Further Readings and References

Deleuze, G., & Guattari, F. (1987). Micropolitics and segmentarity. In B. Massumi (Trans.), *A thousand plateaus: Capitalism and schizophrenia.* Minneapolis: University of Minnesota Press.
Foucault, M. (1977). *Discipline and punish* (A. Sheridan, Trans.). New York: Vintage Books.
Proudhon, P.-J. (1923). *General idea of the revolution in the nineteenth century* (J. B. Robinson, Trans.) (pp. 293–294). London: Freedom Press.

MIDDLE POWER

In international relations (IR) theory, the concept of middle powers is used to categorize a group of states based on their power capabilities and the relative position they hold in the international power spectrum. This conceptualization is important to identify a specific foreign policy behavior associated with that position, often described as "niche diplomacy." As an analytical tool, the concept of middle powers is not recent—its origins date back to the writings of Milan's archbishop, Giovanni Botero, in the sixteenth century. Even though the concept of middle powers seems at a first glance a relatively straightforward theoretical construct, there is disagreement among IR theorists about how middle powers are defined and how they act in world politics. Middle powers are identified based on a combination of their military strength, capabilities, and geostrategic position, or as a result of their leadership ability. Their leadership capabilities are associated with the perceptions that they are liberal, are democratic oriented, and have legitimate concerns in international politics. The former conceptualization stems from the realist paradigm and the latter from the pluralist paradigm as the two main paradigms of international relations are divided over how to differentiate middle powers from the rest of the actors in the international system.

Recent work suggests that middle powers are categorically different because of their reliance on diplomacy and the specific conditions under which they pursue foreign policy. Middle powers favor multilateral foreign policy and forming coalitions rather than unilateral decision making in foreign policy, and the diplomacy style used by middle powers is labeled as niche diplomacy, mainly because middle powers have to follow limited foreign policy objectives because of their relatively lower capabilities than great powers or superpowers. However, middle powers do not challenge the status quo at the international system; they are not revisionist or transformatist states. During the Cold War years, the concept of middle powers became empirically stronger as an analytical tool in international relations as a result of a balance of power between two superpowers. States that did not have superpower capability but that still exerted some influence in world politics, such as Canada, Netherlands, and Sweden, were categorized as middle powers in international relations theory. This was to acknowledge the role they played in international relations while analytically differentiating between different types of power. There is also a recent differentiation between types of middle powers in the literature, mainly between traditional and emerging middle powers. An important trait for the emerging middle powers such as South Africa, Malaysia, and Turkey is that they are also regional great players;

however, middle powers that are able to influence and shape world politics are most often the democratically oriented liberal states.

The middle power conceptualization was based on the dominant paradigm in international relations, the realist paradigm; as a result, the basic tool to conceptualize states and their foreign policy behavior was the relative position states have on the power spectrum. Thus, middle powers have been defined traditionally through the lenses of their relative military strength and capabilities, or the geostrategic location they might have had, which in turn gave them power. There was a revision in this theoretical construction when it became apparent that middle powers' main impact on world politics was influence rather than power.

Middle powers shape and influence international outcomes under two conditions: first as a result of their position in the power spectrum, and second as a result of the recognition of their legitimate concerns. The role that middle powers play as legitimate brokers is emphasized in the pluralist paradigm of international relations theory. Middle powers are important players in the creation and maintenance of world order and favor the establishment of international institutions. In that sense, they act as stabilizers in the world system. Middle powers favor institutionalization at the international level because it benefits them; this, in turn, enables the perpetuation of the hegemonic order, which is partly legitimized by middle powers. According to conventional IR theory, hegemonic powers are responsible for the creation of international institutions, but their maintenance and survival depend on the convergence of interests between other players; this is where the role of middle powers is enhanced. Middle powers favor institutionalization and multilateral solutions to international issues partly because international institutions facilitate coalition building. Middle powers concern themselves with issues such as nuclear nonproliferation, international economic order, debt relief, banning of land mines—issues that do not directly involve vital interests of the great powers. In such international problems, middle powers are able to set and influence international agendas, build successful coalitions, and challenge great power hegemony in these issues. For example, middle powers were successful in the Ottawa Treaty negotiations for the banning of land-mines. This role played by middle powers results partly from the perceptions of their legitimate concerns on issues of human security. The intellectual capabilities and their moral positions enable middle powers to take on activist lines specifically in the creation and maintenance of multilateral international regimes. The central question then is what exactly enables middle powers to exercise such an influence in world politics. The two main factors are the diplomatic capability of middle powers and their ability to project a credible, legitimate position, which enables them to act as moral and intellectual leaders. Middle powers possess highly institutionalized foreign services and are able to disseminate their ideas and foreign policy objectives through the relatively wide network of diplomatic missions they maintain. This sets them apart from weak states. In short, middle powers are conceptualized to theorize about foreign policy behavior of a group of states that influence international events because of their diplomatic abilities and leadership role more than their relative power capabilities.

—*Meltem Müftüler Baç*

See also Global Governance; International Regime; Liberal
   Internationalism; Power

Further Readings and References

Cooper, A. F., Higgott, R., & Nossal, K. R. (1993).
   Relocating middle powers. Vancouver, Canada: University
   of British Columbia Press.
Cooper, A. F. (1999). *Niche diplomacy.* London: Macmillan.
Holbraad, C. (1984). *Middle powers in international politics.*
   London: Macmillan.
Jordaan, E. (2003). The concept of a middle power in
   international relations: Distinguishing between emerging
   and traditional middle powers. *Politikon, 30*(2), 165–181.

MIGRATION

Migration is the process by which individuals, families, or groups move from one country of residence to work or settle in another. Originally used to refer to the temporary movement of people to find seasonal or longer-term employment, migration is now more commonly used to refer to a wide range of processes and phenomena that involve movement from one country to another for a variety of reasons. It is also common for individuals to migrate within a country as well as between two states, for example, between rural and urban areas. The academic study of migration therefore involves a wide range of phenomena, such as labor migration and types of forced migration.

Labor migration refers to the movement of individuals seeking employment in another country. A number of trends have historically been associated with this term, among them the movement of rural populations to urban centers during the process of industrialization in Western Europe and the United States, the movement of indentured labor during the colonial period for the building of railways or mines, and contemporary migration of workers in high-tech industries that require specialized knowledge and technical skills. Labor migration has also been actively encouraged within some economic areas, such as the European Union (EU), where citizens of member states are granted freedom of movement to work in other European countries.

Another prominent area of migration is that of forced migration. This term refers to the migration of people who may be fleeing persecution, civil war, or humanitarian crises such as genocide; people who have been smuggled or trafficked; and those fleeing natural disasters such as flood or famine. Forced migration is commonly used to refer to all these cases and is concerned with individuals as refugees, asylum seekers, or internally displaced people (IDPs) rather than as migrants. The right to asylum and refuge from instances of persecution and crisis is guaranteed under the 1951 Geneva Convention and is overseen by the UN High Commissioner for Refugees (UNHCR). Individual states and regional organizations such as the EU draw on UN conventions in formulating their own immigration and asylum policies. Individuals may also be forced to migrate within their own states and are referred to as IDPs. UNHCR estimates that twenty-five million IDPs have been displaced by conflict, persecution, and humanitarian crises of various kinds.

Migration is sometimes used synonymously with immigration, but the two should not be confused. Many different types of migration refer to more complex phenomena than the process of leaving one country to settle in another.

—Sarah Parry

See also Border Theory; Citizenship; Guest Workers; Immigration

Further Readings and References

Borjas, G. J., & Crisp, J. (2005). *Poverty, international migration and asylum.* Basingstoke, UK: Palgrave Macmillan.

Castles, S., & Miller, M. J. (2003). *The age of migration: International population movements in the modern world* (3rd ed.). London: Palgrave Macmillan.

Spencer, S. (2003). *The politics of migration: Managing conflict and change.* Oxford, UK: Basil Blackwell.

MILITARY NECESSITY

Military necessity is the claim that, because of extreme circumstances, security concerns override competing considerations. A proposed course of action ought therefore be pursued despite the considerable costs exacted by its execution. Though the term can be used to describe any instance in which political, social, or economic calculations are superseded by reasons of war, it is most commonly employed in situations in which security considerations are said to trump ethical restraints on the conduct of war. The claim of military necessity is usually invoked when an actor defies the principles of just war theory, such as a state claiming that extreme military circumstances have forced it to abandon the principles of discrimination or minimum force.

Any declaration of military necessity entails two separate and equally problematic claims. First, it assumes that the proposed military course of action is inevitable, such that a failure to take the action would lead to certain defeat. Second, it assumes that the goal pursued is indispensable, such that failure to achieve the goal would have disastrous implications. In other words, an actor claiming military necessity is suggesting both that success is necessary and that the proposed course of action is the only way to achieve that success. The resort to military necessity thus exaggerates the foresight available to decisionmakers and circumvents debates concerning the moral and political necessity of the goal pursued. Such use obscures the availability of alternatives and the calculations of costs, benefits, and risk that ought to characterize decision making in war.

The response of just war theorists is characterized by two extreme positions. Absolutists reject the concept of military necessity as a farce, concocted by elites or military organizations to justify whatever is necessary to win a war, reduce the risks of losing, or even reduce the costs of war. Absolutists argue that moral considerations always trump cost-benefit calculations, no matter how extreme the circumstances. Utilitarians, on the other hand, conceive of military necessity as entirely compatible with the laws of war. Though the concept does define the limits of those laws, it has also acted as a restraint in war by limiting transgressions to those acts that are truly indispensable for securing the ends of war.

Between these two extremes are those who want to strike a balance between the requirements of humanity and those of military necessity. They require that transgressions of the rules of war be preceded by calculations that take into account the reasonable risks that military actors can be expected to assume, the value of victory, the costs of defeat, and the extent to which moral precepts are placed in jeopardy. These moderate critics do leave room for justifications of military necessity in cases of extreme emergency, such as threats to the survival of a community, as opposed to mere defeat or even occupation.

—Ron E. Hassner

See also Post-9/11; Private Military Companies

Further Readings and References

Downey, W. G., Jr. (1953). The law of war and military necessity. *American Journal of International Law, 47*(2), 251–262.

Walzer, M. (2004). Emergency ethics. In *Arguing about war.* New Haven, CT: Yale University Press.

MILITARY OCCUPATION

An occupation is a contested occurrence. Even the word occupation creates controversy: One person's military intervention is another's peacekeeping effort; charges of illegality or resource-grabbing imperialism are bandied about. At times, the most common attribute is that the intervening group vociferously rejects the label's applicability, even when it is following the international legal conventions: No one wants to be labeled the occupier.

Definitional criteria differentiate between occupations in their origin, duration, resolution, and involved parties, among other qualities. Agreement, however, coalesces around just a few key descriptive features. An occupation implies that a foreign military has displaced the sovereignty of another state. At the most basic level, the occupied state no longer has an exclusive monopoly of force over its territory, is unable to protect its territory and people, and cannot unilaterally carry out its own policies.

Basic definitions of an occupation invariably entail a reference to international legal conventions, which have evolved over time and constitute a minimum standard. These legal concepts and codes are closely tied to the international rules of war that themselves have developed over time: from the brutal spoils of conquest in ancient times, to nineteenth century concerns about the restoration of the status quo, to early and mid-twentieth century concerns about sovereignty. Today, the legal concept of an occupation encompasses concepts of self-rule and self-determination as well as the protection of individual human rights. The need to respond to international terrorism, ethnic conflicts (including genocide), or regional destabilization is an omnipresent challenge.

Occupations can be analyzed through the following analytical lenses: (1) as international law, (2) as a place on the "just war" continuum, (3) as statecraft, (4) as public policy process, (5) as social transformation, and (6) as legacy. Although not definitive, these categories offer critical perspectives on occupations.

International Law

This lens focuses on the legal possibility of armed occupation relative to international law. Initially, the definitions focused on occupation as the result of victory in an armed conflict (including a declared war), which led to physical control over another sovereign's territory. Occupation is legitimate under international law (as set forth in the 1899 Hague Regulations). The international conventions provide that territory will be returned upon signing a negotiated peace settlement. The emphasis is on the temporary acquisition of territory, unlike earlier times when occupation meant permanent acquisition. Until the post–World War II period, the occupier was expected to interact minimally with the citizenry of the occupied country, reflecting the focus on state sovereignty. Today, there are more variations in outcomes. Within the international community, changes in legal expectations were both gradual and dramatic. A major change occurred when individual rights and self-determination became the modus operandi of the international community. This change can be traced in the 1907 Hague Regulations (especially Articles 42–56) and the 1949 Geneva Conventions IV (especially Articles 47–78). These codifications of the law of belligerent occupation have become a branch of international humanitarian law. The welfare of the individual is likely to remain at the forefront of international concern.

A Place on the Just War Continuum

To integrate the just war literature into an examination of occupation is to link the analysis to ethics. The major proponent of just war theory is Michael Walzer. The goal of Walzer and others is to recognize occupation as a continuation of military intervention—a post-conflict phase. Simply, this is a phase where one needs to focus a people's efforts toward ethical closure as well as locating a just future for a war-torn area and its people. It entails assigning responsibilities to the winners and the losers in both monetary and nonmonetary terms. With this approach, one sorts out the aftermaths with a focus on enforceable solutions, long-term stability, and the righting of any wrongs.

Statecraft

Occupation is studied as a political transformation with a focus on process. In this statecraft approach, the emphasis is on the structure of the post-conflict government and institutions. There is setting forth of positive and negative attributes of both the occupier and the occupied. The analysts often advocate certain institutional arrangements. Commonly referenced is the need for and nature of civil liberties in the occupied country. During an occupation, civil liberties often coexist side-by-side with strategic policy that tends to focus on internal and regional stability. This juxtaposition of stability with civil liberty has consequences because civil liberties can be compromised. For example, nondemocratic tools such as censorship can be used to stabilize and consolidate legitimacy in the reemerging state. This statecraft approach often involves the need to consider what the occupied feel and think about the military occupation of their country, especially for the success or failure of an operation. In addition, the "hearts and minds" of all the parties (the occupant, occupant's people back "home," and the occupied) must be discussed when one wants to identify the stable, successful result. Security is often a focal point. It becomes synonymous with stability, and in turn, stability becomes linked to certain institutional arrangements. Experts on political parties, for example, may analyze the stability implication of particular plans for electoral representation. Within the statecraft approach are scholars who embrace nation building—a hands-on, applied version of the statecraft lens. Much of the analyses of the current Iraqi "occupation" apply the democratization literature in this manner to either bolster or refute the U.S. position. Hence, within this approach, one finds scholars who advocate a prescribed course to democratization as well as those who critique the chosen course.

Public Policy Process

The focus is on the internal dynamics of policy making and implementation. Occupations have not typically been studied as part of a general policy process. Thus, it may be fruitful to see an occupation event or related events not as an anomaly but as part of discussion of the mechanics of the general policy process. Policy windows, overlapping jurisdiction,

agenda setting, coalition building, and linkages of policy issues should be the focus of this analytic view of occupations. The ultimate success or failure of an occupation may be linked to internal public policy issues. The limited quantitative work on occupations indicates that successful occupation costs lots of money, but monetary considerations do not necessarily guarantee success. Success may lie elsewhere; that is, the small details of an administrative process may determine the success or failure of an occupation policy and cumulatively the larger occupation.

Social Transformation

This type of analytic lens on occupations would advocate that research energy be directed at neglected areas such as improvements in the status of women and minorities. More traditional scholarship on occupations is not generally concerned with these groups. Particularly when the emphasis has been on security matters, these areas are neglected. Or, worse yet, when an occupation becomes coded as a success, the completeness of certain reforms remains unexamined. In addition, not all social problems have their origins in the occupation experience—many endure beyond it. An occupation may exacerbate existing social ills or lay the groundwork for future difficulties. Understanding Okinawa's place in Japan's defense policy would be incomplete without an exploration of Allied occupation and the heritage of Okinawa. In the social transformation approach, the roles and status of minority groups or women are essential to understanding the nature of the occupation as well as the quality of life after the occupation.

Legacy

This lens is locked on the long term; that is, years after an occupation, the researcher assesses an occupation in its totality and its parts. Within each occupation, there can be more than one legacy. Often, in these kinds of studies, the contemporary issues of today are traced back to decisions made during the occupation. Moreover, examination of the historical record suggests that with the passage of time the public's perception of an occupation can change. Hence, assessing the success or failure in the midst of an occupation is precarious at best. Although historians have largely dominated this legacy approach to occupation (especially in country-specific studies), policymakers use this historical "record" to craft future occupation plans and supporting programs. In the realm of public policy, the careful study of occupation and its legacies reveals an understanding that an occupation is a dynamic process for working out political, social, and economic solutions. Will the governance of post-conflicts yield closure and opportunities for change, or leave a nation and people mired in enduring continuities with the past?

Ideally, an occupation moves quickly beyond armed conflict to focus on issues of governance. From onset to resolution, an occupation is marked by high uncertainty. With this assortment of analytical frameworks, the researcher can more fully capture the complexity of the post-conflict event, the occupation.

—Suzanne Breese Ryan

See also Humanitarian Intervention; International Law and Treaties; Military Necessity; Neocolonialism; Peace Process; Realism and Neorealism

Further Readings and References

Benvenisti, E. (2004). *The international law of occupation.* Princeton, NJ: Princeton University Press.

Edelstein, D. (2004, Summer). Occupational hazards: Why military occupations succeed or fail. *International Security, 29*(1), 49–91.

Roberts, A. (1984). What is a military occupation? *British Year Book of International Law, 55,* 249–305.

Walzer, M. (2004). *Arguing about war.* New Haven, CT: Yale University Press.

Millennium Development Goals

The eight Millennium Development Goals (MDGs), agreed to at the September 2000 UN Millennium Summit consist of eighteen targets and forty-eight progress indicators that identify a number of development priorities dedicated to vastly improving the quality of life for millions of the world's poorest. These are subject to annual progress reports, and 2015 has been set as the final assessment year. The MDGs are

1. to reduce by fifty percent the number of the world's population currently living on less than $1 per day, and to reduce by the same amount the number of people suffering from hunger;

2. to ensure that all children complete primary schooling;

3. to promote gender equality by eliminating disparities at all levels of education;

4. to reduce by two-thirds child mortality among children under five;

5. to improve maternal mortality health;

6. to effectively combat a number of the world's major diseases, such as AIDS, malaria, and measles by improving access to affordable drugs;

7. to ensure protection of the environment by placing sustainability at the top of development programs, reducing by fifty percent the number of people currently without access to safe drinking water and improving the quality of life for the inhabitants of the world's worst slum areas;

8. to establish and consolidate a global development partnership; a transparent, rule-based global and multilateral economic system that promotes principles of good governance and poverty reduction addressing the particular problems faced by less-developed countries (LDCs) and heavily indebted countries (HICs), including more development assistance, debt relief or cancellation, technology transfer, and market access.

The MDGs have established themselves as important benchmarks for UN development programs as well as for other global governance institutions, and donor and recipient states and nongovernmental organizations (NGOs) are using the MDGs as reference points in their own poverty reduction strategies. A number of key international institutions concerned with development, such as the International Monetary Fund (IMF) and the World Bank, contributed expert advice to the design of the MDGs and are involved in formulating strategies aimed at reaching the targets and assessing progress toward them, and the Organisation for Economic Co-operation and Development (OECD) plans to integrate the MDGs systematically into the Development Assistance Committee (the principal body through which the OECD deals with issues related to cooperation with developing countries).

It is widely believed that the MDGs significantly contribute to the fight against global poverty. Acknowledging collective responsibility for formulating development strategies and meeting explicit quantitative targets, the MDGs are claimed to represent a significant commitment by all countries and major international private and public institutions to the millions who have been marginalized from global economic growth and prosperity in recent years. In setting these targets, politicians at the highest level have identified a set of harmonized and integrated strategies geared toward securing outcomes that can be precisely monitored by National Millennium Goals Reports (in addition to standard UN General Assembly reports and conferences) and tracked by a plethora of NGOs, and against which these politicians can therefore be held accountable.

Yet, the MDGs have elicited a number of criticisms. First, some of the targets are set at such a low level they are easily achieved and make little progress toward addressing global poverty. For example, there is concern that, despite the fact that overseas development assistance (ODA) to the least developed countries fell significantly during the 1990s, funds promised for assistance will not use new money but, rather, will take funds from current aid budgets, re-jigging existing development finances rather than providing substantive new amounts. On the other hand, there are clearly significant obstacles in the way of realizing some of the targets, such as ensuring access to richer country markets in agricultural produce or providing sustainable debt relief.

Second, despite this low threshold for claiming success, some observers believe that many of the targets will not be met because of fundamental policy disagreements among the variety of actors involved in developing strategies for addressing the development challenge. For example, some academics and more radical NGOs have expressed concerns that the targets

themselves may serve as merely another set of conditions and rules with which LDCs and HICs must comply if they are to benefit from the program.

The concern is that the MDGs will not be met (indeed, will be undermined) if the preferred method of reaching them is a narrow range of policies based on market-led initiatives seeking to harness the pursuit of profit by private corporations. The argument is that, policy-wise, the MDGs are mildly reformist at best and lack ambition because of a failure to engage in serious discussion about economic policies and underdevelopment/poverty reduction. These disagreements underline the difficulties involved in establishing and coordinating new mechanisms of global governance.

—*Stuart Shields*

See also Nongovernmental Organizations; Poverty Reduction; Sustainable Development; United Nations

Further Readings and References

United Nations. (2000). *UN millennium development goals.* Retrieved from http://www.un.org/millenniumgoals/index.asp

United Nations. (2005). *UN millennium development goals report of 2005.* Retrieved from http://unstats.un.org/unsd/mi/pdf/MDG%20Book.pdf

MINISTRY

See GOVERNMENT DEPARTMENT

MINORITIES

See MULTICULTURALISM

MONETARISM

Monetarism is a neoclassical economic theory that focuses on the causal relationship between the money supply and inflation. The central claim of monetarist theory is that inflation can be controlled or eradicated by regulating the growth of the money supply in line with the growth of economic output. Monetarist ideas became increasingly popular in Western capitalist nations in response to growing political and economic difficulties during the 1970s. The success of monetarist policies in practice, however, has been mixed.

Monetarism in Theory

The theory of monetarism is derived from a range of neoclassical thinkers, the most prominent of which are Milton Friedman and Friedrich von Hayek. Monetarist theorists contend that inflation is the result of an excessive growth in the supply of money in relation to the growth of economic output. This is based on the assumption that a free market capitalist economy will tend toward a stable and harmonious equilibrium if left undisturbed. On this basis, monetarists argue that any political interference that produces an artificial expansion of the money supply to achieve social objectives, such as a lower rate of unemployment or faster economic growth, will prove to be self-defeating and will lead to rising economic and political instability.

In its simplest form, the inflationary process is typically thought to begin when the government initiates an unsound monetary expansion, such as an unwarranted reduction in interest rates or an excessive rise in public expenditure. If such measures are not anticipated by the market, then this monetary expansion will lead to a rise in consumption and to a subsequent increase in trade, output, and employment as the economy grows to meet the extra level of demand. As this process continues, however, a growing scarcity of labor eventually leads to rising wage costs as workers seek to capitalize on their improved bargaining position. This undermines profit margins, so businesses respond by curtailing their activities or by raising prices. As a result, inflation grows, consumption falls, the economy contracts, and output and employment both start to decline.

According to monetarists, this course of events will continue until the economy restabilizes at its previous level of economic activity and employment, though now with higher prices and wages, or until the government embarks on another monetary expansion in an attempt to engineer renewed economic growth. However, because inflationary expectations will have now risen, any subsequent expansion will have to be progressively larger than that anticipated by the market if it is to produce the desired effects, thus leading to escalating inflation and increased macroeconomic instability.

Given the apparent futility of political intervention in the operation of the market, monetarists therefore argue that the government should restrict its economic policy objectives to the provision of a sound and stable monetary framework by keeping the growth of the money supply in line with the growth of output. To achieve this, monetarists contend that the government needs to establish a credible policy "rule" that binds their future economic policy behavior, such as a self-imposed constraint on the growth of the money supply, or inflation targeting by an independent central bank. By limiting the government's discretionary control of monetary issues in this way, monetarists argue that such measures can help preclude any political manipulation, can constrain market expectations, and can thereby help maintain macroeconomic stability and avoid an unwarranted rise in inflation.

Monetarism in Practice

Monetarist ideas in one form or another have provided the dominant framework for economic policy making in major capitalist states for much of the period since the nineteenth century. This began with a widespread adherence to the classical gold standard and to its reconstructed variant during the interwar period, which provided an automatic and a depoliticized means of regulating the growth of the money supply in line with economic output. Following the collapse of the gold standard and the depression of the 1930s, however, monetarist ideas gradually succumbed to the advance of Keynesian economic theory. The popularity of monetarist ideas was revived during the 1970s as Keynesian ideas faced the apparently insurmountable problems of rising unemployment, high inflation, and economic stagnation. In contrast, monetarism seemed able to provide both a theoretically coherent account of these difficulties as being the result of excessive state intervention, as well as a means of successfully resolving them.

The introduction of monetarist policies in major capitalist nations during the 1980s, however, produced mixed results. The implementation of measures such as high interest rates frequently conflicted with other (politically motivated) policies, such as cuts in taxation and higher public spending, and the money supply itself proved difficult to control or even measure with any degree of certainty. Furthermore, the expected relationship between the growth of the money supply and inflation did not conform to empirical realities. In Britain, for example, a fall in inflation was accompanied by a rise in the money supply, whereas in Japan the onset of a deflationary recession during the latter half of the decade proved immune to a series of deliberate monetary expansions.

Despite these difficulties, monetarist ideas have nevertheless continued to dominate the economic policy-making framework of Western capitalist states. Since the 1990s, the most popular model has proved to be an independent central bank operating according to an inflation target. The success of this model, however, has also been mixed. Although inflation has remained generally low, many parts of the world have continued to struggle against the effects of a global economic recession since the turn of the millennium.

—*Steven Kettell*

See also Business Cycle; Keynesianism; Liberal Market Economy; Monetary Policy

Further Readings and References

Clarke, S. (1988). *Keynesianism, monetarism and the crisis of the state.* London: Edward Elgar.

Friedman, M. (1991). *Monetarist economics.* Oxford, UK: Basil Blackwell.

Kindleberger, C. P. (1985). *Keynesianism vs. monetarism and other essays in financial history.* London: Allen and Unwin.

Smith, D. (1987). *The rise and fall of monetarism: The theory and politics of an economic experiment.* London: Penguin.

MONETARY POLICY

Monetary policy became an issue of economic governance in developed capitalist economies in the 1980s. Until then, the conduct of interest rate, money supply, and exchange rate policies was considered to belong to "the art of central banking," more of practical than scholarly interest. The watershed is symbolized by the so-called "Volcker shock," with which the U.S. Federal Reserve (under Chairman Paul Volcker and during the administration of President Jimmy Cater) ended an accommodating stance that had led to rising inflation rates. Other central banks followed suit. Researchers closely scrutinized goals, instruments, and the desirable degree of activism in monetary policy.

Monetary policy has essentially two goals: price stability and low unemployment. In practice, these are difficult to operationalize and quantify. Price stability is compatible with some rise of the price level, an index of money prices, but not with a spiral of rising prices, driven by windfall profits or supply shocks, and rising wage demands. Low unemployment means, somewhat circularly, an employment level that is compatible with price and wage stability so that all unemployment is frictional or seasonal rather than cyclical. Central banks typically react to deviations of these goals from a desired value or long-term trend by raising or lowering the interest rate. This behavior has been found a robust empirical regularity by estimating the so-called Taylor Rule (named for John Taylor) that shows how strongly a central bank can respond to deviations from these two goals of monetary policy.

The instruments of monetary policy consist, in principle, of the short-term interest rate at which banks can get credit from the central bank (discount rate policy) and of money supply that the central bank can manipulate by selling and buying bonds in the money market (open market policy). These instruments are used to manipulate transmission variables such as the long-term interest rates, stock prices, exchange rates, or the volume of credit. These transmission variables are the economic indicators that ultimately account for the spending and saving decisions of economic agents and the competitiveness of firms. This transmission is fraught with uncertainty.

Monetarism has strongly advocated abstaining from manipulating the interest rate as an ambiguous indicator of how lax or strict credit market conditions are. It advocated instead using monetary aggregates such as M1, M2, or M3, which added to central bank ("high powered") money other means of payment that households dispose of in the form of banking accounts of different maturities. Yet, virtually all central banks now use the short-term interest rate only whereas money growth rates are only one set of indicators among many. The use of monetary aggregates is reliable only if monetary demand is quite stable, but this is not the case, largely because of the internationalization and deregulation of financial markets.

Monetary policy is an issue of governance because it raises the question of how far a key economic policy should be delegated to an independent agent. The independence of central banks is a time-honored topic, mainly asking to what extent the monetary authority should be instrument-independent and goal-independent. Although virtually all independent central banks react to deviations from employment and inflation goals with changes in the short-term interest rate, there is now debate whether a central bank should pre-commit to quantified and announced goals and thus follow an explicit rule and to what extent it should use discretion.

The literature on the credibility (or "time-consistency") of economic policy sparked this debate about how best to ensure an effective and coherent monetary policy through institutional design. A credibility problem of monetary policy arises when the central bank is believed to change a policy, at present planned for the future, as times goes by. The inducement to revise a plan, typically to "inflate" the economy despite the promise to keep price stability, stems from the authorities' policy preferences being different from those of the representative private agent. Dynamic inconsistency then occurs because the central bank would benefit from a revision of policy whenever the private sector acts according to the inflation goals as presently announced. Yet, this incentive

of monetary policymakers is rationally expected by the private sector, which adjusts its pricing decisions accordingly. Thus, the authorities do not succeed, and the economy ends up in the worst of all possible worlds, which typically means higher inflation with no gains in employment.

Various proposals have been made to tie central banks' hands and overcome this problem of time-inconsistency or lack of credibility in monetary policy. One proposal is to make central banks obey strict rules such as announcing a monetary growth target in line with the inflation goal. Yet, it is not clear what should happen if the central bank misses the rule because the bank's independence is incompatible with government discretion in hiring and firing central bank governors. One way around this is to pay central bankers according to their performance. Another, and arguably more plausible, solution is to appoint central bankers who are more conservative than the median voter who votes for the government. This would ensure that price stability would not be sacrificed for short-term employment goals. An irony of such propositions is that the underlying rationale assumes an ability and willingness of central banks to fine-tune the economy that the same scholars otherwise deny. Practitioners of monetary policy consider the issue of time-consistency and the governance problems it raises as a largely academic debate of little relevance to their daily work.

—*Waltraud Schelkle*

See also Business Cycle; Economic Governance; Monetarism; Monetary Union; Political Business Cycle

Further Readings and References

Barro, R. J., & Gordon, D. B. (1983). Rules, discretion, and reputation in a model of monetary policy. *Journal of Monetary Policy, 12,* 101–121.

Blinder, A. S. (1997). Distinguished lecture on economics in government: What central bankers could learn from academics—and vice versa. *Journal of Economic Perspectives, 11*(2), 3–19.

Taylor, J. B. (1993). Discretion versus policy rules in practice. *Carnegie-Rochester Conference Series on Public Policy, 39,* 195–214.

MONETARY UNION

A monetary union involves an agreement between two or more states creating a single currency area. This involves the irrevocable fixation of the exchange rates of the national currencies existing before the formation of a monetary union. Historically, monetary unions have been formed on the basis of both economic and political considerations. A monetary union is accompanied by setting up a single monetary policy and establishing a single central bank, or making the already existing national central banks the integrative units of a common central banking system. Usually, a monetary union involves the introduction of common bank notes and coins. This function, however, might be split among the participating states. They may either be granted the right to issue coins or bank notes on behalf of the common central banking system, or the respective national currencies become denominations of an invisible common currency.

The most prominent and recent example of a monetary union is the creation of a single currency among European Union (EU) countries—the euro. This example demonstrates the interplay of economic and political factors in the process of setting up a monetary union. From an economic point of view, a monetary union helps reduce transaction costs in an increasingly integrated regional market. It also helps increase price transparency, thus increasing inner-regional competition and market efficiency. In addition, a monetary union was seen to be an essential step toward the further political integration of the EU.

A monetary union may also have adverse effects on the participating economies. In the case of the euro, some economists raised doubts about whether the EU could be regarded as an "optimum currency area." Economic diversity and the inflexibility of labor markets were seen as the major obstacles for EU member states to exploit to the full the benefits of monetary union. Monetary integration was seen to leave some economies particularly vulnerable to asymmetric (external) shocks, as national decisionmakers are no longer in control of nominal interest rates.

As a result, the creation of a monetary union also represents a particular challenge to monetary and economic governance both at the domestic and supranational levels. It raises the question of the institutional design of a common monetary policy and the necessity of a simultaneous integration of macroeconomic policies. Because these issues touch on core aspects of national sovereignty, monetary unions are sometimes associated with the transition of a confederation of states toward a federal system. However, as the example of the European Economic and Monetary Union demonstrates, a centralized monetary policy may be compatible with a decentralized economic policy framework. In this framework, national governments remain solely responsible for economic policies but are required to engage in policy coordination. They also must respect a set of common rules for the conduct of their fiscal policies. This notably includes the rule to avoid excessive government deficits.

—*Uwe Puetter*

See also European Union; Foreign Exchange Market; Monetary Policy; Regional Governance

Further Readings and References

De Grauwe, P. (Ed.). (2001). *The political economy of monetary union.* Cheltenham, UK: Edward Elgar.

Gros, D., & Thygesen, N. (1992). *European monetary integration.* Harlow, Essex, UK: Longman.

Howarth, D. (Ed.). (2004). Revising the rules: The stability pact and the construction of European economic governance [Special issue]. *Journal of European Public Policy, 11,* 761–936.

MONOPOLY

The standard definition of monopoly is a single seller of a product or service. In the economic sphere, monopoly generally has a negative connotation. Under competitive conditions with many buyers and sellers, prices are bid down to the cost of production and, in the absence of externalities, such as pollution, this yields an efficient allocation of resources. In the absence of competition, producers have incentives to restrict supply and raise prices above competitive levels. Beyond the perceived unfairness of high monopoly prices, the gap between price and marginal cost misallocates resources because of the restricted supply.

The harm done by a monopoly can vary widely, depending on the extent of its market power, which could derive from either demand or supply conditions. On the demand side, where there are many close substitutes for the monopolist's product, the demand facing the monopolist will be highly elastic, and hence, the scope for profitable price increases will be small. However, where substitutes are few, as with a necessity, demand will be inelastic and the scope for price increases will be large. Pricing power may be limited by geographical considerations: A single general store in a small town will find little scope for raising prices if it is cheap to go to the next town for supplies. Likewise, a country with only a single producer of automobiles will find that free trade limits the possibilities for monopolistic pricing. Consequently, economists generally focus on the scope for profitably increasing price above marginal cost as the most appropriate measure of market or monopoly power.

A common misconception is that bigness, or firm size, is a good measure of the extent of its monopoly power. Thus, a Marxist view of monopoly capital will often label any large firm as a monopoly capitalist. It is quite possible, however, for a government of a small country with valuable natural resources to have more effective market power than the small groups of large multinational corporations that are competing for access to the resource. Where corruption is present, one or more of the multinationals may collude with government officials to stifle competition and exploit consumers. In the same vein, a company's country of origin is not the relevant basis for assessment of its monopoly power. Thus, it is a mistake to identify a large firm as a monopolist just because it is based in one of the leading economies, say, in the United States or Japan.

In some instances, monopoly may be useful as a method of calling forth innovation. Thus, patents offer a monopoly for limited periods. Likewise, so-called natural monopolies are traditionally regulated by government on both price and quality issues. The creation of artificial monopolies has often been a source of government revenue and was a major instrument in the heyday of mercantilism. Such blatant monopoly creation has gone out of fashion, but restrictions on entry are still a frequent goal of lobbyists.

—Thomas D. Willett and James A. Lehman

See also Economic Governance; Market Failure; Political Economy

Further Readings and References

Carlton, D. W., & Perloff, J. M. (1999). *Modern industrial organization* (3rd ed.). New York: Longman.

Tirole, J. (1988). *The theory of industrial organization.* Cambridge: MIT Press.

Willett, T. D., Sweeney, R. J., & Tower, E. (1977). The ranking of alternative tariff and quota policies in the presence of domestic monopoly. *Journal of International Economics, 7*(4), 349–362.

MOST-FAVORED NATION PRINCIPLE

Since Bretton Woods, the most-favored nation (MFN) principle has been identified with the nondiscrimination obligation contained in Article 1, Paragraph 1 of the General Agreements on Tariffs and Trade (GATT). Although a number of exceptions limit its scope, this bedrock of international trade law requires that national trade policy afford equal treatment to the products of all World Trade Organization (WTO) members.

The MFN is often seen as an indispensable component of liberal practice because it facilitated the GATT negotiations that have steeply reduced global trade barriers since 1948. Because the "multilateralism" of the MFN eliminates the preferential bilateral arrangements that contribute to tensions among trade competitors, it also has been embraced as a step toward international peace by advocates of the argument known as pacific liberalism.

It is therefore ironic that the MFN clause has been a common component of international trade treaties since at least the early seventeenth century, when it was adopted as an element of mercantilism, not liberalism. Representative is Article II of the first commercial treaty of the United States, signed with France in 1778, in which the parties "engage mutually not to grant any particular favor to other nations, in respect of commerce and navigation, which shall not immediately become common to the other party." In that era, in which trade agreements were bilateral and episodic, the clause protected the signatory of one agreement from the erosion of benefits by a later treaty that conveyed more favorable treatment to another trade competitor. In effect, it was used jealously to guard the status of a most-favored nation by guaranteeing that it would automatically receive privileges at least as favorable as any other.

As it became embodied in global treaties with an increasingly universal membership, and as the exceptions to it multiplied, MFN status became a misnomer. For example, members of regional trade organizations such as the European Union (EU) and North American Free Trade Agreement (NAFTA) enjoy tariffs lower than those of so-called most-favored nations. So, too, do most poor countries under provisions of the Generalized System of Preferences permitted as part of the differential treatment accorded them by GATT since the 1960s. Rather than guaranteeing the best treatment, MFN now merely prevents the worst. In 1998, for example, legislation changed the designation in American trade policy to normal trade relations (NTR), status denied a mere handful of nations by specific legislation: Cuba, Laos, and North Korea. Under U.S. trade law, all nations possess NTR status unless specifically exempted, and even then, waivers are frequently granted. The most famous were the annual U.S. Congressional votes that authorized NTR for China before its eventual accession into the WTO, usually after extensive airing of various grievances concerning Chinese human rights and trade practices.

—*Bruce E. Moon*

See also European Union; North American Free Trade
    Agreement; World Trade Organization

Further Readings and References

Vagts, D. F., Dodge, W. S., & Koh, H. H. (2003). *Transnational business problems.* New York: Foundation Press.

MULTICULTURALISM

Multiculturalism refers to the position that cultures, races, and ethnicities, particularly those of minority groups, deserve special acknowledgement of their differences within the dominant political culture. This acknowledgement can take the forms of recognition of contributions to the cultural life of the political community as a whole, a demand for special protection under the law for certain cultural groups, or autonomous rights of governance for certain cultures. Multiculturalism is both a response to the fact of cultural pluralism in modern democracies and a way of compensating cultural groups for past exclusion, discrimination, and oppression. Most modern democracies comprise members with diverse cultural viewpoints, practices, and contributions. Many minority cultural groups have experienced exclusion or the denigration of their contributions and identities in the past. Multiculturalism seeks the inclusion of the views and contributions of diverse members of society, while maintaining respect for their differences and withholding the demand for their assimilation into the dominant culture.

Multiculturalism as a Challenge to Traditional Liberalism

Multiculturalism stands as a challenge to liberal democracy. In liberal democracies, all citizens should be treated equally under the law by abstracting the common identity of "citizen" from the real social, cultural, political, and economic positions and identities of real members of society. This leads to a tendency to homogenize the collective of citizens and assume a common political culture that all participate in. However, this abstract view ignores other politically salient features of the identities of political subjects that exceed the category of citizen, such as race, religion, class, and sex. Although claiming the formal equality of citizens, the liberal democratic view tends to underemphasize ways in which citizens are not in fact equal in society. Rather than embracing the traditional liberal image of the melting pot into which people of different cultures are assimilated into a unified national culture, multiculturalism generally holds the image of a tossed salad to be more appropriate. Although being an integral and recognizable part of the whole, diverse members of society can maintain their particular identities while residing in the collective.

Some more radical multicultural theorists claim that some cultural groups need more than recognition to ensure the integrity and maintenance of their distinct identities and contributions. In addition to individual equal rights, some advocate for special group rights and autonomous governance for certain cultural groups. Because the continued existence of protected minority cultures ultimately contributes to the good of all and the enrichment of the dominant culture, these theorists argue that the preserving of cultures that cannot withstand the pressures to assimilate into a dominant culture can be given preference over the usual norm of equal rights for all.

Examples of the Impact of Multiculturalism

Some examples of how multiculturalism has affected the social and political spheres are found in revisions of curricula and the expansion of the canon. Curricula from the elementary to the university levels have been revised and expanded to include the contributions of minority and neglected cultural groups. This revision is designed to correct what is perceived to be a falsely Eurocentric perspective that overemphasizes the contributions of White European colonial powers and underemphasizes the contributions made by indigenous people and people of color. In addition to this correction, the contributions that cultural groups have made in a variety of fields have been added to the curricula to give special recognition for contributions that were previously ignored. The establishment of Black, Latino, and Asian History Months are examples of this

movement. The addition of works by members of minority cultural groups to the canons of literary, historical, philosophical, and artistic works further reflects the desire to recognize and include multicultural contributions to the broader culture as a whole.

Challenges to Multiculturalism

There are two primary objections to multiculturalism. One, multiculturalism privileges the good of the certain groups over the common good, thereby potentially eroding the common good in favor of a minority interest. Two, multiculturalism undermines the notion of equal individual rights, thereby weakening the political value of equal treatment. Other questions arise with the claim of multiculturalism. There is the question of which cultures will be recognized. Some theorists worry that multiculturalism will lead to a competition between cultural groups all vying for recognition and that this will further reinforce the dominant culture as dominant. Further, the focus on cultural group identity may reduce the capacity for coalitional political movements that might develop across differences. Some Marxist and feminist theorists worry about the dilution of other important differences shared by members of a society that do not necessarily entail a shared culture, such as class and sex.

Relation to Governance

Multiculturalism is closely associated with identity politics, or political and social movements that have group identity as the basis of their formation and the focus of their political action. These movements attempt to further the interests of their group members and force issues important to their group members into the public sphere. In contrast to multiculturalism, identity politics movements are based on the shared identities of participants, rather than on a specifically shared culture. However, both identity politics and multiculturalism have in common the demand for recognition and a redress for past inequities.

Multiculturalism raises important questions for citizens, public administrators, and political leaders. A prominent trend in democratic theory and governance has been a call for inclusion and increased participation in public life by previously oppressed groups. By asking us to recognize and respect cultural differences, multiculturalism provides one possible response to the question of how to increase such participation.

—Jennifer L. Eagan

See also Asia-Pacific Economic Cooperation; Indigenous Governance; Pluralism; Social Inclusion; Social Justice

Further Readings and References

Cornell, D., & Murphy, S. (2002). Anti-racism, multiculturalism and the ethics of identification. *Philosophy and Social Criticism, 2*(4), 419–449.

Gutmann, A. (Ed.). (1994). *Multiculturalism: Examining the politics of recognition.* Princeton, NJ: Princeton University Press.

Kymlicka, W. (1995). *Multicultural citizenship.* Oxford, UK: Oxford University Press.

Okin, S. M., & respondents. (1999). *Is multiculturalism bad for women?* Princeton, NJ: Princeton University Press.

Taylor, C. (1992). *Multiculturalism and "The Politics of Recognition": An essay.* Princeton, NJ: Princeton University Press.

MULTILATERALISM

In its simplest form, multilateralism refers to a process of organizing relations between groups of three or more states. Beyond this basic quantitative aspect, multilateralism is generally considered to comprise certain qualitative elements or principles that shape the character of the arrangement or institution. These principles are an indivisibility of interests among participants, a commitment to diffuse reciprocity, and a system of dispute settlement to enforce a particular mode of behavior. Multilateralism has a long history but is principally associated with the U.S.–led post–World War II period, during which there has been a burgeoning of multilateral agreements. The organizations most strongly embodying the principle of multilateralism are to be found in trade (the World Trade Organization [WTO]) and

security (North Atlantic Treaty Organization [NATO]), although there are an increasing number of multilateral environmental institutions.

Indivisibility

To better understand the nature of multilateralism, it is useful to contrast it with bilateralism, a good example of which is the commercial policies of Nazi Germany, in which the German government negotiated bilateral agreements with other countries specifying which goods and services were to be traded, their prices, and the quantities to be exchanged. Through this, a significant number of nations were connected by trade agreements, with Germany acting as a central hub. By contrast, the multilateral commercial regime, centered on the General Agreement on Tariffs and Trade (GATT), used the principle of most-favored nation (MFN). Under German bilateralism, third parties were excluded from interstate arrangements, whereas in the GATT, third parties were treated in a more inclusive manner and were granted equal treatment by virtue of the MFN clause. Thus, the German system was built around systematic discrimination, whereas the GATT assured nondiscrimination for all contracting parties.

In security arrangements, the principles of multilateralism are best embodied in a collective security system such as NATO, in which a war against one state is automatically considered to be a war against all states, ensuring that any act of aggression against a member of the collective system is met with a response from all members. By contrast, a bilateral arrangement only ensures that A comes to the aid of B in the event of an attack by C. It would not ensure that C receives similar protection from A in the event of an attack on C by B. In this instance, the system discriminates against C. Bilateral security arrangements are, therefore, like their counterparts in commercial policy, inherently discriminatory, whereas multilateral arrangements have a more inclusive character in which all participants are afforded equal treatment.

In both these examples, there is a notion of the indivisibility of interests. In security arrangements, peace is treated as being indivisible, such that no participating member can be at war while others are at peace. In commercial policy, the norm of MFN makes the trade system an indivisible whole. Bilateralism, by contrast, necessarily fragments relations between states. Indivisibility is therefore the first core principle of multilateralism.

Diffuse Reciprocity

Along with, and related to, the principle of indivisibility of interests, multilateralism is considered to give rise to expectations of diffuse reciprocity among participants. In situations characterized by diffuse reciprocity, there is an expectation that there will not be an equivalence of obligations or concessions in any one exchange but, rather, a balance is expected over an ongoing, potentially indefinite, series of exchanges with a group of partners. For example, in the collective security system outlined previously, members do not expect to be compensated for the military resources they may expend in defending a threatened member country. Their recompense lies in the knowledge that should they be attacked, they too will benefit from a collective response to that attack. By contrast, bilateralism is more associated with specific reciprocity and an explicit balancing of obligations between each pair of actors, as with the commercial relations of Nazi Germany.

These relationships between bilateralism, multilateralism, and their respective forms of reciprocity can be seen to flow from the aforementioned indivisibility of interests. By its nature, the indivisibility of interests associated with multilateral arrangements gives rise to an expectation of diffuse reciprocity and its greater sense of inclusiveness, whereas the fragmentation and divisions of bilateralism lends to it an expectation of specific reciprocity.

Dispute Settlement

For the states to feel assured of the returns of treating their interests as indivisible, multilateral arrangements tend to incorporate some mechanism for ensuring that countries act in accordance with the expected norms. This principle of dispute settlement forms the third principle associated with multilateralism. A variety of

methods for ensuring compliance are available, such as through peer review, which may suit more informal arrangements, or the creation of a formalized body to which grievances may be taken. Having a system of dispute settlement enables participating countries to treat their interests as indivisible and to accept relations of diffuse reciprocity: They know that should the expected benefits not be forthcoming because of noncompliance by other participants, there is a mechanism through which redress may be sought.

Institutionalization

These three principles taken together form an "ideal type" of multilateralism. Although there has been a huge growth since World War II in the number of multilateral institutions, they do not always fully conform to all aspects of this ideal model. Such institutions have undoubtedly played a significant role in postwar global governance. More controversially, it has been argued that multilateral institutions may be inherently more stable than other forms of organization, in that the principles underlying them appear to be more durable than other arrangements and more able to adapt to external changes. Thus, despite the perceived decline in U.S. hegemony since the 1970s, the multilateral institutions that the United States played the primary role in creating, such as NATO and the GATT/WTO, show little sign of decline and continue to play an important role in shaping the international system.

—*James Scott*

See also Global Governance; Liberal Internationalism; Reciprocity

Further Readings and References

Keohane, R. O. (1990). Multilateralism: An agenda for research. *International Journal, 45,* 731–764.

Ruggie, J. G. (1992). Multilateralism: The anatomy of an institution. *International Organization, 46,* 561–598.

Ruggie, J. G. (1993). *Multilateralism matters: The theory and praxis of an institutional form.* New York: Columbia University Press.

Wilkinson, R. (2000). *Multilateralism and the World Trade Organization: The architecture and extension of international trade regulation.* London: Routledge.

MULTILEVEL GOVERNANCE

Multilevel governance is an approach that, for academics from a range of subdisciplines of political science, captures the increasingly fragmented and complex nature of decision making in a number of settings. Multilevel governance draws on frameworks and concepts from across subdisciplines, particularly from European Union (EU) studies, international relations (IR), and public policy. As such, multilevel governance contributes to a growing awareness that many contemporary issues and problems cannot be understood without crossing traditional academic boundaries. Most specifically in this case, multilevel governance crosses the traditionally separate academic domains of domestic politics and international politics. The distinction between what is domestic politics and what is international politics is challenged by empirical developments, particularly in the European context, where the EU has taken on an increasing number of functions previously undertaken by nation states. It is no coincidence that multilevel governance first emerged from studies of the EU.

For many, the EU is not really like traditional international organizations or domestic political systems. It is something unique and, as such, defies explanation purely from approaches applied either to "politics within states" (domestic) or "politics between states" (international). Multilevel governance was first developed to capture the changing nature of EU structural policy following a major reform in 1989, and was subsequently applied to EU decision making more broadly.

Until the mid-1980s, theorizing about the EU had been dominated by approaches derived from the study of IR. From the IR tradition of pluralism, neofunctionalism was developed to understand European integration, whereas those in the state-centric IR tradition applied intergovernmentalism. The concern of theorists in these traditions was with explaining the nature and pace of European integration. Neofunctionalists argued that national governments were increasingly caught in a web of interdependence with nonstate actors, EU institutions, and other governments that took them further along the road to integration than they intended. By contrast, intergovernmentalists emphasized the degree of control national governments retained in the process as gatekeepers over the key decisions.

From the reenergizing of the European integration process in the 1980s, symbolized by agreement to the completion of the single European market and the Mediterranean enlargement, the EU began to take on more functional responsibilities and develop more effective decision-making mechanisms. In particular, qualified majority voting displaced unanimity voting in a range of policy areas. This change occurred primarily to expedite swift agreement to the measures needed to complete the single market, but had implications beyond market integration. This shift limited the ability of individual governments to veto proposals that they believe are against their national interest.

The relaunch of the integration project and the related institutional reforms sparked a new wave of thinking about the EU, which drew parallels with domestic systems. Subsequently, a range of tools and concepts were increasingly applied to the EU from the study of domestic and comparative politics, and new concepts were developed. The development of multilevel governance was part of this new wave of thinking about the EU. Its origins in the study of EU structural policy provide useful insights into the nature and development of the concept.

EU Structural Policy and Multilevel Governance

EU structural policy aims to promote social and economic cohesion across Europe. Much of its focus is on assisting the development of disadvantaged regions in the context of market integration. In the context of moves to complete the single market, and to assimilate Greece, Portugal, and Spain into the EU, the European Commission and its allies in the European Parliament won support from governments for a major reform of structural policy in 1989. Largely as a side-payment to poorer member states for the anticipated consequences of the internal market program, governments agreed to double the amount of funding spent through structural policy and to reform its governing principles.

As part of the desire to ensure effective use of these funds, governments—some reluctantly—accepted the commission's proposal that funds be administered through partnerships established within member states, consisting of national, subnational (regional or local) and supranational (commission) actors. This decision gave subnational actors a formal role in the EU policy-making process for the first time. In subsequent years, the commission pushed for and secured agreement to the greater involvement of nonstate actors (nongovernmental organizations, trade unions, environmental groups, etc.) within these partnerships.

The concept of multilevel governance was developed from a study of these developments. Initially, the study highlighted "continuous negotiation" among governments "nested" at different territorial levels. The analysis drew on the policy networks approach to highlight the territorial overarching networks in which governments found themselves increasingly enmeshed. Although not a theory of integration, the approach had strong neofunctionalist antecedents in its argument that supranational actors and interest groups were significant in shaping the commission's decisions and that this challenged the role and authority of national governments. Increasingly, multilevel governance scholars paid attention to nonstate as well as government actors.

Thus, multilevel governance has both vertical and horizontal dimensions. The former (multilevel) refers to the increasing interdependence of actors situated or nested at different territorial levels—supranational, national, and subnational; the latter (governance) refers to the increased role of nonstate actors in decision making. In short, therefore, the rise of the subnational level and acknowledgement of the significance of policy networks combined to stimulate the initial conception of multilevel governance in EU studies.

If the initial trade in concepts had been from the study of domestic politics and IR to EU studies, the development of multilevel governance offered the possibility of concept trading in the other direction. Over the period since multilevel governance was first developed, internationalization and decentralization/devolution have accelerated as trends, as has the growing participation of nonstate actors in public policy making. As such, scholars from different academic traditions seeking to understand increasingly contested jurisdictional and territorial boundaries both within and beyond states have used multilevel governance.

Two Types of Multilevel Governance

In clarifying the concept, Liesbet Hooghe and Gary Marks distinguished between two types of multilevel governance. Type 1 multilevel governance resembles federalism. It sees the dispersion of authority as being restricted to a limited number of (non-overlapping) jurisdictional boundaries at a limited number of territorial levels. Here, jurisdictions are general purpose with those jurisdictions at the lower territorial levels nested into higher ones. In this typology, the distribution of authority is seen as relatively stable and the focus of analysis is on individual governments or institutions rather than on specific issues or policies.

Type 2 multilevel governance presents a picture of governance that is more complex, is more fluid, and consists of innumerable jurisdictions. These jurisdictions often overlap each other and tend to be flexible as governance demands change. They are focused around specific policy sectors and issues and devised to secure optimal policy-making efficiency. In this typology, the distribution of authority is less stable and the focus of analysis is more on specific issues and policy areas than on individual governments or institutions.

These types of multilevel governance are not viewed as mutually exclusive but can (and do) coexist. General-purpose jurisdictions exist alongside special-purpose jurisdictions: Formal institutions of government operate, and indeed create, special-purpose bodies to carry out particular tasks or address particular problems. There may be tensions between the two, for example, in relation to issues of accountability over particular decisions and outcomes. But such tensions are a characteristic feature of multilevel governance.

Different Uses of Multilevel Governance

Although multilevel governance was developed as an analytical framework to analyze developments in the EU empirically (to explain how things are), the concept has also been adopted in normative debates about how public decision making should be arranged. The phrase has indeed been adopted by the European Commission in its policy documents and has been debated normatively by academics. We deal with the analytical and normative uses in turn.

Analytically, the most controversial aspect of multilevel governance has been the interpretation that it suggests that the nation-state is in irreversible decline. This may be something of a parody of multilevel governance. Although the concept undoubtedly highlights new challenges to state power, there is also recognition in the literature that states remain important both because they often hold nodal positions within networks and because they have democratic legitimacy that other actors do not possess.

Different authors emphasize different outcomes from the challenges to state power presented by multilevel governance. Although some are keen to emphasize the loss of state power, others argue that power should not be conceptualized as zero-sum and that the rising importance of other actors does not necessarily mean the transfer of power away from states. Indeed, some scholars suggest states can set the ground rules for multilevel governance to frame favorable outcomes and can mobilize other actors to help them achieve state objectives more effectively.

That multilevel governance can be used in a variety of ways by different scholars may be seen as an advantage, but it may also illustrate a weakness: that its theoretical content is weak and it is mainly a descriptive term. It is criticized for not generating clearer expectations about the role and influence of "new" actors in the policy process and, related to this, how the role, authority, and power of states are affected.

A particular problem is that multilevel governance to some extent equates governance with the mobilization or participation of new actors in public policy making, irrespective of whether this mobilization or participation leads to any shifts in power between different actors. Put differently, it refers to increasing interdependence between actors but categorizes both the weakest, most asymmetrical relationships of interdependence and the strongest, most symmetrical relationships in the same way.

Normatively, multilevel governance is seen by its advocates to have advantages in its scale flexibility; that is, that jurisdictions can be designed to involve particular actors to meet particular challenges on a particular scale to fit particular preferences. This may be either Type 1 or Type 2 multilevel governance. This custom-built approach is thought to lead to efficient and effective decision making, to have problem-solving capacity.

Critics suggest that the perceived gains in efficiency and effectiveness may have costs. In particular, the proliferation of such jurisdictions and the increase in cross-sectoral participation risk reducing transparency and obscuring accountability to citizens. As such, there may be a trade-off in which gains in efficient decision making are at the expense of democratic accountability, unless new mechanisms of accountability are developed alongside the new forms of governance.

However, not all see complex governance arrangements as an inevitable threat to democracy. From pluralist perspectives on democracy, there may be safety in numbers in complex governance arrangements, preventing any single actor or institution from dominating decision making. Of course, as suggested previously, the evidence of broad participation does not equal diffuse power. Empirically, weaker social groups tend to be marginalized in such processes unless measures are taken to develop their capacity to engage effectively.

Taking Stock

Multilevel governance captures complex decision making in a range of settings. It has an intuitive appeal for many scholars, but although providing an attractive description of decision making, multilevel governance would be stronger if it generated clearer expectations in relation to the implications for the role, power, and authority of actors involved in policy making. Normatively, multilevel governance offers advantages for efficient decision making. However, in some of its manifestations, there are concerns that the virtues of multilevel governance in efficiency and effectiveness are traded for the virtues of democratic legitimacy.

—*Ian Bache*

See also Center-Local Relations; Complexity; European Governance; European Union; Global Governance; Heterarchy; Interdependence; Political Exchange; Regional Governance; Social Network Theory; State-Society Relations; Sustainable Development

Further Readings and References

Bache, I., & Flinders, M. (Eds.). (2004). *Multilevel governance.* Oxford, UK: Oxford University Press.

Hooghe, L., & Marks, G. (2001). *Multilevel governance and European integration.* London: Rowman & Littlefield.

Hooghe, L., & Marks, G. (2003). Unravelling the central state, but how? *American Political Science Review, 97*(2), 233–243.

Hooghe, L., & Marks, G. (2004). Contrasting visions of multilevel governance. In I. Bache & M. Flinders (Eds.), *Multilevel governance* (pp. 15–30). Oxford, UK: Oxford University Press.

Marks, G. (1992). Structural policy in the European community. In A. Sbragia (Ed.), *Europolitics: Institutions and policymaking in the "new" European community* (pp. 191–224). Washington, DC: Brookings Institute.

Marks, G. (1993). Structural policy and multilevel governance in the EC. In A. Cafruny & G. Rosenthal (Eds.), *The state of the European community: The Maastricht debate and beyond* (pp. 391–411). Boulder, CO: Lynne Rienner.

NARRATIVE THEORY

Narrative theory is an umbrella term for various word-based approaches to the study of human acts, including acts of or associated with governance. These include such approaches as discourse analysis, the analysis of stories or storytelling, or more broadly, interpretive social science, in which narrative analysis may be a part. Narrative approaches draw their theoretical substance primarily from philosophy, developmental psychology, and literary theory. They are part of the late twentieth-century "turns" in the social sciences—turns away from various forms of quantitative, behavioralist approaches to the analysis of human behavior toward more meaning-focused analytic approaches, including the so-called interpretive turn, the linguistic turn, and the argumentative turn. Narrative theories argue for the centrality of expressiveness in human acts and in reasoning about those acts, rather than seeing instrumental rationality as the central human orientation. This is seen as holding for collective selves (e.g., organizations and polities) as much as for individual selves.

Theoretical Roots

Narrative theories in governance and other social scientific applications typically draw on one or more of three sources for their theoretical orientation: philosophy, psychology, and literary theory.

Hermeneutic Philosophy and Texts

Early to mid-twentieth-century hermeneutic philosophy (articulated, e.g., in the work of Edmund Husserl and Hans Georg Gadamer) made the argument that the principles of textual analysis that had been developed earlier in traditional hermeneutics for the study of biblical texts could be usefully applied to the analysis of the meanings of contemporary, non-biblical texts. Such contemporary texts, they argued, could include such things as fiction and poetry; by extension, one could apply hermeneutic analysis to painting, architecture, and other linguistic and physical artifacts of human creation. Later some twentieth-century philosophers, notably Charles Taylor, argued that these analytic techniques could also be applied to human acts: Producing written versions of observed acts and interactions for purposes of social scientific analysis (as in ethnographic field notes) renders them analogous to texts, and they may then be subjected to analytic reading to discern their meanings in ways similar to that used for literal texts. In the spirit of Gadamer's argument that the hermeneutic circle describes processes of learning in general (and not just text study), one might also argue that everyday interpretations-in-action of human acts, including the nonverbal, are done hermeneutically.

In governance-related analyses, literal texts might include such documents as government policy drafts and bills, agency correspondence and annual reports, newspaper coverage of events, Web pages of special interest groups, and so on. Oral and visual presentations, such as parliamentary and stump speeches, media broadcasts, policy-relevant films, and other such recorded and transcribed events, could also be subjected to narrative analyses. Two sorts of interpretive research methods for generating data produce other forms of word-based evidence that can usefully be analyzed as forms of narrative: in-depth, conversational interviews that gather stories told about governance-related acts or events or interactions and participant-observation and ethnographic analyses, in which researchers produce field notes documenting their observations of acts, events, and interactions.

Psychology and Identity

Phenomenological hermeneutic philosophy argues that these various artifacts are the concrete projections and embodiments of human meaning made visible and observable. Central to this argument is the assumption that human acts are not just a matter of goal-oriented, instrumental rationality, but that humans are also meaning-making beings and their acts are, or can be seen as, expressive of meaning. Expressive acts, in other words, do not just constitute the communication of information for instrumental purposes. They are tied in, also, to expressions of identity—acts of meaning. Narrative theory posits that humans express what is meaningful to them in narrative form. That makes attention to these narratives requisite for a social science that is serious about engaging questions of meaning in its analyses.

In contemporary psychotherapeutic practice, individual self-narrative is encouraged as a way of identifying what the individual considers meaningful, how she constructs herself, and how she reasons about and explains events in her life. This sort of reasoning underlies researchers' efforts to get street-level workers to tell stories, for example, about events that transpire in the course of the everyday workplace. The hypothesis is that such stories reveal core values, such as fairness, that lie at the heart of administrative practices.

Collective expressions of values—such as the signs that city councils place along their streets declaring

the cities to be "nuclear-free zones"—are ways in which polities express and communicate their identities to themselves and to one another, as well as to other, potentially more-distant publics, from passersby to governmental officials at a remove. From a perspective that focuses on the centrality of meaning to human political (and other) activity, the fact that these policies are unimplementable is less important than the act of identity expression.

Literary Theory and Narrative Forms

Whereas philosophical and psychological theories attend to the substance and purpose of expression seen narratively, literary theories attend to the forms of narrative exposition. Narratives are understood as following their own internal logical order. Their structures may be chronological; they may be spatially ordered (e.g., describing an event's setting from top to bottom or from right to left); they may be structured according to some order of relationship among the actors in the narrative (e.g., kinship or rank); or they may follow some other structure that makes sense to the narrator as an ordering device for the elements of actor, act (plot), setting, purpose, and tool (Kenneth Burke's pentad).

Narrative accounts typically have beginnings, middles, and ends, but these need not be chronological (and what is beginning and what is the end may be culturally specific). Movement from one part of the narrative to the next is set in motion by the plot and its elements—the sequence of acts that address the implied or stated question, and then what happened, and which glue together the sections of the narrative. Narratives also feature actors, including, at times, the narrators themselves. And narratives often describe the settings for actions and actors: neighborhoods, agency buildings and offices, city hall chambers, and courthouses. In this sense, narrative theories adapt dramatistic theories for the analysis of political and other social acts.

One common application of narrative theory in governance-related research is story (or storytelling) analysis, used in conjunction with in-depth, conversational interviewing, either as a distinct method or as part of an ethnographic or participant-observation study. For example, clients of programs implemented by local government agencies may be asked to relate stories from their experiences as recipients of these programmatic efforts. Street-level implementers may be asked to narrate organizational stories that circulate within their agencies concerning experiences interacting with clients in delivering governmental services or the workings of their agencies with respect to these programs (or both). Agency directors and midlevel administrators may be asked to tell organizational stories about intergovernmental relations. Other analyses scrutinize policy drafts, successive version of bills, transcripts from legislative sessions, or agency documents and acts for narratives—key words or phrases in their contexts, including policy or organizational metaphors—that express policymakers' and implementers' values, beliefs, or feelings concerning the subject(s) of pending or existing legislation.

Narrative as Semiology

What these several approaches share in common is a presupposition that narratives of all sorts—whether historical accounts or individuals' stories—contain their own ontological status. That is, narrative theory does not draw a distinction concerning validity between "what really happened" and a story about what happened. For narrative theory, the narrative itself is what matters, as it embodies what is real for its narrator and, therefore, has its own "truth status." Narratives, in this sense, are also epistemological in that they are understood as providing evidence of the character of their narrators' knowledge about the narrated world. Numerical accounts, then, may also be treated as narratives: They are ways of worldmaking through numbers, where the relationships among numerical entries constitute a plot that gives an account of their subject matter.

It is in the semiological sense that narratives are understood to be universal forms of human discourse. Given their centrality for the communication of meaning, analyses must, then, also explore the efforts and abilities of more- and less-powerful groups to air their narratives and to control the possibilities for such expression by others.

—*Dvora Yanow*

See also Dilemma; Discourse; Interpretive Policy Analysis; Interpretive Theory; Situated Agency; Tradition

Further Readings and References

Bevir, M., & Rhodes, R. A. W. (2003). *Interpreting British governance*. London: Routledge.

Bevir, M., & Rhodes, R. A. W. (2006). *Governance stories*. London: Routledge.

Bruner, J. (1990). *Acts of meaning*. Cambridge, MA: Harvard University Press.

Burke, K. (1989). *On symbols and society* (J. R. Gusfield, Ed. & Introduction by). Chicago: University of Chicago Press.

Czarniawska, B. (1997). *Narrating the organization*. Chicago: University of Chicago Press.

Taylor, C. (1971). Interpretation and the sciences of man. *Review of Metaphysics, 25,* 3–51.

Yanow, D. (2000). *Conducting interpretive policy analysis*. Thousand Oaks, CA: Sage.

NATION

What is a nation? Ernest Renan famously defined it as solidarity between a group of people constituted by a mutual desire for, and preparedness to contribute to, the continuation of a distinctive way of life. But what is the basis of this distinctive form of life? What are the consequences of these commitments and sentiments? Why do nations matter, morally speaking, if indeed they do?

Is a nation a natural kind, or is it more closely related to psychological phenomena and thus more mutable and negotiable? According to the former, nations are constituted by people that share certain objective properties or characteristics, such as race, language, a common ethnic descent, or that are shaped by a distinctive climate and homeland. According to the latter, a nation is, above all, the product of subjective belief, that is, a common bond of sentiment. Most political theorists have opted for the second as opposed to the first model, fully aware that the actual uses to which nationhood and nationalism have been put has often appealed to the language of natural kinds. Many have done so precisely because they think it is important to save the idea of the nation, as well as nationalism, from the terrible crimes perpetrated by many nationalists. Others do so in order to point out the fictitious and ultimately bogus status of nations and thus cast into doubt the philosophical respectability of nationalism in general.

It is important not to run together the idea of a nation with two other related but distinct concepts, namely ethnic groups and the state. Ethnic groups and nations are undoubtedly historically closely connected. Both are aggregates of people that share certain common features and that engage in forms of mutual recognition. It has been argued that, in fact, all nations have deep, though often obscured, origins in ethnic communities. But an ethnic group is tied much more closely to the idea of kinship and descent than a nation. Every ethnic group might potentially become a nation, but it need not. Many nations might have their origins in particular ethnic communities, but they can, and often do, branch out to encompass more than one. Similarly, although many states today are nation-states, the two are not identical. (Some critics say it is unfortunate the largest global association of states is called the United Nations, for it is clear that its members are neither united nor made up of nations but rather states.) Many nations may aspire to statehood, but they need not (e.g., indigenous peoples). And many states, if not most, contain more than one nation. So there is no necessary logical connection between nationhood and statehood. This has enormously important consequences for normative arguments about nationalism.

It is often suggested that nations, at least as we understand them today, are a product of modernity, and especially of the nineteenth century, and thus have specific preconditions—such as an integrated economy and common social institutions—which are then used to promote a common language or culture. On this reading, nationalists in control of these institutions and resources produce nations, not vice versa. However, although these preconditions help promote the common bond of sentiment central to nationality, they aren't necessary conditions, because we can find nations without the apparatus of modern industrial states, and in non-Western contexts as well. Also, the language of nationhood as a specific form of political argument has a much older lineage than the nineteenth century, to be sure; we find references to nations as political units as far back as the fourteenth century. But there are indeed important changes that emerge in the modern era. In the early modern period, and especially by the French Revolution, the idea of a nation is increasingly associated with the notion of a people acting collectively to exercise (or at least oppose) political authority. To have the idea of a people possessed of a will, you need some way of conceiving of them as a collective body—as a people. Here the older ideas of nationhood involving a shared culture, language, or homeland are overlaid with an explicit commitment to a shared political project of self-government or popular sovereignty. Because modern political communities are not structured along kinship lines, or based on intimate face-to-face relations, what holds them together, in part, are beliefs about a common political project transmitted through a shared language made manifest in the various modes of mass communication in that society (its books, newspapers, and other media).

Do nations matter, morally speaking? Many argue they should not, and the debunking of the objective account of nationhood is meant to contribute to this possibility. Nations are not real, but the political construction and manipulation of the imaginary aspect of nationhood is. No one looking at the history of the twentieth century, in particular, can fail to appreciate the force of this argument. Nationalism, as a claim about the moral and political consequences of belonging to a nation—that the political and national unit should be congruent, that one ought to identify with a nation, and that one ought to privilege the obligations associated with one's membership in that political community above other obligations—has been used to justify terrible deeds. But we shouldn't reduce the idea of a nation to its most distorted expression. Insofar as human beings are social and political animals, they will seek to live in collectivities bound by sentiments often found among conationals. But these sentiments can be expressed in different ways, albeit shaped as they are by existing institutions and relations of power. Thus, a defense of the moral relevance of nations would have to link the sentiment of nationality to the promotion of values such as freedom, justice, and equality, as well as to inclusive debates about the very nature of that identity. And it would have to integrate the obligations that supposedly flow from identifying with the common political project of a nation to those we owe to each other regardless of nationality. If nations are constructed, then they can be deconstructed and reconstructed. Nevertheless, history suggests that their appeal, however modulated, can never be fully immunized from the dangers nationalism can unleash.

—*Duncan Ivison*

See also Ethnic Groups; Nationalism; Postcolonialism; Regime; Sovereignty; State; Territoriality

Further Readings and References

Anderson, B. (1991). *Imagined communities: Reflections on the origins and spread of nationalism.* London: Verso Books.
Beiner, R. (Ed.). (1999). *Theorizing nationalism.* New York: SUNY Press.
Gellner, E. (1983). *Nations and nationalism.* Oxford, UK: Basil Blackwell.
Miller, D. (1995). *On nationality.* Oxford, UK: Oxford University Press.
Renan, E. (1939). 'What is a nation?' In A. Zimmern (Ed.), *Modern political doctrines.* London: Oxford University Press.
Smith, A. (1986). *The ethnic origins of nations.* Oxford, UK: Basil Blackwell.

NATIONALISM

Nationalism is a set of beliefs in the distinctiveness of a group (a nation) and its right to practice self-determination. The group in question need not share any observable ethnic, linguistic, religious, or racial traits, merely a collective sense of itself as a national political community. As Benedict Anderson puts it, nationalism is the sense of belonging to a community where many of its members may never come into contact with one another. Nationalism creates concepts of nationality or national identity—belonging and owing loyalty to the nation. For these reasons, nationalism is a key source of social integration as a well as disintegration. It provides an important foundation for social and political solidarity and mobilization. The rise of French nationalism in the nineteenth century enabled Napoleon to revolutionize militaries and overrun Europe, as he replaced mercenaries with citizen armies inspired by nationalism. Without nationalism as a sort of social glue, large integrated states could not survive or mobilize their inhabitants. Examples of nationalism as an integrating force include the creation of new nation-states arising out of the breakup of the Austro-Hungarian Empire and the unifications of Germany and Italy. More recently, nationalism is associated with disintegrative processes, such as violent conflicts between minority and majority groups and the collapse of multinational states. Examples include Nazi Germany, fascist Italy, and the collapse of the Soviet Union and Yugoslavia along national lines.

Nationalism is often thought of in reference to the rise of the modern state, when theories of popular sovereignty began to replace monarchical divine right as the basis for political rule. This conception of nationalism as popular government guided the American and then the French in their eighteenth-century revolutions, and American President Woodrow Wilson in his call for national self-determination as a principle of the post–World War I international order. Nationalism is thus something that is peculiarly modern and demarcates the modern era from the premodern.

Nationalism is distinct from and broader than the concepts of ethnicity or ethnonationalism. Ethnonationalism refers to an ethnic group within a state or crossing state borders that seeks a greater degree of political self-government, for example Chechens in Russia or Hungarians in Romania and Slovakia. Nationalism refers to a sense of belonging to a nation that may include many different ethnic, religious, linguistic, and other minority groups. Rather, nationalism may encompass all these groups. For example, American nationalism refers to a set of beliefs that Americans (including Native Americans, African Americans, Irish Americans, Arab Americans, Asian Americans) constitute a distinctive group, and that the group has the right to govern itself. Nationalism is contrasted with cosmopolitanism, a set of beliefs that individuals make up a global rather than a national community.

—*Anne L. Clunan*

See also Citizenship; Cosmopolitanism; Ethnonationalism; Nation; Postcolonialism; Self-Government

Further Readings and References

Anderson, B. (1991). *Imagined communities.* London: Verso Books.
Calhoun, C. (1993). Nationalism and ethnicity. *Annual Review of Sociology, 19,* 211–239.
Haas, E. B. (1997). *Nationalism, liberalism, and progress.* Ithaca, NY: Cornell University Press.

NATURAL RESOURCE MANAGEMENT

Natural resource management refers to the ways in which societies manage the supply of or access to the natural resources upon which they rely for their survival and development. Insofar as human collectives are fundamentally dependant on natural resources, ensuring the ongoing access to or a steady provision of natural resources has always been central to their organization. Historically, this access has been organized through a range of schemes varying in degrees of formality and involvement from the central authorities (or state). Thus, natural resource management goes to the heart of governance, if by governance we mean the regulatory schemes by which societies organize themselves. Specific governance issues include, for example, establishing hierarchies between the different resources or deciding which ones are "strategic" and need to be secured as a priority.

A "natural" resource is one that is afforded by nature without human intervention; hence the fertile lands or the minerals within them, rather than the crop that grows on them, comprise a country's natural resources. Although what is considered a "resource" (or, for that matter, "natural") has varied over time and from one society to another; resources are riches provided by nature from which some form of benefit can be derived, whether material or immaterial. However, only those natural resources that can renew themselves, and whose exploitation relies on these regenerative capacities, properly necessitate management. For example, oil is not considered a subject of natural resource management, whereas forests are. Management seeks to balance out the demands of exploitation with a respect for these regenerative capacities. Thus, natural resource management, in its generic sense, bespeaks the degree to which societies are embedded in the natural environment, and what is being managed is this basic dependency as much as the resources themselves. More specifically, however, the term *natural resource management* has historically coincided with the increasing formalization of these schemes of access to (or provision of) natural resources that accompanied the rise of the modern bureaucratic state. The most fundamental challenge to natural resource management was posed by the encounter with the earth's limits: The realization that natural resources, contrary to implicit assumptions, were not in fact in endless supply. This is the challenge that shifted natural resource management from a simple governance issue, concerned mainly with questions of efficient resource allocation, to an issue of environmental governance.

Origins

The emergence of a rational, systematic management of natural resources can be traced back to the phase of accelerated industrialization of the late nineteenth century. In a period of unprecedented industrial growth, the pressures brought to bear on the supply of raw materials and natural resources by an unrelenting demand intensified the need to rationalize their utilization, so as to eliminate an increasingly costly waste and to allocate them more efficiently. This coincided with a broader tendency toward rationalization, a general social pattern identified by the sociologist Max Weber that emerged in modern industrial societies in response to the large-scale reorganization of production, and whereby goal-oriented rationality was increasingly infused into the organization of social activities. Natural resource management was born at the conjunction of rationalization and its twin process of bureaucratization, which yielded the first bureaucracies to manage nature. Of course, there are huge variations in both the rates and degrees to which the different states became involved with questions of natural resource management—the French state, for example, took a heavy hand in forestry management as early as the seventeenth century, when wood became a strategic resource at a time of accelerated, mercantilist (export-oriented) growth that relied primarily on maritime transportation (boats). These local variations aside, overall it took a certain kind of state, the modern bureaucratic state, to steer the exploitation of natural resources toward principles of scientific management. In the United States, natural resource management was made a federal matter for the first time under the presidency of Theodore Roosevelt. At that time, principles of scientific management, which combined notions of rational management with in-depth scientific knowledge of the resource itself, were promoted by key figures such as Gifford Pinchot, the founder of the National Forestry service in 1896 and the Yale School of Forestry, who was supported by Roosevelt himself. In Europe, a similar concern with rational resource exploitation transpired around the same period, for example, at the International Conference on the Exploration of the Sea that assembled in 1899, with northern European countries sharing concerns around maritime exploitation. It was effectively one of the first international conferences on a natural resource management question, and there, too, science was entrenched as a basis for exploitation of the seas, laying the grounds for future arrangement for the management of collective resources.

Encountering the Earth's Limits

The twentieth century saw natural resource management increasingly projected at a supranational level, where it was also collectivized. A first major impulse toward the internationalization of natural resource management was brought by the post–World War II context, with its pervasive spirit of cooperation on the one hand, and its specific problems of food shortages on the other. Countries came together to address the issues of damaged capacities and insufficient production—in other words, insufficient use of available resources. This context yielded the Food and Agricultural Organization (FAO) in 1945, the International Whaling Commission in 1946, and later the International Fund for Agricultural Development (established in 1977 to specifically tackle problems of agricultural production in developing countries). The problem was seen to lie in the management, rather than in the resources. Therefore, the solution was to develop common solutions to management problems that were widely shared from one country to the next: In other words, how to create international regimes that would disseminate better management solutions, and thus enable each country to make better use of its resources.

In a second phase, problems with the resources themselves shifted the focus toward the global level, or rather, to problems with a different type of resource altogether, that is, the basic resources of the globe itself, the seas, the air, and the diversity of species. They were brought to attention by the realization that these essential resources, hitherto taken for granted and thus the issue of needing to manage them had simply never been posed, were in fact limited, like the other resources. The encounter with the earth's limited resources occurred through two successive crises. First was the new awareness that we had reached a global environmental crisis, which triggered a second wave of bureaucracies to manage nature at both the national and international levels. At the international level, the United Nations Environment Programme (UNEP) was established in 1972, and at the national level, environmental ministries (in Europe) or agencies (in the United States) flourished in developed countries in the early 1970s. Significantly, the issue that popularized the environmental crisis was an issue of failed global resource management: the overexploitation of whales, which threatened certain species with extinction. This initial awareness was rapidly compounded by the 1973–1974 world energy crisis. At this precise juncture, natural resource management was recast as an issue of environmental governance, and it was connected to the new environmental discourses taking shape, such as sustainable development.

The issue of the earth's limits is an unsettled question, not least because of the sheer diversity of natural resources and the difficulty in assessing them scientifically. However, the remaining controversy revolves, not around the idea that the earth's resources are limited, but rather around its regenerative capacities (its "resourcefulness"), which in turn determines how these limits are to be considered. If they are relative, the question becomes one of regulating the access to the resource more stringently or of adapting the activity relying upon it so that it can use a more abundant primary resource. If the limits are absolute, then merely switching the activity from one dependency basis to another is simply insufficient, especially if such dependency continues to expand overall.

Some Conceptual Approaches to Natural Resource Management

Natural resource management ties in with applied concepts such as maximum sustainable yield (MSY) and optimum utilization. Every natural resource has its optimum utilization, or acceptable levels of use that are established scientifically and according to which management authorities regulate its exploitation. Such a concept presupposes scientific knowledge as a basis for management and also a regulatory authority (whether national or international) capable of enforcing the exploitation of the resources in accord with such scientific knowledge. The MSY is a regulatory concept that translates laws of population dynamics into a management tool. Population studies have shown that when the deaths among a given population increase as a result of harvesting (exploitation), reproduction rates start to rise (as if compensating for the deaths). This resultant surplus production can be harvested sustainably, providing the harvest is consistently maintained under the MSY, which is specific to each population (rather than to the

species as a whole). This is the peak level, beyond which the surplus production starts to decline because the negative effect of decreasing numbers on the overall population starts to exceed the positive effect of increased reproduction rates. Subsequently, the population as a whole (and not just the harvestable surplus) begins to decline. On the other hand, maintaining exploitation levels below the MSY creates an efficient use of the resources' regenerative capacities, thus, in principle enabling exploitation to continue indefinitely. The use of this tool, which was first developed in fisheries, has been extended more broadly, notably through its incorporation into the 1982 Convention on the Law of the Seas. However, it has tended to be associated with species-specific management regimes.

Another way to think about natural resource management is to think about what the management is for. The management objectives are determined, in turn, by what the resource itself is used for: as a primary resource, as a raw material or fuel, as a source of food, or as a recreational resource, a more recent but rapidly increasing type of use. These uses fall into two broad categories, consumptive and nonconsumptive. Consumptive utilization implies a once-only form of use; that is, it refers to activities where the resource is effectively consumed or used up, such that it cannot be utilized by another party. Hence, the possibility of future exploitation relies on the resource's ability to regenerate itself. Nonconsumptive utilization also uses the resource to generate economic value, but without using up the resource itself. This category encompasses most recreational uses of natural resources. In the case of consumptive uses, management implies balancing out exploitation with a respect for the resource's regenerative capacities, as we have seen in the discussion of MSY. In nonconsumptive uses, management is about regulating the way in which humans interact with the resource and containing the negative effects of those interactions on the resource. In either case, management is always about resolving a tension between the potentially conflicting objectives of protection and exploitation. Sometimes the use of a resource may change over time or from one part of the globe to the next. The overexploitation of whales is a case in point: Initially, it was a primary raw material and fuel in the West until the mid-twentieth century; today, it is considered a recreational resource in the West and a food in other areas. This coexistence of different forms of use around the same resource has generated conflicts.

Another strand in natural resource management literature focuses on the difficulties in managing collective resources, that is, either resources not contained within specific territorial boundaries (such as the sea or air) or resources whose management at the local level has global repercussions, such as forests. According to one line of argument, known as the tragedy of the commons, collective resources lack the incentives inherently built into a privately owned resource to self-limit their exploitation so as to ensure they will last. There, the tendency is for individual users to consume as much of the resource as possible before others can get to it, resulting in the overall loss of the resource for all. Also at stake in the discussion is the issue of private versus communal management, a question that goes to the heart of environmental governance.

—*Charlotte Epstein*

See also Ecosystemic Approach; Endangered Species Protection; Environmental Governance; Precautionary Principle; Sustainability; Sustainable Development; Tragedy of the Commons

Further Readings and References

Dryzek, J. S., & Schlossberg, D. (2005). *Debating the Earth: The environmental politics reader.* Oxford, UK: Oxford University Press.

NEGOTIATION

Negotiation embraces myriad roles, strategies, and tactics exercised to influence agreement in efforts to create value, solve problems, and resolve disputes. Bargaining encompasses a broad array of simple, two-party to complex, multiparty encounters, both domestic and international.

Optimally Distributive and Integrative

When the average person envisions negotiation, they see what is referred to in negotiation literature as the distributive dance. The field of negotiation stresses distributive bargaining, a simple linear model, with what is termed a fixed pie, or limited resources to be divided, such as water. Negotiating the price of a good further exemplifies straightforward distributive dynamics. The buyer or seller begins with an opening offer or position. The other party responds with a counteroffer or demand. Through a series of moves and countermoves, the parties proceed to split the difference—the distance between the two offers, with a predictable dance of proportional and responsive concessions until they reach agreement through compromise.

Most negotiations, however, do not merely involve a fixed pie to be divided. They encompass complex layers of interests and needs to be explored, identified, and satisfied, rather than split. Integrative in contrast to distributive bargaining assumes interdependence. It is designed to handle complexity. It expects that different stakeholders will define desired outcomes in their own subjective ways. It does not equate such difference in frameworks with distributive positioning. Instead, diverse perspectives are mined and reframed in search for options maximizing satisfaction, without requiring change in mandate. Negotiating different perceptions of risk and value, for example, such as the worth of endangered species and thousands of jobs or reduced infant mortality versus tons of ore, requires integrative bargaining. Integrative parties might ask: How can we generate ore and protect infants simultaneously?

Roger Fisher, founder of the Harvard Negotiation Project, introduced and popularized interest analysis as an alternative to positional, or power-based, bargaining. Rather than expecting political leaders to abandon their postures, they are analyzed. The principals' underlying interests provide an explicit framework for stimulating creative problem solving.

In contrast, framing a complex conflict with linear logic as a simple either/or, win-lose paradigm can polarize. Overly confident distributive moves risk escalating hostility, eroding trust, and otherwise inciting unproductive moves, particularly with conflict involving groups. A seminal study of U.S. lawyers described the least effective lawyers with words like arrogant, stubborn, unethical, and egotistic. A recent study of multicultural leadership of conflict process in four parts of the world likewise described the least effective leadership as closed minded, judgmental, insensitive, negative, and indifferent. Even if a party succeeds in forcing its desire, the agreement is unlikely to last. The risk of public scrutiny and negative publicity is high.

Distributive bargaining in the international arena makes most sense with true fixed pies. Even then, it must be exercised with skill and strategy to avoid incurring the costs previously described.

United Nations and other international case studies evaluating negotiation indicate that integrative approaches as a whole generally result in superior outcomes. Simple logic advocates that agreements reached by consensus are more sustainable and easier to implement than those imposed. Mediators, or facilitators of negotiation, are increasingly recognized as contributing sophistication when parties lack knowledge and experience with integrative bargaining. In the global study of multicultural leadership previously mentioned, careful listening alone was instrumental to progress, particularly with cross-ethnic negotiation.

A student of conflict resolution, whose family immigrated to the United States from Afghanistan shortly after his birth, attributes the coming together of ethnic factions in Afghanistan to integrative bargaining. His intriguing perspective asserts that after a long history of distributive failures, resolution was only possible after finally attempting integrative negotiation for the first time.

Proven Research and Theories

Most negotiation research and resultant theories are criticized for not translating into pragmatic usefulness. Short-term laboratory studies fail to simulate complex conflict. Howard Raiffa, renowned game theorist, in working as an international administrator had an opportunity to test his paradigms' practicality and found that negotiators often fail to act in rational, coherent ways.

A few studies, however, are noteworthy exceptions. They demonstrate that while many rational models and theories are not capable of predicting diverse cultural as well as irrational behavior, they can provide insight capable of making critical difference.

Robert Axelrod, as one example, initiated extensive mathematical research attempting to identify optimal strategy for transforming aggressive tactics to collaborative bargaining. The results indicate the following. Beginning negotiation cooperatively and giving generously builds goodwill. Otherwise, a defensive, hostile climate is created. Transforming broken trust is harder than beginning in ways that earn and build trust. The other's good will, however, cannot be assumed. Negotiators must be vigilant—alert and prepared to respond strategically to each countermove, move by move, like a game of chess. If an opponent responds aggressively, it is recommended to respond in kind to the degree necessary to inform one's opponent that the proponent is not vulnerable to attack. At that point, offering an olive branch gives the opponent an opportunity to collaborate once again. If the invitation is accepted, hostility has been successfully transformed to cooperation, at least for that moment. If an opponent stubbornly persists in aggression, however, the negotiator must resist.

Neil Rackham's research is another example. Scrutinizing labor-management negotiations, Rackham found that the most effective negotiation, judged so by all parties and demonstrated through durable agreement, involved these behaviors. The best were excellent gatherers of information, asking many more questions than less-effective negotiators. They listened actively. They zealously sought common ground and creative options. In contrast, the less-effective negotiators frequently demonstrate unstrategic attack.

—Nancy Erbe

See also Conflict Mediation; Game Theory; Interdependence; Peace Process

Further Readings and References

Axelrod, R. (1990). *The evolution of cooperation*. London and New York: Penguin.

Erbe, N. (2003). *Holding these truths: Empowerment and recognition in action: An interactive case study curriculum for multicultural conflict resolution*. Berkeley: Berkeley Public Policy Press, Institute of Governmental Studies, University of California.

Rackham, N. (2003). The behavior of successful negotiators. In R. J. Lewicki et al. (Eds.), *Negotiation: Readings, exercises, and cases* (4th ed., pp. 169–181). Boston: McGraw-Hill.

Raiffa, H., Richardson, J., & Metcalfe, D. (2003). *Negotiation analysis: The science and art of decision making*. Cambridge, MA: Harvard University Press.

Schneider, A. (2002). Shattering negotiation myths: Empirical evidence on the effectiveness of negotiation styles. *Harvard Negotiation Law Review, 7,* 143–233.

NEIGHBORHOOD ASSOCIATION

The term *neighborhood association* (or *community association*) refers to the relatively formally organized group whose aim is to address local issues, such as education reform, crime, or homelessness, to promote or prevent planned reforms and investments that are perceived as significantly influencing life in the local community/neighborhood. Therefore, neighborhood associations strengthen the link between residents and policymakers. They mobilize residents into political activism and create opportunities for direct communication within the local community and between the local residents and local officials. Unlike professional, lifestyle, or interest-focused associations that group individuals by their occupational characteristics or similar lifestyle or interests, neighborhood associations group individuals that share concern for the good of the local community.

Research shows that while citizens' participation in most types of voluntary organizations is beneficial for the quality of democratic government, neighborhood associations have a particularly positive influence on the functioning of political and economic institutions. Neighborhood associations act as "schools of democracy," in which citizens are socialized into activism and political participation. They facilitate communication among various local actors and institutions and stimulate articulation of citizens' interests and expectations. They contribute to the emergence of the sense of community among local residents. They increase individuals' and communities' civic capacity. As a result, neighborhood associations contribute to the empowerment of neighborhood communities and lay the ground for local and national policy efforts.

Individuals with larger resources (such as skills and money) are more likely to join voluntary associations, but research shows that neighborhood associations that have more resources are less active than less-affluent associations. However, this may be due to the fact that that they operate in the wealthier areas facing fewer social problems, thus requiring less action on their part. It may also be a result of replacing the needs-driven approach, focusing on the problems of a local community, with the asset-based approach that concentrates on utilizing the strengths of even deprived communities, and thus on transforming "clients into citizens."

The late twentieth century has brought a widespread concern about the loss of community in modern Western societies. Anonymity of urban environments, technological advances, and increased mobility are among the main factors blamed for the erosion of formal and informal networks among local residents. Therefore, in attempts to create opportunities for the emergence and development of neighborhood initiatives, governmental and nongovernmental agencies promote policies aimed at improving the quality of life in local communities and strengthening citizens' links with their neighborhoods.

—*Natalia Letki*

See also Association; Civic Capacity; Civic Engagement; Civil Society; Common Good; Communitarianism; Community Organizing; Policy Development; Self-Government; Social Capital

Further Readings and References

Berry, J., Portney, K., & Thomson, K. (1993). *The rebirth of urban democracy*. Washington, DC: Brookings Institution.

Chavis, D. M., & Wandersman, A. (1990). Sense of community in the urban environment: A catalyst for participation and community development. *American Journal of Community Psychology, 18,* 55–81.

Edwards, B., Foley, M., & Diani, M. (Eds.). (2001). *Beyond Tocqueville: Civil society and the social capital debate in comparative perspective.* Hanover, MA: Tufts University.

NEOCOLONIALISM

Neocolonialism can be defined as the control of less-developed countries by developed countries through an indirect means. The term was first used after World War II to refer to the continuing dependence of former colonies on foreign countries. Its meaning soon broadened to apply, more generally, to places where the power of developed countries was used to produce a colonial-like exploitation, for instance, in Latin America, where direct foreign rule had ended in the early nineteenth century. The term is now widely used to refer to a system of global governance in which transnational corporations and global and multilateral institutions combine to perpetuate colonial forms of exploitation of developing countries. Neocolonial governance has been broadly theorized as a further development of capitalism that enables capitalist powers (both nations and corporations) to dominate subject nations through the operations of international capitalism, rather than by means of direct rule.

The term *neocolonialism* was originally applied to European policies that were seen as schemes to maintain control of African and other dependencies. The event that marked the beginning of this usage was the European Summit in Paris in 1957, where six European heads of government agreed to include their overseas territories within the European Common Market under trade arrangements that were seen by some national leaders and groups as representing a new form of economic domination over French-occupied Africa and the colonial territories of Italy, Belgium, and the Netherlands.

Neocolonialism came to be seen, more generally, as involving a coordinated effort by former colonial powers and other developed countries to block growth in developing countries and retain them as sources of cheap raw materials and cheap labor. This effort was seen as closely associated with the Cold War and, in particular, with the U.S. policy known as the Truman Doctrine. Under this policy, the U.S. government offered large amounts of money to any government prepared to accept U.S. protection from communism. This enabled the United States to extend its sphere of influence and, in some cases, to place foreign governments under its control. The United States and other developed countries have also ensured the subordination of developing countries by interfering in conflicts and helping in other ways to install regimes that are willing to act for the benefit of foreign companies and against their own country's interests.

However, neocolonial governance is seen as generally operating through indirect forms of control and, in particular, by means of the economic, financial, and trade policies of transnational corporations and global and multilateral institutions. It operates through the investments of multinational corporations that, while enriching a few in underdeveloped countries, keep those countries as a whole in a situation of dependency and cultivates them as reservoirs of cheap labor and raw materials. It also operates through international financial institutions such as the International Monetary Fund (IMF) and the World Bank, which make loans (as well as other forms of economic aid) conditional on the recipient nations taking steps favorable to the financial cartels represented by these institutions, but detrimental to their own economies. Thus, while many people see these corporations and institutions as part of an essentially new global order and a new form of global governance, the notion of neocolonialism directs our attention to what, in this system and constellation of power, represents continuity between the present and recent past.

—*Sandra Halperin*

See also Dependency; Humanitarian Intervention; International Monetary Fund; Third-World Debt; World Bank; World Trade Organization

Further Readings and References

Bhatt, A. J. (2003). Asian Indians and the model minority narrative: A neocolonial system. In E. M. Kramer (Ed.), *The emerging monoculture: Assimilation and the "model minority"* (pp. 203–331). Westport, CT: Praeger.

Hoogvelt, A. (2001). *Globalization and the postcolonial world: The new political economy of development.* Baltimore: Johns Hopkins University Press.

Werbner, R. (Ed.). (1996). *Postcolonial identities in Africa.* Atlantic Highlands, NJ: Zed Books.

NEOLIBERALISM

Neoliberalism is a policy paradigm that emphasizes the need for free market competition. It is both an ideology (that is, an organized set of ideas) and a practice (that is, a set of policy prescriptions). Although there is considerable debate as to the defining features of neoliberal thought and practice, it is most commonly associated with *laissez-faire* economics. In particular, neoliberalism is often characterized in terms of its belief in sustained economic growth as the means to achieve human progress, its confidence in free markets as the most efficient allocation of resources, its emphasis on minimal state intervention in economic and social affairs, and its commitment to the freedom of trade and capital.

Despite their similar titles, neoliberalism is distinct from new liberalism. Both have their ideological roots in the classical liberalism of the nineteenth century, which championed the freedom (or liberty) of the individual. But liberalism has evolved over time into a number of different (and often competing) traditions. New liberalism has evolved from the social liberal tradition, which focuses on individuals' freedom to achieve fulfillment through state intervention (such as the right to free education and health care). By contrast, neoliberalism is closely related to economic liberalism, which emphasizes individuals' freedom from state intervention (for example, in terms of the right to own private property and to enter into contracts). This variant of liberalism is often associated with the economist Adam Smith, who argued in his 1776 book, *The Wealth of Nations,* that markets are governed by an "invisible hand" and thus should be subject to minimal government interference.

Classical liberalism was highly influential in the late nineteenth and early twentieth centuries in which the industrialized economies pursued trade liberalization and *laissez-faire* economics. However, with the advent of the Great Depression in the 1930s and then World War II, many Western governments pursued a much more interventionist role in economic and social affairs. From the late 1960s onward, the postwar economic order experienced a series of crises, including the international recessions of 1966–1967 and 1974, the collapse of the Gold Exchange Standard in 1971, and the oil crises of 1973–1974 and 1979. For many, this demonstrated the power of markets and the impotence of governments. The collapse of the Soviet Union in 1989–1991 and the crisis of the East Asian "developmental states" in 1997 was seen further to reinforce this.

Thus, neoliberalism is closely associated with globalization, with heightened flows of trade and capital often seen to have shifted the balance of power from states to markets so that governments have little choice but to adopt neoliberal policies in order to achieve economic competitiveness. Yet, as a variety of scholars have noted, social democratic countries have fared just as well under conditions of globalization as their neoliberal counterparts, and many developing countries have failed to flourish—despite following the neoliberal dictates of the Washington Consensus. Indeed, for many critics, neoliberalism is the cause of, not the solution to, social inequality across the world.

—*Nicola Smith*

See also Asian Financial Crisis; Capitalism; Communitarianism; Competition State; Development Theory; Globalization; International Monetary Fund; Market; Post–Washington Consensus; Poverty Reduction; Privatization; Regime Theory; Washington Consensus

Further Readings and References

Castels, M. (1998). *End of millennium.* Oxford, UK: Basil Blackwell.

Robbins, R. (2005). *Global problems and the culture of capitalism* (3rd ed.). Boston: Allyn & Bacon.

Smith, A. (1991). *Wealth of nations.* Buffalo, NY: Prometheus Books.

Neo-Marxism

Marxism is divided into different, often conflicting, tendencies and groups, none of which can, without problem, claim to be the sole, true heirs of Marx. Some writers argue that there is no longer a single theory of Marxism and that we must talk instead of Marxisms in the plural. Others maintain that Marxism should be seen as a concrete and complex historical tradition that contains within it many different schools and theories. Neo-Marxism describes a loose movement of political and social theorists that interpreted Marxism with an emphasis on the humanism and idealism of Karl Marx's early works. Contrary to the orthodox (or traditional) Marxists, neo-Marxists sought to explain why political revolution did not take place as Marx predicted and thus explored the phenomena of psychological coercion and liberation.

Orthodox Marxism

Orthodox Marxism focuses on political economy, exploring the contradictions inherent between the base (the means of production) and the superstructure (conditions of material life), particularly in a capitalist economy. The characteristics of the base determine the nature of the superstructure. The development of the forces of production brings them into conflict with the relations of production, and these conflicts are reflected in class struggle. Such conflicts are the basic motive principle of history. Their specific development within capitalism creates not only the economic conditions for revolutionary change, but also its agents, the industrial working class. History is divided into distinct stages or modes of production. The capitalist mode of production is a transitory form, destined to be superseded by a higher socialist stage of society.

Austro-Marxism

The Austro-Marxists, such as Max Adler and Otto Bauer, were particularly inspired by neo-Kantian philosophy of science and then-nascent positivist philosophy that was the rage in Vienna. In the Austro-Marxian perspective, the Marxian system was a system of sociological inquiry, or, rather, a system of economic theory that was embedded in a more general social theory, which gave a central position to economic relationships. In contrast to the Germans, the Austrians were less concerned with the issue of revolutionary strategy and more concerned with the issue of the Marxian theoretical analysis. This permitted them to embrace a quasi-revisionist attitude. The Austro-Marxists were also contemporaries of the then-prominent neoclassical Austrian School and thus were forced to take the theoretical and economic aspects of Marx a bit more seriously and listened to the neoclassical critiques more carefully. Of particular importance were the criticisms on the Marxian theory of value by the neoclassical economists Vilfredo Pareto and Eugen von Böhm-Bawerk. These economists claimed to have detected inconsistencies in Marx's "labor theory of value," and, in particular, they identified the famous "transformation problem" of converting labor values into prices of production.

Marxist Humanism

Marxist humanism emerged partly as a result of disillusionment with the state socialism of the Eastern European states, including Yugoslavia. It was first articulated by Eduard Bernstein in 1899, who challenged the Marxist idea that economic breakdown was inevitable. Marxist humanists usually base their positions on the early humanist writings of Karl Marx, especially the *Economic and Philosophical Manuscripts of 1844.* The focus on the early works is not exclusive; but generally speaking, Marxist humanism defines itself in opposition to objectivist tendencies in social theory, reflected in orthodox interpretations of historical materialism in which the agent of history is not human beings, but either abstract entities such as "laws of history" or inanimate entities such as "means of production." Therefore, Marxist humanists emphasize human agency and subjectivity and place greater emphasis on the ethical rather than social-theoretical problems of Marxism.

Structural Marxism

Structural Marxism is an approach to Marxism primarily associated with the work of the French philosopher Louis Althusser, although the work of Lucien Goldmann is sometimes seen as a precursor. It was influential in France during the late 1960s and 1970s and also came to influence philosophers, political theorists, and sociologists outside of France during the 1970s. Several of Althusser's theoretical positions have remained influential, though he sometimes deliberately overstated his arguments to provoke controversy. Althusser's essay *On the Young Marx* draws a term from a great "epistemological break" between Marx's early Hegelian writings and his later, properly Marxist texts. His essay *Marxism and Humanism* is a strong statement of antihumanism, condemning ideas like "human potential" and "species-being," which are often put forth by Marxists as outgrowths of a bourgeois ideology of humanity. In Althusser's view, Marx did not simply argue that people's needs are largely created by their social environment and thus vary with time and place; rather, he abandoned the idea that there could be an a priori theory about human nature.

Neo-Marxism continues to be important because many of its criticisms of capitalism and liberal democracy continue to find resonance. Structural Marxism, for example, has remained influential in theorizing how social conditions determine human behavior and thus argues against the powerful Western idea of free will. Humanist Marxism is evident in contemporary calls for international labor rights and human self-actualization. Marxist and neo-Marxist ideals have played a role in socialist democratic forms of governance, as well as in critiques of liberal democratic structures of governance.

—*Lisa A. Zanetti*

See also Communism; Critical Theory; Hegemony; Marxism; Political Economy; Regulation Theory

Further Readings and References

Althusser, L. (1996). *For Marx* (B. Brewster, Trans.) (Reprinted ed.). London and New York: Verso.

Gorman, R. (1982). *Neo-Marxism: The meanings of modern radicalism.* Westport, CT: Greenwood.

Gorman, R. (1985). *A biographical dictionary of neo-Marxism.* Westport, CT: Greenwood.

Koakowski, L. (2005). *Main currents of Marxism: The founders, the golden age, the breakdown.* New York: W. W. Norton.

Marx, K. (1959). *Economic and philosophical manuscripts of 1844* (M. Mulligan, Trans.). Moscow: Progress Publishers.

NEOTRADITIONALISM

Neotraditionalism is the deliberate revival and revamping of old culture, practices, and institutions for use in new political contexts and strategies. It entails a degree of contestation over culture and memory, can serve as a strategy of political legitimation, and is deployed in different ways by both elites and ordinary people. It is especially salient in contexts of rapid social change or when people question the nature or benefits of that which is presented as "developmental" or "modern." Neotraditionalism suggests that regime forms, the nature of law, the means for checking the arbitrariness of rulers, and other forms of state-society interaction should take into account or resonate with local definitions of authentic culture and historical memory.

As a concept, neotraditionalism breaks with primordialist notions of deeply rooted cultural essences or characterizations of static, antimodern tradition. An approach focusing on neotraditionalism instead follows historians in the "invention of tradition" school, neo-Marxists concerned with hegemony, and social theorists in the constructivist vein to treat seemingly historic institutions, practices, and values as moldable resources, subject to ongoing social and political contestation. In this sense, one cannot speak of politically salient, extant, and unproblematic "traditions" of, for example, democratic participation (e.g., *panchayat* village councils in India, *pancasila* democracy in Indonesia, consensual village decision making under the African "talking tree"), but rather of specific efforts to identify and promulgate particular, often reified, always modified, versions of remembered culture and institutions as neotraditions.

Neotraditions serve political goals and are the subject of political contestation over the definition of historical memory and "authentic" culture. They can be especially useful tools for the consolidation of group identity in circumstances of rapid and confusing social change. Thus, Eric Hobsbawm described the invention and deployment of neotraditions surrounding the mythic hero Ossian, bagpipes, and kilts in constructing a new Scottish national identity at a time of rapid class transformation, urbanization, and the decline of feudal forms of social solidarity. Likewise, in southern Africa, historians have shown how the massive migration of men to mines and factories around the turn of the twentieth century precipitated new understandings of "traditional" culture, emphasizing women's subordination, powerful elder male chieftaincy, and rigid customary land laws. These neotraditional customs and institutions enabled absent men to retain control over key resources (especially their wives and their farms). Neotraditionalism has also been used as a powerful tool of political legitimation in postcolonial settings, whereby authoritarian elites from Mobutu Sese Seko in Zaire to Suharto in Indonesia sought to justify single-party authoritarian regimes as "democratic" because one-party rule supposedly revived and updated precolonial traditions of village-level, inclusive, consensus decision making.

Neotraditional analysis does not suggest that the story of Ossian, powerful elder male chieftaincy, or village democracy are fabrications and simple instrumentalist manipulations of an entirely plastic and moldable culture. Rather, it accepts that some forms of these stories, practices, and informal institutions represent ethnographic and historical realities, but that there is a political process in which actors filter and select particular elements of remembered culture as the central and salient definitions of "tradition" in any given moment.

Although often monopolized by state-level postcolonial elites as legitimating cultural patina, neotraditionalism by definition need not serve authoritarianism nor operate only in the hands of dominant groups.

Thus, the much-celebrated Grameen Bank and other systems of revolving credit can be understood as neotraditional redeployments of historically rooted practices of intergroup solidarity and trust (which compel borrowers to repay loans so that kin or neighbor can receive their credit) in new, more modern circumstances. Likewise, small- and medium-sized specialty manufacturers in West Jutland, Denmark, and Emilia Romagna, Italy, redeployed and revamped old practices of cooperation, some rooted in agrarian practices, to achieve economies of scale and international competitiveness. In these cases, social actors at various levels, not state elites, reformulated tradition for new purposes, crafting new institutional solutions that enjoy the benefit of social familiarity and apparent embeddedness in a local culture. Thus, analysis of neotraditionalism in governance demands that we understand not simply how culture and memory are recrafted, but who does so, with the application of what degree of power and in pursuit of what interests.

In an era of rapid globalization of trade and communication, as well as the standardization of liberal democratic politics and free-market economics, neotraditionalism represents an important mode of localist response or resistance to perceived external domination or cultural homogenization. Thus, xenophobic nationalists and religious fundamentalists redeploy visions, values, practices, and modes of social organization of a purportedly more authentic, uncorrupted past as a means to critique the alienation and "mongrelization" associated with the dominant liberal democratic capitalist order. Likewise, some communitarian activists, proponents of "indigenous" rights, and environmentalists (especially social and deep ecologists) evoke historic patterns of social capital, holism, and harmony with nature as neotraditional alternatives to the perceived irresponsibility, materialism, imperialism, and unsustainability of the same liberal democratic capitalist order. Neotraditionalism provides a language, a mode of sociocultural legitimation, and a basis for political mobilization for many forms of critique of "high modernity."

The differences between Afghanistan after 2001 and Iraq after 2003 might offer a quasi-experiment in the political impact of neotraditionalism. In the former case, constitution and regime building after the U.S.-led invasion were grounded on an institution many participants considered traditional, yet was clearly being redeployed and revamped for new purposes (the *loya jirga* council of clan and ethnic group leaders). Regime reconstruction and constitution writing in Iraq after the 2003 U.S.-led invasion benefited from no such deployment of a neotraditional institution and, to date, has proved less legitimate and durable than the process in Afghanistan.

—*Dennis Galvan*

See also Discourse; Interpretive theory; Postmodernism; Social Constructivism; Tradition

Further Readings and References

Amsele, J.-L. (1998). *Mestizo logics: Anthropology of identity in Africa and elsewhere.* Stanford, CA: Stanford University Press.

Brubaker, R., & Cooper, F. (2000). Beyond 'identity.' *Theory and Society, 29,* 1–47.

Hobsbawm, E., & Ranger, T. (1992). *The invention of tradition.* Cambridge, UK: Cambridge University Press.

Kuper, A. (2003). The return of the native. *Current Anthropology, 44*(3), 389–402.

Vail, L. (1991). *The creation of tribalism in southern Africa.* Berkeley: University of California Press.

NETWORK

Between Adam Smith's invisible hand of the marketplace and Max Weber's structured bureaucratic organization, there exists the concept of networks. At its broadest definition, a network is a group of interdependent actors and the relationships among them. Unlike a properly functioning market system, networks do not assume that members have complete information, nor do they assume that every individual with money may choose to be a member. Unlike a bureaucratic organization, a network may operate without clearly defined leadership, without a hierarchy, and even without employees.

At a personal level, networks may be about an individual's social connections, while at an organizational level, networks are about the recognition that organizations' actions seldom stand alone in the world. Human beings can, indeed, achieve more through coordinated, collaborative efforts than through individual efforts. Definitions of networks abound, however, and the term is used to mean very different things.

What is important to understand is that networks are not fuzzy, soft concepts. In fact, they may be either loosely or tightly institutionalized, and so some scholars have started referring to them as "networks and network structures." Thus, when governance networks are being studied, the question is not merely how informal contacts change the functioning of organizational relationships. Instead, the question is what relationships have been structured between two or more programs or organizations that enable them to leverage the strengths and minimize the weaknesses of the collectivity. Networks are distinct social structures in that they involve multiple organizations, they do not need to involve hierarchical or contractual arrangements, there may be significant power differentials or size differences between the various actors, all the organizations are dependent on each other in at least some important aspect, and information or specific skills may be key sources of power rather than just financial and jurisdictional power.

Networks are often defined as interdependent structures linking several organizations, without hierarchy and absent of critical leverage. This definition is useful because it is seemingly general enough to incorporate a vast body of research since the mid-1970s on policy networks, policy communities and policy complexes, advocacy coalitions, social networks, policy issue networks, intergovernmental networks, interorganizational networks, and issue networks. The common threads of these approaches are that they represent a growing field of interorganizational theory as well as the evolution of interest group theories. Research on networks typically highlights the assorted interactions among parties with diverse or narrow interests struggling over the allotment of values. The development of this concept of a network is in keeping with general trends toward systems theory and toward flexible, collaborative organizational models.

Thinking in terms of networks runs the risk of devaluing the status of governments. Governments are responsible for making decisions in the public interest—broadly defined—and networks may narrow the definition of public interest considerably if such networks become the primary sources of input for politicians, diplomats, or administrators. On the other hand, rather than devaluing government, developing clear descriptions of how networks function may be useful as a heuristic device to identify specific potential problems in democratic administration. If all relevant interests are not included in a network, then democratic administration may have been derailed by the power of selected interests. How administrators working on a specific issue define "relevant" may be an important clue as well.

Types of Networks

Policy networks, network management, intergovernmental networks, interorganizational networks and network structures, and issue networks are the five leading network models, although they frequently cross paths in the literature. Table 1 makes some basic comparisons among these five types of networks.

A shared body of knowledge and a common allegiance to professional norms and the scientific process distinguish policy networks. Policy networks are closely knit, stable networks, and they tend to have a limited or controlled membership. They focus on a narrow policy issue, such as energy policy. Frequently, they focus even more narrowly on, to stick with the energy policy example, wind energy, power regulation, or privatizing electrical distribution. Members are generally highly trained and educated professionals from industry, think tanks, academia, and government agencies.

Network management, a newcomer compared to policy networks, is focused on how political leaders and public administrators can manage existing networks. In this model, public management is frequently directly related with network management—managing systems of interdependencies—and is not associated with the new public management of privatization, deregulation, and contracting out. The view of "public management as network management" comes full circle from the original views of policy networks research, which primarily focused on explaining that government policies frequently failed because experts and self-interested groups had special access to the policy-making arena (i.e., vested interests blocked legitimate proposals for change). Network management is still about policy networks, but the focus shifts toward actively controlling policy networks rather than explaining how they constrain policy development.

Intergovernmental networks have focused on local, regional, state, and national governments as key actors in interdependent relationships. These networks are quite interdependent, although power may frequently be lopsided because national governments are usually coming to the table with

Table 1   General Comparisons of Five Network Types

	Policy or Administration as Main Focus	Breadth of Focus (Narrow, Moderate, Broad)	Natural or Deliberate Design	Stability of Network (High, Medium, Low)
Policy networks	Policy	Narrow	Natural	High
Network management	Holistic	Moderate	Both	Medium
Intergovernmental networks	Administration	Narrow	Both	High
Interorganizational networks and network structures	Holistic	Broad	Both	Medium or High
Issue networks	Policy	Broad	Natural	Low

Source: Adapted from Mingus, M. S. (2001). From subnet to supranet: A proposal for a comparative network framework to examine network interactions across borders. In M. P. Mandell (Ed.), *Getting results through collaboration: Networks and network structures for public policy and management* (p. 34). Westport, CT: Quorum Books, Greenwood Publishing Group.

money to spend. They typically are quite stable due to a high degree of interaction and trust that is built up over many decades. Therefore, the general focus is on management and joint program implementation more than on public policy or advocacy.

The approach of interorganizational networks and network structures tends to focus on managerial or implementation issues as well and originated in organizational theory and development. While interorganizational networks started with a business administration or generic administration focus rather than a public or governmental focus, examples of this approach now abound in public administration, especially community development programs such as workforce development, economic development, and community-based substance abuse prevention. An identifying characteristic of this approach is that networks are frequently created by design to achieve specific intended purposes, whereas the policy networks model generally assumes that a network is a naturally occurring phenomenon that can be explained by thorough research.

In contrast to these four approaches, issue networks assume rapidly changing, dynamic networks that ebb and flow in a quantumlike manner. Issue networks are a symbol of the onset of the information age, where a shared knowledge base is what brings people or organizations or both together to focus on a particular issue or problem. Power is commensurate with the information and knowledge one can bring to the table in an issue network, rather than with responsibility, titles, role in a defined hierarchy, and so forth. In a rapidly changing information society, well-informed activists come from many corners, and their knowledge is valued, in part, because of a strong perceived need on the part of government to be right when making decisions.

Key differences of this approach include that non-professionals may have extensive influence and that the focus is on broad policy concerns rather than a narrow policy subfield. An issue network might be concerned about protecting consumers from the mythical "all-powerful, multinational corporation," whereas a related policy network might be focused on deregulating the electrical distribution system to create a more efficient economy. There is a need for the policy network model to replace the traditional progressivist model in public administration.

Issue networks are looser than policy networks; thus, this model does not assume that either trust building or value sharing occurs. This model discounts the possibility that personal interaction of issue network participants might help them communicate better, learn from one another, and alter their values over time, thereby moving intractable policy issues toward closure. In addition, issue networks do not fall neatly within the concept of interorganizational networks and network structures because organizations may still be working separately to get their own needs met and also because the focus is on power more than on building trust.

Comparative Network Theory

This maze of terms and models represents a critical problem for developing a field of comparative network theory. Identical terms are regularly used to describe different concepts, and the same concepts are described in different ways because of the interdisciplinary nature of scholarship on this topic. Table 1 broadly draws from the literature to make comparisons between these five network models in terms of four meaningful categories.

1. *Policy or Administration as Main Focus*—Do networks generally focus on policy issues or on management and implementation issues? Obviously policy networks focus heavily on policy issues, but so do the much more loosely structured issue networks. Intergovernmental networks, on the other extreme, are usually built around program implementation issues and are therefore highly administrative or managerial. The newer models—especially intergovernmental networks and network management—are frequently focused on implementation and administrative issues rather than on public policy. This might show an evolution in the application of the concept of networks.

2. *Breadth of Focus (Narrow, Moderate, Broad)*—Are networks generally highly focused (i.e., oil policy), moderately focused (i.e., energy policy), or broadly

focused (i.e., natural resources and the environment)? Policy networks and intergovernmental networks are generally narrow in their focus, while interorganizational networks and network structures may focus on a broader issue, such as community development for an entire urban center, and issue networks may also focus broadly on a topic, such as adjusting regulatory processes in the age of automation.

3. *Natural or Deliberate Design*—Are networks mostly a naturally occurring form of social organization or are they usually created and designed to accomplish specific tasks? Much of the work on policy networks and issue networks assumes that these systems emerge naturally as people and organizations seek to get their own needs met, while the other three models assume that a network can be developed by design as well. This raises numerous questions around design issues, such as "Can we design a more functional intergovernmental network for implementing a federal program such as the community development block grants?"

4. *Stability of Network (High, Medium, Low)*— How resistant to change are networks? Policy networks are thought to be quite stable because paid professionals with career commitments to a particular policy issue are the driving force. Likewise, intergovernmental networks are quite stable as long as the programs they are designed to implement continue to receive funding. When these networks drift into a policy focus, it is likely to support continued or increased funding. On the other end of the spectrum, issue networks are probably the least stable because they are loosely structured and the participants may not share a specific professional or programmatic commitment.

Subnets and Supranets

In examining cross-border networks, we might distinguish subnet and supranet to ask how subnets interact across borders to form supranets. Essentially, a supranet is a cross-border network of networks, while the within-border networks are termed *subnets*. The language is simple and allows for an easier discussion of regional and international issues because subnets

may be contributing toward a common purpose and may share numerous characteristics, such as a narrow policy focus, yet may also have numerous characteristics that are not shared among the supranet. For example, the subnets may exist under different regime types and may still involve professionally trained individuals to solve a common policy problem.

A supranet might be something focused and concrete, like the Pacific Salmon Commission established by a treaty between the United States and Canada, or something much broader such as foreign nations and international aid organizations seeking to reduce the consequences of hunger in sub-Saharan Africa. With the increasing use of this concept to compare networks from different nations and to discuss regional international networks, these terms can provide some clarity to the discussion.

Characteristics for Comparing Networks

Typologies are often used in academia to enable comparisons to be made, often with the intent of unifying a field of study with a clear classification schema. Two issues plague the development of a universal typology for networks: (1) Should it include one type of network (i.e., policy networks) or should it include multiple types of networks (i.e., a continuum from issue networks on one end to policy networks on the other end)? (2) What are the key characteristics to differentiate a specific network from any other similar or dissimilar network? These issues are interconnected because if a typology includes just one type of network, then the list of characteristics must include elements that help distinguish among the main types of networks.

Common variables or characteristics that have been used in various classifications of networks in the past twenty years include the following:

- Membership size
- Range of member interests (broad or narrow; diverse or similar)
- Frequency of member interaction (in-person, telephone, or electronic; among members or as a whole)

- Decision-making style (consensus, majority vote, veto members, etc.)
- Network continuity or stability
- Resource distribution within the network
- Ability of members to regulate actions of their organizations
- Ability of networks to regulate actions of their members
- Power balance (positive-sum or zero-sum game)
- Legal structure
- Structural focus (implementation/management, policy, or holistic focus)
- Level of management focus (street level, departmental, or organization wide)
- Regime type (military dictatorship, theocracy, unitary democracy, federalist democracy, etc.)
- Locus of power within government (administrative, diplomatic, or political)
- Level of government with primary control (national, subnational, local)

—*Matthew S. Mingus*

See also Advocacy Networks; Association; Coalition; Collaborative Governance; Disintermediation; Heterarchy; Hierarchy; Informal Organization; Interdependence; Interest Group; Interorganizational Coordination; Policy Network; Social Network Theory; State-Society Relations; Trust

Further Readings and References

Agranoff, R., & McGuire, M. (1999). Managing in network settings. *Policy Studies Review, 16*(1), 14–41.

Mandell, M. (Ed.). (2001). *Getting results through collaboration: Networks and network structures for public policy and management.* Westport, CT: Quorum Books.

Marsh, D. (Ed.). (1998). *Comparing policy networks.* Buckingham, UK: Open University Press.

Miller, H. T. (1994). Post-progressive public administration: Lessons from policy networks. *Public Administration Review, 54*(4), 378–385.

Mingus, M. S. (2001). From subnet to supranet: A proposal for a comparative network framework to examine network interactions across borders. In M. P. Mandell (Ed.), *Getting results through collaboration: Networks and network structures for public policy and management* (pp. 30–48). Westport, CT: Quorum Books.

Mingus, M. S. (2004). Validating the comparative network framework in a Canada/United States context. *Journal of Comparative Policy Analysis: Research and Practice, 6*(1), 15–37.

O'Toole, L. J., Jr. (1997). Treating networks seriously: Practical and research-based agendas in public administration. *Public Administration Review, 57*(1), 45–52.

Rhodes, R. A. W. (1997). *Understanding governance: Policy networks, governance, reflexivity, and accountability.* Buckingham, UK: Open University Press.

NETWORK SOCIETY

Network society refers to the argument that a global form of society is emerging where new communications and information technology media have enabled a significant increase in the capacity of networks of relationships to form that are no longer bounded geographically. The networks of the network society are composed of a series of complex and interacting information nodes, markets, organizations, knowledge, and individuals. The approach has conceptual affinities with macrosociological work on reflexive modernization.

The concept of the network society challenges traditional notions of governance and has been explored in various levels of global competitiveness. When applied to governance, the idea challenges classical notions that levels of government, from small-scale local to regional, national, and ultimately international levels can remain relevant to a newly emerging global society. The emerging society that is the network society is composed of a complex of networks adapting and changing. Many of these networks cut across the old organizational structures of civil society, rendering traditional lines of governance irrelevant. Top-down approaches to governance dissolve, and new forms of political action occur at many different levels. For example, it is argued that the centrality of party politics is challenged and, in some cases, the media become a new political force generating issues that can emerge as new frameworks for the organization of further networks of action.

Governance in a network society is governance under the conditions of a sustained and widespread challenge to centralized planning. It is argued that we no longer live in an era of certainty and that subsequently politics must continue under the conditions of a radical uncertainty. Under these conditions, new arrangements for governance are sought that involve a continuous approach to problem solving and an adversity to risk.

Other complicating themes for governance associated with the network society include finding pathways through the languages and discourses of difference. The implication is that new configurations for governance will emerge involving, for example, a role for politics as a generator of trust. It is when the notion of trust is discussed that its partner term *reciprocity* emerges. Both these concepts seem to direct attention toward the underpinning function behind networks that they are mediators of reciprocal relationships. Governance associated with the condition of such relationships, we are told, needs to grasp the potential for an enhanced democracy through alternative approaches to participation that ideally seeks to enhance autonomy and involvement.

—*Barry Gibson*

See also Association; Collaborative Governance; Interdependence; Social Network Theory; Sociocybernetics; State-Society Relations

Further Readings and References

Castells, M. (2000). *The rise of the network society*. Oxford, UK: Basil Blackwell.

Hajer, M., & Wagenaar, H. (2003). *Deliberative policy analysis: Understanding governance in the network society*. Cambridge, UK: Cambridge University Press.

Messner, D. (1997). *The network society: Economic development and international competitiveness as problems of social governance*. London and Portland, OR: Frank Cass.

NEW INSTITUTIONALISM

In the 1980s, new institutionalism developed in reaction to the behavioral perspectives that were influential during the 1960s and 1970s. Stressing structure over agency, new institutionalists show how values, norms, ideas, rules, routines, and roles that are derived from social contexts guide or channel behavior.

As new institutionalists use the term, institutions are symbolic and behavioral systems containing rules that are linked to regulatory mechanisms that impact individuals by stimulating certain roles, routines, and calculations. New institutionalists unpack symbolic and behavioral systems, spell out their rules, analyze their relationship to regulatory mechanisms, and, ultimately, demonstrate how they make human behavior regular and predictable.

New institutionalists come from disciplinary backgrounds in sociology, economics, and political science, and differ in what they emphasize. "Old" institutionalists focus on values and norms. New sociological institutionalists emphasize cognitive and symbolic systems of meaning, particularly how these give rise to certain identities, roles, and routines. New economic institutionalists emphasize rules and enforcement systems, particularly how these affect individuals' cost-benefit calculations. Historical institutionalists emphasize the macrolevel, national consequences of institutions over time and are primarily interested in comparing national political, social, and economic systems.

Old Institutionalism

The original organizational institutionalists saw institutions as a means of control and coordination. For them, institutions were structures infused with value and valued for their own sake beyond their usefulness in reaching other goals. As an organization becomes institutionalized, it changes from an expendable tool into a valued source of personal satisfaction. Institutions, distinct from normal organizations, operate smoothly without relying on coercion or appealing to utilitarian individual self-interest to coordinate individuals' behavior. Because individuals value the organization for its own sake, they obey organizational norms voluntarily and often even without consciously deciding to do so.

Institutionalists argue that leaders consciously create organizational norms and values to achieve organizational ends. Institutionalization is described as a purposeful process undertaken by organizational elites to motivate the key personnel to internalize chosen social values. The Forest Service leadership overcame powerful centrifugal forces—a geographically scattered, diffuse, and independent workforce—by infusing individual forest rangers with the Forest Service's mission of science in the public interest. The Forest Service's leadership achieves this value infusion in several ways: selective recruitment, extensive training, closed promotion practices, and regular rotation to prevent rangers from "marrying the natives." The Forest Service became an institution itself, to be valued and served.

New Institutional Economics

In the late 1980s, some economists that were dissatisfied with the traditional liberal economic assumption that markets are naturally efficient began to examine how social rules and legal constraints aided markets and exchange. Accepting the fundamental economic assumption that individuals will engage in self-interested behavior, or act to maximize their preferences, economists nevertheless argue that markets are not naturally efficient because opportunistic behavior, asymmetries of information, and enforcement problems lead to transaction costs. In other words, in a truly free market, it is too easy to cheat, which makes truly free markets too inefficient to work. Any transaction involves risk—that the service will not be provided as specified or that the product will not be as promised. The more this risk increases, the more costly enforcement mechanisms become and the less likely exchange becomes. The solution is to create laws, rules, norms, and other constraints on individuals' behavior to prevent cheating and thus reduce risk. For new institutional economists, then, institutions are absolutely necessary for efficient economic exchange and markets.

Institutions reduce the uncertainties involved in human interaction and exchange in particular by acting as constraints, or rules with an enforcement mechanism. They are the rules of the economic game. New institutional economists think of institutions formally as laws, rules, and contracts and informally as patterns of behavior, norms, and roles.

By linking institutions to risk and cost, new institutional economists hope to unpack the black box of the firm and show what decision making looks like within businesses. It can be argued that transaction costs, the costs involved with preventing cheating and ensuring the exchange occurs as agreed, make up the majority of the costs of doing business. In each transaction, from buying supplies to hiring labor to supervising manufacturing to securing distribution, risk is involved. The degree of risk determines how costly that project will be to undertake. Institutions help determine level of risk. The stronger the institutions, the lower the risk and transaction cost, and the more likely markets will not fail. In that case, firms will choose to buy products and contract out services. The weaker the institutions, the higher the risk and costs, and the more likely that firms will choose to produce the service or product in-house.

New institutional economists also view institutions as a means of overcoming principal-agent problems. In any situation in which a principal contracts with an agent to carry about the principal's will, there is an inherent problem because agents will always have better information and usually superior expertise about their work. Because they lack knowledge, information, or expertise, principals will struggle to efficiently ensure that their agents are really doing their jobs. Institutions reduce that uncertainty by imposing penalties and norms against noncompliance. As a result, a principal can afford to have more agents, each with his or her own specialty, allowing for a far more efficient means of achieving goals.

For new institutional economists, institutions persist because they become hierarchically nested. Informal institutions, such as norms and roles, become tangled with formal institutions, such as laws, rules, and contracts, to create an interlocking, reinforcing web of constraints on individual behavior. Changing one constraint requires changing many others. Informal institutions, in particular, have tenacious survival ability and can act to reinforce more easily changed formal institutions.

As a result, institutionalization is difficult to reverse and institutions persist. Change is almost always marginal and incremental. However, new institutional economists argue that institutional change can and does occur as a result of a change in relative prices or a change in tastes. Institutions are fundamentally tools to facilitate rational exchange, and if the rules no longer work properly, players will change the rules. A price or taste change alters the payoff structures of transactions, which calls for new guarantees against uncertainty and new institutions for reducing transaction costs. In other words, changes in prices or tastes can throw institutional constraints into such disarray that they actually increase transaction costs. After enough players lose enough money, they will organize to change laws or professional norms until the hierarchical web of institutions begins to untangle and reform.

New Sociological Institutionalism

While new institutional economists emphasize how rules affect the calculus of self-interested behavior, new sociological institutionalists emphasize how cultural and cognitive systems shape behavior, often subconsciously. Instead of stressing risk and cost, new sociological institutionalists stress legitimacy and appropriateness. Institutions are normative and cognitive frames that individuals use to make sense of the world and to decide how to act in it. New sociological institutionalists work to show how macrosocial structures and systems affect individuals by showing how expectations, roles, and routines develop in response to a desire for legitimacy and appropriateness.

New sociological institutionalists argue that institutions directly shape organizational structure. Institutions indicate what is legitimate behavior, and under certain conditions—poorly defined goals, difficult to evaluate technology, and weak governance structures—organizations will closely respond to institutional expectations. Under these conditions, it is difficult for an organization to prove it deserves necessary resources, such as money and personnel. So organizations such as schools work to appear legitimate in order to prove they are deserving of scarce resources.

The new sociological institutionalists' argument is extended by describing exactly how organizations and individuals conform to institutions. The simplest way is by imitation. When technical processes are uncertain and evaluation difficult, organizations tend to imitate legitimate practices, roles, and structures indicated by institutions because they are unsure of what to do and find imitation easier than experimenting through trial and error on their own. In a second, more complex way, institutions shape behavior normatively by conferring identities and roles on actors, by creating classification systems, and by determining what is worthy of attention. In a given situation, institutions indicate to individuals who they are, how they should act, and what should be important to them. Professions, through groups such as the American Medical Association or American Bar Association, play a powerful role in transmitting and perpetuating these normative belief systems across organizations and among individuals. Finally, echoing new institutional economics, institutions can act coercively as the rules of the game. To ensure efficient and secure transactions, authorities make informal rules and formal laws, which become binding institutions.

New sociological institutionalists also emphasize how institutions produce routines and roles that pervasively shape individual behavior. As cognitive and normative systems, institutions make sense of the world, framing experiences to make them intelligible and manageable. In fact, institutions are so necessary and ubiquitous that individuals take them for granted. For example, with a single glimpse at a room with rows of desks facing a chalkboard, an adult, and many children, one will become quiet and watchful, perhaps imagining what class it is, who is the class clown, and who is the teacher's pet. Because we have experienced so many years of schooling and have seen so many movies or read so many books about schooling, the cognitive frame of school guides our thinking and behavior until we see what we expect to see. In fact, individuals can even become who they expect to become. Exposed to the same schooling institutions, children may take on the role of class clown or teacher's pet, and the teacher and other students may reinforce those roles. The roles are reproduced over time and across geography because they are seen as appropriate to the situation.

New sociological institutionalists believe institutions persist because they are necessary for individuals and organizations to function. People are loath to abandon routines and roles because what lies beyond is a blooming, buzzing confusion. In fact, new sociological institutionalists argue that individuals and organizations will follow institutional routines and roles even when it is not obviously in their narrow self-interest to do so. They thus describe institutions as "sticky" because environments change more rapidly than institutions. It is less clear if and how institutions change once they are socially embedded.

Historical Institutionalism

Historical institutionalists come from several disciplinary backgrounds, though primarily from political science and sociology. They differ from their counterparts by taking a macroview of institutions, focusing not on individuals or organizations but on nations, societies, and economies. Historical institutionalists seek to explain the distinctiveness of national political and economic outcomes as well as the inequalities that characterize the outcomes. Institutions are formal and informal procedures, routines, norms, and conventions embedded in political, economic, and social structures. Historical institutionalists see institutions as closely related to rules created and enforced by formal organizations and the state in particular. They emphasize power and ideas in the creation and perpetuation of institutions and show how institutions produce unintended consequences, path dependence, and critical junctures in national historical development.

Because they do not self-consciously work from micro building blocks, historical institutionalists' approach is not as consistent as new institutional economists and new sociological institutionalists, which makes summarizing the approach difficult. We can, however, generalize four general themes. First, historical institutionalists deal directly with power. Unlike new institutional economists, they do not see neutral structures that facilitate free individual exchange, but structures that systematically disadvantage some groups and privilege others. Interactions and conflicts do not take place on a level playing field but within contexts shaped by past struggles.

Second, historical institutionalists argue that nations will take on a historical trajectory over time, as the accumulated weight of past outcomes that are embodied in institutions produces a path or set of paths along which polities, societies, or economies continue. This occurs because institutions encourage social groups to organize along certain lines (for example trade versus enterprise unions), to adopt particular identities (British versus European), and, of course, to develop coalitions to support existing policies (social security). As winners are created, they work to consolidate their gains, institutionalizing rules into laws, treaties, and new government agencies. The same process occurs informally, as practices and beliefs become institutionalized in routines, beliefs, and assumptions.

Third, as countries travel along paths, they develop in ways that policymakers never intended. Historical institutionalists emphasize how many outcomes are the result of unintended consequences, either as circumstances change around institutions or, more likely, as institutions and policies interact in ways policymakers did not foresee. Thus, at any given point in time, current institutions are not necessarily efficient or even effective.

Finally, historical institutionalists distinguish relatively short unsettled periods, sometimes called critical junctures, from normal periods when institutions change only incrementally. During critical junctures, institutions have been shaken, most typically through a crisis, such as a war or depression, and substantial institutional change can take place, creating a branching point to a new historical path.

Evaluating New Institutionalism

All three new institutional approaches gained popularity in the 1980s and 1990s because they provided a means to link individual behavior with social context. To a large extent, the three varieties differ because they explain different things. They provide different analytical tools for different analytical tasks.

New institutional economists focus on risk and cost because they want to explain the behavior of firms in the real world. Their assumptions work best under conditions approximating a market, where actors of roughly equal power are accustomed to strategically bargaining. New sociological institutionalists focus on appropriateness and legitimacy because they want to understand how and why so many individuals and organizations do not behave in a way economists would call rational but which is still predictable, or at least understandable. Their assumptions work best under conditions of poorly understood technology, strong norms, and difficult objective evaluation—in other words, conditions farthest from a market and most like a community. Finally, historical institutionalists focus on power and history because they want to understand conflict over time and across countries. Their assumptions are most difficult to discover because of their eclectic inductive approach, but would seem to apply best when social or political change is incremental, and then sudden.

—Keith A. Nitta

See also Development Theory; Economic Sociology; Institutionalism; Market; Path Dependence; Policy Learning; Social Learning

Further Readings and References

DiMaggio, P., & Powell, W. (Eds.). (1991). *The new institutionalism in organizational analysis.* Chicago: University of Chicago Press.

Evans, P., Rueschemeyer, D., & Skocpol, T. (Eds.). (1985). *Bringing the state back in.* Cambridge, UK: Cambridge University Press.

Hall, P., & Taylor, R. (1996). Political science and the three new institutionalisms. *Political Studies, 44*(5), 936–957.

Kaufman, H. (1960). *The forest ranger: A study in administrative behavior.* Baltimore: Johns Hopkins University Press.

Meyer, J., & Rowan, B. (1977). Institutionalized organizations: Formal structure as myth and ceremony. *American Journal of Sociology, 83,* 340–363.

North, D. (1990). *Institutions, institutional change and economic performance.* Cambridge, UK: Cambridge University Press.

Selznick, P. (1957). *Leadership in administration.* New York: Harper & Row.

Steinmo, S., Thelen, K., Longstreth, F., Lange, P., Bates, R., Comisso, E., et al. (Eds.). (1992). *Structuring politics: Historical institutionalism in comparative analysis.* Cambridge, UK: Cambridge University Press.

Williamson, O. (1989). *Operationalizing the new institutional economics: The transaction cost economics imperative.* Berkeley: Center for Research in Management, University of California, Berkeley School of Business.

NEW POVERTY RESEARCH

The new poverty research emphasizes interpreting research on poverty and social welfare policy by placing that research in historical and social context. It involves understanding the problems of social welfare policy in any one era as associated with a particular regime of practices. In the current era, where the ideology of neoliberalism celebrates participation in a globalizing economy, poverty management is being transformed to be more punitive. The new poverty research focuses on the extent to which the Keynesian welfare state is being replaced by a combination of both neoliberal and paternalistic regimes. The new regime offers less monetary aid to low-income families and more discipline for the adults in those families. Significant changes include (a) decreased financial aid to and increased work enforcement on the unemployed, (b) decreased rehabilitation and increased incarceration for those who commit crimes, and (c) decreased child welfare services to birth families and increased removal of children to foster families.

Further, welfare policy implementation is being devolved from the nation-state to subnational governments, where privatization has led to the growing role of for-profit vendors. As a result, new forms of governance operate on different levels and provide new ways for managing and disciplining the poverty population. This means that the welfare state is not being limited, but instead being eliminated—welfare policy is being decentralized and privatized to provide new programming focused more on regulating the poor to regiment them into local and regional, low-wage labor markets.

Work enforcement is the most pervasive development. Welfare states throughout the developed world are under growing pressure to make this shift, though they continue to vary in the extent to which they have complied. Facilitating this process has been a reframing of social welfare policy in terms of "welfare dependency" in the United States or "labor activation" in Europe. The United States has led the way in reframing issues of poverty and welfare to emphasize enforcing low-wage work on the poor. European countries have varied in the extent to which they have adopted similar policies but none is as draconian in its approach as the United States. Some countries are developing more supportive forms of labor activation that provide substantial training and education supports and income supplements. With immigration, European countries face becoming more like the United States, where the low-income population is disproportionately nonwhite and a disciplinary approach to the poor is more accepted.

Labor activation policies are often justified in terms of helping the unemployed overcome their social exclusion. Yet, the emphasis of workfare programs is to get the unemployed to make rapid attachment to the paid labor force, even if it means taking low-wage jobs. As a result, labor activation policies risk helping the poor overcome their social exclusion in ways that reinscribe their subordination.

The punitive turn in poverty management means that social welfare policy is increasingly associated with new forms of governance that are focused on inculcating habits of mind and levels of motivation that will be consistent with this overriding objective of integrating the poverty population into low-wage labor markets. Social welfare policy becomes more therapeutic in its orientation. In particular, social welfare provision is converted from a form of income redistribution to the social policy equivalent of a twelve-step program that medicalizes welfare dependency as if it were akin to other dependencies, such as a drug dependency. Recipients are screened, diagnosed, and treated for their dependence on welfare. Clients are increasingly evaluated for the personal barriers that prevent them from getting and keeping a job. The new disciplinary practices associated with the punitive turn in poverty management is implemented via a discourse that inverts the meaning of barriers to no longer be external social structures that block the economic mobility of individuals. Instead, now barriers mean something internal to the low-income individual that must be addressed through treatment that helps him or her develop the personal discipline to become self-sufficient via the wage labor market.

The new poverty research helps put this renewed focus on the individual in a new light. It goes beyond the study of welfare recipients that in the past too often relied strictly on human capital models to determine which individuals were likely to be vulnerable to remain poor and why. The new poverty research, in particular, is keen to contextualize welfare recipient behavior in terms of the new forms of governance that are operating to discipline individuals. This contextualization involves paying attention to how discourses of globalization are, on the one hand, encouraging the uncritical acceptance of globalization as a *fait accompli* and, on the other hand, are discouraging consideration of alternative ways of imagining social welfare policy in a new era. The new poverty research enables us to see how welfare reform discourse simultaneously helps legitimate the idea that globalization inevitably requires welfare state revision that treats those who are disadvantaged by globalization as deficient people that need to be subject to new disciplinary practices to fit them into the emerging economic order. The new poverty research also creates the critical resources for challenging that fatalism.

—*Sanford F. Schram*

See also Poverty Reduction; Social Democracy; Social Inclusion; Social Justice; Unemployment; Welfare Reform

Further Readings and References

Handler, J. (2004). *Social citizenship and workfare in the U.S. and Western Europe: The paradox of inclusion.* Cambridge, UK: Cambridge University Press.

Morgen, S., & Maskovsky, J. (2003). The anthropology of welfare reform: New perspectives on U.S. urban poverty in the post-welfare reform era. *Annual Review of Anthropology, 32,* 315–338.

Peck, J. (2002). Political economies of scale: Fast policy, interscalar relations, and neoliberal workfare. *Economic Geography, 78*(3), 331–360.

Schram, S. (2006). *Welfare discipline: Discourse, governance, and globalization.* Philadelphia: Temple University Press.

Wacquant, L. (2001). Deadly symbiosis: When ghetto and prison meet and mesh. In D. Garland (Ed.), *Mass imprisonment in the United States* (pp. 82–120). London: Sage Ltd.

NEW PUBLIC MANAGEMENT

The label *new public management* (NPM) is widely used as an umbrella term covering a broad range of managerial reform strategies that have dominated the secular trend of public-sector change since the early 1980s. Despite the considerable degree of variation among the broad church of NPM-inspired reform measures, the import of microeconomic thinking and methods into the management of public organizations, as well as the leaning toward private-sector management as a normative ideal, can serve as a common denominator. Although the NPM doctrine does not prescribe a well-defined enumerative list of reform steps, the stereotypical toolbox includes measures such as privatization, deregulation, contracting out of public services, the use of competitive tendering and internal competition in service delivery, breaking up of formerly monolithic organizations into semiautonomous result- or service-centers, and—particularly in view of central and federal government reform—the proliferation of executive agencies, introducing result-oriented performance standards and measures, strengthening the role of service consumers, increased emphasis on professional management in the public sector, and the use of noncareer staff in senior civil service positions. More fundamentally, protagonists of the NPM reform agenda share highly optimistic views of the steering capacity of the market as the preferred mechanism of social and economic coordination. As a corollary, the shift toward greater competition is seen as a key remedy to increase the efficiency and responsiveness in the provision and delivery of public services.

By now, an established reform approach, the life cycle of the NPM program includes phases of reform euphoria, but has also gone through fiercely critical debates. In the interim, the missionary zeal and almost naïve reform enthusiasm have given way to a more sober evaluation of the realistic achievements of administrative modernization and of the potential shortcomings and conceptual deficits of the NPM agenda. In particular, the concept of governance has arisen as a strong rival on the stage of public-sector reform, promising to broader the hitherto more narrowly defined debate on markets and competition as major levers of reform to include more participatory elements and network approaches.

New Public Management as an International Reform Movement

NPM-driven reform activity in the public sector is now widely dispersed and has, in many cases, resulted in far-reaching and long-lasting changes that go far beyond the import of a temporary fad or fashion. NPM has become a widely popularized code for a group of loosely coupled ideas that have effectively shaped the discourse on administrative modernization in most Organisation for Economic Co-operation and Development (OECD) countries and beyond. Since its first appearance on national reform agendas some twenty-five years ago, the NPM message has spanned the globe. Although the political traditions and administrative cultures of the Anglo-Saxon family of nations have proven most susceptible to the market-oriented component of the NPM doctrine, the aftershocks caused by the NPM tremor have also been felt in administrative systems shaped in a more collectivist and state-oriented mold. The first waves of the NPM reform movement swept across classical Westminster systems of government with the United Kingdom and New Zealand as their epicenters. The "modernization movement" has also taken firm root in other Anglo-American countries. For example, NPM-driven reform initiatives have been mushrooming in Australia, the United States (as epitomized, for example, by the "reinventing government" debate), and—to a lesser extent—in Canada. The modernizing trend in the public sectors of those "core reform countries" was quickly heeled by comparable reform agendas in an ever-increasing number of European states. The Scandinavian countries and the Netherlands have most notably been riding the wave of public-sector modernization, while the larger continental European nations such as France and, in particular, Germany have been much more hesitant to embark on sweeping administrative reform projects along the lines of new public management. Although in a moderated fashion, NPM ideas have also spread to Asia, where Japanese and South Korean reformers have presented their plans for administrative modernization in NPM parlance. The proliferation of NPM as a blueprint for reform has come near completion when public-sector change in transitional and developing societies come under its influence through the active support from international organizations, such as the OECD, the World Bank, or the International Monetary Fund (IMF). In spite of the more- or less-uniform rhetoric of administrative modernization, however, the degree of variation across nations, levels of government, and policy sector-specific reform programs should not be underestimated.

Theoretical and Conceptual Background

The NPM movement is intellectually nourished by various lines of thought. Rather than being entirely cut from the same cloth, the emperor's new clothes are more the result of a patchwork design. Frequently described as a "paradigmatic shift" away from a bureaucratic type of old public administration rooted in long-standing continental European administrative traditions, the new public management is primarily embedded in the Anglo-American intellectual history. It is largely inspired by the tenets of neoinstitutional economics, public choice–based political theories, and a pragmatic notion of managerialism ("let the managers manage") often tinged with a strong dose of neo-Taylorist concepts.

Against this background, the NPM approach calls established practices and doctrines of old public management into question. This applies to the macrodimension of public management, that is, the overall size and structure of the public sector, as well as to the microlevel of internal management of public organizations. The first concern is with the range and depth of government activities. The proponents of NPM measures tend to argue in favor of a stop if not a reversal of government growth. In contrast to the seemingly ever-expanding role of the bureaucratic welfare state, the NPM creed calls for a refocusing on so-called core competencies and turns to the analysis of transaction costs, property rights,

and principal-agent relations for conceptual guidance (e.g., with regard to "make or buy" decisions). Second, from this theoretical vantage point, the bureaucratic mode of conduct typified by rule-bound behavior and hierarchical order is seen with the greatest of skepticism. Rather, the new focus is on designing the most cost-effective incentive structures and contractual arrangements between supposedly rational actors. The third conceptual lever of administrative change seeks to pull the barriers between public and private management. At this point, the economic school of institutional choice meets pseudoacademic managerialism. The scholarly roots of the managerialist trend can be traced back to the scientific management school in the tradition of Frederick Taylor. This lineage brings a strong technocratic flavor to NPM prescriptions as they tend to emphasize quantitative measures of performance and formal reporting systems. This peculiarly mixed bag of intellectual heritage, of course, is a potential source of tension between NPM measures. However, the lack of internal consistency does not appear to have diminished the widespread appeal of NPM as a convenient code for public-sector modernization.

The New Public Management in Action

Pruning Back the State

Generally, the creed of the reform movement has been to redraw the boundaries of state activities to downsize the public sector, to unleash market forces, and to accord more weight to private-sector parties in rendering public services. Although privatization and deregulation are widely considered hallmarks of recent projects of public-sector modernization, the starting positions, underlying reform strategies, as well as the nature and sequence of reform steps, differ considerably across national boundaries. In spite of the downsizing rhetoric and the decrease in state ownership, the overall range and scope of state activities have remained on relatively high levels, and new forms of state intervention, such as reregulation as a consequence of privatization, seem to be on the rise.

The Growth of Agencies

In the wake of NPM reforms, national government bureaucracies worldwide have found themselves in a period of far-reaching organizational changes. Most notably, many central governments—as typified by the British "Next Steps" initiative—have placed higher emphasis on separating executive functions to peripheral agencies that are to be steered at arm's length according to the principal-agent model.

Human Resource Management

Hand in hand with restructuring the architecture of the central state, the quest for reorganizing the body of public personnel (civil service) has gained new momentum. In particular, the drive for efficiency and the introduction of private management techniques (performance-related pay, open competition for top posts, and enhanced mobility between the public and private sectors) have put significant pressure on the established civil service systems. Most notably, new human resource management techniques are also likely to change the relationship between political appointees and career officials.

Output Orientation and Performance Measurement

An integral element of new public management has been increased emphasis placed on market forces and output orientation in the public sector (as exemplified by the introduction of Compulsory Competitive Tendering in the United Kingdom and the creation of quasi- or internal markets in a wide range of public service domains). To be sure, the success of the new managerialism largely depends on adequate performance measurement in order to assess service delivery and resource use.

Consumerism

Consumerism flows from the emphasis on marketization and individual choice that public-sector reforms under the NPM heading seek to strengthen the customer or consumer roles rather than the citizen role. However, critics increasingly question the wisdom of the citizen-as-consumer model and call for revitalized citizen participation—both in decision making and service production—and strengthened communitarian values.

Explaining the Emergence and Proliferation of New Public Management

How can we account for the explosion of NPM-inspired reform initiatives? In order to understand the advent of new public management as a new paradigm in public-sector reform, we can take a few pointers from the social, economic, and political forces that might have propelled the NPM program into action.

One should be quick to point to the fiscal and budgetary considerations that have prompted a great deal of interest in new public management in many countries. The drastic budgetary crunches in the wake of the global economic recession brought a definite end to decades of stable and high economic growth rates and ever-expanding government spending. The dramatic order of the fiscal constraints made budget officials also painfully aware of the limited use of traditional retrenchment and cutback management. It does not come as a surprise to see that greater emphasis on hands-on professional financial management, cost-cutting exercises, selling publicly owned industrial assets, or the implementation of time-honored private-sector management tools—all part of the standard NPM regimen—had a lot of appeal to budget officials and policymakers alike. Moreover, the increased international economic competition also puts additional pressure on national reformers as they seek to turn cost-efficient public services and better regulation into a comparative advantage over their international economic rivals.

Clearly, party political, if not ideological, factors played a major role, particularly in those countries where radical reform proposals were propagated with almost missionary zeal, as in Thatcherist Britain or in the United States under the Ronald Reagan administration. More generally, the formative years of the NPM movement coincided with a series of government changes that brought right-of-center parties or party coalitions back in power. However, the overall picture is more ambivalent as Social Democratic or (New) Labour politicians (e.g., in New Zealand, Scandinavia, and New Labour in the United Kingdom) have also been known for subscribing to the NPM reform agenda.

Fertile ground for NPM reforms to flourish has also been provided by a number of social and cultural changes that appear to support some of the core tenets of the NPM program. In terms of popular sentiments toward the established public sector in most Western societies, support for traditional public institutions has been dwindling. Also, in an era characterized by increasingly heterogeneous and individualized lifestyles, the standardized and uniformly delivered goods and services provided by established, large welfare bureaucracies leave a lot to be desired. Consequently, the growing share of disgruntled citizens and dissatisfied clients of public bureaucracies lends further support to the new public management doctrine. Finally, the promise of more market incentives, greater managerial flexibility, and less-paternalistic, old-style bureaucracies seems to bode well with a population whose values and attitudes since the 1970s have shifted toward the postmaterialistic end of the spectrum, thus ranking self-actualization and individual rewards over the long-term prospect of material security and a stable social order as offered by established civil service careers in hierarchical organizations.

New Public Management and Its Critics

In assessing the consequences and possible future prospects of NPM, we shed some light on related discourses that can be interpreted as a critical response to the NPM-driven overhaul of established civil service systems. This concluding section looks, in turn, at three potentially tense relations between the major thrust of the NPM agenda, on the one hand, and essential concepts and values of public administration on the other: the impact on public-service ethics, the problems of accountability, the tensions between the role of citizens and customers.

Public Service Ethics

After more than two decades of NPM in action, scholars and practitioners alike seem to be rediscovering the value of having a distinct—though in hindsight often romanticized—public service ethic. Recent empirical findings have given rise to a growing concern about increased unethical behavior—such as more widespread cases of corruption—among employees delivering public services. Is there a need to rebalance the more recently highlighted values, such as value for money, cost efficiency, or managerial discretion, against time-honored principles of probity, equity, or due process? Confronted with contracting resources, far-reaching structural changes, and increasingly blurred boundaries between the public and private sectors, we seem to have lost sight of the normative dimension guiding public-sector decision making. What are the legitimate principles and values on which public decisions ought to be based? How do they differ from private-sector management?

Accountability

Initially, the NPM hype sparked a new interest in the question of accountability, primarily understood as a matter of explicit performance goals, indicators of success, and a corresponding system of controlling and reporting. However, a closer look also reveals an increasing self-serving tendency of the newly introduced accountability regime. It seems to have become a goal in itself, whereas other mechanisms of holding public officials accountable have been partially transformed and potentially weakened (such as the doctrine of government accountability). The increased coproduction of public goods and services by public as well as private commercial or nonprofit organizations poses additional challenges to any system of public accountability. The questions at the center of the discourse are: Who is being held accountable for what and by whom? What are the legitimate roles of legislative bodies, the judicial system, the courts of account, and how do citizens fit into this puzzle?

New Public Management and Citizenship

Revamping the executive machinery of the state is by no means a purely technocratic or managerial exercise, but has far-reaching political and constitutional implications. Closest to the heart of democracy are, of course, the rights of citizens. In the orthodoxy of the NPM creed, the concepts of political and social citizenship are void of any meaning. In principle, it is the role of the customer that is exclusively highlighted by NPM reform programs. However, can our public role as members of democratic societies be legitimately reduced to that of a person who shops around for goods and services? Rather than pitting democratic theory and managerial reform against each other, the challenging question is how to reconcile the two concepts with one another. A more nuanced view, for example, even allows for mutually reinforcing combinations of both customer and citizen rights (by means of Freedom of Innovation legislation or through elements of user democracy).

—*Eckhard Schroeter*

See also Bureaucracy; Contracting Out; Effectiveness; Governance; Internal Market; Localization; Market; Marketization; Neoliberalism; Performance Measurement; Public-Private Partnership; Purchaser-Provider Split; Service Delivery; Virtual Agency

Further Readings and References

Barzelay, M. (2001). *The new public management.* Berkeley: University of California Press.
Christensen, T., & Laegreid, P. (Eds.). (2001). *New public management: The transformation of ideas and practice.* Aldershot, UK: Ashgate.
Flynn, N., & Strehl, F. (1996). *Public sector management in Europe.* New York: Prentice Hall.
Hood, C. (1991). A public management for all seasons? *Public Administration, 69,* 3–19.
Peters, B. G., & Savoie, D. (Eds.). (1998). *Taking stock: Assessing public sector reform.* Montreal, PQ, and Kingston, ON: McGill-Queen's University Press.
Pollitt, C., & Bouckaert, G. (2004). *Public management reform: A comparative analysis* (2nd ed.). Oxford, UK: Oxford University Press.

NEW REGIONALISM

New regionalism refers to the observed resurgence of regionalist projects, beginning around the mid-1980s, and the marked differences that this process had in substance to an earlier rise in regionalist developments, beginning around the 1950s. This qualitatively different phenomenon has been observed by scholars in the fields of international relations (IR) and international political economy (IPE) to coincide with the end of the Cold War and a period of increasing global economic integration. New regionalism has led to regional organizations that are more open with respect to trade than those formed in the previous era.

Aspects of New Regionalism

With the advent or reformulation of regional organizations, such the Association of South East Asian Nations (ASEAN), the Asia-Pacific Economic Cooperation (APEC) forum, the European Union (EU), the North American Free Trade Agreement (NAFTA), and the Southern African Development Community (SADC), among many others, the mid-1980s and early 1990s saw an increase in such regional political and economic activity. This activity prompted a reinvigoration of academic interest into the phenomenon of regionalism, which led to the argument that what was being observed was a new form of regionalism from the type prevalent immediately following World War II. Scholars identified several contours of new regionalism within the context of the political and economic world order that was emerging.

First, this new form of regionalism was occurring toward or after the end of the Cold War; the bipolar world context had shifted and was becoming increasingly multipolar. This shifting of the balance of power, it is argued, may have provided at least the perceived incentive for the increase in the number of regional organizations and their membership. In addition, the regional organizations formed in the earlier Cold War context were shaped by the interests of the dominant superpowers. In the new context, regionalist projects were increasingly shaped "from below" by the interests of actors, such as domestic civil society, in addition to states themselves.

Next, with regard to the global economy, the old form of regionalism tended toward protectionist economic blocs, where trade between member countries was encouraged but trade with countries outside the bloc was discouraged by external trade barriers. In contrast, the new regionalism was of a more open form, where the preferential treatment accorded to member states was also open to countries from outside the region. In this context, it is argued that this open form offers regional industries exposure to global competition and, together with other means of encouragement, the strategically necessary incentives to compete in the global marketplace. By this argument, scholars have concluded that instead of presenting obstacles to the process of increasing global integration, these new regionalist projects assist in furthering this objective.

New regionalism has also given rise to regional organizations that have a wide-ranging set of stated policy objectives. Whereas previous forms of regionalist projects were concerned with economic or security policies, the policies adopted by regional institutions formed or reinitiated in the late 1980s and early 1990s encompassed environmental and social policy, as well as policy to encourage transparency and accountability in governance. With regard to the regional projects initiated by poor countries, such as the SADC in the southern cone of the African continent, these regional organizations include explicit developmental objectives extending beyond trade and monetary policy, considering the concept of development, instead, as a multidimensional process. As such, organizations like the SADC have included health, education, poverty eradication, and gender equality strategies, for instance, among their stated development objectives.

Finally, new regionalism is a process interacting with the force of globalization. Unlike old regionalism, which was oriented more toward the interactions between states, new regionalism involves a variety of state and nonstate actors involved in a process of transformation of the world order. Thus, the social processes of globalization have an effect on shaping the new regionalism, and this regionalism, in turn, has an effect on shaping the process of globalization. The forces of globalization have had an impact on the restructuring of the social, political, and economic aspects of regions, while states and societies have adjusted to these impacts by furthering, changing, or reversing the effects of globalization through the processes of regionalism. Therefore, new regionalism, with its greater openness to the global economy and to global political forces, is seen as a process by which states are furthering their insertion into the existing world order. While the regional arrangement formed during the period of old regionalism proved to be unsustainable, it is argued that these new regional institutions are becoming an integral aspect in the definition of the current, and potential future, world order.

—*Stephen Buzdugan*

See also City-Region; East Asian Economic Grouping; Globalization, Mesoregionalism; Open and Closed Regionalism; Regionalism, Substate Regionalism

Further Readings and References

Fawcett, L. (2004). Exploring regional domains: A comparative history of regionalism. *International Affairs, 80*(3), 429–446.

Gamble, A., & Payne, A. (1996). Conclusion: The new regionalism. In A. Gamble & A. Payne (Eds.), *Regionalism and world order*. Basingstoke, UK: Macmillan.

Hettne, B. (1999). Globalization and the new regionalism: The second great transformation. In B. Hettne, A. Inotai, & O. Sunkel (Eds.), *Globalism and the new regionalism*. Basingstoke, UK: Macmillan.

Payne, A., & Gamble, A. (1996). Introduction: The political economy of regionalism and world order. In A. Gamble, & A. Payne (Eds.), *Regionalism and world order*. Basingstoke, UK: Macmillan.

NONGOVERNMENTAL ORGANIZATION

A nongovernmental organization (NGO) is what it claims to be: a group defined by its autonomy from the state. An NGO is a constitutive element of civil society that, in theory, stands separate from, if not necessarily in conflict with, the state. In democratic polities, NGOs are the mainstays of pluralism and of government accountability to its citizens.

Although nongovernmental organizations generally exist to organize, mobilize, and represent like-minded individuals, not all operate with an explicit connection to governance and state-society relations. Some NGOs, such as bowling leagues or quilting bees, exist purely within the societal realm to bring individuals together to pursue their purposes privately. More relevant to a governance context are NGOs that bring their interests or beliefs to bear on the public realm by making claims on behalf of private or public interests. Some NGOs exist to influence policy in a way that accrues benefits to their own members (private interest), while others seek to accrue benefits to society as a whole (public interest).

Most scholars, when discussing NGOs, focus on groups that make claims with respect to the public interest rather than private interests. As such, although they are societal actors, we do not typically think of business enterprises as NGOs because their governance goals involve benefits that accrue only to them (or to their sector). Rather, we tend to identify organizations such as religious, environmental, scholarly, or aid groups as NGOs because they promote some view of the collective interest and seek benefits that accrue to society as a whole. Indeed, some NGOs provide public goods, such as relief services, when formal governance mechanisms break down.

However, there are certainly gray areas in this definition of NGOs. One difficult case is labor organizations: Are the goals they promote self-interested or public interested? While one could argue that labor organizations represent only their own members in promoting goals such as high wages, one could also claim that other labor goals, such as full employment and corporate accountability, are public goods. More problematic are radical organizations that promote and use violence. Like NGOs, they are societal and typically have goals that involve society at large rather than simply their own members. However, the term NGO is generally reserved for organizations that pursue their goals nonviolently, even if they seek to bring broad changes to society. The term NGO can apply both to social movement organizations as well as those that broadly accept the status quo, but groups that seek to overturn both state and society through violent means stand outside the mainstream conception of what constitutes a nongovernmental organization.

Given these parameters, there remains wide variation in the types of NGOs that exist in the world. NGOs vary in the scope—whether local, national, or international—of their operations or ambitions. This scope guides the level of government they engage: local NGOs engage local governments, national NGOs engage national governments, and international NGOs engage international institutions. However, these distinctions of scope have blurred as advances in information and communications technologies have reduced the effects of distance, allowing local, national, and international NGOs with similar agendas to coordinate with one another in informal networks. Indeed, one attribute that makes NGOs so interesting to students of governance is that, unlike national governments or international organizations, NGOs are "glocal"—that is, capable of using their networks to operate simultaneously at the global, national, and local levels.

This network form of organization typical of relationships among NGOs is significant both in defining their own organizational structure and in embodying their views with respect to governance more generally. Many NGOs, such as the World Wildlife Fund or Amnesty International, are formally glocal in that they operate throughout the world with offices at the local, national, and international levels. These groups are notable for their minimal vertical integration: Their international offices serve merely as umbrella organizations, coordinating local and national efforts but in no means dictating operational strategies. This organizational structure reflects a general conviction, particularly among international NGOs, that governance should involve coordination among societal groups and policymakers with common goals, rather than the imposition of a single set of goals through hierarchical command and control.

NGOs attempt to achieve their governance goals though appeals to both elites and citizens. Like traditional interest groups, NGOs lobby policymakers to enact policies that reflect their own goals. However, as grassroots organizations, NGOs may also attempt to shape societal attitudes through activities intended to reshape the public discourse. These "direct actions," such as public demonstrations and media campaigns, often allow NGOs to affect policy from below by generating a groundswell of support for certain goals, whether for animal rights or against the World Trade Organization. This is a favorite approach of NGOs that specifically consider themselves social-movement organizations, whose preferred means of effecting social change is from the bottom up.

Beyond their unique glocalness, there are two main reasons why the study of NGOs is so compelling to social scientists today. The first is simply that NGOs are increasingly prevalent—particularly internationally—and thus are potentially more important actors in shaping the terms of governance. At the international level, NGOs are potentially part of an emerging "global civil society" consisting of multinational enterprises and international organizations as well as states.

The second reason why NGOs are an important object of study is more normative: In an era advancing democratic norms, we tend to see NGOs as "good." That is, if NGOs are civil society organizations, and if pluralism and democracy in governance are desirable, then naturally the emergence of NGOs as participants in governance is a good thing. This line of thinking reflects a social capital perspective, in which an active civil society sector is crucial to the maintenance of effective democratic governance. It also reflects a sense that the participation and influence of NGOs confers legitimacy on governing institutions, by providing an effective voice for relevant stakeholders and increasing government accountability to them. However, NGOs are not themselves elected representatives, and the arguments of some NGO critics that claim they hinder the effective operation of institutions underlie the complexity of normative arguments regarding NGOs and governance.

—*Edward A. Fogarty*

See also Civil Society; Coalition; Corporate Codes of Conduct; Corruption; Global Civil Society; Glocalization; Group of 7; Interest Group; Millennium Development Goals; Sociology of Governance

Further Readings and References

Almond, G. A., & Verba, S. (1963). *The civic culture.* Princeton, NJ: Princeton University Press.
Keck, M. E., & Sikkink, K. (1998). *Activists beyond borders.* Ithaca, NY: Cornell University Press.
Putnam, R. D. (1993). *Making democracy work: Civic traditions in modern Italy.* Princeton, NJ: Princeton University Press.
Risse, T. (2002). Transnational actors and world politics. In W. Carlsnaes, T. Risse, & B. A. Simmons (Eds.), *Handbook of international relations.* London: Sage Ltd.

NONPROFIT ORGANIZATION

In the United States, a nonprofit or not-for-profit organization is legally delineated from firms in the for-profit sector by its tax-exempt status. Outside of the United States, the legal framework defining the government, business, and nonprofit sectors can be less distinct, depending on the country. International nonprofit organizations are more often referred to as nongovernmental organizations. Nonprofit organizations are active in a large array of activities, from education to poverty relief and music to political advocacy. They have grown tremendously in number and in resources throughout the world in the latter half of the twentieth century. In response to their growing role in governance, the term third sector has been increasingly used over the past decade to describe nonprofit and nongovernmental organizations.

The nonprofit sector provides many opportunities for civic participation, as citizens join with others to pursue mission-oriented goals collectively. Examples range from groups centered around a pastime, such as a local choral group, to advocacy organizations centered on health, environmental, or other policy issues. Demographic groups that are disenfranchised, such as ethnic minorities, can form nonprofit organizations and develop a collective voice in the polity that is stronger than their voice in traditional representative governments. Individuals can develop leadership skills within the realm of the nonprofit sector, and then transition to active participation in decision making in their community. Public participation in nonprofit organizations is limited in some organizations where funding is largely from commercial sources (for example, hospitals). Other organizations involve the public mainly through payment of an annual membership fee. In contrast, many nonprofit organizations depend heavily on volunteer labor and extensive involvement of community members to carry out mission-related programs.

Despite creating opportunities for enhanced civic participation, a strong nonprofit sector can dilute the mandate of the voting public in several ways. First, nonprofit organizations are run not by elected officials, but by community members that have the time and wherewithal to devote themselves to the cause—which often means the community elite. Second, as government agencies contract out their services to be produced by nonprofit organizations, those services are now produced by organizations with multiple stakeholders, including board members, staff, and donors. The clarity of command, from the taxpaying and voting public down to the direct service provider, becomes less distinct. Governance that is clear and unquestioned at the government level, such as the separation of church and state (or in another country, the unified church-state), can be modified to accommodate differing points of view when the government funds a nonprofit organization to produce a service. Finally, an external funder, such as an overseas foundation, can finance activities that either the home government cannot afford to produce or may not want to produce.

Nonprofit Organizational Structure

Decision making in nonprofit organizations is complex due to the multitude of stakeholders involved in organizations. A board of directors convenes at regular intervals to review the finances of the organization and to provide administrative guidance for the organization's staff. In smaller organizations, the administrative role of directors, other volunteers, and paid staff is blurred as volunteers perform substantial administrative tasks. Indirectly, funders also participate in decision making as nonprofit organizations work with foundations, governments, and individuals

to define future programs that fit both the organization's intended purpose and attract revenue. When funding streams appear to influence the organization to change its mission-related activities, nonprofit organizations describe this phenomenon as "mission creep."

Recent Growth of the Nonprofit Sector

From colonial days in the United States, citizens have actively participated in voluntary associations, and the roots of the U.S. nonprofit sector extend back to this preference for association outside of the purview of the government. Colonial leaders expressed distrust of the potential power of voluntary association leaders to sway public opinion. Distrust of nonprofit organizations has surfaced repeatedly throughout history, as lawmakers sought to limit political advocacy and other activities of foundations and other nonprofit organizations. On the other hand, governments have turned to nonprofit organizations, especially since the 1980s, to deliver a vast array of public services that were once provided by public agencies.

Nongovernmental organizations are expanding in influence worldwide. Particularly in developing nations, nongovernmental organizations have developed their capacity over the past two decades to work in partnership with home governments to alleviate poverty and other pressing problems. International human rights organizations have also gained stature, for example, working with the United Nations in addressing international human rights violations. It is their presumed lack of country-specific bias that gives their voice credibility in the international policy arena.

With the current political preference for market-oriented enterprise, governments have relinquished much of their service provision role in favor of managing networks of subcontractors, including both for-profit and nonprofit firms. Some forms of subcontracting benefit nonprofit firms directly, such as a hunger relief organization carrying out a government-funded contract. Other forms of subcontracting benefit nonprofit agencies indirectly by providing demand-side subsidies to consumers, who may choose nonprofit agencies to provide the service. A prominent example of a demand-side subsidy is Medicare and Medicaid payments for health care in the United States.

The tremendous increase in health and human service sector payments to the nonprofit sector, one should note, paints a picture of a sector that has rapidly transformed from reliance on donations to reliance on commercial fees in the past two decades. However, outside of the health and human service sectors, nonprofit organizations are still strongly dependent on donations from individuals, not commercial revenues. Over the past several decades, nonprofit organizations that rely heavily on donated revenues have increasingly turned to high-wealth individuals for major gifts, in comparison to broad-based funding mechanisms seen in previous decades (such as the March of Dimes campaign to end polio). In theory, if a greater proportion of donations come from high-wealth individuals, then decision making in that nonprofit organizations will be more influenced by high-wealth donors than by the rest of the organizations' members and stakeholders.

—*Renee Irvin*

See also Association; Civil Society; Sociology of Governance; Third Sector

Further Readings and References

Salamon, L. (Ed.). (2002). *The state of nonprofit America.* Washington, DC: Brookings Institution.
Smith, S. R., & Lipsky, M. (1993). *Nonprofits for hire: The welfare state in the age of contracting.* Cambridge, MA: Harvard University Press.

NORMAL ACCIDENT THEORY

Normal accident theory describes organizations and technologies that are so complex that accidents are to be expected as a normal outcome. In *Normal Accidents,* Charles Perrow examined such high-risk technologies as nuclear power, petrochemical plants, and air travel (as well as the organizations managing

them), and concluded that it is the combination of complex interaction and tight coupling among the subparts of these systems that makes them accident-prone, regardless of the precautions taken.

Different technologies are marked by varying types of interaction among the parts. At one end of the spectrum lie systems that are linear, where each event in the sequence of production or operation is only linked to those steps immediately preceding and following it. This implies that operators and designers of such systems can easily comprehend what would happen if something were to go wrong with a given part. The opposite type of interaction is complex. In complex systems, connections between parts are multiple, indirect, and unclear. As a system moves toward the complex end of this spectrum, the ability of operators, managers, or even designers to predict or understand possible interactions becomes increasingly difficult.

In addition, technological systems may be tightly or loosely coupled, a term that refers to the amount of slack between components or subsystems. The characteristics of tight coupling include time-sensitive processes, invariant sequences, and a unique production path. In terms of explaining the causes and scale of accidents, tight coupling is important because it reduces the ability of operators (or the system itself) to recover from a failure, thereby making minor breakdowns more likely to become catastrophic accidents.

In Perrow's analysis, falling at the extreme of either of these variables does not necessarily spell doom for an organization; it is only in the combination of tight coupling and complex interaction that the danger of a system accident arises. System accidents are labeled as such because they result directly from the structural makeup of the system (organizational and technological), rather than from the skills, attention, or motivation (or lack thereof) of those operating it.

In response to the normal accidents literature, a number of scholars have attempted to look into the theoretical reasons why many organizations using high-risk technology, which Perrow would predict to have had catastrophic accidents, have not witnessed such accidents. Specifically, analysts have looked at what they have termed *high-reliability organizations—* organizations that must be highly reliable in order to provide their most basic services or accomplish their most fundamental tasks.

Applications of normal accident theory (and its counterpart) to political processes have been limited, but include a few important examples. Scott D. Sagan's work on the prevalence of near-accidents with nuclear weapons during the Cold War demonstrates the usefulness of these approaches to important problems of political science.

—Jordan Branch

See also Crisis Management; High-Reliability Organization; Organizational Culture; Organizational Structure; Organization Theory; Risk

Further Readings and References

La Porte, T. R., & Consolini, P. M. (1991). Working in practice but not in theory: Theoretical challenges of "high-reliability organizations." *Journal of Public Administration Research and Theory, 1,* 23–49.

Perrow, C. (1999). *Normal accidents: Living with high-risk technologies.* Princeton, NJ: Princeton University Press.

Sagan, S. D. (1993). *The limits of safety: Organizations, accidents, and nuclear weapons.* Princeton, NJ: Princeton University Press.

NORMS

Norms make governance in society possible, as they are guides for social behavior and constitute the identities of social actors. Scholars argue that norms reduce uncertainty about how actors will behave and stabilize collective understandings of appropriate conduct and which actors have particular rights, obligations, and authorities.

Despite recognition of their importance, there is not yet a universal agreement on what norms are, how best to study them, and how they evolve and change over time. Many of the disagreements about norms arise out of whether norms are merely patterns of behavior (normal practices) or whether they are collective understandings of behavior and identity that confer a moral or prescriptive status. Even among those that agree that norms are collective understandings, there is debate over whether norms are merely regulatory or also constitutive. Others argue that norms are normal practices, which are distinct from normative or moral practices. This debate is captured in a broad categorization of regulatory or behavioral norms versus constitutive norms.

Regulatory or Behavioral Norms

Most scholars agree that norms are collective expectations of how actors will behave under certain circumstances. For example, when an elderly person gets on a subway car, in many countries it is expected that younger people will give up their seat so that the older person may sit down. Norms of seniority govern the appointment of positions in the U.S. Senate. This enables smoother transfers of authority than would occur if each position had to be contested openly. Norms of diplomatic protocol provide a code of behavior that ensures that foreign diplomats do not inadvertently insult one another and unintentionally spark international disputes. Norms form a web of expectations that guide actors' behavior, even when there is no formal government or other centralized means of enforcing conformity. Even formally anarchic systems, such as the international system, are governed through norms.

Norms are considered to be regulatory in that they define and prescribe what behavior is appropriate in particular conditions. Regulatory norms are behavioral guides or signposts. Regulatory norms function to maintain social stability by guiding how people behave in particular situations. They create part of the social environment or structure that actors face when they make choices about strategies to pursue to achieve their goals.

Orthodox behavioralists and positivists dissent from this view of norms as collective expectations and argue that norms can only be defined as dominant or normal practices (i.e., an observable pattern of behavior). For many behavioralists and positivists, the power of norms lies not in the content of the norms themselves, but in the social sanctions or powerful actors that back them up. These theorists argue that the threat of penalties for noncompliance are what make behavioral norms matter and what shapes actors' calculations of how to behave in a given situation.

Regulatory Norms and Governance

Regulatory norms contribute to governance by facilitating dispute resolution. Norms can prevent disputes from arising in the first place by providing behavioral guidance, as in the norms of diplomatic protocol. Norms also structure actors' choices regarding compliance. They can provide disputants with the bases for evaluating disputed conduct (for example, norms of what counts as inappropriate behavior, valid evidence, and a fair trial). They can also offer potential solutions to the conflict. In some circumstances, the dispute may be resolved by the norm of apology, whereas in other cases, a norm of fair compensation may apply. In addition to facilitating conflict resolution, norms can also be the source of conflict. Actors who reject a prevailing norm, such as the practice of slavery or the separation of church and state, may struggle to change that norm and put their own norm in place. This struggle produces a new or altered norm, which then goes on to govern subsequent behavior.

Regulatory norms clarify the choices of actors. If one mode of behavior is contrary to the norm, then the costs associated with that strategy are raised. If the mode of behavior conforms to the norm, then the costs of acting in that manner are lower and there is an additional benefit of being seen to conform. Norms thus make it possible to establish reputations about which actors conform with and which deviate from the norm. Diplomats that choose to ignore the norms of protocol understand that this is a costly choice, as it may establish their reputation as an unpredictable, and therefore unreliable, partner.

Constitutive Norms

Beyond this general agreement on norms as behavioral guides, interpretivist, pragmatist, and constructivist scholars suggest that norms are also constitutive. Moral norms or normative beliefs fall within this category. Constitutive norms are the collective meaning of particular actions and the identity of actors. They specify what behavior can be socially recognized as counting as policing and teaching, as well as which actors have the collectively understood authority to act in particular ways (as a policeman or teacher). Constitutive norms specify what set of practices make up a particular social category and which actors have roles derived from those categories.

This deontic view of norms, in which norms empower an entity or an actor with moral or obligatory status, takes us beyond the rational-functional view that norms are merely regulatory instruments and into pragmatist, constructivist, and interpretivist approaches. Norms are constitutive because they create reasons for acting (it is a good thing to do, it is one's duty to do it), not merely because they channel the choices among actions by creating costs and benefits (it is the cheapest thing to do). The norms of promise keeping and truth telling create a reason for acting in a particular way (it is the right thing to do), even when doing so may conflict with a rational calculation of the material benefits of doing so.

Constitutive Norms and Governance

Governance would not be possible if groups did not share understandings about what particular actions done by particular actors mean. Constitutive norms create authority to act by constructing certain identities (president, treasurer, football referee, judge, professor, parent, soldier). They define what counts as a particular activity and a particular identity. For instance, there is a general regulatory norm against killing people. Behind this norm is another constitutive norm that constitutes or creates the identity of "murderer" and a category of action called "murder." If actors did not create a norm in which some people have a duty and therefore a right to kill other people in certain situations (for instance, soldiers on a battlefield), then society could not distinguish soldiers from murderers. The norm that duty sometimes requires soldiers to kill enables others to expect soldiers not to kill unless they are in battle and to accept that they will kill in battle. Similarly, these norms govern soldiers' behavior toward others, determining when it is appropriate to kill (when the person is a combatant in battle) and when it is not (when the person is not a combatant). The sense of obligation that constitutive norms create is essential to systems of social governance, without them regulatory norms would not create the costs and benefits that constrain actors' choices. Scholars writing in this tradition suggest that the entire utilitarian notion of rational calculation requires constitutive norms that define what counts as utility and rationality, as well as regulatory norms that tell actors what rational behavior is. They apply the same logic to positivist scientific methods: Norms define what counts as science and how to properly do science.

Explaining the Contribution of Norms to Governance

The study of norms and their contribution to governance has traditionally occurred in those disciplines most directly concerned with social order: social psychology, sociology, and law. Recently, the analysis of norms has taken off in other disciplines as well, particularly in international relations. International relations theorists have long been concerned with the problem of international governance or how order can be created in a formally anarchic environment. Despite the dominance of positivist neoutilitarian theories of international relations in the United States since the late 1970s, scholars have long studied the normative sources of international order and, more recently, global governance. International regime theory, which placed norms at its center, brought to the fore that collectively held understandings, such as international regimes, provide order within international politics. This led scholars to study not only norms, but also related concepts such as identity and other ideational phenomena. Behavioralists and rationalists have sought to include norms in their models, but constructivists and other interpretivists have done much of the recent work on norms. These theorists explain that how and why norms emerge, spread, and causally operate do matter (usually through some theory of institutionalization, internalization, or socialization).

Theories of norms can be broadly classed according to four logics: functional, structural, intentional, and constructivist theories. The boundaries of these groups are not well-defined, and scholars will often combine different logics in their theories. Behavioralists, rationalists, and positivists tend to favor functional and structural theories, whereas interpretivists, constructivists, and pragmatists generally employ structural, intentional, and constructivist theories. Functional theories of norms explain the causal importance of norms in a consequentialist manner. Norms exist because they serve some function, and norms matter to the extent that they alter the consequences of different ways of acting. Here, norms are often treated as instruments employed by actors to achieve their goals. The United States creates and maintains norms for open markets because generating social pressure for compliance with its interest in increasing U.S. exports to foreign markets is less costly than coercing compliance on its own. In situations where actors need to act together, norms create a common knowledge. Therefore, norms can serve as rules of thumb or focal points that make coordination or cooperation easier and of longer duration. For example, norms against interracial marriage clarify the consequences of one's choice of a spouse. Traditional parents use these norms to socialize their children to marry within their racial or religious group. Children are taught that nonconformity has costs (ostracism, diluting group purity, etc.). Norms in this sense function as part of sanctioning systems that guide actors' behavior by imposing penalties and rewards. Norms also serve to facilitate simple learning through the creation of reputations. For example, once someone acquires a reputation for violating the norm of keeping promises, others will learn to avoid depending on that person, and will instead seek out people with better reputations. Groups of actors that have an interest in cooperating will create norms in order to coordinate their behavior, create monitoring and sanctioning systems, and generate reputations. All of this serves to reduce the costs of their transacting with one another, as emphasized in new institutional economic theories. Other instrumental theories of norms focus on how rational individuals manipulate or promote norms in order to achieve some nonnormative end; alternatively, they cynically justify self-interested behavior in normative terms. For these theorists, whether the norm in question is a dominant behavioral pattern or a prescriptive or moral norm, regulatory or constitutive, matters little. What is emphasized is the effect of the norm on actors' abilities to attain their desired ends. For these theorists, there is no difference between norms and other resources that might serve as tools to guide actors' choices and facilitate their collective action. In these theories, norms exist, are created, and are used to further the existing interests of actors. Their use will spread or shrink in line with their usefulness to actors.

Structural theories characterize norms as part of social structures that determine how actors behave in social settings. In the language of game theory, norms are part of the game structure, a given that does not change but which does limit what actors can do. In a more sociological vein, norms are structural constraints on human action and freedom as they restrict the range of options available and the choices that individuals can make. In this view, norms are what maintain social stability and enable societal governance. Stability is created as actors reproduce normative structures through their conformity to what is socially deemed appropriate. A structural theory would emphasize how the norm against interracial marriage constrains an individual's decisions regarding matrimony and stabilizes societal interactions along racial lines. Until the late twentieth century, the norms that only states have international legal personality and are immune from prosecution prevented individuals from suing states for human rights violations. The normative structure of the international legal system did not recognize the rights of human beings against sovereign states. This normative structure therefore limited what humans could do to protect themselves against the actions of state officials. Theories of how these norms arise generally focus on how a particular set of norms becomes institutionalized in legal, social, or economic structures, creating particular forms of governance. Structural theories of norm creation usually employ a power argument,

suggesting that powerful actors create and impose certain norms to structure society in ways that benefit themselves. These norms, once institutionalized, become causal structures in their own right. Structural accounts of norm diffusion often rely on a logic of isomorphism or mimesis (the emulation of successful or powerful others) or a logic of environmental "fitness" to explain why norms spread.

Intentional theories focus on how actors committed to the content of particular norms strive to achieve those norms. These theories are related to, but distinct from, instrumental theories in that norms are not means to an end, but the end themselves. In intentional theories, committed actors use methods of persuasion, ethical argumentation, shaming, and galvanizing external pressure to get political actors to adopt their norms. Intentional studies have focused on the spread of human rights norms, taboos on the use of certain types of weapons, and norms concerning abolishing crimes against humanity and outlawing torture and slavery. They all rely, for their causal explanation, on morally committed actors' intentions of changing a normal set of practices and to replace them with a new prescriptive norm.

Constructivist theories of norms combine instrumental, intentional, and structural approaches. Constructivist theories of norms accept that norms become social structures that constrain behavior and channel action. But in rejecting the limits that such structures place on human freedom, constructivists focus on how human beings create and alter these structures on an ongoing basis. In contrast to structural theories, constructivists view norms and other social facts as enabling and empowering actors, not only constraining them. The process of creating and altering norms may be driven by instrumental ends or intentionality, but the end result is the same: social facts that intentionally or unintentionally create the identities of particular actors and generate frames for understanding social action. Rather than viewing norms as instruments to an end, ends in themselves, or social structures, constructivists see society as a tapestry of norms, whose threads are constantly being added and subtracted or woven in new directions by human beings. Constructivists focus not only on how agents, acting either for instrumental or normative reasons, create or alter social norms, but on the implications such norm change has for wider changes in the fabric of social order. Norms generate identities and therefore interests. Changes in norms lead to changes in what actors' interests will be and what means are deemed acceptable to pursue those ends. For example, scholars argue that the norms of peaceful dispute resolution and compromise embodied in Western international organizations changed the identities of Western countries. This shift in identities created common interests in collective security and economic management and created a zone of liberal democratic peace. Norms are important not only because of their effects on the costs and benefits of particular courses of action. Their normative content matters as well because they change actors' behaviors and change the reasons for actors' behaviors. For example, the norm of racial equality made South Africa's minority white government an international outcast, subject to international sanctions. The United States did not adopt this norm because it would materially gain from it, but because its leaders were persuaded that going against the norm was immoral and unacceptable for a country that identified itself as the leader of the free world. Norms can change actors' conceptions of what is right and wrong, and they therefore can alter the way individuals and societies interact with one another.

—Anne L. Clunan

See also Game Theory; Hegemony; Institution; Organizational Learning; Rule; Social Constructivism; Tradition

Further Readings and References

Axelrod, R. (1986). An evolutionary approach to norms. *American Political Science Review, 80*(4), 1095–1111.

Kratochwil, F. V. (1989). *Rules, norms, and decisions.* Cambridge, UK: Cambridge University Press.

Raz, J. (1999). *Practical reason and norms.* Oxford, UK, and New York: Oxford University Press.

Ruggie, J. G. (1998). What makes the world hang together? Neo-utilitarianism and the social constructivist challenge. *International Organization, 52*(4), 855–885.

North American Free Trade Agreement

The North American Free Trade Agreement (NAFTA) permits trade between Canada, Mexico, and the United States on an unrestricted basis. It was signed in 1993 and came into effect on January 1, 1994. It was unprecedented in that it involved two developed countries and a developing country. The agreement is also significant in terms of its comprehensiveness. It contains provisions on market access (including oil and energy sectors, agriculture, and auto industries), new investment rules (including the arbitration of private investor/government disputes by the World Bank), intellectual property rights, dispute resolution procedures, and two side-accords on environmental and labor standards.

NAFTA was presented by the three negotiating governments in the context of regional trade developments in Europe and the Asia Pacific and as a means of ensuring North American competitiveness. Since its implementation, it has been viewed as a preliminary experiment en route toward the Free Trade Area of the Americas (FTAA) and, ultimately, complete hemispheric integration. Initially, the prospects for all three countries were positive. The agreement was to facilitate growth in trade of capital-intensive exports and plant machinery from Canada and the United States and in labor-intensive exports from Mexico. With the final tariff reduction between Canada and Mexico coming into effect on January 1, 2003, supporters of NAFTA argue that manufacturers in all three economies can better realize their full potential by operating in a larger and fully integrated North American economy.

However, several developments have added to the controversy surrounding NAFTA since its implementation. The effects of Mexico's financial crisis of 1994–1995 were only attenuated after the U.S. government—eager not to jeopardize the future of NAFTA—lent its support to a US$17.8 billion credit agreement negotiated with the International Monetary Fund (IMF). In the aftermath of the crisis, Mexican trade surpluses have reduced support among workers in the United States and Canada, who fear the migration of jobs to Mexico and an influx of migrant labor. In Mexico, NAFTA has been just as controversial. In preparation for NAFTA, the government of President Carlos Salinas de Gortari passed agrarian reforms that fomented political unrest among Mexican peasants and triggered the Zapatista rebellion in the state of Chiapas. The agreement is also held responsible for the increase in the number of export-processing plants along the U.S.-Mexican border. These *maquiladora* plants tend to rely upon low-paid, largely female, labor for their cost advantages and have been accused of fostering exploitative working conditions. Furthermore, critics have also pointed to the reliance upon such industries as precluding the attainment of competitive advantage or the increased technological capacity in Mexico.

—Greig Charnock

See also Arab Integration; Economic Integration; Free Trade Area of the Americas; Hemispheric Integration; Mercosur; Most-Favored Nation Principle; Rules of Origin

Further Readings and References

Porter, T. (2000). The North American Free Trade Agreement. In R. Stubbs & G. R. D. Underhill (Eds.), *Political economy and the changing global order* (2nd ed., pp. 245–253). Oxford, UK: Oxford University Press.
Smith, P., & Chambers, E. (Eds.). (2002). *NAFTA in the new millennium.* Edmonton, Canada: University of Alberta Press.

NORTH ATLANTIC TREATY ORGANIZATION

The North Atlantic Treaty Organization (NATO) is a military alliance of twenty-six countries from Europe and North America that is based on the 1949 North Atlantic Treaty. Its role is to ensure the freedom and security of its members by both political and military means. NATO members offer each other a mutual security guarantee (Article 5), meaning an attack on one is treated as an attack on all. Its tasks are to ensure

security within the NATO area based on the growth of democratic institutions and a commitment to peaceful resolution to conflict, to act as a transatlantic forum for discussion of issues affecting the vital interests of members, to provide defense and deterrence against attacks from outside, and to enhance the security and stability of the wider Euro-Atlantic area through partnership with nonmembers and contributing to crisis management. Moreover, NATO is seen as more than just an international organization, it is also viewed as a security community and as a transatlantic community of states with shared values.

During the Cold War, with Europe split into two opposing security blocs—NATO and the Warsaw Pact—NATO's mission was clear cut: territorial defense. Since the end of the Cold War, NATO has sought a new role in crisis management as the transformation of the security situation in Europe made its original purpose seem dated. The Euro-Atlantic Partnership Council, the NATO-Russia Permanent Joint Council, and the NATO-Ukraine Commission, not to mention successive enlargements to include former–Warsaw Pact and even Soviet states as NATO members, have meant that NATO members are now working closely with their former common enemy. After it agreed on a new strategic concept in 1991, NATO also accepted that security has nonmilitary dimensions and has moved to incorporate these into its policy formulation with initiatives, like the Mediterranean Dialogue and the Istanbul Cooperation Initiative, aiming to enhance stability in its neighborhood through dialogue and cooperation. NATO forces have also engaged in out-of-area military interventions, notably in Kosovo in 1998.

However, despite reform and enlargement efforts, NATO's long-term role remains unclear. While there is little threatening the NATO, or indeed the notion of a transatlantic security community, the sense of a transatlantic community based on shared values is receding. While transatlantic cooperation on international terrorism and other security issues remains strong, the European Union is now developing its own security capabilities with its Common European Security and Defense Policy, and, notably since the election of U.S. President George W. Bush in 2000,

European and American thinking on some aspects of security policy seems to have diverged. In particular, the American-led invasion of Iraq in 2003 was divisive for NATO and has led to further calls for a recasting of the transatlantic relationship.

—Jocelyn Mawdsley

See also Baltic State Cooperation; Regional Governance; Security; Security Community

Further Readings and References

NATO Office of Information and Press. (2001). *NATO handbook.* Brussels, Belgium: Author.

Sloan, S. (2003). *NATO, the European Union and the Atlantic community: The transatlantic bargain reconsidered.* Lanham, MD: Rowman & Littlefield.

North-South Regionalism

North-south regionalism refers to the creation of a regional arrangement between developed and developing countries. As with other examples of economic regionalism, the level of integration in a north-south regional project can vary from the loose ties of a preferential trading agreement to the deep linkages that point toward an European Union-style union. The particular point of interest in a north-south regional project is the question of power asymmetry between the member countries. Where a north-north or south-south regional project is likely to see a certain degree of imbalance in the relative power of countries negotiating an agreement, this imbalance is markedly heightened in a north-south region. The northern country generally occupies a clearly predominant position and, as such, is able to substantially dictate the terms of the regional agreement.

There are a number of reasons why north-south regional projects have emerged over the last fifteen years, which can generally be grounded in the changes in the international political economy caused by the end of the Cold War and the acceleration of globalization in the early 1990s. In the late 1980s and the early 1990s, the dominant thinking in international economic relations posited the rise of three megablocs centered on Japan, Europe, and the United States. Within the context of the Cold War, developing countries had been able to play on global ideological tensions to obtain preferential access to one of these markets, a strategy which became obsolete after 1989. A central policy concern preoccupying leaders in developing countries thus became one of locking in guaranteed and preferential access to developed-country markets, ensuring that they were not ignored in the rise of competition between the three industrialized megablocs. The need to do this was magnified by changes in multinational corporation production techniques, which saw the transnationalization of just-in-time production techniques and the distribution of manufacturing processes across the north-south divide, particularly through *maquiladora*-style export processing zones. A concomitant transformation in the domestic political economy of developing countries took place, leading to the rise of new, export-oriented policy coalitions grounded in locally owned export assembly firms and agro-industrial combines. The result was a shift in the external context for many developing countries, making the formation of a region with a northern country a logical strategy for proactively defending the market access necessary to maintain the new patterns of national economic growth.

The imperatives pushing developed countries into a north-south regional project differ substantially from those seen in developing countries. A need for guaranteed market access is significantly less important given the preexisting patterns of economic dependence that continues to mark north-south relations. Instead, the ambition is one of exporting particular conceptualizations of the neoliberal model of globalization and using the carrot of region membership as a device for addressing the new security issues that dominate the north-south frontier. A particularly notable aspect of the north-south regional projects highlighted by U.S. policy is the expansion of northern trade laws and regulations into the south, in this case Mexico, Central America, and the Caribbean basin. While this does provide a high degree of regulatory homogeneity amenable to transnational U.S.

firms, of greater importance is the subtle dissemination of a particular pattern of addressing global trade liberalization, pointing to a new ideological element in the region formation process. This becomes especially important in the context of hemispheric and world trade talks, where a principle of one country, one vote operates in consensus-driven negotiations. In this context, north-south regionalism becomes a strategy for propagating a "commercial fifth column," creating a natural alignment of national interests by binding the economic elite in the developing country to firms in the developed country. The result is the formation of an implicit consensus on how the neoliberal model should be conceptualized and pursued. Active acknowledgement of the competing version of the neoliberal ideology does play a role in interregional talks seeking the formation of north-south regions, with Mercosur's parlaying of U.S. and European Union (EU) attentions emerging as an example of developing countries seeking a better agreement by playing one side against the other.

The utility of regional agreements as a device for disseminating regulatory and legal structures is also important in the new security agenda embedded in north-south regionalism. During the bargaining process to form the regional arrangement, the northern country is able to use the carrot of guaranteed access to its market as encouragement for reforms in areas such as environmental protection, labor regulation, as well as democracy and human rights. Indeed, inclusion of human rights and democracy provisions plays a central role in the draft texts and conditions that the EU sets for both expansion of the bloc and formation of interregional agreements. A consistent and forceful

element of the long-running talks on Turkish membership in the EU focuses upon democracy and human rights. The formation of a north-south regional arrangement can also play a central role in attempts to control or redirect illegal migration flows by extending the opportunities of northern countries to residents of southern countries. Both NAFTA and EU agreements with North Africa contain an element of immigration diversion within their founding logic. Finally, the prospect of membership in a regional agreement can be used to encourage support in other policy areas. For example, support of military action by a dominant northern country might be rewarded with a new trade deal or the furthering of a regionalist project. In sum, although the pursuit of north-south regionalism has important economic underpinnings, the economic rationale is equally likely to be used as camouflage for an underlying political project.

—*Sean W. Burges*

See also Development Theory; Regional Governance; Security

Further Readings and References

Fawcett, L., & Hurrell, A. (Eds.). (1995). *Regionalism in world politics: Regional organization and international order.* Oxford, UK: Oxford University Press.

Gamble, A., & Payne, A. (Eds.). (1996). *Regionalism and world order.* New York: St. Martin's.

Grugel, J., & Hout, W. (Eds.). (1999). *Regionalism across the north-south divide: State strategies and globalization.* New York: Routledge.

Hettne, B., Inotai, A., & Sunkel, O. (Eds.). (1999). *Globalism and the new regionalism.* New York: St. Martin's.

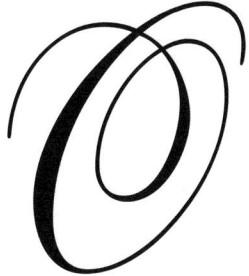

OCCUPATION

See MILITARY OCCUPATION

OFFSHORING

Offshoring refers to the practice of relocating business functions and practices to foreign locations in order to benefit from differential costs. Usually, offshoring entails the switching of jobs to locations where labor costs are lower. While firms are attracted to offshoring as a means of increasing productivity and competitiveness, the practice has proven to be politically sensitive as jobs in advanced economies are outsourced abroad.

This form of outsourcing has been taking place in manufacturing sectors since the 1960s, when a number of American firms switched more routine assembly operations to low-cost labor locations. By the end of the 1960s, for example, many American firms had switched production to the *maquiladora* plants along the U.S.-Mexican border. These processes have since intensified with agreements such as the North American Free Trade Agreement (NAFTA). The impetus behind offshoring in the United States was created by the need to remain competitive as new firms entered the market.

More recently, offshoring has involved moving service–sector, white-collar jobs in advanced economies overseas to locations predominantly in India and Asia. The current trend in offshoring computer-programming and call-center jobs, for example, has been facilitated by developments in information technology and communications. It is now possible to shift the location of service providers to low-cost locations without the end user being aware.

Advocates of offshoring argue that it benefits the firm by reducing costs, improving employee productivity, and allowing firms to focus on core research and development activities. This allows for increased competitiveness and benefits the firm by producing higher profits. Some of this can be reinvested in higher value-added activities. This contributes to the higher average productivity of the domestic economy, raises incomes, and benefits the consumers, who can enjoy lower-cost, reimported goods and services.

However, critics of offshoring argue that the longer-term gains enjoyed by firms and the economy as a whole are countered by the effects upon those domestic workers whose jobs are outsourced. Offshoring is accused of creating job insecurity and downward pressures upon wages. The recent trend in outsourcing white-collar jobs has made offshoring a significant political issue in the United States. During the 2004 presidential elections, offshoring was an issue of frequent debate and was blamed in some quarters for the phenomenon of "jobless recovery." Advocates of offshoring have dismissed such claims as stemming from a "protectionist" political agenda and have argued that only a small percentage of white-collar jobs are affected by offshoring. They have also argued that the reverse practice of "insourcing"—foreign firms switching high-end jobs to advanced countries like the United States—is compensating the economy as a whole.

—Greig Charnock

See also Export processing Zones; Fordism and Post-Fordism; Foreign Direct Investment; Globalization; International Division of Labor; Production Chain; Production Network

Further Readings and References

Bivens, L. J. (2006, May). *EPI issue guide: Offshoring* [Electronic version]. Retrieved from http://www.epinet.org/content.cfm/issueguide_offshoring

Yourdon, E. (2004). *Outsource: Competing in the global productivity race.* Indianapolis, IN: Prentice Hall.

OIL CRISIS

Oil provides the main source of energy for advanced industrial economies. A sudden rise in the price of oil due to, for example, speculation or to a severe disturbance in the existing relationship between supply and demand can therefore create an oil crisis. This can endanger economic and political stability throughout the global capitalist economy. In the postwar period there have been two major oil crises. The prospects for further crises cannot be discounted.

The first major oil crisis of the postwar era occurred in 1973. This was caused when Arab members of the Organization of Petroleum Exporting Countries (OPEC) decided to quadruple the price of oil to almost $12 a barrel. Oil exports to the United States, Japan, and Western Europe, which together consumed more than half the world's energy, were also prohibited. This decision was made in retaliation for Western support for Israel in the Yom Kippur War with Egypt and in response to a persistent decline in the value of the U.S. dollar (the denominated currency for oil sales), which had eroded the export earnings of

OPEC states. With the global capitalist economy already experiencing difficulties, these actions precipitated a steep recession accompanied by rising inflation. This forced capitalist nations to embark on a process of economic restructuring in order to reduce their dependency on oil and prompted fears that the United States might take military action in order to secure free access to its energy supplies. Although the oil embargo was lifted in 1974, oil prices remained high, and the capitalist world economy continued to stagnate throughout the 1970s.

The second major oil crisis occurred in 1979 as a result of the Iranian revolution. High levels of social unrest severely damaged the Iranian oil industry, leading to a large loss of output and a corresponding rise in prices. This became even worse following the outbreak of the Iran-Iraq War, which further added to the level of instability throughout the region. In 1981, the price of oil was stabilized at $32 per barrel. By 1983, however, with major capitalist economies having adopted more efficient methods of production, the problems of the 1970s had been transformed into a relative oversupply of oil rather than a shortage.

At the present time, world oil prices have reached record levels. This is primarily due to political instability in the Middle East and to a growing demand for oil from developing nations. Despite this, the emergence of another severe energy crisis has so far been averted. This is due to the historically low levels of interest rates being maintained in advanced capitalist economies in response to the onset of a world recession from the turn of the millennium. Nevertheless, the prospect of a future crisis cannot be discounted, especially given the ongoing expansion of the international economy coupled with the finite stock of world oil.

—Steven Kettel

See also Organization of the Petroleum Exporting Countries; Political Economy

Further Readings and References

Clark, J. G. (1991). *The political economy of world energy: A twentieth-century perspective.* Chapel Hill: University of North Carolina Press.

OLIGOPOLY

See IRON LAW OF OLIGARCHY

OMBUDSMAN

The ombudsman was created by the King of Sweden in 1806 in order to control the application of laws by the administration. By the second half of the nineteenth century, it became an institution by which the Swedish Parliament could exert more control over the executive branch of government. It was only during the twentieth century that the ombudsman came to provide citizens with a way of fighting against the arbitrariness of bureaucracy. The Office of Ombudsman spread from Sweden to the other Nordic countries (Finland 1919, Denmark 1955, Norway 1963), and then on to Commonwealth countries in the 1960s and the majority of Western democracies in the 1970s and 1980s. It has taken various names: *Defensor del pueblo* in Hispanic countries, *médiateur* in French-speaking countries, and *Provedor de Justiça* in Portuguese-speaking countries. Its success has been such that many ombudsmen have also been created at regional and local political levels, in numerous administrations or specialized parts of the state, and in parts of the private sector, including banks, telecommunications, transports, insurance companies, energy companies, television stations, and newspapers.

The creation of the ombudsman has been the subject of various interpretations. Some have seen it as a political strategy to democratize the administrative work that is continually spreading and appearing opaque and arbitrary to citizens. Others have analyzed it as a political gadget intended to produce greater legitimacy for institutions in crisis. In the particular case of European institutions, some researchers have interpreted the ombudsman as a way for the weak European Parliament in Strasbourg to control the powerful community administrations in Brussels.

Naturally, ombudsmen vary in their status and in the ethical principles that they seek to apply. Their independence, their competence, and their powers to carry out investigations also vary across countries.

The ombudsman is presented as independent in relation to the political and financial powers and the administrative hierarchy. It is presented as affirming its impartiality and as guaranteeing the confidentiality of any information that is brought to its attention. These ethical principles of independence, impartiality, and confidentiality sustain its legitimacy. In practice, however, these ethical principles can prove less clear-cut than one might like, as, for example, when an ombudsman is appointed by the very administration whose activities it is meant to oversee.

Complaints to the ombudsman are generally submitted directly by the citizens, although in some states, such as France and the United Kingdom, complaints must pass through a member of Parliament. As a general rule, ombudsmen cannot investigate complaints until they have been raised with the public agency concerned, because most agencies have internal procedures for handling complaints. The complaint system is flexible, without formal requirements and free of charge. The field of competence of the ombudsman can be broad and related to conflicts with all administrations or narrower and limited to only some of them.

The ombudsman's means of investigation and action can be ample (capacity to introduce legal claims, to carry out surveys on its own initiative, to sanction) or they can be confined to the request of the citizens and the formulation of recommendations. Thus, for example, the ombudsman can give an opinion in the event of injustice caused by maladministration. This concept is not easy to grasp. It covers the questions of delay, incompetence, giving wrong information, arbitrariness, discrimination, and neglect. These criteria must be related to what would have been fair and reasonable in the circumstances of the case.

The effectiveness of the action of the ombudsman is often analyzed in quantitative terms. In all countries one notices the continued increase of its activity since its creation, which surely suggests that it corresponds to a real social need. Nonetheless, it is probably the symbolic dimension of the ombudsmen that is of most importance. The ombudsman is presented as the "white knight" of democracy against bureaucracy, the defender of the citizen mistreated by blind technocratic machinery. From this point of view, the ombudsman is less a mediator (whose ethic obliges him or her to be impartial) than a defender and an agent of moralization and institutional change. Thus, for example, its decisions set precedents, building up guides to "good practices" and expressing a philosophy of good administration and good governance.

Finally, one can think of the ombudsman as not only a plumber fixing communications between citizens and the administration, but also as playing a genuine role of political control and as a vector of democratic change. The intensity of its impact depends naturally on its status and capacities, as well as on its degree of independence. These variables define the legitimacy that is allocated to the ombudsman in each national or local political and administrative culture.

—*Jacques Faget*

See also Accountability; Bureaucratic Politics Approach; Conflict Mediation; Oversight; Regulation

Further Readings and References

Magnette, P. (1999). *La citoyenneté européenne: Droits, politiques, institutions* [European citizenship: Rights, policies, institutions]. Brussels, Belgium: Editions de l'Université de Bruxelles.

Marias, E. A. (Ed.). (1994). *The European ombudsman.* Maastricht, Netherlands: European Institute of Public Administration.

OPEN AND CLOSED REGIONALISM

Open regionalism and *closed regionalism* are terms that refer to the degree of outward or inward orientation, respectively, of regional trading agreements to the multilateral trading system. This topic has received much attention in the fields of international political economy (IPE) and economics, particularly due to the sharp increase in the number of new regional organizations formed toward the late 1980s and early 1990s. The debates in these fields have

focused on whether these new agreements would act as barriers or catalysts to deeper global economic integration.

Closed Regionalism

Closed regionalism is characterized by trade agreements that lower or eliminate barriers to trade among member states of a regional organization, which are not extended to external countries. Closed regionalism is typically associated with the first wave of regional integration initiatives (or "old regionalism") that started during the 1950s. These initiatives mainly took the form of free trade areas (FTAs), which eliminate internal barriers to trade and customs unions (CUs), which include harmonized external tariffs among member states. Among countries in Africa and Latin America, for instance, FTAs and CUs, such as the Latin American Free Trade Association (LAFTA), were combined with industrial planning to implement a development strategy known as import substituting industrialization (ISI). The ISI strategy called for the deliberate discouragement of imports into the region so that these countries could take advantage of the increased size of the regional market and develop their domestic industries. Many of these agreements were unsustainable for various political and economic reasons and by the end of the 1970s had not continued forward.

Open Regionalism

Open regionalism, by contrast, is more outward oriented to where intraregional trade preferences are extended to countries outside the region in a movement toward greater trade liberalization. Open regionalism is the form taken by the second wave of regional activity (or "new regionalism"), which began in the mid-1980s and sharply increased after the end of the Cold War. While these new regional developments raised concerns that the global trading system was witnessing a repeat of the rise of protectionist blocs prevalent in the first wave of the 1950s, the more open nature of these recent projects has instead shifted the debate toward whether or not these regional trading arrangements are impediments, rather than barriers, to increased multilateralism. Examples of open regionalism may be found in the Mercado Común del Sur (or Mercosur/Southern Common Market), although with limits, and the Asia Pacific Economic Cooperation (APEC) forum.

Trade Creation and Trade Diversion

One of the central concerns expressed by economists with regard to closed and open regionalism is that of the welfare-oriented effects of trade creation and trade diversion. Jacob Viner, in his seminal work on the topic, *The Customs Union Issue,* defined trade creation as occurring when countries within an FTA or a CU are able to shift production from the highest-cost to the lowest-cost producer within the region as a result of eliminating internal trade barriers. In this instance, it is argued that welfare increases for both those countries in the area and in the world. However, if the lowest-cost producer is not one of the countries within the area, but one outside of it, and the FTA or CU, through its external tariffs, causes production to shift from the lowest-cost to a higher-cost producer within the region, trade diversion occurs along with an associated decline in regional countries' and world welfare.

Regionalism and Multilateralism

Many neoclassical economists have expressed concern over the phenomenon of regionalism with regard to the multilateral trading system. In terms of trade creation and trade diversion, they argue that a multilateral system versus a system comprised of regional trading blocs increases overall welfare through the shifting of production to the lowest-cost producers on a global scale. With regard to the closed regionalism of the 1950s and 1960s, these economists argue that the increases in external trade barriers led to short-term welfare losses due to trade diversion. Furthermore, they argue, protection from external competition may have led to high-cost regional producers not having the incentives for more efficient production.

In the case of open regionalism, however, it appears that through strategic trade initiatives, where regional industries are exposed to external competition while receiving other incentives to produce more efficiently for export, the global trading system is not experiencing the pattern of protectionist trade blocs observed in the first wave of regionalism. While it is unclear for certain, it is argued that a short-term decline in welfare may be experienced as a result of trade diversion within these regions. However, unlike the closed form of regionalism, it is also argued that this new form may be furthering the process of global economic integration and may perhaps lead to an increase in multilateral trade in the near to long-term future.

—*Stephen Buzdugan*

See also Asia-Pacific Economic Cooperation; Globalization; New Regionalism; Regionalism; Resource Dependency Theory; Substate Regionalism

Further Readings and References

Bhagwati, J. (1993). Regionalism and multilateralism: An overview. In J. de Melo & A. Panagariya (Eds.), *New dimensions in regional integration.* New York: Cambridge University Press.
Page, S. (2000). *Regionalism among developing countries.* Basingstoke, UK: Macmillan.
Viner, J. (1950). *The customs union issue.* New York and London: Carnegie Endowment for International Peace & Stevens and Sons.

OPEN GOVERNMENT

Open government is best regarded as the technique or techniques through which the principles of openness and transparency are given effect. It is now a truism that these principles are essential to the development of governance, which is responsible, accountable, and responsive to citizens. This perception has developed in the light of what some regard as the democratic deficit in national and supranational jurisdictions: Greater transparency has been seen as a corrective to governance that is too complex and remote.

But if there is little dispute about the desirability of the underlying principles, the consensus has often broken down when it comes down to their translation into practice. Aside from anything else, an open government regime is potentially challenging to established modes of government. It has two principal strands:

1. Greater access to information for citizens. This may be further subdivided into reactive and proactive release of information. The first is typically delivered through Freedom of Information (FOI) laws, which give citizens a right of access, which is subject to exemptions and under the oversight of an independent adjudicator. In parliamentary systems, these rights are often supplemented by the right of elected members to obtain information from the executive branch of government. Proactive release is less commonly subject to legislation. To implement such a regime, a public authority has to exceed its customary obligations to produce policy papers or to meet the requirements of legislators and regulators. The objective is to inform public debate through the release of research, background analysis, and the like—without the need for FOI requests.

2. Greater access to the decision-making process. Good-quality, timely information may be an essential condition for greater openness, but it is not sufficient by itself. Citizens and their proxies must have the opportunity to engage with officials throughout the policy-making process and beyond. Attempts have been made to regulate this strand of open government. For example, the United States introduced statutory rights of access to government meetings—subject to exceptions—through the government in the Sunshine Act of 1976. But it is inherently difficult to put a legislative framework around the policy and implementation processes. The real prize is to encourage behaviors that build a dialogue between citizens and government—in short, to develop a culture of openness in which officials seek to draw citizens into the process without being forced to do so on pain of sanction.

—Andrew McDonald

See also Data Protection; Electronic Records; Freedom of Information; Information Access Laws

Further Readings and References

Hood, C., & Heald, D. (Eds.). (2006). *Transparency: The word and the doctrine.* London: British Academy.

OPTIMAL DECISION MAKING

A decision maker is said to behave optimally with respect to a given set of preferences or objectives whenever he or she chooses an alternative that is weakly preferred to (i.e., at least as good as) the other alternatives on the menu of available options. When the relevant objective is easily understood from context—as in the case of a manufacturer who wishes to minimize production costs—the decision maker is often said simply to behave optimally.

Scholarly work on optimal decision making can be usefully divided into two broad and overlapping areas of study. The engineering discipline known variously as decision analysis, management science, or operations research focuses on well-specified problems involving a clear objective and usually adopts an explicitly prescriptive outlook. Within economics, on the other hand, the principle of consumer sovereignty, which states that the social scientist should not impose his or her own tastes or values on the individuals under investigation, has led to a tradition of axiomatic work that links assumptions about preferences with conclusions about the associated optimal behavior, but that, for the most part, remains in the descriptive mode. (Also in this mode there is an enormous amount of literature in psychology documenting and seeking to explain the observed suboptimality of actual human choice behavior in precisely the types of scenarios in which the techniques of decision analysis might be profitably applied.)

As an illustration, consider the problem of choosing whether or not to proceed with a particular business or public policy proposal, such as building a new factory in Malaysia or setting aside land for a state park. Here, management science would explain how to construct the appropriate "decision tree" diagram showing the chains of events that might lead to different possible consequences of the two available options; it would suggest how to assess the costs, benefits, and probabilities relevant to the choice; it would show how to combine all of this information to form estimates of the expected values of the alternatives; and it would recommend proceeding only if the estimated value of doing so exceeds that of the status quo. Such an analysis would draw upon results from axiomatic choice theory that characterizes normatively justifiable behavior over time and in the presence of uncertainty. And in a "rational choice" model in which the fate of the proposal in question were to be decided by a particular corporate executive or public servant, this agent might be presumed to act according to the decision-analytic prescriptions previously described.

In strategic settings, the appeal of an alternative to a given agent will depend upon the actions taken by one or more other agents. Optimal decision making in situations of this sort is the province of game theory.

—*Christopher J. Tyson*

See also Bounded Rationality; Decision Making; Game Theory; Groupthink; Rational Choice Theory; Revealed Preference; Satisficing Behavior

Further Readings and References

Fishburn, P. C. (1970). *Utility theory for decision making.* New York: Wiley.

Raiffa, H. (1968). *Decision analysis: Introductory lectures on choices under uncertainty.* Reading, MA: Addison-Wesley.

OPTIMUM CURRENCY AREAS

Economies form a currency area if they use the same legal tender or have their exchange rates irrevocably fixed. An optimum currency area is a theoretical notion, which suggests extending the size of a currency area to the point where the benefits of using a common currency just outweigh the costs of giving up one's own currency. The literature on what determines the possible benefits and costs flourished until about the mid-1970s and then fell into oblivion.

European monetary integration led to a renaissance of the theory of optimum currency areas (OCA), culminating in the 1999 award of the Nobel Prize to Robert Mundell. His seminal article in 1961 framed the problem of forming a currency area in purely economic terms. It amounts to a cost-benefit analysis of irrevocably fixing the exchange rate. Countries that form a currency area lose, on the one hand, the exchange rate as a presumably effective instrument of adjustment to shocks that affect these economies differently. On the other hand, the member countries of a currency area benefit from lower transaction costs of switching between currencies. The optimum size is reached when the loss from higher adjustment costs are equal to the gains from using fewer currencies.

The benefits of lower currency transaction costs were straightforward and did not arouse much interest, while the determinants of rising adjustment costs became an ever-longer list. Increasing adjustment costs are of less concern, first, if shocks affect the countries or regions in similar ways so that a devaluation or revaluation of the exchange rate would not help. This is the case if the countries in question have a diversified or a similar economic structure. If shocks are asymmetric, however, the costs of forming a currency area can still be manageable if, secondly, other adjustment instruments can substitute for the exchange rate. These other adjustment mechanisms—or "OCA criteria," as they are called by scholars in the field—comprise labor mobility and to a lesser degree capital mobility, flexible prices or monetary wages, and fiscal federalism. Whenever a member of the currency area suffers more from unemployment or inflation as a consequence of a shock, these market mechanisms or government policies would replace exchange-rate changes that otherwise could have led to rising employment (devaluation) or the easing of price pressures (revaluation).

Obviously, no existing currency area is "optimal" in the sense of this theory because none has ever been determined by equating macroeconomic costs and microeconomic benefits. The renaissance of the OCA theory in the 1980s was all the more remarkable, as two developments in economics had questioned two basic assumptions of OCA theory. First, modern conceptualizations of the exchange rate raised doubts in regards to the effectiveness of the exchange rate as a reliable and effective adjustment instrument. In fact, the occurrence of self-fulfilling currency attacks implied that there was no such thing as an irrevocably fixed exchange rate. Second, the rational expectations revolution in economic methodology suggested that evaluating the various OCA criteria *ex ante* suffers from a fundamental flaw. The Lucas critique of econometric policy evaluation states that rational economic agents anticipate and respond to policies; their behavior and therefore the "structure" of markets cannot be taken as given. This implies that the OCA criteria will change with monetary integration itself; they are "endogenous" and cannot be evaluated *ex ante*.

This latter insight is the core of the "new" theory of optimum currency areas. It explores, for instance, whether economic structures converge or diverge due to intensified trade and increasing competition that comes with more price transparency. In theory, this could give rise to a paradox: If the member economies become more specialized and thus more susceptible to asymmetric shocks, a currency union that satisfied the OCA criteria *ex ante* may become suboptimal *ex post* for the very reason that it has been formed.

The insights of the new OCA theory can be instrumentalized politically. This was arguably what gave this rather simplistic economic theory a new lease on life in the late 1980s when European monetary integration was conceived. If structural characteristics of member countries change with monetary integration, policymakers could argue that labor markets had to become more adjustable and prices and money wages more flexible because there would no longer be an exchange rate that could devalue in order to compensate a loss in competitiveness. The evaluation criteria for an optimum currency area can thus be presented as norms for the currency area to be formed. This turns the original argument on its head. It allowed making an economic case for stirring up the corporatist arrangements in many European member states that were held responsible for high unemployment ever since the 1970s.

However, the theory did not prepare governments for the intricacies of central banking and policy coordination in a monetary union without fiscal federalism. This suggests that it was not its sound economic argument but a political strategy to restructure socioeconomic governance in member states that made

OCA theory so popular in the development of the Economic and Monetary Union (EMU) of Europe.

—*Waltraud Schelkle*

See also European Union; Monetary Union

Further Readings and References

Johnson, H. G. (1969). The "problems" approach to International Monetary Reform. In R. A. Mundell & A. K. Swoboda (Eds.), *Monetary problems of the international economy* (pp. 393–399). Chicago: University of Chicago Press.

Mundell, R. A. (1961). A theory of optimum currency areas. *American Economic Review, 51*, 657–665.

Tavlas, G. (1993). The "new" theory of optimum currency areas. *The World Economy, 33*, 663–685.

Organisation for Economic Co-operation and Development

Created in 1961, the Organisation for Economic Co-operation and Development (OECD) is a forum where advanced industrialized democracies seek to promote cooperative solutions to the world's economic and social problems. To this end, the OECD (a) collects, analyzes, and disseminates data; (b) provides a setting where officials from national governments can meet to exchange ideas and experiences; (c) promulgates codes and standards of best practice across a whole spectrum of policy areas including *inter alia,* the environment, trade, taxation, investment, tourism, energy, employment, and development (member states are expected and nonmember states are encouraged to comply with these directives); (d) undertakes ongoing surveillance and periodic peer review to ensure members are adhering to the OECD's strictures; and (e) facilitates the work of other international organizations, principally the WTO and the G7, through the provision of analytical and ideological support and acting as a venue where states can prenegotiate or resolve issues that are proving intractable in larger multilateral institutions. In recent times, the OECD has shown some ambition to become a standards enforcer. These intentions have been thwarted by the absence of any coercive instruments available to the OECD and challenged as both illegal and illegitimate.

The OECD was erected on the foundations of its predecessor, the Organisation for European Economic Co-operation (OEEC). The OEEC was founded in 1948 to administer the Marshall Plan and won acclaim for helping to restore the health of the postwar European trading system through dismantling quantitative barriers and providing credit facilities through the European Payments Union (EPU). However, by the late 1950s it was decided that a new transatlantic organization was required where industrialized states could meet on equal terms (as opposed to the donor-recipient structure personified by the OEEC) and which acknowledged the obligations of rich, industrialized countries to developing economies. The European label was dropped, a development dimension was added in the form of the Development Assistance Committee (DAC), and the OECD was inaugurated. As of 2004, the OECD had 30 members. Originally an exclusively transatlantic organization, today the OECD boasts members from all but the African continent. In the 1960s and 1970s, the organization welcomed its first Asian and Australasian members with the accession of Japan (1964), Australia (1971), and New Zealand (1973). A second wave of expansion in the 1990s saw the accession of the first Latin American country, Mexico (1994), a second Asian country, South Korea (1996), and four of the former communist countries of Eastern Europe: the Czech Republic (1995), Hungary (1996), Poland (1996), and the Slovak Republic (2000). Theoretically, membership of the OECD is open to any country committed to the principles of a market economy and pluralistic democracy but in practice membership appears to have been driven by the geostrategic imperatives of U.S. foreign policy.

The bulk of the OECD's work is carried out by a labyrinth of committees and working groups supported by the Secretariat, housed at the organization's Paris headquarters. There are some 200 committees and working groups at the organization composed of officials from national capitals and representatives from permanent delegations to the OECD. Their task is to undertake peer reviews of member state policies to evaluate their performance, encourage improved policy making in the future, and to check compliance with standards and principles agreed on by the OECD. The Secretariat, numbering some 1,670 in 2003, supports the work of committees and working groups by managing the overall peer review process, providing documentation and analysis, catalyzing discussions, and providing institutional memory.

Today, the OECD is facing formidable challenges to its authority. First, the OECD is facing intensified institutional competition from the G7, the European Union (to which 19 of the OECD's members belong), and a proliferation of private think tanks and international meetings, such as the World Economic Forum. These institutions duplicate the roles played by the OECD and mimic the restricted membership, ideological predisposition, and informal approaches pioneered by the organization. This problem is exacerbated because the OECD roams across many different policy areas and lacks clear bureaucratic ownership in national capitals. Second, the absence of a number of major economies, particularly China, India, Indonesia, Russia, South Africa, and Brazil, has undermined the OECD's claims to be the preeminent club where industrialized countries can resolve tensions. Third, the OECD has been tarnished by high-profile policy failures, most notably the abortive attempt to introduce the Multilateral Agreement on Investment (MAI) and the impasse now facing the Harmful Tax Competition Initiative. Critics observe that while OECD countries are economically dominant, representing sixty percent of the world's Gross National Income, they are home to only nineteen percent of the global population, damaging any aspirations it may have to be a genuinely global standards setter. Under the stewardship of Donald Johnston, the OECD Secretary General since 1996, the OECD has embarked on a reform strategy to strengthen its authority and legitimacy. The OECD has streamlined and restructured its committee system to better reflect the changing global environment, sought to strengthen relations with civil society actors via the creation of the Annual Forum, and is presently devising a strategy to enlarge its membership and consolidate relations with nonmember countries. However, this reform program is beset with contradictions and ambiguities and may be too cosmetic to tackle the problems facing the organization.

—Richard Woodward

See also Corruption; Data Protection; Development Assistance Committee; European Union; Group of 7; Health Care; International Organization; World Trade Organization

Further Reading and References

Cohn, T. (2002). *Governing global trade: International institutions in conflict and convergence.* Aldershot, UK: Ashgate.

Sullivan, S. (1997). *From war to wealth—Fifty years of innovation.* Paris: OECD.

Woodward, R. (2004). Global monitor: The Organisation for Economic Co-operation and Development. *New Political Economy, 9,* 113–127.

ORGANIZATIONAL CULTURE

Commonly, an organization's culture is defined from an integrative perspective where it is believed to consist of those beliefs, assumptions, values, norms, artifacts, symbols, actions, and language patterns shared by all members. In this view, culture is thought to be an acquired body of knowledge where the common interpretation and understanding of shared meanings among members give the organization its identity and its members a sense of identity. An integrative approach assumes clarity and organization-wide consensus among members and discounts ambiguity.

However, organizational culture can also be viewed from at least two other perspectives. A differentiation perspective takes a more decentered view. The analysis centers not on the whole, but rather on consensus as it is arrived at only within the boundaries of subcultures, which often conflict with each other. Outside the confines of the subcultures, ambiguity and inconsistency exist organization-wide (e.g., where members may say one thing and do another). A fragmentation approach discounts consensus and consistency or inconsistency

as defining characteristics of culture and focuses on ambiguity as the essence of culture. Here, agreement and disagreement are constantly changing and no stable organization-wide or subculture consensus exists.

Understanding and interpreting organizational culture is important as it affects organizational development, productivity, and learning at all levels. The underlying, often taken-for-granted cultural assumptions can both enable and constrain what an organization is able to do.

Culture as Organizational Personality

Organizational culture has been referred to as an organization's psychological assets. It can be viewed as holistic (or more than the sum of its parts), historically determined (a collection of rituals and symbols), socially constructed (or created and preserved by the group who form it), and difficult to change. A culture contains patterns of assumptions that lead to behaviors that work for the organization. Many of these assumptions are underlying, unquestioned, forgotten, and may, for the most part, be unconscious to organization members. Even so, these collective beliefs shape organizational behavior. Therefore, people's actions and preferences may not always be their own, but, rather, are largely influenced by socialization processes based in the culture or subcultures of the organization to which they belong. Behaviors are controlled by the beliefs, norms, values, and assumptions rather than being restrained by formal rules, authority, and the norms of rational behavior. As a result, an organization's "personality" may be more important to performance and motivation than the exercise of rewards and sanctions.

Constructing Organizational Culture

An integrative framework for understanding organizational culture is often constructed to depict three layers of organizational interaction. The outermost layer, and the most visible, consists of cultural symbols and artifacts, such as the language used (jargon), ceremonies, stories, rewards, symbols displayed, heroes remembered, and history recalled. Heroes, real or imagined, alive or dead, often serve as models for behavior. Also included are the visible organization structures and processes. The middle layer consists of values and beliefs, or what members believe "ought to be" in the work of an organization. These values may be unconscious to those who hold them, often are automatically assumed, seldom discussed, and can only be inferred by the way people act in various circumstances. Ideologies, attitudes, and philosophies are found in this layer as well. Finally, the innermost and deepest level of culture consists of basic assumptions that capture the fundamental notions of how members are to relate to the environment and to each other. They are often taken for granted and are below the level of consciousness for most members of the organization. These basic assumptions, usually invisible to the outsider and taken for granted by the insider, can only be made known through interpretation, which is often imperfect and incomplete. It is thought that at this level the unconscious, taken-for-granted beliefs, perceptions, thoughts, and feelings are the ultimate sources of values and what motivates behavior.

Manifestations of Organizational Culture

Culture can manifest itself in a number of ways. Visible, but often indecipherable, are the behavioral regularities in the way people interact. Examples include the language used, customs and traditions practiced, and rituals employed in a wide variety of situations. Next and also visible are those publicly announced principles and values the group claims to be trying to achieve and the ideologies and broad policies that guide a group's actions. They may represent a formal philosophy presented to employees and stakeholders alike, as well as the implicit rules for getting along in the organization ("the way we do things around here"). Also included in this level is the climate or the feeling conveyed by the group in physical layouts and the way members interact with each other, stakeholders, and outsiders. Less visible manifestations include habits of thinking; shared mental models that guide perceptions, thought, and language used by the group; and shared meanings and symbols that include ideas, feelings, and images that may not be appreciated consciously by members.

Organizational Culture and Change

An organization's culture can be strong or weak, functional or dysfunctional. In an organization with a long history, stories and heroes may more strongly reflect its values. For instance, in organizations with strong cultures, such as the military and others with long traditions, the indoctrination of its members is standard and enduring; values are continuously reinforced in terms of rituals, symbols, and rules or expectations for patterns of behavior. These features of culture are internalized throughout a person's membership in the organization and perhaps beyond. In such organizations, when its members are faced with uncertainty, they can often make decisions without direction and take action consistent with the mission. Conversely, strong cultures can inhibit organizational transformation where greater flexibility and adaptation are required to respond to changes in the external environment.

Organizations need to be agile and able to adjust to the rapid and exceedingly high degrees of technological change in order to maintain their effectiveness. Organizational change may require cultural change. Therefore, recognition and understanding of the patterns of basic underlying assumptions that guide behavior in an organization are essential.

—*Richard F. Huff*

See also Informal Organization; Leadership; Organizational Field; Organizational Learning; Organization Theory; Professionalism

Further Readings and References

Hofstede, G. (1997). *Cultures and organizations: Software of the mind.* New York: McGraw-Hill.

Khademian, A. M. (2002). *Working with culture: The way the job gets done in public programs.* Washington, DC: CQ Press.

Martin, J. (1992). *Cultures in organizations: Three perspectives.* New York: Oxford University Press.

Schein, E. (2004). *Organizational culture and leadership* (3rd ed.). New York: Wiley.

ORGANIZATIONAL FIELD

An organizational field can be defined as a social area where organizations interact and take one another into account in their actions. Organizational fields contain organizations that have enduring relationships to each other. While these relationships can be cooperative or hierarchical, most fields have a power structure such that those organizations with the most resources dictate the rules of the game. Organizational fields are governed by shared rules and meanings. Rules define conventions that can be normative or consensual. Actors in organizations have cognitive frameworks that incorporate these shared cultural understandings of the rules and allow them to make sense of the behavior of other organizations in the field.

A stable organizational field can be thought of as a game where players have fixed positions and interact to contest or reproduce a given social order. They signal their intentions to one another and respond in turn. Organizational fields take the substantive forms of industries, markets, regimes, or policy domains. The idea of organizational field has proved useful in political science, sociology, and economics. There are a number of ambiguities in the use of the idea of organizational field. It is often difficult to determine exactly who is and who is not a member of the field. Broad definitions of organizational fields can include organizations that are not directly involved with the activities in the field. Therefore, suppliers, customers, and states may or may not constitute members of a field, depending on the case being studied.

The idea of organizational field originated in organization studies. Scholars were interested in trying to capture the socially constructed nature of organizational environments. This led them to postulate that organizations had "enacted" environments and that groups of organizations came together to form sectors. The idea of organizations forming a field with a certain set of social relationships that created a system of governance based on shared rules and meanings began to emerge in the 1980s.

The dynamics of organizational fields are a matter of great interest. Organizations try to create a field where they can promote the survival of their organization. The formation of organizational fields presupposes that there is an opportunity for such a field to come into existence. Most scholars agree that fields are more likely to emerge when there are organizations with lots of resources, where governments ratify or help organize fields, where there are entrepreneurs who propagate a conception of what the field should be, and where it is possible to build a coalition of organizations to produce a social order.

By definition, radical change in a field would imply that organizations disappear and the social order is transformed. Change usually occurs when there is a crisis in existing field relations where the positions of dominant organizations are no longer easily reproducible. Because there is always a certain amount of uncertainty in fields, it is often hard to see when a field is about to undergo radical transformation. Organizations will continue to defend the old order as long as they can. Changes to fields will often come from challengers or invaders into the field. These organizations propose a new conception of the field, and if they can find sufficient allies, they will transform the rules and relationships in the field.

—*Neil Fligstein*

See also Organizational Culture; Organizational Learning; Organization Theory; Social Network Theory

Further Readings and References

Fligstein, N. (2001). Social skill and the theory of fields. *Sociological Theory, 19*(2), 105–125.
Fligstein, N. (2002). *The architecture of markets.* Princeton, NJ: Princeton University Press.

ORGANIZATIONAL LEARNING

Organizational learning is the process by which an organization gains new knowledge about and responds to its environment, goals, and processes. Despite general agreement that organizations can learn and that learning is vital for organizations to survive in dynamic environments, there is little agreement about several central questions: Who learns, organizations or individuals in organizations? What is the learning process? What is learned?

Organizational learning is not simply the aggregation of individual learning, nor is it something that occurs in the absence of individual learning. Herbert Simon wrote in 1997 that an organization's collective knowledge (both facts and procedures) is composed of two subsets, knowledge in the minds of its individual members and knowledge in its files and records. Learning is how the organization acquires this knowledge. Learning happens when an organization discovers that its actions have led to an intended outcome or when the organization identifies and corrects a mismatch between intended and actual outcomes. In both conceptions, individuals perform the actions that lead to learning, but it is the organization that develops roles, a culture and structure, routines, and values to direct its members' decision making.

Organizational learning can be thought of in a number of ways, depending on how an organization is conceived. If it is thought of as a group, learning is the acquisition of facts through the interaction of individuals performing a task. If it is a collective actor, learning is the development of action plans and the incorporation of information into its files. If an organization is a formal structure, it learns by adapting its roles and responsibilities to shifts in its environment. If it is a culture, learning is a process of socialization or the development of shared norms, values, and decision premises.

Another way to distinguish types of organizational learning is by what is learned. The frequent distinction here is between single-loop and double-loop learning (though the analogy should not be carried too far). Single-loop learning occurs when a mismatch between the intended and actual outcomes is observed and corrected without questioning the assumptions or values that gave rise to the actions and the expected outcomes. A common analogy for this kind of learning is a thermostat that reads air temperature and, if necessary, generates the proper airflow to reestablish the desired equilibrium. The mismatch may occur because a task demanded more time and energy than expected or because performance falls short of a priori expectations. In response, an organization may learn new facts about the state of the world, new procedures to accomplish the desired task, new methods of communicating about current states of the world, or new methods for coordinating members' actions.

Double-loop learning occurs when the underlying assumptions or values are questioned by the organization. If the thermostat were to ask why it was programmed to maintain a temperature of 70 degrees or why it was programmed to monitor air temperature and not air quality, then it would be engaged in double-loop learning. Double-loop learning leads to new understandings of causal relationships, new norms or values to guide member behavior, and new organizational goals. The process of questioning assumptions may happen because of conflict among individuals and subgroups within the organization or because of pressure from outside the organization.

Many models of organizational learning assume that the process of learning is at least semirational and directed—organizations perceive problems and work to correct them. Some scholars argue that when an organization perceives a disjoint between the current state of the world and its preferred state of the world as a result of some exogenous shock, it searches for ways to adapt its behavior so as to achieve desired states of the world. The search process is probabilistic: The organization starts with likely solutions (related to its current procedures or ones that have worked for similar problems in the past) and continues until it has found a solution that is good enough. Although this perspective might allow for the possibility of adapting goals and aspiration levels, it generally assumes that organizations have essentially fixed preferences.

However, organizational learning may not be as ordered a process as most models assume. Organizations often simultaneously learn about what they want to do (their goals), what is possible for them to do (their performance expectations), and the best ways to achieve their goals. Some organizations may never have even semifixed ideas about their goals, expectations, or methods. Moreover, learning may not be a conscious process; it may just happen. The organization or its members may not consciously choose to alter their behaviors in response to a perceived problem (if one is perceived at all). Learning may be continuous, in which case the organization is always searching for problems and solutions or incrementally changing its behavior through a process of unconscious adaptation. Or learning may be episodic, in which case the organization learns only when it experiences an intolerable amount of stress. Finally, learning requires interpreting past actions and their outcomes, a process of interpretation that may not lead to clear answers.

—Keith W. Smith

See also Communicative Action; Communicative Rationality; Crisis Management; Norm; Organizational Culture; Organizational Field; Policy Learning; Sensemaking

Further Readings and References

Argyris, C., & Schön, D. A. (1978). *Organizational learning.* Reading, MA: Addison-Wesley.

Argyris, C., & Schön, D. A. (1996). *Organizational learning II.* Reading, MA: Addison-Wesley.

Cyert, R. M., & March, J. G. (1963). *A behavioral theory of the firm.* Englewood Cliffs, NJ: Prentice Hall.

March, J. G., & Olsen, J. P. (1979). *Ambiguity and choice in organizations* (2nd ed.). Bergen, Norway: Universitetsforlaget.

Simon, H. A. (1997). *Administrative behavior* (4th ed.). New York: Free Press.

ORGANIZATIONAL STRUCTURE

Organizational structure encompasses the relationships of authority and communication, both formal and informal, that exist within an organization, as well as the rules, procedures, routines, norms, and other practices that guide and constrain the behavior of organizational participants. Organizational structures comprise both social structures and rational-legal structures that are independent of any particular social actor. The latter get passed down from one generation to the next, enabling an organization to survive despite changes in participation. The way in which organizational structures are designed is important because different designs can either facilitate or impede the ability of an organization to pursue its goals. Additionally, organizational structures can be highly dependent upon and influenced by their external environments.

Types of Organizational Structure

Scholars have conceptualized organizational structure in different ways. The most important is the "hierarchy," which is generally characterized by a top-down authority structure, centralized coordination, and vertical communication. There are different views about how relationships are organized within a hierarchy. Max Weber described hierarchies in terms of their command and control functions—one person at the top directs and coordinates everyone below. Herbert Simon, on the other hand, conceptualized the hierarchy as a system of interrelated subsystems organized from top to bottom. In this model, each person at any given level is connected to many people within that level, but relatively fewer people between levels. Aside from the hierarchical model, scholars have also conceptualized organizational structure as: mechanistic (characterized by high task specialization, vertical coordination and control, and management by plan and command), organic (characterized by multitasking, lateral coordination, and facilitative leadership), matrix (characterized by project-oriented teams comprising individuals detailed from other divisions), and M-form (characterized by multiple divisions organized according to the type of output they produce).

Elements of Organizational Structure

Regardless of the form it takes, organizational structure consists of both formal organization (the rules, procedures, and routines that guide and constrain behavior) and informal organization (the patterns of social relationships that exist "outside" the formal structure of the organization). The most important types of social structures within any organization are the authority and communications structures. The former concerns the relationships of authority, both formal and informal, by which organizational leaders exercise control over other participants. Authority structures are commonly conceived as hierarchies, but they can also take other forms. In some organizations, authority is vested in individuals who that possess highly specialized knowledge; in others, authority may be delegated informally to individuals who occupy no formal position of authority.

Communication structures are principally concerned with the flow of information through an organization. When an organization is functioning optimally, decisionmakers have access to as much of the information as they need to make well-informed decisions. As scholars have observed, however, organizational participants do not always have the motivation or incentives necessary to ensure that information is disseminated in an efficient manner.

Organizational Structure and Rational Decision Making

When an organization's authority and communication structures are working optimally, with the right balance between formal and informal organization, the organization's structure can be said to help individuals approximate rational decision making. Organizational participants are, at best, boundedly rational, with little choice but to make the best decisions possible under conditions of limited cognition and incomplete information. Although complete rationality may not be possible at the individual level, it can be approximated by building rationality into the structure of the organization, using such devices as standard operating procedures, roles, formal rules, and training. Within such a framework, organizational participants are able to make decisions using a variety of means that help them to overcome their human limitations.

Organizational Structure, Uncertainty, and the Environment

Organizational structure also mitigates the effects of uncertainty. According to structural contingency theory, there is no one best way to organize, but not every organizational structure is equally effective. As a result, organizational leaders should give serious thought to the design of their organizations. As uncertainty increases, for example, the amount of information that needs to be processed increases substantially, which necessitates the building of effective communication channels into an organization's structure. Some scholars go even further, arguing that organizations contain multiple interdependent components and organizational structure provides the means through which these interdependencies are coordinated.

Organizational environments can pose the most serious challenges to organizational structure. As resource dependence theorists have argued, the environment is the most important factor influencing an organization's structure. Underlying this assertion is the assumption that organizations are continually fighting to survive. In this view, an organization is only able to survive to the degree that it is able to manage, or adapt to, the demands of outside actors on which the organization depends for resources and support.

Scholars disagree about the extent to which organizational structures facilitate rational adaptation. Population ecology theorists view organizational structure as potentially inhibiting adaptation. They thus describe a type of structural inertia. Inertial forces that make organizations slow to adapt can come from within (e.g., sunk costs, internal political dynamics) or from the environment (e.g., legal restraints, incomplete information, and pressures to maintain legitimacy). Ultimately, those organizations that are not able to compete with other organizations in their environment are "selected" out and die. Not surprisingly, the organizations that survive are those with structures that have been optimized for a particular environment.

In contrast to population ecology, which concerns itself with explaining why so many different organizational structures exist, institutional theory seeks to explain why there is so much homogeneity of organizational forms and practices. Institutionalists typically explain such homogeneity by arguing that organizational structures tend to become similar to each other through a process of isomorphism within a particular organizational field. Competitive isomorphism describes the homogenization that occurs in fields with free and open competition between organizations. Institutional isomorphism, on the other hand, occurs in fields where there is competition not just for scarce resources, but also for power and legitimacy.

—*Angelo J. Gonzales*

See also Authority; Formal Organization; Institutionalism; Organization Theory; Rationality; Resource Dependency Theory; Structural Contingency Theory

Further Readings and References

Cyert, R. M., & March, J. G. (1963). *A behavioral theory of the firm.* Englewood Cliffs, NJ: Prentice Hall.

DiMaggio, P. J., & Powell, W. W. (1983). The iron cage revisited: Institutional isomorphism and collective rationality in organizational fields. *American Sociological Review, 48,* 147–160.

Hannan, M. T., & Freeman, J. (1977). The population ecology of organizations. *The American Journal of Sociology, 82,* 929–964.

Pfeffer, J., & Salancik, G. R. (1978). *The external control of organizations: A resource dependence perspective.* New York: Harper & Row.

Thompson, J. D. (1967). *Organizations in action: Social science bases of administrative theory.* New York: McGraw-Hill.

ORGANIZATION FOR SECURITY AND COOPERATION IN EUROPE

The Organization for Security and Cooperation in Europe (OSCE) is the world's largest regional security organization with fifty-five participating states from Europe, Central Asia, and North America. It originates from the 1975 Helsinki Final Act agreement establishing a Conference on Security and Cooperation in Europe (CSCE), which aimed to promote comprehensive security through a three-basket approach. Basket one promoted a system of cooperative security within and between OSCE participating states. Basket two primarily focused on economic dimensions. The third basket related to the human security dimension, specifically human rights, and so established the right of CSCE states to interfere in one another's internal affairs to protect human rights. In 1990, to mark the transition from the Cold War period, the CSCE gained a permanent structure with a small secretariat and formally became the OSCE in 1994. Today, the OSCE is active in the promotion of human rights and the establishment of democratic structures, early warning, conflict prevention, crisis management, and postconflict rehabilitation.

The OSCE has evolved from simply setting the normative standards necessary to fulfill its comprehensive vision of security to an organization with most of its staff engaged in field missions. These missions are designed to deal with specific issues at a local level by building partnerships and dealing with potential conflicts before they spiral out of control. It is claimed that such missions have helped to rebuild civil society in Bosnia and Kosovo, which included fostering security sector reform, ending civil war in Tajikistan, and preventing or limiting conflict in Moldova, Georgia, Macedonia, and Ukraine.

The OSCE faces a difficult future. It is increasingly argued that it duplicates the work of other European institutions, such as the European Union (EU) and the Council of Europe on conflict prevention and human rights, particularly as the EU becomes a security actor. Similarly, NATO's search for a post–Cold War role is leading it into areas where the OSCE is active. NATO and EU enlargement has meant that the OSCE's initial role as a confidence builder between East and West seems irrelevant. Moreover, the OSCE has suffered some organizational problems. Its rotating political leadership has been inconsistent and variable in quality, and it has some superfluous institutions. A lack of consensus among participating states about its precise role has led to unclear or overambitious mission goals being set and subsequently not being achieved. Important members such as Russia appear to have lost interest. Nevertheless, the OSCE has some valuable features that are not duplicated elsewhere. It includes among its members states that are unlikely ever to join the EU or NATO, often in conflict-prone regions like Central Asia. It is also widely trusted, which makes the OSCE a potentially valuable partner for dealing with current security challenges, such as organized crime, people trafficking, terrorism, the illegal arms trade, and the repression of human rights, where military preemption is unlikely to succeed.

—Jocelyn Mawdsley

See also European Governance; European Union; Security

Further Readings and References

Barry, R. (2002). *The OSCE: A forgotten transatlantic security organization?* BASIC research report 2002 [Electronic version]. Retrieved from http://www.basicint.org/pubs/Research/2002osce.pdf

Freire, M. (2003). *Conflict and security in the former Soviet Union: The role of the OSCE.* Aldershot, UK: Ashgate.

ORGANIZATION OF AFRICAN UNITY, THE

The Organization of African Unity (OAU) was established by thirty-two independent African states on May 25, 1963, in Addis Ababa, Ethiopia. The formation of the OAU was in response to Pan-Africanist political ideology that came to dominate a decolonizing Africa. The OAU was established to promote African sovereignty and unity through increased cooperation among independent states. This purpose was based upon principles of freedom, equality, justice, understanding, peace, and international cooperation with the United Nations and the Universal Declaration on Human Rights. Membership of the OAU was extended to any independent African state.

The aims and institutions of the OAU were enshrined in the organization's initial charter. Article II states the main objectives of the OAU as: promotion of unity and solidarity; defense of sovereignty and independence; territorial integration; eradication of all forms of colonialism; and political, economic, cultural, transport, diplomatic, health, scientific, educational, and security cooperation. The aims of the organization were to be carried out by four main institutional bodies: the Assembly of Heads of State and Government; the Council of Ministers; the General Secretariat; and the Commission of Mediation, Conciliation, and Arbitration. Each member state had one vote within the Assembly of Heads of State and Government and the Council of Ministers and decisions were based upon a two-thirds majority vote.

Since its creation, the OAU has faced many institutional difficulties and has failed to respond to changes within Africa and an enlarged membership of fifty-three states. Tensions existed over member-state sovereignty, increased cooperation, and the interpretation of contentious issues such as human rights. Issues of peace and security became undermined by internal conflict and warfare. Despite forming a Committee on the Review of the Charter in 1979 to respond to such changes, the OAU lacked any substantive institutional change concerning efficiency, action, and integration.

The final problem faced by the OAU was the 1994 formation of the African Economic Community (AEC) under the Abuja Treaty that sought to strengthen African economic cooperation, harmonization, and integration. The AEC presented the OAU with the problem of reconciling the political objectives of the postcolonial era with modern economic and development issues. The OAU responded with the 1999 Sirte Summit, "Strengthening OAU Capacity to Enable It to Meet the Challenges of the New Millennium." The declaration of this summit signaled the end of the OAU and the establishment of the principles of an African Union. The implementation of the African Union was discussed at the OAU/AEC summit in Lusaka in 2001 and was finally inaugurated in July 2002. The African Union encompassed the purposes of the OAU and AEC by enshrining the Abuja Treaty as expressed in the Sirte Declaration. In so doing, the central aim of the African Union was increased economic integration and social development that would subsequently result in political unity. The union moved away from the state-centric notions of the OAU to stress the role of governments, business organizations, civil society, and labor unions within the organization.

—Sophie Rose Harman

See also African Governance; Economic Community of West African States

Further Readings and References

Makoa, F. K. (2004, May). African union: New organisation, old ideological framework. *Strategic Review for Southern Africa, 26*(1), 1–14.

Onwuka, R. I., & Sesay, A. (1985). *The future of regionalism in Africa.* London: Macmillan.

Tieku, T. K. (2004). Explaining the clash and accommodation of interests of major actors in the creation of the African Union. *African Affairs, 103,* 249–267.

ORGANIZATION OF THE PETROLEUM EXPORTING COUNTRIES

The Organization of the Petroleum Exporting Countries (OPEC) was founded by the Baghdad Conference in September 1960. It is an intergovernmental agency that aims to coordinate oil policies among its members and to ensure a stable, yet regulated, supply of oil to the international market.

OPEC was founded in the wake of the nationalization of oil-producing companies in several developing countries following their political independence. These countries wanted to counter the hegemony of large multinational companies (commonly referred to as the "Seven Sisters") that controlled the oil market and set the international prices of petroleum.

Starting with five founding states, OPEC has continually expanded and currently holds eleven members that control over two-thirds of the global oil reserves. Despite the fact that non-OPEC countries supply over half of the oil traded on the international market, the organization still yields a major influence over the direction of oil prices and is by far the largest regulatory agency in the field of oil production.

The influence of OPEC was dramatically felt during the oil embargo imposed on several Western nations during the 1973 Arab-Israeli War. The embargo, implemented by the Arab member states against countries seen as supporting Israel in the conflict, caused a major supply crisis and a sharp increase in the world's oil prices. Since then, OPEC has played a mitigating role in the oil market by increasing production in the face of high demand and limiting it during periods of oversupply. OPEC policies were remarkably successful in avoiding energy crises and price fluctuations during phases of instability that occurred in oil-producing regions. OPEC stepped in to compensate for the loss of production resulting from the Iran-Iraq War (1980 to 1988), the Second Gulf War (1990), and the American-led invasion of Iraq in 2003.

The major tool used by OPEC to regulate its members' production is through the use of production quotas. Member delegations meet twice a year and set future production policies based on forecasts of global demand and supply. Every OPEC conference sets new production levels that are divided proportionately among the member states.

Commitment to production quotas has not always been consistent, and several OPEC members regularly exceed their quota limitations, especially the smaller producers. Large OPEC members, especially Saudi Arabia, have tended to cut their production in order to compensate for the excessive supply by other members. Crashes in oil prices in the mid-1980s and late 1990s were attributed to the lack of commitment to the quota system.

OPEC members were not always in agreement as to the oil-production and pricing strategies, and disagreements among members often reflected larger political differences. For example, since the 1979 Islamic revolution, Iran has been continually calling for higher prices, which have been resisted by Saudi Arabia and other pro-Western member states. Iraq's invasion of Kuwait in 1990 was partially motivated by Iraq's dissatisfaction with Kuwait's overproduction, which contributed to lowering the international prices of petroleum.

—*Amer Mohsen*

See also Oil Crisis; Third-World Debt

Further Readings and References

Amuzegar, J. (2001). *Managing the oil wealth: OPEC's windfalls and pitfalls.* London: I. B. Tauris.

Yergin, D. (1993). *The prize: The epic quest for oil, money and power.* New York: Free Press.

ORGANIZATION THEORY

Organization theory refers to a large and multidisciplinary body of scholarly work that focuses on understanding organizations. Most of this work has been written by scholars in the disciplines of sociology, business management, and economics. These scholars have focused most of their attention on analyzing and theorizing about business firms and, more recently, associations and nonprofit organizations. Scholars in this field have aimed at developing a general theory of organization and analytical tools that are designed to apply to all types of formal organizations, including those in the public sector.

Organization theory literature is primarily concerned with explaining organizational structure, performance, and survival. Scholars addressing these questions may adopt one of a variety of units of analysis. They may focus on individual organizations, sets of related organizations, or entire populations of organizations. They may also focus on relationships both within and between organizations. A large number of competing theoretical approaches exist. While there is no consensus on how precisely to classify the various theories, seven approaches are especially prominent: structural contingency theory, resource dependence theory, population ecology, economic approaches, sociological institutionalism, network theory, and postmodern and critical approaches.

With regard to the analysis of governance structures and processes, the literature on organization theory offers a set of potentially useful theoretical approaches. It also offers a particular overarching perspective as well. From the vantage point of organization theory, the world consists most fundamentally of organizations and interorganizational relationships. An organizational approach to the study of governance thus focuses on analyzing the organizations and interorganizational relationships on which governance structures are constructed and that animate governance processes. While some scholarship on governance does explicitly adopt an organizational approach, the political scientists that dominate this research area have not engaged extensively with organization theory.

Scholars in the discipline of public administration have tended to narrowly focus on the functioning of government organizations, eschewing a broader engagement with the main body of organization theory.

Development and Scope

Modern organization theory developed within and continues to be anchored in the disciplines of sociology, business management, and economics. Max Weber's pathbreaking analysis of bureaucracy inspired the growth of a major subfield within sociology focusing on formal organizations. In economics and business management, in the early part of the twentieth century, scholars began studying the modern business firm. The goal was partly to understand its role in the economy, but much of the focus was on helping managers run firms more efficiently and effectively. Over time, organization theory emerged as a coherent multidisciplinary field of research. Scholars in this field have consistently aimed at crafting a general theory of organization, a science of organizations that applies equally well to all sorts of formal organizations. A key assumption in the field is that there is no fundamental difference between public and private organizations. However, the sociologists, business school professors, and economists that dominate organization theory have focused most of their empirical research on business firms in the United States. Thus, it is unclear how well these theories apply to public organizations. Partly for this reason, scholars in political science and, to a much lesser extent, public administration have tended to regard organization theory as irrelevant to their research on political processes and government organizations. In recent years, however, research by scholars in these disciplines on social movements, the state, and government administration has begun to engage with organization theory to a greater extent than before.

Key Questions, Units of Analysis, and Debates

Organization theory is focused on understanding how organizations work, why they come to be structured in particular ways, and why some organizations are more successful than others. Researchers have addressed these questions by employing a variety of units of analysis. One strand of research examines individual organizations—looking, for example, at how internal structure or organizational culture affects performance. Another strand focuses on relationships among organizations, examining interactions either among a small number of organizations or within a specific "field" of mutually interdependent organizations. This view allows one to understand, for example, how powerful organizations shape others within a field and how organizations come to rely on one another. Other research looks at entire populations of organizations, using statistical tools to see how a population changes over time as some organizations flourish and others die. Overall, a large proportion of work in organization theory centers on organizational relationships and the interaction between an individual organization and its external environment.

Three perspectives appear to dominate within organization theory. The rational system perspective focuses on the formal structures of an organization and sees the organization as a group of people who work together to pursue specific goals. The natural system perspective advances the idea that informal and interpersonal structures within an organization are more important than formal structures. People within an organization have multiple interests, and consensus-building or conflictual processes drive organizational action. Last, the open system perspective argues that one cannot look at an individual organization in isolation. In this view, organizations are intertwined with their environments to the extent that the organization-environment boundary is indistinct.

We might also identify three dominant debates or issues within the field of organization theory. The first concerns whether efficiency and the quest for efficiency are the main determinants of organizational structure, performance, and persistence. While some maintain that the most efficient organizations persist and prosper, others argue that organizations can succeed through the use of other strategies. For example, an organization may do well because it is perceived to have great legitimacy or because it has formed alliances with powerful actors. A second debate concerns the degree to which organizations can actively change or co-opt their environment. Does the environment represent a "hard" structure to which organizations must adapt or die, or is the environment malleable, making it possible for organizations to manipulate it? A last debate focuses on the question of whether or not organizations are able to adapt in the face of environmental change. While some research shows that managers can change their organizations in the face of challenges, other research suggests that it is rare for adaptation to be carried out successfully.

Major Theoretical Approaches

A wide variety of competing theoretical approaches have emerged in organization theory. They differ in terms of the unit of analysis that is employed and the perspective that is taken on major debates in the field. While scholars have organized the field in various ways, most would agree that seven theoretical approaches have proven highly influential: structural contingency theory, resource dependence theory, population ecology, economic approaches, sociological institutionalism, network theory, and postmodern and critical approaches.

Structural (or strategic) contingency theory and resource dependence theory can be grouped together under the rubric of the rational adaptation perspective. This view of organizations emerged out of early generations of work, in particular the decision and behavioral theories associated with James G. March and Herbert A. Simon. These focused on decision-making processes in organizations, examining how managers promote the achievement of organizational goals under conditions of bounded rationality. Structural contingency theory centers on the idea that managers can and do adjust their organization's structure to fit the changing demands of the environment. Structure and performance are thus the result of managers' efforts to act strategically to meet environmental contingencies and to minimize the uncertainties faced by their organization. Resource dependence theory shifts the focus more explicitly to how an organization's dependence on its environment for resources shapes its behavior and structure. Organizations are embedded in a web of interdependencies that must be managed but that cannot be fully controlled. Organizational leaders must focus their attention on managing interdependencies with other organizations by attempting to enhance their power and autonomy.

The population ecology approach represents a reaction to the idea that organizations can adapt to their environment. The focus here is instead on how the environment selects certain organizations—only those that fit into a particular niche can survive and adaptation to the environment is not possible. Organizations rarely change; instead, organizational change occurs within a population as organizations ill suited to an environment die and new, better-adapted organizations emerge. Thus, research using this approach looks at entire populations instead of individual organizations.

Economic approaches in organization theory represent the application to organizational studies of general approaches developed in economics. The two most influential are transaction cost economics and agency theory. In the former, organizations are conceived as structures designed to minimize transaction costs. In the latter, organizations are viewed as sets of contracts between principals and agents. Organizational structure and performance are seen as the results of efforts, given the particular conditions that an organization faces, to reduce transaction costs or make principal-agent relations more efficient. In any specific situation, organizations that have the most efficient ways of dealing with transaction costs or principal-agent relationships will be most successful. A third economic approach, evolutionary theory, focuses on how organizations develop in a path-dependent way, with only incremental change occurring.

Sociological institutional approaches look at how interaction among a set of organizations results in the emergence of a socially constructed "organizational field." Powerful organizations shape the field in critical ways. Indeed, this approach emphasizes how organizations are able to shape (or "enact") their environments. An environment, or the organizational field, encompasses a set of normative understandings, and organizations are driven primarily by the need to enhance their legitimacy by conforming to these understandings. Organizations also seek to decrease the uncertainties that they face. Overall, this approach stresses how political, cultural, and normative processes critically shape organizational structure and behavior.

Network theory examines relationships among people within and across organizations. Researchers collect data on these social ties and (usually) use quantitative techniques to analyze them. The result is a map of relationships that can show, for example, which organizations are most central and what kind of network structures are prominent. Network analysis has tended to be primarily descriptive, but researchers have increasingly tried to show how the character or structure of networks affects interorganizational relationships and processes.

Last, postmodern and critical approaches break with the positivist and scientific orientation of most theorizing about organizations. Both approaches seek to expose the processes of domination that are inherent in organizations. Yet they differ in fairly fundamental ways, and each encompasses diverse strands of thinking. Critical scholars aim, through their research, to create a more just organizational world and to discover how individuals may transcend the domination of organizations. By contrast, postmodern theorists argue that instead of focusing on the search for objective facts and large-scale theories, researchers should instead engage with the messy multiplicity of discourses, identities, and power relations that shape life. Postmodern approaches reject the notion of progress and the advancement of knowledge, arguing that the point of research is to deconstruct conventional wisdoms and approaches.

Another way of organizing the field of organization theory is by substantive research area. For example, coherent bodies of scholarship exist on topics such as organizational learning, organizational psychology, organizational development, and organizational decision making.

Organization Theory and Governance

The literature on organization theory has developed in relative isolation from related research fields found in the disciplines of political science and public administration. Scholars in these disciplines have tended not to use or engage with this literature. Instead of trying to explain organizational structure and functioning, political scientists have focused on understanding political processes and political outcomes. Moreover, many scholars have viewed public organizations as fundamentally different from private-sector organizations, leading to the development of approaches designed specifically for the analysis of government organizations.

The relatively new focus in a number of disciplines on governance as a perspective and research area has opened up greater possibilities for the use of organization theory in political and administrative analysis. Organization theory offers a particular perspective on governance structures and processes, namely that analysis should focus on the organizations and interorganizational relationships on which governance structures are constructed and that animate governance processes. Because organization theory has aimed at developing approaches suitable for the analysis of all kinds of organizations, it offers the opportunity to analyze the wide variety of organizations that participate in governance within a single framework. Moreover, whereas most studies of governance either focus on political processes or on governance outcomes, organization theory aims at the relatively distinct goal of drawing conclusions about organizational structure, performance, and behavior.

Organization theory is especially relevant to a number of areas of research related to governance, including the behavior of government agencies, the policy-making process, and the various phenomena that link together governmental and nongovernmental actors (such as the contracting out of services and participatory modes of governance). For example, the dynamics of interorganizational relations in emergent governance systems might be fruitfully examined in terms of efforts by individual organizations to manage resource dependencies. Another tack is to look at the development and functioning of organizational fields in particular areas of governance. Last, theories of organizational learning and development can be

applied to advance understanding of the evolution of the organizations involved in governance.

—*Kenneth W. Foster*

See also Contracting Out; Economic Sociology; Formal Organization; High-Reliability Organization; Organizational Culture; Organizational Field; Organizational Structure; Political Party; Problem Structure; Resource Dependency Theory; Sociology of Governance; Structural Contingency Theory

Further Readings and References

Aldrich, H. (1999). *Organizations evolving.* Thousand Oaks, CA: Sage.

Clegg, S. R., Hardy, C., Lawrence, T., & Nord, W. R. (Eds.). (1996). *Handbook of organization studies.* London: Sage Ltd.

Farazmand, A. (Ed.). (2002). *Modern organizations: Theory and practice.* Westport, CT: Praeger.

March, J. G., & Simon, H. A. (1958). *Organizations.* New York: Wiley.

Pfeffer, J. (1997). *New directions for organization theory: Problems and prospects.* New York: Oxford University Press.

Powell, W. W., & DiMaggio, P. (1991). *The new institutionalism in organizational analysis.* Chicago: University of Chicago Press.

Rainey, H. G. (2003). *Understanding and managing public organizations.* San Francisco: Jossey-Bass.

Scott, W. R. (1998) *Organizations: Rational, natural, and open systems* (4th ed.). Upper Saddle River, NJ: Prentice Hall.

Shafritz, J. M., Ott, J. S., & Jang, Y. S. (Eds.). (2004). *Classics of organization theory* (6th ed.). Belmont, CA: Wadsworth.

OUTSOURCING

See CONTRACTING OUT

OVERLOAD

The overload thesis became popular in the 1970s. It offered a diagnosis of the crisis afflicting the advanced liberal democracies at the time. Drawing on public choice theory, it identified a set of ongoing processes that it suggested had increasingly served to render the advanced liberal democracies "ungovernable." In this context, the concern of the overload theorists was to demonstrate the need for a withdrawal of a monolithic and overbearing state from its stifling regulation of the economy, civil society, and the public sphere. This account proved extremely influential, decisively shaping the manner in which the crisis of the 1970s came to be understood and the nature of the (largely neoliberal) response.

Drawing on rational choice assumptions, the overload thesis identified a self-reinforcing tendency for the politicization of the economy and civil society. Enticed perhaps by the promise of the scientific management of the economy and society offered in particular by Keynesianism, the state of the postwar period came to claim for itself an ever-greater range of responsibilities. In so doing, it sanctioned ever-spiraling social expectations. The state now claimed to bend an ear to all concerns. The result was to reward those organized political interests that were most active and strategic in lobbying the state. This was to provide a powerful incentive for heightened pressure group activity. The unintended consequence, in turn, was to establish a political marketplace in which the parties would vie for votes, yet one lacking the discipline provided by formal market mechanisms.

In such an undisciplined political market, fiscal irresponsibility is rewarded electorally. Political parties seeking only to maximize votes are encouraged to "buy off" a sufficient share of the electorate by promising to accede to the demands of an ever-greater range of interests, thereby raising the "price" of a vote and the stakes of fiscal irresponsibility. Once established, such logic is cumulative—a crisis of overload and ungovernability is inevitable. For the overload theorists, the result was a profound crisis of democracy—government's capacity to respond fell far short of demands placed upon it.

The image was a simple one: A vicious political whirlpool out of whose clutches political parties can only escape at considerable cost to their electoral prospects, but which could not fail to produce economic irresponsibility and political insolvency. The

solution, however politically unpalatable one might think to an electorate that had come to conceive of government as a simple relay for its preferences, was simple: A severe bout of fiscal austerity, tight monetary control, and a programmatic withdrawal of an overloaded, overburdened, yet beleaguered state.

Despite its appeal and influence, the overload thesis contains a series of profound internal contradictions and tensions. On the one hand, its proponents conjure the impression of a cynical and self-serving electorate responsive only to political bribery and looking to the state to satisfy its every whim and desire. Yet this depiction of the electorate as greedy, unprincipled, opportunistic, and, above all, simply too stupid to consider the costs (both economic and political) of their unrealistic expectations, stands in marked contrast to the empirical evidence. This suggests that the principal factor determining success at the polls throughout the postwar period (particularly since the mid 1960s) has been the perceived state of the economy and not the ability of parties to outvie one another through ever-spiraling public expenditure commitments. Once it is considered that reelection is likely to prove conditional upon perceived fiscal probity, the incentive to court interests with promises that cannot be realized seems to evaporate and with it much of the credibility of the overload thesis. Moreover, in its call for a decisive break with the practices that have led, supposedly, to overload and ungovernability and, in particular, in its advocacy of welfare and state retrenchment, the overload theorists appealed to precisely the good sense of the electorate that they had previously dismissed.

The overload thesis also displays a certain disdain for democracy itself. It is, for instance, somewhat unclear whether the crisis of democracy that Micheal Crozier, Samuel Huntington, and Joji Watanuki identify in their report to the Trilateral Commission in 1975 is really a crisis of democracy at all or a fiscal crisis to which their preferred solution is a significant attenuation and curtailment of liberal democracy and its economic contradictions. Given that for them, and indeed for many of the theorists of overload and ungovernability, this is the heart of the problem, it is difficult not to suggest that given the choice between democracy and governability, most would happily trade the former for the latter.

In one sense, however, such contradictions and tensions are insignificant. To assess the contribution of the overload thesis purely in terms of its intellectual cogency is to ignore altogether its most important contribution—the political debate of the time. The thesis offered a compelling, highly influential, and ultimately persuasive narration of the events of the crisis as it was to develop in the late 1970s. It would steer and mold perceptions not only of the crisis and its culprits and villains but of the necessary response to a condition of political overload. In this, its simplicity, its flexibility, its nostalgia for a deferential past that arguably never existed, and perhaps even its internal contradictions were a significant advantage.

—*Colin Hay*

See also Governability

Further Readings and References

Brittan, S. (1975). The economic contradictions of democracy. *British Journal of Political Science, 5*(2), 129–159.

Crozier, M., Huntington, S., & Watanuki, J. (1975). *The crisis of democracy.* New York: New York University Press.

Douglas, J. (1976). The overloaded crown. *British Journal of Political Science, 6*(4), 483–505.

King, A. (1975). Overload: Problems of governing in the 1970s. *Political Studies, 23*(2/3), 284–296.

Rose, R., & Peters, B. G. (1978). *Can government go bankrupt?* London: Macmillan.

OVERSIGHT

Oversight is a broad term used to describe a variety of actions related to management and supervision in accountability relationships. Oversight is often associated with efforts of a congress or parliament to manage agencies that implement policy. The actions that legislatures take in this process, such as investigations and hearings, are referred to as legislative oversight.

This use of oversight is firmly rooted in conceptions of the unitary state, in which power clearly flows in one direction within a bounded institution. In governance, however, more complex accountability relationships are recognized and, consequently, oversight takes on a broader definition. An example of nonstate uses of the term are arrangements for nongovernmental organization (NGO) oversight of working conditions in private firms, which illustrate the wide spectrum of accountability relationships to which the term *oversight* is applied.

Oversight strategies have been parsed into two main forms, police patrol and fire alarm oversight. Police patrol oversight consists of active surveillance by a centralized body to ensure accountability. For example, in principal-agent relationships, police patrol oversight involves the principal actively sampling the agent's actions to detect and deter transgressions. This model has limitations due to the high costs and difficulties of monitoring.

The fire alarm model relies less on active monitoring by a central authority than police patrol oversight and instead opens up channels for information to be passively gathered from third parties that may also be empowered to take their own action. In this model, third parties, such as NGOs, identify problems and either bring the problems to the attention of power holders or seek redress themselves. Fire alarm oversight is more decentralized than police patrol oversight. It allows for, and depends on, action by a multitude of actors. For example, a politician can choose not to review the actions of an agency regularly, but to investigate after its constituents complain about a problem at the agency. Using this strategy, the politician oversees the agency without actively monitoring the agency's action. Fire alarm oversight is more consistent with governance than police patrol oversight, as it deemphasizes the role of the state and focuses on the importance of nonstate actors. Institutions can be designed specifically to engender fire alarm oversight without any intervention by the centralized authority. For example, many environmental policies in the United States have provisions allowing for oversight by nonstate actors, which are also empowered to take action through the courts after identifying deficiencies in implementation.

Thus in governance, the relatively simple action of oversight, as an effort to supervise and manage, becomes more complex than a simple hierarchical relationship. Oversight takes on a multitude of forms and engages a variety of types of actors in the task of management and supervision.

—Matthew Amengual

See also Accountability; Audit; Ombudsman; Regulation

Further Readings and References

Jensen, C. (2004). Inspecting the inspectors: Overseeing labor inspectorates in parliamentary democracies. *Governance: An International Journal of Policy, Administration, and Institutions, 17*(3), 335–359.

McCubbins, M., & Schwartz, T. (1984). Congressional oversight overlooked: Police patrols versus fire alarms. *American Journal of Political Science, 38,* 165–179.

PACIFIC ISLANDS FORUM

The Pacific Islands Forum is the main organization of regional governance in the Pacific. It was founded in 1971 as the South Pacific Forum and changed its name to Pacific Islands Forum in 2000. The seven founding members were Australia, the Cook Islands, Fiji, Nauru, New Zealand, Tonga, and Western Samoa. These countries wanted to look at shared issues with a regional perspective, cooperate in areas of political and economic concern, and express their joint political views to the international community. Since 1971, the founding countries have been joined by Niue, Papua New Guinea, Kiribati, Tuvalu, Vanuatu, Solomon Islands, Republic of the Marshall Islands, the Federated States of Micronesia, and Palau. Member countries have to be self-governing or independent states. Pacific island territories on a path to becoming self-governing or independent can be forum observers. Current observers are East Timor, French Polynesia, New Caledonia, and Tokelau. In 2005, the forum decided to introduce a new membership category called associate membership to extend cooperation with nonsovereign Pacific territories.

The forum holds an annual meeting of heads of government. Key areas of discussion are trade and economics, the environment, education, good governance, and security. A Post-Forum Dialogue is held after the heads of government meeting. The Post-Forum Dialogue was established in 1989 and is a meeting of the forum with nonregional parties. The dialogue partners are Canada, China, the European Union, France, India, Indonesia, Japan, Korea, Malaysia, Philippines, the United Kingdom, and the United States. This dialogue is an opportunity for the forum to express their collective views to an international audience.

The forum's administrative arm was established in 1972. It is currently known as the Pacific Islands Forum Secretariat. Previously, it had been named South Pacific Bureau for Economic Cooperation and South Pacific Forum Secretariat. The Pacific Islands Forum Secretariat is based in Suva, Fiji. The governing body of the Secretariat is the Forum Officials' Committee. This committee consists of representatives of all the forum governments. It holds its own annual meeting prior to the heads of government annual meeting. The Secretary General of the Secretariat chairs the Council of Regional Organizations in the Pacific (CROP), which represents ten regional organizations in the Pacific region, including the Secretariat and others such as the South Pacific Tourism Organization, Forum Fisheries Agency, and the University of the South Pacific. CROP primarily aims to ensure that its member organizations collaborate efficiently and effectively without replicating each other's activities.

—*Mark Bevir*

See also Asia-Pacific Economic Cooperation; Australasian Governance; Regional Governance

Further Readings and References

Fry, G. (2004). *Whose Oceania? Contending visions of community in Pacific region-building.* Canberra: Australian National University.

Shibuya, E., & Rolfe, J. (Eds.). (2004). *The Asia Pacific: A region in transition.* Honolulu, HI: Asia-Pacific Center Security Studies.

PARETO OPTIMALITY

Pareto optimality is a concept originated by the nineteenth-century marginalist economist Vilfredo Pareto. As it has come to be used throughout economics and political science, it refers to a joint social state in which no single individual's condition can be improved without detracting from one or more other individuals' conditions. In a free market system, the phrase captures the idea that all possible voluntary exchanges of goods between individuals are exhausted. Otherwise, if two individuals' states could be improved, they would trade goods, and the former state could not be considered "optimal."

Deriving as it does from marginalist economics, Pareto optimality is a technical, mathematically defined term that has since found usefulness in philosophical discussions addressing justice. The concept is technical because identifying the state under which an individual's condition may be said to have improved or declined is objectively defined in precise terms. This is achieved by identifying individuals by their preferences over various bundles of commodities, and also by their budget constraints. Because it is presupposed in the model that individuals always prefer more goods to less, any subtraction of one type of asset must be offset by an addition of another type of asset with more value to the agent, if that agent's state has improved. This reflects the standard view that, given original endowments and exact property rights, market transactions optimally improve the overall individually estimated well being of a population without recourse to nonvoluntary redistribution. Pareto optimality does not assume that individuals have numerically expressed, or cardinal, preferences over commodity bundles. Nor does it specify one superior social state, but rather it refers to numerous possible resource allocations that fit its definition. Most importantly, it is widely acknowledged that even if it is accepted that a Pareto optimal state is superior to a suboptimal state, Pareto optimality provides no indication of the satisfactoriness of the overall resource allocation from a distributive standpoint. A state could be Pareto optimal in which one percent of the population owns ninety-nine percent of the society's resources.

Although originally developed in the context of early twentieth-century neoclassical economics, in which individuals express preferences over personal commodity bundles, Pareto optimality has been restated to have relevance to contemporary social choice and game theory. In the latter, agents have preferences over global end states that specify everyone's status. The strict Pareto condition applied in social choice theory stipulates that if all individuals in a group prefer state x to state y, then the group may be said to prefer state x to state y. Another version of Pareto optimality is also used in social choice and game theory to identify as socially preferred state x over state y for the case in which some number of individuals of a group (at least one) prefer outcome x to outcome y and none of the remaining members prefer y. The latter version does not require that group members unanimously prefer state x over state y to identify x as socially preferred, but permits indifference between the two end states for some subset of the group's members.

Pareto optimality, sometimes referred to as Pareto efficiency, has become a routinely used term in theories of commutative and distributive justice. Although the concept itself contains normative assumptions, it is widely supposed that these assumptions are so minimal that, all other things being equal, a Pareto optimal state is obviously better than any suboptimal state. These assumptions hold that individuals have complete and transitive preferences, that individuals' preferences are indicative of their welfare, that the welfare of a society only depends on the preferences of its members, and that the intensity with which individuals hold preferences cannot be compared across individuals. In some situations, these assumptions could be construed to suggest that heroin addicts and alcoholics are better off when intoxicated; that a community whose members are individually tired of a hard-fought siege is better off surrendering, and that a society in which many do not have sufficient drinking water, and few have property holdings with large private bodies of water, is better off than one with redistributive public water usage laws. As well, depending on how it is applied in a social choice or game theory context, the Pareto principle may assume a status quo endowment of resources as the starting point from which to evaluate other possible social states.

Commutative justice addresses the adjudication of well-defined rights, whereas distributive justice addresses the distribution of rights. Some theorists endorse the use of Pareto optimality to make a case for commutative justice upholding strict rights to personhood, property, and contract. Since Adam Smith's *Inquiry into the Nature and Causes of the Wealth of Nations,* some economists have argued that exchange in accordance with absolute property rights, without redistribution, results in a socially preferred state. Pareto explicitly argued that a competitive equilibrium based on free market exchange guarantees an optimal allocation of resources. Whereas neoclassical economics assumes private property with budget constraints, social choice and game theory consider choices over social states that may include positions on respecting private property. In the game theoretic prisoner's dilemma model of exchange, which assumes that each has an ever-present incentive to cheat the other, private property rights are irrelevant to individuals' choices of actions: It is assumed that agents will violate property rights when it serves their interest to do so. Using the prisoner's dilemma, an argument for commutative justice is made by appealing to the state of mutual cooperation as Pareto optimal over the state of mutual defection. By this reasoning, applying coercive force to uphold property rights through legal sanctions is in everyone's best interest.

By contrast, in his *Theory of Justice,* John Rawls starts from the premise of rational egoism to make an argument that distributive justice is socially preferred to solely relying on commutative justice. Rawls argues that rational egoists, contemplating the ordering principles of their society at a preconstitutional stage, would not accept the neoclassical Pareto principle as it permits ever-increasing discrepancies of wealth without concern for society's poorest members. His difference principle, which endorses some form of redistribution, was formulated to counter the acceptance of neoclassical Pareto optimality, upholding strict private property rights, as the last statement on a superior distribution of resources in a society. Rawls argued that citizens who have no clear idea of the specific role they will play in society would prefer a society that goes beyond neoclassical Pareto optimality by ensuring that society's least-well-off members benefit to some degree from any social institution predicated on inequalities of opportunity or income.

—*S. M. Amadae*

See also Game Theory; Impossibility Theorem; Prisoner's Dilemma; Rational Choice Theory; Social Choice

Further Readings and References

Buchanan, J. M. (1975). *The limits of liberty: Between anarchy and Leviathan.* Chicago: Chicago University Press.

Hargreaves Heap, S., & Hollis, M. (1992). *The theory of choice: A critical guide.* Oxford, UK: Basil Blackwell.

Hausman, D. M., &. McPherson, M. S. (1984). Economics, rationality, and ethics. In D. M. Hausman (Ed.), *The philosophy of economics: An anthology* (2nd ed.). Cambridge, UK: Cambridge University Press.

Lockwood, B. (1987). Pareto efficiency. In J. Eatwell, M. Milgate, P. K. Newman (Eds.), *The new Palgrave: A dictionary of economics.* London: Macmillan.

Rawls, J. (1999). *A theory of justice: Revised edition.* Cambridge, UK: Belknap Press of Harvard University.

PARTICIPATION

Participation in governance involves the range of formal and informal ways in which members of a political community make their values, interests, and policy preferences known. The concept of popular participation is primarily a concern for democratic systems, although there is growing recognition that it is a key element in facilitating policy acceptance in other nondemocratic schemes. The concept of participation implies involvement in public decisions, as distinguished from other forms of community involvement. Public decisions are those in which the entire community has a stake in the outcome. Different democratic traditions organize participation in distinct ways in an effort to emphasize certain elements over others. For example, a republican form of government filters citizen participation through representatives, while dialogic democracy relies more heavily on direct involvement. At its core participation is the means by which the *vox de popularis,* or the voice of the people is heard. New forms of governance reinforce the need to examine the underlying assumptions about the roles, expectations, and outcomes of participation in public decisions.

How varied traditions view participation is explained by the tensions between competing values of legitimacy and competency. These components are reflected in the ways and extent to which participation does or does not guide policy formulation and implementation. Although each tradition defines legitimacy and competency in dissimilar ways, there is common agreement that both are important. A government without any form of participation is not valid. Similarly, a government without the capacity to perform its core functions is pointless. To further illustrate these differences of emphasis, it is useful to compare the liberal and participatory traditions to two broad streams of thought in which participation is organized differently.

Liberal and Participatory Traditions

Under the broad umbrella of the liberal tradition is the notion that individuals seek their own private good absent explicit regard for the public well-being. As a result, the role of government is to mediate and build compromises among competing values and interests in an attempt to formulate decisions that serve the whole. This tradition relies upon the wisdom of representatives

elected in open processes. Liberal democratic regimes focus primarily on the procedures of participation, which must be fair and equal. Participation is judged by the extent to which the process was justly administered. In this tradition, citizen rights are supremely important, such as the right to vote and the opportunity to provide input. This makes the design of participatory practices central to good governance. Good participatory procedures ensure that one interest does not have primacy over another. In that goal, participation should be limited but well structured where competition among interests is encouraged. While the outcomes of these processes will produce winners and losers, over time all members of a political community will have the capacity and opportunity to make their voices heard. This system places elected leaders in the position of choosing the wisest course of action. The linkage between competence and elected representatives should not be understated, as some policy choices, such as national security, demand decisive action where deliberation is not feasible. The liberal tradition places a greater value on competent policy as a way to ensure that the interests of the whole are realized.

In contrast, more participatory theories of democracy put faith in the capacity of individuals to reconcile their interests with the public good. The role of government in a more participatory democracy is to educate citizens and create meaningful forums for individual dialog. In this view, some argue that government no longer simply represents citizens, but instead has become a steward of the public process, facilitating the ability of citizens to more effectively engage. The role of citizens focuses on the obligations of participation, as distinguished from rights. Citizens are encouraged to engage in face-to-face conversations out of which discussion and action are born. In this tradition, equity is judged by the extent of ownership and agreement within the process itself. As a result, the design of participatory mechanisms is judged by the extent to which opportunities are expanded and where negotiation over substantive values can occur. Legitimacy is the dominant value inherent in more participatory forms of democratic decision making. Indeed, legitimacy becomes the key difference between more representative or more direct forms of democracy. Each stream of democratic theory emphasizes degrees of competence and fairness on one hand, and legitimacy and openness on the other. These process values can be seen in the variety of mechanisms by which citizens participate in a democratic community.

Participatory Mechanisms

The process values of competence, fairness, legitimacy, and openness are reflected in five broad mechanisms of popular participation: electoral, group, citizen-government, direct participation, and activism. Activism is a distinct form of participation that seeks to influence decisions and policy outside formal political structures. Each of these participatory mechanisms is explored in the following sections.

Electoral Participation

Electoral participation is a formal mechanism for making preferences known. Voters elect representatives that act as trustees for the public good. Participation through voting generally relies on the capacity of the individual to perform minimal duties, such as registering in order to exercise one's right to vote. Electoral participation is also reflected in the right of citizens to make financial contributions that ensure a successful campaign. This demands little of citizens, who simply influence decisions by showing up or writing a check, albeit in a rather blunt manner. It does not ensure that specific decisions or policies will be favored or adopted. This form of participation reflects the value of procedural fairness by constructing equal rules of campaigns, contributions, and voter eligibility. Despite this emphasis on fairness, electoral participation is ripe with problems in its implementation, both globally and in the United States. Equal access to voting is not universally ensured, as a result of poverty, lack of education, or by blatant limitations of gender or class.

Direct Forms of Participation

In more direct forms of participation, individuals take responsibility for getting personally involved in making policy, running for office, sitting on boards, or by proposing legislation. Direct participation is also reflected in the initiative and referendum processes. While these terms are perhaps unique to the United States, they are important tools for direct participation. Initiative and referendum processes put in place procedures by which citizens can propose and vote on state constitutional amendments. This is a fairly powerful tool of popular participation that has the power to bypass state legislatures in the policy formulation process. Although an important tool for citizens, interest groups have discovered this process as a means to push specific policy agendas, with the expectation of success if well funded. The initiative and referendum processes were a result of the populist movement in which citizens sought to create the mechanism for increased access to governing decisions. These forms of direct participation seek to enhance the legitimacy of the state by opening the political process to control by citizens.

Citizen-Government Interactions

A third broad mechanism for participation is citizen-government interaction. This type of participation is primarily used during the implementation stages of policy, where elected and bureaucratic officials seek the advice of citizens. It is an attempt to ensure participation in specific policies and actions. A variety of mechanisms support this citizen-government interaction. For example, in the United States, the Administrative Procedures Act of 1946 set "notice and comment" requirements that create opportunities for interested parties to participate in formulating and implementing administrative rules. Many other mechanisms support citizen-government engagement as well. For example, public meetings, hearings, citizen surveys, consensus-building processes, and a host of other methods seek to involve the public in decisions. A range of input devices are recognized as being important to citizen-government interaction and are as simple as providing public information or as complex as actively seeking input through face-to-face public meetings. Scholars point to the importance of coproduced policy as meeting both tests of legitimacy and competency because these processes value both citizen and bureaucratic input. While citizen-government interactions are considered a key element of participation, there are certain risks in this approach. This approach depends upon the capacity of citizens to fully engage in government. Not all citizens are equally prepared in this regard and require the education and the resources to be successful in making their voices heard. In addition, the legitimacy of a governing system is tested as opening citizen-government interaction implies that the government will listen once they've developed the processes to do so. More damage to legitimacy will occur if the superficiality of participation is apparent. Still, the varieties and forms of citizen-government interaction are gaining global interest due to its promise of producing workable and broadly accepted policies. In particular, international development organizations are focused on ways to enhance this type of participation. These engagement activities are increasingly successful in all types of political regimes, ranging from communist China to relatively new regimes in Eastern European Bloc countries.

Group Participation

A fourth means for involvement structures involvement through group participation where individuals feed their preferences through an organization or body that acts as a mediator to express their interests. These groups, often called mediating institutions, act as a buffer between society and the individual, collecting values and preferences while also structuring individual behavior. Neighborhood associations, churches, and local civic organizations are examples of mediating institutions, a concept made popular by Peter Berger and Richard Neuhaus. Group participation is especially important in a more networked type of governing structure, which relies upon the legitimacy of the group to negotiate values. While group participation may allow for more equal representation of disadvantaged voices, this mechanism is also fairly risky. There are three reasons for this: (1) Groups are not equally accountable to all citizens but respond to their own constituencies, (2) groups are not necessarily guided by community principles, and (3) not all community interests are represented by groups. On the other hand, group participation offers the advantage of legitimacy and openness where substantive dialogue and agreement are most likely to occur at a scale large enough to impact policy decisions.

Activism and Dissent

Finally, activism and dissent are a less-commonly recognized mechanism for participation. Activism rejects the need for government to structure involvement. It can take many forms, ranging from benign letters to the editor to radical dissent. These tools are often used in combination with other forms of participation in an attempt to push policies in a desired direction. Activist movements respond to local policy as well as global concerns. For example, international organizations, such as Greenpeace and Amnesty International, use a variety of confrontational and peaceful tactics to influence environmental and human rights abuses, such as distributing publications and conducting demonstrations. But, because global governance also involves big business, activist movements increasingly focus on influencing large corporations, through such esoteric mechanisms as shareholder activism, which use the voting power of shareholders to influence corporate investment and business choices. Higher education has been a center for activism where student-led intellectual and political movements have sought greater influence in political decisions. These movements exist worldwide, from China to Prague and from Seattle to Washington, DC. Engaging in activism, whether peaceful or confrontational, they require that certain freedoms exist. In particular, freedom of speech and a free media are essential tools. The role of the media in providing space for the range of activities described here allows for open expressions of will and allows movements to develop. The Internet has offered new possibilities for providing a vehicle for activism by providing instant and relatively inexpensive access to information. Globally, there is considerable variation in the extent to which the media is free; resulting in more subtle and underground movements. A free media and tolerance of activism allow for greater transparency in government, which is a crucial aspect of openness.

Requirements for Participation

Each of the mechanisms of participation requires that a governing system strive for procedural clarity, openness, competence, and individual liberty. Procedural clarity attempts to create a level ground for competition among interests by ensuring that citizens have equal access to decisions. The openness also attempts to ensure equality of access whereby decisionmakers are accountable for their actions. Competent public officials are also important, as participatory mechanisms are structured and maintained by the work of bureaucratic officials, such as administration of elections, facilitating rulemaking procedures, and hosting public meetings. In this way, competent administrators are stewards of the public trust, teaching and facilitating meaningful involvement. Finally, liberty in the form of freedom of speech and freedom of the press is essential to ensuring popular participation in the affairs of the public.

The concept of participation is tied to notions of citizenship, which tries to deal with the sometimes-competing values of a legitimate and competent government. Participation is also tied to the structures of participation, which are designed to reflect regime values. Who participates and how various schemes account for ensuring the *vox popularis* are essential to democratic decision making.

—*Margaret E. Banyan*

See also Citizenship; Civic Engagement; Civic Republicanism; Dialogic Public Policy; Human Capital; Legitimacy; Liberalism; Participatory Democracy; Public Opinion

Further Readings and References

Berger, P. L., & Neuhaus, R. J. (1996). To empower people: From state to civil society. In M. Novak (Ed.), *To empower people* (2nd ed., pp. 145–208). Washington, DC: Free Press.

Box, R. C. (1998). *Citizen governance: Leading American communities into the twenty-first century.* Thousand Oaks, CA: Sage.

Dahl, R. A. (1961). *Who governs? Democracy and power in an American city.* New Haven, CT: Yale University Press.

King, C. S., & Stivers, C. (1998). *Government is us: Public administration in an anti-government era.* Thousand Oaks, CA: Sage.

Kweit, M., & Kweit, R. W. (1981). *Implementing citizen participation in a bureaucratic society.* New York: Praeger.

Morgan, D., Bacon, K., Cameron, C., & Deis, R. (1996). What middle managers do in public organizations: Stewardship of the public trust and the limits of reinventing government. *Public Administration Review, 56*(4), 359–366.

Morgan, D., & Vizzini, D. (1999). Transforming customers into citizens: Some preliminary lessons from the field. *Administrative Theory & Praxis, 21*(1), 51–61.

Thomas, J. C. (1995). *Public participation in public decisions: New skills and strategies for public managers.* San Francisco: Jossey-Bass.

Warner, B. E. (2001). John Stuart Mill's theory of bureaucracy within representative government: Balancing competence and participation. *Public Administration Review, 61*(4), 403–413.

PARTICIPATORY DEMOCRACY

The concept of participatory democracy refers to democratic arrangements and practices that allow for direct individual and collective participation of citizens in public decision making. The origins of the concept in democratic theory can be situated in the 1970s, especially in the work of Carol Pateman and C. B. Macpherson, who developed their ideas as a New Left model of democracy, incorporating some elements of the developmental model of republicanism and libertarian Marxist positions. The core principle of participatory democracy is that people have equal right to liberty and self-development, which can only be achieved in a society that fosters a sense of political efficacy, nurtures a concern for collective problems, and contributes to the formation of a knowledgeable citizenry capable of taking a sustained interest in the governmental process. The key features of participatory democracy include the direct participation of citizens in the regulation of the key institutions of society, including the workplace and the local community. Against this background, the term *participatory democracy* can be used to cover various types of democratic arrangements, notably associative democracy and deliberative democracy. In associative democracy, citizens exercise self-governance in associations in nonpolitical domains, such as housing, education, and public health. Deliberative democracy is nowadays one of the most influential models in the literature and inspires various experiments in democratic practices, such as citizen juries, round table conferences, and online policy exercises. In this contribution, we focus on the deliberative arrangements, in particular at the local level.

We define democracy as a political system in which the members of the *demos* have an equal effective input into the making of binding decisions. On the basis of this definition, it can be convincingly argued that representative democratic institutions have to be supplemented by arrangements that allow for direct participation of citizens in concrete decision making. The participation should at least include the phases of agenda setting and policy formulation, but could extend to the phases of policy implementation and evaluation as well.

Historical Background

The historical background of the current popularity of the mostly government-initiated practices of participatory democracy can be traced back to the 1990s. Decreasing electoral turnouts, in particular at the local level, triggered many public authorities to counteract the apparently decreasing citizens' trust in government and traditional politics. Local politicians perceived a legitimacy crisis of local government. New forms of political participation had to be offered to the more self-confident citizens. It was also acknowledged that modern citizens possessed valuable local knowledge and experience expertise, which should be mobilized to improve the quality of public policies.

Moreover, representative democracy suffers from several limits and failures. First, in modern network societies, a decentering of collective decision making has taken place. Politics has been relocated to networks of (semi) public agencies, spanning different levels of government, (semi) private organizations, civil societies, and companies. This development has

been designated by the concept of governance, which refers to the management of interaction and cooperation in networks. Governance brings about less formal modes of decision making that become uncoupled from the official institutions of representative democracy. The centrality of the representative democratic institutions has become eroded, and this also means that other channels have to be created for effective citizens' input in collective decision making. Second, there is a growing distance between the lifeworld of citizens and the system of representative democracy, resulting in feelings of alienation of voters toward politicians and voter apathy. There seems to be a severe lack of responsiveness of political decision making toward the citizens' wishes and concerns. An inherent feature of representative democracy, at least in multiparty systems, is the need of making compromises between the political parties, which are going to form the administration. Moreover, during incumbency new issues will come up, which cannot be foreseen in these election programs and were not discussed during the election period. If the citizens perceive these new issues as important, other forms of decision making providing for direct citizens' participation should be considered.

Against this backdrop, a revitalization of representative (local) democracy was envisaged, with new forms of communication and cooperation between public administrators, civil servants, and citizens, and with new roles for the politicians.

Participatory Democracy: Practices

Citizens' participation has several forms. Therefore, many authors make use of a so-called participation ladder in order to distinguish the scope of different kinds of participation and, also importantly, to distinguish forms of participation in which citizens act as co-decisionmakers and forms in which they are merely consulted.

The scope of participation and the amount of potential power of the participants obviously decrease when descending the ladder. One can add different democratic models to this overview. The first three modes of participation are then connected to more participative and deliberative democracy models, the

Table 1 Participation Ladder

Participation Form	Citizens' Roles	Governments' Roles
1. Self-governance	Initiators, self-governance of communities or groups	Supporter (financially or offering facilities)
2. Partnership	Equal partners, coproducing plans and policies	Equal partners, coproducing plans and policies
3. Delegated co-decision making	Delegated co-decision makers, within policy lines previously set by governmental actors.	Main policy makers, leaving lesser abstract decisions to (groups of) citizens
4. Open advice	Advisors, all kinds of problem definitions and potential solutions may come to the fore during the policy-making process	Requesting advice by formulating open questions
5. Consultation	Consultant, advising on rather closed set of questions, formulated by governmental actors	Consulter, asking advice on limited and controlled questions

Source: Adapted from Arnstein, S. R. (1969). A ladder of citizen participation. *Journal of the American Institute of Planners, 35*, 216–224.

fourth and fifth ones with representative democracy. (See Table 1.)

When facilitation of self-steering is the main form of participation, citizens themselves, or groups of citizens, take the initiative. For example, they decide to improve their neighborhood or to build sports facilities in their district. People organize themselves and make plans. They may need some assistance from governmental agencies. Government may give support to the initiative by offering expertise (e.g., how to build those facilities in a safe way), facilities and equipment (e.g., for getting rid of garbage, for cleaning the streets, or offering places for tolerated graffiti), or money. There surely will be some other governmental activity as well; government will still have to check the acceptability of the initiative according to legal and policy criteria. It, too, will have to safeguard the interests of nonparticipating residents and surrounding districts.

When participation takes the form of cooperation, citizens' involvement does not go as far. The initiative

may come from citizens or government. They both take an equal share in the decision making as equal partners. Government and sports organizations and/or parents may cooperate in creating sports facilities in the district.

Government may decide to opt for delegation of decision making to citizens. A city may, for instance, create a business zone especially designed for information and communication technology companies. It may already have planned roads, waterways, and the kind and size of buildings in the area. It then may leave the rest to interested parties to build the offices, to consider the appearance of the streets, the facilities, the kind of trees, and so on. All of this is within the guidelines set by the government, though still with a considerable amount of policy discretion for the participants.

This latter example will no longer be the case in those situations when government requests open advice. Citizens no longer are co-decisionmakers, the government makes the decisions according to its own principles and procedures. Nevertheless, citizens play a significant role. They are invited to give whatever advice they want. The government poses a rather open issue and formulates rather open questions. It may, for example, want to restructure a neighborhood. The residents are then invited to give their opinion. Their opinions on the problems and even the perceptions of the problems may prove to be relevant. The same holds for their ideas on solutions. The policy-making governmental agencies will consider all advice and decide which they think relevant. The final decisions are governmental ones.

An even less-significant role citizens play is consultation. In that case, the government formulates concrete plans, elaborated as if the implementation is about to begin. The proposal will be made public, and citizens will be invited to share their thoughts and views. They may express their opinions as far as they want to, but government is allowed to ignore everything.

Experiences and Evaluations

Governments seem reluctant to introduce radical forms of citizens' participation. Many authorities seem to prefer consultation and open advice, few opt for other forms and acknowledge a bigger say of citizens.

On the other hand, governments sometimes too hastily, and maybe too enthusiastically, decide to let citizens participate in whatever form. Citizen participation needs due consideration. As far as evaluations are available, a number of factors can be formulated that influence the success and failure of participatory policy making. Lessons to be learned are as follows:

1. Setting the stage is important. Governments as well as citizens willing to participate will have to consider the kind of involvement they prefer and which kind is suitable. One of the distinctive decisions to be made is which roles citizens and governments are to play. Setting the stage is a hazardous activity. It is a role for which elected representatives seem to be the more suitable match, that is, members of parliament or regional or local councilors.

2. Openness and access. Participation can only flourish when all participants prevent having hidden agendas. Those who participate have created mutual trust. If there is no trust, it will be hard for everyone to express wishes, to negotiate, and to codecide.

3. Governments will have to express their confidence in the participatory process. If government officials hesitate, or show disinterest, citizens will easily opt out. Participating citizens will have to have the feeling that what they are doing is relevant and useful. Government officials will have to take citizens seriously.

4. Suitable topic. Not every subject is suitable for involving citizens to a large extent. Solving the world's poverty problem may not be the best issue for inviting citizens, whereas improving the neighborhood may.

Future Developments

First of all, one may expect an increasing need for participation. Many people seem to feel alienated, mainly due to ongoing internationalization and globalization. Another effect is that people identify more and more with what appears to be nearby and recognizable. In both cases, stressing participation will be a necessity for the survival of formal democracy.

A second development might be increasing tension between formal representative democracy and participatory democracy. Both democracy models have their decision-making procedures, and they are not the same ones. Representative democracy is based on decision making by representatives, by a political elite mandated to do so by the electorate. Participatory democracy, on the other hand, advocates far-reaching involvement of citizens in the decision-making processes. To put it differently, a struggle is going on between the primacy of politicians and the primacy of the citizenry. On the other hand, the two democracy models can hardly survive without each other; a mutual dependence exists between the two. Without representatives, who will perform the perilous task of safeguarding participation procedures such as openness and access? And without participation, what will compensate for the inherent imperfections of representation? A new balance between representation and participation will have to be found.

Finally, because citizens' ability to participate in an adequate way may be questioned, empowerment of citizens might be a final development. In some cities this has already happened. Citizens were offered training in order to enable them to understand the complexity of decision making in the modern world.

—Linze Schaap and Arthur Edwards

See also Civil Society; Collaborative Planning; Communication; Communicative Action; Communicative Rationality; Deliberative Democracy; Democratic Theory; Dialogic Public Policy; Local Governance; Participation; Pluralist Democracy

Further Readings and References

Arnstein, S. R. (1969). A ladder of citizen participation. *Journal of the American Institute of Planners, 35,* 216–224.

Chambers, S. (2003). Deliberative democratic theory. *Annual Review of Political Science,* 307–326.

Held, D. (1996). *Models of democracy.* Cambridge, UK: Polity Press.

Hirst, P. (1994). *Associative democracy: New Forms of Economic and Social Governance.* Cambridge, UK: Polity Press.

Macpherson, C. B. (1977). *The life and times of liberal democracy.* Oxford, UK: Oxford University Press.

Pateman, C. (1970). *Participation and democratic theory.* London: Cambridge University Press.

PATH DEPENDENCE

Path dependence is an approach to understanding how organizations, institutions, or technologies become "locked in" to particular choices as a result of their structural properties or beliefs and values. Path dependence begins with a straightforward assertion that "history matters" in studies of governance and then attempts to explain exactly how history matters through studies of the means through which constraints on normal behavior in organizational life appear and the form that these constraints take. It has been used to study how the QWERTY keyboard became dominant (despite its suboptimality in terms of typing speed on today's computers) through how studies of policy change in health care and welfare systems.

Path dependence is most often used as a concept by studies based around the historical institutionalist approach to political science, with its attendant focus on how institutions come to constrain organizational life. It has become a key concept to explain why institutions in political life don't change as much as we might expect if adopting, for example, a rational choice approach to human agency would suggest any continuity results from careful calculation of the costs and benefits faced in a particular decision-making process. Instead, path dependence tends to suggest

that policymakers work within a series of more limited assumptions about their world, learning less frequently and being rather more cautious.

In common with social learning approaches to policy (both share the common heritage of historical institutionalism), studies of path dependence demonstrate that governance processes are often subject to considerable amounts of inertia. Several recent studies of changes in the welfare state suggest that change can only be effected in exceptional situations in embedded welfare regimes. Studies of how technologies become path dependent suggest that "externalities" resulting from supplier and customer preference can lead to the dominance of one particular video recorder over another, even where the technology that "loses" might be superior.

A singular problem with uses of path dependence comes in its careless use—it can often appear in studies as a mere assertion that "history matters" in a particular case with little attempt to explain why or how. In order for the concept to have some theoretical credibility, a number of authors have suggested that it might be based around a particular form of technological and institutional development that has particular defining features.

For a path-dependent system to be in place, three elements need to be present. First, there is the need to demonstrate that at the creation of the institution or technology we are analyzing, a contingency or series of contingencies occurred that led to the selection of one outcome over another, which, given another set of initial conditions, might have led to another outcome having been selected instead. In other words, there is a strong element of contingency in the model—chance can end up as a deciding factor. Second, we need to demonstrate how, after a particular technology or organization form has appeared, feedback mechanisms appear to allow it to become insulated to some extent from change. These feedback mechanisms may be positive (where mechanisms lead to, for example, greater dominance from advocates of the path dependent organization or technology) or negative (where mechanisms interfere with attempts at change from alternative organizations or technologies). We should note that the precise feedback mechanisms involved in path dependence are subject to some controversy. Paul Pierson appears to suggest that path dependence is about positive feedback mechanisms only, following the hard science of the subject in original contributions by Kenneth Arthur and W. Brian Arrow. But other writers appear more relaxed, accepting the possibility of both positive and negative feedback mechanisms when the approach is adapted to the study of political systems.

Feedback mechanisms "lock in" the system under investigation along a particular path and might be either cognitive in form, in which policymakers come to see the world only through the view of a particular idea, ignoring elements that do not conform to it, or else institutional, where the structural properties of institutions constrain actors within them so that they are unable to act in particular ways, even if they are not subject to the cognitive limitations as previously suggested. This is not to suggest that path dependent institutions are stupid—they may be extremely sophisticated in their behavior, but only within defined behavior limits. Path dependence suggests that human behavior has limits, both cognitive and institutional, which have profound implications for the way that governance operates.

Finally, a model of path dependence must specify how change is possible, given the feedback mechanisms identified in the second stage of the analysis that have come to dominate. In cases where historical analysis is being pursued, case analysis will show how change has been effected from a situation where a path dependency no longer exists, or, where the case is more contemporary, the analyst might examine the system under investigation for contradictions or problems that might eventually lead to the establishment of a new policy or technology pathway.

Path dependence is an illuminating and powerful means of analyzing policy continuity and change, but its careless use can lead to bland assertions about the importance of history. Equally, critics of the approach are often concerned that it is somewhat incompatible with forms of institutional analysis based around rational choice approaches. This need not be a problem because, as has been previously noted, one of the

key features of path dependence is its discomfort with rationalistic assumptions of behavior and the suggestion that much of human behavior is rather less reflexive than this.

—*Ian Greener*

See also Complexity; New Institutionalism; Social Learning

Further Readings and References

Arrow, K. (2000). Increasing returns: Historiographic issues and path dependence. *European Journal of the History of Economic Thought, 7,* 171–180.

Arthur, W. (1989). Competing technologies, increasing returns, and lock-in by historical small events. *Economic Journal, 99,* 116–131.

Jessop, B. (2002). *The future of the capitalist state.* Cambridge, UK: Polity Press.

Mahoney, J. (2000). Path dependency in historical sociology. *Theory and Society, 29,* 507–548.

Pierson, P. (2000). Increasing returns, path dependence, and the study of politics. *American Political Science Review, 94,* 251–267.

Torfing, J. (1999). Towards a Schumpeterian workfare postnational regime: Path-shaping and path-dependency in Danish welfare state reform. *Economy and Society, 28,* 369–402.

PATRIMONIALISM

Patrimonialism is a term used to designate a form of political organization. It is more often used in the Latin-based languages (e.g., French, Italian) than in English. The key focus in the model is the extent to which legitimate authority is based primarily on personal power exercised by the ruler, either directly or indirectly. The ruler may act alone or as a member of a powerful elite group or oligarchy. The ruler is not viewed as a tyrant. The structure of the Roman Catholic Church today is still patrimonial. Direct rule involves the ruler and a few key members of the ruler's household or staff maintaining personal control over every aspect of governance. If rule is indirect, there may be an intellectual or moral elite of priests or office holders as well as a military. The priestly group may invoke deity for the leader. The king, sultan, maharaja or other ruler is able to make independent decisions on an ad hoc basis, with little if any checks and balances. No individual or group is powerful enough to oppose the ruler consistently without, in turn, becoming the new patrimonial ruler. The ruler is recognized as the chief landholder and, in the extreme case, all of the land and its people are his domain. The legal authority of the ruler is largely unchallenged; there is no recognized body of case law or formal law, but there may be notions of etiquette and honor.

The term *patrimonialism* is often used in conjunction with patriarchy, since the earliest form of governance in small groups may have been patriarchal. There is a relationship of personal dependence between an official and the ruler, so that the ideology is one of a large extended family. The idea of an early matriarchal society—as distinguished from matrilineal descent—is largely discredited. A "Big Man" chiefdom system is characteristic of many indigenous peoples and transition from patriarchy to patrimony is probably common historically around the world. As the size of the organizational structure switches from an extended family to a larger geographical area, particularly in agriculturally based civilizations, we move to the kind of patrimonialism that was probably characteristic of many early agrarian civilizations based on irrigation systems.

The relevance of the term *patrimonialism* for the study of governance and domination was popularized by Karl Ludwig von Haller (1768–1854), a Swiss conservative from Berne who was an opponent of the French Revolution. Haller attacked the ancient regime but, like Edmund Burke, was also opposed to Romanticism and violent revolutionary change. Haller argues that the state can and should be viewed as the patrimonium of the ruler. In his *Patrimonialstaat* concept, the prince is responsible only to God and natural law. Max Weber picked up on the term in 1922, modified it significantly, rejected the natural law argument, and uses it as a label for his Ideal Type Model (ITM) of Traditional Authority (*Herrschaft*). No doubt the fact that many European thinkers would have associated the term with a conservative stance may have helped Weber make his argument clear.

Weber describes forms of patrimonialism. Patrimonial-prebendalism is the more traditional form; it involves a ruler who practices indirect rule and uses officials. Those office holders are maintained by their prebends. Prebends are essentially premodern bureaucratic offices characterized by the payment of a tribute or labor to the office holder. The Anglican Church still utilizes the term. A prebend is like a stipend, but it is rarely a cash payment. A prebend is always held simply on the basis of the ruler's whim or grace. It can be revoked at any time and it cannot be inherited. Patrimonial feudalism is the more exceptional type because it involves the existence of an order of fief holders, mostly landed nobles and members of the clergy. They constitute a feudal network that has some power separate from the ruler. The key difference between a prebend and a fief is that a fief can be inherited. With primogeniture, it is the first legitimate son who becomes the lord, although women can hold feudal rights if there are no male heirs. Weber argues that the prebendal and the feudal forms of patrimonialism tend to oscillate, with those rulers who are able to maintain a highly centralized form of rule able to withstand the centrifugal forces of a more feudal system. Centripetal force is exercised by the ruler and the ruler's retinue traveling throughout the domain. In feudal settings, the ruler's domain often becomes more circumscribed, but it may still be considerable. Some writers simply posit a difference between patrimonial and feudal forms, but Weber's theory acknowledges the deep similarity between prebendal and feudal aspects of patrimonialism. Norman Jacobs has interpreted classical Indian society as patrimonial rather than feudal, but has also argued that the Marxist notion of an Asiatic Mode of Production does not fit the Indic case.

Patrimonialism is a Weberian model based on comparative-historical idealization that can help avoid various arguments about uniqueness (*Sonderwegen*) and at the same time avoid transcultural and transhistorical dialectical materialist arguments about inevitable evolutionary paths. As an ITM, it helps avoid some of the errors of Marxist work on a more narrow view of feudalism and the Eurocentric notion of a specifically Asiatic Mode of Production. The crucial distinction between the use of the term *patrimonialism* and contemporary terms, such as *totalitarianism* (and *authoritarianism*), is that the patrimonial form tends to be associated with traditional, premodern, precapitalist societies. But aspects of both the arbitrary use of power by rulers and also the employment of mercenaries and retainers can be found again in contemporary totalitarian societies. Similarly, contemporary patron-client systems are often remnants of earlier patrimonial clientism. Whether or not it is useful to speak of nation-states in the twenty-first century as having elements of neopatrimonialism is disputed.

—*Johannes Iemke Bakker*

See also Authoritarianism; Leadership; Power; Sociology of Governance

Further Readings and References

Bakker, J. I. (1988). Patrimonialism, involution, and the agrarian question in Java: A Weberian analysis of class relations and servile labour. In J. Gledhill, B. Bender, & M. T. Larsen (Eds.), *State and society: The emergence and development of social hierarchy and political centralization* (pp. 279–301). London: Unwin Hyman.

Burke, E. (1999). *Empire and community: Edmund Burke's writings and speeches on international relations* (D. P. Fidler & J. M. Welsh, Eds.). Boulder, CO: Westview.

Eisenstadt, S. N. (1973). *Traditional patrimonialism and modern neo-patrimonialism.* Beverley Hills, CA: Sage.

Haller, K. L. von. (1834). *Restauration der Staats-Wissenschaft oder Theorie des naturlich-geselligen Zustands* [Restoration of political science or theory of the natural-informal condition]. Gottingen, Germany: K. G. der Wissenschaften.

Jacobs, N. (1989). *Patrimonial interpretation of Indian society: Contemporary structure and historical foundations.* Delhi, India: Chanakya.

Weber, M. (1968). *Economy and society* (C. Wittich & G. Roth, Trans.). Berkeley: University of California Press.

PEACE PROCESS

In the broadest and simplest practical terms, a peace process can be understood as an effort made by interested parties to achieve a lasting solution to a conflict. In stronger moral terms, it is an undertaking made to replace the psychologically and socially debilitating effects of destructive, bloody, human interaction with the creative benefits of all that civilized behavior has to offer. But what is peace, what are the necessary elements of such a process, who are the interested parties, and what must they do to achieve a lasting solution?

If peace is understood as merely an absence of war, then a military or security solution may be all that is required to implement a peace process. In this most narrow definition of peace, a tyrant could undertake a peace process by imposing his or her will on a society through repressive and draconian measures. Although security measures may be a necessary element of a peace process, establishing peace in the modern world of international norms requires the establishment of a society in which the citizens can enjoy the protection and freedom afforded to them by humanitarian and human rights law.

Peace, then, can be understood as both good governance and an absence of war, and a peace process must seek to achieve these ends through a combination of security measures and a program of social and political reform. These might include a peacekeeping force, policing in compliance with international standards, and the establishment of democratic institutions that can deliver rights and freedoms to all sections of society, with particular reference to those people or communities who previously resorted to violence in an attempt to obtain political or social justice. Such peacekeeping measures, of course, are almost everything from the application of economic, social, and cultural rights without discrimination to the right to life, freedom from torture, an effective criminal justice system, and a constitution that delivers political equitability, perhaps through some form of power sharing.

In practice, the interested parties to a peace process may be limited to those who will be economically or politically advantaged through the establishment of peace. This would hopefully include the parties to the conflict themselves; states neighboring the conflict with historical, ethnic, or economic ties; and other international players with a regional, global political, or economic strategic interest. In principle, however, the interested parties should also include those states with regional and global responsibilities for the maintenance of peace and the application of human rights with regard to the parties in conflict. This, of course, is almost everyone from the aggrieved citizen and victim of the conflict to his or her state, the state's immediate neighbors, and relevant regional and global intergovernmental organizations (IGOs). However, given the limited effectiveness of these IGOs, an array of nongovernmental organizations (NGOs) can also be expected to be interested parties and participants in any peace process.

So, in principle, everyone should do everything they possibly can to advance a peace process by leading parties in conflict away from violence to good governance and all that it implies. In deeply divided societies, this can include bottom-up peace-building activities aimed at improved community relations and reconciliation, such as interschool activities, common history texts, interfaith education, integrated schools and contact groups for children, youths, trade and professional organizations, and so forth. From the top-down, such peace-building activities must be supported by the state with guidance and material support from experienced NGOs and IGOs. But "top-down, bottom-up" is in practice a false dichotomy, as each requires the support of the other to be truly effective.

The very top the United Nations (UN) system has a number of agencies to work on different aspects of a peace process. Similarly, many of these functions can be undertaken by regional organizations, such as the European Union and the Organization for Security and Cooperation in Europe (OSCE) in the European theater. The relevant NGOs are too numerous to mention here, and many of them are created on an ad hoc basis to work on a specific peace process, particularly at the domestic level.

Ultimately, the state or states in conflict must take on board the political guidance and material support that is offered by the international community. If this is not done and there are gross violations of human rights, such as genocide, or if the conflict threatens its neighbors or provides, perhaps as a failed state, a base for international terrorism, then an intervention (legal or otherwise) might be expected. If sanctioned by the international community, such an intervention is arguably part of a peace process. Unilateral action is more problematic, as it may be considered aggression in law or in practice.

Restrictions on effective remedial action, particularly those imposed by a lack of security or the vagaries of the political attention of the international community and the limited resources of IGOs and NGOs, will often condemn peace processes to cycles of relative peace and recurrent violence. A systems approach to social, cultural, and political phenomena would predict little else for a conflict deeply embedded in all aspects of life. However, if the system can be overwhelmed by working on all aspects of a conflict together, then a rigorous, joined up government approach to conflict prevention and management has the greatest possible potential for success.

One cornerstone of any successful peace process is agreement, which in turn implies successful negotiations. This aspect of the peace process has five essential criteria: the protagonists are willing to negotiate in good faith, the key actors are included, negotiations address the central issues in the dispute, force is not used to achieve an objective, and the negotiators are committed to a sustained process. To these five criteria we might add the imperative of consensus building achieved by including the people in the decision-making process. In this circumstance, the prospects for long-term stability are greatly enhanced.

The Northern Ireland peace process, over many years, gradually took on board many of the most desirable characteristics of peace processes as briefly reviewed here, so that, in the end, it was successful. But most peace processes fail because the conditions for favorable interests and positive action cannot be met. Additionally conflict and the requirements of conflict management have now gone global in the post-9/11 world of the war on terrorism. Events on one side of the planet impact on and, in turn, are affected by events on the other side of the planet. Perhaps, if all the lessons of successful peace processes are now applied internationally, such complex problems can be solved. But, at present, no such concerted effort has been made by those states with sufficient power and influence to make the necessary difference.

—*Colin Irwin*

See also Crisis Management; Ethnonationalism; Failed State; Humanitarian Intervention; Human Rights; Negotiation; Second-Track Diplomacy; Security Community; Terrorism; United Nations; United Nations Security Council

Further Reading and References

Darby, J., & Mac Ginty, R. (Eds.). (2000). *The management of peace processes*. Basingstoke, UK: Macmillan.
Darby, J., & Mac Ginty, R. (Eds.). (2003). *Contemporary peacemaking: Conflict, violence and peace processes*. Basingstoke, UK: Macmillan.
Irwin, C. J. (2002). *The people's peace process in Northern Ireland*. Basingstoke, UK: Macmillan.

PERFORMANCE MEASUREMENT

Despite the prominence of performance measurement, there is no single universally accepted definition for measuring the performance of governments and public organizations. Performance measurement has been described as a process for the monitoring, assessing, and reporting of accomplishments to assist better management, but it can also include the broader notions of productivity, economy, efficiency, effectiveness, impact, quality, timeliness, and safety. Performance measurement can be directed toward either individual or collective performance or a combination of both.

The origins of performance measurement date to the early twentieth century when ideas about scientific management and specialization were documented by Frederick Taylor and operationalized by Henry Ford. These ideas were extended to the public sector as a means of improving the administrative efficiency of government. By the 1980s, performance measurement had become an embedded aspect of public-sector management. Many developments within performance measurement have been driven by the results orientation of new public management and have impacted on the way public goods and services are delivered by the state.

Why Measure Performance?

Governments seek to measure performance for a range of reasons—managerial, organizational, political, and for public accountability. They can measure performance on an ad hoc basis or as a part of a larger ongoing evaluation regime. Performance measures can be used to improve the internal management of organizations through the setting of benchmarks and indicators. They can generate the information necessary to assess whether an organization's goals and objectives are being obtained and the level of resources being consumed by an organization's activities. In particular, performance measures can inform managers about the resources used to deliver services, the quantity of services provided, and the achievement of goals and objectives.

Performance measurement can also improve lines of communication within individual organizations and between the various apparatuses of the state. In circumstances where actors are unlikely to share information or experiences, performance measures can be vital in facilitating dialogue and cooperation. Such cooperation can assist governments to overcome horizontal or whole-of-government service delivery problems, facilitate strategic planning, and encourage long-term policy making. Alternatively, performance ratings can facilitate competition between various providers and create behaviors that mirror the benefits of the market. Enhanced competitiveness can be a vital element in ensuring that public programs are delivered in the most efficient and cost effective manner.

In some instances, a dedicated proportion of appropriated budgets may be earmarked for mandated performance assessments that form the basis of future political decision making. Politicians have also embraced performance measures as a basis for decision making, as a way of demonstrating value for money and to enable them to assess the effectiveness and impact of public programs.

Finally, performance measurement addresses an external accountability function, providing transparency and allowing for programs to be evaluated. Results reporting plays a crucial role in informing constituents about the use of public resources and in providing an assessment of public activity. Furthermore, performance measurement can offer a more complete picture of program performance than can be achieved through traditional information provision (e.g., budgets or financial statements). In some countries, performance measurement is even mandated by legislation. For example, federal government organizations in the United States are legally bound by the *Government Performance and Results Act of 1993* to provide Congress with performance information on an annual basis.

Types of Performance Measures

Performance measures typically provide governments and their constituencies with information on outcomes, outputs, and quality. Composites of these measures can be integrated to provide a holistic evaluation of public-sector activity.

Outcome measures indicate the overall effectiveness of organizational activities to achieve desired goals. These measures seek to ask whether an organization is doing the right thing in relation to its stated goals and objectives.

Output measures inform governments and stakeholders about the efficiency and effectiveness of an organization's activities. These results focus on products and deliverables from particular organizations or programs. Typically, they are target driven and can be used to assess optimal performance—both financial and nonfinancial indicators are reported.

Quality measures, by comparison, tend to focus on whether the activities of an agency meet the requirements of its clients and stakeholders. Quality measures tend to focus on satisfaction (meeting client expectations), timeliness (an indication as to whether goods and services can be delivered on time and in accordance with the expectations of clients and stakeholders), and safety (indications as to whether organizational activities impact on the health of employees, customers, and the physical environment), but can also include notions of durability, longevity, reliability, customization, and availability.

Critical Issues in Performance Measurement

The critical issues in performance measurement can be distilled into four categories based on the themes of measurability, complexity, judgment, and distortion. First, many important aspects of human or organizational activity are often not measurable or extremely difficult to measure. Often what is measured is largely a consequence of what is easily quantifiable or able to be counted. Aspects of public activity, such as defense readiness, community well-being, and a more just society, are just a few of the numerous examples where reliable measurement is problematic if not impossible.

Second, measuring performance can be complex and produce contradictory information. There is often a lack of consensus on what should be measured, which, in some instances, leads to the development of costly and time-consuming performance measurement regimes. The complexity of human activity can also offer paradoxical advice to organizational managers and decisionmakers undermining the value of performance measures. For example, assessing the role of senior civil servants in policy development may reveal little about how they use their time and whether their activities contribute to better policy making.

Third, performance measurement can show some dimensions of individual or organizational activity, but offers little indication as to how performance information can or should be used. The use of performance measurement for decision making is often a matter of judgment that bears little significance to the content of the information collected. For example, recent research on budgetary decision making has continually demonstrated the limited impact of performance information on the allocative functions of governments, despite its prominence in the budgetary process.

Fourth, the act of measuring performance can distort the activities of individuals and organizations. It can narrow the scope of behavior over time by focusing on what is counted and what is attempted by individuals and organizations. The more tangible aspects of public activity (such as community service obligations) tend to be overlooked in favor of activities that can be more readily measured and identified. Such distortion undermines the usefulness of performance measures as a tool of contemporary governance.

—*Alexander Gash and John Wanna*

See also Benchmarking; Efficiency; Government Performance and Results Act; Institutional Performance; New Public Management; Transparency

Further Readings and References

Government Accountability Office. (2005). *Performance measurement and evaluation: Definitions and relationships.* Washington, DC: Author.

Halachmi, A., & Bouckaert, G. (Eds.). (1996). *Organizational performance and measurement in the public sector: Toward service, effort, and accomplishment reporting.* Westport, CT: Quorum Books.

Hatry, H. (1999). *Performance measurement: Getting results.* Washington, DC: Urban Institute Press.

Mayne, J., & Zapico-Goni, E. (Eds.). (1997). *Monitoring performance in the public sector: Future directions from international experience.* New Brunswick, NJ: Transaction.

McDavid, J., & Hawthorn, L. (2005). *Program evaluation and performance measurement: An introduction to practice.* Thousand Oaks, CA: Sage.

Morley, E., Bryant, S., & Hatry, H. (2001). *Comparative performance measurement.* Washington, DC: Urban Institute Press.

PHYSICAL CAPITAL

The term *capital* is used to refer to a factor of production within economics, one of three primary building blocks (along with land and labor), that in combination can be used to produce goods and services. Although suggesting homogeneity, capital as a term has no fixed conceptual definition, and different schools of economic thought through classical and neoclassical economics have defined it differently. Physical capital is a subset of capital, with other subsets including financial or money and the recently developed human, social, and knowledge capital. However, this subdivision does not result in making physical capital a homogeneous substance, and both its definition and measurement remain problematic.

Since the birth of capitalism and mechanized production, physical capital has been considered a stock of capital goods. Economic production functions, which model production processes using factor inputs, assume this definition. National accounting statistics, however, subtly alter the definition to one of produced assets, which do not necessarily have to be factors of production. A nation's physical capital or capital stock consists of fixed capital assets. The Organisation for Economic Co-operation and Development (OECD) suggests that most countries use a derivation of the United Nations System of National Accounts (SNA) to determine which sorts of goods to include in the fixed capital stock. According to the OECD, the goods included are durable (if lasting longer than one year), tangible (not patents and copyrights), fixed (mobile equipment excluded, but inventories and work in progress included), and reproducible (natural forests and land and mineral deposits are excluded). This provides a relatively clear definition, but means, for example, that items such as housing stock and artistic originals may be included, in contradiction to the economic definition.

Both definitions of physical capital suffer from a problem of measurement. Joan Robinson first raised the problem of how heterogeneous physical capital stock was to be measured in 1954. She argued that a physical measure is impossible if we are dealing with different goods, and a price or monetary measure invokes circular reasoning. This is because the theoretical price of a capital good is a measure of its total future profitability in current money. Yet profits are determined by the quantity of capital used in production; therefore, the quantity of capital cannot be determined by the amount of profit generated without circular reasoning. This is highly problematic for aggregate measures of physical capital, as well as for economic theories that depend upon them as inputs. National statistics ignore the problem by using average historical purchasing prices to calculate quantity of capital. Price is treated as an exogenous variable, independent of future profitability and therefore quantity of capital. Textbook economic theories also ignore the problem when invoking aggregate production functions. More radical approaches, utilizing institutional and evolutionary methods, reject the reduction of production to quantifiable factor inputs and therefore challenge not only the definition and measurement of physical capital, but also how the concept is deployed.

—Paul C. Lewis

See also Human Capital; Political Economy; Social Capital

Further Reading and References

Economic Statistics and National Accounts Division of the Statistics Directorate, Organisation for Economic Co-operation and Development. (1992). *Methods used by OECD countries to measure stocks of fixed capital.* Paris: OECD.

Hodgson, G. M. (1994). Capital theory. In G. M. Hodgson, W. J. Samuels, & M. R. Tool (Eds.), *The Elgar companion to institutional economics.* Aldershot, UK: Edward Elgar.

Robinson, J. (1954). The production function and the theory of capital. *Review of Economic Studies, 21,* 81–106. Reprinted in *Collected economic papers of Joan Robinson* (Vol. 2). Oxford, UK: Basil Blackwell.

PLANNING

Planning is the rational pursuit of goals by actions. Planning normally involves either explicitly or implicitly the following stages: identification of goals, objectives, and targets; development and evaluation of alternative strategies to achieve goals; identification of the preferred strategy; implementation; monitoring; and adjustment of plans based on monitoring results.

Within this broad definition there are many variations of planning. Before reviewing variations, it should be cautioned that the large number of planning types and inconsistencies in terminology preclude developing a comprehensive typology. However, it is useful to organize discussion of planning typology around four themes: the scope of decision-making strategies, political responsibility for planning processes, mechanisms for planning implementation, and the subject matter of planning.

Decision-Making Strategies

Commonly identified decision-making strategies in planning include rational, comprehensive, systems, incremental, and strategic. The rational comprehensive model of planning proposes consideration of all goals and all ends for achieving goals. Ends are assessed for all possible consequences and the ends are chosen that maximize social welfare. The founding assumption of comprehensive planning is the ability of experts to use rational scientific analysis to identify and implement appropriate actions to achieve the public interest. Comprehensive planning is based in part on systems theory, which views society as being comprised of interdependent components whose relationship and behavior can be understood and modeled. The modeling of the system can identify key levers of control that can be used to affect system behavior and achieve desired outcomes. An example is monetary and fiscal policy, which can be used to affect economic performance.

Critics of comprehensive planning suggest it is naïve and counterproductive to attempt comprehensiveness. Goals are too diverse and conflicting, and systems are too complex to understand or manage. A more realistic model, according to some, is incremental planning. Incremental planning focuses on short-term problem solving based on considering only limited ends and limited means. Choices are made by agreement among competing political interests as opposed to rational methods of evaluation.

Most empirical analysis of planning concludes that incremental planning is one of the most commonly used models. However, criticisms of incremental planning are that it ignores interdependencies and responds to problems instead of preventing problems. Consequently, incremental planning is not very effective. A third planning strategy that attempts to combine some of the benefits of the comprehensive model while recognizing the constraints is strategic planning. Strategic planning tries to provide a comprehensive framework focusing on the large, key issues.

A vision is created of the desirable future, the environment is scanned to identify major trends, and a strategy is devised for achieving the desired outcome. The strategic plan provides the framework that identifies key priorities and issues that require more intensive comprehensive planning to address.

Political Responsibility for Planning

A second feature distinguishing types of planning is political responsibility for decision making. Commonly identified models of political responsibility for planning include technocratic, advocacy, mediation, collaborative, and postmodern structuralist.

Technocratic planning delegates planning control to experts that use scientific analysis to prepare plans. In its most extreme form, technocratic planning gives experts control over the setting of goals and the preparation of means to achieve goals. For example, providing basic public services, such a clean drinking water, setting pollution emission standards, and setting allowable harvest levels for natural resources, are often viewed as decisions that should be made by independent experts above politics. In the 1960s, however, this more extreme model of technocratic planning came under increasing criticism for its failure to acknowledge that planning attempts to achieve goals that are based on the values of citizens, not the values of experts. Decisions by experts, such as building freeways through poor neighborhoods, building urban renewal projects that displace the poor, and setting resource harvesting rates for forests that failed to protect other environmental values, illustrated the political nature of planning. It was increasingly acknowledged that planning goals should be articulated through a democratic process, not expert judgment. Under this less-extreme form of technocratic planning, experts are relegated to evaluating appropriate means to achieve goals that are provided by democratic processes. Democratic processes for determining goals include direction from politicians as well as direct consultation with affected citizens.

The acceptance of the value-based, goals-oriented nature of planning stimulated development of new models designed to integrate citizen preferences into the planning process. It was soon recognized that citizen involvement should not be restricted to just setting goals, but should include the evaluation of means. This led to the development of various methods to involve citizens in planning, such as providing information, obtaining feedback through open houses, public meetings, and ongoing consultation by using citizen advisory committees. Several new models of planning emerged from this effort: advocacy planning, mediation planning, and collaborative planning.

Advocacy planning is based on different interest groups having their own experts to prepare plans and advocate on behalf of their clients in the same way as lawyers do in a courtroom. Advocacy planning assumes that planning is an inherently interest-based process in which decisions reflect the preferences of different groups. By having stakeholders and their experts argue the merits of their respective plans in an open public forum, advocacy planning can improve planning outcomes by ensuring consideration of all interests.

The criticism of advocacy planning is that it assumes that planning experts that are advocating on behalf their clients will affect the decision. However, advocacy planning does not suggest how the decision will be made among these competing planning interests. By default, advocacy planning assumes that the decision can still be made by the same powerful interests that are able to ignore the rational arguments of competing experts.

Mediation and collaborative planning try to address this deficiency of advocacy planning by proposing consensus-based decision making achieved by face-to-face negotiation among competing interest groups, often with the aid of professional facilitators. The difference between mediation planning and collaborative planning is that mediation planning normally reacts to an existing conflict among stakeholders, while collaborative planning is normally proactive by creating a consensus-based mediation process at the start of a planning process. By delegating responsibility for planning to stakeholders who reach decisions by consensus, mediation and collaborative planning can ensure that plans reflect the interests of all parties. Collaboration also generates more creative options through interactive dialogue among stakeholders. Consequently, plans developed by collaboration are more likely to be in the public interest. Plans developed by consensus are more likely to be implemented because they have the support of all stakeholders that helped develop the plan. Mediation and collaborative planning also develop skills, knowledge, and better relationships among stakeholders, which make future planning easier and more effective.

Mediation and collaborative planning also pose challenges. Effective use of mediation and collaborative planning requires that those controlling planning are willing to delegate power to other stakeholders, that there are well-organized stakeholder groups that cover the spectrum of competing interests, and stakeholders are able to reach a consensus decision. These conditions are not always met. Defenders of collaborative planning emphasize that while failure to meet these conditions can reduce effectiveness, collaboration is still more effective under imperfect conditions than alternative models of planning. For example, collaboration that does not reach consensus will still result in better decisions by improving understanding of relevant interests.

Postmodern, structuralist planning is more a theory of how society functions as opposed to a normative theory of how planning should be done. Although there is wide variation in the postmodern planning theories, there are several common themes. According to postmodern structuralists, there is no objective knowledge, no value-neutral techniques for determining what is in the public interest, and little opportunity to rationally choose how society will develop. Instead, outcomes are largely controlled by independent structural forces beyond rational control or by the needs of the most powerful interests in society. In this model, rational planning to achieve the public interest does not exist.

Planning Implementation

A third dimension to planning typologies is the way that plans are implemented. Planning implementation strategies can be categorized along a spectrum from indicative, to market, and to regulatory, depending on the intensity of implementation. Indicative planning is based on providing information to decisionmakers to allow them the freedom to make informed, rational choices. No compulsion is present. For example, environmental plans may inform the public of emissions of various types of automobiles in the hope that they choose lower-emitting vehicles. Market-based implementation alters relative prices of goods and services to implement plans. For example, taxes may be reduced on low-polluting automobiles to encourage consumers to buy more relative to high-polluting vehicles. Again there is no compulsion. Regulatory implementation uses laws and enforcement to mandate outcomes. For example, laws can be passed that prohibit automobile emissions beyond a certain level. Regulatory planning is sometimes referred to as command planning.

Subject Matter of Planning

A fourth dimension to planning typologies is the subject matter of what is being planned. Planning is divided by both spatial and functional characteristics. Common spatial divisions of planning include neighborhood, city, region, and national. Planning at these different levels is usually based on political jurisdictions. Common functional divisions include social, economic, environmental, land use, transportation, and public infrastructure. Within these broad divisions there are numerous categories. Social planning, for example, can be broken down into numerous subcategories, such as health, day care, education, social services, and so on. In the comprehensive planning model, the attempt is made to coordinate all the different spatial and functional categories of planning to achieve consistency.

A recent international trend in planning is the emergence of sustainability planning. Sustainability is defined as meeting the needs of the current generation without sacrificing the needs of future generations. The interest in sustainability planning is increasing with the growing awareness of broad environmental trends such as global warming that challenge the integrity of the earth's ecological systems. Sustainability planning is ushering in a new era of comprehensive, international planning based on the recognition of interdependencies between national systems. Many countries have committed in international agreements to prepare sustainable development strategies that integrate social, economic, and environmental objectives.

Conclusion

In sum, planning has a common theme: the attempt to achieve goals by rational implementation of strategies. Within this broad theme there is significant variation in the meaning of planning. This variation can best be understood as a multidimensional matrix organized around themes of decision-making strategies, political responsibility, implementation strategies, and spatial and functional subject matter. The emphasis on planning type within this typology varies with time, circumstance, and the dominant ideology of the society. Current trends point to increasing emphasis on collaborative planning and international and national sustainability planning to preserve integrity of ecological systems. While the future of planning as a rational attempt by humans to affect their future is assured, the specific planning styles that will dominate remain uncertain.

—*Thomas Gunton*

See also Collaborative Planning; Dirigisme; Strategic Planning; Urban and Regional Planning

Further Readings and References

Allmendinger, P. (2002). *Planning theory*. New York: Palgrave.
Campbell, S., & Fainstein, S. (Eds.). (1996). *Readings in planning theory*. Oxford, UK: Basil Blackwell.

PLURALISM

Understood most broadly, pluralism is a belief in more than one thing or a tendency to be, to hold, or to do more than one thing. As applied to political systems, pluralism recognizes the existence of multiple, often overlapping, and potentially conflicting characteristics within a political community. The central concern of pluralism in a democratic society is how public decisions are to be made and action taken given the multiplicity of, and likely conflict between, legitimate interests. Pluralism stands in contrast to monism, which claims the possibility of a unity of theory and practice running from epistemology and ontology all the way down through specific instrumental policy proposals and decisions.

Political Pluralism

Several related strands of pluralist thought have emerged as the focus of intellectual development over the last one hundred years. In the United States, the works of David Truman and Robert Dahl represent one of the primary perspectives associated with the related concepts of political pluralism, pluralist democracy and interest group pluralism. The foundations of political pluralism can be found in the works of Harold Laski and G. D. H. Cole, who moved pluralism and its understanding of the state away from the abstract and idealized treatment in philosophy to a more concrete, instrumental analysis that recognized corporations and associations as independent formations and interest sets. Having embraced the move of pluralism out of philosophy, Truman's work made a further shift, in this case away from the dominant focus on descriptions of institutions and structures that characterized the study of American political processes at the time, and focused instead on developing an understanding of how interest groups shaped political and policy activities. Pluralist theorists of this vein sought to locate the stability of the political system in the interactions of the local, immediate, and small, consistent with the perspectives articulated by Alexis de Tocqueville. Political pluralism argues individual rights and interests are protected by an ongoing process of negotiation and renegotiation between interests such that no single group holds the dominant power position, power is always shifting, and individuals can influence policy making through being active in one of these power groups. In this way, Truman moved away from both the politics of social class and the large-scale political projects of the Left, as well as the notion of inclusive or unitary interest in favor of the bargaining of competitive interest groups as the source of public policy.

Dahl further contributed to the development of political pluralism by including conflict in his analysis. Starting from the position that the existence of conflict is unavoidable, he works to develop an understanding of how political communities respond to and resolve that conflict. Dahl identified the problem of conflict as a central one in the debates over the writing and ratification of the Constitution. Looking to James Madison's *Federalist 10,* he identified the source of conflict in the diverse interests of those in the political community. One of the fundamental questions thus becomes, what are the means of resolving conflicts in a way that will enable community to be possible? That is, what are the structures and processes by which the diverse interests of factions can be successfully negotiated? To answer this question, Dahl recounted the debate between aristocratic and democratic forms of government and notes that while there are difficult challenges associated with democratic forms of government, it is a better response than aristocratic forms. Once democracy is selected, a balance between the dangers of faction and the need for the consent of the governed must be achieved. The dangers of faction, whether minority or majority factions, cannot be limited simply through the exercise of self-restraint. Instead, drawing again on Madison, Dahl looked to the creation of processes through which the consent of the political community can be established. Establishing the consent of all is important because of its consistency with personal freedom, human dignity, and respect, as well as being a means of enhancing the durability of the political system. The political processes that emerge represent a model of pluralism. Rather than relying on a single center of sovereign power, pluralism demands that there be many centers of power, none of which is or can be wholly sovereign. Although in the United States, "the people" are the source of legitimate sovereignty, from the perspective of American pluralism, even the people should never be an absolute sovereign. Moreover, no part of the people, even a majority, should be absolutely sovereign. The existence of multiple centers of power, none of which is wholly sovereign, will help—or may in fact be necessary—to secure the consent of all and to settle conflict between interests without resorting to coercion or outright violence. The basic concept is the idea of setting power against power as a means of ensuring that it will be tamed, civilized, controlled, and limited to decent human purposes, reducing the use of power and coercion to the lowest possible level. Further, because all interests, even the smallest minorities, can contribute to decisions and, in some cases, can even have the opportunity to veto solutions they strongly oppose, the consent of all can be established in the long run. Last, because ongoing negotiation between interests and centers of power is necessary for decision making, leaders will develop requisite capacity to deal with conflict to the mutual benefit of all involved in conflict without the use of coercive power.

Gabriel Almond and Sidney Verba extended the work on political pluralism by shifting the focus of their analysis away from the institutions and processes of government and instead highlight the importance of the broader political culture within which the processes take place. For them, democracy requires a particular kind of political culture that is tied not only to the formal institutions of governance, but also to the experience of community and social and family life—interests generated outside of politics. Building on theses elements, a pluralistic culture shaped by communication and persuasion emerges. This culture is one that elevates consensus and diversity and is one that allows for the possibility of change, but moderates that change, recognizing that too much politics can be dangerous.

The same processes operate at the agency and interagency level as well. There are likely to be overlapping missions between agencies as well as multiple purposes within agencies. These dynamics are expressed in the presence or representation of multiple and competing social, political, and economic interests. The result is pluralist competition or negotiation in and across agencies.

This political conception of pluralism explains how interest groups translate individual concerns into political action and eventually public policy. Interest groups represent and give voice to actors and provide a means of influencing political elites. Memberships in multiple interest groups and divided loyalties lead to compromise and integration of proposed actions. Liberal democracy is well suited to the wide range of interests emerging from a pluralist system without leading to political instability. In addition to retaining stability, pluralism supports the legitimacy of the state, which is both authoritative and responsible and simultaneously requires influential and deferential citizens. Interest group politics or pluralism helps the state act in a consumerist environment consistent with the post–World War II period of economic growth and moderate social reform.

Value Pluralism

In addition to political or interest group oriented pluralism, others, including Isaiah Berlin and John Rawls, have conceived concepts of value pluralism that also influence the principles and practice of government in a liberal democracy. Isaiah Berlin developed an understanding of value pluralism wherein values are conceived of as human creations or social constructs, as opposed to universalistic entities to be deduced or derived from nature. Despite the claim that values are social constructs, they are, according to Berlin, objective in that they are facts about the people who hold them. Therefore, belief in certain values is an objective reality of human nature. Value pluralism emerges from the argument that each value compels particular actions by virtue of its own requirements, rather than on the basis of some other, universal value. As such, there is no common or universal measure for evaluation or judgment between two or more values.

To Berlin's notion of value pluralism is added his conception of negative and positive liberty. Negative liberty is understood as freedom from constraints, while positive liberty is understood as the freedom to pursue ends as an autonomous actor rather than being dependent on others. The connection between value pluralism and liberty is the critical importance of choice to both. The ability to choose between values and the courses of action they imply is at the core of the connection between value pluralism and liberty.

The implication is that there is no single or best way to live, but rather, governance and social processes are oriented toward maintaining a balance of values—preserving individual liberty while at the same time recognizing the need, for example, to in some cases restrict that liberty in order to promote justice or equity. For Berlin, concepts of value pluralism and liberty are central to both his understanding of the nature of human agency and the governance processes required to protect human agents.

Value pluralism is also a central element of John Rawls's conception of justice and his shift in the understanding of justice from metaphysical to political. That is, in modern democratic societies, diverse and incommensurable notions of the good (values) are an empirical fact. The fact is not a law of nature, but rather is relative to individual policies and specific social institutions. It is possible in these conditions to establish universal social agreement only through the use of coercive power by the state. A commitment to both noncoercion and individual liberty is inherent in the first component principle of Rawls's theory of justice—each person has equal right to the most extensive liberty compatible with a similar liberty for others. This, along with the difference principle would, according to Rawls, be accepted from the perspective of the "original position" under the veil of ignorance. In combining these elements into his political conception of justice, value pluralism becomes a driving factor in the governance processes and ultimately, the decisions and actions of political communities.

Cultural Pluralism

Although the concept of political pluralism developed in the United States largely moved political inquiry away from a concern with class and power, these concerns do figure into some understandings of cultural pluralism. The literature on cultural pluralism tends to describe the conditions in which two or more cultures come into contact with one another, typically within the boundaries of a single political entity. This work tends to examine the extent of multiculturalism or cultural diversity as well as the social divisions and resource inequities that manifest between groups. Some strands of cultural pluralist study have continued to focus specifically on the issues of class and power and their relationship to issues of democracy and governance. For example, in addition to examining the relationships between cultures within a single political community, J. S. Furnivall's description of cultural pluralism detailed the conditions of instability, inequity, and uncertainty that often characterized colonial situations. M. G. Smith extended the examination of power such that contemporary understandings of cultural pluralism include attention to both the degree of differentiation between groups and the allocation of status, resources, and ultimately, power among subgroups. As such, these accounts of cultural pluralism often imply a redistribution of political and economic resources in a way that is consistent with liberal elements of the political and value pluralism previously described.

Postmodernism and Pluralism

Structuralist and neo-Marxist perspectives that emerged in the 1970s criticized the version of American pluralism that emerged in the 1950s and 1960s as being concerned with superficial behavior rather than pervasive or deep structures, lacking rigorous theoretical or paradigmatic grounding, and generally being a complacent form of liberalism. Perhaps ironically, postmodern critiques of structuralist perspectives have returned to some attributes of pluralism—ever-changing groups of citizens that form, separate, and reform in new ways, emphasis on increasing individual liberty and freedom of choice. The denial of universal truth claims, monism, and the affirmation of heterogeneity and difference are recurrent themes in postmodern discourse. For example, while Michel Foucault never claimed to be a pluralist, his exploration of power and governance processes revealed some of these pluralist characteristics. Foucault moved from a modernist examination of the question of what power is, to an analysis of what functions the state serves. In doing so, power becomes a microlevel phenomenon that permeates both official institutional settings as well as social relations. His notion of governmentality revealed the existence of multiple and distinct modes of pluralization of modern government. That is, in contrast to unified or monistic theories of the state, Foucault argued for the existence of many processes by which the state and society interact. This analysis is consistent with the emphasis on individual liberty and freedom of choice in that it suggests plural avenues of resistance and contestation.

Criticisms of Pluralism

A number of criticisms have been leveled at pluralism and its connections to liberalism. One criticism is the assessment that the extent of the competition between competing interests may be more apparent than real, as can be seen in the existence of long-standing, stable political coalitions and the practice of logrolling. A further critique is that public agencies often operate as interest groups in their own right. Doing so creates tension between the agency's function of policy implementation on the one hand and its efforts directed toward securing resources on the other hand. A related concern is the possibility of agency capture, or the possibilities that public organizations with regulatory responsibilities become unduly influenced by the interests they are supposed to regulate. Another criticism is that political executives have become dominant in the agenda-setting process, further reducing the extent of negotiation between interest groups.

Marxist critics point out that social class essentially vanished from the political pluralist discourse, despite evidence that those dominant interests that proceeded through the pluralist process to become operationalized in public policy were strongly influenced by economic interests. In other words, in liberal, capitalist democracies, the state does not merely provide a neutral framework within which the plurality of interests vie for position on a level playing field. So while consumerist attributes of pluralism suggest that individual preferences, interests, and their pursuit largely fall outside the political system, Marxists argue that the state privileges forms of private property or capital acquisition such that the interests of business are necessarily granted a position of advantage in the struggle between interests.

While even some advocates of political pluralism acknowledge discomfort with the economic inequities and political failings of pluralism in the late twentieth century, they neither develop a theory of value that would enable a critical analysis of various distributions of economic and political power nor do they articulate the sort of structural reorganization championed by Marxists. It can be argued that the Madisonian position, which posits that the passions of the masses are held in check by apathy or deference to either elites or the rules of the game, has become untenable. At the same time, the claim that economic elites are constrained by internalized democratic values, political institutions, periodic elections, and overlapping interest groups has similarly collapsed. These claims began to fail with the mass political involvement and activity of the civil rights, antiwar, feminist, and other political movements in the 1960s and 1970s, as well as the changing economic conditions of the late Cold War period. In the aftermath of the fall of the iron curtain and with the growing emphasis on global capitalism, Marxist critiques appear to have lost some of their currency in the popular political discourse, though they have yet to be replaced in that broader political discourse by postmodern or poststructuralist approaches.

—*Eric K. Austin*

See also Association; Civil Society; Interest Group; Liberalism; Marxism; Multiculturalism; Pluralist Democracy; Polyarchy; State Capture

Further Readings and References

Almond, G., & Verba, S. (1965). *The civic culture*. Boston: Little, Brown.

Bellamy, R., & Hollis, M. (1999). *Pluralism and liberal neutrality*. London: Frank Cass.

Berlin, I. (1969). *Four essays on liberty*. New York: Oxford University Press.

Dahl, R. (1967). *Pluralist democracy in the United States: Conflict and consent*. Chicago: Rand McNally.

Hirst, P. (Ed.). *The pluralist theory of the state: Selected writings of G. D. H. Cole, J. N. Figgis and H. J. Laski*. London: Routledge, 1989.

Manley, J. F. (1983). Neo-pluralism: A class analysis of pluralism I and pluralism II. *The American Political Science Review, 77*(2), 368–383.

McLennan, G. (1995). *Pluralism*. Minneapolis: University of Minnesota Press.

Rawls, J. (1985). Justice as fairness: Political not metaphysical. *Philosophy and Public Affairs, 14*(3), 223–231, 234–239, 245–248.

Runciman, D. (1997). *Pluralism and the personality of the state*. Cambridge, UK: Cambridge University Press.

Seidman, H. (1970). *Politics, position and power*. New York: Oxford University Press.

Simpson, J. C. (1995). Pluralism: The evolution of a nebulous concept. *American Behavioral Scientist, 38*, 459–477.

Truman, D. (1951). *The governmental process*. New York: Knopf.

Pluralist Democracy

As a concept, pluralist democracy is highly relativistic, ranging from a potentially broadly defined condition to a narrowly defined, nearly corporatist model. Arguably, both conditions or states could be said to be pluralist within an overarching democratic political system.

In theory, the United States' model of pluralist democracy is built on the founders' desire to simultaneously promote the rights of citizens to organize into factional interests while also preventing individual citizen liberty from falling prey to factional influence; in essence, an attempt to find a middle ground between the absolutism of monarchy and what was seen as potentially deleterious and chaotic majoritarianism. Nevertheless, the existence of faction, and hence pluralist democracy, was seen as a natural and essential element in free society, consistent with human nature and the desire to express differences.

Scholars have repeatedly addressed the human tendency to promote group interests, at times at the expense of individual rights and liberties. Diversity of perspective was looked upon as being an important element in the maintenance of democratic pluralism and one that required constant monitoring and consideration. Issues of diversity and scope of participation are seen as particularly important to the protection and maintenance of civil liberties in a pluralist democracy. Simultaneously, there must be some shared values in pluralist democracy, an acceptance of institutions and the recognition of individual rights. Diversity was of particular interest to late nineteenth- and also twentieth-century scholars such as William James, who focused on individual diversity in relation to participation in the public dialogue, while other scholars have focused on the elevation of the individual in relation to participation in organizational life, public and private.

The issue of diversity has continually plagued pluralist democracy. Looked upon from a broadly defined view, the greater the number of positions represented in a pluralist democratic process, the more likely that a diverse set of perspectives are being represented and expressed, but scholars are careful to point out that even though there is a great number of positions represented or expressed does not mean that the positions are equally represented, expressed, heard, or acted upon. In a dynamic model of pluralist democracy and over several iterations of the democratic decision-making process, outcomes may not represent the diversity assumed to exist. In a narrowly defined view where very few interests exist, pluralist democracy is likely to lack the diversity of viewpoint that James and others believed to be so critical to public dialogue.

Recent historical events and scholarly treatments have shown that the problem of diversity promotion with pluralist democratic dialogue tends to be endemic in both established democratic nations as well as newly emerging democratic regimes in Africa, Asia, the Americas, Europe, and the Middle East. Group-based identity may serve as a limiting factor in shaping the potential to engage in dialogue. Depending upon the nature of groups, it is possible that an orthodoxy of positions may be fostered at the expense of the very diversity of viewpoints within democratic dialogue that may be desired or desirable.

A second dilemma that has been of concern to scholars has been the true nature of democratic pluralism. As pluralism requires a proper respect for the diversity of citizens, the status of racial and ethnic minorities, as well as the status of women and the economically underprivileged and socially disenfranchised, is of particular concern to the linking of pluralist theory with practice. Robert Dahl, for instance, argues that two of the basic requirements

for a pluralist democracy are: consent and political equality, neither of which were or are available to all citizens or denizens; but Dahl goes further in pointing out that pluralist democracy exists on a continuum between authoritarianism and pure democracy—he refers to this status as polyarchy, challenging theorists and practitioners to consider pluralism along a range rather than as an absolute concept. In essence, this second dilemma revolves around the issue of social pluralism, not only the variant of positions but also a focus on the individuals (particularly, their socialization and exposure to pluralist traditions) that hold these positions.

Concern with the underprivileged and disenfranchised is one of the major differences between a simply pluralistic condition and democratic pluralistic tradition—the former is more likely to be described as an atomistic condition, while in theory the latter is concerned with a basic set of principles that govern human rights above and beyond differences in preferences and viewpoint—socially or economically. An understanding of basic principles governing human rights, however, remains a central part of the dialogue about pluralist democracy, particularly when sociocultural, racial, gender, and economic barriers establish biased visions of consent. Furthermore, political equality has been shown through social scientific research to be directly related to social equality. Dahl's two basic requirements may be ideals that cannot be reached, serving rather as possible benchmarks to be pursued ad infinitum, directly feeding into the third major dilemma discussed in the following paragraphs.

In many ways related to concerns of social pluralism is the nature of collective acceptance of basic principles, namely, the locus of agreement in relation to conflict. According to William Galston, there is an inherent conflict between value pluralism and the concept of individual freedom. John Gray, for instance, argues that negative freedom—that is, an individual's right to disassociate from others and from the values of others—is inversely related to the promotion of value pluralism. In essence, Gray is arguing for a liberal democracy in which public action is governed by the pursuit of individual freedom, a movement away from the values of Dahl's polyarchy, which focuses to a greater extent on groups. Galston argues that while there is a moral bottom, a locus of basic value premises is not relativistic—beyond this there is an emphasis on diversity of shared values and beliefs governing pluralist democracy, processes, and outcomes. Yet, other scholars reinforce the need to remain cognizant of the primacy of the individual and his or her needs.

The proper balance between individual rights, the promotion or acceptance of pluralistic conflicts, and Dahl's concerns for cooperation remains a central concern as the concept of pluralist democracy evolves and as the conditions within and surrounding nation-states change. In recent decades, for instance, Germany faced the likely long-term challenge of reunification. Political traditions and values in former East Germany differed significantly from West Germany, influencing views on individual rights, pluralist conflict, and the nature of cooperative enterprise through the political process.

In more recent studies, pluralism has evolved in terms of its meanings and emphasis. There is a growing need to focus on its complexity in order to fully realize its meaning and lasting importance. Scholars have increasingly emphasized the need to explore the full meaning of pluralist conflict, dialogue, compromise, and cooperation through the use of non-traditional methods of participation. Through the exploration of meaning, it is believed that pluralist processes will be more inclusive, emphasizing group and individual notions of political and social justice.

The scope and meaning of pluralism in the late twentieth and early twenty-first centuries has, at times, led to a greater focus on the structural inequalities in society created by early conceptions of pluralism. Neopluralism places greater emphasis on substantive outcomes, focusing more on class and distributions of wealth and power. Neopluralism also questions the prerequisite for (and value of) capitalist liberal democracy in the promotion of promised substantive pluralist outcomes. The identity of individuals and groups, therefore, is focused to areas outside of traditional concerns, with more generally constructed measures of racial, ethnic, gender, and economic-based measures of diversity.

Until quite recently, classical liberal traditions within the pluralist democracy dialogue were built on the notion of the individual operating within a pluralist democracy. As individuals, consent was centered on individual rights and liberties within the political process. The neopluralist argument was dismissed or countered with a marketplace metaphor in tandem with a conception of the individual actor rationally operating within the political sphere. Pursuing individual self-interest within a set of governing principles regarding individual rights and liberties was seen as the best way to maintain the system and to promote unbiased outcomes.

In the early twenty-first century, both neopluralist and classical liberal traditions related to pluralist democracy have, to some degree, floundered on the shoals of the political and social realities of fundamentalism in its multifarious forms. Aspects of the neopluralist tradition are provided some support through the recognition of racial, ethnic, and gender-based measures rather than simply considering the individual and individual rights bereft of such considerations—in essence, the concept of the individual separated from the aforementioned factors is entirely incomplete and the promotion of pluralist democracy without such consideration is likely rendered useless. Simultaneously, aspects of the classical liberal tradition within the pluralist democracy dialogue critique an overemphasis on grouping factors in the consideration of liberal democracy. Scholars within the classical liberal tradition find that neopluralist emphases may actually promote skewed distributions of power and effectively weaken individual consent by focusing on grouping factors rather than on individual choices and association within a pluralist tradition.

The current status of pluralist democracy is challenged by two different sets of forces. In one sense, there is a rapidly accelerating movement away from particular notions of collective action assumed by scholars for quite some time—in essence, the model built on the assumption that individuals from across the spectrum of a broadly defined society with similar possibly secular (in the broadest sense of the word) interests would form groups to pursue individual and collective interests through the democratic process.

Technology and a greater emphasis on private market-based solutions within a commodified environment form the foundation of individually based solutions, rather than collective action through democratic pluralism. Therefore, pluralism is left to promote the interests of two general groups: often-powerful economic interests that benefit directly from a corporatist or quasi-corporatist relationship with government; and sociocultural-based cause groups that often promote what may be viewed as almost unbending principles rather than relative preference sets to be considered in relation to other preference sets. The latter two conditions within the pluralist tradition—perhaps of greater concern to scholars in the tradition of Theodore Lowi—effectively limit the basic assumption of diversity, instead promoting a potentially pernicious (in terms of pluralist democratic tradition as discussed thus far) and secondary force—a form of economic, social, and political fundamentalism, a term alluded to previously.

A final challenge to democratic pluralism is that it is possibly not as natural a concept as theorists have often assumed, as seen in the case of many newly emerging nation-states. With the end of the Cold War and the dissolution of the Soviet Union, many nations in Eastern Europe and in Central Asia have entered into the democratic pluralism dialogue in a period of political, social, and economic change. The issue of individual rights was often not part of the political or social lexicon. A concept that is not recognized or understood may not be easily employed. Certain assumptions about the relationship between the individual and government must be considered and consented to before democratic pluralism can be applied in any form. Democratic pluralism may not be natural. Rather, it may be seen as simply a more desirable approach in lieu of alternative and possibly undesirable arrangements.

Much of the work and consideration of democratic pluralism has been done within the context of particular social, economic, and political conditions: current challenges are, to a lesser degree, concerned with its meaning and, to a much larger degree, concerned with its applicability or even legitimacy built on evidence or assumptions regarding desirability. Pluralism—in an unvarnished sense—tends to be based in the pursuit of individual or group "wants," while democratic pluralism tends to imply the pursuit of "wants" in the context of "obligations," the meaning of which may be either narrow or expansive; the latter proves to make a discussion of democratic pluralism much more complex than a discussion of pluralism per se. Democratic pluralism will likely continue to evolve as challenges to its meaning and applicability arise, or it may face potential marginalization in a changing world.

—*Christopher A. Simon*

See also Association; Democratic Theory; Marxism; Participatory Democracy; Pluralism

Further Readings and References

Bickford, S. (1999). Reconfiguring pluralism: Identity and institutions in the inegalitarian polity. *American Journal of Political Science, 43*(1), 86–108.

Dahl, R. (1972). *Democracy in the United States* (2nd ed.). Chicago: Rand McNally.

Dahl, R. (1978). Pluralism revisited. *Comparative Politics, 10*(2), 191–203.

Galston, W. (1999). Value pluralism and liberal political theory. *American Political Science Review, 93*(4), 769–778.

Gibson, J. (1990). Pluralism, federalism, and the protection of civil liberties. *Western Political Science Quarterly, 43*(3), 511–533.

Gray, J. (1986). *Liberalism.* Minneapolis: University of Minnesota Press.

Lowi, T. (1969). *The end of liberalism.* New York: W. W. Norton.

Rohrschneider, R. (1996). Pluralism, conflict, and legislative elites in united Germany. *Comparative Politics, 29*(1), 43–67.

Schlosberg, D. (1998). Resurrecting the pluralist universe. *Political Research Quarterly, 51*(3), 583–615.

POLICY ANALYSIS

Policy analysis is primarily concerned with the consideration of a number of different policy alternatives that are expected to produce different policy consequences or outputs, varying the quality or quantity of policy output for a given amount of resources to be used. Policy analysis requires careful systematic and empirical study. Policy analysis focuses on all aspects of the policy process, from the early stages of policy adoption and formulation to the implementation and evaluation of public policies.

The complexities of policy analysis have contributed to the development and growth of policy science, which applies the variety of theories and tools of hard sciences (e.g., biology and chemistry), social sciences (e.g., sociology, psychology, and anthropology), and humanities (e.g., history and philosophy) in an effort to better understand all aspects of human society, its problems, and the solutions to those problems. Policy analysis is important in a modern complex society because public policy is so vast, public problems are sophisticated and are often interconnected, and public policies have tremendous social, economic, and political implications. Additionally, public policy is a dynamic process, operating under changing social, political, and economic conditions. Policy analysis helps us to understand how social, economic, and political conditions change and how public policies must evolve in order to meet the changing needs of a changing society.

Public policy analysis is an integral part of the policy-making process, from the initial stages of decision making to the evaluation of public policies that are implemented. Policy analysis requires an interdisciplinary approach—a solid understanding of the theoretical developments within a variety of science and social scientific disciplines and the practical applications of the information available. In that sense, public policy analysis helps us to bridge the gap between developing an understanding of what government ought or ought not do and what government does or does not do. Policy analysis is involved in determining who will get what, when, and how.

As government grows and policy challenges become more numerous, more complex, and more interrelated, policy analysis plays a larger role in making certain that decisions in one policy area are consistent or at least compatible with decisions made in other policy areas. Government development and growth tends to parallel population growth and the heterogeneity of needs associated with a diverse population. Therefore, policy analysis must also seek to overcome the complexities of consumer needs, yet advance equal policy outcomes.

Policy analysis first plays a role in policy formulation. When a proposed policy is first considered by elected officials, it is often difficult to frame the policy issue in a way that is tangible and understandable. Policy analysts help define the proposed policy and outline the goals for the policy. In the policy process, elected officials often consider a number of different policies; again, it proves difficult to compare these alternatives without a thorough analysis of their similarities and differences. Policy analysts approach this second part of the analysis process carefully, comparing the expected outcomes to estimated costs. Many public policies are designed to solve both current and future problems. While policy is often designed to deal with contemporary issues, it must be able to adapt to future needs. Policy analysts attempt to forecast future needs based on past and present conditions. Policy outcomes can be found in a variety of different forms—tangible outputs and less tangible outputs for which the impacts are more difficult to measure. In many cases, it is difficult to determine if the policy itself resulted in desired change or other exogenous or external factors were the most direct cause. Nevertheless, it is important to determine if policy is responsible for the desired change—otherwise, there would be no need for the policy. Policy analysts often use theoretically grounded statistical models to determine if the policy will have the desired impact. In a final stage of policy analysis, analysts collate the information gathered to determine which policy alternative will best meet present and future needs.

There are two types of empirical analysis: qualitative studies and quantitative studies. Qualitative studies involve a variety of different tools. Some qualitative studies involve archival analysis, studying policy history and determining what has been done in the past to solve certain policy problems. Qualitative studies might also involve personal interviews, asking individuals to describe in words a variety of issues surrounding the policy process—from policy agendas to formulation, implementation, and evaluation. Interviews with policymakers and with the clientele being served by a particular policy may provide valuable information about policy goals, processes, and outcomes.

Archival analysis is particularly important in public policy analysis. Through studies of policy history—what was done in the past, why it was done, and how much it cost—policy analysts can learn important lessons from earlier times and apply these lessons to current or future problems and goals. A new policy goal may sound highly innovative and cost effective and promise to meet worthy goals; but archival research may illustrate the hidden costs and pitfalls that might result in policy failure. Accounting for the hidden costs and steering clear of potential problems might result in a different understanding of the policy innovation and improve the possibility of success.

Personal interviews are also an important method of improving current public policy and building better policies in the future. Public policy is formulated and implemented by professionals working in government, oftentimes for an entire career. Through their individual experiences in particular policy areas, the experiences of elected and appointed officials become key policy artifacts. When these individuals leave government service, their experience and wisdom are often lost. It has been said that the best way to see into the future is to understand the past. With a diminished understanding of the past, younger government officials may find themselves traveling in uncharted waters, having to establish a sense of what government can and can not do through public policy. One way to alleviate some potential policy fumbling is to document the informal lessons or experiences of senior elected and appointed officials. Personal interviews are perhaps the most effective method of accomplishing this goal, largely because a personal interview technique will allow for greater flexibility in information collection.

Quantitative studies are also of tremendous value to policy analysts in their continual efforts to address important policy issues. Quantitative analysis involves the use of numbers to describe phenomena. The analysis of numbers can simplify the study of public policy, in large part because numbers have assigned values that may have a more universal meaning. In the strictest sense, monetary values are often understood by all individuals who encounter them. Other numerical values have meanings that are more ephemeral and often socially constructed, a function of a particular set of values that may or may not change over time. Increasingly, government policy analysts use quantitative tools to shape public policy. Qualitative methods, while potentially quite valuable, require significant amounts of time and resources, and data collected cannot be easily accessed and uniformly stored. Due to the growing data storage and processing capabilities in society, numbers can be more readily collected and stored and are readily accessible and transportable.

Cost-benefit analysis is one of the most common forms of policy analysis. Such analysis requires that the analyst have a solid understanding of both economic theory and statistics. Cost-benefit analysis is primarily concerned with comparing the amount of expected or known benefits produced from a particular policy choice with the expected or known costs associated with that choice. Of the two elements of the equation, the determination of costs is often more easily computed. Costs are most often measured in monetary terms—labor and supplies are easily converted to dollar costs. While there are always hidden costs associated with any policy decision, those costs can be estimated given previous experiences in prior public policy endeavors. Opportunity costs—the costs associated with choosing a particular policy over an alternative policy—can also be estimated.

Benefit calculation is oftentimes a difficult endeavor. In order to complete the cost-benefit calculation, benefits must be assigned a numeric value; most frequently the numeric value is made in monetary terms. Yet, most aspects of public policy benefit are not easily measured in monetary terms. Individual clientele of a policy and individual officials fulfilling policy goals have a tremendous influence on the quality of a policy outcome or output; but, the calculation of a benefit is often measured and aggregated in a manner that fails to capture those nuances.

Despite limitations in estimation, benefits must be measured in monetary or unit output terms for a cost-benefit calculation to proceed. Policymakers may determine benefit estimates through survey research by asking clientele of a policy to indicate how the public policy has impacted their lives. Policymakers also view the benefit in terms of the output of a policy, that is, the number of individuals that were served. In higher education policy, for instance, policymakers will conduct surveys of alumni to determine the impact of their higher education experience on their salary level and to also inquire about their positive and negative experiences at the university or college. Additionally, policymakers will conduct a headcount of the number of student credit hours generated and the number of university or college graduates to measure policy output and equate it to a benefit.

Of course, the determination of cost-benefit ratios is not a one-time event. Public policy is dynamic and requires that policymakers adjust policy to changing conditions and needs. When change of policy direction or emphasis occurs, it usually requires increased resource expenditures. For example, if a public school's administrators determine that many of the students' reading disabilities are impeding their general progress in school, it might be necessary to increase resources devoted to reading programs. The goal would be to increase benefit as a result of increased expenditure on a particular facet of a public policy. The increased benefit is called a marginal benefit, while the increased cost is known as a marginal cost. In cost-benefit analysis, it is important marginal increases in cost that are justifiable in terms of increased benefits. If a benefit does not increase at a rate greater than cost increases, then the marginal policy changes are economically inefficient.

The dynamic quality of public policy is also considered in a procedure known as discounting. The value of a particular resource (e.g., money) does not remain the same over time. For example, money that is not spent may grow in value, simply by gaining interest or investment value. Once money is spent for a particular policy, that interest or investment value potential is lost. The longer money remains invested, the greater potential value can be generated. Therefore, current resources frequently have greater potential value than resources collected or retained in future years—not all money is equal once time is factored into analysis. The discounting procedure allows policymakers to compare

monetary values on an equal basis, thereby making the cost-benefit analyses more accurate in terms of both present and future costs associated with a policy.

The ability to conduct accurate and complete cost-benefit analyses is often hampered by a variety of other factors that play a role in public policy. Policy risk is always a factor in cost-benefit analysis. When one chooses to move or not to move in a particular policy direction, there is the risk of policy failures. Those risks might mean that resources that were spent with good intentions never produced an expected benefit; thus, policy efficiency might be nil or at the very best deemed inefficient. Oftentimes, the risks of failure are so great that policymakers avoid potential political ire by simply not choosing to take on high-risk (yet, potentially valuable) policy goals.

Existing public policy often carries with it a lower level of risk than newer public policies. Frequently, there are unforeseen indirect start-up costs associated with new policies. Additionally, public policies are often vague and require the establishment of rules and procedures for day-to-day operations. These costs of implementation cannot always be determined before a public policy is put into place; but they must be factored into cursory cost-benefit analysis to determine the feasibility of a particular prospective public policy.

Whether government is considering a new direction for public policy or simply implementing existing policy, the changing nature of society's needs must be continually monitored. People migrate, economic and social conditions change, and the nature of public problems continually evolves. Demographic data helps policy analysts determine if social and economic change is occurring in an equitable manner. Demographic analysis played an important part in documenting the rise of economic and social inequality that arose in the post–World War II era. While the analyses were interpreted by political conservatives and liberals in different ways, the findings themselves played an important role in developing public policies intended to remedy the inequities, the impacts of which could be studied in future demographic analysis.

Policy analysts use decision theory to plan for contingencies that arise in policy formulation and implementation. Decision theory is an attempt to explore all possible contingencies extant in a particular policy. The approach is especially useful after a particular policy has been adopted by government. Following policy adoption, the details of policy practice must be explored in full. For the most part, policy adoption means that a particular set of general policy goals have been recognized as being a function of government. Government agencies in charge of meeting those goals frequently must determine how to deal with a variety of alternative decisions that will have to be made and what outcomes (and the value of those outcomes) are likely from each of those decisions. Decision theory involves determining the probability that various events will occur and factoring that probability into decision analysis.

Policy analysts may use experimentation to cost-effectively "test" public policy alternatives. Experiments are one the most effective methods of determining a causal connection between the presence of a public policy and particular outcomes. The use of policy experiments may face ethical challenges: Denying a policy benefit to those outside of the experiment may be harmful. Conversely, subjecting individuals to a bad policy may also face ethical challenges.

The outcomes of public policy analysis are highly varied. In one sense, policy analysis provides elected and nonelected government decisionmakers the opportunity to develop a greater understanding of a policy problem and possible solutions. Through policy analysis, it is possible to gain a greater understanding of the projected costs and possible benefits that will emerge from the adoption of a particular policy alternative. Decisionmakers often seek the most economical alternative possible—the alternative that offers the most in the way of benefit and the least in the way of cost. Government is asked to deal with a number of policy goals with limited resources; therefore, it is wise to stretch tax dollars. Policy analysis can help decisionmakers make more rational decisions.

—*Christopher A. Simon*

See also Cost-Benefit Analysis; Evidence-Based Policy; Governability; Groupthink; Policy Cycle; Policy Implementation; Policy Learning; Policy Predictability; Program Evaluation

Further Readings and References

Harberger A. C., & Jenkins, G. P. (Eds.). (2002). *Cost-benefit analysis.* Northampton, MA: Edward Elgar.

Simon, C. A. (2007). *Public policy.* New York: Longman.

POLICY CYCLE

Like astronomy (solar cycles), biochemistry (DNA sequences), or economics (Kondratiev cycles), political scientists also use cyclical reasoning. In the field of policy analysis, a cycle refers to the set of constituent phases of a policy. These elements follow one another according to an invariable order and recur in accordance with the renewal of public policies. The concept of policy cycle is an intellectual tool that constitutes neither a method nor a theory. This means that the choice of the theoretical point of view is crucial because it determines the form and the substance of policy cycles.

Features of Policy Cycles

From an ontological perspective, a policy cycle is made up of three complementary characteristics. First, it is linear in the sense that its different steps are chronologically consecutive. These stages act as categories that constitute the whole policy. They are jointly exhaustive and mutually exclusive. Their evolution is ruled by a relation of necessity and not by a causality effect. Second, a policy cycle is recurrent because it repeats itself when a policy is implemented. Thus, the end of a cycle is always the beginning of another cycle. This feedback capacity engenders the emergence of policy loops that are free from temporal and spatial contingencies. The analysis of policy cycles fits all types of public policies (social, industrial, etc.) irrespective of their context and allows these patterns to be compared by structural homology. Third, policy cycles have the same properties as fractals. Theoretically, the elements of a policy cycle can be infinitely divided into subelements. In practice, the only limit to this division lies in the analysis of the individual interests of the agents.

The policy cycle concept has three advantages. First of all, its linear feature imposes a certain order beyond the chaos of raw data. As it orders and organizes facts into hierarchies, it becomes a useful analytical tool. Second, recurrence facilitates the constitution of similar stages, which are the first step before elaborating unities of comparison. Finally, its fractal nature allows research to go beyond the conception of public policies as defined by the law. This sociological dimension allows the decision process black box to be opened. However, the qualities of the policy cycles model can also restrict analysis if they are considered from a rigid position. Actually, an excessively linear study can quickly become a teleological analysis. Indeed, a mechanistic vision of cycles introduces a metaphysical bias into the analysis. In the same way, the repetition of stages can create an illusion of homogeneity and overlook the specificity of local public policy implementation. Last, the division of cycles into stages and substages can favor the study of the form to the detriment of the substance by focusing on the structuring of the phases.

Related Concepts

Policy cycles are one of the first analytical tools of policy studies. Their nature is intimately connected to the context during which they emerged. Created in the 1950s in the United States by Harold D. Lasswell, policy cycles were durably influenced by the seminal works of the dominant functionalist and behaviorist authors of that time. This explains the universal vocation of the initial cyclical analysis. This innovation had great success in the academic community and led to an increase in cyclical analysis but also to a fragmentation of the original model. Some authors favored the openness of the cycle vis-à-vis the environment by integrating several peripheral agents at the risk of losing consistency, while others preferred considering a restrictive core of decisionmakers to keep more coherence to their work. Despite the vast quantity of literature regarding policy cycles, there is a relative consensus to consider the taxonomy of Charles O. Jones as the standard model. He divides a policy cycle into five phases: agenda setting, policy formulation,

decision implementation, policy evaluation, and policy termination. This division is open to criticism. Nevertheless, it is relatively balanced and it permits the inclusion of nongovernmental actors in the agenda setting and implementation stages while maintaining sufficient coherence by limiting the study of governance processes through time and space.

Policy cycles are closely related to the method of sequential analysis of public policies. This framework is usually opposed to the cognitive analysis developed some years later. However, the stages of the policy cycle are just an abstract ideal type, whereas the sequences of the sequential analysis are an empirical representation of reality. Beyond this confusion, the sequences differ from the stages by their dependency with regard to the context because a sequence only makes sense in a given situation. It follows that a sequence is not linear because every change alters its path; it is not recurrent either because of its irreversibility; and it is not fractal because there cannot be two identical sequences.

The Paradox of Policy Cycles

The recent evolution of the concept of policy cycles is paradoxical. On one hand, after a long intellectual sedimentation process, this notion has become a deep-rooted part of the collective consciousness of policy researchers. On the other hand, few authors still explicitly use this concept, as it is often considered to be an old-fashioned idea just as sequential analysis has been labeled. In fact, recent literature demonstrates that a large number of defenders of the cognitive approach still have recourse to the notion of policy cycle in a latent way by focusing on one of the key concepts such as agenda setting, policy formulation, and others.

—*Jean-Baptiste Harguindéguy*

See also Policy Analysis; Policy Development; Policy Implementation; Policy Learning

Further Readings and References

Jones, C. O. (1970). *An introduction to the study of public policy.* Belmont, CA: Duxbury Press.

Lasswell, H. D. (1956). *The decision process: Seven categories of functional analysis.* College Park: University of Maryland Press.

May, J. V., & Wildavsky, A. B. (1978). *The policy cycle.* Beverly Hills, CA: Sage.

McCool, D. C. (1995). *Public policy theories, models and concepts: An anthology.* Englewood Cliffs, NJ: Prentice Hall.

Policy Development

Policy development can be defined as a process that consists of the identification of public issues, the transformation of these issues into political problems through the governmental agenda, and the elaboration of solutions to resolve these problems. Policy development constitutes the core of the activity of governments and the first step before the implementation stage of laws and regulations and their evaluation. Despite this simple definition, the concept of policy development is an extremely complex political process that relates to general issues of state governance. From the moment of the recognition of public needs and the solving of these needs, many externalities can occur. The policy development process frequently meets three related problems: identification of the general context of application, identification of main actors, and identification of rationality patterns that rule the interactions.

Policy Development in Context

The notion of policy development is intimately linked to the stages approach of public policies. This approach is crossed by many debates on the number of stages constituting the concept of policy development. Harold D. Lasswell, in 1956, was the first to elaborate such a distinction. His dichotomy was based on seven stages (intelligence, promotion, prescription, invocation, application, termination and appraisal). Nevertheless, the most frequently adopted scheme was defined by Charles O. Jones in 1970. This scheme is based on five stages with their own logics of action: agenda setting, which consists of the integration of a public issue by a political agenda; program development, when a problem is converted into a policy; program implementation, when government physically organizes the solving of the problem; program evaluation, which is an a posteriori analysis of the whole process; program termination, which supposes the end of the process and the beginning of another policy development.

The principal interest of these analyses is to introduce an order into a chaotic situation by dividing policy development and implementation into clear and logical stages. In reality, each policy involves frequent feedbacks and reformulation of political issues during its development. That is why many authors prefer an explanation of policy development in terms of cognitive process, focusing on the collective elaboration and diffusion of interpretations of policy issues.

Related Concepts

Notions such as policy cycle or implementation are related to the concept of policy development. However, the latter conserves its own identity vis-à-vis the former. The main difference between the notions of policy development and policy cycle is that a cycle is an analytical tool of public policies that proposes a complete view of the policy process. In turn, the notion of policy development only constitutes the beginning, the first stages of the whole process. For example, drawing on the model defined by Charles O. Jones, this means that the addition of the stages of policy development, implementation, evaluation, and termination constitute a whole policy cycle.

This also means that the concept of policy development depends on the analytical framework adopted to study the evolution of state governance. As an essentially descriptive notion, policy development is interpreted in different ways by state theorists. Thirty years ago, it was commonly assumed that the most important actors of policy development were those who worked for public institutions. Elected people, civil servants and state experts were more legitimate to act at the global level than the rest of society. However, this elitist conception of policy making has been under attack since the 1970s. Many authors demonstrated that the erosion of borders between state and civil society allowed the involvement of a growing number of actors into the policy development process. Pluralists stressed the integration of many participants, such as private advocates, companies, lobbies, and media. A new perspective was opened up during the 1980s through the success of the literature dedicated to the study of policy networks in policy making. Beyond the opposition between elitism and pluralism, policy networks analysts focus on the links between public and private actors (horizontal dimension) at different tiers of governance (vertical dimension).

The Ambiguity of Policy Development

As a descriptive concept of public policies, policy development is also highly dependent on the theoretical framework adopted by researchers. Rational-comprehensive models have dominated the analysis of public policies for thirty years by assuming that policy making consisted of identifying all possible solutions to a problem and selecting the best alternative. The introduction of the model of bounded rationality allowed research to reintroduce contingency into the analysis. In this case, policy makers are supposed to act in an incremental way instead of choosing the best solution. Policy developers only try to satisfy their electors by selecting the first alternative that suits the largest number of people because of time and information constraints. At the opposite side of the continuum, constructivist authors state that rationality largely depends on the context. As a social construction of reality, policy development is produced by (and produces) interactions. Then, the outcomes of policy development become more difficult to predict.

—Jean-Baptiste Harguindéguy

See also Bureaucratic Politics Approach; Civic Capacity; Governance; Neighborhood Association; Policy Cycle; Policy Implementation; Program Evaluation

Further Readings and References

Jones, C. O. (1970). *An introduction to the study of public policy).* Belmont, CA: Duxbury Press.

Kingdom, J. W. (1995). *Agendas, alternatives, and public policies.* New York: Harper.

Lasswell, H. D. (1956). *The decision process: Seven categories of functional analysis.* College Park: University of Maryland.

Lindblom, C. E. (1993). *The policy-making process.* Englewood Cliffs, NJ: Prentice Hall.

Sabatier, P. A. (Ed.). (1999). *Theories of the policy process.* Boulder, CO: Westview.

Policy Implementation

Concisely defined, policy implementation is what occurs after a legislature has acted and a bill becomes law. Legislatures typically are unable to consider all that must be undertaken when they envisage a program or initiative and so rely on implementers (or administrators) to flesh out the details once a statute has been enacted. Those particulars are often heavily freighted with political portent or carry with them far-ranging responsibility to develop new technologies, invent or refine approaches to problems, or mediate important conflicts. For example, when the National Environmental Policy Act was created in 1970, it was expected to work with industry to develop technologies to limit and hopefully to remediate air and water pollution. But there was no consensus in industry or among experts, as it began its task, concerning which technologies to employ or whether certain technologies out of those available were more effective than others. Similarly, the Department of Health and Human Services was charged by law (Section 504 of The Rehabilitation Act of 1973) with securing access to public transportation for the wheelchair bound (among other things)—a process that took some twenty years, cost millions of dollars in litigation-related fees, and involved multiple federal agencies, state and local governments, and the nation's courts as these entities wrangled over what constituted a most practicable technology and what manner of cost was reasonable to impose for this purpose. These examples illustrate the importance of this phase of the policy process and suggest the centrality of administrators to policy outcomes. Plainly put, actual outcomes for citizens are often determined during program implementation.

Policy implementation is indeed a critical phase of the nation's public policy process and one that is necessarily political as administrators use their discretion to make important choices that often have significant consequences for those receiving services or who are otherwise affected by public programs. Implementation decisionmakers work to make statutory pronouncements real for the populations affected. If a program for the shut-in poor is created, for example, that choice demands that the implementing agency take necessary steps to locate targeted individuals in affected jurisdictions, decide how to contact them—whether to send a letter to potential participants, at what grade level to write that note, whether the message should be sent only in English or in other languages—and so on. Alternately, perhaps it would be more effective to send Boy Scouts and Girl Scouts to knock on the doors of those potentially eligible to provide them information about the new program? These implementer choices make the difference in who is served and how they are assisted. Choices that affect service quality, equity, and effectiveness are the everyday stuff of policy implementation. Importantly, these decisions are typically made with only general guidance from lawmakers who often cannot foresee important program concerns or who otherwise wish to be absolved of responsibility for addressing them. Their nearly unavoidable exercise of discretion makes administrators ready targets for lawmakers that often blame implementers for policy outcomes, even when it is arguable that poor policy design or other factors well within the purview of the legislators were the proximate cause of a less-than-ideal outcome. Hurricane Katrina may provide an example, as many in Congress moved to blame the Federal Emergency Management Agency (FEMA) as well as state and local authorities for the ineffective response to the disaster, even as some experts are contending that legislative decisions not to provide the necessary funds for levee upkeep and repair allowed the breaching to occur in the first place. Whatever the appropriate explanation or combination of explanations in this instance, the broader point is that implementation agents operate in a regime structure of separated powers and often find themselves held responsible for all dimensions of policy outcomes regardless of whether they could reasonably have been expected to control those results. Because they work for three different political masters (congressional, executive, and judicial), implementers have little formal recourse to complain about this state of affairs. Their place, in short, within our regime framework is paradoxical—administrators are critical, but their efforts are unlikely often to be rewarded, much less revered.

The self-conscious study of policy implementation is said to date to the early 1970s, although, like much else related to this subfield of inquiry in political science and public administration, that argument is contested. Indeed, there is little about this terrain that has gone unchallenged, including whether the field of inquiry itself remains relevant. It is emblematic of this literature that some scholars have recently declared its demise, even as others have suggested its apogee. One way to consider such a restless intellectual landscape is to chart it against the phenomena that it examines. This brief essay does so around three critical challenges and a number of concerns that arise naturally from them, dubbed the three C's: Context, Contentiousness, and Constraints. These categories are not parsimonious. Nor do they constitute a theory or analytic framework by which to describe policy implementation dynamics or the range of tools governments employ to implement programs. Instead, these categories serve to point to many of the core concerns confronting both analysts and agents of implementation.

Inevitably, policy implementation processes and outcomes are shaped by the broader political economy in which they are ensconced. The emergence of the self-conscious study of policy implementation began in earnest even as the women's and civil rights movements were at or near their peak and the tide of neoliberal claims concerning the proper role and reach of government was also rising. The ascendancy of the latter in particular is neatly symbolized by former President Ronald Reagan's famous declaration in his first inaugural address that governmental intervention was not a solution. While the women's and civil rights movements sought equitable representation in government and governance, that trend was accompanied by a broader political mobilization of disaffection. That is, American governance was increasingly characterized by demands for action from these and other groups, but those concerns were often met by profound skepticism of the efficacy of government and a companion call that it be replaced (or avoided whenever possible) via action through civil society institutions or for-profit entities. Overall, the pace of government growth has not changed markedly during this period, but a majority of the citizenry has, nonetheless, supported claims that its government's actions on behalf of the public weal are likely to prove insufficient or worse unless implemented in partnership with for-profit or nonprofit institutions or otherwise left to nonstate actors. This skepticism is not new in U.S. culture or politics. Americans have always been chary of their national government's reach and authority and have always demanded that their agents implement programs through the states or other entities whenever possible. Nonetheless, the general population has shown a growing unwillingness to countenance direct national service provision, even as demands for government action have grown.

One primary consequence of this shift in the public zeitgeist is that government action by contract has become ubiquitous during these decades at both levels of the federal system, as has government by implicit partnerships, such as the uneasy and shifting alliance in medical care insurance provision between public and private providers. Even defense, that most classic of public goods, is now the province of large contracts to for-profit providers that provide everything from onboard weapons systems expertise for the nation's nuclear attack submarines to food service and motor vehicle maintenance for its troops in the field. None of this is good or bad per se, but it certainly implies a much more complex administrative responsibility for those who must write and oversee the contracts that animate these relationships. This also is true for those who must manage them when they often lack any real capacity to replace the service provider or to deliver services in its stead when it falters.

In addition to these concerns, it is clear that it is innately more difficult for government officials to implement a policy through other actors than it is to do so themselves. And so a paradox has emerged during this period: A conflicted citizenry continues to demand public services but often deeply mistrusts its elected agents' capacity to deliver on those claims. Accordingly, government is now more enmeshed than ever in for-profit and nonprofit sectors as it seeks to deliver many public programs through such intermediaries and across political-economic lines. That is, the aims of neoliberalism notwithstanding, government is now larger and more interconnected with all sectors of society despite two decades of policy making that have declared it a noxious weed that must be controlled. The paradox is profound. Rube Goldberg could not have devised such a complex set of relationships by which to seek to secure public aims, as have the nation's policymakers during this period of particular disquiet over the reach of government. A skeptical social and political context has created implementation structures of enormous complexity that, paradoxically, now affect a larger sphere of society than ever before.

That fact points to the second "C" of implementation studies, contentiousness. Implementation analysts have had to grapple with the reality that much public action in our era can only occur when managers and leaders successfully find ways to reach across organizational, political (as in nation to states or states to localities), or sectoral lines (as in public entity to nonprofit or for-profit organization), or all of these at once. This reality has demanded that researchers confront the fact that organizational actors are hardly autonomous and the equally cruel reality that their parent organizations and governments are not either. Efforts to understand how and why cooperation or coordination occurs in interorganizational implementation structures have resulted in large subliteratures concerning exchange and transaction dynamics, as well as trust and boundary spanning. This imperative suggests that to deliver services in the indirect ways we have adopted is virtually to guarantee conflicts during policy implementation, even when political leaders broadly agree on policy aims. That fact implies, in turn, that these must somehow be managed effectively, if not overcome, in order for services to reach their intended targets. Policy implementers must be master conflict mediators and managers, as well as being superbly adept at understanding what incentives will yield sufficient alignment across organizational lines so as to secure a modicum of effective action. And, to be successful, they often must accomplish this feat at multiple analytic scales: individual, organizational, interorganizational, and sectoral.

Therefore, conflict might be regarded as a central constraint, the third "C" of implementation studies, on both how the nation has chosen to implement many of its policies and on efforts by analysts to understand and model those dynamics. But this nation has also imposed another double-barreled sort of constraint on its would-be implementers. It has, at once, sharply limited the resources available for many public programs, even as it has raised public expectations concerning the possibility of those initiatives. That is, elected leaders have often mobilized majorities to the polls with the argument that significant change would occur with the passage of proposed legislation or policies, even as those self-same leaders, aware of the unpopularity of taxes and the public's general skepticism of the efficacy of public action (a paradox to be sure), have severely limited resources for implementation of those programs. The result is an odd conflation of difficulties for policy implementers. Not only is the operating environment innately difficult due to its structural and social complexity, but those challenges also are compounded by the reality of often-continuously inadequate resources as against political claims. The resulting scenario is one in which implementers confront daunting obstacles to action, let alone to effective action, and they must pursue those efforts with thin political support.

This discussion suggests several conclusions. First, its critics notwithstanding, policy implementation studies are a necessary field of inquiry. They must be if researchers are to chart how the public is seeking to conduct its affairs and why, as well as to understand more fully how it might better affect that business. Such work continues apace. Second, understanding the relationship of the administrative challenges

endemic to these processes demands an understanding of broader contextual, or even cultural, trends and forces. Third, that finding implies that if scholars are to develop even an adequate descriptive theory of policy implementation (none now exists), it must be contextually driven—at whatever relevant analytic scale is selected for examination. Finally, complex network governance structures demand peculiarly gifted managers and leaders, individuals with strong intellectual imaginations and equally vigorous conflict management capacities, and these gifted people must find the incentives to work with others across organizational and sectoral spaces literally to make our implementation structures act. We not only need theory to describe what these talented people must do, but we also need well-conceived and challenging college- and graduate-level curricula that will help to equip them to address these difficult responsibilities.

—Max Stephenson, Jr.

See also Policy Analysis; Policy Cycle; Policy Development; Policy Learning; Policy Network; Policy Predictability; Policy Style; Policy Transfer

Further Readings and References

Barrett, S. M. (2004). Implementation studies: Time for a revival? Personal reflections on 20 years of implementation studies. *Public Administration, 82*(2), 249–262.

Hill, M., & Hupe, P. (2002). *Implementing public policy: Governance in theory and practice.* Thousand Oaks, CA: Sage.

O'Toole, L. J., Jr. (2003). Intergovernmental relations in implementation. In B. G. Peters & J. Pierre (Eds.), *Handbook of public administration* (pp. 234–244). Thousand Oaks, CA: Sage.

Saetren, H. (2005). Facts and myths about research on public policy implementation: Out-of-fashion, allegedly dead, but still very much alive and relevant. *Policy Studies Journal, 33*(4), 559–582.

POLICY LEARNING

Policy learning consists of a process of acquiring knowledge, skills, habits, or tendencies through the experience of policy making. The concept of learning was transferred from the field of cognitive psychology to policy analysis during the 1970s. In a context of bounded rationality, this notion implicates an implicit capacity of learning by policymakers and goes beyond the mechanistic-behavioral vision of public policy that limited the action of participants to the couple stimuli/reaction. Thus, policy making is more an incremental process than a series of radical shifts.

Policy Learning in Context

One of the first authors to use the notion of policy learning was Hugh Heclo (in 1974). In his book on social policies in Great Britain and Sweden, he demonstrated that politics also integrates an intellectual dimension and cannot be reduced to conflicts of power. Actors try to reduce the context of uncertainty through a learning process and the integration of policy advocacy. The latter allows reusing and modifying past routines and experiences with respect to a new situation.

The concept of policy learning varies in intensity through space and time. On the one hand, the policy learning process involves four dimensions. The first one consists of the introduction of new information, the second is a new interpretation of past policies, the third can be the involvement of new ideas, and the last one is based on a change of policy context. On the other hand, learning also leads one to take into account the time dimension. Learning can involve short-term or long-term modifications. These changes depend on the capability of adaptation of policymakers to a new context. As said before, this continuous adaptation makes policy making an incremental process ruled by marginal adjustments with respect to external pressures.

Related Concepts

The concept of policy learning differs from the notions of political inheritance. The former defines the capacities of transformation of actors. It is an essentially active concept that stresses the free will (even if limited) of participants and the possibility to adopt an alternative route among different available options. In turn, political inheritance (or policy legacy)

refers to pressures exerted by context on policymakers. In this second case, participants act in a passive way. They are totally constrained and have no margins of action. They have only one course to choose; no alternatives are available.

In the same way, policy learning and policy transfer—or lesson drawing—share a common background. Both concepts refer to the selection and the adaptation of the best solutions to public issues in a context of informational asymmetry. Nevertheless, policy transfer (from another government or to another government) is just a modality of policy learning that relates to a larger process.

The Ambiguity of Policy Learning

The notion of policy learning is a theoretical tool of analysis that is strongly linked to a cognitivist vision of public policies. It is based on two related interrogations: the question of actors involved in the learning process and the question of levels of learning. First, the identity of policy learners is not always clearly defined. Elected people, civil servants, and state experts are at the core of the learning process. By accumulating experience under the pressure of political events (at the domestic and international levels), these actors progressively change the structure of state policies. However, this elitist vision contrasts with the pluralist approach, which includes new participants such as trade unions, associations, lobbies, companies, and media. Since the 1980s, the thinking about policy learning also includes research on policy networks and has demonstrated the interaction between public and private sectors at different tiers of governance. From this point of view, learning is a changing process involving common thinking on the past and future, and where the state is just another (even if fundamental) part of the whole.

Second, the level of policy learning is a decisive feature of works on cognitive aspects of public policies. Many authors make a distinction between technical and global changes imposed by learning. Nevertheless, many scholars now assume that both technological and ideological changes can occur. Drawing on the 1987 work of Paul A. Sabatier, many authors have argued that the cognitive core of policies is more difficult to modify than the periphery. In the case of the economic policy shift that occurred in the United Kingdom between 1970 and 1989, Peter A. Hall suggested in 1993 that this change is produced in three steps. A first change concerns the level of objectives of economic tools. After that, a second change occurs at the level of macroeconomic instruments themselves. Finally, a third change completely modifies the economic paradigm. The first and second changes effectively respond to a process of policy learning where state actors modify their behaviors with respect to a changing environment. However, the third change refers to the monopolization of the head of the state by a neoliberal coalition, and the successive replacement of Keynesian policies by the monetarist *doxa*. The limits of the notion of policy learning are based on this use of power. The learning thesis is valid as far as a coalition can maintain power by adapting to circumstances. Nevertheless, policy learning models have had difficulties in explaining the replacement of the actors themselves.

—*Jean-Baptiste Harguindéguy*

See also Advocacy Networks; Incrementalism; New Institutionalism; Organizational Learning; Policy Analysis; Policy Cycle; Policy Implementation; Policy Network; Policy Style; Policy Transfer; Social Learning

Further Readings and References

Bennett, C. J., & Howlett, M. (1992). The lessons of learning: Reconciling theories of policy learning and policy change. *Policy Sciences, 25*(3), 275–294.

Etheredge, L. M. (1987). Government learning: An overview. In S. L. Long (Ed.), *The handbook of political behavior, Vol. 2.* New York: Pergamon.

Hall, P. A. (1993). Policy paradigms, social learning and the state: The case of economic policy-making in Britain. *Comparative Politics, 25*(3), 275–298.

Heclo, H. (1974). *Modern social politics in Britain and Sweden: From relief to income maintenance.* New Haven, CT: Yale University Press.

Rose, R. (1991). What is lesson-drawing? *Journal of Public Policy, 11,* 3–30.

Sabatier, P. A. (1987). An advocacy coalition framework of policy change and the role of policy-oriented learning. *Policy Sciences, 21,* 129–168.

POLICY NETWORK

Policy networks consist of governmental and societal actors whose interactions with one another give rise to policies. Typically, these actors are linked through informal practices as well as formal institutions, or even instead of such institutions. Typically, they are interdependent; they can secure the outcomes for which they hope only by collaborating with one another. Policy networks can vary widely, however. At one extreme, we find "policy communities." Policy communities have a limited number of participant groups, with some others being deliberately excluded. The participants share broad values, beliefs, and preferences. They usually meet frequently, with all of them interacting closely on any topic related to the policy area. All of them have significant resources or power, so their interactions consist of institutionalized forms of negotiation and bargaining. They are usually organized hierarchically so the leaders can secure the acquiescence of the members in whatever policies are agreed upon. At the other extreme, we find "issue networks." Issue networks typically have far more participants. The participants disagree with one another so conflict, not consensus, is the norm. They also have unequal levels of power and widely varying degrees of access, so their interactions are often primarily consultative.

Concepts such as policy network, policy community, and issue network all refer to government links with other state and societal actors. Other related concepts include epistemic communities, iron triangles, and policy subsystems. All these concepts can be situated within a broader research program of network analysis, which can be found throughout the social sciences. Network analysis has been used to discuss diverse phenomena, including the information revolution, technological innovation, and urban villages. Policy network analysis is the species of network analysis most relevant to governance. It emphasizes how networks decide which issues will be included and excluded from the policy agenda, shape the behavior of actors, privilege certain interests, and even substitute private forms of government for public accountability.

Governance as Networks

Accounts of governance often concentrate on policy networks. Governance has been described as rule by and through networks. Indeed, governance has become the most widely accepted term for describing the patterns of government or rule that arise from the interactions of multiple organizations within networks. One common account of governance emphasizes its contemporary nature. In this view, governance has arisen with a recent proliferation of networks. There has been a shift in the organization of the state from hierarchy—the bureaucracies of the traditional welfare state—by way of the market reforms of the New Right to a contemporary era of networks. The role of the state has changed from making policy decisions to coordinating the delivery of services. The state has become increasingly dependent on other actors; perhaps it can get its way only through negotiations with other actors in all sorts of networks. In this view, governance through networks constitutes an alternative to hierarchies and markets as a way of allocating resources and securing coordination. Networks rely on trust and cooperation, whereas hierarchies rely on administrative orders, and markets rely on price competition. Networks are characterized by diplomacy, reciprocity, and interdependence.

Equally, we might take governance through networks to be a ubiquitous pattern of rule. The allegedly special characteristics of networks also appear, we might suggest, in hierarchies and markets. The rules and commands of a bureaucracy do not have a fixed form; rather they are constantly interpreted and made afresh through the creative activity of individuals. Similarly, the operation of markets depends on the contingent beliefs and interactions of interdependent producers and consumers that rely on trust and diplomacy, as well as economic rationality, to make their decisions. In this view, once we stop reifying hierarchies and markets, we find that many allegedly unique features of governance through networks are actually ubiquitous. Power and administrative rationality are always dispersed among diverse practices, technologies, and networks.

A concept of governance by and through networks draws on themes from the earlier literature on policy networks. One such theme is networks as interorganizational analysis. The predominantly European literature on interorganizational analysis emphasizes the structural relationship between political institutions as opposed to the interpersonal relations between individuals within those institutions. These structural relations are taken to be the crucial element in any given policy network. The focal organization of the network tries to manage the more dependent organizations using diverse strategies, while the other organizations use similar strategies to attempt to manage each other and the focal one. Therefore, a network consists of numerous overlapping relationships, each of which depends to a greater or lesser degree on the others. This concept of an interorganizational network has been used to describe and analyze interactions among diverse political actors, including parties, ministries, unions, business associations, and interest groups.

The concept of governance by and through networks also draws on earlier studies of networks as interest intermediation. The predominantly American literature on interest intermediation is part of a broader tradition of pluralism that has devoted much attention to subgovernments. Pluralists disaggregated the study of policy making into subsystems within which bureaucrats, members of Congress and their staff, and the representatives of interest groups interacted with one another. These clusters of individuals were said to make most of the routine decisions in any given area of policy. Typically, the pluralists concentrated on a few elite groups who had especially close ties to government and who often excluded other groups from access. In this view, government confronts innumerable interest groups. Some groups are considered to be extreme and unrealistic; they are kept away from the policy process. Others are deemed significant and responsible; they become insiders upon whom government relies to ensure its policies work appropriately. Over time, the interactions between government and the insiders become institutionalized. An "iron triangle" develops between the central agency, the Congressional Committee, and the elite interest group; they develop an almost symbiotic relationship to one another.

Although concepts of governance draw on the earlier literature on policy networks, they also transform important aspects of this literature. Earlier studies of policy networks typically concentrated on analyzing relations of power around the central state. In contrast, concepts of governance are often tied to the idea of a decline in the power of the central state. Accounts of governance usually focus on the boundary between state and civil society rather than on policy making in specific areas. They explore the increasing diffusion of state power and authority to other organizations. *Governance* is a broader term than *government* because it points to the diverse ways public services are delivered by any combination of public, private, and voluntary sector organizations. Similarly, concepts of governance often invoke international factors that contributed to the decline in the power of the central state. Whereas earlier studies of policy networks concentrated most commonly on policy making in national policy sectors, concepts of governance are more likely to point outward to transnational networks. However, this last difference is perhaps not that great; after all, transnational policy networks have long been recognized as a feature of policy making, especially in the European Union.

Network Theory

There has been considerable debate about policy network analysis. Some critics complain that the concept of a network is little more than a metaphorical description; it does not do explanatory work. At times, they also complain that the approach fails to adequately specify causal relationships between the characteristics of a network and policy outcomes; it lacks, in particular, a microtheory capable of accounting for change over time. We might distinguish four approaches to network theory, each of which offers a different response to such criticisms. These approaches, each of which appears to some degree in studies of governance, are: power dependence, rational choice, dialectical, and decentered.

The power dependence approach unpacks policy networks as made up of resource-dependent organizations. Their relationships are such that any organization depends on others for resources that they thus have to exchange to achieve their goals. Each organization within the network deploys its resources, whether these are financial, political, or informational, in order to maximize its influence on outcomes. Although one might suggest that the relationships between organizations thus resemble a game rooted in trust and regulated by rules, advocates of the power dependence approach rarely explain outcomes by reference to rational behavior within a game. Instead, they explain differences in outcomes in a network and variations between networks by reference to the distribution of resources and the bargaining skills of participants.

Rational choice approaches to policy networks have flourished, in particular, in the work of Renate Mayntz, Fritz Scharpf, and their colleagues at the Max-Planck Institut für Gesellschaftsforschung. Scharpf explains how policy networks operate in terms of an actor-centered institutionalism that combines rational choice with the new institutionalism. Networks are institutional settings in which public and private actors interact. They consist of rules that structure the opportunities for actors to realize their preferences. Actors adopt strategies to maximize their satisfaction and their resources within the context of such rules. It is arguable that this rational choice approach differs from the power dependence approach mainly in the extent to which it uses formal game theory to analyze and explain rule-governed networks.

Advocates of a dialectical approach to policy networks oppose the methodological individualism associated with the rational choice one. They argue that network structures and the agents within them have a mutually determining effect upon one another. At the microlevel, networks are comprised of strategically calculating subjects whose actions shape network characteristics and policy outcomes. However, the beliefs and interests of these actors are products of the macrolevel nature of the relevant networks and their contexts. These macrolevel factors are understood, in turn, to be ones of power and structure—terms that often carry a Marxist echo—rather than rules of a neutral game.

Decentered theory shifts our attention to the social construction of policy networks. It eschews the search for generality, correlations, and models found among the other approaches. Policy networks are seen as the contingent products of the actions of diverse individuals, where these individuals might act on different beliefs and understandings informed by conflicting traditions. At the microlevel, we can explore networks in terms of the behavior of a host of everyday policymakers—citizens and junior public servants as well as politicians, senior bureaucrats, and members of interest groups. At an aggregate level, we can explain the behavior of clusters of everyday policymakers by reference to the traditions and dilemmas that inform their webs of belief. Change within networks arises because people change their patterns of action in response to various dilemmas.

Networks as Reform

The study of policy networks has contributed to the transformation of contemporary governance. Networks are no longer a metaphor for changes in government or a site for theoretical debate; they have become a live issue in public-sector reform.

Some strands of network analysis emphasize the virtues of networks as a form of organization. Networks are said to be flexible and responsive: They are proposed as a response to the problems of coordination and control associated with hierarchies. They are also said to promote innovation and dynamism: They are proposed as ways of promoting competitive advantage within the new knowledge-based economy. Many elite political actors have accepted these claims on behalf of networks. At times, they have attempted to reform the public sector to encourage networks and partnerships in grand visions of holistic governance or joined-up governance. Public-sector bodies are supposed to collaborate within quality networks to better deliver services and tackle problems that cut across traditional functional divisions. They are also supposed to form partnerships with private and voluntary bodies to gain access to resources and to encourage greater diversity and flexibility in the delivery of policies.

Just as policy network analysis has inspired public-sector reforms, so it has informed strategies for managing the products of such reforms. Indeed, recognition of the ways networks constrain the state's ability to act has fueled research on how the state can manage policy networks effectively. We might distinguish between three approaches to network management in the public sector: the instrumental, the interactive, and the institutional. The instrumental approach to network management is a top-down form of steering. It concentrates on ways in which government can exercise its legitimate authority. As such, it typically presumes a governmental department to be the focal organization within a network. The central state is then to devise and impose tools that foster integration in and between policy networks and so enable the state to better attain its objectives. One problem with this instrumental approach is, of course, that it relies on government being able to exercise effective control when the whole study of networks and governance has exposed the ever-present problem of control deficits. The interactive approach to network management moves away from hierarchic modes of control. It presumes the mutual dependence of actors in networks: Collective action depends on cooperation, with goals and strategies developing out of mutual learning. Management thus requires negotiation and diplomacy; there is a need to understand others' objectives and build relations of trust with them. Chief executive officers in the public sector are urged to develop interpersonal, communication, and listening skills. This interactive approach is often costly; cooperation is time consuming, objectives can be blurred, and outcomes can be delayed. The institutional approach to network management focuses on the rules and structures against the background of which interactions take place. Management strategies seek to change relationships between actors, the distribution of resources, the rules of the game, and even values and perceptions. The aim is incremental changes in incentives and cultures. One problem with this approach is that institutions and their cultures are notoriously resistant to change.

Governance in and through networks is a complex pattern of rule, and the complexity is such that no management strategy is likely to be fully effective. Any widely accepted strategy is thus liable to appear striking only in its banality. The successful management of policy networks requires one to communicate well, to be creative, to use interpersonal skills, and to create incentives.

—*Mark Bevir*

See also Bottom-Up Approach; Collaborative Governance; Differentiated Polity; Interdependence; Network; Policy Implementation; Policy Learning; Political Exchange; Social Network Theory

Further Readings and References

Kickert, W., Klijn, E.-H., & Keppenjan, J. (Eds.). (1997). *Managing complex networks: Strategies for the public sector.* London: Sage Ltd.

Knoke, D. (1994). *Political networks: The structural perspective.* New York: Cambridge University Press.

Marin, B., & Mayntz, R. (Eds.). (1991). *Policy networks: Empirical evidence and theoretical considerations.* Frankfurt, Germany: Campus Verlag.

Marsh, D. (1998). *Comparing policy networks.* Buckingham, UK: Open University Press.

Rhodes, R. (1997). *Understanding governance.* Buckingham, UK: Open University Press.

Scharpf, F. (1997). *Games real actors play: Actor centered institutionalism in policy research.* Boulder, CO: Westview.

Thompson, G., Frances, J., Levacic, R., & Mitchell, J. (Eds.). (1991). *Markets, hierarchies, and networks: The coordination of social life.* London: Sage Ltd.

POLICY PREDICTABILITY

The policy field represents two diametrically opposite views about the predictability of policy. One approach to this topic is rooted in the belief that policy developments can be viewed as a science, where a rational process of deliberation and analysis leads one to gather information that seeks to address social, political, or economic problems. The opposite approach emphasizes the unpredictability and uncertainty of both the political processes as well as the range of actors with multiple values that are a part of the decision-making process.

The scientific approach to this topic seeks to analyze decisions and situations that produce specific policy outcomes. There are various lenses that have been used in this analysis, including attention to the stages of the policy process (usually defined as agenda setting, formulation, adoption, implementation, and evaluation), economic approaches that involve the calculation of benefits to the participants in the process (who are expected to maximize their interests), and the values and agendas of the participants in the decision-making process. These and other lenses have been employed, to respond to crisis situations and also to prevent problems and anticipate decisions.

The early stage of the policy analysis field rests on this set of assumptions. Policy analysts in the 1960s usually attempted to pursue objective and rational solutions to policy problems and find ways to employ market metaphors and public choice theories in this search. The classic model of policy making employed by rational actor policy analysts calls on individuals to identify objectives, devise alternative courses of action to achieve these objectives, predict the consequences of each alternative, and select an option that best achieves the objectives.

The alternative approach to this topic rests on a model of political reasoning that assumes that organizations and institutions make decisions in a chaotic and unplanned manner. For some, this decision-making process approaches anarchy, and these commentators are unable to specify the institutions or even the processes that lead to decisions. Others are willing to define the agendas, ideas, institutions, and processes that lead to decisions within a constantly changing environment. John Kingdon has identified three streams that interplay to produce policy outcomes—problems, policies, and politics. His analysis begins with the assumption that policy ideas come from multiple and unpredictable sources, which then are tossed into a messy and complex policy process. He notes that the three streams only come together when a "policy window" is opened, providing a limited opportunity for various participants in the three streams to present their agendas.

Deborah Stone emphasized a related approach. She notes that policy comes out of a political environment that defines people in and out of a conflict. She notes that issues are designed to attract support and to forge alliances. Like Kingdon, she noted that the relationship between ideas and alliances is constantly changing and problems are never really solved.

These two views about policy predictability have such diverse approaches and assumptions that it is extremely difficult to define a middle ground on which policy participants can engage with one another.

—*Beryl A. Radin*

See also Policy Analysis; Policy Implementation; Policy Style; Public Choice Theory

Further Readings and References

Kingdon, J. W. (1994). *Agendas, alternatives and public policies* (2nd ed.). New York: HarperCollins.
Stone, D. (1997.) *Policy paradox: The art of political decision making.* New York: W. W. Norton.

POLICY STYLE

More than two decades ago, Arnold Heidenheimer posed a fundamental question to comparative policy analysts. He noted that there are many discrete differences in the way in which nations handle the various challenges facing them, but asked to what extent can these habits and experiences be subsumed under consistent national models of policy making (and) are these models applied similarly in most policy areas or do the various sectors develop their own policy-making characteristics? These questions address the issues raised in Theodore J. Lowi's still-seminal 1964 article in which he suggested that different types of policy promote different types of political activity. He maintained that the link between policy and politics is clear and that distributive policies are patronage policies that produce a dependence relationship between the agency and clients. Regulatory policies and redistributive policies produce politics that are a great deal more conflictual and tend much more to encourage an autonomous, aggressive, and healthily competitive relationship between government and the individual.

Countries tend to regulate, say pollution, in much the same way (style) as they regulate other policy sectors. Lennart Lundqvist noted the differing regulatory styles of pollution control in the United States and Sweden, arguing that undisturbed by citizens' suits and court orders, the Swedish administrators could engage in negotiations with polluters to find an acceptable formula for policy implementation. France also differs from the United States in its regulatory style; what appears highly suspect in the United States because of susceptibility to undue influence is viewed in France as the unavoidable integration of relevant interests in the formulation of results.

These observations suggest that there is indeed a French, a German, or a British "way of doing things" that can override differences in policies.

National Policy Styles

An alternative to viewing policies as determining politics is to attempt to identify national procedural patterns. Thus, nations often develop standard operating procedures for making public policy that may have strong dampening effects on cross-sectoral differences. It is argued that we need to move our focus from decisions to systems of decisions.

Rather than address the question of the differences in the politics produced by different types of policies, it is possibly more important for the study of comparative public policy to ask whether it is possible to identify national characteristics of policy processes. If nations have a characteristic set of standard operating procedures for public policy making, what we term *policy styles,* then it might prove possible to predict how they will respond to a given problem.

Since the original formulation of the concept of policy style in 1982 there has been much debate about its utility in comparative public policy. On one hand, it is seen as not a new concept at all, but merely another variant of (vague) cultural explanations—like culture, a "residual" category. On the other hand, it is seen as a theory in the sense that it has predictive value—once a national style has been identified, one can predict outcomes in particular policy situations. At worst, it is merely "armchair generalizations," and, at best, a "systematic comparative tool." In fact, concepts are neither true nor false: They are more or less useful.

The original concept of policy style was extremely simple. Indeed, the simplicity might explain why policy style is still often used by empirical researchers. In the original typology of policy styles, it was suggested that it is useful to describe policy processes according to two main factors. The first factor is a government's approach to problem solving. Some governments have appeared to adopt an anticipatory/active attitude toward societal problems, while others have seemed to adopt an essentially reactive approach to problem solving. The second main factor is a government's relationship to other actors in the policy-making and implementing process. For example, how do governments deal with the interest groups in society? Is government accommodating and concerned about reaching a consensus with organized groups, or is it more inclined toward imposing decisions notwithstanding opposition from groups?

These two factors should at least be generally accepted as central aspects of the policy system in any one country, even if readers would see other factors of equal importance. Certainly, it would be easy to justify extending the list because selecting only two factors may fail to capture the richness, complexity, and diversity of policy processes. For example, it is argued that degrees of centralization, openness, and deliberation should be added as central features of a policy process. However, simplicity has the advantage of increasing the heuristic value of the typology in comparative terms; one should avoid a country-specific typology if it is to be used for comparative analysis. A country's policy style is therefore defined as the interaction between the government's approach to problem solving and the relationship between government and other actors in the policy process.

Such a definition enables societies to be categorized into four basic policy styles:

1. Some societies seem to be located in a category that we might see as emphasizing consensus and a reactive attitude to problem solving.

2. Others appear to be located in a category also stressing consensus but with a set of normative values that emphasize an anticipatory or active approach to problem solving.

3. Others are seemingly less concerned with consensus but see the role of the state as being rather active and willing to impose policy in the face of opposition from organized interests.

4. A fourth category is where governments are increasingly reactive rather than anticipatory in their approach to problem solving, and if any policy change is to be achieved, it has to be enforced against the resistance of at least some organized groups.

By concentrating on two main factors in the policy process, a simple basic typology of policy styles, as shown in Figure 1, produced what we term *policy styles*.

Sweden might reasonably be seen as having been (for most of the post–World War II period until the early 1990s) located in the upper-left quadrant of the figure because it placed great emphasis on policy innovation and an anticipatory style, yet emphasized the need to reach consensus. France might be seen as much more inclined toward an active policy style in which solutions are often imposed against resistance—neatly captured in the French saying that if you want to drain a swamp, you do not first consult the frogs! Great Britain, in sharp contrast, may be best characterized (for most of the post–World War II period until Margaret Thatcher's election in 1979) as having a policy style that has placed great emphasis on bargaining in the context of a reactive approach to problem solving. Germany, in the postwar period, also

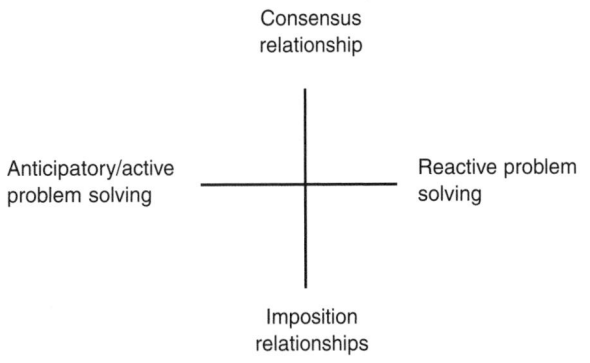

Figure 1   National Policy Styles

Source: Richardson, J. (Ed.). (1982). *Policy styles in Western Europe* (Chap. 1). London: Allen and Unwin. Reprinted with permission.

emphasized an active policy style to be achieved through consensus. In the late 1970s, however, policy became more reactive, as the active policy style posed problems to consensus building, especially in the energy sector.

Thus, the policy style concept does not imply total stability of standard operating procedures, although it was assumed that styles were strongly embedded and "sticky." However, under certain circumstances, policy could be determined via a different style if necessary. More importantly, under certain circumstances, the predominant national policy style might itself change over time. As pressures for more participation developed from the mid-1960s onward, and as more interest groups emerged, there seemed to have been a tendency for most societies to be increasingly reactive rather than anticipatory and for policy change to be blocked because of the difficulty of reaching consensus. As the problems of reaching consensus increased, so-called "reform deficits" developed. Essentially, the gradual shift toward a more reactive policy style eventually weakened the capacity of governments as problem solving institutions. At various times, governments decided to tackle some of these reform deficits and to adopt a more impositional policy style. In Europe, Margaret Thatcher's administration was the classic example of a shift in policy style. The irony of her government was that it was elected on a slogan of having less government but became one of the most interventionist governments of the postwar period, often imposing tough reforms on hitherto powerful interests. Other countries seemed to follow suit sooner or later.

Conclusion

The history of the policy style concept has been rather odd. It was certainly simple indeed, hence the jibe that is was merely armchair generalizations. Yet it had a degree of plausibility about it. As travelers, we do know that nations have easily recognized "styles" of various kinds, such as architecture, food, and clothing. Looking back, the criticized simplicity of policy style perhaps was what nowadays is often seen as a virtue. To use the current fashionable jargon, it was parsimonious. It was

also flexible enough to become a generic concept, which allowed researchers to select their own set of variables, from which a national style could be constructed. Thus, it is not uncommon for authors to use the term *policy style* without any reference to the original work. For example, Colin Bennett's excellent review of the policy convergence literature floats the idea that, in addition to the convergence of actual policies, there might be a convergence of policy style, a more diffuse notion signifying the process by which policy responses are formulated (consensual or conflictual, incremental or rational, anticipatory or reactive, corporatist or pluralist, etc.). His use of policy style is close to the original formulation, without actually citing it. Other authors have found the basic concept of style useful, but use different variables to capture the essence of the style and apply it to particular sectors, such as legal regulation. We leave it to the reader to decide whether the enduring attraction of the policy style concept is likely to be fatal or whether we are likely to see bigger and better versions of policy style in the future.

—*Jeremy Richardson*

See also Policy Implementation; Policy Learning; Policy Predictability; Policy Transfer

Further Readings and References

Bennett, C. J. (1991). Review article: What is policy convergence and what causes it? *British Journal of Political Science, 21,* 215–233.

Feick, J. (1990). L'analyse comparative des politiques publiques: un chemin vers l'integration des résultats? [Comparative analysis of public politics: A way toward the integration of the outcome?]. *L'annee sociologique, 40,* 179–225.

Freeman, G. P. (1985). National styles and policy sectors: Explaining structured variation. *Journal of Public Policy, 5,* 467–496.

Hayward, J. (1982). Mobilising private interests in the service of public ambitions: The salient elements of the dual French policy style? In J. Richardson (Ed.), *Policy styles in Western Europe* (pp. 111–140). London: Allen and Unwin.

Lowi, T. (1964). American business, public policy, case studies and political theory. *World Politics, 16*(4), 677–715.

Lundqvist, L. (1980). *The hare and the tortoise: Clean air policies in the United States and Sweden.* Ann Arbor: University of Michigan Press.

Richardson, J. (Ed.). (1982). *Policy styles in Western Europe.* London: Allen and Unwin.

Van Waarden, F. (1997). Persistence of national policy styles: A study of their institutional foundations. In B. Unger & F. Van Waarden (Eds.), *Convergence or diversity? Internationalisation and economic policy response* (pp. 333–372). Aldershot, UK: Averbury.

POLICY TRANSFER

The term *policy transfer* covers processes through which the framework of political, institutional, and cognitive actions are used or readjusted for the development of action frameworks within other political systems, often foreign.

Analysis in terms of policy transfer is increasingly observed as a matter of analysis and discussion at the level of studies on public policies, international relations, as well as at the level of administrative and legal spheres. A model of public action and a concept for analysis, today policy transfer is a more highly relevant object of analysis dealing with major questions such as globalization and convergence.

A Framework for Analyzing a Variety of Processes

A large number of terms are used to qualify processes of transfer: policy transfer, lesson drawing, legal transplantation, policy learning, and institutional transfer, to name a few. If each of these expressions represents a particular analytical approach, each emphasizing different institutional issues, actors, or various degrees of obligations, they all aim to describe the same phenomenon and participate in the understanding of various fields of governance. From these different perspectives it is possible to determine some elements of definition, each of which are potential research subjects.

First, it is essential not to reduce policy transfer only to ideas or political objectives, but to also to consider the exchange of instruments, practices, and programs of governance between "exporter" and "importer" systems.

Second, the dynamics of transfer cover several forms: direct and total transfer of a model, a process of opening up to an external idea, and hybridization of various models.

Third, policy transfers can be voluntary, forced, or totally imposed. These different mechanisms of legal obligation or imposition are essential to the understanding of such processes.

Finally, the link between policy transfer and success or failure represents an important dimension. Taking into account the cases where the transfer of solutions or models failed also enables one to reveal the transfer mechanisms by focusing particularly upon factors that facilitate or block transfer.

One of the main interests of this concept is certainly its flexibility, which allows research to describe a wide range of phenomena. Through analyzing the various degrees and methods of transfer, this concept enables one to understand the mixtures present in certain models. Concerning the question of mechanisms of obligation, it can also establish a continuum between cases where the model is wanted and cases where the model is imposed from outside.

The Agents: Policy Transfer and Organizational Analysis

Understanding the processes of policy transfer means retracing the logical progression (cognitive interactions) and the social progression (social interactions) of recipes exchange and policy-making ideas. The objective is to question the manner in which exchanges or the circulation of some political solutions occurs between different systems or levels of action.

The study of actors, their strategies, and their resources provides an essential tool of understanding. Agents participate in processes of construction, legitimation, and distribution, which lie at the origin of the dynamics of import-export. In the case of social policies transfer between the United States and Great Britain (in the mid-1980s), several types of facilitating factors were identified. If the existence of a common language and a shared ideology constitute facilitating factors, they are not sufficient to explain the dynamics of exchange. Personal relations and the essential role played by some think tanks or policy entrepreneurs showed the importance of social interactions.

International actors or national representatives circulate different models of public action between institutions and therefore spread values and discourse that open the way to transfers.

Literature that studies transfers strongly insists on the necessity of making precise sociological analyses of the actors and the role of socialization (regional, international institutions, political parties, governmental or nongovernmental institutions, pressure groups). Such research enables one to understand the mechanisms of policy making and why and how some systems come to be set up as models. Taking into account the actors' representations and perceptions also plays an important role both to explain policy formulation and to study the results of policy transfer (success or failure). By studying the methods and instruments that support the exchange of ideas and information, it is possible to show the manner in which the promotion of a common language occurs that leads to the emergence of common definitions of policy-making's meaning.

Finally, policy transfer can raise two questions about current governance that constitute important research areas based on this concept: convergence and the technicity of policy making.

Any transfer process leads to adjustment and adaptation phenomena, depending on the institutional and political configurations where it is applied. Policy transfer does not necessarily imply convergence between exporter and importer systems. In some cases, renationalization processes occur where the transferred model is influenced by the national environment and readjusted accordingly, because of reception, translation, and appropriation mechanisms. This question also introduces the issue of domination between policy systems.

Through the processes of policy transfer, it is also possible to identify a phenomenon of policy-making's depoliticization. Instrumentalization of governance's categories can lead to a shifting from a political approach to a highly technical approach. The consequence of this trend is to evacuate the divergent political interests that could constitute obstacles to transfer. Processes of policy transfer thus contribute to a logic of rationalization of public action, thereby meeting the expectations of what many practitioners qualify as good governance.

—*Antoine Mégie*

See also Benchmarking; Good Governance; Policy Implementation; Policy Learning; Policy Style

Further Readings and References

De Jong, M., Lalenis, K., & Mamadouh, V. (2002). *The theory and practice of institutional transplantation: Experiences with the transfer of policy institutions.* Boston: Kluwer Academic.

Dolowitz, D. (2000). *Policy transfer and British social policy: Learning from the USA?* Buckingham, UK: Open University Press.

Rose, R. (1993). *Lesson-drawing in public policy.* Chatham, NJ: Chatham House.

POLITICAL BUSINESS CYCLE

Political business cycle generally refers to the fluctuation of economic activity that results from an external intervention of political actors. Mainly, it is used to describe the stimulation of the economy just prior to an election in order to improve prospects of the incumbent government getting reelected.

It is assumed that expansionary monetary and fiscal policies have politically popular consequences in the short run, such as falling unemployment, economic growth, and benefits from government spending on public services. However, the same policies, especially if pursued to excess, are found to have unpleasant consequences in the long term, such as accelerating inflation and damaging the foreign trade balance. Thus, they can harm the long-term growth potential of the economy. Thought to be rational actors with short-term horizons of calculation, the politicians will pursue popular expansionary monetary and fiscal policies immediately before an election. However, being aware of adverse effects of expansionary policies, they will not intend to keep these measures after they get elected. Thus, after the election is over, the politicians will reverse course, which may include cutting spending, slowing the growth of money supply, and allowing interest rates to rise. As a result, the regular holding of elections will produce cyclical fluctuation of economic activity because of recurring patterns of government stimulus and restraint in order to induce an artificial boom in the election time.

Politicians' rational preference of short-term political concerns over macroeconomic calculation in economic policymaking is assumed to have consequences on the general monetary and fiscal policy setting as well. The politicians will try to drive up the natural or equilibrium rate of employment. Thus, the rate of inflation and interest rates will be higher than they need to be.

Likewise, there is a political cycle found in welfare regimes. Accordingly, the state officials will tend to make the welfare system more generous in the pre-election period, restoring restraint and incentives to work afterward.

Moreover, nondemocratic leaders also have incentives to allocate budgets and credits to their strategic partners. But without regular elections, they will have few reasons to engage in opportunistic manipulations of fiscal or monetary policies. However, their time horizons may be shortened by immediate threats to survival, such as war. In general, theorists of the political business cycle believe that democratic politicians will manage monetary and fiscal policy less responsibly than the nondemocratic leaders or politicians in the regimes with less political competition.

Explaining the Political Business Cycle

The theories of political business cycle are based on several assumptions. First, it is generally agreed by the economists that there is a short-term trade-off between the level of utilization and employment in the economy and the rate of inflation. Second, it is assumed that politicians are rational actors, prioritizing their short-term political objectives. In the run-up to elections, they will trade inflation for lower levels of unemployment. Third, the people referring to the political business cycle often think that there is a single best policy solution in a given situation that is in the general interest. This solution leads to a natural equilibrium between inflation and unemployment. Very often, the understanding of such equilibrium is counterinflational.

There are two streams of theories in the political business cycle literature. First, partisan theories stress the difference of fiscal and monetary preferences between parties. While Leftist parties are expected to boost real economic activity (employment), the Rightist parties are thought to focus on fighting inflation. Second, the political business cycle models concentrate on the manipulation of policy instruments by politicians who seek to get reelected.

There are four basic models of the political business cycle found in recent scholarly discourse: William D. Nordhaus's model of the political business cycle; the model of a rational political business cycle of Torsten Persson and Guido Tabellini; Douglas Hibbs's partisan theory; and Alberto Alesina's rational partisan theory. Despite numerous attempts to establish their existence, the empirical evidence of political business cycles remains rather equivocal.

Political Business Cycle, Institutional Design, and Depoliticization of Monetary Policy

According to the theorists of political business cycle, the political competition systematically affects fiscal and monetary policies in a way that is adverse to the general economic well-being. Governments have policy preferences that are inconsistent with the needs of the economy; therefore, they cannot be trusted to deliver appropriate monetary and fiscal policy. If policy credibility is to be achieved, the public authorities need to be able to make a monetary and fiscal precommitment independently of political competition. This entails an institutionally guaranteed depoliticization of monetary policy. This can be achieved by an independent central bank constitutionally mandated to deliver a specific inflation target. This is assumed to deliver monetary and fiscal policies appropriate to the conjuncture, for example keeping a natural rate of unemployment. Independent central banks have been relatively rare until the past decade. More recently, advanced capitalist states have tended to increase the autonomy of the central bank and depoliticize monetary policy. This has also become an integral part of the developmental panacea of the Washington Consensus.

The trend of depoliticizing monetary policy by making central banks independent of political struggle raises serious concerns about public accountability of respective policymakers. Some people think that this may pose a threat to democracy as it limits the scope of policy that can be pursued by publicly accountable politicians.

—*Jan Drahokoupil*

See also Business Cycle; Keynesianism; Monetary Policy; State; State-Society Relations; Unemployment; Washington Consensus

Further Readings and References

Alesina, A. (1992). *Political models of macroeconomic policy and fiscal reforms*. Washington, DC: Country Economics Department, World Bank.

Gärtner, M. (1994). The quest for political cycles in OECD economies. *European Journal of Political Economy, 10*, 427–440.

Gasiorowski, M. J. (2000). Democracy and macroeconomic performance in underdeveloped countries: An empirical analysis. *Comparative Political Studies, 33*, 319–349.

Hibbs, D. A. (1992). Partisan theory after fifteen years. *European Journal of Political Economy, 8*, 361–373.

Nordhaus, W. (1975). The political business cycle. *Review of Economic Studies, 42*(2), 169–190.

POLITICAL COMMUNICATION

Political communication is concerned with the role of communication within the political process. Consequently, the development of new forms of mass media at the turn of the twentieth century foreshadowed significant changes in the study and practice of this phenomenon. This was also the period when there was significant growth in adult literacy as well as a major expansion of the electoral franchise among the most advanced industrial societies. The arrival of (near) universal suffrage alerted political elites to the limitations of their traditional interpersonal forms of address and of the increasing need for them to be able to address a much enlarged, more heterogeneous public. Political communication through different media then became the norm for campaigns that increasing went beyond simply trying to inform or publicize an issue or candidature to seeking to engage and persuade a mass audience.

Pioneering theorists with an interest in political communication recognized that sometimes emotive imagery would increasingly become prominent in what passed for public debate as competing politicians particularly sought to attract the attention and support of the large numbers of new voters. The resulting forms of address were far removed from the kind of rational debate that many critical theorists argue is a central component of a healthy functioning public sphere. The debasement and "refeudalization" of the latter took place with the rapid growth of commercially driven forms of communication, such as advertising and public relations.

Contemporary public intellectuals active in interwar politics were among those keen to welcome and explore the potential interplay between mass media and mass democracy. It is no coincidence that the 1920s saw the publication of important books with major relevance to the development of strategic communication including Charles Higham's on advertising and Walter Lippmann's treatise on public opinion, which promoted the desirability of elites manufacturing consent. Similar sentiments underpinned Edward Bernays's popularization of the concept and practice of public relations as a means of influencing mass opinion through the solicitation of favorable coverage from a range of news media outlets with large audiences.

Lippmann and his fellow practitioners and theorists of political communication held to patrician notions of an essentially benevolent party and media elites managing debate and influencing the popular will. Their complacency was seriously challenged by the destruction of many European democracies during the

1930s. The Nazi takeover, in particular, was conceived of as a response to economic and civil crises but also as the result of a concerted campaign that demonstrated the power of mass propaganda. The perceived success of this debauched strategy contributed to a belief in the "hypodermic needle" model, which suggested an influential media coexisted with a largely passive, suggestible audience. The idea of this strong effect was reinforced by other, more-discreet and less-disturbing incidents, such as Orson Welles's notorious 1938 broadcast of *War of the Worlds,* in which he caused panic in the rural Midwest with his all-too-vivid radio dramatization.

The strong effects model encouraged the pioneering work of early political communication scholarship involving Harold Lasswell and his colleagues at the Institute of Propaganda Analysis. Their attempt to develop typologies of the different kinds of manipulative activity was superseded by Paul Lazarsfeld and others' attempts at researching the relationship between media consumption and voter participation. These and other studies led to the forging of an influential limited effects consensus that argued the primary influence of the media over voters was reinforcement not change.

The inherent difficulties in accounting for the impact or not of different forms of political communication shaped postwar research and led to the flourishing of other debates as to the relationship between politicians, voters, and media. Most obviously, there were attempts to conceptualize a more sophisticated understanding of how audiences actually read, watched, and listened to politics and how they perceived and responded to events and personalities through their exposure to news coverage, campaigns, or other messages. Consequently, there were moves to identify other less-general effects and how different groups of citizens and voters responded to communications and especially those tailored to them by electoral strategists. Some of this work came to the plausible conclusion that those with less formal education and little interest in politics, but who were also above-average media consumers (especially of television) were more susceptible to being influenced by campaigning.

A discernible trend among researchers toward going beyond the "voter persuasion paradigm" led to the revisiting of debates begun in earnest by Lippmann and others during the interwar years as to the strategic role and function of political communication in a democracy. Much work was devoted to understanding how media and campaigns attempted to set the agenda or frame issues in a way that was presumed to have an impact on public understanding. Unlike other subjects, these functions were perceived to be important because for many citizens politics was still a remote topic of only periodic interest to them.

Neoliberalism has had an obvious impact on the public and private sphere if judged by the rise of rapacious consumerism and the significant growth in the size and reach of the marketing industry. Democratic debate has not been immune to these trends, and there has been a notable marketization of political communication apparent in the excessive attention now devoted to electoral advertisers (image makers), public relations consultants (spin doctors), and opinion researchers (pollsters). Although each of these actors has long played a role in various campaigns, the growing influence of these electoral professionals toward the end of the twentieth century had a major impact on the organization of parties, the state, and interest groups. It is then no coincidence that the most image-aware and marketing-conscious creations, such as the New Democrats and New Labour, were born out of a response to defeats by New Right opponents who pioneered the more integrated use of the communication techniques that they eventually copied. Central to this approach is an excessive focus on a few target voters at the expense of all others, which helps resolve the apparent paradox as to why turnouts are falling in spite of the use of the most supposedly professional political communications.

—*Dominic Wring*

See also Communication; Communicative Action; Interpretive Theory; Media Freedom; Translation

Further Readings and References

Bernays, E. L. (1923). *Crystallizing public opinion.* New York: Boni and Liveright.

Corner, J., & Pels, D. (Eds.). (2003). *Media and the restyling of politics.* London: Sage Ltd.

Deacon, D. (2003). Holism, communion and conversion. *Media Culture & Society, 25,* 209–231.

Higham, C. (1925). *Advertising, its use and abuse.* New York: H. Holt.

Kaid, L. L. (Ed.). (2004). *Handbook of political communication research.* Mahwah, NJ: Lawrence Erlbaum.

Lasswell, H. D., & Kaplan, A. (1950). *Power and society.* New Haven, CT: Yale University Press.

Lazarsfeld, P. F., Berelson, B., & Gaudet, H. (1944). *The people's choice.* New York: Knopf.

Lippmann, W. (1922). *Public opinion.* New York: Macmillan.

Negrine, R. (1996). *The communication of politics.* London: Sage Ltd.

Sproule, M. J. (1997). *Propaganda and democracy.* Cambridge, UK: Cambridge University Press.

POLITICAL ECONOMY

Political economy has never been more central, nor has it been seen to be more central, to the nature and trajectory of the reform of governance (at whatever level) than it is today. That this is so is due largely to the influence of a set of powerful processes that have tended simply to be termed *globalization.* Globalization, however understood, is invariably seen to pose significant governance challenges. These relate to the need for and nature of institutions of governance at the international level capable of regulating and steering the process of globalization itself just as much as they do to the imperatives unleashed at the domestic and other levels by the largely untamed and unguided process of globalization. In this way, debates about the reform of existing institutions of governance and about the need to develop genuinely new transnational institutions of governance are linked—by a common concern to negotiate and, to some extent, to manage the process of globalization. Political economy lies at the heart of these debates; indeed, the political economy of governance has largely become synonymous with these debates. For, in so far as globalization is seen to unleash a powerful set of constraints on policy-making latitude and autonomy at the regional, domestic, and local levels, these constraints are principally seen to be economic in nature. Similarly,

in so far as globalization is seen to call forth the need for new and genuinely transnational institutions of governance, this is largely because of the anticipated environmental and political consequences of an unconstrained global market.

Given this, it is perhaps unremarkable that there is no topic in the contemporary literature on governance, public administration, and public policy more contested or controversial than the impact of globalization. The balance of opinion would certainly suggest that there is a strong *prima facie* case for seeing globalization and the capacity for governance itself as antagonistic—the extent of globalization, for many, being an index of the retrenchment of public policy, at least at the national level. A variety of more or less plausible mechanisms for this tension between globalization and the public nature of governance can be pointed to. In particular, globalization is seen to challenge the deliberative nature of (domestic) public policy by summoning a series of nonnegotiable, external, and largely economic imperatives that must be appeased in a technically proficient manner if good economic performance is to be maintained, whatever the cost in terms of democratic accountability. Chief among these is that of competitiveness. The reform of governance institutions is now seen to be circumscribed and increasingly driven directly by considerations of competitiveness. In an era of ever-more-intense global competition, each and every reform of an institution of governance must either arise directly out of a consideration of the imperatives of competitiveness or be exposed to an exacting audit in terms of its potential contribution to such competitiveness. It is only if potential reforms to governance institutions can be demonstrated as competitiveness enhancing or, at worst, neutral with respect to competitiveness that they can seriously be contemplated. Is it any wonder that Philip G. Cerny should talk of the emergence of a competition state in place of the welfare state of the postwar period?

Similarly, globalization is seen as the enemy of domestic governance, public or otherwise, in the sense that it is seen to dictate policy choices while itself being beyond the capacity of domestic political actors to control. Yet none of this is uncontested. In this overview of the political economy of contemporary governance, the aim is to unpack the notion of globalization, considering the diverse ways in which globalization might be seen as antithetical to public governance before turning to a review of the empirical evidence and the debate that it has generated. The conclusion suggests that although globalization and public governance can be seen as antithetical in a variety of respects, this is less a consequence of the direct and necessary constraints imposed by the political economy of globalization than it is a consequence of more political and contingent factors. I also suggest that if globalization is antithetical to governance, public governance especially, then this is only at the domestic level; arguably it merely reinforces the need for effective and democratic governance at the transnational level. If it is problematic or at least premature to suggest that the public and democratic character of domestic governance is a casualty of globalization, it is no less problematic to overlook the opportunities and need for governance at the transnational level that globalization generates.

In most conventional treatments, globalization and public governance at the domestic level are counterposed. Invariably, in such accounts, globalization is seen to intensify the competitive struggle among nations for global market share, driving states to subordinate public policy considerations to economic imperatives, thereby exposing their public sectors to an exacting "competitive audit." Yet, however familiar, this is by no means the only mechanism by which globalization might be seen as in tension with domestic public governance. Indeed, at least four rather different sources of such tension might be identified:

1. Globalization is held to necessitate a certain privatization and technicization of governance, rendering it less publicly accountable. Here, it is the distinctly public character of domestic governance that is potentially seen as a casualty of globalization. By virtue of time-space compression and the complex interdependencies that ensue, globalization is seen to render policy deliberations so technical and involved as to necessitate significant changes in the conduct—and notably the legitimation—of public policy. In the face

of the speculative dynamics unleashed by financial market integration, for instance, it is argued that monetary policy must be removed from political control and rendered both predictable and rules bounded rather than discretionary. Globalization, and the complexities and interdependencies that are seen to characterize it, are here associated with powerful tendencies to the depoliticization, privatization, and technicization of macroeconomic governance. If valid, this is an important development, for it implies that in a context of globalization, such institutions cannot be held to account publicly (and, hence, democratically) to the extent to which we have become accustomed. Such claims rest on the notion of a significant and perhaps growing trade-off, in a context characterized by complex interdependencies, between effectiveness and accountability in public policy, and that we should resolve any such trade-off in terms of the former. It is suggestive, moreover, of a potentially troubling explanation for the growing and widely identified lack of trust in public officials and associated discontent and disengagement with formal politics.

2. Globalization is seen to necessitate an internalization by the state of the preferences of capital and an associated squeezing of the "fiscal space" for public policy. We move from governance for the people to governance for accumulation. This is perhaps the most conventional sense in which globalization is seen to be antithetical to public policy. As will be discussed in more detail, the mechanism invoked here is relatively simple. Globalization is treated as synonymous with the mobility of capital. In order to retain high levels of investment, on which economic growth and high levels of employment are predicated, states must increasingly provide an investment climate conducive to profit maximization or, more to the point, conducive to the anticipation by potential investors of profit maximization. Their regimes of governance must, in short, internalize the preferences of capital. Such preferences are conventionally assumed to be, for a lightly regulated marketplace, relatively free from public policy interventions and characterized by low levels of taxation. The mobility of capital is seen,

both directly and indirectly, to exert strong downward pressures on public policy—directly, because globalization enhances the effective bargaining power of capital and capital is seen to exert a strong preference for market mechanisms, as opposed to public regulation; and indirectly, because globalization effectively squeezes the fiscal base out of which public policy is funded.

3. More generally, globalization is seen to diminish the capacity for governance of the nation-state, resulting in a displacement of functions from public to quasi-public bodies (such as independent central banks) and from national to transnational institutions (such as those associated with the process of European integration and, more obviously, global institutions such as the IMF, the WTO, and the World Bank). Clearly this third sense in which globalization and governance capacity at the national level are seen to be antithetical is not unrelated to the points already discussed—indeed the displacement of functions from public to quasi-public bodies almost directly parallels the privatization and technicization of economic governance previously discussed. Yet the emphasis is, again, slightly different. Here commentators highlight what they identify as an increasing disparity between the level at which policy problems emerge and must effectively be dealt with and the still predominantly national/domestic character of the institutions from which such responses are initially sought. In short, they note, in a context of globalization, the nation-state's increasing lack of fitness for purpose. Of course, to identify a proliferation of global/transnational problems that the nation-state is not well placed to deal with is not necessarily to point to a shortfall in governance capacity, especially if the global/transnational policy-making capacity is enhanced in parallel with the proliferation of problems at this level. Yet, it is the gap between the pace at which the problems proliferate and the governance capacity increases that prompts contemporary concerns. Invariably, it seems, global problems have failed to prompt coordinated global solutions—environmental degradation providing an ever-more-alarming case in point. As this already serves to indicate, many of our most pressing contemporary challenges are to devise effective and democratic institutions of global governance—an effective policy-making capacity for dealing with problems of global public policy.

4. Globalization is seen as driving a process of convergence, thereby diminishing both variations between states in public policy and the significance of variations in public policy as variables in the explanation of comparative performance. Questions of convergence, divergence, or continued diversity have provided a key focus for students of governance in an era of globalization, provoking considerable controversy. In most conventional accounts, for reasons already discussed, globalization is seen to promote convergence, as governance regimes have been revised to internalize the preferences of capital. Yet in recent years, a rather more institutionally differentiated view has developed. This so-called varieties of capitalism perspective predicts dual rather than simple convergence. It sees globalization as an agent of convergence, but suggests that it is likely to have different impacts on coordinated and liberal market economies, reinforcing rather than undermining their distinctiveness. Yet even in this more subtle, differentiated, and increasingly influential perspective, globalization heavily circumscribes the space for and nature of governance regimes. In liberal market economies, for instance, it essentially imposes market-conforming governance, raising questions again about the extent to which public policy can be held publicly and democratically accountable.

As this already serves to indicate, the dominant themes in the existing literature all point to an adversarial relationship between globalization and governance—in which the former is seen to select strongly for the depoliticization, privatization, and technicization of the latter. Yet before rushing to endorse such a pessimistic conclusion, it is important to acknowledge that most of the themes of the literature already discussed rest on strong assumptions as to the nature, extent, and consequences of globalization. Whether acknowledged as such, these are unavoidably empirical claims and, moreover, empirical claims that do not always stand up to a close consideration of the available evidence.

Indeed, although the contemporary period is invariably referred to as one of globalization, and although globalization is invariably seen as placing stringent constraints on the size of the public sector, in aggregate terms, states consume a larger share of global GDP than at any previous point in their history. Of course, such evidence is not in itself sufficient to refute the globalization thesis, nor is it especially difficult to see how the globalization thesis might accommodate such ostensibly unsupportive data. Yet it certainly suggests the importance of a rather more detailed consideration of the empirical evidence than characterizes much (though by no means all) of the current literature. The frequently hyperbolic nature of much of the globalization debate and its tendency to extrapolate wildly from anecdotal illustrations where empirical evidence is appealed to at all necessitates a more thorough empirical review.

The Impact of Globalization

In the political economy of governance, globalization is seen to summon four separate sources of external imperatives. Each is seen to have significant governance implications.

1. Trade—the free mobility of goods leads to pressures to enhance economic competitiveness.

2. Foreign direct investment—the free mobility of investment capital (and, in many accounts, already-invested capital) leads to pressures to enhance and retain "locational competitiveness."

3. Finance—the free mobility of virtual or digital capital leads to an essentially constant audit by international investors of monetary and fiscal policies and the institutions (for instance, independent central banks) responsible for their delivery.

4. Environment and the global commons—the mobility of pollutants and the global nature of risks with high consequences leads to the need to pool sovereignty in institutions of effective global governance.

In what follows, each mechanism is considered in assessing the plausibility of the assumptions and the evidential basis for both the assumptions and the consequences inferred from them to discern the likely consequences for public policy arising from each.

Trade Integration

Most accounts of the consequences for economic governance of globalization start from a consideration of trade integration. Pointing to a near exponential rise in openness (conventionally expressed in terms of imports plus exports as a share of gross domestic product, GDP) since the 1960s, they seek to derive a series of competitive imperatives for domestic economic governance from heightened trade integration.

In rather stylized terms, such accounts frequently counterpose the supposedly closed national economies of the advanced liberal democracies until the 1960s and 1970s with the open integrated world economy that, they suggest, has developed subsequently. In the former, closed national economic world, competitiveness is of no great consequence, because only a relatively small proportion of GDP is traded and domestic consumption can be assumed to be satisfied by domestic production, thereby facilitating a series of domestic management techniques such as Keynesianism.

Under open economy conditions, things look different. Keynesianism is no longer effective because the injection of demand into the domestic economy will only serve to boost imports, worsening the trade balance. More significant, domestic economic growth is now predicated upon success in international markets—in other words, competitiveness. Competitiveness, moreover, is frequently understood in rather narrow and cost-centered terms—the capacity to produce, distribute, and ultimately sell a given commodity in international markets for less than the competition. Consequently the imperatives of competitiveness that (global) trade integration brings tend to be seen in terms of cost-saving measures—the elimination of burdensome regulations, the reduction in nonwage labor costs (such as those out of which welfare states are funded), and the exertion of downward pressure on labor costs (by, for instance, scaling back workers' bargaining power and removing the institutional settings in which it might be exercised).

The mechanism is a clear one, lubricated by the heightened mobility of goods in a more globally integrated world market (an improvement in the aggregate terms of trade within the world economy).

Yet, compelling and influential though it is, the necessity of the competitiveness-enhancing, cost-saving "race to the bottom" that it predicts is not so easily reconciled with the empirical evidence. As already noted, state-related activity continues to account for a high and, in fact, rising share of global GDP, suggesting at minimum that in the face of such competitive imperatives public institutions funded out of taxation receipts have proved remarkably resilient. Moreover, as a growing body of literature testifies, there is a positive and, indeed, strengthening relationship between public spending and economic openness—the most open economies in the world are also those, in statistical terms, with the largest public sectors. That historical relationship shows no signs of being eroded. Finally, however high contemporary levels of trade integration are, a significant body of scholarship suggests that such levels are by no means unprecedented. Indeed, it suggests there is still some way to go before pre–World War I figures of trade integration, at least for the world's leading economies, are exceeded.

The empirical evidence also suggests a number of reasons why the anticipated deregulatory "race to the bottom" is, at best, a simplifying distortion of a far more complex reality. First, as already noted, markets, not least those for traded goods, are far from perfectly integrated—and, on balance, distortions from perfect market integration tend to serve to protect the most advanced and affluent economies (those with the largest public sectors) from competitive undercutting. Second, it is only a relatively small proportion of potentially tradable commodities whose cost is determined to a significant extent by direct labor costs and indirect nonwage labor costs (such as payroll taxes). Consequently, the competitive undercutting predicted in the globalization thesis, even though it certainly goes on, is more confined to certain sectors of the world market than the model assumes. Third, to a considerable extent, the advanced capitalist economies compete less in terms of cost than they do in terms of the distinct qualities of the goods they export. And quality competitiveness, in contrast to cost competitiveness, is often enhanced and supported by high levels of public spending and quite interventionist regimes of economic and industrial governance.

Fourth, as already noted, regionalization tendencies that are often ignored in the overly general literature on globalization may significantly alter the real terms of competition that economies face, giving rise to rather different competitive dynamics to those assumed to drive a deregulatory race to the bottom.

Foreign Direct Investment

Scarcely less significant in accounts of the consequences for economic governance of globalization is the role of foreign direct investment and the (assumed) mobility of international investors. The significant, indeed at times exponential, growth in both the accumulated stock of invested foreign capital (total fixed capital formation) and fresh foreign direct investment is seen, in conventional accounts of globalization, to impose upon domestic governance regimes a series of additional competitive imperatives. Here, it is not so much the competitiveness of the domestic economy *qua* domestic economy that is the focus of attention (important though this is), but the "locational competitiveness" of the economy as a site for new or continued investment.

The picture created is of potentially footloose and fancy-free investors choosing from a vast array of potential investment locations the one that offers the best anticipated return on their investment—that is, until a new and better opportunity arises elsewhere. In order to attract investors in the first place, then, governance regimes must essentially internalize and approximate as closely as possible the preferences of mobile capital. Those preferences, in turn, are anticipated to be for attractive investment incentives at the point of initial investment, flexible labor markets, low rates of corporate taxation, a flexible regulatory regime, and lax environmental standards. Good governance is assumed to be minimal governance.

Equally intuitive though such a view is, it is again at some considerable odds with the available empirical evidence. A number of points might again be noted. First, the mobility of invested capital is grossly exaggerated in such stylized accounts that invariably discount the costs borne by investors of carrying through an "exit" threat to the point of disinvestment. Having invested and often built a plant in a particular economy, foreign direct investors acquire a variety of generally irredeemable sunk costs. For, to relocate production is, essentially, to sacrifice the lion's share of the capital value of the initial investment (assuming no new investor is prepared to take the place of the old), while bearing the significant costs of building and equipping a new plant, to say nothing of the intervening period of nonproduction. For this reason, while it may well be rational for hypothetically mobile investors to threaten "exit" whenever they wish to bargain for concessions or changes in policy from their host government, it is seldom in their interests to exercise their hypothetical mobility, even in the absence of such concessions. This is presumably why the much-vaunted exit option is, in fact, rather less frequently exercised than the model of free capital mobility would predict. Second, there is quite simply no inverse relationship, such as the model would lead us to anticipate, between volumes of inbound foreign direct investment and levels of corporate taxation, environmental and labor-market regulations, generosity of welfare benefits, or state expenditure as a share of GDP. This would merely seem to underline the point of the previous section that competitive advantage is not necessarily secured by cost-minimization strategies. Finally, as is again now well documented, the vast majority of the world's outward foreign direct investment (over ninety percent between 1980 and 1995) is sourced from within the so-called triad (North America, Europe, and Pacific Asia) and the vast majority (between seventy-five and eighty percent over the same period) of inward foreign direct investment is invested within the triad. This staggering concentration of foreign direct investment is hardly consistent with the predictions of the simple globalization model, a point reinforced by the observation that the most significant factor determining investment location is not the availability of investment incentives but geographical proximity and access to a sizable market.

Financial Market Integration

The third in the triumvirate of sources of external economic constraints on economic governance comes from the anticipated consequences of financial market integration. Once again, the assumption in much of the literature is of perfectly clearing and fully integrated global markets—here, financial markets, with near instantaneous investment decisions lubricated by new digital technologies are operating in an effectively postgeographical environment. In such a context, vast financial resources can be unleashed by institutional investors in speculative attacks on the currencies of states incurring the investors' displeasure. The forcible ejection of the British pound from the European Monetary System (EMS) in 1992 at the hands of George Soros and others is a classic case in point. Within such models, portfolio investors, in particular, are seen to display a clear interest in, and preference for, strong and stable currencies backed both by implacable independent central banks with hawkish anti-inflationary credentials and governments wedded in theory and in practice to fiscal moderation and prudence. Any departure from this new financial orthodoxy, it is assumed, will precipitate a flurry of speculation against the currency and a hemorrhaging of investment from assets denominated in that currency.

Once again, this is a familiar and intuitively plausible proposition that would seem to be borne out by a series of high-profile speculative flurries against rogue governments in recent decades. It is, however, an empirical claim and one that a growing body of scholarship reveals to be considerably at odds with the empirical evidence. For capital markets do not seem to be as perfectly integrated as the globalization literature invariably assumes. In particular, the anticipated convergence in interest rates, which one would expect from a fully integrated global capital market is simply not exhibited. Moreover, financial integration has also failed to produce the anticipated divergence between rates of domestic savings and rates of domestic investment, which one would expect in a fully integrated global capital market—the so-called Feldstein-Horioka puzzle, as conceived by Martin Feldstein and Charles Horioka in 1980. Finally, though the liberalization of financial markets has certainly increased the speed, severity, and significance of investors' reactions to government policy, capital market participants appear far less discriminating or well informed in their political risk assessment than is conventionally assumed. Consequently, policy makers may retain more autonomy than is widely accepted. Speculative dynamics are, in fact, rarely unleashed against currencies and, at least as far as the advanced liberal democracies are concerned, the range of government policies considered by market participants in making investment decisions is, in fact, extremely limited. Financial markets, it seems, are neither as highly integrated as we are accustomed to thinking, nor as exacting in the audit of fiscal and monetary policy that they are frequently assumed to engage in.

Environmental Degradation

Thus far, we have focused almost exclusively upon mechanisms identifying economic globalization as the key contemporary constraint on public policy-making autonomy. We have also questioned, in so doing, the extent to which contemporary economic trends are well captured by the term *globalization*. Yet at least equally compelling is a rather more political mechanism that refers unequivocally to issues that are genuinely global in their scope and scale. Strictly speaking, this does not so much point to the diminished capacity of domestic governance in an era of globalization as to the globalization of the problems to which governance regimes must find solutions—and to the inability to date to deal with such problems.

The classic example here is the problem of high consequence global environmental risks. This is well expressed in the so-called tragedy of the commons first identified by Garrett Hardin in 1968. Hardin provides an intuitively plausible and all-too-compelling description-cum-model of the seemingly intractable problem of environmental degradation in contemporary societies. The systematic exploitation and pollution of the environment, it is argued, is set to continue because individual corporations and states, despite a clear collective interest, choose not to impose upon themselves the costs of unilateral environmental action. Their logic is entirely rational, though potentially catastrophic in its cumulative consequences. Such actors know that environmental regulation is costly and, particularly in an open international economy, a burden on competitiveness. Accordingly, in the absence of an international governance regime capable of enforcing the compliance of all states and all corporations, the anticipation of free riding is sufficient to ensure that corporations and states do not burden themselves with additional costs and taxes. The long-term effects for the environment are all too obvious, preventing as it does a global solution to a genuinely global problem.

The extent to which the narrowly perceived self-interest of states and governments can subvert the development of effective mechanisms and institutions of global governance is well-evidenced by the George W. Bush administration's withdrawal from the 1997 Kyoto Protocol (committing signatories to staged reductions in greenhouse gas emissions); and, for its critics, by the fact that such a protocol, even if fully implemented, would only serve to slightly reduce the pace of an ongoing process of environmental degradation.

This is a most important example, and a number of broader implications might be drawn from it. First, the tragedy of the commons is indicative of a more general disparity between the need for and supply of effective institutions and mechanisms of global governance. For while it is easy to point to genuinely global problems requiring coordinated global responses for their resolution, it is far more difficult to find examples of the latter. Second, while the proliferation of genuinely global political problems does point to the incapacity of a system of sovereign states (capable of exercising veto power) to deal with the challenges it now faces, it does not indicate any particular incapacity of domestic public policy to deal with the problems and issues it has always dealt with. This is, then, less of a story of a loss of capacity than of the proliferation of issues that domestic governance regimes have never had the capacity to deal with.

Conclusion

This overview began by pointing to the pervasiveness in the existing literature of a significant tension between economic globalization and economic governance. The preceding sections have sought to demonstrate that however influential this trade-off is seen to be, it is deeply problematic—both theoretically and empirically.

Indeed, as the final section hopefully serves to demonstrate, the greatest challenges faced in reforming existing institutions of governance today do not come from domestically internalizing the competitive imperatives unleashed by economic globalization. Rather, they lie in developing the global and transnational governance capacity to deal collectively with the environmental and other consequences of processes of complex economic integration. The challenge is to devise and construct effective institutions of global governance capable of holding the process of globalization democratically accountable. Rather than economic globalization reining in domestic governance capacity, we must develop the global governance capacity to control economic globalization.

—*Colin Hay*

See also Convergence and Divergence; Coordinated Market Economy; Dirigisme; Environmental Governance; Global Governance; Globalization; Global Market; Liberal Market Economy; Market; Physical Capital; Social Democracy; Third Way; Tragedy of the Commons

Further Readings and References

Bairoch, P. (1996). Globalization myths and realities: One century of external trade and foreign investment. In R. Boyer & D. Drache (Eds.), *States against markets: The limits of globalization.* London: Routledge.

Berman, S., & McNamara, K. R. (1999). Bank on democracy: Why central banks need public oversight. *Foreign Affairs, 7,* 2–8.

Brewer, T. L., & Young, S. (1998). *The multilateral investment system and multinational enterprises.* Oxford, UK: Oxford University Press.

Cerny, P. G. (1997). Paradoxes of the competition state: The dynamics of political globalization. *Government and Opposition, 32*(2), 251–274.

Cooke, W. N., & Noble, D. S. (1998). Industrial relations systems and U.S. foreign direct investment abroad. *British Journal of Industrial Relations, 36*(4), 581–609.

Dalton, R. J. (2004). *Democratic challenges, democratic choices: The erosion of political support in advanced industrial democracies.* Oxford, UK: Oxford University Press.

Feldstein, M., & Horioka, C. (1980). Domestic savings and international capital flows. *Economic Journal, 90,* 201–220.

Garrett, G. (2001). Globalization and government spending around the world. *Studies in Comparative International Development, 35*(4), 3–29.

Giddens, A. (1990). *The consequences of modernity.* Cambridge, UK: Polity Press.

Hall, P. A., & Soskice, D. (Eds.). (2001). *Varieties of capitalism.* Oxford, UK: Oxford University Press.

Hardin, G. (1968). The tragedy of the commons. *Science, 162,* 1243–1248.

Hay, C. (2005). Globalization's impact on states. In J. Ravenhill (Ed.), *Global political economy.* Oxford, UK: Oxford University Press.

Hirst, P., & Thompson, G. (1999). *Globalization in question* (2nd ed.). Cambridge, UK: Polity Press.

Marquand, D. (2004). *Decline of the public.* Cambridge, UK: Polity Press.

Mosley, L. (2003) *Global capital and national governments.* Cambridge, UK: Cambridge University Press.

O'Brien, R. (1992). *Global financial integration: The end of geography.* London: Royal Institute for International Affairs.

Rodrik, D. (1996). *Why do more open economies have bigger governments?* (NBER Working Paper No. 5537). Cambridge, MA: National Bureau of Economic Research.

Wilensky, H. L. (2002). *Rich democracies: Political economy, public policy and performance.* Berkeley: University of California Press.

POLITICAL EXCHANGE

Governance requires an exchange of resources because resources that are necessary to govern societies are controlled by different actors. In contemporary differentiated societies, governance involves different kinds of actors—such as politicians, bureaucrats, experts, or interest representatives—composing networks of governance and exchanging different kinds of resources, such as money, information, trust, competence, or legitimacy.

From Tradition to Modernity

Political exchange refers to situations where resources are exchanged between individuals and the collective, as well as public and nonpublic actors taking part in the policy process. The nature of such an exchange depends on the political context and on the institutional setting in which it is embedded. One major form that is described as prevalent in traditional societies is clientelism, also called patronage: Politicians, once in power, reward those voters or militants whose support was necessary for their election with particularistic benefits, such as jobs in public administration. Clientelism as a form of political exchange where votes or partisan loyalty are traded with exclusive "club goods" differs from another related form of political exchange, which is corruption: The latter is based on money as a medium (e.g., firms use bribery of civil servants or politicians to acquire privileged access to public procurement) and is illegal. Clientelism (and of course corruption) is also a feature of contemporary, advanced societies, but the personal relation that it traditionally implies between clients and patrons ("bosses") is typically replaced by an exchange between mass parties capable of providing state resources ("cartel parties") and broader electoral constituencies. Also, theories inspired by economics (primarily Mancur Olson's solution to the free riding problem in collective action) point out that organizational leaderships have to provide "selective incentives" of a clientelistic nature to ensure that the rank-and-file will effectively mobilize. Collective adherence to a common cause is not a sufficient condition, simply because in order to maximize the benefits of mobilization it is rational to externalize its costs (time investment, risk taking, etc.). And the more modern—that is, secularized—a society is, the more likely that societal actors will resort to these kinds of calculations.

Political Exchange in Arenas of Partisan and Interest Representation

The major reason why actors must engage in exchange relations is that they have competing interests but are at the same time caught in relations of interdependence. In differentiated societies, pluralistic political contexts or fragmented institutional settings (checks and balances) and the support of several actors with frequently divergent interests is necessary for decision making. This is mirrored in log-rolling practices between parties in governmental behavior,

which are often required for the achievement of a majority by coalition building. In log-rolling an actor agrees to make concessions to another actor on issues that are secondary to the former but crucial to the latter, under the condition that the actor benefiting from these concessions will in the future make similar concessions on points that are of marginal interest to it but of central concern to the other actor. Log-rolling presupposes that the preferences of actors can be weighed in terms of their intensity and requires an institutional context to make interactions durable (e.g., government committees), which, in turn, favor the building of trust between actors. Similar forms of political exchange resting on "differed gratifications" were found in so-called neocorporatist summit agreements between the leaderships of organizations representing business and labor interests. Business has a blackmailing power vis-à-vis labor as it provides jobs, whereas labor's blackmailing power resides in its capacity to generate turbulences through strikes and other forms of collective action. To avoid a stalemate, labor representatives agree to moderate their claims for higher wages, having obtained assurances from business representatives that full employment will be preserved. For such agreements to be enforced, interest organizations must secure control over and compliance from their members, which is more likely when the organizations are encompassing enough to be preserved from competition for the representation of interests (representational monopolies).

Political Exchange in Network Governance

Most contemporary advanced societies are not centrally steered by a unique state body, but governance is the domain of policy networks where public and nonpublic actors (elected politicians frequently representing different decisional bodies and levels, administrators coming from various services, nongovernmental organizations, private firms, experts) have to coordinate their action and cooperate with each other, in spite of frequently diverging interests and world views. Political exchange thus refers to the bargaining strategies deployed by these actors in networks in order to reach mutually beneficial compromises in the formulation or the implementation of policies. The foregoing applies to governance across levels in the European Union and its member states, but even more so to governance in the transnational sphere, where political regulation is the object of concerted action in the absence of a central sovereign body, and where private forms of regulation abound.

The success of negotiation practices rests on a number of prerequisites:

• Durability—not only does it offer more opportunities for reciprocity and help create mutual trust, the fact that the "game" is, in a sense, repeated also has disciplining effects favorable to cooperation. When actors are embedded in durable (and frequently face-to-face) relations, they are subject to increased peer pressure that, through "blaming and shaming," raises the costs of "cheating."

• Selectivity—if policy networks are overly pluralistic, overcrowding can impede the search for solutions between competing options. This consequently raises the transaction costs of compromise seeking and can impede efficient problem solving. Therefore, exchange in networks is often the task of elites imperfectly mirroring societal or organizational pluralism.

• Informality—bargaining is more easily achieved when actors are not exposed to the scrutiny of their constituencies, their rank-and-file, or the media. Such an exposure reduces the ability of negotiators to reach compromises, for fear of being blamed as traitors or being called chicken. Hence, political exchanges frequently take place behind closed doors in a nontransparent way and in informal settings that sometimes supplement the official decision-making circuits.

Limitations and Problems of Political Exchange

Political exchange can contribute to governability, as policy solutions require the contribution of, and support from, various actors who are likely, if they do not cooperate, to undermine the effectiveness and the acceptance of decisions through the resources each of them possesses. However, political exchange faces two major limitations:

1. Bargaining is much more difficult on issues of the either-or type, or that are not strictly interest based but involve actors' identities too.

2. Political exchange, in fact, replaces authoritative allocation through a form of more horizontal contractual decision making. Decisions are not imposed by policymakers on policy takers; rather, in a sense, they coproduce them. On issues entailing the redistribution of resources, such procedures confer a voice to potential losers and are biased toward the status quo.

Political exchange—though necessary in fragmented societies where majority rule can be dangerous for specific interests—may undermine democratic legitimacy. Prerequisites, such as selectivity and opacity, can lead to limited pluralism and deprive official representative institutions of their power. To what extent is bargaining between powerful actors compatible with democracy? As political exchange requires a narrow elitist sphere, it is open to contestation either by the basis of organizations or by organizations that, as a whole, are excluded from or decide not to enter the negotiations arena (e.g., the increasingly successful antiestablishment and populist parties). In order to benefit from political exchange, one must indeed have something substantial to offer, and this property is unevenly distributed. Political exchange can thus be criticized for leading to collusiveness between "distributive coalitions" mainly motivated by rent seeking. This is likely to put into question not only its normative legitimacy—as it would perpetuate power inequalities—but also its social acceptance, and thus its contribution to socially legitimate governance.

—*Yannis Papadopoulos*

See also Accountability; Clientelism; Collaborative Governance; Collusion; Complexity; Corporatism; Corruption; Free Riding; Governability; Interorganizational Coordination; Legitimacy; Multilevel Governance; Policy Network; Power Sharing; State Capture; Steering

Further Readings and References

Olson, M. (1965). *The logic of collective action.* Cambridge, MA: Harvard University Press.

Olson, M. (1982). *The rise and decline of nations.* New Haven, CT: Yale University Press.

Papadopoulos, Y. (2003). Cooperative forms of governance: Problems of democratic accountability in complex environments. *European Journal of Political Research, 42*(4), 473–501.

Piattoni, S. (Ed.). (2001). *Clientelism, interests, and democratic representation.* Cambridge, UK: Cambridge University Press.

Pierre, J., & Peters, B. G. (2000). *Governance, politics and the state.* London: Macmillan.

POLITICAL PARTY

Do politics matter? This founding issue of modern political science questions the functions of politics in modern political systems. In democratic regimes, it has often been posed differently: Do parties matter? The role of political parties, competing for votes to reach power, is undoubtedly problematic given recent changes in governance. But, the question of the influence of political parties is far from new. In fact, for a long time, contrary to traditional or economic theories of democracy, many scholars have advocated the idea that political parties have no impact at all on the government of society. The reasons are numerous and have changed over time.

In democratic theory, whether traditional or economic, people vote in accordance with policy preferences, and political parties propose and try to implement specific policies for instrumental or intrinsic reasons. Hence, the identity of the governing parties or the proximity of elections should matter in policy making. Two famous models of political business cycles were built on this assumption: The opportunistic one considers that parties in government try to win elections by stimulating the economy just before elections, and the partisan one predicts that the change of governmental parties induces changes in policy reflecting the distinct political preferences of succeeding governmental parties. Much of empirical research supports the general perspective of partisan influence on policy making, including the level of welfare provision or the size of government.

In contrast, however, other studies postulate and provide evidence that political parties do not affect governance. For example, for some scholars, the welfare state expenses depend on economic growth and demographic variations. More recently, renewing the industrial society convergence theory, scholars explained that globalization, the increasing levels of complex interdependence and international capital mobility, sharply decrease the probability of partisan influence. An exhaustive historical work on British policies confirms that parties do not matter in policy making.

In short, there are two essentially divergent views on the relationship between political parties and governance. One way to overcome this contradiction is to reformulate the question: When do parties matter for governance? To answer it, we have to focus on the conditions of partisan influence in the general process of governance: The interaction between partisan variables and institutional or socioeconomic variables. For example, the impact of capital mobility on partisan policies is neither null nor univocal, but changes according to whether there is a fixed or floating exchange rate regime. In this issue area, therefore, parties could and do have a clear impact on tax and monetary policies. Furthermore, convergence among parties on traditional macroeconomic demand-side policies coincides with divergence on supply-side economic strategies: Conservative parties give priority to private provision of production factors (fixed and human capital formation), whereas social democratic parties favor the public provision of production factors.

—*Sylvain Brouard*

See also Elections; Iron Law of Oligarchy; Organization Theory

Further Readings and References

Boix, C. (1998). *Political parties, growth and equality.* Cambridge, UK: Cambridge University Press.

Franseze, R. (2002). *Macroeconomic policies of developed democracies.* Cambridge, UK: Cambridge University Press.

Oatley, T. (1999). How constraining is capital mobility? The Partisan hypothesis in an open economy. *American Journal of Political Science, 43,* 1003–1027.

POLITICS-ADMINISTRATION DICHOTOMY

The politics-administration dichotomy posits a clear distinction between practices of governance that belong to the realm of the political on the one hand, and those that belong to that of bureaucracy on the other hand. The contribution of this dichotomy to the field of public administration has been periodically debated in the literature throughout the twentieth century. In recent years, however, the original intentions of scholars like Woodrow Wilson and Frank Goodnow have been reexamined, and their views were found to be not as two-dimensional as history had alleged. Simply put, the dichotomy holds that progressive reformers at the turn of the twentieth century sought to separate the corrupt practices of political party bosses, especially those in large metropolitan areas, from the day-to-day administration of the public's affairs. By creating an impenetrable wall between the two spheres, reformers could transform government and make it operate more like a business—efficiently, effectively, and honestly. "Politics" then became the exclusive sphere of elected officials that debated the ends of government, concerned themselves with choices among competing values, and performed the thinking of government, while "administration" was conducted by appointed officials that made choices among the means by which government ends might be achieved and focused exclusively on accomplishing goals or the doings of government. Administrators were accountable to the people through elected officials that set policies, provided funding, and were themselves accountable to the people through elections. At the same time, this barrier served to protect administrators from partisan politics. The politics-administration dichotomy thus came to symbolize these dualisms, while administration itself was reduced to mere instrumental rationality.

Opponents of the dichotomy argued that it was neither possible nor desirable to separate politics from administration so absolutely. Indeed, they contended that those who advocated such a bifurcation, often under the auspices of science, were not only misleading citizens but deceiving themselves as well. Values, and thus politics, were embedded in virtually all administrative actions and it was preferable to recognize this openly rather than to pretend that administration could, indeed, be neutral. The reexamination of early public administration writings in the 1980s and 1990s revealed that most of the founders had held more nuanced views of the relationship between politics and administration than they had been given credit for. While these findings lent support to critics of the dichotomy, the administrative ground on which the argument was based was also beginning to change.

Public agencies, especially those at the federal level, have always subcontracted portions of their work. Yet devolution in the 1980s and reinvention in the 1990s meant that many of the agencies historically responsible for providing services were no longer directly involved in doing so. Instead, they began contracting out their responsibilities to others—be they state or local agencies or private (both profit and nonprofit) organizations. Increasingly, then, the performance of traditionally governmental tasks, the doings of government, was not conducted by public employees. Instead, the agencies responsible for the work became parts of complex networks where they made every effort to ensure that the ends of government were achieved through oversight techniques, not unlike those employed by legislators. Some administrationists have countered that a distinction still remains between program and policy outcomes, with administrators being concerned with the former and politicians the latter. But increased organizational complexity and the dynamics of globalization have meant that public administrators are also taking on new roles, engaging citizens and other stakeholders in deliberation, negotiating service contracts, and otherwise involving themselves in mediating roles in the policy continuum. Maintaining accountability under such complex and fragmented conditions appears more likely to occupy public administrationists in the immediate future than the now-dated and overly simplistic politics-administration dichotomy.

—*Susan H. MacDonald*

See also Accountability; Agency; Bureaucracy; Elections

Further Readings and References

Lynn, L. E. (2001). The myth of the bureaucratic paradigm: What traditional public administration really stood for. *Public Administration Review, 61*(2), 144–160.

Svara, J. H. (2001). The myth of the dichotomy: Complementarity of politics and administration in the past and future of public administration. *Public Administration Review, 61*(2), 176–183.

POLYARCHY

Central to any definition of democracy is electoral representation by means of free elections and representative government. The concept of polyarchy (i.e., rule by many) is an attempt by Robert Dahl to develop an empirical definition of the process of democratization as well as elaborating a set of normative criteria for deciding whether or not a political system can be counted as a democracy. Polyarchy, as presented by Dahl, should be understood as a process developing a set of institutions that comes close to what one could call the ideal type of democracy. Therefore, that public power is essential and authority is effectively controlled by societal organizations and civil associations (e.g., interest groups and political parties). Hence, in Dahl's view, the extent to which these societal actors can and do operate autonomously, as well as independently from the state, will enhance the democratic quality of a polity. Obviously, central to the adequate functioning of polyarchy is not only the existence and working of institutions, but also the existence and actual room for maneuver of societal groups and their organization. The institutionalization of the democratic process of accountable government is a prerequisite, not yet the establishment of a regime as a fully fledged democracy, as many students of democracy appear to think. These necessary institutions are, according to Dahl:

- universal suffrage and the right to run for public office;
- free and fairly conducted elections for all adults;
- availability and observance of the right to free speech and protection to do so;
- the existence and free access to alternative information (not controlled by government);
- the undisputed right to form and to join relatively autonomous organizations, in particular, political parties (and, crucially, parties in opposition);
- responsiveness of government (and parties) to voters and accountability of government (and parties) to election outcomes and government.

This set of institutions taken together distinguishes polyarchy from other regimes. The coming about of these institutions can then be seen as the process toward democratization. The enduring existence and observance of the whole set is the hallmark of an established democracy.

Dahl's concept of polyarchy is not only a seminal contribution to (normative) democratic theory, but has also been a powerful incentive for empirical analysis. Almost by definition, this type of research has been of a comparative nature and has induced a great number of attempts to measure polyarchy as well as its performance according to the democratic ideals. It is therefore important to distinguish between the operationalization of polyarchy aiming at the process of democratization and those that measure the level of democratization.

The concept of polyarchy is currently one of the most widely used terms in political science because it has prescriptive qualities—enhancing democracy as ideal government—combined with empirical options. Both help analyze extant democracies and how they can be further developed.

—*Hans Keman*

See also Democratic Theory; Democratization; Heterarchy; Hybrid Organization; Marxism; Pluralism; Rule of Law

Further Readings and References

Dahl, R. A. (1971). *Polyarchy: participation and opposition.* New Haven, CT: Yale University Press.

Dahl, R. A. (1998). *On democracy.* New Haven, CT: Yale University Press.

Keman, H. (Ed.). (2002). *Comparative democratic politics: A guide to contemporary theory and research.* London: Sage Ltd.

POOLED SOVEREIGNTY

Pooled sovereignty means the strengthening of a country's resources by combining them with those of partner countries. Pooling sovereignty is the conceptual answer to a realization of weakened and permeated sovereignty. The classical concept of state sovereignty assumed the autonomous ability of decision making as the ultimate expression of a country's independence. In light of the European experience with nationalism (conflict and self-destruction), as well as in light of the changed character of contemporary challenges to society and statehood, European countries have begun to pool their individual sovereignty by transferring autonomous state rights to the level of the European Union (EU).

After five decades of European integration, this transfer of sovereignty has affected all three central areas of modern state sovereignty: monetary sovereignty, internal security, external defense. Pooled sovereignty does not mean that member countries of the EU revoke their statehood and its sovereignty. Pooled sovereignty means the development of a multilayered system of governance by which the national and the European level—in federal systems also the regional level within a member state of the EU—are jointly involved in political decision making.

The limits of autonomous national decision-making powers (inherent in the character of most contemporary political challenges) are dealt with by the ambition of political actors involved in the process of European integration to strengthen their joint performance under the umbrella of the EU. This logic applies to the creation of a single European market with monetary and currency union, including a common currency, the EURO; it also applies to efforts in pooling resources, for instance, in order to establish European police coordination (EUROPOL), a common migration policy, and a European Border Force; it finally includes the sphere of foreign and security policy based on a common security strategy of the EU, with a joint response to the threat of terrorism and with joint military operations in peace keeping by the EU (such as in Macedonia and Bosnia-Herzegovina)

and joint postconflict operations (such as in Aceh, Indonesia and, most spectacularly, in supervising the border opening between the Gaza Strip and Egypt in late 2005).

In the meantime, the European integration experience has also been studied by other regional integration schemes worldwide in order to emulate some of the fundamental European insights in the context of other regional circumstances with their specific conditions and potentials (i.e., MERCOSUR, Andean Community, Central American Integration System, ASEAN, Gulf Cooperation Council, African Union).

—*Ludger Kühnhardt*

See also European Governance; European Union; Sovereignty

Further Readings and References

Soldatos, P. (1989). *Le système institutionnel et politique des communautés européennes dans un monde en mutation: Théorie et pratique* [The institutional system and politics of the European communities in a world in mutation: Theory and practice]. Brussels, Belgium: Bruylant.

Soldatos P. (Ed.). (1990). *Federal and international relations.* Oxford, UK: Oxford University Press.

POSITIVE POLITICAL THEORY

Positive political theory is a variant of rational choice theory initiated by William H. Riker. In understanding the relationship between positive political theory and rational choice theory, it is sufficient to understand that both are committed to positive as opposed to normative political theory, and that both presuppose purposive action. However, not all the models of political phenomena studied by positive political theorists are developed in terms of rational choice theory. The hallmark feature of positive political theory is its adherence to the scientific method of building up descriptive generalizations, or universal laws, from minimalist intuitive assumptions. Often relying on the formal language of rational choice theory, these general laws are deduced from axiomatic systems that can be tested against actual human behavior. Positive political theory eschews making normative claims about how political agents or systems should function and instead emphasizes building explanatory and predictive models that serve as the basis for a progressive study of political phenomena. Positive political theorists study elections, legislative behavior, political institutions, and the formation of international alliances.

Riker coalesced positive political theory from what are now recognized to be canonical texts in the rational choice tradition of research: John Von Neumann and Oskar Morgenstern's *Theory of Games and Economic Behavior* (1944), Duncan Black's "On the Rationale of Group-Decision Making" (1948), Kenneth J. Arrow's *Social Choice and Individual Values* (1951/1963), and Anthony Downs's *An Economic Theory of Democracy,* Riker's *Theory of Political Coalitions,* along with James M. Buchanan and Gordon Tullock's *Calculus of Consent* (1962), and Mancur Olson, Jr.'s *Logic of Collective Action* complete the early rational choice canon that spans public choice and social choice theories as well. These results progressively build on each other, realizing the hope of positive political theorists that formal deductive models tested against empirical phenomena yield a growing body of knowledge. Von Neumann and Morgenstern's innovative treatment of game theory provided the basis for a new study of politics directly relating numerous individuals' strategically rational decisions to collective outcomes. Importantly, they developed the idea of equilibrium strategies that, when played against each other, yield predictable, law-like outcomes that exhibit stability.

Black's and Arrow's late 1940s research addressed electoral processes for reaching collective decisions. Both researchers used the eighteenth-century Condorcet voting paradox as a point of departure for their investigations. According to the Marquis de Condorcet's analytic assessment of voting, it is possible for three individuals voting over three alternatives to reach deadlock if their preferences are structured such that, as an example, Alex prefers candidate Zeus to Athena to Hercules, Loren prefers Athena to Hercules to Zeus, and Pat prefers Hercules to Zeus to Athena. When the votes are tallied over pairs, the

collective preference has the form that Zeus is preferred to Athena, who is preferred to Hercules, who is preferred to Zeus. This circular statement of a collective preference order was recognized by Condorcet, Black, and Arrow to be cyclical, and therefore irrational and unstable. Black contributed to the analytic study of election procedures by demonstrating that in the case in which voters' preferences over three outcomes are single peaked—that is, outcomes may be represented in a linear order with two distinct poles and no voter least prefers the middle outcome—then cyclic stalemate outcomes can be avoided. Arrow worked in the opposite direction of Black in developing his impossibility theorem. He proved that the cyclic instabilities that Condorcet alerted us to characterize voting procedures of *n* individuals selecting from *n* alternatives more generally. In the 1950s, Riker pursued these results to empirically investigate if actual voting procedures tend to result in unstable, cyclic outcomes. Riker's research indicated less cyclic outcomes than are anticipated by the theoretical models of voting.

Riker also responded to Downs's medium voter theorem. Downs relied on the idea of rationally self-interested politicians and voters to demonstrate that in order to win elections, candidates must shape their platforms to appeal to the median voter, thereby securing necessary votes. Riker amended Downs's theory by arguing that rational candidates will develop political platforms to appeal to the median voter only to the extent that is necessary to achieve a minimum winning coalition.

Although there has been considerable advance along the lines of positive political theory in understanding collective action problems, public goods problems, and international treaty formation, much of the ongoing effort has been devoted to refining knowledge of democratic decision making and political institutions. Major advances have focused on agenda setting and structure-induced equilibria in legislative settings. Given that empirical cycling occurs less frequently than theoretically predicted, research focused on explaining this discrepancy. Agenda control was determined to be one feature of democratic decision procedures that contributes to their robustness as a direct counter to cyclic instability. As well, it became understood that the institutional structures shaping democratic decision procedures also play a role in securing stable outcomes. Thus, the voting rules themselves are crucial for not only deciding outcomes, but further for contributing to the rationality and hence acceptability of outcomes, given that irrational outcomes are those that exhibit cyclic instabilities. Another vein of research combats concerns over the irrational nature of democratic will formation as elucidated by the impossibility theorem, arguing that if citizens rely on voting to throw politicians out of office, rather than to manifest a Rousseuan general will, then elections can be seen to constitute a firm basis for Madisonian liberalism.

Positive political theory has polarized departments of U.S. political science. If an identifying characteristic of a successful research program is its generation of fruitful debate over methodological assumptions and of research findings, then positive political theory could not have been more prosperous. At the root of these debates is the question whether a purely positive approach to political phenomena does justice to human agents as reflective beings that intentionally animate political institutions. With its heavy reliance on game theory and rational choice theory, positive political theory often accepts that individuals are strategic agents that promote their self-interest in accordance with their personal preferences. It remains unclear, however, whether this model of human action, which requires that all rational expressions of the human will must conform to well-ordered personal preferences, is sufficient. Competing theories of human agency and democratic politics emphasize that political legitimacy may be the result of aspects of agency, such as commitment, loyalty, duty, or fair play, that cannot in principle be reduced to the language of preferences. Much hangs in the balance of this debate because at the present time it remains unclear if a positive political theory allied with rational choice theory can propose a political philosophy that deviates from "might makes right."

—*S. M. Amadae*

See also Collective Action; Equilibrium Theory; Game Theory; Impossibility Theorem; Public Choice Theory; Rational Choice Theory; Social Choice

Further Readings and References

Amadae, S. M. (2003). *Rationalizing capitalist democracy: The Cold War origins of rational choice liberalism.* Chicago: University of Chicago Press.

Amadae, S. M., & Bueno de Mesquita, B. (1999). The Rochester School: The origins of positive political theory. *Annual Review of Political Science, 2,* 269–295.

Black, D. (1948). On the rationale of group decision making. *Journal of Political Economy, 56,* 23–34.

Riker, W. H. (1982). *Liberalism against populism: A confrontation between the theory of democracy and the theory of social choice.* San Francisco: Freeman.

Riker, W. H. (Ed.). (1993). *Agenda formation.* Ann Arbor: University of Michigan Press.

Post-9/11

On September 11, 2001, four airliners were hijacked after taking off from airports in New York and Boston. They were seized by men linked to the radical Islamist group, Al-Qaeda. Two planes were flown into the World Trade Center in New York City. One plane was flown into the Pentagon in Washington, DC. Another crashed into a field in Pennsylvania, following a fight between the passengers and hijackers. Over 3,000 people died.

For analysts of politics, numerous questions arise from these events. Two are of particular significance. First, did 9/11 (as the events soon became known) instantiate or symbolize a radical break in the dynamics of global politics? Many journalists, public commentators, and politicians argue that the world has changed irrevocably, that we live in a new era. The West, so it is claimed, has finally awoken to the fact that it is under attack from assorted terrorist organizations (usually grouped together under the heading of Islamic fundamentalism) and it is consequently essential to defeat this enemy through a new global war: the war on terror. Accordingly, the old rules and norms of the international system—based on respect for state sovereignty as the basis of international law and generally excluding policies such as preventive war—no longer hold.

The second main question relates to the appropriate balance between liberty and security within states. The war on terror has entailed a significant clampdown on civil liberties throughout the world. Not only have various rights been curtailed (most obviously by the USA PATRIOT Act of 2001), but also heightened levels of anxiety have meant that public debate over such policies is often perfunctory or nonexistent. Moreover, a number of states (including Israel, Russia, and Indonesia) have employed the rhetoric of the global war to legitimate their actions in long-standing conflicts. Critics have accused governments of either overreacting to the threat posed by terrorism or of deliberately utilizing the new climate of anxiety to instigate otherwise-controversial measures and legislation.

For politicians, civil society activists, and scholars of politics, the analysis of and response to the events of 9/11 will continue to present a pressing challenge for years to come. However, it would be premature to draw concrete conclusions about the "meaning" of 9/11. While it is possible to discern significant shifts in political language, in the levels of anxiety felt in many parts of the world, and in the actions and attitudes of a number of political administrations, it remains to be seen whether there has been a fundamental change, rather than a transient shift, in priorities and perceptions.

—Duncan Bell

See also Crisis Management; Human Security; Liberal Internationalism; Military Necessity; Terrorism; War on Terrorism

Further Readings and References

Calhoun, C., Price, P., & Timmer, A. (Eds.). (2002). *Understanding 11 September.* New York: New Press.
Dudziak, M. (Ed.). (2003). *September 11 in history: A watershed moment?* Durham, NC: Duke University Press.
Waltz, K. (2002). The continuity of international politics. In K. Booth & T. Dunne (Eds.), *Worlds in collision: Terror and the future of global order.* London: Palgrave.

POSTCOLONIALISM

Postcolonialism refers both to a specific historical period or state of affairs—the aftermath of imperialism—and to an intellectual and political project to reclaim and rethink the history and agency of people subordinated under various forms of European imperialism. It signals a possible future of overcoming colonialism, yet also new forms of domination or subordination that can come in the wake of such changes, including new forms of global empire. It should not be confused with the claim that the world we live in now is actually devoid of colonialism.

Modernity comes to the world outside of the orbit of Western capitalist democracies in different ways and generates different responses. Thus, postcolonial theorists and historians have been concerned to investigate the various trajectories of modernity as understood and experienced from a range of philosophical, cultural, and historical perspectives. They have been particularly concerned to engage with the ambiguous legacy of the Age of Enlightenment—social, political, economic, scientific, legal, and cultural thought beyond Europe itself. The legacy is ambiguous according to postcolonial theorists because the Age of Enlightenment was also an age of empire, and the connection between these two historical epochs is more than incidental.

From Decolonization to Postcolonialism

Although there were and are many different kinds of imperialism and thus of decolonization, two of the most important periods for postcolonial writers include the British disengagement from its second empire (of the nineteenth and twentieth centuries) and the decolonization movements of the 1960s and 1970s in Africa and elsewhere. It was during the latter era, in particular, that many of the international principles and instruments of decolonization were formally declared (although the history of their emergence and formation goes back much further), and the language of national self-determination applied to liberationist movements within former colonial territories (see especially the United Nations' *Declaration on Friendly Relations*). The processes triggered by these struggles were not only political and economic but also cultural. Previously subjugated people sought to assert control over not only territorial boundaries—albeit ones carved out by the imperial powers—but also over their language and history.

The language of postcolonialism is also sometimes used to refer to the struggles of indigenous people in many parts of the world today. However, given the interpretation of the principles of self-determination and self-government within the current international system, along with their minority status and vulnerability even within decolonized states, the term is perhaps less apt. Indigenous people have been denied even the modest gains extended by the United Nations and the international system of states to the various decolonized territories in the 1970s. Moreover, the history of imperialism is complex. European imperialism between the sixteenth and eighteenth centuries in the Americas, West Indies, Australasia, and South East Asia was substantially different from that of the nineteenth and twentieth centuries. Still, one of the central themes of postcolonial scholarship has been both the persistence of empire in human history but also resistance to it.

Thus, on the one hand, the legacy of the Enlightenment forms an indispensable and unavoidable feature of the present, whether European or otherwise. The universal categories and concepts at the heart of much Enlightenment thought have been put to work by both European and non-European intellectuals and activists to criticize the injustices of their societies, as well as imperialism itself. There is a tradition of anti-imperialist criticism that extends as far back as the sixteenth century, and yet on the other hand, some of these very same commitments were not only compatible with, but were often used to justify, imperial domination. The theoretical tools provided by the Enlightenment, combined with an often-unrelenting cultural Eurocentrism, informed the political and economic practices of imperialism throughout the nineteenth and twentieth centuries. Still, many of the most powerful local and indigenous critics of empire in the twentieth century were themselves deeply influenced by European social and political theory, as much as they were deeply critical of it. The seminal work of C. L. R. James, Aimé Césaire, Albert Memmi, Frantz Fanon, Edward Said, as well as by the group of historians associated with the editorial collective of *Subaltern Studies,* all exemplify this complex inheritance. It derives in part from the fact that there is no such thing as "the" Enlightenment, but rather, multiple Enlightenments shaped by different historical and political contexts. And also because the bundle of concepts and ideals to which "the" Enlightenment refers are plural and capable of a wide range of elaboration.

What Is the Subject of Postcolonialism?

As a general domain of intellectual inquiry, postcolonialism refers to those questions that emerge in relation to the aftermath of imperialism. And one of the most important features of the history of imperialism in the last 500 years has been the emergence of states, either from the consolidation of territories and polities or from the dissolution of empires (or some combination thereof), and along with it, new conceptions of international order. In this sense, to be concerned with postcolonialism is to be concerned with a set of questions at the heart of modern political thought.

However, in recent years postcolonialism has also become closely associated with a more specific set of questions, and although it shouldn't be reduced to them, they have proved to be enormously influential. One of the most prominent has been the relation between imperialism and identity. Frantz Fanon presents one of the most searing and provocative analyses of the relation between colonized and colonizer in *The Wretched of the Earth* (1963), as well as in his earlier *Black Skin, White Masks* (1953). Fanon is perhaps best known for his explosive justification of violence in *The Wretched of the Earth* (highlighted in Jean-Paul Sartre's famous preface to that work), where it is cast as the appropriate response to the violence perpetrated by colonialism, and also as the mediation through which the colonized can begin to reclaim their self-conscious agency. This is a deeply unsettling argument, shaped undoubtedly by the brutal period of colonial rule and war in Algeria between 1954–1961, which Fanon experienced first hand. Violence was inevitable and necessary, Fanon seems to be saying, but also has to be overcome. One has to move from reaction to the construction of something new, which for Fanon included overcoming the binary oppositions imposed on the colonized by the geopolitical structures of the Cold War. It is here that we find the foreshadowing of some important themes that have become central to postcolonialism today. For example, Fanon combines a material and psychological analysis of the consequences of colonialism, which looks to both the micro- and macroeffects and experience of colonial governance. Both the colonized and the colonizer are implicated in the horrors of imperialism and both will have to be decolonized. The colonized have to find a way of overcoming the imposition of alien rule not only over their territory but also over their minds and bodies. Seeking recognition from an oppressor in terms that the oppressor has set hardly provides a genuine liberation from the grip of colonialism (this anticipates an important debate in contemporary political theory over the "politics of recognition"). But the colonizers also have to make sense of how the brutality of colonialism relates to their own apparent humanism. At times, Fanon combines, often worryingly, the idioms of Marxist revolutionary, psychoanalyst, and ethnonationalist, deeply committed and involved as he was in the struggle for Algerian independence. But at other times in *The Wretched of the Earth,* as careful readers have pointed out, he is well aware of the pitfalls of a purely reactive nationalism. Here he tries to link the struggle for national liberation to the emergence of a new humanism, one that departs from what he saw as the bad faith of liberal humanism, as well as the forced choice between socialism and capitalism, but still reaches toward the universal.

In Fanon's work we encounter the complex relation between imperialism and nationalism that has remained a critical focus of much postcolonial writing. The aspiration for self-determination at the heart of anticolonial struggles has proved difficult to institutionalize democratically in existing postcolonial states (about which Fanon was remarkably prescient). Most postcolonial theorists, whether writing about Africa, South Asia, or elsewhere, have been critical of nationalism, but also equally critical of the "nativism" and romantic communitarianism often supposed to be alternatives to it. They have been concerned to investigate the ways in which European conceptions of the political, as well as assumptions about secularism and historical time more generally, have been used to describe and locate non-European peoples' forms of collective action and modes of self-understanding along a continuum that terminates with the ideas and institutions of modern Europe. They have also been critical of the assumption, often made by liberals, that what is needed is simply the extension of existing liberal universals, this time in good faith, to those to whom they were previously denied (or never seriously intended). For some postcolonial theorists, the problem is not simply one of a lack of consistency on the part of liberalism, but lies more deeply within the structure of the universal principles themselves. The conditions attached for the ascription of rights, for example, or the distribution of liberties, were often grounded in narratives of social or cultural development that justified denying rights and freedoms to those deemed too backward or uncivilized to exercise them properly. John Stuart Mill's justification of the denial of Indian self-government is a classic instance of this kind of assumption, however much he thought it was best for the well-being of Indians themselves.

The Critique of Historicism

A central *topos* of postcolonialism is the problem of historicism. One basic question many postcolonial writers have asked is: How does the non-European world write its own history? Some Indian historians associated with *Subaltern Studies,* for example, although deeply influenced by Marxism, have also sought to rescue the collective agency of Indian peasants from the category of the "pre-political" to which they had been assigned by Marxist historicism. This puts into question the very idea of theories of social and historical development in which entire peoples or cultures are located somewhere on a scale between "primitive" or "archaic" and "civilized." The critique of historicism and its relation to the elaboration of various concepts central to Marxism and liberal democratic theory is, however, complex. Could peasants be genuine political actors if they didn't use the language and practice of rights or sovereignty in the way that European political thought—differentiated as it is—conceived of it? Was the collective action of Indian peasants, or Aboriginal Australians, prepolitical or "backward" because oriented around "religious" or kinship relations, for example, as opposed to class or universal human interests? And how should we describe and make sense of those alternative sociabilities anyway?

Thus, postcolonialism has been associated with skepticism about the historicism of Marxist and liberal historiography. For some, this means abandoning any form of essentialism whatsoever in thinking about the representation of subaltern collective action in time or, at least, that any identity is always ultimately heterogeneous and must be theorized as such. Here, the influence of the work of Michel Foucault has been significant. For example, in Edward Said's groundbreaking book *Orientalism,* Foucault's subtle conception of the constitutive relation between power and knowledge provided a critical angle from which to investigate the way representations of non-European culture and thought were shaped by a web of institutional and political forces connected to the justification and practice of Western imperialism.

Foucault's work has also proved influential in trying to make sense of the ambiguous legacy of the Enlightenment, as previously mentioned. In *Discipline and Punish,* he argued that the legal and administrative reforms put in place during the eighteenth and nineteenth centuries in England and France as instances of self-consciously enlightened progressivism were also used to regulate and "discipline" the population in more sweeping and yet also more efficient ways than ever before. Although he was less interested in colonial contexts himself, Foucault's arguments and methodology have provided a remarkably productive set of critical tools for postcolonial theorists looking at the different forms of power at work in eighteenth and nineteenth century imperialism, as well as today. The postcolonial critique of contemporary state-sponsored multiculturalism as a form of ongoing colonial domination—albeit more subtle and indirect than previous forms—is deeply indebted to his work.

The notion of "unmasking" the Enlightenment has been a powerful theme in this strand of postcolonial writing. The critique has tended to generate two kinds of claims. First, certain modes of Enlightenment thought are inherently Eurocentric and thus deeply problematic when applied in non-European contexts, or presented as offering genuinely neutral principles of political association or justice. But second, and perhaps more interestingly, despite the legacy of empire, the humanism and universalism of much Enlightenment thought is still indispensable for addressing the challenges faced by those on the sharp end of contemporary global inequality. Indeed, this kind of ambiguity can be found in Foucault's own work, insofar as he understood the Enlightenment to represent not just a set of doctrinal commitments or principles, but also a particular philosophical ethos and attitude committed to permanent critique and self-reflection. Postcolonialism suggests that as dominant and important as the European process of modernity has been, there have been and will continue to be multiple modernities, and thus important questions about how best to understand the relations between them.

Postcolonialism and Governance

If postcolonialism raises basic questions about the representation of non-European people in history, as well as about the entanglement of Enlightenment thought with the justification of empire, is there an alternative vision of the postcolonial? One influential account of the nature of postcolonial identity has emphasized the hybridity and "in-betweenness" of the postcolonial, poised between various categories and forms of self-understanding associated with "native," "minority," "citizen," and "subject." This work, associated most closely with Homi Bhabha, has pointed to the centrality and unavoidability of a particular conception of difference—nonhierarchical, fluid, overlapping, multiform, and complex—at the heart of any possible postcolonial conception of justice. However, the general approach is oriented primarily to literary and cultural studies, the political and institutional consequences of which remain unclear.

What are the consequences of postcolonialism for thinking about the nature of governance? One strand of postcolonialism, drawing on the critiques of historicism and Enlightenment humanism previously examined, suggests a radical critique of liberalism, and thus of various forms of liberal democracy, as inherently unjust. But another strand of postcolonial thought takes a different tack, in line with the complexity of Enlightenment thought itself, and seeks to combine a critique of Eurocentrism with the attempt to rethink and yet also put to work new conceptions of equality, global justice, and human rights. And here, postcolonialism points to the difficulty—and yet the necessity—of trying to think simultaneously with and also against dominant conceptions of sovereignty, justice, and the state. This strand of postcolonial theory takes aim, in particular, at the state-centric assumptions of much cultural, legal, and political discourse, and especially the way non-European political agents are forcibly assimilated into or excluded from an international order organized around a particular idea of statehood and radically unequal forms of economic development. The fundamental orientation of this strand of postcolonialism is to point to the essentially contested nature of political modernity, and thus of some its basic structures of thought—including the idea of humanity—without necessarily abandoning them. With new forms of transnational and global relations of power at work in the world, as these theorists suggest, we need to think differently about not only the nature of cultural and political identity, but also the political and institutional forms in which to realize freedom and equality given these complex circumstances. In this sense, postcolonialism remains a vital aspect of the ongoing debate over the nature of sovereignty and global justice.

—*Duncan Ivison*

See also Indigenous Governance; Nation; Nationalism; Postmodernism; State; Tribal Governance

Further Readings and References

Bhabha, H. (1994). *The location of culture.* London: Routledge.
Canny, N. (Ed.). (1998). *The Oxford history of the British empire, Volume 1: The origins of empire.* Oxford, UK: Oxford University Press.
Chakrabarty, D. (2000). *Provincializing Europe: Postcolonial thought and historical difference.* Princeton, NJ: Princeton University Press.
Dirlik, A. (1997). *The postcolonial aura: Third world criticism in the age of global capitalism.* Boulder, CO: Westview.
Fanon, F. (1953). *Black skin, White masks.* New York: Grove Press.
Fanon, F. (1963). *The wretched of the Earth.* New York: Grove Press.
Foucault, M. (1979). *Discipline and punish.* New York: Vintage Books.
Guha, R. (Ed.). (1983–1993). *Subaltern studies in Indian society and history.* Oxford, UK: Oxford University Press.
Said, E. (1978). *Orientalism.* London: Penguin.
Said, E. (1994). *Culture and imperialism.* New York: Vintage Books.
Young, R. (2001). *Postcolonialism: A historical introduction.* Oxford, UK: Basil Blackwell.

POST-FORDISM

See FORDISM AND POST-FORDISM

POSTMODERNISM

Postmodernism is a theoretical orientation often associated with deconstruction, the linguistic turn, neopragmatism, contextualism, contingency, irony, pluralism, social constructivism, antiessentialism, and the decentered self. While the term shares the skepticism toward religious supernaturalism that inheres in Enlightenment liberalism, it also carries with it a critique of modernity—its foundationalism, essentialism, universalism, monism, and word-fact correspondence. Postmodernism is often described as incredulity toward metanarratives.

Modernity was buttressed by a triumphant instrumental rationality, the value predisposition of modern organizations whose task it is to dominate and control pertinent aspects of nature and life. Modern systems assume for themselves a potentially all-encompassing universalistic view. The postmodern word for this way of assembling reality is metanarrative. Examples of metanarratives include logical positivism in the philosophy of science, the canons of analytical logic in philosophy, the materialist dialectic in Marxism, and structural functionalism and systems theory in anthropology, sociology, and political science.

Postmodern critique casts doubt on the so-called foundations of public policy/administration. Representative democracy assumes that the sovereign people express their will through the democratic accountability feedback loop, whereby elected representatives elaborate the public will through rules that are enforced through the chain of command. Postmodernism regards this loop model of governance as implausible; sovereignty, the people, and representation are all rendered problematic through postmodern interrogation.

A second tendency flowing from postmodern thought is to expose supposed neutral instruments and procedures as technologies of power—the tactics deployed in the control and care of the population. Typical concerns of government include disease prevention and the control of epidemics, the food supply, water supply, public sanitation, shelter, education, and so forth. Postmodern thinkers are interested in how government goes about these tasks. Certain technologies of category construction and distinction making are deployed for the care and control of the population. These technologies of normalization and individualization are put into place and function as coherent political technology, a form of political power that exercises itself through social production and social service. For example, individuals are counted as members of the population. We are classified as citizen and noncitizen, for instance. If classified as citizen, one is eligible for military service, is called upon to participate, to grow, and to develop. One's vote is counted. On the other hand, one is forced into things. A timetable and a time card for some of us, soldiers march to the drum, and others join the rush hour traffic. The body manipulates the machine on the factory floor just so. It is forbidden to waste time. Time becomes linear and serialized (successive activities). These are technologies of discipline, the practices of governmentality. Governmentality, a term coined by Michel Foucault, gives sociopolitical meaning to governmental rationality, a meaning that is not necessarily attached to a government office.

By problematizing governmentality, postmodernism also problematizes the categorization process that presents itself as "scientific." Processes that statistically define the population, for example, are all about governmentality. This kind of governing emerged in sixteenth-century Europe and was made possible by the creation of specific expert or professional fields of knowledge. Hence, governmentality came into being concurrently with the societal construction of experts and disciplinary knowledge.

Postmodern thinkers subscribe to the view that reality is a social construction. The names that interactive human groups give things are ultimately arbitrary. Names and symbols are not so much denotative of something as they are socially agreed-upon gestures, various shorthand significations for commonly accepted phenomena for which significance has been mutually developed. Humans are born into a world already rich in meanings, which they internalize. In so doing, they re-create or reproduce them, although never exactly identically, for the present and into the future.

Words, signs, and symbols are not self-evidently connected to factual, denotative reality, as would be the case from a modernist perspective. Denotative signs were long thought to be the essential building blocks of realism, communication, and science. Language, by this view, was anchored by direct one-to-one representations of objects. Language had the capacity to mirror nature. Strictly denotative signs, having one-to-one correspondence to reality, are no longer considered plausible. This is because denotative signs, once uttered, have already-connotative implications that depend on the context in which they are used. Words connote more than mere empirical facticity. Even the photograph, the denotative medium that never lies, is understood now to be possibly posed, in a manipulated setting, to connote certain moods or appearances.

In postmodern thought, there is no final arbiter. There is no universal reality against which truth claims may be verified. Any imagined reality is transient, unstable, and mutates over time. While any version of reality may gather local adherents and culturally affiliated subscribers, with respect to one another these realities are incommensurable, or, more optimistically, contestable within pluralistic public discourse.

—*Hugh T. Miller*

See also Governmentality; Interpretive Theory; Neotraditionalism; Postcolonialism; Power; State-Society Relations

Further Readings and References

Foucault, M. (1994). Governmentality. In J. D. Faubion (Ed.) & R. Hurley et al. (Trans.), *Michel Foucault: Power*. New York: New Press.

Lyotard, J.-F. (1984). *The postmodern condition: A report on knowledge* (G. Bennington & B. Massumi, Trans.). Minneapolis: University of Minnesota Press.

Miller, H. T. (2002). *Postmodern public policy*. Albany: State University of New York Press.

Miller, H. T., & Fox, C. J. (2006). *Postmodern public administration: Revised edition*. Armonk, NY: M. E. Sharpe.

POST–WASHINGTON CONSENSUS

The post–Washington Consensus (PWC) is a term used to define a shift away from a more starkly neoliberal policy agenda, encapsulated in popular understandings of the Washington, DC consensus. The key distinctions of the PWC are the following:

- *An interest in institutions.* It is not self-evident that free markets flourish merely as a result of the roll back of state intervention. For markets to work, it is necessary to ensure that they exist in the appropriate institutional context. This means largely that states need to establish robust legislative contexts for a market economy. It also means exploring the possibility of more networked forms of governance as underpinnings of marketization.

- *An interest in information.* The nature of a market or economic sector crucially depends on the topography of its information flows. Fluid and transparent forms of information allow markets to work more effectively. It is poor or limited information

flows that contribute to financial crises, poorly executed privatizations, or localized monopolies.

- *An interest in public goods.* Related to the previous ideas, economists within the PWC tradition have highlighted the importance of public goods, especially at the global level. These public goods include security and order in the first place; thereafter, one could add predictable and transparent trade regulations and various forms of data or information sharing. These kinds of goods are seen as central to ensuring that economic globalization works efficiently.

- *An interest in policy execution.* Rather than focusing on economic liberalization as a single, unified project to be executed as rapidly as possible—even through shock therapy—the PWC pays attention to the scheduling and rolling out of new economic policies. This concern was largely the product of the poor performance of privatization programs in various transition economies.

Taken collectively, we can see the PWC as an intellectual development from neoliberalism. The idea that an abstract (free) market would always prove to be the best possible way of organizing economic life has been replaced by a moderate caution toward the market, in which the latter's functioning is significantly conditioned by a set of interrelated contexts.

These ideas are actually not particularly new. They derive from some classical theories of the market economy as well as some contemporary developments in theoretical economics, with its growing algebraic complexity. Hence, we can only fully understand the PWC as a political construct. In this sense, obviously, the PWC reflects a desire to generate distance from the Washington Consensus and its perceived failure.

It is certainly the case that neoliberal policy agendas throughout the world did not produce strikingly healthy results by almost any criteria. In this respect, the PWC constitutes an attempt both to move beyond the Washington Consensus but also to salvage aspects of the neoliberal policy raft and rethink their application.

The key intellectual figure here is Joseph Stiglitz, former World Bank Chief Economist and Nobel Prize winner. Throughout the 1990s, his writing on institutions and information fed into World Bank policy, moderating its desire to promote the free market. After his resignation from the World Bank—itself a highly charged political event—he wrote scathingly about the International Monetary Fund, representing it as an unreconstructed neoliberal fundamentalist. Thus, the PWC has become part of the World Bank's repositioning through the 1990s, a useful intellectual hook to see the World Bank through a range of criticisms of its previous policies.

—*Graham Harrison*

See also Neoliberalism; Poverty Reduction; Washington Consensus

Further Readings and References

Fine, B., Lapvitsas, C., & Pincus, J. (Eds.). (2001). *Development policy in the twenty-first century: Beyond the post-Washington Consensus.* London, Routledge.

POVERTY REDUCTION

One of the most urgent global development challenges is the continued existence of widespread poverty. A recent estimate suggests that in 2001 there were 2.73 billion people in the world living on less than US$2 per day. This represents more than half of the total population of the developing world. The current context of globalization has made people increasingly aware of the existence of poverty. Many argue that the continuation of absolute poverty is likely to lead to greater political tensions, both at the national and the global levels.

In response, over recent years, a substantial level of agreement has developed on the need to reduce poverty. World leaders adopted the Millennium Declaration at the United Nations (UN) in 2000, which pledged to cut the incidence of extreme poverty in half by the year 2015, in contrast with 1990 levels. However, there is much less of a consensus among interested parties on how this is to be achieved. The major difficulty in devising a strategy for poverty

reduction is that poverty, however we choose to define it, can be caused by a number of different factors. Although the vast majority of the world's poverty is found in the Global South, it is an issue that faces every country in the world, whether developed or developing.

What Is Poverty?

Before we can begin to think about how best to approach the task of poverty reduction it is important to appreciate the contested nature of the term *poverty* itself. How we define poverty is vital to how we conceive of the bigger problem of reducing it. Historically, poverty has been understood in a rather limited sense as being a substantial lack of income. Absolute measures of what it meant to be living in poverty differed from country to country because it was judged in relative terms to the standard of living within individual societies. National governments have often drawn a "poverty line" to mark where they judge the minimum income necessary to be able to live a satisfactory life. Over recent years, the publication of data that uses purchasing power parity has made meaningful international comparison much simpler.

The orthodox understanding of what poverty is has broadened somewhat in recent years. Rather than reflecting a simple measure based on a lack of economic wealth, it is now viewed by many as something that also includes a number of socioeconomic factors. A good example is the human poverty index (HPI) that was first published in the annual *United Nations Human Development Reports* in 1997. The HPI is a measure of poverty based on the experience of individuals and is calculated by focusing on the proportion of citizens that are below certain basic levels of health, education, life expectancy, and access to clean water. It is expressed as a percentage, but it should be noted that different criteria are set for the HPI of developing countries and high-income countries.

All these measures of poverty are objective. That is to say, they are based on observable criteria and most of the debate over what constitutes poverty is confined to what are the most suitable criteria to include. However, we could view poverty in a subjective fashion. This would involve appreciation of whether individuals actually consider themselves to be living in poverty. Orthodox interpretations of poverty do not include the nonmaterial aspects of life, which are far less quantifiable. The general consensus today is that those living a life based on subsistence agriculture are more likely to be living in poverty. However, this view could be seen as representative of Western notions of development and modernity.

Alternative Strategies for Poverty Reduction

Different strategies have been developed to achieve poverty reduction. In part, they reflect the differences of opinion over what poverty is. How the problem is defined often dictates the type of strategies that are developed. The most dominant theoretical approach to poverty reduction over recent decades has been the neoliberal strategy. This reflected a shift in the dominant economic thinking within a number of major states in the West in the early 1980s. According to the neoliberal model, poverty reduction is to be achieved through the achievement of high levels of economic growth. It is argued that economic growth will be maximized by allowing the market to operate as freely as possible, with only minimal state interference. For developing countries, this has meant an approach centered on the growth of exports. It is argued that there is a strong correlation between sustained economic growth and poverty reduction, and that the benefits of this growth will trickle down to the poorest members of society. In essence, maximizing the growth of the global economy is argued to be the best way to solve the problem of global poverty.

The neoliberal model understands poverty as a lack of income. It makes no reference to the levels of inequality within societies. An alternative view would suggest that there is actually a direct link between inequality and poverty. If we were to adopt this approach, then the goal of greater income equality would be prioritized over economic growth. Put simply, poverty could be reduced by a redistribution of existing resources and is not wholly reliant on the generation of further wealth. Proponents of this model

point to the fact that the income gap, both between states and also within states, has widened over recent decades.

Many of the debates over poverty reduction have centered on whether economic growth is a sufficient condition. There is evidence to suggest that it is possible to achieve economic growth without reducing poverty. Other critics have pointed to examples that indicate the outcome of a neoliberal strategy has actually resulted in an increase in poverty. Here, the focus on the role of the state is revisited. It could be argued that specific policies and institutions are needed to harness the benefits of economic growth for poverty reduction. This view emphasizes how poverty encompasses a number of components, which may not be provided by a complete reliance on market forces. It is suggested that to reduce poverty, we also need to improve access to health care, education, and vital resources, such as clean water.

Two other issues have also had an impact on recent debates over poverty reduction. A significant proportion of those people living in poverty are women, some estimates being as high as seventy percent. Here, it is argued that the social construction of gender roles is directly linked to the existence of poverty, and that these need to be deconstructed for the development of effective poverty reduction strategies. Such inequalities in gender have an effect on the experience that men, women, and children have of poverty. To a limited extent, such views have been incorporated into mainstream policy making. The World Bank, for example, now claims to include issues of gender in its approach to poverty reduction.

Others argue that we should put the environment at the center of our approach to poverty reduction. The centrality of economic growth is questioned in this view and the need for sustainability is often put forward. This concept of sustainable development is interpreted in different ways. The mainstream view is that there is an inescapable link between economic growth and poverty reduction. From this perspective, the main cause of environmental degradation is poverty. In contrast, more radical interpretations link these two problems with the economic system and argue that alternative models, often small-scale developments, are needed to reverse environmental decline.

Development Policy and Poverty Reduction

The neoliberal approach dominated policy making during the 1980s. Increasingly, the market was viewed as the only means to reduce poverty and promote development. The impact of this model on the developing world was criticized on a number of fronts. The main problems were identified as a lack of concern for the poorest sections of society, and the imposition of polices from above that incorporated little discussion with host country governments and civil society.

In response to these criticisms, changes have occurred. The World Bank in particular has responded to these challenges. There has been a marked shift in the stated approach of the World Bank to development since the mid-1990s. The origins of this shift are to be found in the *World Development Report, 1990* and its focus on poverty. Previously, poverty had been viewed as just one of a number of issues related to development policy. The central component of the approach had been economic growth, and any other development indicators, such as those measuring health or education levels, were seen as secondary outcomes of this main target. Increasing criticism of this approach led to a rethinking in the World Bank, particularly after James Wolfensohn was appointed the new president on June 1, 1995.

It appeared that there was growing uncertainty within the World Bank over its development policy. There were two key reasons for this: first, the World Bank's 1993 report on East Asia, which moved it away from a market-led approach to development to a market-friendly view; second, the difficulties encountered in defending the poor record of the World Bank's policies in Africa. In October 1998, at the World Bank/International Monetary Fund (IMF) Annual Meetings, President Wolfensohn outlined his new vision. He called for a more balanced interpretation of development and suggested that it was not just about economic adjustment. The concept of a partnership approach to World Bank development policy

was also mentioned in response to the criticism of conditionality. The culmination of this period of internal soul searching in the World Bank was the Comprehensive Development Framework (CDF), which was launched on January 21, 1999. This has moved the World Bank toward a concern for poverty reduction and away from a view of development based purely on economic growth.

The CDF was soon followed by the launch of Poverty Reduction Strategy Papers (PRSPs) in September 1999. These were jointly adopted by the World Bank and the IMF and can be seen as in line with the new thinking adopted in the CDF. The World Bank emphasized that PRSPs should be centered on a process led by the country involved, with the full and active participation of civil society, and should be concerned with the comprehensive nature of the causes of poverty. The message of the PRSPs appears quite clear. The new focus should be poverty, and the policies designed to achieve this should be created in partnership with developing countries.

The adoption of PRSPs has had a major impact beyond just the policies of the World Bank and IMF. They have increasingly become a general measure of the suitability of developing countries for either debt relief or further lending. The European Commission has noted how PRSPs have become a central part of the European approach to development policy. Debate has ensued as to whether the overall approach of the World Bank has drastically changed or not. They created a new instrument called the Poverty Reduction Support Credit (PRSC), which was explicitly designed to support the implementation of PRSPs. However, traditional adjustment loans continued alongside the new PRSPs.

The renewed focus of the World Bank on poverty reduction is actually nothing new. During the 1970s, the World Bank adopted its "basic needs" approach, which had similar aims. However, one of the most notable aspects of current development policy is the level of harmonization of approach among most of the key actors. There is significant agreement on the central role of poverty reduction within the World Bank, the European Union (EU), and many of the governments in the developed world.

A brief survey of the current policy of the UK government demonstrates the existence of similar themes to those of the World Bank. The Labour government published the first white paper on international development by a UK government in over two decades in 1997. The Department for International Development (DFID) then published another in 2000 titled *Eliminating World Poverty: Making Globalisation Work for the Poor.* Both these documents sought to highlight the centrality of poverty reduction to the development policy of the UK government.

Of course, such harmonization does not happen by accident. The new centrality of poverty reduction to development policy is reflected in the Millennium Development Goals (MDG). They provide the framework within which all development policy is now located. This new model has been termed the post-Washington Consensus, in contrast to the dominant neoliberal approach of the 1980s and early 1990s, which was labeled the Washington Consensus. A number of recent meetings have since reinforced this consensus. The United Nations Conference on Financing for Development, held in Monterrey, Mexico, in 2002 was followed by a meeting in Rome in February 2003, at which all the major bilateral and multilateral actors of the international development community met and signed a declaration on harmonization. Here, the commitment to poverty reduction and partnership was restated. For some commentators, it remains a matter of opinion as to how much of a change in policy has actually taken place.

—Stephen R. Hurt

See also Development Theory; Global Civil Society; Millennium Development Goals; Neoliberalism; New Poverty Research; Post–Washington Consensus; Sustainable Development; World Bank; World Development Indicators

Further Readings and References

Allen, T., & Thomas, A. (Eds.). (2000). *Poverty and development into the twenty-first century.* Oxford, UK: Oxford University Press.

Booth, A., & Mosley, P. (Eds.). (2002). *New poverty strategies: What have they achieved? What have we learned?* Basingstoke, UK: Palgrave.

Cammack, P. (2004). What the World Bank means by poverty reduction, and why it matters. *New Political Economy, 9,* 189–211.

Department for International Development. (2000). *Eliminating world poverty: Making globalisation work for the poor.* London: HMSO.

Sen, A. (1999). *Development as freedom.* New York: Alfred Knopf.

United Nations Development Programme. (annual). *Human development report.* New York: Oxford University Press.

Wade, R. H. (2004). On the causes of increasing world poverty and inequality, or why the Matthew Effect prevails. *New Political Economy, 9,* 163–188.

Weber, H. (2002). The imposition of a global development architecture: The example of microcredit. *Review of International Studies, 28,* 537–555.

White, H. (2001). Will the new aid agenda help promote poverty reduction? *Journal of International Development, 13,* 1057–1070.

World Bank. (1990). *World development report, 1990.* New York: Oxford University Press.

World Bank. (2000). *World development report 2000/2001: Attacking poverty.* New York: Oxford University Press.

POWER

Within human governance, power refers to the ability of a given individual, corporate body, political organization, or political system (broadly defined) to further interests, shape behaviors (positively and negatively), and inform strategies for action. Often improperly taken as a synonym for authority or control, the term is more closely tied to influence. As such, power is relational, existing only among sets of actors: everything from the family to interstate conflict and cooperation. The nature of these relationships may vary in strength, duration, and complexity, but power is a causal factor in all interactions. While omnipresent, the myriad of divergent and occasionally intangible forms in which power is realized makes it all but impossible to develop a universal definition for the term that is precise and measurable. Faced with these challenges, the following discussion generally outlines the dimensions and manifestations of power so that it may be identified, disaggregated, and meaningfully analyzed.

The first step to understanding power's empirical manifestations comes by appreciating the three ways in which the term is typically employed in discussions of social, economic, and political relations. While useful for illustrative purposes, in practice, the distinctions between these three manifestations of power are frequently blurred or indistinguishable.

The first view takes power as something possessed by an organization, group, or individual due to personal characteristics or from being associated with an office or social role. The powers of a political office are one example. The focus here is on direct influence over others, although inscribed forms of power can exist even when commands are not made. For this reason, state leaders retain the power to make decisions affecting others (granting pardons, for example) even when they choose not to do so. Moreover, they may indirectly discourage others from contesting issues.

The second perspective takes power as a resource that can be used at will. The focus here is less on direct influence over others, but rather evaluates power as the ability of an actor (again, a group, individual, organization, or state) to achieve a consciously defined objective. In the final conception, power is taken to be a system of strategies, practices, and techniques. The latter view does not deny that power takes on the forms previously described, but rather, demands a relational perspective that explicitly recognizes how the exercise of power depends on the institutional and social contexts. More important, it illustrates how with others' individual actors' strategies and techniques interact to create forms of power that at once comprise actors, but outside of direct individual and collective control. As discussed further in the following paragraphs, these more amorphous manifestations of power are critical to understanding the complexity of power and governance in contemporary societies.

All three perspectives previously outlined describe the exercise of power without identifying the means that endow actors, however defined, with the ability to pursue their objectives or influence others. Amitai Etzioni's neo-Weberian study of compliance within formal organizations addresses this paucity by identifying three primary sources of power, each corresponding to a critical concept in Weber's own writing: coercion or violence (power, for Weber), material resources (class), and values and identity (status).

Coercion or violence—"power" per se for Weber—refers to the use, or threat thereof, of physical confinement or removal, torture or the application of pain, physical destruction of the means for survival, or death. Power in this form also includes other indirect forms of coercion (e.g., taxation, law making) that at least implicitly rely on the threat of force. Niccolo Machiavelli's assertion that it is better to rule by fear than love is a clear, normative statement on governance drawn from a perspective that makes coercion the preeminent form of social power. Reflecting a Machiavellian skepticism of anything other than coercion (especially values and norms) as an effective disciplinary force, contemporary realists typically base their analyses (and normative recommendations) on the exercise of organized violence: Everything from the use of state resources to maintain domestic order, the exercise of intrastate conflict, genocide, or even violence within the home and workplace. Indeed, for scholars who analytically privilege coercion, the other sources of power described in the following paragraphs are typically taken as an outgrowth of physical power or as means of enhancing it.

Structuralist approaches to politics, which include many forms of Marxism, typically privilege the material bases of power, which includes control over natural resources, commodities, and the allocation—by whatever means—of remuneration for labor, services, or a willingness to refrain from action. Therefore, power can emerge from influence in the market (as in capitalism), the state (as in socialism), or networks of patronage, corruption, and violence, as in kleptocratic (greedy or corrupt) or clientelistic (political machine) regimes. As with all bases of power, material power not only exists when goods are being actively distributed or withheld, but also as a potential force. An actor's mere possession or control of resources (or the ability to convince others of such control) can itself serve as a form of power, although this must often be supplemented by the kinds of nonmaterial sources of power described in the following paragraphs. Whereas those privileging coercion typically portray material accumulation as a means of bolstering physical power, this perspective posits the pursuit of material gain as the primary motivation for violence in all its forms. Vladimir Lenin's assertion that capitalists' quest for new markets drives imperialism and military expansion is one of the most explicit statements of this position and continues to influence work on trade, international relations, and economic development.

A third, autonomous source of power is potentially derived from coercion or control over material resources, values, identities, and symbols. As with the other types, normative power appears in multiple forms, from the mundane (e.g., brand loyalties), the personal (e.g., love), to the utopian and violent (e.g., cosmopolitanism, patriotism, and nationalism). Nonmaterialist perspectives on power do not assume the inherent desire to accumulate wealth or expand military influence but, rather, suggest that people's desires for particular goods or social ends are embedded in and derive from systems of values and norms. Similarly, the ends to be achieved through violence are derived from a social definition of what is individually desirable or in the interest of a collective actor, be it a state, liberation movement, or terrorist organization. Even those who identify coercive power as the foundation of the modern state typically recognize that the sustainability of social structures and ruling elites depends on the degree to which they are legitimized through nonmaterialist appeals. Constructivist scholars who focus on norms and institutionalized behaviors exemplify this approach in explaining everything from ethnic mobilization to interstate relations as systems of values. Similar perspectives appear among those who, albeit on a smaller scale, focus on symbolism, socialization, and "appropriate" behavior within families and the workplace.

Two critical points emerge when exploring the varied sources of power in governance. First, although a particular source of power may be foremost within a defined set of social relations, actors' abilities to dominate, influence, or achieve a desired end are almost always conditioned by all three sources. For this reason, even governments ruling through fear (e.g., those with vast armies) or patronage will typically seek to legitimate their rule through appeals to values,

mythology, and ethics, as do leaders of private companies. Conversely, even organizations and individuals whose primary source of power stems from value and belief systems (e.g., clergy) must still rely on some degree of coercion or material incentives to retain their positions of authority, to maintain group cohesion, and to propagate their message. Georg Hegel's assertion of the need for human recognition in even those relationships primarily characterized by violence (e.g., master-slave) highlights the interplay and interdependence of the various sources of power.

Hegel's comment draws attention to a second concern, that compliance and influence are premised on the recognition that all actors—however small or grand—possess power in some form: Workers control their labor, soldiers their ability to fight (and their weapons), and (in democratic political systems) voters control the ability to confer legitimacy through the ballot. These dynamics allow even the most visibly downtrodden to exert influence, as individuals or collectives, over their physical and social surroundings. Labor mobilization and public protests are visible examples, although passive resistance by peasants, factory workers, and prisoners is another way in which the seemingly dispossessed are able to exert influence on those in structurally superior positions. Conversely, Peter Bachrach and Morton Baratz note how elites may exercise power in limiting the scope of debate and contestation, even without undertaking specific actions to do so.

These two points—that all sources of power are mutually present and that all actors possess control over some source of power—provide sources of dynamism in explaining social change. Challenges to systems of patron-client rule, for example, may not only come from elites' shifting economic fortunes (e.g., changing terms of trade or shifting product preferences), but may also derive from the growing legitimacy of radical discourses (e.g., a belief in individual rights, land distribution, or the growth of secularism), which undermine the normative foundations buttressing those relations. Post–World War II independence movements, for example, owed much of their success to the colonies' declining economic viability and the strengthening discourse of self-determination. As in this case, change may emerge from multiple sources as power shifts in complex and sometimes unpredictable ways.

Disembodied Power

Much of how we understand power focuses on its exercise by discrete actors in identifiable relations, often within formal governing parameters (e.g., laws and institutional structures). These include not only masters and slaves, but also employees and employers, household members, parties in armed conflict, or relations between officials and citizens (or among citizens themselves). The idea that power is levied by one actor (or set of actors) against or over another is useful—and affirms the view that power is necessarily relational—but often overlooks the historically configured expressions of power that define those actors and condition their relations.

Returning to the view of power as a system of strategies, practices, and techniques, one begins to see that the emergence of discrete actors, their relations to others, and their relative control over the sources of power comes about as much by accident as design. Rather, actors and their endowments emerge through the interactions, language, and the sharing of symbols that may themselves be the unintended by-products of efforts to achieve other ends. Historically, informed discussions of ethnic formation and conflict highlight the resources, strategies, and coincidences that typically precede the emergence of what later appears as a unified group. The unintended consequences of economic, political, and institutional reforms also demonstrate how strategies dedicated to achieving one goal can generate opportunities and resources in forms other than those originally envisioned. Moreover, once established, discourses, values, institutions, and past patterns of action continue to exert an influence on current behavior.

Revealing the often hidden, historical precedents for the formation of these webs of power has been central to Michel Foucault's archaeologies of knowledge, his idea of governmentality, and to much of the work his scholarship has inspired. Building on the invisible face of power Bachrach and Baratz identify, one sees a similar acknowledgment in Anthony Giddens's idea of structuration, in Michael Mann's discussion of infrastructural power, or in other analyses of the constraints and opportunities facing actors embedded in social networks. From this we see how the exercise of power has increasingly shifted away from easily identifiable or explicit hierarchies founded on coercion, to social stratification enforced through diffuse forms of internalized, normative power. Within such structures, it is all but impossible to identify either a single source of power or the complete range of influences accounting for individual actions. Critically, these diffuse forms of power may become effectively invisible or taken for granted, even to those who ostensibly exercise it.

That power is dynamic, derives from multiple sources, and exists in both easily identified relations among actors and within systems of thinking and social organization means that the study of power must itself be ecumenical in its approach. Individual scholars may productively examine power relations between two actors or within a narrowly defined spatial and historical context, but understanding governance means situating such analyses within a broader context of dynamic conglomerations of historically constituted actors linked through various forms of power. Scholars must similarly be aware of forms of power that are not immediately visible and those embedded in the language used in daily interactions or in the language and concepts scholars use to describe them.

—Loren B. Landau

See also Coercion; Hegemony; Middle Power; Patrimonialism; Postmodernism; Power Sharing; State-Society Relations

Further Readings and References

Allen, J. (1997). Economies of power and space. In R. Lee & J. Wills (Eds.), *Geographies of Economies* (pp. 59–70). London: Arnold.

Bachrach, P., & Baratz, M. S. (1962). Two faces of power. *The American Political Science Review, 56,* 947–952.

Dahl, R. (1957). The concept of power. *Behavioral Science, 2,* 201–215.

Etzioni, A. (1961). *A comparative analysis of complex organizations.* New York: Free Press.

Hirschman, A. O. (1970). *Exit, voice, and loyalty: Responses to decline in firms, organizations, and states.* Cambridge, MA: Harvard University Press.

Lukes, S. (1997). *Power: A radical view.* London: Macmillan.

Poulantzes, N. (1975). *Political power and social class.* London: Verso Books.

Rose, N. (1999). *Powers of freedom: Reframing political thought.* Cambridge, MA: Cambridge University Press.

Scott, J. C. (1985). *Weapons of the weak: Everyday forms of peasant resistance.* New Haven, CT: Yale University Press.

Weber, M. (1922). The distribution of power within the political community: Class, status, and party. In *Economy and Society.* Berkeley: University of California Press.

Power Sharing

Power sharing results when governments or civil society actors elicit cooperation in actions undertaken by one another. Power sharing also results from passive acquiescence in such undertakings. More extensive in representative democracies, power sharing also occurs in other governmental systems. Also, democratic transitions are marked by increased power sharing—planned and unplanned.

The diversity of social organization often prevents otherwise dominant official governments from monopolizing governance. Resources available to national and local governments may not suffice to carry out tasks expected of them. Thus, power sharing complements and modifies useful insights from power elite, social class, and interest group pluralist theories. For explaining decision making in presidential systems, power sharing is a more nuanced alternative to checks and balances.

Power sharing manifests itself in the day-to-day bureaucratic politics in and between government departments. In nonelectoral activity, power sharing occurs almost continuously between governments and well-positioned individuals and organizations. Official governments may also be understood as larger, more powerful interest associations. One of many among plural centers of power, official government agencies and departments compete and negotiate with business and trade associations, veterans' organizations, educational groups, news media, and antiwar movements to get their business done. From the perspective of political actors, therefore, power sharing occurs both willingly and unwillingly, skillfully and ineffectively.

Policy narratives answer the questions of where, when, and how skillfully power is shared. The details of these case studies can explain why government officials or civil society organizations succeeded or failed to achieve their preferred futures. Top-down consultation with individuals and nongovernmental or civil society organizations is one kind of power sharing. Inclusion of minority political parties in the cabinet of national governments is another. The quality of power sharing also explains how small, seemingly weak social movements sometimes prevail dramatically in achieving policy objectives, despite opposition from large and powerful established governments.

Intragovernmental power sharing in federal systems is premised on domestic division of sovereignty. Within federal and unitary states, regional autonomy for indigenous people is further power sharing. It also occurs between national or local governments of two or more countries, for example, with international treaties between independent states. More broadly, growing collaboration in the European Union, and the Association of South East Asian Nations implies power sharing and unacknowledged surrender of a degree of sovereignty. Power sharing between government agencies of one country and people and organizations in another has become an increasingly common form of crossnational pressure politics and lobbying. Trade negotiations between the United States and Japan in the 1980s and 1990s are a good example of this.

Among other implications of power sharing, representative democracies co-opt protest activities more efficiently than do authoritarian systems. But whether lobbying, educational, and protest activities designed to elicit power sharing from official governments by civil society associations are more effective in parliamentary or presidential systems is debated.

—*Vincent Kelly Pollard*

See also Dialogic Public Policy; Interdependence; Political Exchange; Power

Further Readings and References

Parenti, M. (2002). *Democracy for the few* (7th ed.). New York: St. Martin's.

Pollard, V. K. (2004). *Globalization, democratization and Asian leadership: Power sharing, foreign policy and society in the Philippines and Japan.* Aldershot, UK: Ashgate.

PRAGMATISM

Pragmatism is a school of philosophy developed by American philosophers Charles Peirce, William James, John Dewey, and George Herbert Mead and extended by philosophers such as W. V. O. Quine, Nelson Goodman, Hilary Putnam, and Richard Rorty. It is difficult to give a concise definition of pragmatism, because it ranges so widely across logic, education, moral theory, social psychology, aesthetics, political theory, and other fields. However, the central preoccupation of pragmatism is with how we can know the world and then act upon that knowledge. Pragmatism argues that knowledge is created when we use symbols, concepts, and ideas to solve problems we encounter in our everyday lives. Pragmatists reject a theory of knowledge that sees knowledge as a mere reflection of the natural world. Instead, knowledge is a social product of communities engaged in dialogue about common problems. Conflicting perspectives are useful for advancing knowledge, but fruitful conflict requires cooperation to clearly set the terms of joint inquiry. Pragmatism's emphasis on knowledge, dialogue, fruitful conflict, and cooperative inquiry make it an attractive philosophical starting point for many students of governance and provides insight into the character of institutions, public deliberation, and societal problem solving.

The work of John Dewey is a notable touchstone in current discussions about governance. In his major work on political theory, *The Public and Its Problems,* Dewey linked an analysis of the rise of modern organizational and technological society with a critical intellectual defense of a deliberative, communitarian, and participatory vision of democracy. His key analytical concept was the "public," which he argued was being eclipsed with the erosion of local face-to-face community. Successful modern democracy, he argued, required the restoration of a public that could match the scale and scope of modern organization and technology. His analysis anticipates much of Jürgen Habermas's more recent work on the "public sphere."

The revival of Dewey as a defender of a deliberative, communitarian, and participatory vision of democracy is appropriate, though it sometimes leads to a one-sided view of his larger political commitments. For example, Dewey was also an advocate of the positive role of scientific inquiry, and he felt that experts and public agencies had a critical role to play in modern democracy. The apparent antinomies of his thought were, in fact, inherent in the pragmatist vision and were aimed at reconciling a bottom-up, populist approach to democratic governance with a top-down expert-oriented view.

The next section of this entry describes three central themes of the pragmatist vision. The entry then goes on to explore Philip Selznick's use of pragmatist themes in his approach to institutions and then analyzes pragmatist-inspired work on problem solving. The entry concludes with a discussion of the differences between classical and neopragmatism.

Three Core Themes of Classical Pragmatism

One of the basic goals of the founding pragmatists was to escape the dualism that they believed plagued modern thought. They regarded earlier philosophers from René Descartes through Immanuel Kant as having created theories of knowledge that relied too heavily on sharp separations between the mind and the body, the knowing subject and the external world, or the theoretical and the practical, to name just a few of these dualisms. This section examines pragmatism's attempt to overcome three such dualisms with particular relevance to governance: (1) meaning and action (or theory and practice), (2) individual and society, and (3) the plural and the unitary.

A central theme of pragmatism is overcoming the duality between meaning and action. Drawing on Kantianism, on the one hand, pragmatism emphasizes the central role of symbols (concepts) in human behavior. At the same time, influenced by Charles Darwin, pragmatists view humans as adaptive organisms oriented toward concrete problem solving. Integrating these two points, pragmatism emphasizes the instrumental role of conceptual thinking in problem solving, while insisting that abstract concepts only assume concrete meaning when oriented to specific problems.

This stance was part of a larger philosophical agenda. Beginning with Peirce, pragmatism sought to reconcile the competing philosophies of empiricism and rationalism. Rationalism believed that our concepts were mental phenomena that should be understood as prior to experience, thus conceiving of knowledge in deductive terms. By contrast, empiricism saw concepts as inductive generalizations from sensory experience. Alternatively, Peirce proposed "abduction" as a moving back and forth between deduction and induction. This iterative relationship between meaning and action also informs Dewey's argument that "ends" and "means" must be understood as continuously interacting.

Pragmatism's second recurring theme is the attempt to overcome the dualism between individual and society. The pragmatists rejected the individualism they associated with classical liberalism and social contract theories as too atomistic (Dewey called it "old" individualism). But they did not reject individualism, and they would have equally opposed the privileging of society over the individual. Instead, as most fully developed in the work of Mead, the individual and society develop together: Individuals develop into social consciousness by internalizing the norms of society. As this happens, society itself evolves. It becomes a community only with the development of self-consciously "social selves."

Again, symbols are key mediating factors in this coevolution. For Mead, as for the other pragmatists, symbolic exchange—communication—is the central process that relates individuals to society. Habermas draws directly on Mead in developing the idea of communicative rationality, which has become an important concept for contemporary debates about governance.

Pragmatism's third recurring theme is the attempt to overcome the dualism between pluralism and unity. Whether they were talking about scientific inquiry, social psychology, or democratic debate, pragmatists continuously stressed the pluralism of ideas and perspectives. William James, for instance, famously stressed that human attention is highly selective, producing a plurality of perspectives. His analysis of attention later inspired the bounded rationality approach to organizations developed by Herbert Simon. At the same time, pragmatism also emphasizes the possibility for integrative unity to develop out of this pluralism. In the terms of modern complexity theory, this unity is "emergent," developing out of the interaction of contending perspectives. Thus, for Peirce, truth was emergent from the process of scientific inquiry, as "will" emerged out of streams of consciousness for James, and "community" emerged out of the process of communication for Mead and Dewey.

It is certainly in the pragmatist spirit to ask whether these abstract themes have any concrete application for the topic of governance. The following section describes Philip Selznick's perspective on institutions as one important translation of pragmatist ideas into terms useful for understanding governance.

Selznick on Institutions

Although Selznick's intellectual genealogy is complex, he is explicit about the inspiration he drew from Dewey. Selznick pointed out in 1980 that he approached the subject as a "moral pragmatist" who sought to understand how an abstract ideology—grass roots administration—fared when confronted with concrete political realities. Selznick argued that the full realization of this concept of grass roots democracy failed because it was an "unanalyzed abstraction." Consequently, the hopes for direct political participation were co-opted by powerful political forces.

Although working in a tradition that took both Max Weber and Emile Durkheim as classical points of reference, Selznick's pragmatism led him to a different interpretation of modern institutions. Both Weber and Durkheim erected analytical dichotomies—formal versus informal, personal versus impersonal, mechanical versus organic solidarity—that represent just the kinds of modernist dualisms that pragmatists seek to overcome. Selznick's summary statement of much of his thought on institutions, *Leadership in Administration,* demonstrates the differences between his work and Weber's and Durkheim's. Whereas Weber emphasized the centrality of impersonal and formal forces embodied in the rise of bureaucracy and feared that they would empty modern life of meaning, Selznick stressed the importance of personal leadership in institutionalizing meaningful frameworks for organized action. In fact, his well-known definition of institutions equated institutionalization with the process of "infusing value" into the social fabric of the organization. The dichotomy between charismatic leadership and bureaucratic routinization are thereby avoided. Moreover, while Weber saw formal rational-legal authority as driving informal organization out of modern bureaucracy, Selznick viewed successful modern organizations as mobilizing informal organization to support formal organization. The organization becomes an institution, he argued, when it evolves from an "instrument" into a "community."

Selznick's view of modern organization has many affinities with Durkheim's hope that occupational communities will become sources of moral socialization in the modern world. Many of Selznick's prescriptions in *Leadership in Administration* regard socialization—notably the internalization of the organization's mission—as a key management device with important implications for governance. For example, while the Weberian concept of bureaucracy encourages centralization, value internalization permits an important measure of decentralization because employees that have internalized the organization's mission do not require strong hierarchical control. Although Selznick draws on Durkheim to understand socialization, his analysis also has a strong pragmatist spirit. He argued that socialization is about building "character," both at the individual and the institutional level. And character building, in turn, requires building competences that allow moral action. Therefore, successful institutionalization depends on the focusing of social energies on realistic and purposeful organizational missions. Meaning must be aligned with action.

Problem Solving, Knowledge, and Cooperation

Problem solving is a leitmotif for pragmatism, tying together many important themes.

Concrete problem-solving is a process that bridges between theory and practice and, as emphasized by Dewey's educational philosophy, provides opportunities for creativity and learning. Pragmatists suggest that problematic situations produce reflexivity—scrutiny and revision of our basic commitments and beliefs—that allows experimental inquiry and the advancement of knowledge. A shared focus on concrete problems can also produce social cooperation and community and discourage fruitless disputes over abstract meanings. In fact, social conflict can itself be thought of as a problem that requires a strategy of conflict resolution.

This problem-solving focus has many interesting implications for governance, only a few of which can be noted here. In *The Reflective Practitioner,* for example, Donald Schön developed a model of professional problem solving very much in a pragmatist spirit. Against the separation of theory and practice that dominates our contemporary understanding of professional expertise, Schön argued that we ought to instead conceive of professional practice as "reflection-in-action." He argued that highly skilled professionals continuously engage in reflection that probes their past experiences in light of current problematic situations. Reflection allows them to "reframe" the problem or their knowledge so as to devise more appropriate, context-specific solutions. In a later book with Martin Rein, Schön applied a similar model of reflexivity to resolving collective public policy conflict.

Charles Sabel and colleagues have also applied a pragmatist-inspired model of problem solving to public and private collaboration. They argue that successful and creative collaboration requires "learning by monitoring," in which multiple parties appreciate the provisional nature of knowledge and recognize the importance of pursuing mutual intelligibility. Learning-by-monitoring requires parties to adopt an experimentalist stance toward learning and to pursue knowledge through joint inquiry and mutual observation. This learning-by-monitoring model has been used to explore the possibility of new forms of organizational and interorganizational collaboration in both the public and private sphere.

Conclusion

This entry has largely drawn on classic perspectives on pragmatism. In concluding, however, this entry would be remiss if it did not consider more broadly— if too briefly—the place of neopragmatism in contemporary governance. Although the work of Hilary Putnam, Nelson Goodman, and Donald Davidson, among many others, has revived and advanced pragmatism as a philosophical tradition, the work of Richard Rorty has captured particular attention beyond philosophy. Building on Dewey, Heidegger, and Wittgenstein, Rorty presented in 1979 a sweeping argument against the basic "foundational" conception of human knowledge, hence challenging the status of philosophy as the foundational discipline for all knowledge (based, in turn, on a claim about the foundational role of epistemology). Rorty argued that the major distinction between classical and new pragmatism is that neopragmatists do not accept the classical pragmatist's faith in scientific method. The implications of this argument for governance are less specific than those previously described, but possibly more far-reaching. Hugh Miller, for example, argued that neopragmatism provides a better resource for reforming contemporary public administration precisely because it so clearly rejects claims of scientific objectivism. Certainly Rortian pragmatism provides a critical perspective from which to understand the authority claims of scientific expertise in governance.

It also probably complicates Dewey's goal of reconciling progressive models of expertise with populist models of direct democratic participation.

However, beyond these differences, both classical pragmatism and neopragmatism share an openness to the world of everyday politics that allows them to engage with contemporary debates about governance. It is both steadfastly antiutopian and hopeful for social progress.

—*Chris Ansell*

See also Communicative Rationality; Interpretive Theory; Public Sphere; Reflexivity

Further Readings and References

Anderson, C. (1990). *Pragmatic liberalism.* Chicago: University of Chicago Press.

Chisholm, D. (2001). *Waiting for dead men's shoes: Origins and development of the U.S. Navy's Officer Personnel System, 1793–1941.* Palo Alto, CA: Stanford University Press.

Dewey, J. (1927). *The public and its problems.* New York: H. Holt.

Mead, G. H. (1934). *Mind, self and society.* Chicago: University of Chicago Press.

Miller, H. (2004). Why old pragmatism needs an upgrade. *Administration & Society, 36*(2) 243–249.

Rorty, R. (1979). *Philosophy and the mirror of nature.* Princeton, NJ: Princeton University Press.

Schön, D. (1983). *The reflective practitioner: How professionals think in action.* New York: Basic Books.

Schön, D., & Rein, M. (1994). *Frame reflection: Toward the resolution of intractable policy controversies.* New York: Basic Books.

Selznick, P. (1980). *TVA and the grass roots: A study of politics and organization.* Berkeley: University of California Press.

Selznick, P. (1992). *The moral commonwealth: Social theory and the promise of community.* Berkeley: University of California Press.

PRECAUTIONARY PRINCIPLE

The precautionary principle is a principle of environmental policy making that legitimizes the adoption of preventative measures to address a potential threat of severe environmental damage. It was developed in response to two specific problems of international environmental governance: the need to take into account the particular nature of environmental damage, as well as conditions of persisting uncertainty in decision making. It recognizes that some forms of environmental harm, such as the extinction of a species, are irreversible. Furthermore, the full extent of the harm (and thus its reversibility) cannot always be assessed in advance: Thus, uncertainty as to the extent of the damage persists often until after it is committed, when it is sometimes too late (or too costly) to stem the harm. Given such conditions, the precautionary principle prescribes the safest course of action, namely, the suspension of the potentially damaging activity until it has been proven risk free. In precautionary language, it shifts the burden of proof: The risk need no longer be verified in order for policymakers to be able to proscribe a potentially harmful activity. Rather, the onus is upon those who want to pursue the activity (or course of action) to prove that it is not environmentally damaging. The precautionary principle moves environmental governance from a reactive basis (where protective policies are devised in reaction to damage that has already occurred) to a preventative one.

The concept has its roots in 1970s–1980s German environmental law (*Das "Vorsorgeprinzip"*). It emerged into international law at the 1987 International Conference on the Protection of the North Sea. Since then, it has permeated most international environmental conventions: Entrenched by the 1992 Rio Declaration (Principle 15), it was written into the Climate Change Convention and (retroactively) into the Convention on Substances that Deplete the Ozone Layer. Thereafter, it was progressively fitted into the mandate of international organizations concerned with natural resource management: It was integrated into the criteria for the listing of endangered species by the Convention on International Trade in Endangered Species in 1994, and adopted by the Food and Agricultural Organization in 1995. However, despite this widespread occurrence in international texts, the use of the term appears to be geographically circumscribed. It is a cornerstone of European Union

(EU) environmental law, for example, and has been central in determining the EU's position toward genetically modified organisms. The EU has also advocated extending it to other areas, such as food and health issues. Yet it is widely absent from the U.S. context.

One problem with the precautionary principle, related to this disparity in occurrence, is the lack of consensus as to its status, and, consequently, also its forcefulness: The debate is on-going as to whether it should be considered a principle of international environmental law or merely an approach, a guide to policy making. The precautionary principle has been criticized for promoting a risk-averse approach to natural resource management, in contexts where risk is part and parcel of decision making, and the problem of scientific uncertainty especially acute. In natural resource management, the course of management often has to be decided upon despite persisting uncertainty; there the precautionary approach merely risks paralyzing management altogether.

—*Charlotte Epstein*

See also Environmental Governance; Natural Resource
    Management; Sustainable Development

Further Readings and References

Appell, D. (2001, January). The new uncertainty principle. *Scientific American*, pp. 18–19.
Kriebel, D., Tickner, J., Epstein, P., Lemons, J., Levins, R., Loechler, E. L., et al. (2001, September). Commentary: The precautionary principle in environmental science. *Environmental Health Perspectives, 109*(9), 871–876.

PRINCIPAL-AGENT MODEL

The principal-agent model deals with relationships in the public service in terms of various kinds of agreements or contracts between principal (the government or employer) and agent (employee or contractor). The central dilemma investigated by principal-agent theorists is how to get the agent to act in the best interests of the principal when the government or contractor has an informational advantage over the principal and has different interests from the principal.

Principal-agent theory rests on a basis in economics. Principal-agent theory in economics makes these information asymmetries central to the emergence of institutional structures that organize the workplace and management-staff (principal-agent) relations. The more difficult it is for the principal to gain information on performance outcomes, the more likely that contracts will be framed instead in terms of contractor behavior. The more uncertain the outcomes, the more the agent will have an incentive to resist the principal's information-gathering efforts so as to encourage behavioral rather than outcome performance standards.

The principal-agent approach is especially insightful for handling disequilibrium situations and taking into account the role of the information at the microlevel. The principal-agent theory wrestles with the problem of ensuring that agents serve principals in accordance with stated or implied contractual conditions. The essential policy prescription is to clarify and define the relationships between agency heads and top bureaucrats, and between the latter and departmental managers at lower levels.

Principal-agent theory also played an important role in developing the policy framework that underpinned the corporatization and privatization programs in several countries. The dominant state ownership was (still is in some countries) a typical feature of most state-owned economies. This permits us to consider the transition as a change of ownership structure—a radical privatization will transform the whole. From a theoretical perspective, the implications of the change of the ownership structure can be analyzed in the boundaries of the principal-agent model. The model can be used as a theoretical basis for transition economic policy. This theory has been successfully applied to the problems of the interdependence between the competitive market structures, ownership, and economic efficiency. It is also a useful tool for the study of the role of the financial markets and the different techniques of privatization.

Some rational choice scholars argue that politics can be best understood as a chain of principal-agent relationships: The citizenry empowers the elected officials,

the legislature in turn delegates its collective power to its various standing committees, which in turn delegate authority to various government agencies (e.g., department of education, health and human services agency), which are organized internally as bureaucratic hierarchies. From the principal-agent theoretical perspective, the key issue is democratic control. Good government performance will be obtained when each agent receives the proper incentives from its political superiors.

—*Naim Kapucu*

See also Public Choice Theory; Rational Choice Theory

Further Readings and References

Boston, J., Martin, J., Pallot, J., & Walsh, P. (1996). *Public management: The New Zealand model.* New York: Oxford University Press.

Horn, M. J. (1995). *The political economy of public administration: Institutional choice in the public sector.* Cambridge, UK: Cambridge University Press.

Thompson, F. (1998). Public economics and public administration. In J. Rabin, W. H. Hildreth, & G. J. Miller (Eds.), *Handbook of public administration* (2nd ed., pp. 995–1063). New York: Marcel Dekker. Retrieved from http://www.willamette.edu/~fthompso/pubfin/ECON&PA.html

PRISONER'S DILEMMA

The prisoner's dilemma game specific to game theory is widely used to study human interactions from market exchanges and armament decisions to collective action problems. In this game, two players each have a single choice between two symmetrical actions: to cooperate or to defect. There are four possible outcomes: both players cooperate, both players defect, player A cooperates and B defects, or player B cooperates and A defects. The players' preference rankings are symmetrically inverse, with player A preferring, first, A's unilateral defection and B's unilateral cooperation; second, that both cooperate; third, that both defect; and fourth, that A unilaterally cooperates and B unilaterally defects.

The rudimentary logical structure of the prisoner's dilemma is usually embedded in a narrative explaining of what the various outcomes represent. Sometimes the two players are cast as co-conspirators caught by a jailor who wishes that each prisoner confesses to a crime. In this scenario, the payoff matrix is explained to the prisoners such that if both confess, they both get a moderate sentence; if neither confesses, then they both receive a light sentence; if only one confesses, then the other will walk free while the co-conspirator who confesses will stay in jail for life. This game structure demonstrates that, regardless of what the other person chooses to do, it is rational for the agent to choose to confess as walking free is superior to receiving a light sentence and receiving a moderate sentence is superior to receiving a life sentence. Thus, both rational agents select confessing rather than not confessing: In this case the two each achieve a mutually inferior outcome of receiving a moderate sentence instead of a light sentence.

This single-play version of the prisoner's dilemma game exhibits strict dominance for both players because, regardless of what course of action the other adopts, each player gains by the strategy of defecting from cooperation. Even though other outcomes are possible if the prisoner's dilemma was to be played repeatedly, the basic game form has received abundant attention among rational choice researchers for being paradigmatic of many types of human interactions, wherein motivations of coordinating actions to achieve a better mutual outcome reside side-by-side with motivations to better one's own condition at the price of potential collective impoverishment. Even the market, once viewed as reflecting individuals' mutual interest in exchange, is now cast as a prisoner's dilemma in which each would prefer to cheat the other. The free rider and collective action problems rely on the logic of the prisoner's dilemma to demonstrate that in group situations relying on voluntary contributions, each has the ever-present incentive to withdraw support, regardless of what others choose to do.

It is widely thought by rational choice researchers that the prisoner's dilemma is a ubiquitous feature of human society that cannot be resolved through voluntary agreement among community members. Instead it is proposed that external sanctions must be imposed to enforce voluntary compliance so that communities

of individuals are able to achieve the rewards of cooperation instead of paying the price of mutual defection. These external sanctions resolve the prisoner's dilemma by altering the game's payoff structure, thereby transforming it into a different game.

—*S. M. Amadae*

See also Collective Action; Collective Wage Bargaining; Game Theory; Pareto Optimality; Rational Choice Theory; Trust

Further Readings and References

Campbell, R., & Sowden, L. (Eds.). (1985). *Paradoxes of rationality and cooperation: The prisoner's dilemma and Newcomb's problem.* Vancouver: University of British Columbia Press.

Hargreaves Heap, S. P., & Varoufakis, Y. (2004). *Game theory, second edition: A critical text.* London: Routledge.

Poundstone, W. (1992). *Prisoner's dilemma: John von Neumann, game theory, and the puzzle of the bomb.* New York: Doubleday.

PRIVATE MILITARY COMPANIES

Private military companies (PMCs) constitute an important and deeply controversial element of the expanding privatized military industry. This industry provides a full range of military services to national governments, international organizations, and substate actors.

The private military industry provides a wide variety of military services, ranging from basic maintenance support to the provision of combat units. Military consultancies, for example, specialize in advising clients on how to deal with assorted security issues. The largest corporate actors, such as Dyncorp (United States), mainly provide logistical and administrative support (both in home countries and combat zones), including transport, communications, technical, and maintenance provision. This outsourcing of important functions previously monopolized by militaries is occurring throughout the world. It is thought to increase efficiency and to free soldiers for more important military functions. PMCs, on the other hand, specialize in providing combat and protection forces. Their work ranges from running small-scale training missions to providing combat units comprised of up to several hundred highly trained soldiers equipped with powerful weapons platforms, including tanks and helicopter gunships.

The use of military force by private-sector organizations is not new. Mercenaries are a long-standing feature of warfare. The East India Company had at its disposal a large army during the eighteenth and nineteenth centuries. Private-sector actors, meanwhile, have been helping to maintain the hardware of armies for decades. Yet for much of the twentieth century, the outsourcing of combat functions was disparaged, and the employment of military power was restricted largely to the agencies of the state. In the post–Cold War era, this began to change. The end of the Cold War not only flooded the market with military specialists and surplus equipment, it also saw the eruption of numerous small wars, especially in Africa. It was in such conflicts that a number of the PMCs, including Sandline (United Kingdom) and Executive Outcomes (South Africa), made their name (and sometimes their fortune).

The military record of such companies is mixed. They played a key role in a number of recent conflicts, including those in Angola and Sierra Leone. However, they rarely have been tested against well-organized conventional military forces, and consequently their overall effectiveness is still not proven. The main criticism of PMCs is that they lack legitimacy, for they often seem to operate without adequate legal restraints, although there are signs that this is beginning to change. Moreover, it is frequently argued that PMCs, especially those operating in Africa, have been responsible for abuses of human rights.

—Duncan Bell

See also Capitalism; Military Necessity; Privatization; Security

Further Readings and References

Fayemi, K., & Musah, A.-F. (Eds.). (2000). *Mercenaries: An African dilemma.* London: Pluto Press.

Kaldor, M. (1999). *New and old wars: Organized violence in a global era.* Cambridge, UK: Polity Press.

Singer, P. W. (2003). *Corporate warriors: The rise of the privatized military industry.* Ithaca, NY: Cornell University Press.

Privatization

The process of privatization first began after World War II, became increasingly popular since the 1980s as a neoliberal economic reform, and then became increasingly common after the fall of communism in Eastern Europe in the 1990s. Indeed, under leaders such as former President Ronald Reagan and former Prime Minister Margaret Thatcher, privatization was introduced with force and since has transformed into a global phenomenon, with many developed and developing countries adopting this economic strategy.

In its simplest form, privatization is the transfer of control and management away from the government to the private sector. A publicly owned asset is literally sold off to the private market. This can take the form of being traded on the stock market or simply a few companies taking over the industry after buying it from the government. These public-private transfers can and have been implemented in a slew of industries that range from power generation to social services.

At least five arguments are made in favor of privatization. First, the largest and most often-cited benefit of privatization is its efficiency. It is argued that a government is a single entity that cannot adequately provide goods and services in all the different arenas in which they are needed. Privatized entities are generally smaller, more specialized and thus able to provide a much needed level of expertise. They are also well trained and able to handle both day-to-day situations as well as the crises that inevitably arise in different fields. This narrow focus allows for both effective and efficient services to be created and delivered. Second, privatization also encourages market competition. With multiple companies vying to make a profit, there is a new incentive for quality products that was not present when the government was the sole provider. Third, unlike nationalized services and industries, private companies can raise capital however they choose and in a manner that is both more efficient and more lucrative than when carried out by their civic counterparts. These companies' strong financial situation makes it easier to develop and execute novel and creative strategies that can yield better results. Fourth, privatization also helps the state and government remain out of debt or not to fall into deeper debt. Finally, private organizations are outside the sphere of electoral pressure. This allows for the companies to make decisions based on long-term potential instead of instant gratification that politicians seek when constantly thinking about the next election. The removal of public opinion from the decision-making process, many argue, promotes efficient and effective policy and service.

Privatization is not, however, without critiques and dissenters. First, privatization also creates a need for regulation, most often filled not by governments but by independent agencies. These nongovernmental organizations have an enormous amount of potential to intervene in a way that the government simply cannot, but also a disproportionate amount of power that some see as problematic. Second, some commentators believe that a privatized company loses its moral imperative to serve and provide to the greater public. What is left, then, are companies whose sole objective is to profit as much as possible. Opponents argue this profiteering will result in companies pandering to those who can afford to pay while ignoring the needs of the majority. Especially when it comes to providing specific services to society, the greed of a private market can impede the goals of a policy or program. Some argue that while in certain industries, privatization increases efficiency and productivity, in others, such as social services, there must be some form of overarching regulations that supersede the private ownership of a company.

Another common complaint concerns the undemocratic nature of privatization. When the government sells them off, private companies do not answer to elected officials. There is no accountability and the agencies have full control to handle situations however they deem fit. While this fact is what creates many of the advantages of privatization, it simultaneously produces the more abstract, but equally important, dilemma of an undemocratic system. The public neither elects the agencies nor are they held to a standard by those who are elected. The public and its opinion are essentially removed from the process entirely, a fact that concerns many. Public oversight can be a painstakingly slow process, leading at worst to gridlock that many believe hurts the system of delivery. The trade-off for efficiency, however, is a less-than-democratic system in certain arenas. Others contend that a democratic process where the electorate has ultimate control must be seen as the priority.

In summary, private companies can, without doubt, provide certain services in a better fashion than governments. The question posed then, is which industries and services are better off privatized and which should remain in the public domain. Having decisions made outside the electoral sphere has benefits and poses problems that must be weighed accordingly.

—*Michele Margolis*

See also American Governance; Consumption; Hybrid Organization; Neoliberalism; Private Military Companies; Washington Consensus

Further Readings and References

Kikeri, S. (1992). *Privatization: The lessons of experience.* Washington, DC: World Bank.

Megginson, W. L., & Netter, J. M. (2001). From state to market: A survey of empirical studies on privatization. *Journal of Economic Literature, 39*(2), 321–389.

PROBLEM STRUCTURE

A problem structure is a theoretical construct used to explain how one or more individuals understand an issue; it is composed of a starting state and a finishing state. Once problem solvers have settled on the assumptions or causal mechanisms composing the start and finishing states, they turn to formulating the necessary steps required to move from start to finish.

A well-structured problem is one where actors seeking a solution are in agreement on the constraints, the starting point, finishing point, and the steps necessary to progress from one to the other. An ill-structured or fuzzy problem is one where one or more constraints are vaguely defined or unknown by the actors seeking a solution. Pointing to the socialized nature of a problem structure, Herbert Simon argued that, in fact, all problems are ill structured and become well structured only after those seeking a solution reach a consensus on the constraints. The final agreement on the nature of the constraints composing the problem is important because whether the understanding of the problem matches the solution determines the likelihood of success for problem solvers.

The primary determinant of an ill-structured problem is the character of the relevant information. First, the volume of information potentially relevant to the problem may overwhelm problem solvers and prevent agreement on the nature of the problem constraints. Second, the ontological ambiguity of relevant information may prevent agreement on the nature of problem constraints. Third, incomplete information relevant to the problem may prevent agreement on the nature of problem constraints. Information is often discovered or understood only in the process of solving the problem. Encountering new information contradicting problem solvers' given understandings of the start and finishing states is often how agreement is reached on the constraints of the problem structure.

The process transforming an ill-structured or fuzzy problem into a well-structured problem is a combination of cognitive functions and social interaction. Problem solvers' perceptions are the primary determinants of problem constraints. Individuals have a limited cognitive capacity, with the amount of information that each can comprehend often being less than that presented by the external environment. As a result, problem solvers utilize previously established understandings to order, process, and store incoming information. Problem constraints understood by individual problem solvers are a product of selecting and simplifying incoming information, meaning that an understanding of the causal dynamics composing the starting and finishing states is less a description of all

the relevant information than a reflection of what previous experiences have told problem solvers is relevant information. Ultimately, a well-structured problem is the result of social contestation among multiple cognitively limited perceptions of the problem constraints.

—*Zachary Zwald*

See also Decision Making; Garbage Can Theory; Organization Theory

Further Readings and References

Simon, H. A. (1972). The structure of ill-structured problems. *Artificial Intelligence, 4,* 181–202.

PRODUCTION CHAIN

Production chain is an analytical tool to understand the nature of the production process (including production of both goods and services) and its transformations. The production process is understood as a chain of linked functions. It is a sequence of productive activities leading to end use. Each stage adds value to the production sequence. Hence, production chains are often called "value added" or "value" chains. The stages in the chain are connected through a set of transactions. The organizational and geographical structure of the transactions characterize the nature of production.

The concepts of production chain and production network are often used interchangeably. However, at least on the analytical level, it is possible to distinguish between production chain as a characterization of a production process in general, involving various activities within the production system that may be performed by various organizations, and production network as a network of relationships within and between firms.

The structure of the chain may vary between two extremes, which can be characterized along two dimensions. The first refers to the degree of coordination or control over production chain (tight/loose), the second to the geographical location of functions (local/global). Thus, at one ideal-typical extreme, all operations of the chain may be concentrated in a single firm in one place. Here, transactions are organized hierarchically through a firm's organization structure. At the other extreme, each function of the chain may be performed by independent, geographically dispersed firms. In this case, the transactions are organized through the market.

The technological change and liberalization of trade have enabled radical reorganization of the production process in the last couple of decades. They have made possible specialization in each segment of the production process. Once concentrated in one country, the production chain can be parceled out and distributed around the globe. This has led to increases in trade relative to domestic production. Intrafirm trade now accounts for between one-quarter and one-third of total trade. This has sharply raised the proportion of imported inputs in the production processes. Thus, the national economies have become more dependent on trade for domestic production. For instance, the United States has transformed from a virtual self-sufficient economy to an import-dependent one.

The increasing ability to "slice up" the value chain has increased trade between industrialized and developing countries, reinforcing the shift toward a new international division of labor. Whereas in the past, advanced industrial processes tended to be concentrated in developed economies, companies now locate segments of the production process in lower-wage countries or subcontract to local companies in Asia or Latin America.

—Jan Drahokoupil

See also Foreign Direct Investment; Globalization; International Division of Labor; Production Network

Further Readings and References

Dicken, P. (2003). *Global shift: Reshaping the global economic map in the twenty-first century.* London: Sage Ltd.

Gereffi, G., & Korzeniewicz, M. (Eds.). (1994). *Commodity chains and global capitalism.* Westport, CT: Praeger.

PRODUCTION NETWORK

Production network refers to a network of internal relationships within a corporation or network of external relationships between independent or quasi-independent firms. Thus, it refers to the organization of production from the perspective of a firm's strategy. Production network allows us to investigate different strategies of production organization, ranging from transnational corporations and international strategic alliances, through subcontracting links to more independent network forms.

The concepts of production network and production chain are often used interchangeably. However, at least on the analytical level, it is possible to distinguish between production network as a network of internal relationships within a corporation or networks of external relationships between independent firms, and production chain as a characterization of a production process in general, involving various activities within the production system.

In the last couple of decades, technological innovation in the transport and communication media, together with trade liberalization, have enormously enhanced the potential of companies to organize their strategies over vast geographical distances. The technological change also enabled the development of complex organizational technology. In this context arose the transnational corporation (TNC), which can be broadly defined as an organization that coordinates production from one center of strategic decision making when this coordination takes it across national boundaries.

Large business enterprises have largely transformed from a functional form of organization, in which the firm is divided into major functional units, into a divisional form, where they are organized by product. This should enable companies to better cope with product diversity. It relates to the shift from Fordist economies of scale to the post-Fordist economies of scope.

There are four general types of competitive strategy that a TNC may pursue. First, there is an export-based strategy of high geographical concentration of production with loosely coordinated marketing activities. Second, the TNC may pursue a basic global strategy of high geographical concentration of production with tightly coordinated marketing activities. Another option is the complex global strategy of geographically dispersed production with tight coordination between overseas affiliates. Finally, there is a multidomestic strategy of geographically dispersed production with a high degree of local autonomy.

The external networks of relationships between firms include mainly international strategic alliances, international subcontracting, and dynamic networks. The strategic alliances comprise various forms of collaboration in order to share risks or rewards through joint decision making. These alliances often include corporations in fierce competition. Subcontracting is a customer-supplier relation between firms. The subcontractor is required to undertake the production according to the specifications provided by the firm offering the contract. Finally, dynamic networks are flexible forms of organization involving firms performing a specialized role within the coordinated network.

—Jan Drahokoupil

See also Fordism and Post-Fordism; Foreign Direct Investment; Globalization; International Division of Labor; Production Chain; Social Network Theory

Further Readings and References

Dicken, P. (2003). *Global shift: Reshaping the global economic map in the twenty-first century.* London: Sage Ltd.

Henderson, J., Dicken, P., Hess, M., Coe, N., & Yeung, H. W.-C. (2002). Global production networks and the analysis of economic development. *Review of International Political Economy, 9*(3), 436–464.

PROFESSIONALISM

The concepts of professionalism, profession, and professionalization have received considerable and sometimes critical attention in sociology. In early British and American analyses, professionalism was identified as an occupational value that was important for the stability and civility of social systems. In these interpretations, professional relations were characterized as collegial, cooperative, and mutually supportive. Relations of trust characterized practitioner-client and practitioner-management interactions since competencies were assumed to be guaranteed by education, training, and sometimes by licensing.

There is a second more pessimistic interpretation of professionalism, however, which has grown out of the more critical literature on professions that was prominent in Anglo American analyses in the 1970s and 1980s. During this period, professionalism came to be dismissed as a successful ideology, and professionalization as a process of market closure and monopoly control of work and occupational dominance. Professionalization was intended to promote professionals' own occupational self interests in terms of their salary, status, and power, as well as the monopoly protection of an occupational jurisdiction. Professionalization was a process largely initiated and controlled by the practitioners themselves through their professional institutions and associations in order to promote and protect their own interests.

A third and later development has involved the analysis of professionalism as a discourse of occupational change and control—this time in work organizations where the discourse is increasingly applied and utilized by managers. There is an important difference when the discourse of professionalism is constructed "from within" (by the occupational group itself) and "from above" (by managers in work organizations). When the discourse is constructed from within, then the returns to the group can be substantial. The occupational group uses the discourse to construct its occupational identity, promoting its image with clients and customers, and in bargaining with states to secure and promote the occupational control of the work. In contrast, when the discourse is constructed from above, then it is usually a false or selective discourse used to facilitate occupational change and rationalization. The effects are not the occupational control of the work by the practitioners but rather control by the organizational managers and supervisors. Organizational objectives define practitioner-client relations and set achievement targets and performance indicators. Organizational objectives regulate and replace occupational control of the practitioner-client work interactions, thereby limiting the exercise of discretion and preventing the service ethic that has been important in professional work.

Professionalism as an occupational value is currently under threat from the logic efficiency and effectiveness of organizational models of control of work. Talcott Parsons demonstrated in 1951 how the authority of the professions and of hierarchical bureaucratic organizations both rested on the same principles. He went on to argue that the professions, by means of their collegial organization and shared identity, demonstrated an alternative to the managerial hierarchy of organizations toward the shared normative end. In 2001, Eliot Freidson examined the logics of three different ways of organizing work in contemporary societies (the market, organization, and profession). He demonstrates the advantages of professionalism for both clients and practitioners and the importance of maintaining professionalism, along with trust, competencies, and discretion, as the main organizing principle for service work in modern societies.

—Julia Evetts

See also Market; Organizational Culture; Sociology of Governance

Further Readings and References

Evetts, J. (2003). The sociological analysis of professionalism: Occupational change in the modern world. *International Sociology, 18*(2), 395–415.

Freidson, E. (2001). *Professionalism: The third logic.* London: Polity Press.

Parsons, T. (1951). *The social system.* New York: Free Press.

PROGRAM EVALUATION

Program evaluation in government is typically traced to the 1960s and early 1970s when the expansion of government led to demand for assessments of their effectiveness. While the idea of evaluation is, of course, part of daily human problem solving, program evaluation became institutionalized in federal and, eventually, state agencies as policy makers and the public began asking whether the benefits of government programs were worth their costs, and has now become a major bureaucratic activity. Program evaluation is widely employed as a means of identifying the costs and benefits of policies and programs and assessing their effectiveness. Despite its common sense roots, it is nevertheless often a controversial enterprise, because the conclusions drawn from program evaluation may clash with political demands and expectations, and there is an inherent conflict between the expectation of scientific, neutral assessments and the need to satisfy political imperatives. Program evaluations that take on powerful political interests run the risk of being rejected and ignored, regardless of how thoroughly and professionally they are executed.

Central to the policy-making process is the ability of policy makers to assess the strengths and weaknesses of existing policies and alter them when necessary. Models of the policy process typically identify five main stages in the process. First, through a variety of ways, some problems become defined as policy concerns and find a spot on the policy agenda. Second, policy advocates and analysts generate options in response to the framing of the policy problem. Policy analysis in general rests on the expectation that the technical assessment of competing policy options will be separated from the political calculations of the policy makers, and that there will be an objective, nonpolitical assessment of policy options before the inevitable political calculations shape the decisions that are eventually made. In theory, careful policy analysis precedes the application of narrow political pressure and ensures that policies producing the greatest net gains in social welfare will be pursued. In practice, of course, policy analysis is a political exercise, and public organizations are caught in the middle of the political tug of war over evaluating and reshaping public policies. The third step is policy selection, authorization, and appropriation: The governing body selects the policy option to be pursued and provides funding to carry it out. In theory, policy makers allow those responsible for implementing a law the flexibility to make the adjustments necessary to solve evolving problems and to learn from trial and error. The fourth step is policy implementation, where government agencies are expected to carry out the intent of the body that authorized the policy effort. Implementation is often a long, complicated procedure that includes interpreting legislative intent, balancing statutory and executive priorities, creating administrative structures and processes, reviewing congressional or parliamentary debates on policy formulation as regulations are devised, and building political support for enforcement of regulatory requirements.

The final step in the policy process is program or policy evaluation. Unlike the analysis that occurs throughout the entire process, policy evaluation focuses on the extent to which the policy effort achieves its goals. Policy evaluation requires clear goals and standards against which policy implementation efforts can be measured. But that kind of clarity is often lacking, making policy evaluation itself a political, rather than an objective, scientific exercise. Program evaluation by program administrators is expected to be rooted in politically neutral, professional judgment, but policy evaluation also occurs by legislators and other political officials who are motivated by a range of factors. Once program evaluation occurs and changes are recommended, the policy process begins anew with the evaluation serving as the basis for a reframing of the problem.

Max Weber was among the first to contribute to the idea of an objective social science that could help evaluate options for achieving goals through scientific analysis. Harold Lasswell, a leader in the development of the field of policy sciences, emphasized the role of policy scientists in planning, analyses for decision making, and policy evaluation. The Great Society programs of the 1960s spawned program analysis and evaluation research in federal agencies, and the development of statistical techniques and models to measure policy outcomes and changes in behaviors and correlate them with policy actions. By the 1980s, criticism of government programs came to permeate politics, faith in free markets grew, and program evaluation became heavily influenced by related modes of analysis.

Implementation studies, for example, have often concluded that government is destined to fall short in achieving its policy goals because of administrative complexity. Pressman and Wildavsky found that the complexity of requiring participation by so many political actors destined most policies to failure or at least to delays and distortions. The assumption that implementation meant policy making could come from the top down, that agency heads could impose controls from above on a host of actors below them was simply unrealistic. Subsequent studies of implementation have concluded that governments can successfully implement programs and have suggested factors that appear to be associated with different outcomes. Some implementation fails to achieve its objectives because of a lack of political will or agreement. Other efforts suffer from inadequate funding or authority. Policy goals in one area, such as environmental protection, for example, must compete with social welfare, economic, and other policy objectives. Unintended consequences pervade policy implementation efforts. These and other challenges often result in programs failing to achieve the goals established for them.

Program evaluation is an essential part of the policy-making process, but its expectations of objective and scientific analysis are difficult to satisfy.

—*Gary Bryner*

See also Evidence-Based Policy; Policy Analysis; Policy Development

Further Readings and References

Lasswell, H. D. (1977). *Harold D. Lasswell on political sociology* (D. Marvick, Ed.). Chicago: University of Chicago Press.
Pressman, J., & Wildavsky, A. (1973). *Implementation.* Berkeley: University of California Press.
Weber, M. (1947). *The theory of social and economic organizations.* New York: Free Press.

PROPERTY RIGHTS

Property is best understood as a set of rights (or entitlements) to assets. Although most definitions of property follow the Roman tradition in emphasizing the relationship between people and things, it is more accurate to think of property rights as a complex group of relationships among people with respect to things, because property rights impose obligations on nonowners as well as conferring rights (and sometimes obligations) on owners.

Property has taken on a wide range of forms across cultures and across time. In all its forms, however, property is a political institution. It allocates authority over assets to individual people, groups, or legal entities comprised of individuals. Those who possess that authority have greater freedom of action within the range or sphere of their authority than they do outside it as well as greater freedom (within that same sphere) than others.

Property is distinct from possession. Possession is a de facto relationship of control between people and things that need not entail recognition or acceptance by others. Property is a relationship of control, whether legally codified or not, that commands a significant degree—not necessarily complete—of recognition and respect by others.

The most fundamental distinction between forms of property is that between common and private ownership. The Roman historian Tacitus contrasted the system of private property that was developed in Roman society with the German practice of common ownership of land and centralized distribution of livestock. Although the practice of common ownership with respect to some things is culturally widespread and historically persistent, in modern usage the term *property* is usually applied to private property.

Three attributes define a distinctively modern form of private property that is widely viewed as the standard form and sometimes taken to be the only "true" or "legitimate" form of property. In this form, the kind of entitlement that we normally call a property right entails: (a) the right to make use of the things over which one has ownership more or less as one sees fit, (b) the right to exclude others from using the things one owns, and (c) the right to alienate the things one owns by transferring one's entitlements to those things to others.

These three attributes of this form of property rights are distinct from one another conceptually and

separable from one another in practice. Moreover, each of these three attributes can be more or less absolute. For example, an owner may be entitled to absolute discretion in the way in which he or she uses his or her property, or the owner's right to use may be subject to limitations or regulations imposed by others. The same variability in an owner's discretion—in the "absoluteness" of ownership rights—applies to the right to exclude others and the right to transfer one's property to others.

The range of things over which property rights have been held is vast. It is likely that historically, the first substantial kind of asset over which property rights were held was livestock. Roman law, which is a major source of concepts and legal provisions regarding property, restricted the scope of ownership to tangible things, whether movable or immovable, and even today many people associate the notion of property closely with tangible things, especially land. For centuries, land was the preeminent object over which property rights were asserted and it remains one of the most important objects of property claims. During the past several centuries, however, intellectual property (in forms such as ownership of patents and copyrights) and financial assets have come to rival and perhaps surpass land and other tangible assets in importance as objects of property rights. It is also important to remember that for nearly the whole of human history, human beings have been the objects of legally recognized property rights, and that even today, in the absence of formal legal recognition, many human beings are subject to de facto virtual ownership.

Although the range of people capable of exercising property rights is not as great as the range of things subject to ownership, different societies (and the same societies at different times) have adopted dramatically different arrangements for conferring the right to be a property holder. Historically, many human beings have been denied the right to own property by virtue of their caste or official servile status. In Great Britain and the United States in the early nineteenth century, women automatically transferred their rights as property owners to their husbands when they married. Nowadays, legal entities such as corporations that are not human beings (though they are composed of human beings) have the right to own property, and in many business corporations, effective control of property is distinct and separated from the legal right to benefit from property.

The institution of private property has been the subject of both withering criticism and vigorous defenses for centuries. Writers like Thomas More and Leo Tolstoy have suggested that private property is the root of all evil, while John Locke, David Hume, and G. W. F. Hegel have portrayed it—for very different reasons—as an indispensable aspect of any good or fully developed human life. The belief that one of the principal tasks of good government is to protect a clearly and authoritatively defined system of private property rights is widespread today, for good reasons. Property rights that are well defined and secure give people strong incentives to use assets productively. They also make it possible for people to exchange assets efficiently, which helps ensure that resources are put to their best possible use and results in a highly productive division of labor. Yet severe problems are likely to arise if private property rights are treated as if they were absolute or near absolute. The most serious of these problems is that strictly enforced systems of private property rights are virtually certain to lead to highly unequal distributions of assets, which in turn can make it difficult or impossible for people to satisfy their basic needs, especially in societies that are relatively poor or in times of economic contraction. In severe cases, these maldistributions often result in famine and starvation, outcomes that could be prevented by governments by abridging or relaxing the security of private property rights.

—David C. Johnston

See also Capitalism; Human Rights; Liberalism; Market

Further Readings and References

Barzel, Y. (1997). *Economic analysis of property rights* (2nd ed.). Cambridge, UK: Cambridge University Press.
Donahue, C., Jr. (1980). The future of the concept of property predicted from its past. In J. R. Pennock & J. W. Chapman (Eds.), *Property: Nomos XXII* (pp. 28–68). New York: New York University Press.
North, D. C., & Thomas, R. P. (1973). *The rise of the Western world: A new economic history.* Cambridge, UK: Cambridge University Press.
Waldron, J. (1988). *The right to private property.* Oxford, UK: Clarendon Press.

PROTECTIONISM

Protectionism refers to all strategies used by countries to prevent the importation of goods and services, thereby protecting domestic industries and jobs from foreign competition. There is great variety in the methods used by governments to this end, but the most common form is the application of tariffs (taxes applied on goods as they cross national borders). Neoclassical economic theory views all forms of protectionism as economically damaging, other than in exceptional circumstances. Drawing from this theory, a central purpose of the World Trade Organization (WTO) and the General Agreement on Tariffs and Trade (GATT), which preceded the WTO, is the reduction of protectionism by member states. Outside liberal theory, targeted protectionism has been advocated as a means of fostering industrialization through the protection of infant industries until they are able to compete with foreign suppliers.

Neoclassical Economic Theory

In neoclassical economics, protectionism is seen to be economically damaging to both the world economy and to the country applying the protectionist measures, except in limited circumstances. By increasing the prices of imported goods, tariffs raise prices for consumers and raise profits for domestic producers. Protecting inefficient domestic businesses poses a net cost to the country as it diverts investment away from where it would be most productive. Adopting a policy of free trade would allow consumers to purchase cheaper imported goods and would in turn lead, through the market mechanism, to a shift in domestic investment away from inefficient industries to those industries in which the country has a comparative advantage. Liberalization of a country's trade policy is therefore economically beneficial but politically difficult, as the benefits are thinly spread among consumers, while a vocal and frequently politically powerful minority group comprised of the owners of the protected industries and their employees are harmed. The lobbying power of these groups is seen in liberal thinking to be the force behind the introduction and maintenance of trade protection.

Economic Nationalism

Protectionism plays a different role in the school of economic nationalism (sometimes known as mercantilism or just protectionism). Here, economic efficiency is subordinated to other political and economic goals, principally that of fostering industrialization through the protection of infant industries in key sectors. It is generally envisaged that once an industry has been established and is able to compete in world markets, the protection should be withdrawn, although in practice this has not always happened.

This policy was used extensively by the United States in the nineteenth and early twentieth centuries to protect industries unable to compete with British exports. After World War II, developing countries adopted a protectionist strategy in an effort to increase their production of manufactured goods and decrease their reliance on the export of primary products. Two strategies were used: import substitution, particularly associated with Latin America and India, in which imports are replaced by domestic production under the protection of high tariffs or quotas, and export-led growth, pursued by the newly industrialized countries (NICs) of East Asia, in which targeted protection is used to nurture export industries.

Import substitution is widely regarded as having been a failure. Heavily protected industries not subject to foreign competition grew to be inefficient and uncompetitive. Consumers paid more for goods of worse quality than those available on the world market. The NICs, by contrast, saw a rapid rise in living standards and a large growth in their manufacturing industries. These developments led in the late 1970s and 1980s to a shift away from import substitution to a more export orientated method of development.

Types of Protectionism and WTO Regulation

Politicians have traditionally shown great creativity and imagination in developing new forms of protectionism. These include, but are by no means limited to, quantitative restrictions, by which countries set quotas for imports of a given product, traditionally a feature of trade in textiles and clothing; subsidies to domestic producers, a feature particularly of trade in agriculture; voluntary export restraints (VERs), by which a country agrees (frequently as a result of political coercion) to limit their exports of a given product; and legislation favoring domestic producers.

WTO legislation forbids the use of quantitative restrictions and requires that these be converted into tariffs, except under certain limited circumstances, such as Article XII allowing the imposition of quantitative restrictions by a country facing balance of payments difficulties. The use of subsidies is somewhat more complex. Three types are identified: prohibited subsidies, comprised of those that are most trade distorting, such as export subsidies; actionable subsidies, which are permitted but with the caveat that if their use has adverse effects on another WTO member, consultations, countervailing duties, and dispute settlement procedures may be initiated; and nonactionable subsidies, which are not targeted to benefit a specific firm or industry and are, therefore, the least trade distorting.

The early GATT Rounds concentrated on reducing tariffs, with significant success. During the 1960s there was a move by developed countries toward what was termed "new protectionism," characterized by a greater use of nontariff barriers (NTBs), such as restrictively severe health and safety checks, license requirements, VERs, and lengthy administrative procedures. These were directed primarily against the exports of developing countries, partly in response to the challenge posed to developed countries by the rapidly industrializing NICs. Efforts were made to address the use of NTBs starting in the Kennedy Round (1963–1967), but were more substantial in the Tokyo Round (1973–1979) and the Uruguay Round (1986–1994), initiating a significant extension of the coverage of GATT rules away from border issues (i.e., measures applied to products as they cross borders, such as tariffs) to member states' domestic legislation.

—James Scott

See also World Trade Organization

Further Readings and References

Bhagwati, J. (2002). *Free trade today.* Princeton, NJ: Princeton University Press.

Hoekman, B. M., & Kostecki, M. M. (2001). *The political economy of the world trading system: The WTO and beyond* (Chap. 5). Oxford, UK: Oxford University Press

List, F. (1885). *The national system of political economy* (Vol. 2, Chaps. 14–15). London: Longmans, Green.

Rodrik, D., & Rodríguez, F. (2000). Trade policy and economic growth: A sceptic's guide to the cross-national literature. In B. Bernanke & K. S. Rogoff (Eds.), *NBER macroeconomics annual 2000.* Cambridge, MA: National Bureau of Economic Research.

PUBLIC ADMINISTRATION

The term *public administration* encompasses a vast range of issues and activities. One way of grasping this diversity is to distinguish between two sets of questions: How public authorities are organized and how they seek to act within societies through making and implementing public policy. In short, public administration is about the state "in action" and "in interaction." Traditionally the organization and the action of the state have generally been seen as coterminous with the concept of government. Over the last thirty years, however, an increasing number of academics, experts, and practitioners have begun to differentiate between public administration that is government and that which they label governance. According to this view, (Western) societies and economies have been transformed to such an extent that public authorities have been obliged to change both their internal modes of functioning and the way they engage with nonstate actors. More precisely, proponents of the concept of governance consider that it not only encapsulates changes in public administration

itself but acts as a catalyst to the transformation of state-society relations.

These contentions about the relationship between public administration and governance will be examined in two parts. The first sets out to discover how and why governance has so frequently come to be used as a narrative with which to describe, and often rationalize, a range of "new" public policies and state-society relations. The second part of this article looks more closely at how, more recently, governance has been used as a means of explicitly inciting policy and political change. In both parts, the interplay between academic and practitioner usages of governance is highly important. Indeed, in introducing a range of issues that are dealt with in more detail elsewhere in this volume, the principal claim made here is that avoiding confusion between "governance as narrative" and "governance as an agenda" constitutes a central challenge for both public administration as an activity and public administration as an academic discipline.

Governance as a Narrative for Public Administration

As Mark Bevir and Rod Rhodes underlined, public administration can and should be understood in terms of narratives. Such an approach explains social action by identifying the links between beliefs, preferences, intentions, and actions. Indeed, narratives explain actions through analysis of the beliefs and preferences of the actors involved.

From this perspective, governance has most certainly become the dominant narrative within which contemporary public administration has come to be described and analyzed. As such, the term *governance* synthesizes a series of perceived and real changes in the way public authorities are organized and organize themselves to interact with representatives of civil society. In so doing, governance is simultaneously used to explain new modes of public policy making and implementation. Based on both these sets of observations, a central hypothesis in theories of governance is that contemporary politics features an increasingly wide range of public bodies on the one hand and, on the other, more contact between these bodies and representatives from civil society.

Governance as Coordination Within and Between Public Authorities

An initial use of the term *governance* concerns a perceived need for greater intra- and interorganizational coordination.

Within individual public administrations, governance is frequently used by practitioners to describe situations where they are increasingly obliged to inform, consult, and negotiate with representatives of other parts of the same administration. In terms of analysis, this trend can be seen as public authority coming to terms with one of the basic claims of organizational theory: Administrations are differentiated units of collective action that possess bounded rationality, have limits upon their legitimate authority but also contain actors who often contest these limits. In other words, any public administration is fragmented in ways that can hamper its overall coherence and effectiveness. As we shall explore later in this text, over the last three decades, most national governments have tried to mitigate such effects by promoting a variety of new coordination mechanisms. In this respect, as Rhodes has repeatedly underlined using British examples, it is important to focus upon how the discourse of governance has been used to justify reforms made in the name of new public management or "joined-up government." In other words, governance has become a relatively standardized account and even explanation of networking and socialization within individual units of public administration.

If governance has thus been used to understand intra-administrative segmentation and encourage quests for greater cohesion, it has simultaneously been employed in order to encourage more effective coordination between public administrations. More precisely, governance here denotes attempts to improve intersectoral and interterritorial coordination.

Intersectoral coordination has come to be seen as an increasingly serious challenge for public administrations because of the way many public problems have come to be framed. At least according to the governance narrative, until the 1970s, public administration was essentially structured around sectoral policy goals and instruments. For example, the aim of ministries of agriculture was to improve the productivity of farmers while the ambition of ministries of industry was to stimulate that of industrialists. If such targets have not necessarily disappeared, the governance narrative underlines how an increasing number of cross-sectoral issues have made their way to the forefront of political agendas. Among the most prominent of these are the liberalization of markets using competition law, fighting pollution through environmental policy instruments, and improving the physical well-being of populations through public health campaigns, programs, and legislation. Setting up and running polices to attain these goals forces sectoral administrations to work with transsectoral bodies (e.g., environment ministries) and to deal more directly with administrations representing other sectors (e.g., health ministries working with ministries of agriculture). In some cases, the office of the prime minister has been strengthened in the name of intersectoral governance. In other cases quasi-governmental agencies, such as monopolies commissions, have been set up to foster intersectoral coordination. In all such instances, governance is frequently used to describe the greater interdependence and needs for coordination that result when public problems are framed or reframed from an intersectoral angle.

Interterritorial coordination has become an increasingly central part of contemporary politics for two reasons. Firstly, many Western polities have undergone varying degrees of change in their center-periphery relations. Labeled decentralization (France), devolution (the United Kingdom), *autonomisation* (Spain), or new federalism (United States), the relocation of powers and responsibilities that these processes have entailed has engendered the building of new mechanisms for political and policy coordination that have frequently been labeled governance. Second, over the last few decades, many states have become members of "international regions," such as the European Union (EU) or MERCOSUR, the EU's South American equivalent. Coordinating supranational and national administrations is a constant challenge for these new political entities. At least in the EU's case, this challenge is intensified by the need to simultaneously take into account the views of subnational public authorities. In this context of multilevel governance, traditional forms of organizing public administrations are constantly put to the test during both the setting and implementation of public policy.

Governance as Coordination Between Public and Private Actors

However, governance's organizational challenges certainly do not find their roots solely in demand for better coordination between public bodies. Indeed, for most specialists of this subject, governance is even more about managing linkages between public authorities and nonpublic actors in general, and representatives of business in particular.

As the literature on policy networks has consistently underlined, public administrations in Western democracies have always governed in association with groups representing sectoral or transsectoral interests. As the pluralist versus neocorporatist debate of the early 1980s served to highlight, states were engaged with such groups within widely differing patterns of interaction and interdependence. The United States was traditionally seen as the ideal type of pluralist state-society relations, wherein a plethora of interest groups fed political demands into a fragmented state. An opposing, neocorporatist model was provided by 1970s West Germany, where a relatively united state negotiated with a small number of "peak" business and labor organizations. Despite such variations in state-society relations, in nearly all national cases, the level of consultation was such that public policies were often coproduced or even comanaged. In exchange for their expertise and policy-making support, administrations readily provided a select range of interest groups with information and access to decision-shaping arenas. In short, as political science has consistently underlined, public policy making has essentially been carried out by relatively small, closed, and discreet policy networks or policy communities.

Of course, high degrees of collaboration between state and interest group actors have not always been widely and openly accepted. In France, lobbying is officially outlawed and seen by many as a threat to the very authority of the state. In the United Kingdom, between 1979 and 1997, successive conservative governments introduced an initial wave of neoliberalism that often depicted such levels of contact between public administration and interest groups as inefficient and even illegitimate. Notwithstanding these examples of resistance to "horizontal" coordination between agents of public and nonpublic bodies, such practices have increasingly been normalized as part of contemporary democracy. Indeed, the narrative of governance has played a major part in this process of naturalization.

If the governance narrative has allowed and encouraged public administrations to be more open about their relationship with interest groups in general, it also has links with the way in which the involvement of a particular set of interests—those of business—are now publicly acknowledged and discussed. At the municipal level, the role of business in local governance has become an increasingly important subject of debate and analysis. First, local government has increasingly turned to private industry in order to match funding it receives from national or European budgets. Second, real estate companies or building contractors often become partners of local government when engaging in urban renewal projects. Third, in many countries, services previously provided by local authorities have often been privatized or outsourced to private companies operating on medium- to long-term contracts. Indeed, the latter development has also occurred at national levels. For example, ministries of defense in countries such as the United Kingdom have outsourced much of the day-to-day management of resettlement policies, vehicle maintenance, and even the guarding of operational bases.

As representatives of business have come to be considered more acceptable and even desirable voices in public life, in many countries, their overall role in national and international public affairs has been the subject of a new legitimating discourse in which the term *governance* has played a prominent part. For some commentators, this rediscovery of business as a public actor simply reflects the change in economic and social structures that has resulted from the globalization of markets. For others, the views of representatives of business are heard better in public administrations because neoliberal ideology has come to shape what public actors think they can and cannot do.

In summary, governance as a narrative considers that the administration of public affairs has shifted away from vertical hierarchy toward more horizontal forms of coordination. More state, local government, and private actors are involved in this process, each having a more equal public voice. Whether such claims are actually reflected in reality is open to debate. Some actors are still clearly more equal than others. Nevertheless, an increasing number of public administrations have recently committed themselves to moving in the direction of governance, thus setting themselves and other stakeholders a political agenda to which we now turn.

Governance as an Agenda for Public Administration

Over the past ten to fifteen years, governance has increasingly been used by a variety of public bodies as a central part of an agenda for the reform of public administration. By making public decision making more open and accountable, good governance has been used as a synonym for both greater democracy and greater efficiency. Chronologically, this trend stems from analysis of government and governability failure, which began in the 1970s. Following an initial period of diagnosis, governance then came to be seen as an antidote by international organizations such as the World Bank and the Organisation for Economic Co-operation and Development (OECD). It subsequently began to be used in the domestic politics of several nation states (e.g., British local government reform in the late 1990s) before becoming the watchword of the European Commission. Rather than simply list the definitions of governance that have emerged in these different contexts, this section analyzes a number of

common themes that fall under two headings: the way public administration should formulate public policy and the way it is managed in order to implement such goals. As shall be underlined in the following sections, changing the way public officials think about themselves, their respective organizations, and the way they relate to civil society has been striven for not only by spreading a discourse about governance, but also by modifying laws and longstanding organizational practices.

Reforming Deliberation Over Public Policy

According to those who see governance as an agenda for public administration, major changes need to be made in the way public authorities go about setting public policy goals and instruments. Rather than making policy by imposing their views upon other public bodies and private actors, these authorities are instead required to change the way they consult, reflect upon, and discuss public problems and options for action.

Better consultation is the first item usually placed upon this part of the governance agenda. Under this heading, public authorities are supposed to become both more transparent and better able to listen to societal demands. Transparency is to be attained partly by providing more information to both the general and specialized publics about what public authority is doing, would like to do, and why. Web sites are often cited as a means to this end, but many public bodies are now going much further by organizing more public meetings and events that encourage citizens to voice their opinions upon policy issues. Over the last ten years, the European Commission has provided a prime example of an organization that has consistently sought to enhance its legitimacy by becoming more transparent in this way. However, as the example of the Commission again testifies, transparency also means that the decision-making processes of public bodies are supposed to become more open to scrutiny. Rather than decisions being made by secretive committees or cozy policy networks, wider access to negotiating arenas is now supposed to be the norm. In short, although systematic consultation of interest groups is seen as part of transparent governance, this is only so if groups are consulted equitably and all voices, regardless of their respective power resources, can make themselves heard.

Forms of governance that are transparent are, in turn, supposed to foster processes of reflection about public problems and policy options that are informed by more systematic and accurate forms of data than had been the case hitherto. In this regard, over the last thirty years, much faith and public finance has been invested in varying forms of policy evaluation. Introduced massively in the United States since the 1970s, in the United Kingdom in the 1980s, and across continental Europe a decade later, evaluation is now an institutionalized part of the policy process in most Western countries. Ongoing and ex-post evaluations focus upon policy implementation and impacts (see next paragraph). Ex ante evaluations are more focused upon synthesizing existing data, making forecasts, and envisaging scenarios in order to encourage more informed debate over the choices for public policy that need to be made. As part of its better regulation agenda set in 2000, the European Union has even gone so far as to try to systematize this type of evaluation into the way it makes all its policies. Labeled an "integrated impact assessment system," policy development is to be assessed through evaluations of likely economic, social, and environmental impacts. This EU scheme has yet to be fully adopted, but other, equally ambitious, national and local initiatives have already shown that impact assessment implies opening up discussion of the likely effects of public decision making to debate with an increased number of stakeholders. It also means that under conditions of good governance, policy formulation processes should produce sets of criteria, or even indicators, against which the actual implementation of public action could subsequently be measured.

The third and final dimension of the governance agenda devoted to improving public deliberation concerns the actual discussion of options for public policy. In some countries and regions, referenda are now used more frequently in order to actually take decisions. Such set piece events also provide a means of concentrating and organizing public debate, in particular through attracting the attention and use of the media. A second means of encouraging public deliberation is to reinforce the commitments of public administrations to consult the federal government and subnational assemblies. For some actors and commentators, governance is therefore also about revitalizing and modernizing representative democracy. A third means of encouraging more open deliberation during public decision taking is through developing partnerships of public bodies. Under such conditions, each organizational partner contributes in some way to the policy in question (usually through matching funding but sometimes by providing personnel). As their name implies, partnerships are supposed to encourage consensual-type negotiations and the committed engagement of each partner. A prime example of such arrangements is the local monitoring committees, which put the EU's regional development policy into practice. Now part of an EU-wide governance agenda since the reform of this policy in 1988, these committees have been supposed to enhance policy deliberation and give greater responsibility to local actors.

Whether partnerships actually function in accordance with these objectives is open to debate. Indeed, notwithstanding the aforementioned process, changes made in the name of governance, in most instances final decisions over public policy are still usually made in negotiating arenas where public access is limited and attempts to end secrecy usually result in failure. A case in point here is the EU's Council of Ministers. For years, journalists in particular have asked for the right to attend meetings of this body. Although limited access now seems likely to be granted, only the most naïve of commentators believe that key decisions will not, at least in part, be the result of behind-the-scenes bargaining.

In summary, the proponents of governance as an agenda for public administration are firm believers in what has been labeled "the deliberative turn" in contemporary politics. Making public policymaking more of a dialogic process means organizing public administration and its relations with civil society in new and often novel ways. But it also means inventing alternative methods of implementing public action once policy goals, instruments, and targets have been set.

Reforming the Management of Public Policy

Research has conclusively shown that the introduction in many Western countries of a discourse and practices labeled new public management dates from the early 1980s. Administrative techniques initially imported from the private sector have steadily been translated into procedures for managing public organizations and policy programs. Along the way, governance has emerged as a more openly political discourse with which to legitimate and give meaning to changes in implementation procedures that include three processes in particular: contracting, monitoring, and evaluating.

Contracting is a procedure that formalizes processes of negotiation and the commitments made once final decisions are taken. As we have seen in the previous paragraphs, establishing contracts between public administrations and private contractors constitutes legally binding ways of structuring and providing services. Over the last thirty years, however, contracting has increasingly become a technique whereby different public authorities set out new operating procedures that define how they relate to each other. This is particularly so in the case of relations between central and local governments. In many countries, these relations used to organize themselves multilaterally around the annual negotiation of transfers of finance from the center to the periphery. A case in point here has been the British system of block grants calculated essentially on a per capita basis. In polities undergoing processes of decentralization, more individualized forms of negotiation have often emerged and contracting has been their principal method. French examples of state-region and state-city planning contracts provide a clear-cut example of this. Under this form of governance, both local and central partners are supposed to make cases for more or less joint finance on the basis of clearly identified projects, such as the building of roads or schools. In so doing, contracting not only acts as a financial security and

discipline but also allows the "rules of the game" between individual local governments and the center to emerge and consolidate.

Once in place, contracted agreements on public action then give rise to a second technique on the governance agenda: policy monitoring. Of course, public administrations, and central governments in particular, have always sought means of verifying that commitments to implement policy are actually met. What the governance agenda seeks to do is to systematize procedures for following up on policy decisions. In so doing, it frequently finances the setting up of new information collection systems as well as new ways of presenting such data. Under the banner of monitoring, new accountancy methods that are supposed to be more analytical have also often been set up (e.g., the recent French "organic finance" law: *la LOLF*). Often such reforms are introduced by finance ministries in order to save public money. In some instances, monitoring reforms can thus be disguised forms of cutting public expenditure. According to the governance agenda, however, being clearer about how public finance is spent is ultimately about making public administration more accountable to citizens.

A third and final method of public management that has been firmly linked to the governance agenda is policy evaluation. When used during (ongoing) or after (ex-post) implementation, evaluation is supposed to generate data and analysis about the impact of public policy upon societal problems. In theory, the results of evaluations of policy impact should be fed back into the policy-making process in order to both improve implementation and incite informed discussion about whether or not to persevere with the policy instruments concerned. Again, the governance agenda sees evaluation more as a process than as either a formal procedure or an end in itself. Indeed, as specialists of evaluation underline, in order for evaluations to have any hope of influencing decision making, they must be clearly differentiated from financial audits. Moreover, administrators, politicians, and other stakeholders must be made to feel engaged in the evaluation process from the outset and not just as passive recipients of reports concocted by external consultants. In other words, as so often happens under the governance agenda, the question of "ownership" of political processes is implicitly raised whenever public administrations set up evaluations.

In summary, the governance agenda encompasses techniques that modify the way actors within and without public administrations are now expected to behave. In this way, each of these techniques, at least potentially, also involves altering equilibria between actors involved in the implementation of policy. This risk of change arises because the introduction of new public management techniques occurs in contexts of shifting inter- and intragovernmental relations. It also arises because governance as an agenda places all public administrations under pressure to modify the way each of them engages with representatives of interests within civil society.

Conclusion

There is little doubt that, as a narrative of public affairs, governance has changed the way public administration is considered and discussed in many Western countries. Similarly, the term *governance* has been used to set a relatively homogenous agenda for the reform of public administration in many of these polities. Considered from both angles, governance therefore consistently appears both relatively new and to have been a catalyst for change. However, to date, much less evidence exists to show the extent of change wrought under the banner of governance and to what degree its discourse and practice have actually been the prime causes of such change. Notwithstanding its claim to replace vertical and hierarchical government, the narrative and practices of governance cannot bring disequilibria of power to an end. Robert Dahl's question—"Who governs?"—is thus still as pertinent as when his seminal work was published in 1961. Rereading Dahl also reminds us that horizontal or polycentric forms of governance are far from original. Indeed, even in contexts of governance the question "Who governs?" leads quite naturally to two others: "Can one steer contemporary polities?" and "How can such steering be conciliated with the constraints of democracy?" Only in-depth research into the workings of contemporary public administrations

can provide solid answers to these questions. Throughout the rest of this encyclopedia, definitions and interpretations of how governance fits, or fails to fit, with public administration provide valuable signposts with which to encourage social scientists to aim their empirical investigations in this direction.

—*Andy Smith*

See also Audit; Bureaucracy; Executive; Governance; Legislature; Public Sector

Further Readings and References

Bevir, M., & Rhodes, R. (2003). *Interpreting British governance*. London: Routledge.

Callon, M., Lascoumes, P., & Barthe, Y. (2001). *Agir dans un monde incertain: Essai sur la démocratie technique* [To act in an uncertain world: Essay on technical democracy]. Paris: Editions du Seuil.

Dahl, R. (1961). *Who governs? Democracy and power in an American city*. New Haven, CT: Yale University Press.

Dryzek, J. (2000). *Deliberative democracy and beyond: Liberals, critics, contestation*. Oxford, UK: Oxford University Press.

European Commission. (2001). *European governance: A white paper* (EC, COM. 2001 428 final, 25.7.01).

Gaudin, J.-P. (2003). *Pourquoi la gouvernance?* [Why governance?]. Paris: Presses de Sciences.

Hood, C. (1998). *The Art of the state: Culture, rhetoric and public management*. Oxford, UK: Clarendon Press.

Hooghe, L., & Marks, G. (2001). *Multi-level governance*. New York: Rowman & Littlefield.

Jobert, B., & Muller, P. (1987). *L'Etat en action* [The state in action]. Paris: Presses Universitaires de France.

Le Galès, P. (2002). *European cities: Social conflicts and governance*. Oxford, UK: Oxford University Press.

Marsh, D., & Rhodes, R. (Eds.). (1992). *Policy networks in British Government*. Oxford, UK: Clarendon.

Nagel, S. (Ed.). (2002). *Handbook of public policy evaluation*. London: Sage Ltd.

Pierre, J. (Ed.). (2000). *Debating governance: Authority, steering, democracy*. Oxford, UK: Oxford University Press.

Pollit, C., & Bouckaert, G. (2000). *Public management reform*. Oxford, UK: Oxford University Press.

Rhodes, R. (1997). *Understanding governance*. Milton Keynes, UK: Open University Press.

Smith, A. (2003). Multi-level governance. What it is and how to study it. In M. Painter (Ed.), *Handbook on public administration*. London: Sage Ltd.

PUBLIC CHOICE THEORY

Public choice theory is a subfield of rational choice theory that was originally articulated in James M. Buchanan and Gordon Tullock's *The Calculus of Consent* (1962). This school of thought claims that the traditional domain of political theory, that is, constitutional design and electoral processes, is better understood in terms of calculable self-interest. Buchanan and Tullock drew on Anthony Down's median voter theory and Duncan Black's research on single-peaked preferences to put forward their theory that all political processes are best analyzed as the product of the self-interested actions of all agents, whether public officials, voters, or political candidates. They perceived their work as injecting realism into political theory by casting into doubt such concepts as public service and public interest as meaningful motivations animating political action. In the view of public choice theory, any bureaucratic organization is best studied as being comprised of individuals striving to achieve their own ends instead of some larger social goal.

Public choice exists as both a specific school of thought pioneered by Buchanan and Tullock and as a more pluralistic body of scholarship, some of which is published in the journal *Public Choice*. In the early 1960s, researchers met under the name of the Committee for Non-Market Decision Making, which is a telling title for the main thrust of the then-new research initiative: to apply the idea of rational egoism to individuals' choices in political arenas not governed by monetary prices. Since economic science up until that time was concerned with scarce commodities that were exchanged in markets for objective prices, it is important to recognize that public choice theory represents a break with economic analysis. Public choice is doubly innovative: for applying the idea of calculable, rational self-interest to political actors, and for breaking free from the confines of viewing economics as the science of constricted maximization of purchases under a budget constraint.

Much research in public choice has been focused on constitutional design and legislative rules for achieving collective outcomes. Public choice theory incorporates the impossibility theorem, holding that if one starts with individuals' preferences, it is impossible to achieve any collective expression of the public good or public interest. *The Calculus of Consent* subjects decision rules to scrutiny, finding that self-interested rational actors would insist on a procedure of unanimous decision making to establish a constitution. This is because the costs of living under a constitution that do not reflect personal interests would be prohibitive; hence total agreement guarantees each individual that personal interests are secure. On the other hand, for routine legislative decisions, citizens would agree to a less-than-unanimous decision rule because the costs in energy and resources to reach any type of agreement would outweigh the possibly negative repercussions of a decision for any single person.

Public choice has extended its research to many of the problems addressed by political economy and political science: public goods, voting rules, majority voting, two-party and multiparty political systems, rent seeking, lobbying, federalism, and the appropriate role of the state.

—*S. M. Amadae*

See also Game Theory; Impossibility Theorem; Market Failure; Principal-Agent Model; Rational Choice Theory; Social Choice

Further Readings and References

Buchanan, J. M., & Tullock, G. (1962). *The calculus of consent*. Ann Arbor: University of Michigan Press.
Downs, A. (1957). *Economic theory of democracy*. New York: Harper & Row.
Mueller, D. C. (2003). *Public choice III*. Cambridge, UK: Cambridge University Press.

PUBLIC GOODS

The notion of public goods encompasses a range of goods that markets fail to allocate efficiently because they are nonrivalrous and nonexcludable in use. Goods that have these characteristics absolutely are termed *pure public goods*. A good is nonrivalrous when more than one person can derive benefits from its consumption when its supply does not change. As such, prices do not serve their normal allocative function. Further, a good is nonexcludable when its use by one consumer does not preclude its use by another. These two characteristics cause either undersupply by the market, as firms cannot receive a return on the investment needed to produce the good, or congestion, as too many consumers attempt to use the good. Rationally, suppliers will always prefer to allow others to invest in the production of the good and then free ride on the resulting benefits.

A classic example of a pure public good is national defense. Members of society benefit from the production of national defense. However, no consumer can exclude another from receiving the benefits, and each additional tank or plane benefits citizens equally.

Pure public goods are generally rare and economists have created a number of useful subdivisions that describe a good by its excludability and rivalrousness. Nonexcludability and rivalrousness leads to open access, common property resources, and free goods. Excludability and nonrivalrousness characterizes toll goods such as a bridge. Public goods also have a regional quality to them, and economists generally distinguish between local, regional, national, international, and global public goods.

Economists have identified two instances in which public goods may be supplied by the market. In the first case, one consumer would purchase the good no matter the free riding resulting from subsequent benefits accrued by other consumers who cannot be excluded. In the second case, if a group of consumers is small enough, pressure can be brought to bear on those who do not contribute, and each marginal contribution can make a significant difference.

In light of the free-rider problem, there are four possible strategies of intervention. The first involves government provision after collection of contributions from varied consumers in the form of taxes. One problem with this mode of intervention is that it is difficult to ascertain the amount of demand for a good and thus how much to supply. A second strategy involves government subsidies to private firms to encourage them to produce the public good. A third mode involves the

aforementioned privileged group. Fourth, the government can create excludability through legislation. Intellectual property schemes follow this model by prohibiting the free flow of information as a pure public good.

—Karthik Srinivasan

See also Contracting Out; Free Riding; Market Failure

Further Readings and References

Olson, M. (1973). *The logic of collective action.* Cambridge, MA: Harvard University Press.

PUBLIC INFORMATION

Public information, in general terms, refers to that information that is universally available or that is not controlled or limited in its availability for strategic or security purposes. Public information includes records held by a public body, regardless of the form or source. The primary issue associated with the necessity of publicly available information revealing the actions of government is the assurance and maintenance of accountability and transparency, qualities deemed to be critical features of governance in a democracy. Public information allows citizens to examine the activities of a government and is the basis of informed debate about those activities.

Two fundamental tenets of democracy underlie the need for adequate public information disclosing the activities of government: popular sovereignty and the Constitutional scheme of checks and balances. From the perspective of popular sovereignty, the people cannot govern themselves in a democracy if the institutions of government can deny access to information that bears on the issues the public is supposed to decide. Secrecy, or the withholding of information, enables officials to shape policy without the input of outside individuals or groups. Moreover, the demands of checks and balances require adequate information to allow for an oversight function to take place. Secrecy allows agencies to hide mistakes or conceal misbehavior.

The historical development of the notion of public information parallels the development of the administrative state. The executive branch, starting during the Washington administration, established the precedent for the president and agency heads to manage and limit dissemination of information as a way to promote efficient and effective government. Although the systematic practice of record keeping did not become widespread until regulatory and administrative responsibilities grew dramatically in the late nineteenth and early twentieth century, the general practice of tightly controlling the availability of information continued. By the 1940s, the issues of executive secrecy necessitated in some agencies by World War II had too many aspects of administration across a wide range of agencies. Following the end of World War II, a series of federal laws were passed that provided many of the basic mechanisms through which public information regarding the activities of government was to be disseminated.

Legislative Response

Based on the theory that administrative operations and procedures are public property to which the public and not just elites are entitled, the Administrative Procedures Act (APA) was passed in 1946. The APA required federal agencies to publish information about their organization, powers, procedures, and rules in the *Federal Register,* but allowed those agencies to retain information if the public was not concerned or if the information should be, with cause, kept confidential. In 1966, the Freedom of Information Act (FOIA), which provides the basic authority and procedures for the public to petition agencies for otherwise unreleased documents, was passed. While there is a range of exemptions allowed by the FOIA that agencies can use to withhold information, it does provide the judicially enforceable right to access the records of federal government agencies. The Federal Advisory Committee Act (FACA) is intended, in part, to open federal advisory panel proceedings, purposes, memberships, and activities to wider public scrutiny. Finally, the government in the Sunshine Act of 1976 realized the principle of ensuring open discussion prior to decisions being made by further opening government meetings to the public.

The enactment of these federal laws, as well as of their state and local counterparts, was based on and intended to advance a number of characteristics of open government. First, they are based on the presumption that government information, in any of its various forms, should be available to the public unless it is specifically exempted. Second, they build on the notion that formal process should govern the access in terms of timeliness, necessary characteristics of an appropriate request, right of appeal, or review of decisions. Third, they establish a means for a judicial review of denials or refusals that will ultimately resolve disputes. These laws serve the individual citizen by being clearly intelligible in application and effective in achieving the desired results.

Underpinning all these aspects of law and process is a fundamental assumption that the effective functioning of a democracy lies in an alert and articulate public that is active in the affairs of the state. Without that participation, a democratic government cannot be truly said to exist. It is hoped that through such processes, seemingly reasonable decisions can be arrived at, presented, argued, altered, and finally settled. However, a remaining challenge is the legitimate need to protect public information in some situations.

As is the case with many principles associated with democratic governance, tension exists between the necessity of information for ensuring accountability on the one hand, and the need to ensure secrecy or privacy in some circumstances on the other. There is a range of situations where official or public information is legitimately withheld. The need for secrecy with respect to issues of national defense or foreign relations is well established, though since the Vietnam conflict, the tensions between demands for disclosure of military activities and the need for secrecy are quite well known. Further, individuals have a constitutionally justifiable concern that information regarding their personal characteristics, associations, or activities not be universally available. Finally, private organizations expect that proprietary information regarding their operations, such as proposals for contracts, patent applications, and other information that could affect competitive advantage be kept confidential. Although the laws previously noted contain provisions allowing agencies to respond to such privacy needs, and other legislation, such as the Privacy Act of 1974, has also been established for this purpose, the tensions between openness and secrecy will remain.

Public Information and Decision Making

Beyond the use of public information as a tool for ensuring accountability in a democracy, one further treatment of public information should be noted. Here, the issue is the nature and availability of information and the role it plays in decision-making processes. The rationale for arguing that a wide range of publicly available information be available to public bodies for decision-making purposes suggests that secrecy isolates decisionmakers and narrows the knowledge available to them for making decisions. There are at least two aspects to this rationale. First, from the perspective of democratic theory, public information would include the views and opinions of the public and extends the operation of democracy beyond narrow practices of voting. Second, extending the range of public information available to decisionmakers should have the effect of improving the quality of their decisions.

—*Eric K. Austin*

See also Accountability; Informationalism; Transparency

Further Readings and References

Campbell Public Affairs Institute. (2003). *National security and open government: Striking the right balance.* Syracuse, NY: Maxwell School of Syracuse University.

Cross, H. (1953). *The people's right to know.* New York: Columbia University Press.

Feinberg, L., & Relyea, H. (1986). Symposium: Toward a government information policy–FOIA at 20. *Public Administration Review, 46,* 603–639.

Rourke, F. (1961). *Secrecy and publicity.* Baltimore: Johns Hopkins University Press.

Thompson, D. (1999). Democratic secrecy. *Political Science Quarterly, 114*(2), 181–193.

PUBLIC INVESTMENT

Public investment is investment by the state, whether through central or local government, or state-owned industries or corporations, in particular assets. Public investment has arisen historically from state ownership, control and delivery of goods, and infrastructure or services, whose provision has been deemed to be of vital national interest. Public investment has tended to rise as a consequence of the process of industrialization and the demands created for a new infrastructure of goods and services from the accompanying large-scale movement of population from rural areas into densely populated urban communities. During the past decade, the process of privatization of industries, and the accompanying liberalization and deregulation of markets, has witnessed the growth of public investment in goods and services provided by the private and not-for-profit sectors, principally through the development of various public-private partnerships.

Public investment tends to be measured quantitatively, on an annual basis, as a percentage of total national income in a given period. It tends to be divided between capital investment in physical or tangible investment in fixed infrastructure, for example, transport, telecommunications and buildings; human or intangible investment in education, skills, and knowledge; and current investment in the consumption of goods and services, for example, welfare benefits and pensions. Public investment has tended to constitute a relatively small percentage of overall public spending, but frequently a major component of total national capital investment.

Public investment has been justified both on the grounds of economic theory and political ideology. In economics, public investment has been justified because of the existence of certain public goods and natural monopolies that, if held under private ownership, would result in an inefficient allocation of resources because of potential overcharging and underinvestment. Public goods refer to those goods and services that the market would find difficult or impossible to invest in or provide profitably because of the existence of externalities, that is, costs and benefits that could not be captured exclusively by the goods provider. Primary examples of public goods are the maintenance of law and order, the security and defense of a particular territory, and the provision of clean air and a sustainable environment. Natural monopolies are those goods and services for which the cost of provision is so vast that only one supplier can economically invest in the necessary infrastructure of supply and where the costs of market entry are prohibitive for rival suppliers. Primary examples of natural monopolies are the supply of electricity, clean water, and sewage.

In politics, public investment has been justified because of the desire to achieve a variety of political objectives, notably the guarantee of national security, the protection of property rights, and the maintenance of the rule of law, rising educational and health standards, national economic development and full employment, a cleaner environment, collective ownership of the means of production, and greater equality in the distribution of income and wealth.

The growth of public investment was driven during the nineteenth century by the demands of industrialization and the need to provide a physical and human infrastructure to accommodate the rapid movement of population from rural areas into cities. Friedrich List identified the critical importance of public investment for any industrializing economy wishing to develop its national productive powers sufficiently to be able to catch up to its more advanced competitors. Public investment was seen not only as a vital source of investment in factors of production, but also as a prime mover of the independence, power, national unity, and sense of common purpose of the nation concerned.

During the first half of the twentieth century, the role of public investment was expanded by the demands of the warfare state during the two World Wars and during peacetime by the demands of the welfare state and the insights provided by the political economy of John Maynard Keynes. The experience of mass unemployment and poverty during the 1920s that had been exacerbated by the stock market crash of 1929 and the ensuing Great Depression had convinced Keynes that wages, interest rates, and prices would

not spontaneously adjust themselves to deliver full employment. The amount of effective demand in an economy arising from investment and consumption might not be sufficient to yield a level of output sufficient to produce jobs for everyone. Through a large-scale extension of the traditional functions of government, Keynes saw that governments could borrow money to finance public investment, which in turn would have a multiplier effect on the level of private investment, demand, and confidence among firms and consumers.

A Keynesian social democratic consensus about the central role of public investment in delivering postwar recovery, full employment, and enhanced public welfare was prominent in many industrialized economies from 1945 until 1970. At the same time, public investment played a central role in the political economy of the developmental states that shaped rapid industrialization in East Asia. In particular, the World Bank has highlighted the importance of sustained public investment in primary and secondary education as a key agency of high and rising endowment of human capital for rapid economic development and improved productivity in the high-performing Asian economies.

From the mid-1970s, the coincidence of slower economic growth and rising inflation and unemployment fostered an ideological assault upon the principle and practice of public investment in the United States and the United Kingdom from proponents of the New Right as part of a broader political project to roll back the frontiers of the state. Public investment was deemed to have crowded out private investment and promoted a less-efficient allocation of resources than could be achieved by transferring the ownership and control of nationalized industries and public utilities to the private sector. Furthermore, public investment was held to have undermined enterprise, entrepreneurship, and consumer choice, and fostered a dependency culture among the communities and sectors of the economy that had become overly reliant upon it as a source of income.

In theory, by privatizing public assets and transferring responsibility for investment from the public to the private sector, it was held that a number of key policy objectives would be accomplished. First, investment would be depoliticized and new markets would be created for private capital. Second, investment would be allocated more efficiently and more profitably, thereby promoting freedom, consumer choice, and improved national economic performance, through reduced state borrowing and enhanced productivity. Third, the power of public-sector trade unions would be reduced and the frontiers of a property-owning, share-owning democracy simultaneously advanced.

In practice, there is little evidence that the transfer of assets from the public to the private sector has enhanced the overall pattern of investment in public goods and services, especially in mature economies, such as the United Kingdom with a long track record of underinvestment in tangible and intangible assets. Public investment had originated because of a market failure to invest sufficiently. As recently as 1967–1968, public-sector net investment had been as high as 7.1 percent of the gross domestic product (GDP).

The transfer of assets to the private sector simply threatened to repeat the underinvestment of the past. Consequently, following the large scale privatizations of state assets during the 1980s, UK public-sector net investment declined by an average of more than 15 percent between 1991–1992 and 1996–1997, accounting for only 0.6 of GDP in 1996–1997, the lowest level of public investment for more than a decade. Rather than resulting in an increase in overall investment in public services and infrastructure, by 1997 privatization had resulted in a backlog of repairs and maintenance, estimated at around £7 billion in Great Britain's schools and £3 billion in the National Health Service.

Public-Private Partnerships

Although public investment, financed through the conventional taxation of individuals and businesses, remains the principal means of providing public infrastructure and services in the major industrialized economies, the past decade has witnessed an increase in innovative uses of private finance to fund public goods and services.

Public-private partnerships (PPPs) have been introduced with the intention of enhancing efficiency, equity, and accountability in the delivery of public services, and harnessing the skills of the private sector in the design and management of major capital projects. PPPs have taken a number of forms. They have involved the introduction of private-sector ownership into state-owned businesses; the purchasing of public services from private-sector partners, with the latter assuming responsibility for delivering investment in better quality services; and the sale of government services into wider markets with a view to exploiting the commercial potential of investment in government assets.

The dividend for public investment from PPPs, in terms of increased efficiency, value for money, and the transfer of risk from the taxpayer to the private sector, has been limited. Although the private sector has taken on responsibility for major project performance risks (such as cost overruns and delays), nevertheless, the key risks in investment projects have remained with the public sector and taxpayer. Furthermore, the capacity to assess the actual risk transfer has proven problematic because of the multitude of risks to which PPPs have been exposed and because of the sheer complexity of PPP contracts. At the same time, the transfer of investment from the public to the private sector has raised questions about the detrimental impact upon working conditions and terms of employment for public servants involved in PPPs, especially in relation to pension provision.

Under the British government's flagship Private Finance Initiative (PFI), the number and total capital value of PFI projects has increased from nine projects with a total value of £667 million in 1995, to sixty-five projects with a total value of £7.6 billion in 2002. However, during the same period, gross public-sector investment rose from £17.3 billion in 1997–1998 to £33.4 billion in 2003–2004. Thus, conventionally procured public investment still accounts for more than 85 percent of total public investment. The share of private-sector investment in public services remained relatively constant, at between 10 and 13.5 percent of total investment between 1998–1989 and 2003–2004. While the British government has been able to point to a trebling in public-sector net investment from 0.7 percent of GDP in 1996–1997 to 2.1 percent of GDP by the end of 2005–2006, this increase has arisen overwhelmingly from increased investment by the taxpayer rather than from the private sector.

While privatization and the introduction of PPPs may have inflicted measurable short-term damage upon both the quantity of investment undertaken in public services and the overall quality of services delivered, greater and more intangible long-term damage may have been inflicted upon citizenship and the underlying idea of the public domain. The introduction of private-sector management techniques and market-driven reforms into the public domain, and the attendant triumph of consumerism over citizenship may have fatally undermined public confidence in the efficacy of public investment and the broader ethos of public service, equity, and civic duty. Without such public support, a vital source of democratic citizenship and a shared sense of political community may have been lost permanently.

Investment for Development

The role of public investment in the political economy of development has been the source of major contention in recent years. On the one hand, public investment was identified by the United Nations (UN) as a key component of the March 2002 Monterrey Consensus for financing the development of the lesser-developed economies. To further the common pursuit of growth, poverty eradication, and sustainable development, the UN has agreed upon the need for public resources to be mobilized effectively for investing in basic infrastructural needs, such as education, health, nutrition, shelter, and social security programs. Subsequently, the UN's Millennium Project has suggested that, for the poorest countries, an increase in public investment is vital, not only to meet certain critical needs but also to increase private investment held back by the lack of infrastructure, service delivery, and a healthy, skilled labor.

On the other hand, while both the International Monetary Fund (IMF) and World Bank have emphasized the importance for effective structural adjustment of country ownership and participation in recent years, the conditionality attached to their Poverty Reduction Strategy Papers for medium-term development has attached an increasing importance to the privatization of water supply and other public utilities. For example, in 1999, while a civil war in Sierra Leone was still raging, the IMF was advocating the privatization of the country's utility sector. In 2001 and 2002, similar conditionality was attached to Sierra Leone's receipt of aid and participation in debt relief. However, privatization has met with fierce political resistance, both from domestic interests and from nongovernmental organizations, because of their legitimate fear that vital public services such as water and power supply will no longer be affordable.

Despite an increasing emphasis upon the importance of entrepreneurship and investment by the private sector, the role of public investment is still widely seen as being vital if the international community's Millennium Development Goals (MDG) are to be achieved by 2015. To achieve the MDG, the UN has estimated that public investment in Official Development Assistance (ODA) for direct MDG support will need to rise from $16 billion in 2002 to $73 billion in 2006 and $135 billion in 2015. Total global public investment in ODA will need to double from $69 billion in 2003 to $135 billion in 2006 and $195 billion, according to UN figures. The UN Millennium Project has identified the goal of combining public infrastructure investments and human capital with market-oriented economic policies in order to ensure private-sector growth. It has further suggested that, once developing economies become richer, they will be able to finance an increasing share of their core infrastructure services from the private sector. However, the evidence of PPPs in industrialized economies suggests that for the foreseeable future, public investment will remain the primary source of funding for vital public goods.

Public investment therefore remains critical for the provision of the core investments in infrastructure and human capital in both the industrialized and industrializing economies, which will enable people to be empowered with the political, economic, and social rights that, in turn, enable them both to participate in the global economy and promote their own human development.

—*Simon Lee*

See also Citizenship; Investment

Further Readings and References

Heald, D. (1993). *Public expenditure: Its defence and reform.* Oxford, UK: Martin Robertson.

Her Majesty's Treasury. (2003). *PFI: Meeting the investment challenge.* London: HMSO.

Marquand, D. (2004). *Decline of the public.* Cambridge, UK: Polity Press.

Tanzi, V., & Schuknecht, L. (2000). *Public spending in the twentieth century.* Cambridge, UK: Cambridge University Press.

United Nations. (2002). *Report of the international conference on financing for development,* Monterrey, Mexico, March 18–22, 2002. New York: Author.

United Nations. (2005). *Investing in development: A practical plan to achieve the Millennium Development Goals.* New York: United Nations Millennium Project.

World Bank. (1993). *The East Asian miracle: Economic growth and public policy.* Oxford, UK: Oxford University Press.

PUBLIC OPINION

The most popular meaning of public opinion refers to the beliefs, attitudes, and preferences prevailing among the members of a given community. Although public opinion is often personified, it is, in fact, a random aggregation of individual opinions that are lacking any internal coordination. The influence of the concept of public opinion arose with the growth of modern democracies, with their expanding electorates in the twentieth century. Polling citizens' prior to presidential elections in the United States started as early as 1904, but the rapid growth of the industry of public opinion research took place after World War II. Increased literacy, improved means of communication and the emergence of mass consumerism made public opinion research an indispensable tool for politicians, but also for advertising and marketing experts, who needed to know what

most of the public thinks. Nowadays, market research is a multibillion-dollar worldwide industry, and using public opinion polls to monitor satisfaction with government activities and to inform electoral campaigns are standard practices.

Growth of interest in public opinion resulted in the emergence of various methods of interviewing respondents, as well as methods of sampling of who is to be interviewed. Different types of questions and wordings have been invented to most accurately measure subtleties of opinions and beliefs. The most popular surveys are either face-to-face or telephone/mail surveys aimed at random or quota samples. Random polls involve interviewing randomly selected members of a population: As each of them has a known probability of being selected, the error resulting from under- or overrepresentation of certain types of individuals can later be taken into account. Quota polls are based on samples that reproduce the social distribution of individuals in the population. Both methods are aimed at reconstructing opinions that would be representative for the general public. The establishment of *Public Opinion Quarterly* in 1937 brought official acknowledgment of public opinion research as a part of the social sciences. Since then, public opinion surveys are a recognized source of data for research in the social sciences, particularly in sociology and political science.

While the knowledge of public opinion is certainly an important cue for assessing relevancy and adequacy of governmental policies, it is important to remember that public opinion is susceptible to manipulation, especially by the media. So-called persuasion, when the tone of information coverage causes shifts in public opinion, and agenda setting, when media's attention makes the public see a given issue as particularly important, are among the most common strategies of influencing public opinion. It is also known that negative information has a stronger effect on public opinion than positive news, which, in turn, affects the choice of campaign strategies.

—*Natalia Letki*

See also Civic Engagement; Legitimacy; Participation

Further Readings and References

Bradburn, N. M., & Sudman, S. (1988). *Polls and surveys: Understanding what they tell us.* San Francisco: Jossey-Bass.

Vaus, D. de. (2002). *Social surveys* (Vols. 1–4). London: Sage Ltd.

PUBLIC-PRIVATE PARTNERSHIP

While public-private partnership (PPP) is an ancient phenomenon, scholars did not pay serious attention to analyzing it before the late 1980s, probably because its use became widespread in public administration and management during those years in both developed and developing countries. Today, a large variety of PPPs are contributing to the design and implementation of public policies, and it seems there will be a strong trend for greater use of partnership in the future. Even so, there is much debate on this topic, especially regarding what constitutes a genuine PPP and also regarding the costs and benefits of partnerships.

Definitions

At first, it has to be said that *partnership* is one of those catchall terms that may be used to convey all kinds of different meanings. On the one hand, some people consider any kind of relationship to be a partnership, and on the other hand, some genuine partnerships may be designated by other words. In France for instance, in addition to practitioners (in the financial sector in particular), the only academics to have used the expression PPP are economists and town planning specialists. French lawyers refer more willingly to "outsourcing administration of public services" (more restrictive than PPP), and political scientists refer to the "co-production of public policy or negotiation of contractual policies" (which has a broader meaning). However, the expression PPP is becoming more generalized as the phenomenon has grown.

According to dictionaries, partnership's most basic definition is any business or institutional association within which joint activity takes place. A PPP can be discerned from the moment such associations bring together one (or more) public organization(s) and one (or more) private organization(s) of whatever formal status, and they agree to act in concert. PPPs embrace public-sector partnership with both business and organizations in civil society, including community organizations, voluntary organizations, and nongovernmental organizations (NGOs).

The point is that one should not consider partnership as simply an equivalent to any contractual relation. Although such relationships are sometimes labeled partnerships by the parties concerned, when they are based simply on the traditional contracting principles of management, monitoring, and enforcement of a detailed specification contained within a legally binding agreement, they do not constitute genuine PPPs. The main reason for which not every contract between a public authority and a private-sector service provider constitutes a PPP is the following: Genuine partnership implies a triangular relationship binding the public authority, the private-sector partner, and the members of the public concerned with the service (users, customers, citizens). PPP is (or should be) a win-win agreement directed toward a social purpose.

But it is also true that (1) a multiplicity of agreements or contracts, more or less formal in nature and sometimes very informal, may give rise to a partnership; (2) the most institutionalized forms may go as far as the formalization of permanent structures mobilizing a coalition of interests and bringing them together around a common agenda between partners charged with taking policy decisions; and (3) in practice, PPPs produce a layering of practical solutions because it is in the nature of a partnership to develop and to adapt to the special circumstances of its particular field of operation. In this regard, political cultures and traditions have considerable impact. For instance, it is possible to distinguish between substitutive and collaborative forms of partnership. Under substitutive partnership, the private partner replaces the public agency more or less completely, as has happened in the French system of outsourcing public services. However, under collaborative partnership, typical of German organizations, each partner has its specific function that corresponds to a specific profession.

In summary, PPPs are a polymorphous reality that is difficult to conceptualize. Partnership implies a mutual commitment, but is, to some extent, different from other collaborative relationships. Based on the town planning experiences, François Ascher has proposed a definition of PPPs as public and private agencies engaged in long-term risk sharing to carry out a multifaceted process regarding the services, such as housing, amenities, transport, and other services.

Emergence of PPPs

In many countries around the world, the rise of PPPs has been quite spectacular. They are now written into legislation in a lot of developed countries, for example, the United States and United Kingdom (urban policies, economic development policies); France (infrastructure and public transport, urban services and development); Italy and the Netherlands (economic development policies), to name just a few. In the United Kingdom, the Private Finance Initiative (PFI, which is only one of many British PPPs), accounted for more than £8 billion of capital works contracts signed between 1997 and 1999, and at least half of UK local authorities use partnerships as an approach to supplier relationships.

In France, the PPP concept is quite long standing. But since the 1980s there has been a wide application of PPP in almost all areas of public policies. In addition to the industrial and commercial services that have traditionally involved partnerships, social services, and even activities fundamental to and characteristic of the state's authority are opening up to PPP. Local authorities no longer confine themselves to services such as water, trash collection, or household waste disposal; they now seek partnerships, for example, for legal services, communications, or services for the elderly. The state itself is openly contemplating partnerships between national public services and private enterprises. The economic weight of concessions (in which most of the concessionaires, but not all of them, are from the private sector, some of them being from the public sector or mixed-economy companies) is considerable. The annual turnover of water and sewage concessions has been estimated at

5 billion euros, while the treatment of waste and urban transport is worth at least 2 billion euros. Even more important is the fact that if PPP is still not a stabilized part of the framework of political values within French society, it has nevertheless imposed itself on reality because public-sector decisionmakers are using it pragmatically. The choice of management method—direct control or delegation—is now made on the basis of a financial calculation whose objective is to obtain the best service at the best price instead of adhering to an ideological dogma. Indeed, there are as many mayors on the Right opting for public-sector companies as there are mayors on the Left choosing outsourcing. This signifies that PPP has now been taken on across the board, even if this fact is not always advertised.

Recent enlargement of the European Union can only stimulate the demand for PPP further. To take one example, the investment required to install water services in Poland to a standard that meets European norms is estimated at between 15 billion and 20 billion euros over the next ten years. It is reasonable to consider that only PPPs are capable of smoothing the way for increases in tariffs and avoiding the brutal increases that would be inevitable just as they are socially unacceptable.

Concerning the international level and developing countries, partnerships between international donors and nongovernmental development organizations (NGDOs) are essential and rapidly increasing. The World Bank seeks to cooperate with NGDOs as partners, and several reports and evaluations call for improvements in World Bank procedures. Meanwhile, the most lofty partnership rhetoric comes from the United Nations (UN). Kofi Annan, the Secretary-General of the UN, has said that a true partnership between NGDOs and the UN is essential, and identified UN-NGDOs partnerships as vital to enforcing the Universal Declaration of Human Rights. The United States Agency for International Development (USAID) has also undertaken efforts to promote partnership. For example, its New Partnership Initiative (NPI) has produced many reports and guidelines culminating in an intersectoral partnerships handbook to support intersectoral PPPs within the agency.

There are, of course, a wide range of reasons leading to this success of PPPs, partly depending on national characteristics and special contexts. But, generally speaking, the considerable flexibility of a PPP means that it is most often in a position to provide an adequate response to the increasing complexity of public administration. Within developed countries at least, PPP appears to be a formula adapted to the contemporary circumstances of public policies and state intervention, one of the main reasons being the changing nature of public-sector problems. These are no longer restricted to the relatively simple production of goods, facilities, or activities that can be mastered and standardized through the use of technology. Rather, these problems have become increasingly complex as services become more qualitative and participate in the quest for global coherence within each local area. More lateral or horizontal public policies should promote a better environment, achieve the ambitious objectives of urban policy, fight against poverty and exclusion, and so forth in order to generate territorial development. In short, policy has to take into account all issues and agencies involved in the region in which it is developing. As a result, partnership in general—not only, but of course including, PPP—arises in the nature of what can be called modernizing public policy. In addition to these reasons, there are two other key drivers. First, the fiscal problems of the state mean that the mobilization of private funding for public services is no longer a real choice; this is why, in some cases, it is encouraged by national legislation and funding regimes. Second, the exponential rise in interest in e-government drives governments to seek resources from the private companies of the information technology (IT) sector, both to finance massive capital investments and, above all, to access the expertise of these companies. Nevertheless, when, reflecting upon this success, the big question is, What is the additional value of PPP?

PPPs and Governance

Because of the huge diversity of the phenomenon, it is almost impossible to take stock of the results of PPPs as a whole in regard to better governance. On the one hand, partnerships are able to bring real advantages, such as economies of scale in the provision of services or activities, the ability to maximize complementary competences, and provide opportunities for mutual learning between partners. On the other hand, PPP brings much fragmentation of structures and processes, leading to a blurring of responsibilities and of accountability; therefore employees fear losing their jobs or perks, and service users or citizens may fear becoming objects of profit making rather than recipients of public services.

Ultimately, PPPs can produce the best as well as the worst outcomes, depending on the configuration of factors involved in each of them. Generally speaking, PPPs should pay more attention to public governance issues. In the case of partnership between international donors and NGDOs, overcoming administrative or operational obstacles is not enough—the political and economical ramifications of the relationships of NGDOs and donors must be accounted for. PPP offers a favorable framework well adapted to contemporary needs in terms of public policy. It facilitates innovation and experimentation. By definition, it encourages the sharing of responsibility. It imposes increased transparency (in relative terms, depending on the complexity of its operations) in the management of services through contractual negotiations and the process of drawing up specifications. It may give marginalized groups, kept on the fringe of representative institutions (foreigners, women, young people, especially in the inner city) access to negotiations and a certain legitimacy. However, in every instance, PPPs take shape through the actions of the agents involved, with their personal ethics, their varying capacity for taking opportunities, their ulterior motives, their corporate or community culture and the rational expectations they inspire.

—*Pierre Sadran*

See also Contracting Out; New Public Management; Public Sector; Third Way

Further Readings and References

Ascher, F. (1994). Le partenariat public-privé dans le (re)développement. Le cas de la France [Public-private partnership in (re)development: The case involving France]. In W. Heinz (Ed.), *Partenariats public-privé dans l'aménagement urbain* [Public-private partnerships in the urban installation]. Paris: L'Harmattan.

Bovaird, T. (2004). Public-private partnerships: From contested concepts to prevalent practice. *International Review of Administrative Science, 70*(2), 199–215.

Brinkerhoff, D. W., & Brinkerhoff, J. M. (2004). Partnerships between international donors and non-governmental development organizations: Opportunities and constraints. *International Review of Administrative Science, 70*(2), 253–270.

Lorrain, D. (2003). Dix ans de réforme de réseaux: sept enseignements (Des privatisations au partenariat public-privé) [Ten years of reformation of networks: Seven teachings (Privatizations to public-private partnership)]. In J. Y. Perrot & G. Chatelus (Eds.), *Financement des infrastructures et des services collectifs: le recours au partenariat public-privé, les enseignements des expériences françaises dans le monde* [Financing of infrastructures and collective services: Recourse to the public-private partnership, the teachings of the French experiences in the world]. Paris: Presses de l'Ecole Nationale des Ponts et Chaussées.

Sadran, P. (2004). Public-private partnership in France: A polymorphous and unacknowledged category of public policy. *International Review of Administrative Science, 70*(2), 233–251.

PUBLIC SECTOR

The public sector is defined as the portion of the economy composed of all levels of government and government-controlled enterprises. Therefore, it does not include private companies, voluntary organizations, and households.

While the notion of the public sector is often used to classify distinct areas of economic activity, for example, in the area of national accounting, it also implies a definition of public activity that goes beyond the core domains of public administration. The general definition of the public sector includes government ownership or control rather than mere function, thereby including, for example, the exercise of public authority or the implementation of public policy.

When pictured as concentric circles, the core public service in central and subnational government agencies defines the inner circle of the public sector. In this case, the distinction of the public from the private sector is relatively straightforward—it is evident in terms of employment relationships and the right of exercising public power. The next circle includes a number of different quasi-governmental agencies that are, however, placed outside the direct line of accountability within government. Examples range from social security funds to regional development agencies. The outer circle is populated by state-owned enterprises, usually defined by the government's ownership or its owning the majority of shares. Since the 1980s, a number of developed countries have witnessed extensive privatizations of state-owned enterprises, whether in parts or in full (examples range from airlines to the telecom sector), although public ownership continues to be a widespread feature, for example, in the field of local public transport.

The term *public sector* is also used for analytical purposes, in particular, as a contrast to the private and third, or voluntary, sectors. This allows for the mapping of the scope of state activities within the wider economy (also allowing for comparison across space and time). Furthermore, it highlights distinctive patterns and operating procedures within the public sector. This relates to the contemporary interest in cross-sectoral learning, especially the learning of "private" management practices for application in the public sector.

Among the key themes of public-sector research is its growth, and whether growth is inherent to the public sector. For example, William Baumol identified a public-sector "disease," suggesting that those activities characteristic of the public sector were those that could not be "automatized," therefore leading to lower productivity gains in comparison to the private sector. William Niskanen linked public-sector growth to the incentives of budget-maximizing bureaucrats. Others have focused less on public-sector size overall, but on the relationship between the different circles of the public sector. Patrick Dunleavy's "bureau-shaping" model points to incentives among politicians and senior bureaucrats to shuffle institutional responsibilities from the first to the second circle of organizations.

The notion of governance highlights the difficulties in defining what the public sector is. Privatization, delegation of public power (for example, in prisons), the joint public-private provision of services, usually regarded as "public," as well as institutional rearrangements have made the identification of the public sector difficult, especially for purposes of comparative analysis. For some, therefore, the notion of the public sector has lost all conceptual strength, given these problems of defining clear boundaries.

—*Kai Wegrich*

See also Bureau Shaping; Civil Service; Public Administration; Public-Private Partnership; Service Delivery

Further Readings and References

Dunleavy, P. (1985). Bureaucrats, budgets and the growth of the state: Reconstructing an instrumental model. *British Journal of Political Science, 15,* 299–328.

Lane, J.-E. (2000). *The public sector: Concepts, models and approaches.* London: Sage Ltd.

Peters, B. G. (2001). *The politics of bureaucracy.* London: Routledge.

PUBLIC SPHERE

The public sphere is the political arena where citizens discuss issues of common concern. Besides participation in the electoral process, citizens' contribution to public debate represents one of the main avenues open to them to influence the process of democratic decision making. For this reason, an accessible public sphere characterized by robust discussion is considered to be an indispensable element of modern democratic politics.

Given that discussion in the public sphere focuses on issues of general interest, it is less individualistic and less personal than discussions in the private realm. At the same time, public discussion is less rigidly structured than deliberation in such organized political arenas as governments, which have formal rules of order and set membership requirements. Loosely structured, public debate is governed by the laxer standards of general political civility. Formal requirements regulating participation are also absent; ideally anyone concerned with an issue should be able to voice an opinion. Public debate results neither in legislation nor in administrative rules; these remain the purview of government and the state respectively. Instead, public debate generates influence. By mobilizing opinion in the public sphere, citizens have the opportunity to convince their representatives and state officials of the need to take action on an issue or to voice their opposition to government action in a specific policy area. In this way, citizens influence the process of political decision making; they do not directly make the decisions.

While public sphere has spatial connotations, it possesses no precise location. Debate can take place in venues as varied as public squares, political conventions, and the virtual space of the media, including, of course, the Internet. Some argue that the public sphere is also increasingly transnational. Political perspectives that transcend a national frame of reference now frequently characterize public debate. Also public participation has expanded beyond members of the nation-state to include international nongovernmental organizations and representatives of international institutions.

Although consensus exists regarding the public sphere's democratic significance, widespread disagreement persists concerning the rationality of public opinion and its desired scope. Scholars who stress democracy's deliberative quality consider the rational potential of public debate to be high. Thus, they argue that public discussion should play as large a role in political decision making as possible. Others who work with the various permutations of postmodern democratic thought deny that public debate can generate a rational political consensus. Instead, the public sphere is best thought of as an arena of agonistic competition regarding identities and political positions. To the extent that such competition contributes to the dynamism of democracy, it should be encouraged. Finally, a third group argues that the rationality of public debate is limited to finding a balance between competing interest groups. It cannot hope to achieve rational agreement on controversial issues. Given this limited potential and because citizens never possess the policy knowledge of experts, debate in the public sphere should play a relatively minor political role.

—*John Brady*

See also Civil Society; Communicative Action; Democratic Theory; Feminist Theory; Functionalism; Pragmatism

Further Readings and References

Habermas, J. (1974, Fall). The public sphere: An encyclopedia article. *New German Critique, 3,* 49–55.

Marx Ferree, M., Gamson, W. A., Gerhards, J., & Rucht, D. (2002). Four models of the public sphere in modern democracies. *Theory and Society, 31*(3), 289–324.

PUNCTUATED EQUILIBRIUM

Punctuated equilibrium describes a pattern of development in which rapid change occurs during brief periods, followed by longer periods of stasis. Originally proposed in the study of biological evolution, this concept has been applied to the development of political institutions as well.

The concept of punctuated equilibrium was developed by Stephen J. Gould and Niles Eldredge as an alteration of Darwinian theory of evolution. While the latter holds that evolution occurred in a gradual and continuous manner, depending on individual mutation, the theory of punctuated equilibrium argues that change occurs in sudden "fits and starts," followed by long periods of relatively minor changes across species.

Like many other concepts in the physical sciences, the model of punctuated equilibrium has been applied by social scientists to describe patterns of change seen in social and political institutions. Political arrangements often exhibit the same pattern of change involving short periods of major destruction, creation, and transformation followed by longer periods of equilibrium.

Among the numerous applications of this concept to political science, Stephen Krasner's consideration of state sovereignty is an early example. Considering the ways in which the existing institution of state sovereignty and the state system more generally are less than optimal arrangements, Krasner argues that such political institutions exhibit features similar to the biological model: change is difficult, the availability of past institutional models limits the possibilities for new developments, and chance often has a role in determining final outcomes.

Later authors have contributed to the use of the punctuated equilibrium concept by proposing mechanisms to explain what is essentially a description of a pattern of change. For example, the concept of critical junctures offers an explanation for sudden change followed by stasis or path-dependent development. Ruth Berins Collier and David Collier's work on Latin American political development is a major example of this. In another vein, Paul Pierson proposes that the economic concept of increasing returns can be applied to political institutions, arguing that some institutional arrangements can become "locked in" and, hence, be resistant to change, even when the forces behind their creation have disappeared.

On the other hand, punctuated equilibrium has been criticized for overemphasizing stasis and exogenous shocks and for not being able to explain gradual change. Kathleen Thelen, for example, argues that political and social developments actually occur in a more gradual fashion, and that even catastrophic political events (such as defeat in a war) often lead to very little change in major institutional arrangements.

—Jordan Branch

See also Institution; Institutionalism

Further Readings and References

Collier, R. B., & Collier, D. (1991). *Shaping the political arena.* Princeton, NJ: Princeton University Press.

Gould, S. J., & Eldredge, N. (1977). Punctuated equilibria: The tempo and mode of evolution reconsidered. *Paleobiology, 3,* 115–151.

Krasner, S. D. (1988). Sovereignty: An institutional perspective. *Comparative Political Studies, 21,* 66–94.

Pierson, P. (2004). Increasing returns, path dependence, and the study of politics. *American Political Science Review, 94,* 251–264.

Thelen, K. (1999). Historical institutionalism in comparative politics. *American Political Science Review, 2,* 369–404.

PURCHASER-PROVIDER SPLIT

The term *purchaser-provider split* refers to a model of public service delivery where the functions of paying for and delivering goods and services are separated.

The purchaser-provider split model of service delivery entails two components. First, it involves the existence of dedicated purchasing agencies with responsibility for financing services and for ensuring the needs of the population entitled to services that are covered, but who are not directly involved in the provision of services. Providers of services relate to purchasers through contracts rather than direct forms of accountability, and these contracts specify their roles and responsibilities in delivering the public goods or services. The second component involves giving purchasers and providers a degree of autonomy and responsibility with respect to their functions in purchasing or providing services. Both components stand in contrast to an integrated model of service delivery, where a single organization or set of organizations is responsible for financing, planning, and providing services and accountable for the overall structure of the service.

The separation between purchasers and providers of public services has long existed in a number of continental European countries and the United States, where social or private insurers or governmental agencies have responsibility for purchasing services but not directly providing them. For instance, many publicly financed health care systems have been built around a split between social insurers who are responsible for funding health care services and the hospitals and doctors who provide these services but are independent of the insurers.

In recent years, a number of countries that have traditionally relied on integrated models of service provision have introduced purchaser-provider splits in public services. These reforms have been particularly popular in the health care sector, where countries like the United Kingdom, New Zealand, Italy, and Sweden have experimented with them as a way of moving away from an integrated health care delivery system.

However, these reforms have also been introduced in a range of other areas, from child welfare to prison services, and across a range of countries.

The introduction of a purchaser-provider split generally aims to accomplish two sets of goals. First, it is intended to stimulate clearer lines of management accountability by clarifying different functions in the production of public services. Second, it is often introduced as part of a larger movement toward stimulating competition among the providers of services. This move toward competition may occur primarily within the public sector, thus creating an internal market where public providers compete for contracts from public purchasers. However, purchaser-provider splits often occur alongside greater contracting and purchasing from the private sector. These reforms, then are a key component in the marketization of the public sector and are often part of the prescription for public service reform advocated by proponents of new public management. This movement is intended to stimulate a more marketlike governance of services, rather than directing government steering.

—*Jane Gingrich*

See also Internal Market; Marketization; New Public Management; Quasi-Market; Service Provider

Further Readings and References

Jost, T. S., Hughes, D., McHale, J., & Griffiths, L. (1996). The British health care reforms, The American health care revolution, and purchaser/provider contracts. *Journal of Health Policy, 20,* 885–908.

Robinson, J. C. (1997). Physician-hospital integration and the economic theory of the firm. *Medical Care Research and Review, 54*(1), 3–24.

Shackley, P., & Healey, A. (1993). Creating a market: An economic analysis of the purchaser-provider model. *Health Policy, 25,* 153–168.

QUANGO

The term *quango*, an acronym for quasi-autonomous nongovernmental organization, has come into use as a label for a wide range of public bodies and extragovernmental organizations that are responsible for developing, managing, and delivering public policy under largely appointed, rather than elected, governing boards.

The definition of quango has been the subject of considerable dispute. Quangos differ in their size, their funding, their legal and organizational forms, their accountability mechanisms, and their relationships to their reporting ministry. Reflecting these differences, quangos have also been named differently in different countries: service agencies in Canada, independent administrative authorities in France, crown entities in New Zealand, departmental public bodies in the United Kingdom, and independent agencies in the United States. Despite such differences, there seems to be some consensus on three basic features of quangos:

1. They are created as a result of governmental action, although not necessarily directly created by governments, and are considered part of the public domain.

2. They have no direct electoral accountability and operate, to a greater or lesser extent, at arm's length from government officials.

3. While they spend public money and fulfill key public functions—ranging from advising policymakers to commissioning, purchasing, and delivering public services—they are not government departments or even subsections of government departments.

Yet some analysts suggest that the conceptual problem is that the plethora and range of bodies that the term *quango* can refer to, with such broad features, is so wide as to render the term completely worthless, making it difficult to use the term *quango* as an analytical category. One proposition has been to map the field of quangos as a continuum moving away from direct governmental control toward organizations that are clearly in the private sector but perform some public tasks. The location of one organization on the continuum would then depend on several factors including its managerial autonomy, its governance structure, its policy dependence, and its legal structure. This continuum approach, while acknowledging the diversity of quangos, also highlights their dynamic nature and the fact that quangos can change into other types of organizations by adopting new organizational features.

As suggested by many governmental reports and scholarly works, the creation of quangos in modern democracies has been driven by three main objectives:

1. An increased autonomy for public actors. The transfer of functions from elected politicians to

organizations enjoying a degree of autonomy is conceived of as a means of insulating certain activities from political and bureaucratic influence, creating a buffer zone between the spheres of policy formation and policy delivery, and consequently protecting some areas of public administration from the cut and thrust of day-to-day politics.

2. An increased participation in public policy. One of the key arguments for supporting the creation of quangos is their potential to offer new opportunities for involvement and participation. Thus, quangos are conceived of as tools to involve societal actors that are often underrepresented through the electoral process (disabled people, ethnic minorities, women). Quangos are also used as a means of drawing specific groups of people into public services, such as specialized professionals and experts that would not otherwise be attracted to the world of politics.

3. An increased effectiveness and efficiency of public services. The creation of quangos has also been driven by the widespread perceptions of the inadequacies of state-run organizations and the quest for greater effectiveness and efficiency of public services. The rationalization for the disaggregation of large, multifunctional bureaucracies into a range of quasi-autonomous bodies draws upon the assumption that the structural isolation of these bodies from the political arena, their management autonomy, their smaller size, their focused objectives, and the opportunity they offer to separate the roles of purchaser and providers will create conditions for innovations, will generate new incentives, and will make them more responsive, more adaptive, and more efficient.

Although the creation of quangos is an old feature of statecraft strategy and is common to all modern democracies, the rapid establishment in recent years of a range of unelected bodies has raised widespread concerns as to their impact on public governance. A first chief concern relates to the capacity of the quango state to maintain the coherence of public policy. The institutional fragmentation occasioned by an increase of quangos inevitably produces a dispersion of governmental activities and may cause problems of coordination. This creates a challenge to the maintenance of government and policy coherence across a complex network of service bodies. Such a fragmentation may also reduce the strategic capacity of governments due to the growth in the potential constriction points through which each initiative must pass. Another main concern relates to potential threats to accountability. The growth of fringe bodies that are insulated to some degree from direct governmental or political supervision is often perceived of as a retreat from the traditional democratic framework. In particular, there has been much criticism of the lack of transparency surrounding the appointments of quangos' boards and their benefits. In addition, observations have shown that governments and elected politicians may use nonelected bodies as a means of paying political allies or extending their influence over areas of public activity that are politically strategic and difficult to control centrally. In some cases, quangos have been created to replace functions previously performed by local authorities. In such cases, the creation of quangos may be interpreted as a project to substitute new agencies, operating from a centrally determined agenda, for local authorities. Government officials facing difficult political choices may also prefer to create a quango that will take responsibility for possible failures, even though these failures may result from poor policy decisions.

In summary, a great number of public bodies with various degrees of separateness from governments have become integral components of state activities in many countries. Different goals have been pursued through the creation of these extragovernmental bodies. However, the development of these governing institutions is confronted by the challenges of finding the right balance between autonomy and accountability, maintaining the steering capacity of central governments, and preventing conflict with local governments' prerogatives.

—Carl-Ardy Dubois and
Damien Contandriopoulos

See also Global Civil Society; Hybrid Organization; New Public Management; Quasi-Market

Further Readings and References

Flinders, M. (2004). Distributed public governance in Britain. *Public Administration, 82*(4), 883–909.

Greve, C., Flinders, M. V., & Van Thiel, S. (1999). Quangos—What's in a name? Defining quangos from a comparative perspective. *Governance, 12*(2), 129–146.

Organisation for Economic Co-operation and Development. (2002). *Distributed public governance: Agencies, authorities and other government bodies.* Paris: Author.

Payne, T., & Skelcher, C. (1997). Explaining less accountability: The growth of local quangos. *Public Administration, 75*(2), 207–224.

QUASI-MARKET

Quasi-markets, also sometimes described as planned markets or internal markets, are organizationally designed and supervised markets intended to bring us more efficiency and choice than bureaucratic delivery systems while maintaining more equity, accessibility, and stability than conventional markets.

From the viewpoint of economics, a market is an exchange mechanism of commodities that is able to match supply and demand, mostly through price adjustments. In this way, a market can also be conceptualized as a self-adjusting monetary incentive system that influences the behavior of consumers and providers so they agree on terms of exchange. Quasi-markets are also an exchange system that aims to emulate competitive markets' characteristics of being self-adjusting incentive systems that influence consumers' and providers' behaviors. However, those systems are "quasi" markets because they have characteristics both at supply and demand levels that differentiate them from conventional markets.

On the supply side, quasi-markets are a form of market system because there is competition between many providers to attract consumers. However, most of the time, these providers do not merely seek a maximization of their profits. In the public sector, these providers are often quangos or other forms of more-or-less nonowned organizations or NGOs (nongovernmental organizations). Providers can also be components or

sectors of a single organization that internally trade their services inside a specific form of quasi-market called an internal market. Moreover, internal markets are not open markets because providers and their products or services often need a third party or purchaser approbation to enter the market.

On the demand side, quasi-markets are designed to create or enhance consumer choice, obliging providers to be responsive to those choices. However, welfare-state quasi-markets differ from conventional ones because generally, consumers are not directly paying for the service they choose and because price plays only a marginal role, if any, in the consumers' choice. In private sector internal markets, pricing does have a direct influence on internal resource allocation, though it does not directly influence a company's bottom line.

The implementation of any form of quasi-market implies that purchaser and provider are distinct entities and that there is more than one provider. The process by which some entities are granted a purchaser status and the allocative prerogatives that come with it, while other entities are given a provider status and broader latitude in their own governance and strategic planning, is called a purchaser-provider split.

In most welfare-state quasi-markets, while consumers have a level of choice in the services they consume, it is a third party, often a state-based purchaser, who will pay or reimburse the provider for those services. Quasi-market purchasing can be implemented through fee-for-service reimbursements, vouchers, retrospective budgeting, and the like. Hence, while consumers' choices will be made according to such factors as perceived quality of service, waiting time, or availability, price will generally play no role in their choice. However, price will matter for the third-party payer, who is expected to limit consumers' choices to services that have a comparable high value for money. Successful providers are expected to simultaneously respond to purchasers' demands for low price or good value as well as to consumers' demands for quality, availability, waiting time, and the like. However, this implies that the necessary information to make a rational choice of providers and services will be accessible in a timely and usable form to both consumers and purchasers. This involves important transaction costs that are supposed to be compensated for by added efficiency.

At the beginning of the 1980s, a shift in the theoretical foundations of state welfare schemes took place in many countries, while neoclassical economics started to replace some of the Keynesian postulates that once predominated. The main purpose of welfare systems shifted from an enhancement of equity and social justice to a maximization of value for money and consumer choice. Quasi-markets have been one of the principal means used to reform the delivery of welfare in order to achieve those results. Many sectors have been targeted, from education to health care or social housing in countries ranging from New Zealand or Sweden to the United Kingdom. However, the interest in quasi-markets is far from limited to welfare-state interventions, and corporations such as the British Broadcasting Company (BBC), Intel, and British Petroleum (BP) have implemented forms of internal markets in some sectors.

Where they have been implemented, the actual functioning of quasi-markets has often been less conclusive than theory would have predicted. The existing delivery infrastructure often considerably limits the extent of potential competition in the market. For example, if there is only one hospital in a given rural region, for many interventions, the extent of consumers' choice of providers is very low unless they are willing to travel to other regions. Moreover, creating new providers to enhance competition would run opposite to the quasi-market goal of maximizing efficiency.

Even where there are a sufficient number of providers to allow for competition, in many sectors where quasi-markets have been implemented, inter-provider competition has often been below the expected level. Many factors can account for this. First, in the case of welfare interventions, those who consume the most services (the very young, the very old, the very poor, and disabled people) are the least likely to be able to access, treat, or use the information needed to make a rational choice. Second, from the purchasers' viewpoint, many services have intrinsic characteristics that make them difficult to assess in terms of value for money. And, whereas the quasi-market provides at least theoretical incentives to maximize providers' performance, it is not clear what the incentives are that would convince purchasers to make the extra effort needed to compare available services. Finally, the underlying incentive behind the notion of competition is that low-performing providers would either improve or disappear, something that governments have often proved reluctant to see happen.

—Damien Contandriopoulos
and Carl-Ardy Dubois

See also Hybrid Organization; Internal Market; Purchaser-Provider Split; Quango; Service Provider

Further Readings and References

Le Grand, J., & Bartlett, W. (Eds.). (1993). *Quasi-markets and social policy.* London: Macmillan.

RATIONAL CHOICE INSTITUTIONALISM

See NEW INSTITUTIONALISM

RATIONAL CHOICE THEORY

Rational choice theory is a theory of human action that is committed to expectations over probabilistic outcomes and game theory. From its original articulation, this theory of rational decision making was put forward as a new approach to economics, warfare, and social science more generally.

Rational choice theory is often simplistically considered to be a theoretical generalization of either technical instrumental rationality, requiring that an agent adopt the means necessary to realize a chosen end, or of economic efficiency, demanding the effective use of scarce resources as exchangeable means to achieve ends. Instead, rational choice theory represents a unique approach to social science that locates human rationality in an agent's mutually consistent hierarchy of preferences over all conceivable global nonexchangeable end states. Additionally, rational agents are presumed to make decisions (a) in strategic environments in which one agent chooses actions in direct response to the actions that others are calculated to take and (b) in situations with either unknowable

(uncertain) or well-defined (risky) probabilities of what outcomes may result as a consequence of actions.

Elements and Structure of Rational Choice Theory: Expectations and Game Theory

In rational choice theory, agents are described by their unchanging sets of preferences over all conceivable global outcomes, such as whether candidate Smith, Davidson, or Nelson will win an election, whether dinner will consist of chicken, fish, or tofu, or whether a public policy is one of waging war, negotiating a settlement, or relying on the international community of nation states to provide leadership. Agents are said to be rational if their preferences are complete, that is, if they reflect a relationship of superiority, inferiority, or indifference among all pairs of choices; and logically ordered, that is, they do not exhibit any cyclic inconsistencies of the sort: Chicken is preferred to fish, fish is preferred to tofu, and tofu is preferred to chicken. In addition, for choices in which the probabilities of outcomes are either risky, or uncertain, rational agents exhibit consistencies among their choices much as one would expect from an astute gambler. All of these consistency relations among preferences over outcomes are stated in mathematical axioms; a rational agent is one whose choices reflect internal consistency demanded by the axioms of rational choice. Rational choice theory holds that all considerations pertinent to choice (that may include attitudes toward risk, resentment, sympathy, envy, loyalty, love, and a sense of fairness) can be incorporated into agents' preference rankings over all possible end states. Social scientists only have indirect access to agents' desires through their revealed choices; therefore, researchers infer back from observed behavior to reconstruct the preference hierarchy that is thought to regulate a rational agent's decisions.

It is generally not appreciated, but important, that the consistency constraints defining rational choice theory are not equivalent to those specifying maximization of marginal utility under a budget constraint, although formal bridging conditions may be added to achieve congruence. It is also the case that even though many social scientists that use rational choice theory adopt one canonical axiomatized form specified as "expected utility theory," the research paradigm sustains alternative views as well. There are subtleties in probability theory that divide researchers: Are probabilities objective features of the world or are they best regarded as subjective features of individuals' psychology, and what sorts of consistency conditions apply to decision problems that incorporate both attitudes toward risk and unknowable probabilities? The intractability of decision making in uncertain circumstances has lead to the formulation of bounded rationality that grounds rational choice in manageable rule-of-thumb calculations in a series of one-time circumstances. As well, psychologists have observed several prominent and predictable empirical deviations from rational choice theory that has made it possible to identify patterns of what may be termed "folk psychology."

Game theory, which relies on some form of expectations theory, provides a mathematical framework for analyzing individuals' mutually interdependent interactions. These agents are defined by their preferences over outcomes and the set of possible actions available to each. As its name suggests, game theory represents a formal study of social institutions with set rules that relate agents' actions to outcomes. Such institutions may be thought of as resembling the parlor games of bridge, poker, and tic-tac-toe. Game theory assumes that agents are like-minded, rational

opponents that are aware of each other's preferences and strategies. A strategy is the exhaustive game plan each will implement, or the complete set of instructions another could implement on an agent's behalf, that best fits individual preferences in view of the specific structural contingencies of the game. These contingencies include the number of game plays, the sequential structure of the game, the possibility of forming coalitions with other players, and other players' preferences over outcomes.

For social scientists using game theory to model, explain, and predict collective outcomes, games are classified into three groups: purely cooperative games in which players prefer and jointly benefit from the same outcomes; purely competitive games in which one person's gain is another's loss; and mixed games, including the prisoner's dilemma, that involve varied motives of cooperation and competition. Game theory is a mathematical exercise insofar as theorists strive to solve for the collective result of various game forms, considering their structure and agents' preferences. Equilibrium solutions are of the most interest because they indicate, following the Nash equilibrium concept, that given the actions of all other agents, each agent is satisfied with his chosen strategy of play. Equilibrium solutions have the property of stability in that they are spontaneously generated as a function of agents' preferences. Solving games is complicated by the fact that a single game may have more than one equilibrium solution, leaving it far from clear what the collective outcome will be. Moreover, some games have no equilibrium solutions whatsoever.

One perplexing feature of game theory relates to the assumption of reflexivity on the part of agents: Agents must choose strategies in response to their beliefs of what strategies others will choose. This idea of reflexivity leads some researchers to associate methodological individualism with game theory. This is the assumption that the individual is the pivotal unit of analysis for understanding collective outcomes in politics and economics. However, as the use of game theory for understanding interactions in populations studied in evolutionary biology makes clear, the assumption of reflexivity and a view of the individual that could sustain a liberal understanding of politics and economics are not essential. Still, having made this observation, it remains the case that many who adopt game theory in social science find it consistent with individualistic approaches that view the individual as the sole determinant of personal preferences, goals, and values. It cannot be ignored that part of rational choice theory's outstanding successes in the late twentieth century is inseparable from its extensive refashioning of our understanding of how and why markets and democracy function to respect individual choices.

Applications of Rational Choice Theory to Problems of Governance

Bargaining, democratic processes for reaching decisions, the bases of social contracts, various constitutional designs, systems of incentives and punishments, processes for achieving conflict resolution, collective actions and the provisions of public goods, the assignment of rights, and distributive justice have all been studied using game theoretic models. Rational choice theory has become paradigmatic of social science because it has successfully navigated between explanatory and descriptive analyses of political phenomena on the one hand, and has provided useful tools for leveraging social scientific knowledge to better design institutions on the other hand. Thus, supposedly nonnormative findings from rational choice research have been applied to formulating public policies and to designing institutions. Much of the research within the paradigm with direct relationship to political economy and governance has been achieved in one of three schools: positive political theory, public choice, and social choice.

The first result derived from rational choice theory with clear implications for social welfare and democratic theories was the "impossibility theorem" derived by Kenneth J. Arrow in 1951. Starting with the assumption of individuals' rational preferences, the theorem proves that, given minimum conditions that many believe consistent with democratic will formation, regardless of what procedure is used, it is impossible to generate a collectively rational preference ordering over global social states. Given that democracy traditionally drew its legitimacy from claiming to deliver government of,

by, and for the people, the impossibility theorem is a setback for hopes that collective-will formation based on individual preferences can accurately reflect people's preferences. Similarly, the impossibility theorem challenges policymakers' ability to fashion public policies consistent with the public interest, as there is at this time no scientifically credible means to derive a comprehensive statement of the public good or social welfare from individuals' desires. The impossibility theorem thus served to cast the cogency of the paternalistic social welfare state into doubt.

In the 1950s, researchers exploited rational choice and the impossibility theorem to investigate further how individual choice leads to collective outcomes. Duncan Black developed the insight that under special conditions in which individuals' preferences exhibit the characteristic of being "single-peaked," that is, specially arranged from lowest to highest on one universal hierarchy between two poles, then collective-will formation can said to be a valid expression of individuals' interests. The "median voter" theorem, first stated by Anthony Downs, performs an analysis of rationally self-interested voters, finding that in running campaigns designed to win elections, rational candidates will cater to the average voter, as this mathematically ensures receiving the highest number of votes. In turn, William Riker demonstrated a feature the median voter theorem missed: That candidates' motives to cater to the average voter are limited by the extent they must reach to accommodate voters' preferences to establish a minimum winning coalition.

The insight that collective outcomes are best analyzed as the result of individuals' acting on rational preferences was also applied to the question of what types of constitutions such agents would select. Early research suggested that rational individuals would only agree to a constitutional framework as a result of unanimous voting that neutralized any citizen's fear that others' encroachment on personal interests could result. As well, rational choice research scrutinized the standard rule that collective decisions cast in accordance with majority rule are legitimate. Instead, it was proposed by James M. Buchanan and Gordon Tullock that rational citizens would uphold a greater-than-majority threshold for many legislative decisions as a function of a cost-benefit analysis balancing the time and energy costs of reaching any decision against the costs of living under a government whose policies violate personal preferences. Rational choice was also used to define the problems of the "free rider" and collective action by demonstrating that rational individuals cannot easily cooperate to achieve mutually beneficial outcomes. Research on the behavior of rational voters raised the question of why individuals vote in the first place, given that there is only a minute mathematical probability that any single vote will affect the final election outcome.

More recently, the rational choice approach has been used to reconsider central questions in traditional political philosophy. The Western social contract tradition, relying on individuals' consensual agreement to abide by contracts, has been reexamined using the idea that some multiparty, repeated form of the paradigmatic prisoner's dilemma game is characteristic of the state of nature from which government and social contracts must emerge. Political theorists employing game theory revisit Thomas Hobbes's seventeenth-century social contract theory put forward in his work *Leviathan* to understand how social order emerges from the state of nature characterized by a total lack of security consistent with each having the natural right to all things, including each others' person and property. Rational choice theorists ask how it is that individuals can form a sovereign state given their character is governed by rational self-interest. As the prisoner's dilemma suggests, whereas each person can see the prospective gains from cooperation, he or she has the ever-present incentive to cheat, either as a defensive tactic to avoid being the sucker, or as an offensive strategy to gain the most for oneself. It is widely held by game theorists that the prisoner's dilemma captures tensions between individual action and collective outcomes that typify government: Each person calculates better personal payoffs by cheating the system or one's fellow citizen, with the final result that each person is worse off.

Rational choice theorists disregard Hobbes's social contract theory on the basis that it seems to presuppose what is in fact impossible: Agents can contract their way out of a prisoner's dilemma game by

promising compliance with an agreement without an external enforcement mechanism to ensure compliance. As game theorists realize, Hobbes proposed an absolute sovereign that would enforce the social contract by coercive means to ensure compliance. However, it remains unclear how agents can establish a sovereign by mutual contract: If contracting were possible in the first place, then why the need for the absolute sovereign?

Instead of a social contract theory of government, rational choice theorists propose a coordination theory of government. Given that social contracts require third-party enforcement through incentives or punitive measures, and that such a third party cannot be presupposed in a state of nature, rational choice theorists argue that government emerged as a coordination game. In this understanding of social order, parties mutually realize that they are forever caught in the bind of the prisoner's dilemma, with each poised to cheat the other. The only solution to the prisoner's dilemma that is consistent with rational choice theory, leaving aside nonanonymous interactions in indefinitely repeated games more typical of small communities, is for all the parties to agree to establish an enforcement body to ensure individuals' compliance with contracts. Thus, the contract itself is not a solution to the prisoner's dilemma supposed to structure the state of nature. Instead, individuals' mutual acknowledgement of the intractable nature of the prisoner's dilemma is resolved though a more encompassing coordination game in which all parties accept the need for contracts combined with the need for sanctions to ensure compliance. As coordination games are defined by all agents having aligned preferences that reflect their agreement over ends, no recourse to promises, duty, or commitment to principle is required to understand the establishment and maintenance of government. Crucially, then, the social contract is disregarded as means by which stable government is secured.

Along with the social contract, theories of state legitimacy based on consent are also in disfavor among rational choice theorists because legitimacy requires a normative foundation that positive political theory cannot countenance. Instead, rational choice theorists rely on the concept of "mutual best-reply" from game theory to assess whether state institutions are stable. Rather than relying on consent to a set of rules or constitutional principles to indicate their legitimacy, rational choice theorists look to individuals' revealed choice of actions as a clear demonstration of their preferences. In this view, the mere fact that individuals choose their own actions and, therefore, participated in the creation of a given collective end point, indicates their compliance in bringing about that end point. Even though a collective outcome cannot be evaluated for its legitimacy, game theorists do ask whether each agent would choose a different course of action if all other agents' actions remained constant. A stable, self-reinforcing equilibrium is achieved when every agent selects the same action in view of what every other agent selected to do. This is an informal statement of the "Nash equilibrium," which has become prominent for playing a role in political theory that resembles the role that consensual theories of legitimacy played in traditional social contract theory. The idea of consent to a set of governing principles is replaced by the idea that each person is satisfied with his strategy and outcome given what all other agents decide to do.

Rational choice theorists have reformulated the concept of trust, basing it on straightforward coordination, supplemented by sanctions, rather than principled agreement that may at some point in the future deviate from agents' assessments of their personal best interests. In this view, because it is irrational for any individual to go against personal preferences, trust among individuals must always be consistent with preferences in order to be a meaningful social category of engagement. Thus, for example, in a marriage, according to rational choice theory, trust among partners cannot be of the form captured by the traditional oath "for richer or poorer, for better and for worse, in sickness and in health, until death do us part." A viable marriage must, at all times, be consistent with both members' preferences, or it will result in at least one individual defecting from the marriage contract. Trust, in this view, is not predicated on loyalty or commitment through unforeseeable circumstances, but is instead based on moment-by-moment agreement with rational and unchanging preferences.

Other views of trust that invoke an agent suffering in violation of personal expected utility maximization are regarded as naïve and unrealistic.

Commutative and distributive justice have received copious attention from rational choice theorists. John Rawls's 1972 book *A Theory of Justice* was the most path-breaking attempt to develop a robust theory of justice to be wholly consistent with the idea of rational preferences. Rawls's attempt was communicating how useful rational choice theory may be for understanding the implications of constitutional principles of government. Whereas Rawls's first principle of justice, the priority of liberty, is familiar and protects individuals from external interference, his second principle of justice, the difference principle, is novel and was taken directly from game theory. Adapting von Neumann's argument, Rawls suggested that rational individuals, when deciding how to organize society, would adopt a strategy of minimizing the outcome that can be expected in the worst possible scenario in a multiparty game. Rawls maintained that the rationally self-interested individuals, who were selecting constitutional principles unaware of which specific role they would play in the resulting society, would only permit inegalitarian institutions that guaranteed some positive benefit for society's poorest members. Although the inherent rationality of the minimax strategy continues to be debated, it is significant that Rawls and others believed that the entire project of constitutional design could be analyzed as a complex decision-theoretic problem that considers agents' anticipated outcomes in complex social interactions.

Conclusion

As an axiomatic treatment of rational human decision making, and as a method for studying collective decision processes, rational choice theory is studied in philosophy and mathematics departments, as well as throughout the social sciences in political science, economics, sociology, and psychology. The science of rational choice is both research on the abstract conditions, or norms, governing human rationality, and it also encompasses research that explains and predicts outcomes assuming rational agency. There are two views on whether the theory simply represents a descriptive means to model behavior without presupposing that agents actually reason in accordance with the theory, or whether instead it actually describes the decision rules manifested by rational agency. Researchers upholding the first view are content to use the axioms of rational choice to model actions and predict outcomes. The second view maintains that rational actors exhibit purposive action consistent with the behavioral norms of rational choice. The first view is modest by not suggesting anything about the internal thought processes of agents; the second view upholds rational choice theory as a theory that describes the normative foundations of rational decision making. Even though the first view is more restrained, and is sufficient for applying rational choice methods to understanding social and political phenomena, many researchers hold the view that rational choice theory is a powerful analytic tool precisely because it reflects the actual principles that must characterize purposive agency.

Rational choice theory has been central to methodological debates throughout the social sciences because of its adherence to a limited view of human rationality as consistency among preferences that categorically deems irrational modes of conduct not reducible to this description. As with any robust research tradition, intense controversies abound both internally and externally. Debates internal to the field have tended to focus on complex nuances of the formal theory, as well as the suitability of associating consistency of choice with choices characterized by narrow self-interest. Whereas the former is previously touched on, the latter attempt, for example, is to determine if altruistic behavior can be consistent with rational choice. As it currently stands, researchers agree that altruistic preferences can be readily encompassed within rational choice theory, but this leaves open the question of whether a satisfactory concept of altruism can be reduced to agents' preferences over outcomes. Even though it seems widely recognized that any agent whose behavior fully resembles that predicted by rational choice theory would be either a mythical construction at best or a nonfunctional social idiot at worst, it also seems to be widely accepted that

at the current time there is no compelling alternative that better captures what many people now refer to as purposive agency.

Rational choice theory is advanced as a positive as opposed to a normative theory of social science because it obeys what many consider to be a canonical rule of scientific investigation: Build testable theories with observable facts, mathematical relationships, and uncontroversial minimalist assumptions. From its birth in the eighteenth century, social science is believed by many to stand in contrast to philosophy, morals, metaphysics, and religion, specifically because it studies humans as they are and not as they may, in some ideal world, be. Social scientists attempt to describe human agency as it currently exists and do not strive to alter people's underlying motivational rationales. This steadfast commitment among many social scientists to advance value-free theories of human behavior and collective outcomes is consistent with the abiding understanding of many since the Enlightenment, that the individual is the final and sole judge of her own ends, conscience, and rationales for conduct. Many researchers believe rational choice theory to be consistent with this distrust of normative theories of human choice and social formations that purport to tell people how to live their lives or govern their society.

—*S. M. Amadae*

See also Bounded Rationality; Collective Action; Communicative Action; Communicative Rationality; Equilibrium Theory; Game Theory; Impossibility Theorem; Logic of Appropriateness; Optimal Decision Making; Pareto Optimality; Positive Political Theory; Principal-Agent Model; Prisoner's Dilemma; Public Choice Theory; Revealed Preference; Satisficing Behavior; Social Choice

Further Readings and References

Amadae, S. M. (2003). *Rationalizing capitalist democracy: The Cold War origins of rational choice theory.* Chicago: University of Chicago Press.

Axelrod, R., & Hamilton, W. D. (1984). *The evolution of cooperation.* New York: Basic Books.

Binmore, K. (1994–1998). *Game theory and the social contract* (Vols. 1–2). Cambridge: MIT Press.

Elster, J. (1983). *Sour grapes: Studies in the subversion of rationality.* New York: Cambridge University Press.

Hardin, R. (1988). *Morality within the limits of reason.* Chicago: University of Chicago Press.

Hargreaves Heap, S., Hollis, M., Lyons, B., Sugden, R., & Weale, A. (1992). *The theory of choice: A critical guide.* Oxford, UK: Basil Blackwell.

Hargreaves Heap, S., & Varoufakis, Y. (2004). *Game theory: A critical text* (2nd ed.). New York: Routledge.

Luce, D. R., & Raiffa, H. (1957). *Games and decisions: Introduction and critical survey.* New York: Dover Books.

Hausman, D. M. (1995). Rational choice and social theory: A comment. *Journal of Philosophy, 92*(2), 96–102.

Mansbridge, J. J. (Ed.). (1990). *Beyond self-interest.* Chicago: University of Chicago Press.

Mirowski, P. (2002). *Machine dreams: How economics becomes a cyborg science.* Cambridge, UK: Cambridge University Press.

Monroe, K. R. (Ed.). (1991). *The economic approach to politics: A critical reassessment of the theory of rational action.* New York: HarperCollins.

Rawls, J. (1972). *A theory of justice.* Oxford, UK: Clarendon Press.

Satz, D., & Ferejohn, J. (1994). Rational choice and social theory. *Journal of Philosophy, 91*(2), 71–87.

Sen, A. (1982). Rational fools: A critique of the behavioral foundation of economic theory. *Choice, measurement and welfare.* Oxford, UK: Basil Blackwell.

Sen, A. (1987). Rational behavior. In J. Eatwell, M. Milgate, & P. Newman (Eds.), *The new Palgrave: A dictionary of economics* (Vol. 4, pp. 68–76). London: Macmillan.

RATIONALITY

Rationality may be the most contested concept in all of the social and human sciences. Since the European Enlightenment, it has been a primary normative goal of humankind. The empirical view of humans as rational creatures has justified setting us apart from other species, even as it has served as the cornerstone for the most elaborated theories of human behavior. Attempts to cure irrationality have been at the heart of the development of psychology and the goals of social institutions. The attempts to define rational behavior and the question of under what circumstances humans exhibit it have been central to debates among and within the major social science disciplines. Meanwhile, chronicling the folly of man's attempts to act rationally is regularly explored in the humanities. Understanding rationality has even been a key driver in the attempt to use natural science (in the form of neurobiology) to put social science on a firmer basis.

This central role has often brought controversy more than it has led to cumulative theory or research. Whether and in what way man is rational is a central question of philosophy, but it is also the basis for social science, as it defines the way that people will react to others and their environment. The conventional wisdom on the connection of rationality to human nature differs dramatically by discipline. In economics, a purely rational man is often assumed and said to imply self-interested action for personal gain. Though sometimes used as a close approximation rather than a cognitive theory, the assumption of rational man allows the mathematical tractability for the great aggregate theories of social life that drive the creation of the market economy. In sociology, scholars say that people are driven by conformity to social norms about acceptable behavior and react to their position in society. This view is either offered as an alternative to rational man or established as an alternate definition of rationality. In anthropology, rationality is either a Western construct designed to impose our form of knowledge generation on others or a term wide enough to encompass all forms of human learning. In psychology, rationality is either an ideal type of behavior that we should emulate and intervene to create or, instead, one theory of cognition that can be updated or discarded with current knowledge of the brain.

Part of the cause of the wide variety of uses of the word rationality is a lack of clarity about the purpose of invoking it. In psychology and the cognitive sciences, researchers are typically trying to describe the mechanisms of human thinking and the patterns of behavior that arise as a result of cognition. A rational decision-making model may serve as a basis for comparison. In philosophy and the applied social sciences, in contrast, the goals are often normative. There are rational options, and we seek to explain how to find them. In economics, political science, anthropology, and sociology, the cognitive process and the manner of decision making are not the primary object of study. Assumptions about how humans will act allow scholars to build aggregated theories of how humans will act in society, given their interactions with others making similar decisions and the environment in which they interact. To assist theory development, scholars use simplified models of individual decision making and then ask whether models based on rationality best predict the development of social life when compared to other models of human behavior.

Models of rational decision making in the cognitive sciences rely on advances in the study of the brain to examine the mechanisms of thought. They are tied to explanations of the development of human cognitive faculties generated in linguistics and evolutionary biology. These theories ask what kinds of cognitive responses to the environment would have improved survival and thus become a product of natural selection. Many of these theories are explored in simulations and attempts to emulate human thought patterns in computer science. Rationality is often seen as the advance of the human mind that allowed humans to develop language and society. Researchers of artificial intelligence attempt to understand this rationality to copy it for use in new applications.

In philosophy, the use of rationality to explain or endorse human thought has a long lineage. It is intimately tied to the debate over whether reason should be considered the only source of knowledge. Ideas from logic and probability theory are used to defend conclusions by some philosophers and dismissed by others as arbitrary reasons to prefer a particular set of conclusions. Members of the continental rationalism school of thought believe that rationality is the only proper way to build knowledge. The empiricist school, in contrast, argues that the primary source of knowledge is human experience through the senses. To philosophers, how we make decisions is secondary to the debate about how we should see the world.

Rational Decision Theory in the Social Sciences

The theories of decision making used in empirical social science are not as detailed as evolutionary cognitive theories or philosophical ideas about knowledge

generation, though they often appeal to the same notion of rationality. The branch of behavioral theory with the largest set of deductions, rational choice theory, employs a highly specific theory of rationality that builds on utility theory and noncooperative game theory. Other social science theories of rationality typically use this set of ideas, based in economics, as their basis for comparison. In utility theory, individuals have preferences over the state of the world. Those preferences are rational as long as they are (1) complete (they cover the entire spectrum of possibilities), (2) stable (they are not constantly in flux), (3) transitive (individuals do not prefer A to B, B to C, and C to A), and (4) context independent (additional options do not change the preference ordering of the original options). Preferences that meet those assumptions can be assigned utilities and used to predict the decisions of the actor. Individuals are rational if they make the best decision given their desires and beliefs about how their actions will affect those desires. Some authors say that rational actors should also have internally consistent beliefs and desires. In noncooperative game theory, individuals also have beliefs about how other actors will influence outcomes and may have information about the beliefs and desires of others. The term *perfect rationality* is invoked to further hypothesize that people are capable of unlimited deductions from their beliefs and desires to find the rational course of action.

To most practitioners of rational choice social science, these assumptions serve as a baseline for theory building and are not deeply considered. Jon Elster has been a prominent voice in the efforts to consider the logical and empirical problems of these base assumptions. He argues that rationality implies intentionality, that a behavior must be based on a set of cognitions and desires that are used to make a decision in the way that rational choice theory describes. He extrapolates additional conditions from this idea, including internal consistency of beliefs and desires, the optimality of choices given options and beliefs, the appropriate causal relationships between thoughts and actions, and a basis for action in one's cognitions. Others respond with a view of rationality that does not include these additional assumptions or that labels them as convenient fictions rather than hypotheses regarding cognition.

Refinements and Challenges

In applied game theory, ideas about rationality have been refined to include many differences across individuals regarding how they perceive and think about options. We can incorporate differences in individual attitudes toward risk, preferences over time, levels and uses of information, and views of choices. Researchers have also expanded their lists of rational benefits that people may claim as a result of their actions. Rather than economic or self-interested gains, in this view, individuals may obtain reputational and expressive benefits from their actions, or they may behave according to their conception of moral rights. In this view of rationality, people may also be differentially influenced by people in their social networks or with whom they have group ties.

These extensive refinement programs were driven by several problems discovered when applying rational behavior to collective decision making. First, Ken Arrow popularized the notion that collective rationality could not occur from any nondictatorial decision-making system. This finding was of prime importance to those who study committee decisions, where it appeared that no decision would be stable because enough people would always have an incentive to act to change the current decision. However, empirical researchers found many stable social institutions that seemed to imply collective rationality. Second, a strict rational choice theory argued that collective action in large groups would be impossible because everyone would have an incentive to free ride on the activities of others and choose not to contribute to public goods. Again, empirical researchers discovered many examples of collective action that did not seem to include the incentives hypothesized by the theory. Third, many potential equilibrium solutions were found to common noncooperative games. Researchers disagreed about the criteria for selecting the likely course of action in these circumstances; they went about generating reasons to prefer some outcomes over others that imposed additional constraints on rational behavior.

However, the most extensive set of refinements of economic ideas about rationality came in response to common findings in empirical studies of organizations and in experimental social psychology. Herbert Simon studied the way that people make decisions within organizations and identified a large list of limits on the cognitive capability of these individuals. The individuals he studied did not formulate or solve problems the way that rational decision making implies, often because they processed information differently than theory assumes. His set of ideas became known as a theory of "bounded rationality." In the most commonly referenced part of this theory, individuals are said to engage in "satisficing" rather than optimizing; they select the first acceptable option that they find rather than search for the best possible option.

The experimental critiques of common theories of rational decision making were pioneered by Daniel Kahneman and Amos Tversky. They showed that individuals use a large class of heuristics, or shortcuts, in decision making rather than always making the decisions implied by traditional theory. Their experiments showed that individuals assume that the events they see are more representative than they actually are, leading to the use of unrealistic stereotypes in many circumstances, rather than individual assessment of new pieces of information. Further, individuals rely on information that is easily retrieved and matched to current events, rather than all available information. Finally, individuals are influenced by "anchor" values or obvious preexisting ideas that frame their response to new information. Researchers have since found many other examples of similar behavior.

These debates about the kind of information processing that rationality implies occur alongside a long-standing but separable series of critiques about whether individuals act in a self-interested manner. Self-interest is usually compared to altruism, or behavior that acts in the collective interest. More recently, however, researchers have found that many individuals often respond to group-based or class-based interests, even when they have no personal incentive. If behavior is driven by group membership or social network position, it can be defined as rational but may be more difficult to track than traditional rational decisions. When considering these personal, social, and public interests, researchers generally find that people conflate their individual interest with the group interest and the public interest. They are driven to make their normative ideas about how the world should be converge with their self-interested ideas about what outcome would most benefit themselves—they rationalize their altruistic beliefs by implying that the results they favor will be in their own interest in the long run, or they rationalize their interests by changing their normative opinions to match their self-interested motives.

Alternatives

To some researchers, this set of findings presents a more global problem to the rationality thesis than can be accounted for by additional refinements. Rather than continually adjusting decision theory as new challenges arise, sociological theories of rationality generally begin with an entirely different premise. Max Weber argued that rationalization was a general social pattern arising in response to the rise of large-scale organizations in the aftermath of the Enlightenment and the Industrial Revolution. Specifically, organizations tried to institute goal-oriented rationality and move away from traditional reasons for behavior and the blind following of leaders. Rational notions of decision making were infused throughout society. In a more extreme extrapolation of this theory, George Ritzer argues that the move toward rationalization is a period effect; it is part of the nature of current times defined by vivid examples of rationalized enterprises. This view of rationality no longer even implies that better decisions are being made with additional information; they are just decisions that are in line with current thinking.

Several related alternatives to the rationality thesis have come from scholars of political science. Followers of Murray Edelman argue that politics is primarily a fight over symbols, rather than rational choices among options. In this view, people have affective responses to their choices that originate in early life experience; as choices arise, individuals merely categorize incoming choices to make their decisions based on reflexive application of their existing normative ideas. Many political scientists also have inherited sociological theories about acting in response to institutionalized norms or social group and class identities. Researchers of political opinions often combine many categories of motivations for action in one multivariate analysis of a particular decision. These empirical models imply that individuals make decisions based on the perceived consequences of their decisions as well as their membership in groups, their normative ideas, and their attachment to symbols. In this view, we need not define rationality as anything other than how all of these effects combine in the mind to influence behavior. Rational decisions are merely decisions that consider all these potential reasons to prefer each option.

However, to some opinion researchers, this hodgepodge of motivations implies that there is something fundamentally wrong with the general theory of rational decisions. John Zaller and Stanley Feldman argue that people deal with internal conflict concerning their basic values, their allegiances, and their opinions. They change their mind more frequently than one would expect and respond to the framing of questions in ways that imply that they lack consistent and strong views. In Zaller's view, we should think of the human mind as a container for the many different ideas that they find in society. Though some elites are driven to rationalize their views and make them consistent, most people make decisions by accessing some of their conflicting views. Rationality, in the common view, may be limited to elites. Whether or not rationality is in need of major redefinition will continue to be a lightning rod for major debates throughout social science.

—*Matt Grossmann*

See also Bureaucratic Politics Approach; Communicative Action; Communicative Rationality; Deterrence; Groupthink; Planning; Rational Choice Theory; Rationalization; Sociology of Governance

Further Readings and References

Arrow, K., Colombatto, E., Perlman, M., & Schmidt, C. (Eds.). (1996). *The rational foundations of economic behavior.* London: Macmillan.

Chong, D. (2000). *Rational lives*. Chicago: University of Chicago Press.

Edelman, M. (1967). *The symbolic uses of politics*. Champaign: University of Illinois Press.

Elster, J. (1985). The nature and scope of rational-choice explanations. In E. LePore & B. McLaughlin (Eds.), *Actions and events: Perspectives on the philosophy of Donald Davidson* (pp. 60–72). Oxford, UK: Basil Blackwell.

Kahneman, D., & Tversky, A. (Eds.). (2000). *Choices, values, and frames*. Cambridge, UK: Cambridge University Press.

Lash, S., & Whimster, S. (Eds.). (1987). *Max Weber, rationality and modernity*. Boston: Unwin Hyman.

Luipa, A., McCubbins, M., & Popkin, S. (2001). *Elements of reason*. Cambridge, UK: Cambridge University Press.

Ritzer, G. (1996). *The McDonaldization of society*. Thousand Oaks, CA: Pine Forge.

Samuels, R., & Stich, S. (1999). Reason and rationality. In M. Sintonen (Ed.), *Handbook of epistemology*. Dordrecht, Netherlands: Kluwer Academic.

Simon, H. (1947). *Administrative behavior*. New York: Macmillan.

Stein, E. (1996). *Without good reason: The rationality debate in philosophy and cognitive science*. Oxford, UK: Clarendon Press.

Zaller, J., & Feldman, S. (1992). A simple theory of the survey response: Answering questions or revealing preferences? *American Journal of Political Science, 36*(3), 579–616.

RATIONALIZATION

Rationalization denotes the shift from traditional, habitual, and particularistic methods of economic, social, and political organization and administration to methods that are instead calculative, systematic, and universalistic. In contemporary governance, rationalization is often shorthand for streamlining government for the purpose of maximizing the efficient provision of public goods and services. This is accomplished, for example, by introducing uniform standards, applying universal and impersonal rules, enhancing transparency and accountability, eliminating redundant staff and overlapping agencies, and promoting the functional specialization of services.

As theorized by Max Weber, rationalization referred to a process by which rational methods—for example, the calculation of cost and benefit—lead to a devaluation of traditionalism. The sacred and transcendental are replaced by the secular and utilitarian; the particularism of kinship ties is replaced by the impersonal universalism of the market and bureaucracy. By extension, contemporary usage focuses on the application of market rationality to government. This idea is clearly reflected in the "good governance" movement associated with the World Bank, which emphasizes fiscal responsibility, efficiency, transparency, and accountability as keys to good governance.

In the developed world, fiscal challenges emerging from a number of sources over the last thirty years have increased pressure on states to reduce spending. In this context, rationalization is an attempt to reduce spending without abandoning established goals. Efforts to rationalize states and produce more efficient governance may result in governments shifting responsibilities to functionally specialized organizations, such as semiautonomous public agencies (like central banks) or firms and civil society organizations in the private sector. If it does, then rationalization implies a loss of autonomy for states as they are increasingly drawn into wider networks to create and implement policies and achieve their goals.

In the developing world, rationalization implies conflicting trends for states. On the one hand, rationalization implies a trend toward state building and increased state capacity through the creation of bureaucracies and state administrations that displace inefficient and particularistic forms of economic and political organization. On the other hand, rationalization may mean a diminution of state autonomy, if fiscal or other concerns push governments to turn to private firms, nongovernmental organizations (NGOs), and international organizations in order to more efficiently create and implement policies.

Rationalization raises an interesting paradox about the nature of contemporary governance. While efforts to rationalize governments appear to be leading to new forms of network governance, this new governance may itself be irrational. As in the European Union, governing through formal networks can be cumbersome and inefficient. Consequently, the locus of governance may shift to informal networks. While informal networks may facilitate more efficient governance in some ways, they may also be based on particularistic ties, like ethnicity or kinship, with significant potential for corruption and other kinds of inefficiency. What shape will attempts to rationalize these new forms of governance take?

—*Jeremy Darrington*

See also Efficiency; Groupthink; Organizational Structure; Rationality

Further Readings and References

Pierson, P. (2001). Coping with permanent austerity: Welfare state restructuring in affluent democracies. In P. Pierson (Ed.), *The new politics of the welfare state* (pp. 410–456). Oxford, UK: Oxford University Press.

Weber, M. (1955). *The theory of economic and social organization* (T. Parsons, Ed., T. Parsons & J. M. Anderson, Trans.). Berkeley: University of California Press.

REALISM AND NEOREALISM

Realism and neorealism have dominated the post-1945 academic study of international relations (IR). Realists claim to offer both the most accurate explanation of state behavior and a set of policy prescriptions (notably the balance of power between states) for ameliorating the inherent destabilizing elements of international affairs. Realism, at a general level, stresses the centrality of the state, national interest, and military power in world politics. It focuses on the continuity of patterns of interaction in an international system lacking a centralized political authority. This condition of anarchy means that international politics often follow a different logic from domestic politics, which is regulated by a sovereign power. Realists are pessimistic about the possibility of radical systemic reform. Realism is a broad tradition of thought, composed of a variety of different strands. The most significant break is between classical realism and neorealism.

Classical Realism

Realists frequently claim to draw on an ancient tradition of political thought. Their canon includes Thucydides, Thomas Hobbes, Niccolo Machiavelli, Jean-Jacques Rousseau, and Max Weber. Realism as a self-defined tradition of reflection on international politics emerged during the mid-twentieth century, inspired by the British historian E. H. Carr. Carr attacked what he perceived as the dangerous and deluded "idealism" of liberal internationalists and, in particular, their belief in the possibility of progress through the construction of international institutions (especially the League of Nations). He focused instead on the perennial role of power and self-interest in determining state behavior. World War II converted many people to this pessimistic vision. Thereafter, realism became established in American political science departments, its fortunes boosted by a number of émigré European scholars, most notably Hans Morgenthau. It is the realism of Carr, Morgenthau, Reinhold Niebuhr, and their followers that is labeled classical.

Classical realism was not a coherent school of thought: It drew from a wide variety of sources and offered competing visions of the self, the state, and the world. Carr was influenced by Marxism, Niebuhr by Augustinian theology, while Morgenthau drew on Friedrich Nietzsche, Weber, Carl Schmitt, and American civic republicanism. They were united mainly by that which they opposed. Classical realism is a philosophy of limits. Critical of the ambition, optimism, and explanatory focus of liberal internationalists, realists have instead tended to stress the barriers—whether inscribed in human nature, political institutions, or the structure of the international system—to progress and reform. The fortunes of classical realism, grounded as it was in a combination of history, philosophy, and theology waned under the 1960s onslaught of social scientific behaviorism. Its fortunes were revived by the emergence of neorealism during the 1970s.

Neorealism

Associated in particular with Kenneth Waltz, neorealism is an attempt to translate some of the key insights of classical realism into the language and methods of modern social science. In the *Theory of International Politics* (1979), Waltz argued that most of the important features of IR, and especially the actions of great powers, could be explained solely in terms of the anarchical structure of the international system. This was not a new argument, but in systematizing it and attempting to establish it on scientifically defensible grounds, Waltz simultaneously reinvigorated realism and further detached it from its original roots.

The shift from classical realism to neorealism was marked by continuity and change. The changes were along two main axes: the method and the level of analysis. In terms of method, realism was reconfigured as a rigorous and highly parsimonious social scientific theory, drawing in particular on microeconomics. Regarding the level of analysis, Waltz argued that traditional realist arguments about domestic institutions, the quality of diplomacy and statecraft, national morale, and human nature were largely irrelevant. He conceived of states as unitary rational actors existing in a self-help system. Concerned above all with survival, and operating with imperfect information, states are socialized by the logic of the system into similar patterns of behavior. The international system is defined by remarkable continuity across space and time. The trajectory of IR is explained by the distribution of power across the units in the system, and Waltz argued that the most stable arrangement was bipolarity, a balance between two great powers.

Neorealism(s) and Beyond

Both Waltz's conception of IR theory and his substantive arguments proved influential, and debates between neorealists and their critics dominated the field for much of the 1980s and 1990s. While a competing school of neoliberal institutionalists dissented from his claims about the difficulty of cooperation under anarchy, they nevertheless adopted his method and many of his assumptions. Neorealism divided between "offensive" and "defensive" variants. "Defensive" realists, following Waltz, argue that states tend to seek security, and as such a stable international

equilibrium is possible via balancing. This position has been attacked for displaying a status quo bias. "Offensive" realists argue that states seek to maximize power rather than security, making equilibrium harder to achieve. Recently, neoclassical realists, while remaining within a social scientific framework, have refocused attention on the domestic sources (both individual and institutional) of international action.

Neorealism has numerous detractors, including many sympathetic to classical realism. It has been chastised for failing to engage seriously with history, sociology, and philosophy; for falsely claiming scientific credibility; for an inability to account for systemic transformation (including the end of the Cold War and globalization); and for a self-defeating analytical reductionism. Nevertheless, it remains a powerful research program. Recent years have also witnessed a resurgence of interest in classical realism, which its admirers present as a far more complex and radical position than many contemporary realists and their critics allow.

—Duncan Bell

See also Cosmopolitanism; Groupthink; Hegemony; Liberal Internationalism; Mercantilism; Power; Regime Theory; Security; Sovereignty

Further Readings and References

Carr, E. H. (1939). *The twenty years' crisis, 1919–1939.* London: Macmillan.

Haslam, J. (2002). *No virtue like necessity: Realist thought in international relations since Machiavelli.* New Haven, CT: Yale University Press.

Lebow, R. N. (2003). *The tragic vision of politics: Ethics, interests, and orders.* Cambridge, UK: Cambridge University Press.

Mearsheimer, J. (2001). *The tragedy of great power politics.* New York: W. W. Norton.

Morgenthau, H. (1948). *Politics among nations: The struggle for power and peace.* New York: Knopf.

Waltz, K. (1979). *Theory of international politics.* Reading, MA: Addison-Wesley.

Williams, M. (2005). *The realist tradition and the limits of international relations.* Cambridge, UK: Cambridge University Press.

RECIPROCITY

Reciprocity is essentially a principle of exchange. It requires that like be exchanged for like, such that the value of that being exchanged is perceived by participants to be of roughly equivalent value, although it is not an exchange of the same thing. It is most commonly associated with trade agreements. For example, if country A agrees to cut tariffs on a certain product, say clothing, such that country B can export a greater quantity of clothes to country A, country B must then offer tariff cuts on a product of export interest to country A, say computers, such that the value of the increased clothing exports from B is perceived by both countries to be of roughly equivalent value to the increase in computer exports from A.

Diffuse and Specific Reciprocity

We can distinguish two forms of reciprocity—specific and diffuse. Specific reciprocity is characterized by the involvement of a limited number of participants, each known to the others, who exchange items of equivalent value over a finite, delimited period of time. Initial offers are known to all and are made contingent on the granting of concessions of a roughly equivalent value by the other actors.

By contrast, diffuse reciprocity is less precise. Partners are viewed more as a group than as individual actors, and the sequence of exchange is more open. The expectation is not for equivalence of concessions in any one exchange, but rather a balance is expected over an ongoing, potentially indefinite, series of exchanges with a group of partners. A balance of concessions is not required between any two specific participants, but each individual actor expects to have a rough equivalence over time between the aggregate benefits it receives from the group as a whole and the overall concessions it makes. As such, reciprocity in this instance is more diffuse in character.

Relationship to Trade Liberalization

Reciprocity has its intellectual roots in mercantilist economics, in which increased exports are seen to be beneficial because they lead to inflows of foreign exchange and increased imports are conversely seen as harmful because they require an outflow of foreign exchange. Politicians and trade negotiators are generally considered to instinctively embrace mercantilist ideas, seeking each dollar's worth of increased imports arising from the granting of trade concessions to be balanced by concessions from trading partners worth a dollar in increased exports. Liberal trade theory, current economic orthodoxy, by contrast, sees liberalization of one's own trade policy as economically preferable to maintaining protectionist measures, regardless of whether or not one's trading partners reciprocate that liberalization. According to this view, import restrictions cause losses to a country's welfare that exceed the domestic gains. Therefore, neoclassical economists argue that a requirement of reciprocity in trade policy makes no economic sense. Furthermore, reciprocity may lead to higher tariffs being maintained even when those tariffs are economically harmful, as a requirement of reciprocity in trade negotiations encourages countries to stockpile such tariffs for use as bargaining chips in subsequent negotiations.

However, reciprocity can aid the trade liberalization process by creating political support for liberalization agreements. While protected industries will oppose liberalization measures that subject their markets to greater competition, the linking of the liberalization of the domestic market to liberalization by other countries via reciprocity helps to garner support from exporters that stand to gain from increased access to foreign markets. Therefore, reciprocity eases the difficult political process of undertaking trade liberalization by increasing the stake that exporters have in that process, encouraging them to put their political weight behind the trade agreement.

Operation in the GATT and the WTO

This garnering of political support for liberalization has been an important element in the success of the World Trade Organization (WTO) and its predecessor, the General Agreement on Tariffs and Trade (GATT). Reciprocity was used to help prevent countries from free riding on other countries' tariff cuts, which were automatically extended to all members of the GATT through the application of the most-favored nation (MFN) clause. However, a potential exception was made for developing countries contained in Part IV of the GATT agreement, appended to GATT law in 1965 to address their growing discontent with the multilateral trade system, which they perceived to be biased against their interests. Part IV released developing countries from the requirements of reciprocity under some circumstances, although the commitments developed countries took on not to seek reciprocity from developing countries were not legally binding, but served merely to exert a degree of moral suasion in future negotiations.

In subsequent GATT rounds, developing countries used the waiver in Part IV to take advantage of tariff cuts made by developed countries while offering little in return. However, any advantages they gained through this were severely limited because developed countries focused their liberalization on those areas in which they had a strong commercial interest, such as high-technology manufactured goods. Developing countries had little interest in such areas because their principal exports were in raw materials, semimanufactured and low-technology goods. Sectors in which developing countries had the most to gain from liberalization, namely agriculture, textiles, and clothing, were excluded from the GATT framework.

This illustrates the value of reciprocity in trade negotiations. The benefits of liberalization commitments agreed to in successive GATT rounds were concentrated among those countries that themselves made commitments to liberalize, despite the force of moral suasion contained in Part IV. The waiver developing countries had from the requirements of reciprocity meant that they had little influence on negotiations, leaving developed countries to dominate the process and exclude from the agenda areas of commercial interest to developing countries.

—James Scott

See also Generalized Exchange; Human Capital; Mercantilism; Multilateralism; World Trade Organization

Further Readings and References

Curzon, G., & Curzon, V. (1989). Non-discrimination and the rise of 'material' reciprocity. *The World Economy, 12,* 481–499.

Finger, J. M., & Winters, L. A. (2002). Reciprocity in the WTO. In B. Hoekman, A. Mattoo, & P. English (Eds.), *Development, trade and the WTO.* Washington, DC: World Bank.

Keohane, R. O. (1986). Reciprocity in international relations. *International Organization, 40,* 1–27. (Reprinted from *International institutions and state power,* by R. O. Keohane, 1989, Boulder, CO: Westview)

Wilkinson, R. (2000). *Multilateralism and the World Trade Organization: The architecture and extension of international trade regulation.* London: Routledge.

REFLEXIVITY

Reflexivity evokes the explicit acknowledgement of personal sources of bias when describing and acting upon reality. It highlights the fact that in any interaction with the external world, we are simultaneously disclosing something about ourselves. Being reflexive denotes a critical stance that challenges both the traditional scientific ideal of objective inquiry and the modern ideal of a clear-cut separation between individuals and impersonal institutions.

Anthony Giddens, Ulrich Beck, Scott Lash, and others identify reflexivity as an organizing systemic principle in late modernity. Reflexive modernization refers to a recursive turning of modernity upon itself, which is of significant relevance to the concept of governance. According to this thesis, linearity and the following of rules, in consonance with a set of pre-established roles, characterized the functioning of prereflexive modern institutions (e.g., family, ethnic group, and the state). These institutions are now in crisis, and functions that were once taking place at the interface of institution and role are now taking place much closer to the subject. Rigid rules and roles are progressively being denormalized in light of nonlinear reflexivity. Yet the outcome is neither chaos nor irrationality. Instead, the outcome is a reorganization in which the subject relates to institutions by being reflexive, rather than by the strict following of rules and roles.

In late modernity, reflexivity transforms governance by opening institutions toward culture and tying them to the political attributes and capacities of self-reflexive individuals. In this context, cultural governance arises as a political practice of promoting citizens' empowerment and self-discipline. This new governance requires a willingness to learn, to be self-reflexive and question oneself, to seek wisdom, to be accepting of other perspectives and consider what one can learn from them, and to trust others in this process of mutual reexamination. Political and administrative research must reformulate the concepts of government and state them in order to include the various perspectives about how to do politics and govern themselves. Effective governance relies increasingly on the ability to empower lay people and to affect their identities in such a way that they act effectively and self-responsibly for the sake of coherence and integration of the socioecological system to which they belong.

Reflexive governance implies moving to more network-oriented forms of strategic communication. Reflexivity can enhance the dialogue and collaboration among different institutions. It can also help create a process of self-reflection within institutions in which people ask why they do the things they do and how things could be done differently. This kind of reflexive exercise is fundamental not only to understanding and contrasting different versions of reality and situating different perspectives within a wider argumentative context, but also to discussing the alternative courses of action in order to deal with the new risks and opportunities posed by modernity and globalization.

—*David Manuel-Navarrete*

See also Communicative Action; Communicative Rationality; Globalization; Interpretive Theory; Pragmatism; Social Practice; Sociology of Governance

Further Readings and References

Bang, H. P. (2004). Culture governance: Governing self-reflexive modernity. *Public Administration, 82,* 157–190.

Beck, U., Giddens, A., & Lash, S. (1994). *Reflexive modernization: Politics, tradition and aesthetics in the modern social order.* Cambridge, UK: Polity Press.

REGIME

The concept of a regime evokes a system of social control. Simply, a regime refers to an institution with a clear substantive and geographical remit, bound by explicit rules, and agreed on by governments. So, the concept is often preceded by a spatial adjective—international, national, or urban, for example—referring to the area over which it has jurisdiction and can be used to refer to all manner of substantive remits over which it has control—development, environment, labor, trade, and so on. A more detailed definition documents the means through which an institution forms. The emphasis is on the principles, norms, rules, and decision-making procedures around which the expectations of individual actors (normally governments) converge and are institutionalized.

Uses of the regime concept often involve an association with a specific individual (e.g., Nicolae Ceausescu's regime), a particular ideology (e.g., a fascist regime), approach (e.g., a military regime), or political project (e.g., a neoliberal regime). In theory, the term need not imply anything about the particular government to which it relates, and most social scientists used it in a normative and neutral manner. The term, though, can be used in a political context. It is used colloquially by some, such as government officials, media journalists, and policymakers, when referring to governments that they believe are repressive, undemocratic, illegitimate, or simply don't square with the author's own view of the world. Used in this context, the concept of regime communicates a sense of ideological or moral disapproval or political opposition. So, regime change, as for example recently witnessed in the case of Iraq, refers to the overthrow of a government considered illegitimate by an external force, and its replacement with a new government according to the ideas or interests promoted by that force. So, in the case of Iraq, a U.S.-led coalition of national armies led the overthrow of the Saddam Hussein regime and oversaw its replacement by, first, a U.S.-led interim government and then, subsequently, an elected regime.

While not as well-developed as the work on international regimes, two other uses of the regime concept have been advanced, and remove the usage of referring to one national government or another. The first describes supranational agencies, often involved in the regulation of one or more issues. Examples include the International Labour Organization and its regulation of labor conditions, and the European Environment Agency and its regulation of the environment. These have a different set of resources—economic, political, and social—to draw on than national governments, and their activities can either empower or constrain individual nation-states. The second alternative use of the regime concept is in describing the formation of institutions to govern urban relations. Implicit and explicit norms and rules inform the decision-making procedures, in and through which urban regimes make judgments over the types of strategies to be pursued in, for example, balancing the need for cities to be economically competitive while, at the same time, ensuring citizens enjoy a good quality of life.

—*Kevin Ward*

See also Authoritarianism; City-Region; Democratic Theory; Institutionalism; Nation; Urban and Regional Planning

Further Reading and References

Krasner, S. (Ed.). (1983). *International regimes.* Ithaca, NY: Cornell University Press.

Stone, C. (1989). *Regime politics: Governing Atlanta 1946–1988.* Lawrence: University of Kansas Press.

REGIME THEORY

Regime theory emerged within the study of international relations (IR) in the mid-1970s in order to explain cooperation among states that pursue their self-servingly defined interests rationally in the international system, which is characterized by anarchical structures. The most commonly accepted definition of regimes has been put forward by Stephen Krasner. Krasner defined regimes as sets of implicit or explicit principles, norms, rules, and decision-making procedures around which actors' expectations converge in a given issue area. Regimes are usually understood as specific cooperative institutions. In contrast to general institutions, such as organizing principles like sovereignty, regimes are tied to specific issue areas. Unlike organizations, they cannot appear as actors in the international system. Academic interest in the IR regime debate became strong and peaked in the 1980s, In view of the relative American decline in the 1970s, the transformation of the postwar economic order, which was based on U.S. hegemony, generated substantial theoretical and normative challenges for IR scholars. Since the 1980s, the study of local and urban politics has made use of the regime concept. The urban regime concept is more explicit than the original IR regime notion and entails the specification of additional properties. It describes processes and structures of cooperation among public and private actors that form an informal but relatively stable group with access to institutional resources.

Regime Theory and the Study of International Relations

In IR, we can broadly distinguish between three different regime theoretical approaches: interest-based, power-based, and knowledge-based theories. Interest-based (also known as neoliberal) theories have become the leading school of thought in IR regime analysis. Neoliberals, like Robert Keohane, who shaped this approach decisively, draw on microeconomic (or rationalist) assumptions concerning human action and extend these to state behavior. States are depicted as rational egoists, which seek to maximize their gains. However, in contrast to power-based theories, states seek absolute, and not relative, gains. Neoliberals explain regime creation through this orientation toward absolute gains: In situations where states have homogeneous interests that cannot be attained unilaterally, they tend to cooperate in order to achieve gains through collective action, even if other participants benefit to a greater extent from this cooperation. Thus, the impact of regimes is not to change the interests of the participating states. Instead, they function as catalysts of cooperation that leave the interests of states essentially untouched.

The neoliberal approach regimes further contribute to international cooperation through the reduction of transaction costs. The latter are reduced, for example, because regimes offer a framework for negotiation. Cooperation is facilitated as negotiating partners, procedures, and basic objectives are already established. In addition, regimes can reduce transaction costs by providing control mechanisms in order to ensure compliance among cooperative partners and may thus also contribute to reliability in terms of actors' expectations. Cooperation is also facilitated through issue linkage, which increases the scope for trade-offs across different (sub)sectors. Moreover, regimes help define what cooperation entails in the first place. As a result, states can no longer justify breaches of cooperation with the uncertainty as to what international cooperation asks of them. Default becomes more costly because the reputation of being a trustworthy cooperation partner is damaged. This is of particular importance, especially as most cooperation processes are continuous. Game-theoretical models have been applied by neoliberals to simulate different preference constellations that affect the likelihood of regime creation and maintenance. Interest-based theories highlight the significance of international institutions for the structure of the international system and the realization of common interests. Regimes are portrayed as effective and resilient. States can be shown to have an interest in maintaining regimes even after the conditions that brought the regime into existence are no longer operative. Neoliberals primarily stress the objective of economic welfare and have focused, for example, on issue areas of finance and trade, such as the international trade regime (General Agreement on Tariffs and Trade, or GATT).

Power-based approaches, which are also referred to as (neo)realist theories of international relations, share with neoliberals the emphasis on self-interested actors, the anarchical nature of the international system, and the predominance of states within this system, although power-based theories attribute somewhat stronger weight on the last two points than neoliberal approaches. The central determinant of outcomes is not the distribution of interests, but of power; although interest-based theories are not completely insensitive to the latter. The central factor distinguishing power-based from interest-based theories is that states are assumed to seek relative, rather than absolute, gains, that is, greater benefits than their cooperation partners. This makes cooperation among states a difficult undertaking from the realist perspective. Hence, power-based approaches contend that regime creation is mainly dependent on the existence of a hegemon that is willing and able to bear most of the costs for the provision of collective goods necessary for the establishment and maintenance of the regime. This strand of realist regime analysis has also been referred to as hegemonic stability theory. It also holds that the decline of a hegemon or its decreasing supply of collective goods would lead to the gradual disintegration or collapse of the existing order and the regimes it constitutes.

Other than through hegemonic stability, realists see only limited chances for successful cooperation among states that seek relative gains, or at least aim to avoid relative losses. Joseph Grieco views regime creation and maintenance as promising when gains from cooperation can be distributed evenly among the participating states. On the whole, power-based theories attribute considerably less causal importance to international regimes than interest-based approaches. The significance ascribed to international institutions varies within this paradigm. While most neorealists acknowledge that regime-based international cooperation constitutes a real phenomenon and a major puzzle to the realist research program, few (arch)realist scholars do not take international institutions seriously and consider the study of international regimes a false promise. Neorealists attribute particular importance to the goal of (military) security. Thus, their (regime) analysis has especially focused on cooperation in the field of security. But some neorealist authors like Grieco have also analyzed regimes in the economic realm.

Both interest-based and power-based theories are rationalist approaches. They (1) assume strategic and interest-maximizing actors and (2) take strategies and preferences as exogenously given. Knowledge-based, also known as reflexive, cognitive, or social constructivist, approaches generally do not share the rational choice tenet of exogenously given interests. Instead, the normative orientations of actors, their state of knowledge, their perceptions, values, and so forth are taken into account. Cognitive approaches assume that actors' preferences are not fixed but variable entities. The formation of regimes and their development is viewed not as the result of interest maximization or certain power constellations, but as the distribution of knowledge, predominant (and evolving) norms, mutual (often discursive) interaction, as well as socialization and learning processes.

We might distinguish here between weak and strong cognitivism. The weak strand seeks to fill a gap in rationalist theorizing by adding a theory of preference formation. This can be seen as complementary to interest-based theorizing on international regimes. Weak cognitivists, like Peter Haas, emphasize the importance of knowledge and expertise for facing the challenges of international politics. In order to reach decisions in complex issue areas, policymakers often need to resort to transnational professional communities of knowledge-based experts, also referred to as epistemic communities. Haas holds that problems characterized by a high degree of uncertainty from the perspective of decisionmakers; a far-reaching consensus concerning causes, effects, and solutions within the epistemic community; and the latter's access to the political decision-making processes impacts favorably on the formation and development of international regimes. The impact of epistemic communities is estimated particularly high in cognitively complex issue areas, such as environmental, energy, and technology policy, which require substantial scientific expert knowledge as a basis for reaching decisions. Research on epistemic communities has thus focused, for instance, on ozone or climate-change regimes.

Strong cognitivists also contest the other main rationalist assumption pointed out previously, that is, actors and states as utility maximizers. Instead, actors such as states may also be role players, norm followers, or truth seekers. This more maximalist approach emphasizes not only the actors' strategic competence, but also their discursive and argumentative competences. Hence, strong cognitivists, like John Ruggie, have criticized interest-based approaches for failing to adequately embrace the repercussions of institutionalized practices on actors' norms and identities. They view institutions and regimes as not only constraining or shaping but as constituting actors' preferences. Overall, knowledge-based theories ascribe international regimes the strongest significance among the three approaches.

Research on international regimes has undergone a number of different phases. In the early stages of regime analysis, scholars focused particularly on the conditions for regime formation and maintenance. Since the 1990s, the study of international regimes has gradually focused more on questions of implementation, compliance, design, and effectiveness. The issue of regime effectiveness especially has generated a fair amount of scholarship. After many years of research on international regimes, there is little or no doubt that regimes in various issue areas make a certain impact. However, the challenge is to ascertain and measure the extent to which they are effective. One of the foremost scholars on the question of regime effectiveness is Oran Young. He advanced research on this question, for example, by specifying several different dimensions of regime effectiveness. These include problem solving (are the problems that led to regime creation solved?), goal attainment (are the objectives defined for the regime met?), normative effectiveness (are criteria like justice and sustainability fulfilled?), behavioral effectiveness (does the regime change actors' behavior?), and process effectiveness (are the regimes' provisions implemented?). Most of the research on effectiveness has concentrated on effectiveness as problem solving. In recent years, scholars have managed to quantify regime effectiveness. In addition, recent research has begun to focus more strongly on the interaction of different regimes and on the role of nonstate actors and policy networks.

Regime Theory and the Study of Local and Urban Politics

Urban regime theory elaborates the regime concept drawn from the international relations literature. It goes beyond the IR conceptionalization of regimes as cooperative institutions that are characterized through informal or formal structures—principles, norms, rules, and procedures—that contribute to the solution of conflicts. In the study of local and urban politics, the regime concept entails additional properties. Largely following Clarence Stone, the urban regime concept describes processes and structures of cooperation of public and private actors in urban areas and their ability to find access to institutional resources. An urban regime is a relatively stable coalition of actors that has, or seeks to achieve, a sustained role in making governing decisions on the local level. Political power is sought by regimes as the power to act, rather than the power over others. Cooperation is attained through both formal institutions and informal networks. Regimes bridge the divide between popular control of government and private control of economic resources. They are stable because they bring together fragmented resources and manage to establish long-standing patterns of cooperation for the accomplishment of tasks.

The urban regime concept has developed through induction from exemplary case studies. The wide-ranging and multifaceted concept combines, for example, elements of political economy, pluralism, and institutionalism. The urban regime concept bears certain similarities with both elite and pluralist theories. Yet, while these two approaches have the idea in common that urban politics is characterized by struggle concerning the distribution of public goods and income, regime theory stresses the importance of the role played by the cooptation of private interests and the need of combining and commonly using private and public resources in order to implement local policy agendas. Urban regime theory also differs from the concept of policy networks. The latter theorizes at a higher level of abstraction and cannot sufficiently hypothesize which logics spur cooperation in local and urban politics.

Authors have developed a number of different typologies of urban regimes. Stephen Elkin holds that the structural features that define urban regimes stem from the division of labor between market and state. He thus distinguishes between entrepreneurial, pluralist, and federalist regimes. Stone also differentiates between three types of urban regimes that are defined through the properties of governing coalition structure and development outcomes: corporate, progressive, and caretaker regimes. Corporate regimes

are characterized by the central role of private interests. They entail the risk that the preferences of citizens are circumvented. Progressive regimes are based on neighborhood organizations of the lower and middle classes. This type is considered unstable. Caretaker coalitions represent tight neighborhood networks and associations of small firms or minorities. They tend to need the city council or political organizations in order to become operational.

Urban regime theory has covered quite a number of interdisciplinary debates and substantive issues within its research agenda. These include, first, the potential of cross-national comparisons. Comparative research on urban regimes has the potential to break the concept out of its focus on the governing coalition by comparing processes within different contexts. This potentially allows for an explanation of the impact of changes in the larger environment on the formation and evolution of regimes. Second, the importance of business participation in defining urban regimes has been subject to discussion. Some scholars have contested the inclusion of business as a critical element of urban regimes. They contended that Stone's social production model reflects a U.S. bias as American local governments are dependent on the private sector for critical resources. Thus, they called for a broader conception of urban governance. Karen Mossberger and Gerry Stoker, among others, have refuted this view. They suggest that through the broader conception of urban governance, the regime concept would surrender features that have made the concept distinctive, such as the collaboration with business entities. Moreover, there is evidence of government-business partnerships from research on European local politics. A third substantive issue on the urban regime agenda deals with the application of the regime concept to new contexts. Despite the dangers of concept overstretching and creating conceptual muddle, the regime concept has been productively applied to some new areas. For example, its application to the regional level has been promising, not least because many issues that are traditionally dealt with in urban regimes, like economic development, cannot be adequately dealt with within the confines of local government. Limitations of the urban regime concept have been demonstrated concerning noneconomic issues, for example, in the area of identity politics, such as civil rights issues.

—*Arne Niemann*

See also Cooperation; Epistemic Community; International Regime; Internet Governance; Local Governance; Neoliberalism; Pluralism; Policy Network; Realism and Neorealism; Self-Regulation; Social Constructivism

Further Readings and References

Elkin, S. L. (1987). *City and regime in the American republic.* Chicago: University of Chicago Press.

Grieco, J. M. (1988). Anarchy and the limits of cooperation: A realist critique of the newest liberal institutionalism. *International Organization, 42,* 485–507.

Haas, P. M. (1992). Introduction: Epistemic communities and international policy coordination. *International Organization, 46,* 1–35.

Hasenclever, A., Mayer, P., & Rittberger, V. (1997). *Theories of international regimes.* Cambridge, UK: Cambridge University Press.

Keohane, R. O. (1984). *After hegemony: Cooperation and discord in the world political economy.* Princeton, NJ: Princeton University Press.

Krasner, S. D. (Ed.). (1983). *International regimes.* Ithaca, NY: Cornell University Press.

Mearsheimer, J. J. (1995). The false promise of international institutions. *International Security, 19,* 5–49.

Mossberger, K., & Stoker, G. (2001). The evolution of urban regime theory: The challenge of conceptualization. *Urban Affairs Review, 36,* 810–835.

Ruggie, J. G. (1998). What makes the world hang together? Neo-utilitarianism and the social constructivist challenge. *International Organization, 52,* 855–885.

Stone, C. N. (1989). *Regime politics: Governing Atlanta, 1946–1988.* Lawrence: University Press of Kansas.

Young, O. R. (1994). *International governance: Protecting the environment in a stateless society.* Ithaca, NY: Cornell University Press.

REGIONAL AUTHORITY

A regional authority is an administrative body responsible for governing a geographically defined region. Its responsibilities may be general or limited to a given sector of activity, and its autonomy may range from almost autonomous to directly controlled by an upper level of government.

A renewed interest in the regionalization of the state's responsibilities in the 1980s and 1990s at the international level spurred the creation of many new regional authorities and the reinforcement of existing bodies' functions.

Regional authorities are generally established as intermediary governance bodies between local institutions or service providers on the one hand and national or provincial governments on the other. Regional authorities' existence can be explained according to the subsidiarity principle regarding the optimal equilibrium between centralization and decentralization of governance functions. The subsidiarity principle states that each governing task must be carried out at a level that is close enough to production or delivery levels to have a good understanding of local conditions, while controlling enough resources to maintain integration of services, coordination, and economies of scale. The creation of regional authorities may thus constitute a mix of centralization and decentralization, as power and responsibilities are transferred downward from central governments to the regional level, while functions previously performed by local authorities or organizations are shifted to the regional level.

While regional authorities can have broad responsibilities, they are often in charge of sector-specific responsibilities (for example, in health care or education). As intermediate governance bodies, regional authorities' autonomy is never absolute. They can only exist in equilibrium between complete centralization and total decentralization. In a totally centralized governance system, regional authorities would disappear, while they would become privatized organizations— or, at an extreme, autonomous states—in an absolutely decentralized system. In between, their autonomy can range from a simple deconcentration of an upper-governance-level's powers to a complete devolution. In a deconcentration scheme, the regional authority is limited to the regional implementation of centrally established policies and decisions without significant decision-making autonomy. In a delegation scheme, the upper level of government transfers some decisional power to the regional authority. These powers are usually sector specific and limited to a capacity to define the modalities by which policy objectives set by the upper level will be met at the regional level. Both in deconcentration and delegation, regional authorities' legitimacy is mainly, if not entirely, derived from the upper level of governance's own legitimacy. Last, in devolution schemes, the regional authority has its own electoral system and the capacity to levy its own taxes: Thus, it can rely partially on autonomous sources of legitimacy. Devolved bodies are often in charge of multisectoral responsibilities.

At the administrative level, regional authorities are generally accountable to a board of directors. Regional boards can be appointed, elected, or a mix of both. Regional authorities having a devolved status are expected to have a mainly elected board, while deconcentrated regional authorities are expected to have no boards at all or a centrally appointed one.

—*Damien Contandriopoulos*
and Carl-Ardy Dubois

See also Center-Local Relations; Devolution; Intergovernmental Relations; Local Governance; Multilevel Governance; Substate Regionalism

Further Readings and References

Dorland, J. L., & Davis, S. M. (1996). *How many roads? Regionalization and decentralization in health care.* Kingston, ON, Canada: Queen's University.

REGIONAL DEVELOPMENT BANK

Regional development banks are membership-based multilateral development finance institutions intended to assist with economic growth, poverty reduction, industrialization, and social progress in specific regions of the developing world. Their overarching goal is to reduce poverty in the developing countries in their region, and they pursue this objective by financing loans and technical assistance across a range of development activities, including agriculture projects, infrastructure building, social sector improvement, and good governance projects and policy reform. Regional development banks pursue many of the same projects and promote similar objectives at the regional level that the World Bank does for developing countries all over the world.

Regional development banks are a major source of multilateral funds for socio-economic development, poverty reduction, and institutional capacity building in their regions. They provide financing to governments and to enterprises in both the private and public sectors in their developing member countries, which are also their shareholders. Their principal instruments are loans, grants, and technical assistance, intended to support governments in identifying high-priority development programs and carrying out specific development projects. Country assistance strategies are designed in conjunction with government counterparts in member countries to ensure that assistance from regional development banks support development investments that are based on a country's own priorities. The regional development banks also provide differing degrees of policy advice to their member countries, and carry out policy and economic analysis that forms the basis of ongoing dialogue with governments. Some of them provide investment guarantees. In addition, regional development banks facilitate regional integration, promoting cooperation around development issues and helping countries learn from others in their region and at their level of development.

Major regional development banks include: the African Development Bank (AfDB), the Asian Development Bank (ADB), the Caribbean Development Bank (CDB), the European Bank for Reconstruction and Development (EBRD), the Inter-American Development Bank (IDB or IADB), and the Islamic Development Bank (IsDB). These all have slightly differing mandates and operating structures, but the similarities across the group allow us to understand the concept of the regional development bank.

While they work in partnership with the International Bank for Reconstruction and Development (IBRD, commonly known as the World Bank) and bilateral aid agencies, regional development banks are separate and independent institutions. The International Monetary Fund (IMF) and the World

Bank were created at the Bretton Woods Conference in 1944 and are part of the United Nations system. Regional development banks, on the other hand, were created by their regional shareholders at different points in time. Their shareholder membership overlaps partly with that of the Bretton Woods institutions. But, unlike the IMF and World Bank, the majority of regional development bank funds and shareholder power belongs to their developing country members rather than the world's developed countries.

Furthermore, while regional development banks do provide some lending at concessional rates, most of their development loans are made at interest rates based on the cost of raising funds in international capital markets. This differentiates them from the concessional lending that the World Bank's International Development Association provides to the world's poorest countries. It also differentiates them from the bilateral foreign aid programs of governments, such as those managed by the U.S. Agency for International Development, the United Kingdom's Department for International Development, and the Japan International Cooperation Agency, which provide grants for development purposes. The aims of regional development bank and the recipients of their financing are also different from those of institutions that promote a country's exports, such as the Export Import Bank of the United States (Ex-Im Bank).

The first regional development bank was the Inter-American Development Bank (IADB). It was established in 1959 at the initiative of the Latin American countries, designed as a institution with a new mandate and tools for development in the region. In particular, its lending programs and modes of technical cooperation and assistance for socio-economic development were intended to go beyond the strategies common for financing economic projects. In many respects, the IADB became the model for the creation of other regional development banks.

The IADB finances its projects and technical cooperation programs in member countries through market rate or concessional loans. Different entities—including governments, civil society, subregional organization, and financial intermediaries—are eligible for lending, depending on the nature of the

particular project and the specific financing instrument and fund involved. The IADB does not invest directly in private equity itself, but its affiliates invest in private businesses, and the IADB and its affiliates also finance a number of grants for micro- and small business development in the region. When private financial sources lend to the public and private sectors in Latin America and the Caribbean, the IADB can guarantee these loans in order to encourage investment in the borrowing countries.

Similarly, the Asian Development Bank (ADB) promotes economic and social development in its member countries in Asia through a variety of different mechanisms. It designs and provides technical assistance, helps to coordinate and offers advisory services for development programs, and facilitates capital investment in both the private and public sectors through loans, equity investments, and other forms of non-financial support. The Islamic Development Bank (IsDB) aims to foster socioeconomic development in member countries and Muslim communities using financing modes that are in conformity with Shari'a, or Islamic law. It provides financing for development projects in agriculture, industry, and infrastructure, trade, and private sector development, and also offers technical assistance and facilitates technical cooperation among its member countries.

Regional development banks have, like the World Bank, moved over time from a heavy focus on agricultural development and infrastructure building toward a greater emphasis on social sector (health and education) development and strengthening governance and institutional capacity. Both their financial and non-financial interventions now involve non-governmental organizations (NGOs) and other community-based stakeholder groups. Moreover, they have recently moved toward a greater emphasis on providing economic opportunities for poor women and incorporating sound natural resource management and environmental impact mitigation measures in their operations.

—*Naazneen H. Barma*

See also Capacity Building; Regional Governance; World Bank

Further Readings and References

Devlin, R., & Castro, L. (2002, February 19). *Regional banks and regionalism: A new frontier for development financing.* Paper presented at Institute for International Economics Conference on Financing for Development: Regional Challenges and the Regional Development Banks, Washington, DC. Retrieved from http://www.iie.com/publications/papers/devlin-castro0202.pdf

REGIONAL GOVERNANCE

While the nineteenth century and the beginning of the twentieth century could be deemed the golden age of the nation-state, a new process of diversification of levels of governance has changed the political organization of a large number of liberal democracies since the end of World War II. First, a progressive generalization of subnational territorial governance meant that decentralized and federal systems greatly progressed since 1945. More innovatively, however, a certain number of supranational regional organizations also resulted in the emergence of a higher level of governance. Altogether, these new multilevel systems of governance and the crowning of regional governance as a new unit of decision making represented a quiet revolution in the life of many Western democracies, though attempts at regional governance have not been confined to these countries. Nevertheless, it is the case that regional governance is most advanced in Europe and less so outside of the West.

Arguably, the origin of regional governance could be found in the long imperial tradition of the European continent, from the Greek and Roman extended areas of sovereignty to the Austro-Hungarian empire from 1867 to 1914. However, the notion of a nonimperialist form of regional governance that is based on a union of independent sovereign states is not quite as new as one may first suspect. In 1464, the King of Bohemia at the time, George of Podehrady, wrote to his European colleagues suggesting that they unite in a new form of European Union (EU) for the common good of themselves (the monarchs) and of their people and to avoid more unnecessary bloodshed.

Four hundred and fifty years later, in the early twentieth century, other idealists revived the idea of a political unification of Europe that finally stopped to be an abstract dream following the end of World War II. Belgium, Luxembourg, and the Netherlands created the Benelux area of preferred trade, and some leaders tried to think of ways in which the German Zollverein of the early nineteenth century could be replicated at a trans-European level. In the Congress of the Hague in 1948, Western European political and intellectual elites, as well as a number of their liberal colleagues from the center and east side of the continent, decided to launch this political process, which resulted in the creation of the Council of Europe, a cultural organization.

By and large, the unification of the Western European continent became the single most outstanding example of regional governance in the world. Starting as a primarily economic and peace-oriented project, European unification progressively transformed into a fully fledged, quasi-federal political system with its own policies, institutions, citizenship, and constitution. The various treaties that marked the deepening of the European model of regional governance (Rome, Schengen, Maastricht, Amsterdam, Nice) all participated in this profound transformation of our understanding of regional governance.

Indeed, the EU is no longer a simple single market area, but the source of eighty-five percent of the new legislation that applies in every single member state every year. Within the spirit of multilevel governance, an EU citizenship now exists, which allows any citizen from a member state to freely travel, work, or live in any part of the European Union. A unified European Union passport, the direct election of a European Parliament through a single transnational election (nationally organized at the same time across the member states), and the right to vote in local and European elections in one's country of residence have completed this new conception of a European citizenship. Among the institutions of the new supranational political system, apart from the European Parliament and traditional executive (European Commission) and state-representing second legislative institution (the Council of the European Union), a Court of Justice of the European Communities has, by and large, the role of a national supreme court and can be directly solicited by individual citizens, unlike traditional supranational judicial instances. Similarly, a European ombudsman deals with the problems occurring between EU citizens and their institutions.

Following the example of the EU, a certain number of other continents or subparts of continents have tried to initiate processes of regional governance, usually with a primary economic dimension. One can mention the cases of the Association of Southeast Asian Nations, the North American Free Trade Agreement, the Mercosur union in South America, and several attempts of the subparts of the African continent, as well as the Arab League, which has a predominantly political and diplomatic orientation. These new initiatives largely follow from the success of the EU and the new situation it has created, whereby even the largest and most powerful nations may occasionally find themselves undersized when it comes to reasserting their world position in a number of policy areas.

—*Michael Bruter*

See also Commonwealth of Independent States; European Union; Hemispheric Integration; Interregional Relations; Mesoregionalism; Monetary Union; Multilevel Governance; Pacific Islands Forum; Regional Development Bank; Regionalism; Transnational Governance; World Health Organization

Further Readings and References

Bruter, M. (2004). On what citizens mean by feeling "European": Perceptions of news, symbols and borderlessness. *Journal of Ethnic and Migration Studies, 30,* 21–39.

MacLeod, G. (2001). New regionalism reconsidered: Globalization and the remaking of political economic space. *International Journal of Urban and Regional Research, 25*(4), 804.

REGIONALISM

Regionalism has recently emerged as one of the key areas of research and debate in international relations (IR) and international political economy (IPE), together with the nature of the state and of globalization. As with the state and with globalization, regionalism is a complex phenomenon and its definition depends on the theoretical perspective employed within these fields. From a neofunctionalist perspective, regionalism involves the process of integration of nation-states toward regional institutions that possess the authority to provide functional needs. Similarly, neoliberal institutionalists argue that regionalism is a process whereby regional institutions, such as the European Union (EU), assist in reducing the costs associated with collective action and enhance the potential for states to engage in long-term reciprocal relationships. By contrast, neorealists argue that states regionally cooperate in order to balance power against other states or regions in an anarchical world. Economic approaches to regionalism place focus on the market-oriented welfare effects of economic interaction, such as lowering regional trade barriers and harmonizing external tariffs. Other approaches, from the field of "critical" IPE, identify regionalism as a process by which states and state-society complexes interact with processes of globalization to further their insertion into the economic and political world order. Finally, and in a related manner, the new regionalism approach seeks to understand the post–Cold War rise in regional formations as a process emerging from civil society in order to respond to the various challenges posed by globalization.

Theories of Regionalism

Early empirical studies of regionalism focused on the then initial stages of European integration from a mainly neofunctionalist perspective. Neofunctionalist interpretations of regional integration retained the thrust of the functionalist approach, which is that cooperation between nation-states begins with low-level economic and social cooperation, but then shifted their analytical focus from the international to the regional and introduced a utilitarian framework to describe the motives of rational political actors. As such, the neofunctionalist perspective seeks to understand and explain why sovereign nation-states choose to integrate in such a manner as to exchange aspects of their sovereignty for the authority of regional institutions. Proponents of this view argue the explanation lies in the concept of "spillover" and the interests of national and supranational political actors. Through the interdependence inherent in the various sectors of modern economies, integration in one sector "spills over" into other sectors and necessarily leads to sectoral integration. Furthermore, due to the interwoven nature of the economic and political spheres, according to this argument, functional and political spillover induces the processes of regional integration to take place. The result is that supranational regional institutions are created with the jurisdiction over their member states to facilitate these integrative functions.

In a similar manner, neoliberal institutionalists emphasize the role of institutions in the formation of regional organizations. These institutions, it is argued, lower the transaction costs of increased cooperation and thus satisfy the demand of increased interconnectedness at the regional level. Unlike neofunctionalist theories, neoliberal institutionalists focus their analyses on the state as a rational actor in an anarchical international system of states. From this perspective, states seek long-term, absolute gains from cooperation and are discouraged by the actions of states that seek to cheat or defect from their mutual obligations. Regional institutions, it is argued, may provide the transparency, unified expectations, and the mechanisms to inhibit cheating through their coordination role at the supranational level. Thus, for neoliberal institutionalists, as with neofunctionalists, the creation of regional institutions depends on the benefits of cooperation accorded to the regional actors involved. Therefore, these regional institutions are subject to the actions of states and motivated by internal political interest groups and domestic political objectives. The success and longevity of these regional institutions, then, depend on their ability to successfully carry out their coordinating and problem-solving functions.

Neorealist accounts of regionalism, however, while also shifting analytical focus to states as rational actors in an anarchical international system, argue that integration is dependent on their concern for their own security from external threats. Within this context, neorealists emphasize several key criteria with regard to the possibilities and rationale of integration. The underlying constraint to integration, unlike cheating or defection in institutionalist explanations, is that of the relative gains and losses of the states involved. As states are concerned with the relative gains from cooperation, an uneven distribution of gains, where some states experience losses relative to others, will affect their security and hinder efforts to form and maintain regional arrangements. In addition, the role of a hegemonic power (a state with the military and economic resources, as well as the impetus to impose order—both at the global and regional level) may affect the creation and dynamics of regional institutions. Some neorealist arguments point toward the creation of regional economic blocs in the face of the decline in power of a global hegemon, while others have emphasized the role that a hegemonic state may play in strengthening economic and military relations among smaller and medium-sized allied states.

While these theories of regionalism recognize the role of the market and of economic factors that contribute to the creation of regional institutions, they emphasize the political rationales of actors. Theories of regionalism stemming from the field of economics, which have had a dominant impact on the study of regionalism, emphasize the market-oriented economic rationality of actors and the welfare effects of integration. One of the pioneering studies in this regard is Jacob Viner's *The Customs Union Issue,* first published in 1950. A customs union, Viner explained, is created in order to lower or eliminate trade barriers among its members and harmonize tariffs on imports from outside the union. The issue then becomes that of trade creation and trade diversion. Trade creation, which has a positive overall welfare effect for member countries, it is argued, occurs when products from high-cost producers in any one member country are replaced by less-costly output from other member countries (which are freely traded within the union due to the elimination of trade barriers). Trade diversion, which has an overall negative welfare effect, occurs when the common external tariff discourages trade with the lowest cost producers outside the union and diverts trade toward less efficient industries from within the member countries. Extending and refining Viner's arguments, Bela Balassa proposed that economic integration occurs along evolutionary lines, beginning with a free-trade area, where internal tariffs are eliminated among its members; continuing on to a customs union as defined by Viner; progressing, then, toward a common market, where labor and capital are allowed to move freely among member countries; advancing to an economic union, which includes the harmonization of economic policies; and finally, reaching a stage of complete economic integration, with a supranational authority ensuring the unification of all economic policies, including fiscal and monetary policy. These arguments have influenced many important debates among policymakers and academics regarding the benefits of regional integration versus bilateral or multilateral free trade and the role of regional organizations as either building blocks or stumbling blocks to a globalized economy.

Indeed, it is within the context of globalization that the next set of theories seeks to understand the phenomenon of regionalism. Working from within a framework that analyzes current and historical social changes with respect to the interaction of ideas, institutions, and material capabilities at various levels in society, such as state/society complexes and world orders, Andrew Gamble and Anthony Payne set out an agenda in *Regionalism and World Order* that sought to critically explain the renewed interest toward regionalism that had been taking place within the world order since the mid-1980s and early 1990s. From this perspective, this new form of regionalism is understood as a process by which states and state actors politically and economically adjust to the pressures of globalization. Globalization, seen as a social process with a set of evolving structures, may interact with regionalist projects in such a way as to further, change, or set back these processes. Regionalism and globalization, then, are interrelated and, as such, do not seek to exert dominance over one another. Thus, the increased pace of states toward regionalism, from this perspective, does not signify the construction of a protective front in the face of the declining power of a global hegemon, as in the case of neorealist perspectives. Instead, regionalist projects emerge as a means by which these states manage to further their insertion into the existing world order.

In a similar vein, Björn Hettne and his colleagues at the United Nations University/World Institute for Development Economics Research (UNU/WIDER) have sought to understand and explain the rise of new regional formations in the midst of the global structural transformations that were taking place in the mid-1980s. As such, new regionalism theory (NRT), which they have proposed, seeks to explain this process of regionalism, which exhibits qualitative differences from the processes of regionalism that took place soon after World War II. The theory sets its focus on the region as a complex construct, consisting of such attributes as geography, politics, economics, and culture, that is consistently created or reshaped by human agency. In this context, regionalism represents a process with many forms that interact with processes of global transformation in the world order. The NRT outlines five levels of "regionness"—regional space, regional complex, regional society, regional community, and region state—defined as the process by which a region is capable of representing its transnational interests. At each level, the political, economic, and cultural aspects of society become ever more regionally articulated and deepened. However, proponents of this view are careful to point out that this theory of regionalism does not imply stages of regionalism but rather forms of regions constructed and deconstructed by human agents interacting with the forces of globalization.

Regionalism and Regionalization

Beginning with the studies of the new regionalism, scholars in the field of IPE have emphasized that regionalism must be understood in the context of the process of regionalization. Although definitions vary somewhat, regionalization is often compared to, and indeed is argued to act in tandem with, globalization, as a social process of integration that exerts pressure on states and societies. Therefore, regionalism as understood as a state- and society-led process, in the approaches put forward by Gamble and Payne and the UNU/WIDER project, is seen to interact with the forces of regionalization in much the same way as regionalism interacts with the forces of globalization, as a source for social, political, and economic restructuring. While some, such as Hettne, have argued that regionalization acts as a force that encourages political, cultural, and economic homogenization at the regional level, others have emphasized that regionalization, like globalization, may affect regional societies in uneven ways, such as to benefit certain groups of people or certain geographical areas and marginalize others. Thus, it is argued, regionalization may be a force that encourages disintegration through its potential to polarize societies at the regional level, which integrative, state-led regionalist projects may face as a challenge.

Examples of Regional Organizations

As regionalism is a global phenomenon, examples of regional organizations may be found in Europe, the Americas, Africa, Asia, and the Pacific. In Europe, the European Coal and Steel Community, established in 1953 between France, West Germany, Italy, and the Benelux countries, initiated the process of European integration and led to the signing of the Treaty of Rome in 1958, which established the European Economic Community (EEC). By 1992, the Maastricht Treaty on European Monetary and Political Union was adopted, and by 1993, the Community was formally known as the European Union to signify the level of integration that it had achieved (encompassing most of the countries in Western Europe by that point). In the Americas, examples include Mercosur (the Mercado Común del Sur or Southern Common Market), including the countries of Argentina, Brazil, Paraguay, Uruguay, and Venezuela (Bolivia and Chile are associate members), and the North American Free Trade Agreement (NAFTA), including Canada, Mexico, and the United States.

Among the many such organizations on the continent of Africa, the Southern African Development Community (SADC), consisting of the countries in its southern cone, was relaunched in 1992 to promote economic and social development objectives. Finally, in Asia and the Pacific, the Association of South East Asian Nations (ASEAN), which encompasses most of the countries of South East Asia and intends to promote regional political stability as well as economic development, and the Asia Pacific Economic Cooperation forum (APEC), are just two examples. APEC, which was formed in 1989 to promote open free-trade and investment, includes as its members the countries of ASEAN and spans the Pacific to include Japan, South Korea, China, Russia, Taiwan, Hong Kong, Australia, New Zealand, Papua New Guinea, the United States, Mexico, Chile, and Peru.

—*Stephen Buzdugan*

See also Asia-Pacific Economic Cooperation; Baltic State Cooperation; Caribbean Community; Caribbean Governance; Chiang Mai Agreement; Common Market for Eastern and Southern Africa; Coordination; Globalization; Hegemony; Interregional Relations; Mercantilism; Mesoregionalism; New Regionalism; Open and Closed Regionalism; Regional Governance; World Health Organization

Further Readings and References

Balassa, B. (1961). *The theory of economic integration.* London: Allen and Unwin.

Gamble, A., & Payne, A. (1996). Conclusion: The new regionalism. In A. Gamble & A. Payne (Eds.), *Regionalism and world order.* Basingstoke, UK: Macmillan.

Haas, E. B. (1958). *The uniting of Europe: Political, social and economic forces 1950–1957.* Palo Alto, CA: Stanford University Press.

Hettne, B. (1999). Globalization and the new regionalism: The second great transformation. In B. Hettne, A. Inotai, & O. Sunkel (Eds.), *Globalism and the new regionalism.* Basingstoke, UK: Macmillan.

Hettne, B., & Söderbaum, F. (2000). Theorizing the rise of regionness. *New Political Economy, 5*(3), 457–473.

Hurrell, A. (1995). Explaining the resurgence of regionalism in world politics. *Review of International Studies, 21,* 331–358.

Krasner, S. D. (1976). State power and the structure of international trade. *World Politics, 28,* 317–347.

Mansfield, E. D., & Milner, H. V. (1997). The political economy of regionalism: An overview. In E. V. Mansfield & H. V. Milner (Eds.), *The political economy of regionalism.* New York: Columbia University Press.

Marchand, M. H., Bøås, M., & Shaw, T. M. (1999). The political economy of new regionalisms [Special Issue]. *Third World Quarterly, 20*(5), 897–910.

Mattli, W. (1999). *The logic of regional integration: Europe and beyond.* Cambridge, UK: Cambridge University Press.

Payne, A., & Gamble, A. (1996). Introduction: The political economy of regionalism and world order. In A. Gamble & A. Payne (Eds.), *Regionalism and world order.* Basingstoke, UK: Macmillan.

Viner, J. (1950). *The customs union issue.* New York and London: Carnegie Endowment for International Peace and Stevens and Sons Ltd.

REGULATION

Regulation has a variety of meanings that are not reducible to one single concept. In the field of public policy, regulation refers to the promulgation of targeted rules, typically accompanied by some authoritative mechanism for monitoring and enforcing compliance. Accordingly, for a long time in the United States, the study of regulation has been synonymous with the study of the independent agencies enforcing it. In political economy, it refers to the attempt of the state to steer the economy, either narrowly defined as the imposition of economic controls on the behavior of private business or, more broadly, to include other governmental instruments, such as taxation or disclosure requirements. The two meanings share a focus on the state's attempt to intervene in private activities. A third definition moves beyond an interest in the state and focuses on all means of social control, either intentional or unintentional. This understanding is most common in anthropology, sociolegal studies, and international relations because it includes mechanisms such as voluntary agreements or norms that exercise social control outside of the reach of a sovereign state and not necessarily as an intentional act of steering. Thus, different strands of regulation studies share an agreement on the subject of regulation (the state), the object (the behavior of nongovernmental actors), the instruments (an authoritative set of rules), or the domain of application (the economy), but they do not necessarily agree on all of these elements.

Especially in its broader meanings, the concept of regulation resembles the concept of governance: It points to the rules that structure the behavior of individuals within a given political context without postulating where these rules come from and how they are imposed.

The diversity of meanings has led to a certain amount of controversy and misunderstandings between scholars, most notably on the topic of deregulation. In the economic tradition, deregulation refers to the elimination of the specific controls that the government imposed on the market interactions, in particular the attempt to control market access, prices, output, or product quality. However, if regulation is conceived of more broadly as a form of economic governance, it is difficult to imagine the total elimination of state intervention. Moreover, the relationship between regulation and competition seems to be transforming. Previously, regulation was depicted as the enemy of free market interactions. Competition necessarily required deregulation. Today, there is a sense that some regulation facilitates competition, while others impede it. Regulation is no longer the antonym of free markets or liberalization, and scholars increasingly prefer using the terms reregulation or regulatory reform instead of deregulation.

The theoretical debates around the concept of regulation reflect different disciplines and research agendas and can be broadly divided into approaches to regulation as an act of government and perspectives on regulation as governance.

Regulation as State Activity

Two aspects of this particular governmental activity have been studied extensively: (1) the reasons for and (2) the process of regulation. The first question has led to a normative-positive debate about the origins of regulation. The second concentrates on empirical dynamics and analyzes its administrative process.

Public Versus Private Interests?

The original justification of government intervention in economic interactions was public interest. This perspective considers the market as an efficient allocation mechanism of social and economic welfare, but cautions against market failures. Market failures commonly include natural monopolies, externalities, public goods, asymmetric information, moral hazard, or transaction costs, and regulation was considered necessary to overcome these difficulties.

Theorizing regulation as a tool for overcoming market imperfections has been criticized on a number of points. First, with the evolution of economic theory, several scholars have questioned the understanding of market failure underlying the explanation of government regulation. Second, economists have pointed out the often-considerable transaction costs of imposing regulation, which might make it an ineffective policy tool and harmful to social or economic welfare. Finally, the market failure approach argues that regulation is put into place with the goal of achieving economic efficiency. However, this makes it hard to account for other objectives, such as procedural fairness or redistribution at the expense of efficiency.

The Chicago School, or the Virginia School of public choice theory, focused instead on private interests as the source of regulation. The principal aim of this perspective is to understand how private interests and public officials interact. The central claim of these studies is that policy outcomes are most often contrary to societal or public interest because industry representatives lobby the government for benefits they might gain through protectionism or other forms of economic controls. Politicians are susceptible to these demands because they are interested in contributions that business actors can offer. Thus, interest groups compete for specific policies in a setting that has been called the political market for governmental regulation. As long as interest groups exist, we should expect regulation, which impedes the achievement of maximal social and economic welfare.

The theory of economic regulation has been criticized for its risk of tautology. Because regulation is in place because private interests lobbied for it effectively, one can only know who asked for it by looking at who benefits from it. Therefore, a particular industry advantage is the cause and effect of regulation. Furthermore, if regulation is defined in a narrow sense

as specific economic policies aiming at the control of prices or market entry and access, the decrease in regulation of several industries in the United States during the 1970s and 1980s seemingly refutes the theory. Indeed, Sam Peltzman, one of its best known advocates, conceded in 1989 that the theory cannot account for the entry and exit of regulation. Nonetheless, as a model of business-government interactions, the theory of economic regulation directly or indirectly informs a large number of studies in the field of political economy until this day.

Pragmatic-Administrative Analyses

A large number of studies have grappled less with the normative-positive debate about the existence of regulation, but instead with the empirical fact of it. These pragmatic-administrative perspectives shed light on regulation as an act of policy making. The study of the politics of regulations is informed by the tools of public policy analysis, organizational sociology, or political science more generally. In an early study, Marven Bernstein identified the rhythm of regulation in what he termed the life cycle of regulatory commissions. He distinguishes between the gestation, youth, maturity, and old age of agencies in order to analyze the initial activism in the formulation of a regulatory policy approach and the specific management problems that occur in the course of its lifetime. Regulation had been classified as a specific type of public policy, indicating that policies should be categorized according to the degree and application of governmental coercion and separating regulatory policy making from distributive and redistributive policy making.

In the U.S. literature, the administrative study of regulation is often assimilated to the study of independent governmental agencies. Peter Selznick defines regulation as the sustained and focused control exercised by a public agency over activities that are generally regarded as desirable to society. In Europe, the study of regulation is much broader, not least because the elaboration, monitoring, and enforcement of targeted rules are often handled by a multitude of governmental bodies and not just independent agencies. It is considered an act of governmental intervention more broadly, and empirical investigations have looked at its implementation and the politics of its reform.

Furthermore, the study of regulation has aimed at characterizing different policy regimes or, more ambitiously, state capacity. The predominantly European literature on the regulatory state seeks to show that governmental action is increasingly based on the use of authority, rules, and standard setting, rather than distributional or redistributional tasks, such as public service provision. In an extension of this debate to the European level, it has been argued that the governmental capacity of the European Union (EU) is strongly biased toward regulation. As a political system, the EU might therefore develop into a regulatory state, but not into an interventionist welfare state.

Regulation as Governance

In the context of globalization, regulatory studies have moved away from focusing on independent agencies and governmental control of the economy only. The incorporation of different disciplinary perspectives has brought with it a considerable amount of insight, but also leads to theoretical diffusion. Yet, the conceptual expansion appears to be necessary given that recent developments have shown that some interactions of market participants, product standards, or processes are no longer regulated through state intervention, but through international agreements or even self-regulation arrangements between private actors. Because it seems pertinent to address these new modes of economic governance, it has become common to address regulation in the absence of direct governmental authority. Other studies have pointed at patterns that govern the behavior of certain actors without reference to a unitary subject of regulation. Of these studies, we will only consider the French *école de la régulation* to avoid broadening the understanding of regulation unnecessarily.

Regulation Without the State

As in the context of the EU, students of regulatory reform have become interested in regulation at the international level. In certain sectors, such as the e-commerce or telecommunication services, international agreements have been decisive for controlling the market behavior of individuals. Moreover, many studies have pointed out the effect of self-regulation of firms or various sets of public-private partnerships for the elaboration, monitoring, or the implementation of targeted rules. Different forms of private authority structure the economic behavior of firms in sectors as diverse as maritime transport, mineral markets, or financial services.

Yet even at the national level, self-regulation has existed for quite some time. Surveying different forms of sectoral regulation within countries, rule-making structures have been categorized according to the relationship between and the power of governmental and societal actors and distinguish between statism, corporatism, colonization, policy networks, and market dynamics. Sectors with a high degree of state capacity and little implication of private actors are statist. Once important functions are in the hands of societal actors without much state intervention, we find colonization. Public and private actors share roles in corporatism, policy networks, or market dynamics, which can be distinguished by the degree of action capacity of both actors (from high in corporatism to low in a market setting). By studying the varying agents of regulation, the question "Who regulates?" has become an important element of regulatory investigations.

Finally, it is often hard to identify exactly who or what leads to the rise or fall of regulatory reforms. While regulation and deregulation in the United States can be identified closely with specific political leaders and parties, a growing literature investigates what mechanisms lead to the diffusion of regulatory reforms across countries or policy contexts. Animated by the desire to understand regulatory emulation, this new research agenda connects the study of regulation with the ongoing debate about the roots and consequences of liberalization and globalization.

Governance Through Regularization: L'École de la Régulation

The French *école de la régulation* also studies patterns of societal behavior without being interested in concrete governmental action. Yet its insertion into the literature on regulation is more due to translation difficulties than to conceptual proximity, even though it shares with Anglo-Saxon political economy an interest in the governance of the economy. Inspired by Marxist thought, *l'école de la régulation* is a social theory that investigates the mechanisms by which power structures are produced and maintained. The term *régulation* refers here to the often implicit routines, norms, and conventions by which actions become regularized or normalized—an understanding similar to the biological sense of regulation as the reproduction of life forms such as DNA. To distinguish the theoretical focus from the Anglo-Saxon literature, Bob Jessop has suggested translating *régulation* into English as "regularization" or "normalization" to avoid confusion with an analysis of administrative rule making.

In this perspective, regulation is a governance mechanism that helps to reproduce capitalist economic and social relations over time. Through an analysis of the success and failure of Fordist modes of production, scholars have sought to explain economic crises and understand the national forms economic growth and crisis can take. The perspective asserts that (a) capitalism as a mode of production is inherently unstable and characterized by class conflict and antagonism, and (b) the history of capitalism is one of a succession of patterns of economic development and expansion, disturbed infrequently by structural crisis. Therefore, the central question is how capitalism succeeds in being so stable despite the inherent tensions. The answer lies in the way in which capitalism reproduces itself, in other words, in its regularization, which hinges on accumulation as a central mechanism. The approach that emerges from this analysis seeks to understand the variation and transformation of social and institutional forms that contribute to this regularization.

The French *l'école de la régulation* and the regulatory approach that followed it provide an important contribution to the study of state-market relations, but it is unified much more by the questions it poses than by the answers it has yielded. Because it arguably applies to a research area much larger than the transition from Fordism to post-Fordism, it should be viewed as an ongoing research project about the transformation of societal relations rather than a part of the literature on regulation in the Anglo-Saxon meaning.

All different branches of the literature on regulation share an interest in the rules that structure the behavior of individual actors in a given political setting. In the narrowest sense, the making of these rules is an act of governmental decision making, most often over economic interactions. Broader notions also included rule making in the absence of a state or study merely the existence and effect of rules without focusing on their origins, which makes the study of regulation quite similar to certain aspects of the study of governance.

—*Cornelia Woll*

See also Governance; Liberalization; Market Failure; Rational Choice Theory; Regulation Theory; Regulatory Enforcement; Regulatory Negotiations; Regulatory State; Rent Seeking; Self-Regulation

Further Reading and References

Baldwin, R. E., Scott, C., & Hood, C. (Eds.). (1998). *A reader on regulation.* Oxford, UK: Oxford University Press.

Bernstein, M. (1955). *Regulating business by independent commission.* Princeton, NJ: Princeton University Press.

Jessop, B., & Sum, N.-L. (2006). *The regulation approach and beyond.* Cheltenham, UK: Edward Elgar.

Jordana, J., & Levi-Faur, D. (Eds.). (2004). *The politics of regulation: Institutions and regulatory reforms for the age of governance.* Cheltenham, UK: Edward Elgar.

Joskow, P. L., & Noll, R. C. (1981). Regulation in theory and practice: An overview. In G. Fromm (Ed.), *Studies in public regulation.* Cambridge: MIT Press.

Majone, G. (1996). *Regulating Europe.* London: Routledge.

Mayntz, R., & Scharpf, F. W. (Eds.). (1995). *Gesellschaftliche Selbstregelung und politische Steuerung* [Social self-regulation and political control]. Frankfurt, Germany: Campus Verlag.

Peltzman, S. (1989). The economic theory of regulation after a decade of deregulation. *Brookings Papers on Economic Activity, Microeconomics,* 1–41.

Selznick, P. (1985). Focusing organizational research on regulation. In R. G. Noll (Ed.), *Regulation policy and the social sciences.* Berkeley: University of California Press.

Stigler, G. (1971). The theory of economic regulation. *Bell Journal of Economics and Management Science, 2,* 3–21.

Wilson, J. Q. (Ed.). (1980). *The politics of regulation.* New York: Basic Books.

REGULATION THEORY

Regulation theory is a distinctive paradigm in critical political economy. It originated in Europe and North America in the 1970s in response to the emerging crisis of the postwar economy and its mode of regulation, and it has since been applied to many other periods, regions, and contexts. Its name derives from its French originators, who describe it as *la théorie de régulation* (the theory of regulation) or *l'approche en termes de régulation* (the approach in terms of regulation). Similar ideas were developed by other schools. Their common core concern is the contradictory and conflictual dynamics of contemporary capitalism considered in terms of its extraeconomic as well as economic dimensions. In highlighting the latter, regulationists engage with other social sciences. One such affinity is with work on governance, especially economic governance. Indeed, regulation theory has been seen as the European equivalent of American institutionalist interest in macroeconomic and sectoral governance. This is overstated because there are important theoretical differences rooted in the Marxist background of the regulation approach and its focus on the logic of capitalism rather than the broader issues studied by governance theorists.

The various regulation schools examine the role of extraeconomic as well as economic factors in securing, albeit for limited periods and in specific economic spaces, what they regard as an inherently improbable and crisis-prone process of capital accumulation. Overall, while well aware of the invisible hand of market forces in this regard, they also explore how extraeconomic factors embed profit-oriented, market-mediated capitalist production in the wider society and help to tame, displace, and defer its contradictions and class conflicts. This process is associated with alternating periods of relatively stable expansion and crisis-induced restructuring, rescaling, and reregulation. Capitalism is deemed so contradictory and conflictual that crises will periodically trigger a trial-and-error search to find new ways of regularizing capitalist expansion. This provides the basis for regulationist work on different stages and varieties of capitalism.

Starting from real social relations in specific historical periods rather than from the abstract, transhistorical, rationalist assumptions of orthodox economics, all regulation schools largely share four goals: (1) describe the historically specific institutions and practices of capitalism, (2) explain the various crisis tendencies of modern capitalism and likely sources of crisis-resolution, (3) analyze different periods of capitalism and compare their respective accumulation regimes and modes of regulation, and (4) examine the social embedding and social regularization of economic institutions and conduct through their articulation with extra-economic factors and forces.

These goals provide potential links to research on governance. Governance theorists often distinguish among the invisible hand of the market (exchange), top-down management (command), reflexive dialogue and deliberation among equals with different but complementary interests (networking), and unconditional solidarities based on identification with a (real or imagined) community. Regulationists certainly recognize the importance of exchange mechanisms, but they argue that markets alone cannot secure economic growth or stability because they are inherently prone to market failure, especially in capitalist economies. Regulationists also argue that markets assume different forms and functions in different epochs, economic periods, and economic sectors. They also examine the state's role in providing many of the extraeconomic supports—material, institutional, policy driven, and discursive—that enable markets to operate or that compensate for their inevitable failures. They explore historically specific forms and functions of state intervention and insist that these cannot be reduced to purely technical questions but are always shaped by various kinds of social struggle. Therefore, they study the state's forms and activities in terms of successive patterns of institutionalized compromise. Equally significant are the other extraeconomic forms through which capital accumulation comes to be unevenly and provisionally stabilized. Here regulationists discuss the role of networks, interfirm linkages, norms, values, conventions, and other social forces in regularizing capital accumulation.

The dominant Parisian School introduced three major concepts for addressing these questions. An industrial paradigm is a model that guides the development of the technical and social division of labor (e.g., mass production, flexible specialization). An accumulation regime is a specific pattern of production and consumption that can be reproduced over a long period. For example, Fordism involves a virtuous circle of mass production and mass consumption. A mode of regulation is an ensemble of norms, institutions, organizational forms, social networks, and patterns of conduct that can stabilize an accumulation regime. This is the closest equivalent to other work on governance. Parisians generally distinguish five structural axes around which regulation (or governance) must occur in capitalism: (1) the capital-labor relation, broadly conceived; (2) the enterprise form, which includes many aspects of corporate governance, such as the main source of profits, forms of competition, interfirm linkages, and links to banking capital; (3) the monetary and financial systems; (4) the forms, functions, and social bases of state intervention; and (5) international regimes, including the regulation of trade, investment, and monetary flows and the political arrangements that link national economies, nation states, and the world system. Other schools have similar concepts but each has its own distinctive features reflecting its concerns with the sectoral, national, or transnational dimensions of regulation, broadly conceived, and its interest in the market economy or its embedding in a wider institutional and sociocultural context.

While regulation theorists are more narrowly concerned with basic structural features of capitalism and their medium- to long-term constitution and stabilization, more general theories of governance tend to focus on institutions and practices across many different social fields. Nonetheless, there has been a partial rapprochement between regulationist work and studies of economic governance at the sectoral, local, regional, national, and international levels. Thus, regulationists have shown increasing interest in different mechanisms of governance and their role in regularizing the key structural forms of the economy in its inclusive sense. And students of governance have become interested in why different economic sectors have different modes of coordination, in the problems of economic governance at different scales from the local to the global, in the shift from government to governance in the state and interstate systems, and in the rise of networked forms of sociality and network societies. There is certainly scope for continued dialogue and mutual learning in these two traditions.

—*Bob Jessop*

See also Economic Governance; Fordism and Post-Fordism; Governance Failure; Marxism; Political Economy; Regulation

Further Readings and References

Boyer, R., & Saillard, Y. (Eds.). (2002). *Regulation theory: State of the art*. London: Routledge.

Jessop, B., & Sum, N.-L. (2006). *The regulation approach and beyond: Putting capitalist economies in their place*. Cheltenham, UK: Edward Elgar.

Lipietz, A. (1993). The local and the global: Regional individuality or interregionalism? *Transactions of the Institute of British Geographers, 18*(1), 8–18.

REGULATORY ENFORCEMENT

Regulatory systems comprise three components: standard setting, supervision, and enforcement. Enforcement refers to actions undertaken by regulators to penalize or modify behaviors that deviate from the standard set by the system. For example, enforcement tools may be applied by an environmental regulatory agency in response to a firm's disposal of toxic waste, which infringes environmental regulations.

Enforcement is usually discussed with regard to state agencies' actions and business compliance with laws. However, in the age of governance, enforcement further applies to regulation of informal norms by nonstate actors.

The implementation of enforcement varies in the extent to which regulators are inclined toward deterrence or compliance styles. Deterrence style is rule bound and reliant upon formal punitive measures, such as criminal prosecution and civil fines. Compliance style is disposed toward persuasion, education, negotiation, and flexible interpretation of regulatory requirements. Regulators that exercise a deterrence strategy presume that individuals and corporations would not abide by the law unless threatened to do so. In contrast, those preferring a compliance approach assume that most people would voluntarily comply with regulations if they understood their requirements and logic.

The previously mentioned difference in enforcement styles has been explained in both rational choice and sociocultural rationales. From a rational choice perspective, it is arguable that regulators are more likely to manifest a compliance style when they are reliant on their regulated industry for information, technical expertise, and personnel—exchanging lenient regulation for resources. Applying a sociocultural perspective, the difference in regulatory styles is explained as a function of public trust in government and corporations. It is claimed that societies characterized by a high level of mistrust in governments and corporations tend to prefer a rule-bound deterrence style, which allows regulators little discretion. Another sociocultural explanation views the difference in regulatory style as a function of the sociological affinity between regulators and their regulated industries: that is, the scope, frequency, and length of their interaction. It is argued that greater sociological affinity will be associated with a compliance approach.

Going beyond the deterrence and compliance dichotomy, it is recognized that in order to be effective, regulators should vary their enforcement strategies and match the gravity of their enforcement tools to firms' relative resistance to comply. Research has shown that this is how most regulators behave in practice. Accordingly, regulatory agencies a priori prefer communication and persuasion to punishment and employ severe punishment only after less-severe means of attaining compliance have been exhausted. Thus, the difference between the deterrence and compliance styles regards the rate of escalation from persuasion to punishment tools, rather than two extremes.

—*Sharon Gilad*

See also Competition Policy; Regulation; Regulatory Negotiations

Further Readings and References

Ayres, I., & Braithwaite J. (1992). *Responsive regulation: Transcending the deregulation debate, Oxford socio-legal studies.* New York: Oxford University Press.

Hawkins, K. (2002). *Law as last resort, Oxford socio-legal studies.* Oxford, UK: Oxford University Press.

Vogel, D. (1986). *National styles of regulation: Environmental policy in Great Britain and the United States, Cornell studies in political economy.* Ithaca, NY: Cornell University Press.

REGULATORY NEGOTIATIONS

Regulatory negotiations broadly refer to the process of negotiating regulations between particular groups and administrative agencies. However, the term has recently become synonymous with negotiated rule making—a specific process of regulatory rule making in American government that involves all affected groups sitting down with the governing agency and achieving consensus on new regulatory rules. These negotiations supplement the "notice and comment" process of rule making, where agencies construct new rules and affected groups respond with their opinions, as specified by the Administrative Procedure Act of 1946.

Regulatory negotiations are most feasible when the costs and, to a lesser extent, the benefits of regulatory programs are concentrated upon particular groups, as it is then easier to bring representatives of those groups to the bargaining table. The regulating agency must determine who will be affected by the new rule and what information is needed to reach consensus on a new rule. Members of the agency and the affected groups will then form a committee and publicly negotiate a new rule to be issued. The new rule can still be challenged in court later, but proponents of negotiated rule making claim that such challenges are fewer when consensus is achieved.

Many scholars claim that traditional rule making became more costly through the 1970s as procedural hurdles imposed by Congress and the courts delayed completion of new rules and resulted in frequent litigation. In 1982, the Administrative Conference of the United States (ACUS) formally recommended that government agencies utilize Alternative Dispute Resolution (ADR) techniques, such as arbitration and mediation, to elicit feedback from all affected parties in the creation of new rules. The ACUS recommendations provided the intellectual foundation for negotiated rule making, while executive agencies in the Reagan administration served as laboratories.

In 1990, Congress enacted the Administrative Dispute Resolution Act and the Negotiated Rule-making Act, which does not mandate the use of negotiated rule making, but establishes a procedure by which agencies can initiate negotiations with interested parties. In 1993, the National Performance Review issued by Vice President Gore praised negotiated rule making, and shortly thereafter, the Clinton administration started pushing for greater use of the process throughout the federal government. Congress permanently reauthorized the Negotiated Rulemaking Act in 1996. Although many federal agencies engage in regulatory negotiations, the Environmental Protection Agency (EPA) probably employs the procedure more than anyone else, as EPA rules have been frequent targets of litigation.

As the use of regulatory negotiations by federal agencies began to spread in the 1980s, scholars praised it as an ideal supplement to the rule-making process. Proponents claim that the process allows everyone's concerns to be acknowledged, it leads to a more efficient exchange of relevant information, and it makes rule making a less time-consuming and litigious process. Recently, however, some have argued that negotiated rule making does not adequately represent all relevant interests, that it does not save time or reduce litigation, and that participating agencies can issue rules different from those agreed to at negotiation. Despite these criticisms, regulatory negotiations continue today to be widely utilized by all types of federal agencies.

—Colin Provost

See also Regulation; Regulation Theory; Regulatory Enforcement

Further Readings and References

Coglianese, G. (1997). Assessing consensus: The promise and performance of negotiated rulemaking. *Duke Law Journal, 46,* 1255–1350.
Fiorino, D. J. (1988). Regulatory negotiation as a policy process. *Public Administration Review, 48,* 764–772.
Harter, P. (1982). Negotiating regulations: A cure for malaise. *Georgetown Law Journal, 71,* 1–113.

REGULATORY STATE

The notion of the regulatory state suggests that the role of the state in economy and society is shifting from positive intervention to arms-length regulation and arbitration, particularly in advanced industrial economies. The supposed rise of the regulatory state has thus both a policy and an institutional dimension. It signals a formal end of Keynesian demand management as the dominant economic policy paradigm and highlights the creation of new administrative tools to steer market dynamics. It also has an international dimension, as the instruments of the regulatory state—independent agencies, commissions, and courts—engage in transnational governance through regulatory networks. Finally, the rise of the regulatory state poses important questions about the transparency and democratic accountability of governance.

Across the advanced economies, governments are relying less on direct economic intervention through fiscal and monetary tools and increasingly on arms-length regulation to stimulate competition and ensure the provision of social goods. Likewise, they have withdrawn from directly running companies in fields such as transportation, telecommunications, and utilities. In these newly liberalized sectors, the role of government is now one of a neutral watchdog that ensures competition and, where necessary, social protection. What has happened, then, is not a sweeping deregulation, but rather a complex reregulation associated with a redefinition of the state's role in the economy.

While the process of delegating regulatory authority to nonmajoritarian institutions gained widespread appeal with the New Deal in the United States, it has picked up considerable speed in the 1980s and 1990s.

In constructing the regulatory state, governments have developed a set of agencies, commissions, and special courts that develop, monitor, and enforce market rules and that increasingly shape policy at home and abroad. Regulatory agencies may set the policy agenda, specify regulatory statutes, and punish non-compliance. The formal and informal resources delegated and available to these institutions affect the state's capacity to shape political outcomes. Increasingly, these institutions take advantage of their domestic autonomy to work with their foreign counterparts, spearheading a new form of global governance rooted in transgovernmental networks. Thus, the regulatory state is at once the foundation and stimulus of transgovernmentalism.

Although the regulatory state is often heralded as a fast and flexible alternative to the cumbersome and overly bureaucratic strategies of a previous era, its emergence raises several important questions about democratic governance and accountability. Unlike Keynesian policies that were generally proposed and adopted by elected executives and legislatures, market rules are increasingly developed and implemented by unelected technocrats. To advocates, this mode of economic governance takes the politics out of market regulation; to skeptics, this is precisely the problem. Whereas the independence granted to new regulatory institutions is supposed to buffer them from capture by political and business interests, it also threatens to isolate them from direct democratic control. This dynamic has been most pronounced at the international level, where projects such as the European Single Market continue to suffer from a legitimacy deficit that many analysts attribute to the democratic deficit of new arms-length regulatory institutions.

—*David Bach and Abraham Newman*

See also Keynesianism; Political Economy; Regulation; Regulation Theory; State; State-Society Relations

Further Readings and References

Majone, G. (1997). From the positive to the regulatory state: Causes and consequences of changes in the mode of governance. *Journal of Public Policy, 17,* 139–167.

Slaughter, A.-M. (2004). *A new world order.* Princeton, NJ: Princeton University Press.

Vogel, S. K. (1996). *Freer markets, more rules.* Ithaca, NY: Cornell University Press.

RELIGION

Religion has long been considered an effective instrument of governance and social control: Religion can uphold the authority of leaders, bolster the dictates of morality, and contribute to the formation of collective identity. The two primary roles of religion in governance, therefore, are the production of belief and the distribution of services. Along with facilitating governance, it has also long been recognized that religion can produce fanaticism, fundamentalism, and sectarian division. In addition to the long-noticed effects of religion in creating belief, the recent resurgence of public religion has brought renewed attention to the role of religious institutions in administering public services.

While religion is notoriously difficult to define, we might isolate the following five general features: Religion is (1) a symbolic system that (2) instills durable human motivations by (3) codifying and explaining the order of existence (4) authoritatively and (5) beyond doubt. The system of meaning and belief codified in the doctrines of religion and reinforced through the practices of its observance present powerful motivation for the actions of human agents. Religion functions to insulate the beliefs it establishes from criticism. These features lead both to stability and instability. In the post-Reformation era in Europe, powerful and insular religious motivations often led to violence between the adherents of conflicting Christian doctrines. As the forces of globalization continue to bring the disparate regions of the world system into tighter connection, religious belief is again contributing to conflict.

The forms of liberal governance prevalent in the developed world are predicated on a sharp distinction between public and private life. Classically, liberalism consigns religion to a private realm and locates the affairs of state in the public realm. Nonetheless, it is widely recognized that there has been an ongoing global resurgence in public religion since the 1970s. Because of focus on the permeability between public and private administrative functions, governance scholars have a clear view of the impact of religion on administration. Along with the resurgence of religious symbolism in public life, religious institutions are participating in an increasing number of the functions of governance. In addition to expanding roles in education, child care, and elder care, religious institutions are increasingly participating in interest group politics, developing new media outlets, and contributing to the agendas of international development and human rights projects.

—*Matthew Scherer*

See also Confucian Governance; Hindu Governance; Human Rights; Islamic Governance; Liberalism; Multiculturalism

Further Readings and References

Casanova, J. (1994). *Public religions in the modern world.* Chicago: University of Chicago Press.
Geertz, C. (1973). Religion as a cultural system. In *The interpretation of cultures* (pp. 87–125). New York: Basic Books.

Rent Seeking

Rent seeking is the competition for politically protected transfers of wealth. The typical rent-seeking scenario includes a "prize" and a set of actors that create, capture, and finance the prize. The government creates the prize by setting, for example, a public subsidy, an import license, or a monopoly protected by legal entry barriers. Interest groups struggle to influence the government and capture the prize, a contest that may include lobbying, public-relations campaigns, and bribery. Unorganized segments of the public complete the rent-seeking picture, for they are the actors from whom resources are extracted to finance the prize, via taxes or higher, monopolistic prices.

Research has focused both on the consequences and the causes of rent seeking. Major social problems are commonly seen as a consequence of rent seeking, especially decreased economic output. Pioneering work by economists has shown that the political creation of economic rents, in inducing interests groups to fight for political influence, causes a dissipation of resources that is potentially more serious than the waste associated with the rent itself: Groups struggling for the prize invest time and money in the transfer of wealth rather than in the creation of wealth.

The policy implications of this research are clear. Reallocating resources from rent seeking to productive activities should result in a greater economic output, which in turn is a necessary condition for a "Pareto-superior" outcome: The benefits from the larger pie can be split between the parties so that at least one member of society is better off and no one is harmed. This line of analysis provides a theoretical justification for promarket reforms, such as those implemented in many rich and poor countries in the 1980s and 1990s. However, promarket reforms in Eastern Europe and Latin America have shown that the process of privatization and trade liberalization can generate an avalanche of rent-seeking activities among formerly protected groups rushing to control the positions abandoned by the state.

Analyses of the causes of rent seeking have traditionally classified political decisions based on their relative costs and benefits for winners and losers. Governments are more likely to create political prizes and induce rent seeking when such prizes involve (a) large benefits for a small, well-organized interest group and (b) small costs for a large number of consumers or taxpayers in the unorganized public. In such a case, the costs to each consumer or taxpayer of gathering the relevant information and organizing other individuals in the same situation into a comparable interest group outweigh the benefits of dismantling the prize. Conversely, the creation of prizes is less likely when potential losers are well-organized and must bear a high individual cost, while potential winners lack organization and must broadly share the benefits of the prize. Because the creation of prizes depends on the political configuration of winners and losers, levels of rent seeking correspondingly vary across policy realms and countries. Another argument about the causes of rent seeking conceptualizes it as a low-quality trap in a multioutcome coordination game. A further insight is that the decision to establish the political prize—not just the competition for it—is a rent-seeking activity, thus including politicians as rent seekers.

Notwithstanding the increasing separation between the disciplines of economics and sociology, it is clear that the concept of rent seeking, as developed by economists, is a specific example of what classical sociology called political capitalism, which Max Weber differentiated from rational capitalism in terms of the role of political authority in the creation of economic benefits. Weber posited an "elective affinity" between political capitalism and patrimonial institutions of rule and advanced multiple hypotheses about their origins. A dialogue between the Weberian tradition and economists' perspectives may, in the future, yield important gains in our understanding of rent seeking.

—*Sebastián L. Mazzuca*

See also Corruption; Pareto Optimality; Regulation; State Capture

Further Readings and References

Krueger, A. O. (1974). The political economy of the rent-seeking society. *American Economic Review, 64,* 291–303.

Tullock, G. (1967). The welfare costs of tariffs, monopolies and theft. *Western Economic Journal, 5,* 224–232.

Weber, M. (1981). *General economic history.* New Brunswick, NJ: Transaction.

REPRESENTATION

In modern politics, the idea of representation is commonly deployed in relation to three related processes. Representation suggests the forms through which political action can take place in the context of a principal-agent relationship, so that, for instance, a government can be said to act in the interests of its people. Representation identifies the place, or places, through which political power can be exercised responsibly and with a degree of accountability, thus enabling citizens to have both a degree of influence and some control over such power. Finally, representation determines the ways in which political voice can be embodied with a certain degree of equality and recognition; traditionally the right to vote for representatives is considered a simple means and measure of political equality.

It has long been recognized that such processes, and the related meanings of political representation, are both complex and contested. Establishing what representation, or fair representation, is often implies what we want to do with it. In this sense, the idea of representation is related to both its history and its changing applications.

The Meanings of Representation

The English words "representation" and "to represent," and their equivalents in many other modern languages, derive from the Latin: *repraesentatio* and *repraesentare.* The original meanings of these words were not political. Indeed, representation has maintained a rich variety of meanings that do not directly apply to things political. Although independent, the deployment of representation in our political vocabulary maintains, nonetheless, some important conceptual and semantic connections with uses in other vocabularies and areas, so that paying attention to them is not irrelevant.

The original Latin meanings referred to three different acts: (1) payment in ready money, (2) bringing something before the mind, and (3) an image in art. Each of these particular meanings involved ideas of "substitution," "presenting something again," and "presenting something in a different form." How these uses and their more general connotations developed into a constellation of differentiated meanings in unrelated fields is an exceedingly complex story. The crucial period is probably the time between the twelfth and the thirteenth centuries, when more abstract ideas of representation acquired currency and the Latin meanings of the term were variously conjugated with (or used to translate) more philosophically established Greek ideas such as *phantasia* (as the faculty of representation) and *mimesis,* or the process of abstraction through which particular things are related to their "representation" in the mind. The philosophical refinement of the word is important to understand some later uses in political discourse. But equally if not more important is the way in which theological and religious ideas of representation established some of the conceptual paradigms influencing the development of ideas of political representation. In particular, ideas of the vicarious presence of God and Christ through the *corpus mysticum* of the Church, the Pope, and the Cardinals proved decisive to inform political ideas of representation.

Since then, separate uses have developed, informing discourses about "artistic representation" in both figurative and symbolic contexts; practices and theories of "acting" and "impersonating" in theater; and, at some remove from political ideas, conceptions of "mental representation." Representation has also become a central concept in the overlapping discourses of politics, law, and, more recently, social research. As already noted, the connections between political and other uses are not just diachronic but also synchronic, continuously enriching and revitalizing the political understanding of representation. It is less obvious whether a metatheory of representation, encompassing all such disciplinary fields and discourses, is possible. One distinction that originated in the philosophy of "mental representation," that is, between the problem of representations (plural) and that of representation (singular), may have useful applications in politics. Robert Cummings distinguishes between problems concerning the means of cognitive representation (in the plural) and problems concerning the relationship of representation (in the singular): that is, what representations represent. A philosophical approach to political representation may have to do with a similar analytic distinction between an investigation of the institutions of representation and one of the nature of the representative relationship in politics.

The History of Political Representation

The history of political representation in the early modern age can be characterized through two different processes: the establishment of the representative nature of the state and of its institutions and the emergence of "representative government." These two processes are concerned with what Hanna Pitkin has characterized as "formal" views of representation. The former, often associated with Hobbes, is concerned with the act of authorization: Through what processes and to what extent do people transfer their personal power of action or decision to political or legal authorities? By emphasizing the act of authorization, this view of representation insists on the fact that the actions of the representative agent(s) can be ascribed to the principal, and that the represented are bound by such acts. The latter process, the one connected to the emergence of representative forms of government, is instead concerned with the reverse aspect of representation: how and to what extent the representatives can be made accountable to the represented. Therefore, the two views respectively emphasize the initial and the final stage of the representative relationship.

By extreme simplification, one can conceive these two processes as taking place sequentially: one coinciding with the emergence of ideas of sovereign and absolute power in the sixteenth and seventeenth centuries; while the other takes root through the establishment of modern parliamentary institutions and constitutional government in the eighteenth and nineteenth centuries. Institutionally, this meant a gradual passage of the claim of political representation from the more personalized institutions of the monarchy to the more diffuse institutions of modern governments. Socially, this also meant a reconfiguration of the political space, from the more fragmented and hierarchical structure typical of feudal societies to the more unitary and undifferentiated relations underlying modern commercial, and eventually industrial, societies. In the process, the relationship between territory and power was fundamentally transformed, a fact reflected in the attempts to divide the national population in roughly equal territorially based electoral constituencies. However, it is also worth noting that, at least historically, the claim to represent the people advanced by governments was first, and almost invariably, made in the name of the whole body of the legislature and not in that of individual members of it, as representatives of their own separate constituencies. Such a holistic claim directly challenged that of the monarch as the absolute sovereign. Nonetheless, it subsequently became a matter of continuous underlying tension between more strictly "political" views of representation, insisting on the priority of the common good as expressed by the whole government, and "interest-based" views, emphasizing the more discrete nature of representation as reflected by the particular attachments of individual representatives to their constituencies. This opposition became a classical *topos* of the political and constitutional thought of the eighteenth and subsequent centuries and was discussed in terms of the contrast between "free" and "imperative" mandate: Whether the representatives should act with a degree of independence and according to their own personal opinions in their role as government leaders or whether they should act like delegates, following more or less precise directions from the members of their own constituencies. The former opinion has generally prevailed in both the theory and practice of modern constitutional democracies, though the "imperative" mandate has remained an unexpressed principle of more participatory conceptions of democracy.

The Concept of Representation

From this rough historical sketch several conceptual issues have already emerged. On the one hand, representation involves asking the question of how different people and institutions come to advance their claims for governing. On the other hand, it involves the question of what they actually do when they act in such a capacity. Pitkin's distinction between formal and substantive concepts partly captures such a difference of perspectives. As we have seen, formalistic understandings and theories focus either on authorization (by the "principal") or accountability (of the "agent") as the two key factors according to which claims to political representation are assessed. Substantive theories, instead, are concerned with the way in which the relationship works. The dispute over "free" and "imperative" mandate fits here. Pitkin suggested that substantive concepts can view representation either as a way of "standing for" someone or something else or as a way of "acting for" someone or something else. "Standing for" suggests a more passive way of taking

someone's place, while "acting for" indicates a more independent way of doing the same thing. However, such simple characterization can be overdrawn.

In fact, "standing for" can take descriptive and symbolic forms, both of which allow for interpretation and independence on the representative's part. Think, for instance, of the way in which opinion polls (a form of descriptive "standing for" through statistical generalization) can be used to orient government's action. Or think of the way in which activism and political mobilization can take the form of either a symbolic "standing for" or, occasionally, "acting for" the population at large. "Acting for" can also give rise to different understandings of the relationship involved in representing another person. One can act in lieu of someone else by acting as a trustee, a deputed agent, a fiduciary (in the sense of a "free" agent), or an expert. Each of these ways of "acting for" involves different interpretations of the relationship between the representative and the represented and different expectations (and obligations) on the former.

Two things seem to be conceptually relevant here. First, at the core of political representation there is a relational element between the entity that represents and the entity that is represented. The implication is that both sides of the relationship have an "agency" role, both contributing—through their actions, expectations, and interpretations of their respective roles—to determine the nature of the relationship itself. Second, the act of political representation is a "constructed" one, being dependent on both contextual and ideological beliefs. Such socially constructed aspect of representation is evident in all discussions about what is represented in the political process: people, interests, values, characteristics, or any other element of a group.

More specifically, when one looks at the mechanisms of electoral representation as one of the key aspects of modern political representation, it is possible to distinguish between two conceptions of it. One focuses on the more procedural- and input-related processes of electoral representation; that is, the way in which selection processes operate fairly by either reproducing or mirroring the relevant features of the electorate. The other, instead, looks at the output element of the selection process and the way in which the process of representation achieves its end of good and responsive government. This difference of perspectives underlies, for instance, disputes over the merits and failures of proportional versus majoritarian electoral systems, or assessments on the relationship between "descriptive" and "substantive" aspects for the representation of minorities or of other traditionally disadvantaged groups in society.

Democratic Representation and Its Transformations

At the core of the different concepts of representation there is a fundamental ambiguity, in so far as "representation" makes present what in fact is absent. In political discourse, such an ambiguity has come to the fore as "representative government" and "democracy," which have increasingly been treated as synonymous. In the early modern period, arguments in favor of representative government were often directed against a classical conception of direct, participatory democracy, and the former was promoted as a way of tempering the presumed excesses of growing social and political egalitarianism. The practice of democratic government has relied on various forms of representation as a way of introducing aristocratic and elitist components in the fabric of modern democracy. However, with the emergence of mass democracy, a number of representative institutions, such as large popular parties and class-based organizations, have offered opportunities for broadening political and democratic participation. The practice of democratic representation should therefore be seen as a two-faced relationship, amenable as much to exclude from as to include people in politics. This tension between presence and absence in representation is indicative of some more general tensions in modern democracy, as this often stands in between the pitfalls of populism and elitism.

The close connection between the idea of representative government and that of democracy has informed much of the research on modern political representation. The discussion of electoral systems and of the way in which the elected legislators relate to their own constituencies have taken priority, though it has become increasingly evident that political representation in democracies is a rather more complex process, involving more than the one-to-one relationship between legislators and their electors. The most obvious transformation has been the increasing dominance of political parties in both the electoral process and the business of government. Along similar lines, there has been the development of "private interest government," through the proliferation of a neocorporativist structure of informal and semi-informal institutions around the legislative and the executive powers, guaranteeing a more diffuse (though often power-sensitive) representation of interests.

More generally, political representation in modern democracies is not exclusively limited to the direct relationship between citizens and their legislators because the division and balance of power characterizing constitutional democracies give different, and occasionally conflicting, claims of representation to a variety of institutional figures. This is evident in presidential or federal systems, for instance, which provide multiform grounds for representation. In addition, public spheres and civil society organizations perform an important role in the formation and channeling of public opinion so that mechanisms of political representation are diffuse throughout the sociopolitical system rather than exclusively concentrated in the formal relationships between the electors and their representatives.

From a more theoretical perspective, but also in terms of institutional change, the last twenty years have been characterized by the debate on "quotas" and on whether more descriptive and mirroring, rather than generally promissory, forms of political representation may redress entrenched forms of bias and discrimination in the political process (affecting particularly women, but also ethnic minorities), thus reestablishing some kind of political equality. This has reopened the discussion on what "to represent" means and on territorial versus other bases of institutional representation.

Representation and Governance

The weakening of the "territorial" dimension as the primary basis for democratic representation has become evident with the emergence of discourses of governance, signaling the crisis of the paradigms of national sovereignty and governmental control over the decision-making process. Contemporary democracies have evolved in ways that further undermine the adequacy of the standard model of political representation based on the formal relationship of authorization and accountability established between the representatives and their constituency. The emergence of transnational decision-making arenas, where new international and global players operate, tends to escape the reach of the nation-state and its representative institutions. Decision making increasingly requires a specialized degree of knowledge and expertise, while decisions in modern regimes of governance have greater externalities, which are difficult to determine in advance.

These developments have produced more complex practices of representation and brought in new "agents" of political representation both at national and international levels. There has also been a diffusion of more informal structures and opportunities for democratic representation and influence. This development partly reflects the diminishing role of formal political structures in social decision making and also the increasing diversification of the forms of association in modern societies.

As the new institutions of governance change the nature of decision making in politics, the three main processes characterizing democratic representation come into question. The principal-agent relationship is too simplified to provide an account of the democratic dynamic. There is no easy way in which to fix the place(s) where government can be seen to operate responsibly. Finally, there is no longer a single or simple way in which the people can be given voice. In such circumstances, the discourse of political and democratic representation is wide open once again.

—*Dario Castiglione*

See also Accountability; Elections; Governance; Legislature; Representative Democracy

Further Readings and References

Manin, B. (1997). *The principles of representative government.* Cambridge, UK: Cambridge University Press.
Mansbridge, J. (2003). Rethinking representation. *American Political Science Review, 97,* 515–528.
Philips, A. (1995). *The politics of presence.* Oxford, UK: Oxford University Press.
Pitkin, H. (1967). *The concept of representation.* Berkeley: University of California Press.
Plotke, D. (1997). Representation is democracy. *Constellations, 4*(1), 19–34.
Williams, M. S. (1998). *Voice, trust, and memory: Marginalized groups and the failings of liberal representation.* Princeton, NJ: Princeton University Press.
Young, I. M. (2000). *Inclusion and democracy.* Oxford, UK: Oxford University Press.

REPRESENTATIVE DEMOCRACY

Democracy means rule by the demos—or people—as opposed to rule by the one (monarchy), rule by the few (oligarchy, aristocracy), or by the skilled (technocracy, meritocracy). The democratic principle is that individuals have the right to control their own lives. Any other form resulting in rule by the few over the many requires some degree of oppression.

Direct democracy involves citizens participating directly and equally in collective decisions. However, large numbers of people involved in decision making is cumbersome, if not impossible. Likewise the complexity of modern government is beyond the reach of most citizens. Representative democracy resolves the problems of size and expertise.

The challenge for representative democracy is to construct a participative policy process that integrates the diverse preferences of the population. One perspective of representation asserts that representatives must "mirror" the preferences of citizens. An alternative perspective (sometimes known as "agency theory") is that elected representatives make decisions in the "best" interest of the collective, regardless of citizen preferences. Government structures and institutions may support either perspective.

Representation is more challenging with a diverse citizenry. A homogenous group that shares interests, preferences, and beliefs may be represented by a small number of like-minded people. A diverse group must have a way to integrate a variety of perspectives if its decision making is to be representative.

Institutional structures affect representation. They can favor elites, organized groups, large parties, and status quo powers, or they can encourage minority representation and new power configurations. This entry explores how governments may be structured to achieve representative democracy. It examines government structure, election foundations, representative selection systems, terms of office, legislative decision rules, and other factors affecting representation.

Government Structure

In the simplest form of representational government, one person makes decisions for the group. This format may be used by small groups or organizations. However, most groups are reluctant to place absolute power in the hands of a single person. Historically, representative government evolved from groups of aristocrats balancing royal power. These representatives of the people, initially identified by birth and class, were later selected by election from an ever-broadening citizen base. How democratic representation is derived involves a complex variety of factors.

Representation is affected by the relationship between the three core governmental functions of executive, legislative, and judicial authority. These functions can be combined or fragmented in a variety of ways. Concentrated power is more time efficient. Fragmented power limits potential abuse by requiring wider agreement to take action. Election structures concentrate or fragment governing power in several ways.

Parliamentary System

In parliamentary structures, the executive and legislative functions are combined in a representative assembly. The union of these functions results in ease of governability because of less opportunity for opposition. The same institution makes and directs implementation of public policies.

Presidential System

The presidential structure of government separates the executive and legislative functions. This separation limits concentration of power while increasing potential for disputes and delays. The president is normally elected by all citizens (although the position may be appointed by the legislature), and thus represents the entire country, while members of the legislature represent their party or district.

While the legislative function is to set policy, within the presidential form of government this function is further divided between the president and the legislature. A constitution, laws, or legal tradition articulate this division of power. Decisions made by a representative of the whole are less responsive to preferences of individual districts.

Unicameral Versus Bicameral Legislatures

The legislative function may be performed by one (unicameral) or more assemblies, but normally not more than two (bicameral). A bicameral structure divides legislative power, increasing possibilities for representation while decreasing time efficiency. Citizen groups have more legislators available to represent them, but the division of power between the two legislative houses makes agreement more difficult. The bicameral structure may be used to represent different stakeholders or to affect the distance between the legislator and the represented.

Federal or Unitary Structures

The larger the organization or country, the more difficult it is for the people at the administrative center to comprehend the variety of factors involved in local governance. Most recognize that local administrators need to be able to evaluate and act upon local circumstances. In unitary governance this takes place within an undivided organizational structure. There may be some decentralization of power, but ultimately the lines of authority flow uninterrupted from the central executive power to the smallest local jurisdictions.

A federal structure separates power between central and regional authorities. While local discretion may be allowed in unitary structures, a federal division ensures that separation. Federal structures fragment power. They allow for the expression of regional preferences while often limiting the consistency and equality of public policy. Federal structures can also address concerns of minority groups that feel overwhelmed by the will of the majority. Providing minority groups with semiautonomous regional governments often satisfies their need to be represented.

Election Foundations

At the center of representative democracy is the selection of representatives that carry out the legislative, executive, and judicial functions. Their selection shapes the distribution of power, and thus "representativeness." Democratic representation is influenced by voter eligibility, election logistics, representative qualifications, candidate selection, reserved seats, and campaign rules.

Voter Eligibility

Democracy is rule by the people, but the issue of which people or how many people is unspecified. "The people" must be specified before we can turn to the issue of how to represent them in governance structures. There are always limits and qualifying characteristics of who is considered part of "the people." There are differences of opinion on who is capable and who "deserves" to participate.

Every collective grouping specifies the characteristics of their membership. They may be geographical or based on common characteristics or practices (religion, ethnicity, vocation, etc.). Membership in the group often does not guarantee participation in collective decision making. There may be residence or longevity requirements. Participation may require tests of literacy, knowledge, or language ability. There may be limitations based on sex, race, religion, age, and mental or social status. And participation rights may be withdrawn by the collective for violation of rules or determination of incompetence. Democracy, it turns out, is a continuum rather than an absolute.

Election Logistics

The convenience of voting affects who is able and willing to participate in the process. Location of voting sites, dates and hours of balloting, time required to vote, ballot complexity, and voter registration procedures significantly affect who can and will vote, regardless of

other structural elements. Control of election logistics often favors status quo power structures.

Representative Qualifications

Electoral structures also limit who can be an elected representative. One common criteria requires representatives to be eligible voters. Another requires candidates to be residents of the jurisdiction they aspire to represent. Restrictions intend to increase the quality of representation, but any restriction limits citizen choice, perhaps decreasing representativeness.

Candidate Selection

Representativeness is also affected by the selection of candidates. Democracy depends on an underlying freedom of association. Candidate selection must be determined by independent political associations (parties) that identify and support candidates. While unrestricted nominations make a ballot cumbersome and difficult to implement, limits on the ability of groups to place nominees on the ballot supports status quo power structures and impedes democracy.

Reserved Seats

The geographic base of most electoral systems limits representation of interests that are small or scattered. Reservation of seats or offices may represent groups that would not otherwise receive representation. Reserved seats may be based on ethnicity, religion, sex, language, or any other criteria. The number of seats reserved is often based on the proportion of that group in the larger population. Reservation structures assume group interests are not otherwise represented and tend to encourage group solidarity.

Campaign Rules

Democracy can also be subverted by limiting or controlling information dissemination to voters. Campaign or media restrictions can favor one group over another. When access to voters is determined by financial resources, wealthier interests will have an unequal advantage, decreasing fair representation and supporting status quo power structures. Campaign finance laws and mandated media access may increase the quality of representation.

Representative Selection System

Representative democracy is achieved by the selection of representatives. Rules and regulations governing selection have a significant effect on the quality of representation. A variety of complex electoral systems have been created to attempt achievement of fair, equal, and effective representation. These include majority and plurality systems, proportional systems, and district design.

Majority and Plurality Systems

The most basic element of election is how many votes are required to select a representative. Increasing the percentage requirement (threshold) increases those who are represented, but also increases the difficulty in achieving that percentage. Consensus may be achieved in small organizations but becomes impractical as size increases. Requiring two-thirds, three-fourths, or any large percentage increases the representational quality of the elected, but may be difficult to achieve. Election may be achieved by a simple plurality (also known as "first-past-the-post"), meaning more votes than any other candidate. Such an outcome is the easiest to achieve but may lead to a minority of voters controlling one hundred percent of the legislative seats.

If a specified percentage of the vote (threshold) is required, the system must determine what happens if no candidate reaches that threshold. In single member districts, a runoff election is often required between the top candidates.

Runoff elections are costly and turnout is often so low that the winner may receive fewer votes than in the first election. One solution is preferential voting, sometimes called "instant runoff," where voters identify a second (and perhaps third) choice of candidates. If no candidate attains a majority, the votes of the bottom candidate are redistributed according to voters' second choice. This continues until one candidate attains a majority. In such a system, a vote for a minority candidate is never "wasted," thus encouraging minority parties. Single member districts determined by plurality encourage fewer, more dominant parties.

A further modification of this process is found in the electoral college system used in the United States. In this indirect model, citizens select electors from their state who, in turn, vote for the president. The number of electors is a function of the population plus two additional electors for each state, regardless of size (integrating the rural bias of the Senate). The winner must achieve a majority of the electoral votes, which may not be a majority of the popular vote. Indirect voting tends to favor status quo power structures.

Proportional Systems

Proportional electoral systems are the most common method to ensure representation of a broader range of the citizenry. The basic intent is that percentage of votes received equals voting power in the legislature. Such results may be accomplished by voting for parties in addition to, or in place of, voting for individuals.

Representatives are elected from party lists in proportion to the votes received by that party. Lists established by the party strengthen the power of the parties who determine list order. An alternative format allows citizens to select individuals as well as parties. This format deemphasizes the power of the party, but the ballot may become complex. Proportional representation may also be achieved through district magnitude.

Individuals Versus Parties

Whether citizens vote for individuals or parties has a significant effect on representational outcomes. Voting for parties tends to emphasize policies and group identity. Voting for individuals focuses on the personal characteristics of legislators. Voting for parties increases party unity, while voting for individuals limits party discipline and allows more independence of representatives. When legislators are selected by district, rather than a national list, they are more obligated to their respective jurisdiction and are more prone to pursue policies beneficial to their district over concerns of the party or country as a whole.

District Design

District Size

District size can refer to either geographic or demographic divisions. If representation is established by jurisdiction, districts with smaller numbers of people may achieve larger representation per capita. The United States changes federal representative districts after every ten year census to ensure that each district contains a similar number of people. However, the unchanging senatorial districts (states) provide unequal representation for rural populations.

There may also be "shape" restrictions, requiring districts to be of a somewhat symmetrical shape. Without such restrictions, districts may be gerrymandered, or drawn to favor the dominant party.

District Magnitude

District magnitude refers to the number of elected people representing a district. Increasing the number of representatives from a district provides an opportunity for more citizens to select a "winner." For example, a district with three representatives may elect the top three individual vote getters. That provides more citizens with a chosen representative, but also gives citizens who select the less-popular candidate greater voice in the legislature. The top candidate may represent fifty percent of citizens, while the third candidate may represent fifteen percent of citizens, yet both are elected. A variety of formulas for seat determination helps balance this disparity, including party list and preferential balloting, where voters rank their choices.

The United States primarily uses a single district magnitude for national elections, while senatorial districts have a magnitude of two staggered elections, which eliminates any equalizing impact. However, local jurisdictions, such as city councils and school boards, often include district magnitudes of more than one representative, increasing opportunities for representation. Combination systems occur where some candidates represent districts and other "at large" candidates represent the entire jurisdiction. These systems try to balance the positive goal of local representation against the negative result of partisanship and divisiveness.

Multiple Votes

Another variable is the number of votes each citizen may cast. When district magnitude is one, each citizen has a single vote. However, when district magnitude is greater than one, multiple votes may be allowed. Multiple votes for each citizen provide greater opportunities for small groups of citizens to elect the representative of their choice. If the goal of a system is to provide minority groups with representation, cumulative voting may be allowed, giving citizens the right to cast all their votes for a single candidate.

Terms of Office

How long a representative serves has a significant impact on electoral systems. Terms of office range from a single year to life. Variations include life with age limits or limits on the number of terms a representative may serve. Debate about the role of representatives often revolves around whether their votes should directly mirror the changing mood of the electorate or whether elected representatives should make their own judgments about the best interests of citizens. The electoral structure determines the incentives for these alternatives. Representatives with shorter terms (and a desire to be reelected) will continually try to represent their constituents' preferences. Those with longer terms of office have more freedom to deviate from current (and possibly temporary) citizen preferences. The electoral advantages possessed by incumbent representatives can be offset by establishing term limits. Term limits restrict citizen preferences, but tacitly acknowledge that such preferences may be influenced by structural advantages of incumbents.

Staggered Terms

Terms of legislators may expire at the same or different times. In the U.S. House of Representatives, all legislators must run for office every two years. The effect is that the will of the people at any one moment is emphasized. In the U.S. Senate, legislators have six-year terms with one-third expiring every two years. Staggering terms reduce the immediate impact of public preference.

Recall Elections

While a term may be for a particular length of time, electoral structures may allow citizens the option of reversing their choice before the next election. Special recall elections may be possible to end the term of office of the incumbent representative. The process to institute a recall election may be easy or difficult. The effect of the recall option is similar to shorter terms of office. Legislators will be more concerned with the day-to-day preferences of citizens.

Parliamentary No Confidence

In parliamentary systems, a majority of the legislators may pass a "vote of no confidence" in the government, cutting short the term of office and forcing elections. The possibility of no-confidence votes is more likely in multiparty systems, where the ruling party has to establish coalitions with minority parties. This system may keep parties from taking extreme positions (defined as different from the majority views), because a majority of votes of parliament is required to stay in power.

Prime Minister Call for Elections

In most parliamentary systems, the prime minister may unilaterally call for elections at any time. This right strengthens the party in power because they calculate when to call elections based on their own popularity.

Other Factors Affecting Representation

While discussions of representation often focus on how to elect legislative representatives, a variety of other structures and systems affect representation, including legislative scope of power, legislative rules, the judiciary, group preferences, policy implementation structures, and the underlying economic and social systems.

Legislative Scope of Power

Representatives may be democratically elected, but the issues they can address may be limited. There may be divisions of power between levels of government (federalism). There may also be overarching institutions that limit the scope of legislative power. When legislatures are limited, other institutions will fill the gap. Religious, commercial, social, or corporate entities make up the status quo power structure of a community and tend to fill any power vacuum not undertaken by the legislative body.

Legislative Rules

The selection of representatives is a central element of representative governance, but the decision-making rules of the legislative body can offset the balancing effect of election systems. The greater the percentage of votes required to pass legislation, the more broad the representation required, but the less likely legislation will pass.

Legislative bodies often define their own procedural rules. While the electoral structure may elect minority groups, their power will be limited if the majority controls decisions within the legislative body. To balance this possible tyranny of the majority, governments may have constitutional protections for minority groups and individuals that cannot be changed without broad-based support.

Judiciary

Governance representation is also reflected in the judiciary. While judges are charged with acting impartially, they also represent their own particular ideological interpretation of law and policy that may or may not be representative of the preferences of citizens.

The selection of judges may be accomplished through an electoral process involving all the previously described electoral criteria. Alternatively, judges may be appointed by elected officials. Their term of office, as for all elected officials, may range from a short period of time to life and have similar representational effects.

A hybrid variation is found in the so-called Missouri Plan for selecting judges in some states of the United States. Judges are appointed by the governor and subsequently stand for noncompetitive, "approval" election every set number of years.

Special Judicial Districts

Decisions on issues of so-called family law (e.g., marriages, divorces, adoptions, inheritances, child custody) may be determined by religious or ethnic courts, whose jurisdiction is not geographical, but based on group membership. Citizens may or may not have a choice of courts.

Group Preferences

Rules may be established to provide preferential treatment of specified groups, as a reward, or as compensation for inequalities. Besides the reservation of legislative seats previously mentioned, preferences may be established for employment in public positions, for educational or economic opportunities. Such opportunities seek to increase representation of the specified groups that are the social and economic makeup of society.

Policy Implementation Structures

The ultimate impact of policy making is felt through policy implementation. Because of this, control of the civil service is a key determinant of representative democracy. Unelected public managers are not influenced by citizens in the same way as elected representatives, although they may be subject to indirect influence of citizens through the legislative and judicial branches of government. Representation may be structured into the implementation of government policies through institutions of citizen participation and deliberative democracy. The existence or lack of such institutions influences representativeness. The composition of the civil service may or may not reflect the demographics of the population. Quotas,

preferences, and diversity efforts in public employment may increase its representativeness.

Economic and Social Systems

The underlying economic and social systems of a society may be the determining factor controlling equality of representation. Many decisions affecting the collective lives of citizens are not made by governmental institutions, but by economic and social power structures. Any evaluation of the representativeness of a democracy must include analysis of the equality and representativeness of these underlying systems.

Conclusion

Representative democracy reflects citizen preferences and tolerances for chaos, security, freedom, affluence, and equality. Transformation of citizen preferences into public policy is a complex process, and the degree of representativeness is influenced by a wide variety of characteristics, including government structure, electoral rules, policy implementation systems, and underlying social institutions. Any one of these constituent pieces has the potential to shape, bend, or co-opt the policy process, concentrating power and reducing democratic representation.

—Jonathan F. Anderson

See also Collaborative Governance; Deliberative Democracy; Democratic Theory; Elections; Representation; Social Democracy

Further Readings and References

Blaustein, A., & Flanz, G. (1971). *Constitutions of the countries of the world: A series of updated texts, constitutional chronologies and annotated bibliographies.* Dobbs Ferry, NY: Oceana.

Bogdanor, V., & Butler, D. (1983). *Democracy and elections: Electoral systems and their political consequences.* New York: Cambridge University Press.

Dahl, R. (1961). *Who governs? Democracy and power in an American city.* New Haven, CT: Yale University Press.

Farrell, D. (2001). *Electoral systems: A comparative introduction.* New York: St. Martin's.

Grofman, B., & Lijphart, A. (Eds.). (1986). *Electoral laws and their political consequences.* New York: Agathon Press.

Inter-Parliamentary Union. (1993). *Electoral systems: A world-wide comparative study.* Geneva, Switzerland: Author.

Lijphart, A. (1984). *Democracies: Patterns of majoritarian and consensus government in 21 countries.* New Haven, CT: Yale University Press.

Lijphart, A. (1999). *Patterns of democracy: Government forms and performance in 36 countries.* New Haven, CT: Yale University Press.

Rae, D. (1967). *The political consequences of electoral laws.* New Haven, CT: Yale University Press.

Reynolds, A. (2002). *The architecture of democracy: Constitutional design, conflict management, and democracy.* New York: Oxford University Press.

Rule, W., & Zimmerman, J. (Eds.). (1994). *Electoral systems in comparative perspective: Their impact on women and minorities.* Westport, CT: Greenwood.

REPUBLICANISM

See CIVIC REPUBLICANISM

RESEARCH AND DEVELOPMENT

Research and development (R&D) refers to the process of discovering new knowledge about natural and social reality. It is usually related to the application of such knowledge to create new and improved products, processes, and services that fill market needs or improve efficiency and profitability of a production process. Along with human capital accumulation, R&D activity is considered to be a primary determinant of economic growth.

The complexity of research operation has increased during the last couple of decades. Consequently, the length of time to develop an innovation and the costs of undertaking R&D have risen dramatically. Simultaneously, the life span of new innovations has significantly shortened and the rate of technological change has sped up.

In the conventional understanding of R&D as a product development, three phases can be identified in this complex process. The first phase is concerned with applied science or marketing research. Here, the basic need is for access to the basic sources of science and marketing information. The second phase is product design and development. This usually requires large-scale teamwork because it needs a large supply of skilled labor. The third phase is concerned with adjusting product to a particular consumer. This phase requires contact with the user of the innovation.

From the point of view of a position of a locality in the international division of labor, it is crucial to keep or attract R&D activities for local economic development. From the point of view of mobile capital, the major locational criteria for the R&D activities are the availability of highly skilled scientists and engineers, access to the sources of basic scientific and technical developments (usually universities and private research laboratories), and an appropriate infrastructure. So far, R&D has tended to be concentrated in the developed countries, often in a firm's parent country.

With the rise of the so-called knowledge-based economy, there is a new emphasis on the importance of R&D for national competitiveness. Thus, states transform their R&D facilities at the universities to meet the perceived needs of businesses. They engage in different forms of partnership with businesses, which not only increases innovation potential of local capital but also embeds it in the locality, making its departure less likely. However, this may raise serious concerns about the role of the university system in a society, as its priorities are likely to be determined less by the long-term, public interest (e.g., sustainable-development research) than by short-term, private, profit-oriented preferences.

—*Jan Drahokoupil*

See also Competitiveness; Human Capital; Human Capital Mobility; International Division of Labor; Science

Further Readings and References

Jessop, B. (2000). The state and the contradictions of the knowledge-driven economy. In J. R. Bryson, P. W. Daniels, N. D. Henry & J. Pollard (Eds.), *Knowledge, space, economy* (pp. 63–78). London: Routledge.

Pearce, R. D. (1997). *Global competition and technology: Essays in the creation and application of knowledge by multinationals*. Houndmills, UK, and New York: Palgrave Macmillan.

RESOURCE DEPENDENCY THEORY

Resource dependency theory is based on the principle that an organization must engage in transactions with other actors and organizations in its environment in order to acquire resources. While transactions between organizational and environmental actors are advantageous, they also create dependencies that are not. The focus of the theory is on the relationship between resource acquisition and its related organizational behaviors. Resources the organization needs may be scarce, not always readily obtainable, or under the control of noncooperative actors. The resulting unequal exchange generates differences in power, authority, and access to further resources. This leads to a rise in dependencies. To avoid dependencies, organizations develop strategies (as well as internal structures) that will enhance their bargaining position in resource-related transactions. Such strategies include taking political action, increasing the scale of organizational operations, diversification, and developing interorganizational linkages. Strategies, like diversifying product lines, lessen an organization's dependence on other actors and improve its power and leverage.

Dependencies between organizations shift power, influence, and sometimes even administrative control to external agents. As the dynamics of power relationships between organizations change, they adjust their strategies to meet those changes. One of the assumptions of resource dependency theory is that uncertainty clouds an organization's control of resources and makes its choice of dependence-lessening strategies imperative. As environmental uncertainty and environmental dependencies increase, the need for external linkages increases. For example, declining profits may lead to expanding business activity through diversification and strategic alliances with other companies.

Research using resource dependency theory seeks to observe organizational adaptations to dependencies.

Adaptation consists in aligning internal organizational elements with environmental pressures. By internalizing responses for managing dependent relationships, an organization enhances its performance. Organizations also adapt by attempting to alter their environments. This contrasts sharply with classic organizations' perspectives in which firms are seen as closed systems. Closed systems frameworks argue that rational use of resources, personal motivation, and individual capabilities determine organizational success, while other actors in the environment figure minimally. In open systems frameworks, the environment, consisting of other organizations, institutions, professions, and the state, predominates. An organization will be effective insofar as it correctly reads the environment and adjusts its responses to those contingencies.

There are two main strategies for protecting an organization from environmental uncertainty. The first tactic is to protect an organization's technical core from the kinds of environmental dependencies that threaten to disrupt its central activities. These buffering strategies provide a measure of coordination and control over resources that otherwise create greater dependence on external actors. Buffering is accomplished by coding, stockpiling, leveling, forecasting, and adjusting the scale of operations. Buffering strategies aimed at reducing environmental uncertainty involve coding all inputs as appropriate or not, or stockpiling materials. Coding inputs as appropriate or not is not limited to industrial or even for-profit enterprises. Human service agencies and hospitals guarantee organizational control by coding clients and patients into appropriate categories. Stockpiling allows organizations to collect and retain input materials in order to guard against gaps in supply as well as the instability of price fluctuations. Forecasting reduces uncertainty by using statistical techniques to anticipate changes and fluctuations in inputs and outputs. Statistical models of some sophistication are used to forecast changes in the environment. Last, large size translates into the power to dominate production, influence prices, and control decision making throughout the system.

The second adaptive tactic involves trying to manipulate other organizations and actors in the environment through bridging or boundary-spanning strategies. While buffering strategies protect the technical purposes of the organization, bridging strategies are oriented toward protecting the entire organization. To that end, an organization creates linkages with exchange partners, competitors, and regulators. Because organizations are interdependent, bridging strategies involve maintaining control over organizational boundaries. Bridging strategies increase coordination between organizations by balancing out inequalities of power or by reducing other uncertainties in the environment, such as competition. Bridging encompasses bargaining, contracting, cooptation, hierarchical contracting, joint ventures, strategic alliances, mergers, the creation of associations, and political action linked to the state.

Bargaining, contracting, and hierarchical contracting involve negotiating with external actors, such as suppliers and buyers. Hierarchical contracting stipulates a series of rights and mechanisms for resolving disputes. Nonetheless, it undermines the autonomy of some of the contracting parties. Cooptation is a coordinating strategy that includes external actors in the decision-making structure of the organization, often in the form of board memberships, liaison roles, and interorganizational brokers. Nonprofits, for instance, usually have interlocking directorates with individuals on different boards. This increases access to resources, reduces uncertainty, and enhances legitimacy. Strategic alliances are another way in which organizations seek to control their environments. These involve agreements to share information and activities but fall short of redesigning the organization. Joint ventures and mergers are also excellent strategies for stabilizing environmental uncertainty. Mergers are the most dramatic form of strategic intervention in the organizational environment. There are several types of mergers: vertical, horizontal, and diversification. Vertical mergers assimilate needed resources in relation to production, horizontal mergers acquire competitors, and diversification involves combining types of diverse enterprises. Associations allow organizations to work in concert in the form of coalitions, leagues, cartels, and coordinating councils. These structures constitute sector governance systems. Last, organizations may seek to exert their influence on government at the federal, state, or local level. Access to the political and legal system in its various forms is one of the most potent means for eliminating competition, establishing favorable legislation, and lessening environmental dependencies.

—*Matthew E. Archibald*

See also Interorganizational Coordination; Organizational Structure; Organization Theory; Structural Contingency Theory

Further Readings and References

Aldrich, H. E., & Pfeffer, J. (1976). Environments of organizations. *Annual Review of Sociology, 2,* 79–105.

Pfeffer, J., & Salancik, G. R. (1978). *The external control of organizations.* New York: Harper & Row.

Scott, W. R. (2003). *Organizations: Rational, natural and open systems* (5th ed.). Thousand Oaks, CA: Sage.

Thompson, J. D. (1967). *Organizations in action.* New York: McGraw-Hill.

Zald, M. N. (1970). Political economy: A framework for comparative analysis. In M. N. Zald (Ed.), *Power in organizations* (pp. 221–261). Nashville, TN: Vanderbilt University Press.

RESPONSIBILITY

Responsibility is an important concept for governance because it requires individuals and institutions to be answerable for their actions both in the public domain (to specific political authorities) and in the private domain (to themselves and their families). In politics, a balance had to be struck between responsibility, on one hand, and, on the other hand, the notion of individual or collective rights, that is, political and institutional arrangements or particular goods and opportunities that are guaranteed protection by the law, whether domestic or international. Consequently, major political debates have tended to focus upon the identification of the political, moral, and legal principles upon which individual and collective responsibility and rights should be based; the balance that should be drawn between those rights and responsibilities; the extent to which they should be exercised individually or collectively; and whether they should be exercised in the public domain of the state and politics or in the private domain of the market and the family.

Political responsibility has been particularly salient in the English model of parliamentary government. The convention of ministerial responsibility has required individual Cabinet ministers to be answerable to the Westminster Parliament for the actions of all those working within their ministry, even when errors of judgment, conduct, or policy implementation have occurred without the minister's express knowledge. At the same time, under the convention of collective Cabinet responsibility, individual Cabinet ministers have been expected to support the collectively agreed upon policy of the government, even where they have found themselves dissenting from that policy. Only rarely, such as on issues of political or moral conscience (for example, the death penalty and abortion, or major constitutional issues, notably the 1975 referendum on the terms of the United Kingdom's membership of the European Economic Community) has this convention been suspended.

During the 1980s, a series of major environmental catastrophes involving transnational corporations (TNCs) (notably the poisonous gas leak from the Union Carbide Corporation plant at Bhopal, India, in December 1984, and the major spillage from the *Exxon Valdez* oil tanker in Prince William Sound, Alaska, in March 1989) led to increasing demands for corporations to both behave responsibly and be held accountable for their actions. Critics held that there was an essential conflict of interest between the desire of corporations to maximize their profits, in the interests of their shareholders, and the need to behave in an ethical manner to address societal interests. Such demands for the exercise of corporate social responsibility (CSR) were given renewed impetus during 2002, with the respective filing for bankruptcy of Enron, America's seventh largest corporation, and WorldCom, the subject of the largest accountancy fraud in American corporate history. However, the debate over how best to ensure CSR remains unresolved between the advocates of a voluntary approach, based upon corporate self-regulation, and those demanding that corporate responsibility be given a statutory legal framework.

—*Simon Lee*

See also Accountability

Further Readings and References

Paul, F. P., Miller, D., Jr., & Paul, J. (Eds.). (1999). *Responsibility*. Cambridge, UK: University of Cambridge Press.

REVEALED PREFERENCE

A decisionmaker is said to weakly prefer Brie to Camembert if he or she likes the first cheese either more than or just as much as the second. Such a preference is, moreover, said to be revealed whenever the decisionmaker chooses Brie from a menu of options containing both of the cheeses in question. The logic behind this terminology is straightforward: An agent that views Camembert as superior to Brie will never choose the latter when the former is available, and therefore any observed choice of Brie in the presence of Camembert implies a weak preference in the opposite direction.

The concept of revealed preference grew out of the work of neoclassical economists. These neoclassical economists and their contemporaries showed that the standard practice of modeling economic agents as maximizers of numerical "utility" functions did not depend for its validity on any of a variety of questionable auxiliary assumptions about the form of the functions being maximized (such as additive separability in the variables upon which they depend). However, as this independence came to be understood, the logical strength and psychological content of the utility maximization hypothesis became increasingly unclear. On the one hand, had this hypothesis been reduced to a tautology, excluding no logical possibilities and thus capable of "explaining" any pattern of behavior? And on the other, did the new, neoclassical notion of utility continue to reflect the view of human decision making originally adopted by the founders of the utilitarian school?

Working in the context of consumer demand theory, Paul Samuelson sought to identify the "refutable implications" of utility maximization for behavior in market environments. In response to the first question previously listed, he showed that—far from being tautological—this hypothesis has definite implications that can be expressed as a prohibition against the preferences revealed by the decisionmaker's actions coming into conflict with each other. With regard to the second question, Samuelson's contribution made clear that in psychological terms, agents in economic models are typically endowed with both the well-integrated personalities and the substantial cognitive resources needed to behave consistently across different choice problems. Indeed, it is this internal consistency of the decisionmaker's behavior, rather than any assumption about the tastes or values lying behind it, that has come to be seen as the essence of the utility maximization hypothesis.

While Samuelson's definition of a revealed preference was phrased in terms of choices among consumption bundles in a market setting, the idea that opinions or other mental states can be deduced from observed behavior applies much more generally. For example, in the theory of decision making under uncertainty, an agent's assessments of the relative likelihoods of different events (such as a particular company going bankrupt within the next year or a particular political party winning a majority in the next national election) are revealed by his or her choices among bets contingent on the unknown information.

—*Christopher J. Tyson*

See also Decision Making; Optimal Decision Making; Rational Choice Theory

Further Readings and References

Samuelson, P. A. (1938). A note on the pure theory of consumer's behaviour. *Economica*, New Series, *5*, 61–71.
Samuelson, P. A. (1965). *Foundations of economic analysis.* New York: Atheneum.

RISK

In recent years, risk has become a topic of intellectual, political, and social interest. Rarely does a day pass without some coverage of risk issues by the mass media (e.g., Avian flu, mad cow disease, SARS, terrorism). By their very nature these issues are complex and contentious and spawn questions on how risks should be managed or governed. Because risks are ubiquitous, risk governance can be defined as a series of processes for minimizing the probability of exposure to a hazard and the degree of adverse outcomes flowing from such exposure. Within the context of environmental and human health risks, such governance considerations focus on the interface of science and policy, and ultimately involve specifying the design of this interface so as to increase accountability, transparency, strategic vision, participation, and equity. These principles of good governance are essential when dealing with risk issues because risks are intertwined with problems of governance.

Throughout history, risks have presented a challenge to human survival while simultaneously presenting opportunities. A changing environment, the threat of epidemics and pandemics, famine, and human-made threats such as war have invariably presented risks to both individual and collective survival. The formulation of risk-based policy is an intricate process that reveals the influence of multiple actors, abiding societal conditions, conceptual paradigms that predominate in the minds of the public and elites alike, estimates of the resources available, and the perceived costs and benefits of suggested courses of action.

Risk is often defined as the probability of adverse outcomes multiplied by consequences. Technically, the word "risk" refers to situations in which a decision is made whose consequences depend on the outcome of future events having known probabilities. For example, the decision to build or relicense a civilian nuclear power plant involves comparing the risks and benefits associated with this energy source to other sources (e.g., coal, hydroelectric, natural gas, wind) by assessing the veracity of certain assumptions about future impacts on human health, environment, energy security, and so forth. As such, risk is not simply equivalent to hazard, but rather, the possible damage that may result from one's decisions or indecisions. In short, the type, magnitude, and distribution of risks borne by industrialized societies are determined by regulations and the effectiveness of their implementation and enforcement.

In seeking to overcome or manage such risks, democratic societies are obliged to preserve certain fundamental values, such as a citizen's right to comprehend and to take part in governmental decision making. Since risk evaluation is essentially a social process, and all risk assessments are value laden, risks must be managed with recognition that a science-alone approach is incomplete because it ignores many of the ethical and social issues that accompany new technologies. Developments in stem cell technology, human cloning, and xenotransplantation demonstrate the pressing need for a more-inclusive approach to governing risk in an open and transparent manner. Moreover, decision making without a requirement of public participation not only encourages the capture of government agencies by business interests, but also promotes a relatively uncritical acceptance of science on the part of the public. However, creating practical participatory mechanisms for the public is increasingly difficult in a decision-making environment heavily dominated by technical expertise.

By embracing technical definitions of issues, the language of political debate often becomes specialized and has the appearance of being scientifically objective and value neutral. Because science is a social enterprise, and scientists are human actors, it is important to note that relying upon such advice without recognizing how it is shaped by values is folly. As well, the widespread requirement for specialized knowledge in the assessment and management of technologically generated risks raises the concern that the power of public decision making will shift from politically responsible authorities to those that best grasp the technical issues associated with a particular hazard.

As a concept, risk can be used to understand contemporary political conflicts. Risk conflicts are essentially political conflicts where an appeal to folk wisdom and common sense, taking into account historical precedence, is more likely to satisfy a majority of the population than an approach where technical expertise defines the language of political debate and technocratic procedure channels it. Many such conflicts (e.g., antinuclear debates, antibiotechnology movements) can be characterized as a competition between two risk paradigms: a technically inclined, positivistic orientation and a socially constructed, culturally embedded orientation. An awareness of the role that these two competing risk paradigms have in the construction and unfolding of risk debates may enhance the opportunity to understand how risk is subject to social, economic, and political processing. Such an approach also provides an opportunity to explore many of the tensions that exist between the political processes of democracy, economic imperatives of capitalism, and the primacy of scientific knowledge in assessing and managing risk.

The technically oriented way of conceptualizing risk requires that decisionmakers and members of the public trust scientific authority and expertise. Furthermore, there must be a willingness to limit boundaries of analysis so risks can be compared quantitatively to one another in a rational and depersonalized manner. In this sense, risk is the relation between decision and damage, where scientific knowledge claims are true to the extent that they adequately reflect reality. A reliance on expertise and a belief that objectivity and neutrality are possible only through the scientific method ensure that this remains so. In general, the assumption is that risk, treated as an objective phenomenon, can be assessed using scientific techniques that reveal their deepest, most complex secrets to the best scientific minds. Empirical testing, peer review, and internal standards should, in theory, consistently yield the best possible risk estimates. Managing hazards with access to such knowledge should also be a fairly straightforward process. In this case, public input and debate would add little value to these assessments.

Although not directly linked to the erosion of democracy in postindustrial societies, a reliance on a technically oriented approach to risk assumes that liberal, individualistically oriented policy making cannot deal with modern, communal risks. Furthermore, such an approach assumes that the production and distribution of risks are independent from economic and political forces and from public consultation. This is where technocratic decision making shines brightest. If public participation distracts regulators from making the correct choices using the tools of science and scientific modes of thinking, then too much public participation will interfere with the public policy process.

The concept of a public out there somewhere waiting to be heard from implies that those who actually make decisions do so without wide-scale support, and that such decisions are in the interest of an elite that is keen on maintaining control over ever-scarcer resources. As a result, the role of the public in shaping risk-based policy often plays a peripheral function in technical debates that tend to accord greater weight to expert scientific opinion.

Transformations in the physical world most likely stimulated a series of changes in the politics of risk processing and risk-based regulation. Such changes coincided with a sweeping diagnosis of an emergent risk society as proposed by Ulrich Beck. Beck wrote in 1992 that we are nearing the end of an era concerned with building an industrial society and moving into a postindustrial "risk distributing" society, concerned chiefly with controlling environmental risks created by modern technology. For Beck, Western society is in a transition period. His landmark book *Risk Society: Towards a New Modernity* (1992) argued that we are heading toward a second stage of modernity, rather than into postmodernity. As such, the logic of industrial production and distribution is becoming increasingly connected to the logic of the socially produced risk.

According to Beck, in the first stage of modernity, industrial society was concerned primarily with distributing material wealth. A newly emerging second stage of modernity—called the "risk society"—is concerned with distributing risk or harm. In essence, this shift represents a redistribution of "desirable items in scarcity" to a distribution of risks that are undesirably abundant. This new modernity involves replacing traditional values of progress and accumulation with an ethic emphasizing risk avoidance, transfer, denial, and reinterpretation. In this period of acute uncertainty and risk, a reflexive social system (a self-monitoring one) ensures that individuals exposed to particular risks will no longer passively live with them. Consequently, a period of transition exists where the distribution of both wealth and risks overlap.

The failure of science to handle the ever-more-menacing risks of modern industrial life is accelerating an erosion of trust in science and authority. As it becomes more apparent that the management of risk is increasingly reliant on political decisions, new forms of public participation will be demanded. Technocratic decision-making cultures are no longer able to ignore the will of the public when the benefits of industrialization pose socially unprocessed risks.

The developing literature on risk poorly addresses organizational behavior, political processes, and social movements. This is probably due to a tendency to view risk assessment and management as tasks that require logical and rational decision making rather than as forums for addressing the issue of public acceptability and participation. However, the presence of modern-day risks heightens the necessity of rights-based democracy and requires a renewed commitment to equal rights in public dialogue and enhanced citizenship rights within a participatory, communal, and cooperative decision-making environment. Such an environment would evaluate risk in terms of its political and social consequences, such as possible disruptions in the social fabric, rather than by exclusively considering a hazard's possible effects on human health and environment.

This alternative form of decision making is aptly illustrated by a concept of risk that is sensitive to social constructions of reality and an understanding of reality through scientific knowledge. Like all social reality, risks are socially constructed to a certain degree. This is a classic insight of the sociology of science and, more recently, the direction in which research on risk and social movements is headed. In other words, all reality, ideas, and meanings (including ideologies) are socially constructed. A cultural perspective on risk that is sensitive to these social constructions can address larger social issues that its technically oriented counterpart must ignore. Additionally, this approach to risk requires widespread trust in the democratic process because there exists an important difference between public acceptance and public participation. Expanded citizenship rights need to keep pace with change if risk is to be descientized and, consequently, withdrawn from technocratic decision-making environments, where an appeal to expertise is of little help because experts disagree on many scientific questions, let alone social ones.

One of the consequences of orchestrating debates about risk using principles of analysis, which mirror logico-deductive modes of inquiry, is that alternative forms of knowledge carry little or no weight. As such, risk becomes a tangible product that can be sold, traded, or redefined according to the will of politically active members of society that have access to scientific legitimation. Conceptualizing risk in this manner tends to turn risk into a strategy for optimizing sustainable modes of development consistent with existing ones. Therefore, environmental policy becomes a risk strategy that serves to minimize the mismatch between economic development and ecological sustainability under certain future conditions. Risk becomes merely a minor player in determining how to best ensure profitability and continued growth without creating an obviously dangerous situation that presents a direct threat to human health and environmental quality.

In conclusion, the rise of environmentalism, a growing number of arguments for appropriate, manageable technologies, and increasing antipathy toward social institutions are, in part, by-products of this struggle between competing risk paradigms and their respective supporters. Such conflicts suggest that debates about risk are not, in essence, scientific disputes. They are arenas of social conflict in which a poorly articulated debate about values and visions influences the distribution of economic and political power and highlight the importance of good risk governance practices.

—*Michael D. Mehta*

See also Crisis Management; Risk Society; Trust

Further Readings and References

Beck, U. (1992). *Risk society: Towards a new modernity.* London: Sage Ltd.
Boardman, R. (Ed.). (1992). *Canadian environmental policy: Ecosystems, politics, and process.* Toronto, Canada: Oxford University Press.
De Marci, B., & Ravetz, J. (1999). Risk management and governance: A post-normal science approach. *Futures, 31,* 743–757.
Hiskes, R. (1988). Emergent risks and convergent interests: Democratic policy making for biotechnology. *Policy Studies Journal, 17,* 73–82.
Jasanoff, S. (1986). *Risk management and political culture.* New York: Russell Sage.
Leiss, W. (2001). *In the chamber of risks: Understanding risk controversies.* Montreal, PQ, and Kingston, ON, Canada: McGill-Queen's University Press.
Lyall, C., & Tait, J. (Eds.). (2005). *New modes of governance: Developing an integrated approach to science, technology, risk and the environment.* Aldershot, UK: Ashgate.
Mehta, M. (Ed.). (2005). *Biotechnology unglued: Science, society and social cohesion.* Vancouver: University of British Columbia Press.
Mehta, M. (2005). *Risky business: Nuclear power and public protest in Canada.* Lanham, MD: Lexington.
Shrader-Frechette, K. (1991). *Risk and rationality: Philosophical foundations for populist reforms.* Berkeley: University of California Press.

RISK SOCIETY

The risk society concept was introduced in Ulrich Beck's now-canonical 1986 text *Risk Society: Towards a New Modernity.* According to Beck, we are currently living in a transformative moment of the modern era. Whereas previous societies faced life-threatening natural hazards—floods, famines, and droughts—the risks faced by contemporary societies (e.g., nuclear explosion, environmental degradation, toxins, terrorism) are unique in that they are consequences of decisions made by human beings. Beck understands risk as a side effect of industrial progress, but he is clear that the current era is not any more hazardous than the premodern world. The key difference of the modern era, Beck maintains, is that manufactured risks (as opposed to natural disasters) are tied to human activity, rationalistic calculation, and human faith in science and technology.

The significance of the risk society concept as a major theoretical advancement in governance studies became clearer with the publication of *World Risk Society,* in 1999, *Conversations with Ulrich Beck,* in 2004, and a series of highly influential papers by

Beck, Wolfgang Bonss, and Christoph Lau. Beck's argument rests on the distinction between the first and second ages of modernity. In the first, simple age of modernity (industrial modernity), Beck argues that a residual risk society began to emerge from the successes of industrial production. The side effects of the residual risk society (pollution, environmental degradation, resource depletion) stimulated a reflection on industrial modern production to the extent that people were aware of the dangers of industrial production. Still, society maintained a faith in science and technology, and there remained faith in human supremacy and scientific advancement.

According to Beck, as societies enter the second modern period, the unintended side effects of industrial production become a dominant force in society and history. The passive reflection that is characteristic of the first modern period is replaced by an active reflexivity in the second age of modernity. Under conditions of reflexive modernization, modernity itself becomes a problem. But in Beck's view, the conditions of governance in the second modernity are far more complex than a reflexive engagement with risk. Under conditions of reflexive modernization, the manufactured uncertainties of the first modern period configure with trends toward individualization, globalization, and subpolitical relations. Through these processes, the rule-directing linear logic of the first modern period is replaced with a nonlinear, rule-altering logic immersed in contingency and ambivalence. The individual in the first modernity period responded to heightened awareness of risk in a regulative fashion, seeking systemic solutions to catastrophic conditions, but in the second modernity period, the reflexive and cosmopolitan individual confronts the institutional integrity of the first modern period in a constitutive manner.

—*Sean P. Hier*

See also Crisis Management; High-Reliability Organization; Risk

Further Readings and References

Beck, U. (1992). *Risk society: Towards a new modernity.* London: Sage Ltd.

Beck, U. (1999). *World risk society.* Cambridge, UK: Polity Press.

Beck, U. (2005). *Cosmopolitan vision.* Cambridge, UK: Polity Press.

Beck, U., Bonss, W., & Lau, C. (2003). The theory of reflexive modernization: Problematic, hypotheses and research programme. *Theory, Culture and Society, 20*(2), 1–33.

Beck, U., & Willms, J. (2004). *Conversations with Ulrich Beck.* Cambridge, UK: Polity Press.

Lash, S. (2002). Foreword by Scott Lash: Individualization in a non-linear mode. In U. Beck & E. Beck-Gernsheim (Eds.), *Individualization* (pp. vii–xii). Cambridge, UK: Polity Press.

Lash, S. (2003). Reflexivity as non-linear. *Theory, Culture and Society, 20*(2), 49–57.

RULE

A rule is a principle to which action should conform: a widely accepted standard of behavior. The term *governance* is closely linked to the concept of rule making, via the Greek and Latin verbs *kubernan* and *gubernare,* respectively. Modern definitions of governance refer to the stewardship of the formal and informal "rules of the game." The growth of multilevel and multiactor governance makes a focus on rules particularly timely. In this context, the omission of governance-as-process with government-as-organization becomes problematic. The study of governance requires a focus on underlying rules and how they vary over time and across space (governments are just one, albeit an important, player within that game).

Elinor Ostrom has defined rules as prescriptions that define which actions are required, prohibited, or permitted, and specify the sanctions for noncompliance. In the domain of governance, rules shape the behavior of actors—elected politicians, public officials, community leaders, and individual citizens—by making certain courses of action more or less possible and more or less attractive. Rules create "positions" (president, prime minister, committee chair, spokesperson, community representative, voter, consultee), and they determine how participants enter or leave these positions (election, appointment, random selection, patronage, contract), what actions they are permitted to take, and what outcomes they are allowed to affect.

Typologies of modes of governance ascribe a more important role to rules in bureaucratic or hierarchical systems than in market- or network-based arrangements. However, with a more expansive definition, it becomes clear that rules bring an important element of stability, regularity, and predictability to behavior within all governance systems. Rules can be informal as well as formal. Formal rules are consciously designed and clearly specified—as in the case of written constitutions, treaties, laws, contractual agreements, property rights, the terms of reference and standing orders, and so forth. Informal rules are not consciously designed or specified in writing—they are routines, customs, and conventions that are part of habitual action. Informal rules may be as influential as official codes of conduct and written constitutions; indeed, "invisible" rules may be more powerful. Rooted as they are in custom and tradition, informal rules are particularly difficult to change. It is not uncommon for long-standing informal rules to persist in the face of (and in potential contradiction with) new formal rules. Ostrom distinguishes between rules of form and rules of use.

An expansive conception of rules has been criticized on the grounds of nonfalsifiability: All behavior conforms to some rule, even if it has yet to be identified. The concept of "standard operating procedures" offers a helpful way forward: The researcher's aim should be to identify the specific rules of behavior that are agreed upon and (in general) followed by agents, whether explicitly or tacitly agreed to. Informal rules are distinct from personal "rules of thumb": They are specific to a particular governance setting, they are recognized by actors (if not always adhered to), and they can be described and explained to the researcher. Standard operating procedures may be circumvented or manipulated by certain groups of actors, but actors are still able to identify, and reflect upon, the nature of such rules.

Pure rational choice theory tells us that rules are human constructions, designed to solve collective action problems, which can be "undone" when they no longer serve actors' interests—they provide only short-term constraints on individuals' behavior. In reality, of course, rules tend to be self-reinforcing and remarkably enduring. More sophisticated theorists argue that actors will only seek to change rules when the likely benefits outweigh the expected costs of change itself—which include the costs of learning how to operate within new rules, of dealing with new sources of uncertainty, and of engaging in change (which itself presents a collective action problem). Other critical voices note that the rules of the governance game are not technical constructions: They embody power relations by privileging certain courses of action over others and by including certain actors and excluding others. Action to change rules may arise in response to, and become part of, power struggles among different groups.

Normative theorists have a less clear account of why rules are created, but are better at explaining how they persist and evolve over time. It can be argued that rules simplify political life by ensuring that some things are taken as given in decision making. Evolutionary change is endemic as actors engage in a creative process of matching situations to rules. Rules are not always strictly followed; they may be "bent" or even ignored. Rules produce variation and deviation as well as standardization and conformity. There are always areas of ambiguity in the interpretation and application of rules (not least because individuals vary in their own values and experiences) because rules are adapted by actors seeking to make sense of changing environments and to pursue their own interests.

Intentional projects of rule change rarely satisfy the intentions of their initiators. Within governance systems, every set of rules is nested within a hierarchy of more fundamental and authoritative rules. At the same time, governance rules may have deep roots in locally specific cultures and conventions that exhibit remarkable tenacity over time. But because rules express social values and power relationships, the prospect of their redesign will continue to seduce politicians. Such efforts are part of the process whereby actors develop an understanding of what constitutes the good society—even if they are not able to directly achieve it.

—Vivien Lowndes

See also Institution; Institutional Performance; Rule of Law

Further Readings and References

March, J., & Olsen, J. (1989). *Rediscovering institutions.* New York: Free Press.

North, D. (1990). *Institutions, institutional change and economic performance.* Cambridge, UK: Cambridge University Press.

Ostrom, E. (1999). Institutional rational choice: An assessment of the institutional analysis and development framework. In P. Sabatier (Ed.), *Theories of the policy process* (pp. 35–72). Boulder, CO: Westview.

Rothstein, B. (1996). Political institutions: An overview. In R. Goodin & H. Klingemann (Eds.), *A new handbook of political science.* Oxford, UK: Oxford University Press.

RULE OF LAW

The rule of law refers to a mechanism, a process, an institution, a practice, or a norm that secures a particular type of governance. The relevant type of governance is usually defined in opposition to arbitrariness. Arbitrariness typically characterizes various forms of despotism, absolutism, authoritarianism, and totalitarianism, which are widely thought to be evils that the rule of law is supposed to curb. These include even highly institutionalized forms of rule, where atop the apex of a power structure sits some sovereign entity (a king, a junta, a party committee) that can make decisions unconstrained by law when it deems necessary. Ideas about the rule of law have long been central to political and legal thought since at least as early as when Aristotle distinguished the rule of law from individual law. In the eighteenth century, Montesquieu elaborated a doctrine of the rule of law that contrasted the authority of monarchs with the caprice of despots, which underpinned his notion of an independent judiciary (rightly or wrongly with regard to England) and has since profoundly influenced Western liberal thought.

In all, the rule of law implies that the creation of laws, their enforcement, and the relationships among legal rules are themselves legally regulated so that no one—including the most highly placed official—is above the law. The legal constraint on rulers means that the government is subject to existing laws as much as its citizens are. Thus, a closely related notion is the idea of equality before the law, which holds that no "legal" person shall enjoy privileges that are not extended to all and that no one in particular shall be immune from legal sanctions. In addition, the application and adjudication of legal rules by various governing officials are to be impartial and consistent across equivalent cases, made without taking into consideration the class, status, or relative possession of power among disputants. In order for these ideas to have any real purchase, moreover, there should be some legal apparatuses in place for challenging officials to submit to the law.

Not only does the rule of law entail such basic requirements about how the law should be enacted in society, but it also implies certain qualities about the characteristics and content of the laws themselves. In particular, laws should be open and clear, general in form, universal in application, and knowable to all. Moreover, legal requirements must be such that people can be guided by them; they must not place undue cognitive or behavioral demands on people to follow. Thus, the law should be relatively stable, comprised of determinate requirements that people can consult before acting and not retrospectively establish legal obligations. Furthermore, the law should remain internally consistent and, failing that, should provide for legal ways to resolve contradictions that can be expected to arise.

However, despite these basic features, the rule of law has not always had a particularly established or even systematic formulation (not for lack of attempts by jurists and political philosophers). The idea that the law should contribute to beneficial ways of channeling and constraining the exercise of public power is a matter of interpretation that is especially true over time and across different polities. One reason why its meaning continues to be widely contested is that any of the strictly legal or philosophical aspects of the concept points beyond itself also to political and social conditions that are historically and culturally contingent. Another reason for the inherent complexity of the idea is that for whatever empirical particulars are said to fall within the purview of the concept, there is always some larger normative vision about the nature or purpose of law and the legitimate aims and limits of political power that support it, which stand to enjoy even less agreement.

Institutional Arrangements and Legal Culture

For these reasons, the rule of law is best seen not as a blueprint for institutional design but as a value, or cluster of values, that might inform such design, and which can, therefore, be pursued in a variety of ways. Nonetheless, several rather simple and generalizable institutional insights follow from the idea that those who judge the legality of exercises of power should not be the same as those who exercise it. For instance, a typical rule-of-law state will institutionalize some means of shielding legal officials from interference, political or otherwise, that threaten their independence. Accordingly, the institutional separation of the judiciary from other branches of government is commonly thought to be an important feature of rule-of-law states. Other measures to ensure fair access to legal institutions may also be important for rule-of-law regimes. In addition, a binding written constitution is an American innovation that is widely believed to aid the rule of law and has thus been mimicked in other parts of the world.

While certain institutional traditions and conventions as well as written laws may be important to ensure that judicial decisions are grounded within plausible interpretations of existing laws, no single institutional character of a state should be seen as necessary or sufficient to the rule-of-law ideal. The rule of law is tied neither to any one national experience nor to any set of institutions in particular, although it may be thought to be better served in certain nations and by some institutions more than others. Institutional variety and possibilities are likely to be too rich and complex to identify precise institutional

arrangements of the rule of law that could be automatically duplicated or transplanted. Different polities embody their own judgments about how to implement specific rule-of-law ideals, given their particular legal and cultural traditions that influence the character of their institutions. What's more, the initial sociological condition of the rule of law is that most people in society, including those whose profession it is to administer the law, believe that the law does and should count in the first place. In this regard, political and legal institutions are but one factor among many variables that comprise cultural supports for and means of socialization into the rule of law as a value.

Negative and Positive Forms of the Ideal

The basic idea that the rule of law is at odds with arbitrariness has led most legal theorists to view the rule of law as a purely negative ideal, where its value lies mainly in what it shields against. Those who take the view that the rule of law is primarily devoted to "damage control" concentrate especially on the various kinds of damage that might be done at the hands of government. The point of institutionalizing the consolidation of power, then, is to be able to curb it and thereby buttress the citizenry against the potentially intrusive claims of the state. Yet the constant fear that the threat of violence and actual cruelty of those holding a monopoly of power can engender in citizens is not the only perilous alternative to the rule of law. Without the rule of law's promise of fixed and knowable points in the vast field of human interactions that constitute the basis for legitimate expectations and the means of social coordination, the alternative may be widespread chaos, if not paralysis. Hence, many theorists have derived the value of the rule of law by focusing on the disastrous state of affairs that would ensue from the absence of information, security, and legally enforceable obligations that the rule of law provides for ordering and regularizing social relations.

As a solution either to the problem of an all-too-powerful state or the need for order and predictability within modern societies, the rule of law's assurance of constraint by clear legal rules and the establishment of well-defined legal processes is of central importance to a purely negative ideal of the rule of law. As a negative ideal, the rule of law sets out principles of legal efficacy but remains silent on the moral quality or purpose of the law. While it may appear empirically inconsistent for horrific acts to occur under the rule of law, mere formal regularity and procedural justice is quite consistent, in principle, with iniquity in the law's content. Thus, many writers have offered a more affirmative, morally ambitious account of what is required to govern according to the rule of law. A more positive understanding of the rule of law includes some underlying principles of substantive justice and purpose in legal systems in relation to society. In this tradition, formal regularity and attention to process are likewise valued, but they are seen as valuable not merely for their own sake but insofar as they help to secure further goods—such as greater equality and fairness and respect for the dignity and integrity of people or groups. A particular theory about the proper respect for individual rights or a preferred conception of political community and communal goods usually lies at the heart of a more substantive rule-of-law ideal that seeks not only to protect but also to realize specific social goods and human values through the law.

Challenges to the Rule of Law

Anyone who holds that what matters most in politics is having the right people in power and not how power should be constrained will not be convinced of the value of the rule of law. Neither will anyone who believes that institutions of public power are merely instruments of the ruling class that need more than to be constrained but dismantled. For the majority of modern democratic societies, however, the rule of law's requirement that both rulers and the ruled be accountable to the law is of unquestionable value. To be sure, in the modern world, it is the liberal tradition that values the rule of law most highly. Liberals who are concerned with ways of protecting (and realizing) liberty in some form and averting threats to it view the rule of law as an overarching source of security and value. Be that as it may, there is substantial

disagreement even among liberals over what exactly counts as a faithful application of the term, and even when that is pinned down, there is still disagreement on how it is to be accomplished.

In and of itself, the rule of law is not a faithful description of any state of affairs but a complex ideal that is even more complex to realize. Thus, we have reason to be skeptical about whether societies necessarily benefit from all that might be invoked under the term. The independence of the judiciary, for instance, is a murky value at best and clearly a problem if the independence is misused to foster the sectoral privileges of judicial personnel or to allow unchallenged interpretations of the law. Heavy emphasis on the negative aspects of the rule of law, for example, on formal regularity and procedural justice, may distract from the content and consequences of those laws. Critics of a strictly negative conception of the rule-of-law ideal argue that too much attention to legal process generates significant vices of its own, in the form of exaggerated legalism and excessive juridification. The price of excessive veneration of the law and legal procedures may be too high if doing so inhibits independent social assessments of the merits of a given policy proposal or if the official mandate of "blindness" gives legitimacy to actions performed "according to the law," even when most people would oppose such acts. Some writers have charged, moreover, that the increasing domain of judges and lawyers, indeed, their encroachment into areas previously left to politicians and the electorate, entails the loss of much that is politically and democratically valuable.

In short, too much emphasis on procedures for preventing arbitrariness can lead to subverting the doing of justice according to what might otherwise find support in the rule of law, and the legal strictures then become themselves a form of arbitrariness that is no more legitimate. On the other hand, those who defend the negative value of the rule of law object to more substantive understandings of the ideal on the grounds that morally ambitious aspirations about the rule of law threaten to purge the concept of its specificity and usefulness. They argue that to open the concept to a whole host of extralegal considerations about substantive justice and wider societal goals is to conflate ideas about the rule of law with notions about the rule of good law, such that any distinction between the two is reduced to nothing. As a consequence, no separate or practical discussion of the rule of law can take place short of propounding whole rival social philosophies.

To address further challenges to the ideal, a matter of continuing controversy is whether contemporary law associated with the welfare state is compatible with the rule of law. The regulatory activities of modern governments are frequently neither general nor abstract, but are targeted, detailed, and specific. A matter of even longer dispute is whether such formal equalization counts for much if it merely leaves substantive social and economic inequalities to play themselves out with greater effect. Liberals commonly believe that the existence of social inequalities does not necessarily cancel out the worth of the rule of law, for they maintain that inequalities should not confer advantages before the law even if they do so in the world. Those on the political Left disagree and argue that real differences in the world render the blindness or neutrality of the law false, inconsequential, or pernicious.

Therefore, despite widespread consensus in different parts of the world that the rule of law is a good thing, it is neither automatically nor self-evidently so. Like any social value, the rule of law can be a mixed blessing when it conflicts with commitments to other social ideals or because different interpretations of the same ideal or attempts to realize different ideals can require different institutional logics. Where the governing powers of a polity are unconstrained, the negative conception of the rule of law will undoubtedly hold much salutary promise. However, where power is already substantially constrained by law, the rule of law might not only tolerate but require that some space be made for wisdom, judgment, particularity, and substantive justice.

—Naomi Choi

See also Accountability; Civic Republicanism; Constitutionalization; Contract Enforcement; Democratic Theory; Good Governance; Liberalism; Polyarchy; Power; Rule; Sociology of Governance; State-Society Relations

Further Readings and References

Dicey, A. V. (1956). *Introduction to the study of the law of the constitution.* London: Macmillan.

Dworkin, R. (Ed.). (1985). *A matter of principle.* Cambridge, MA: Harvard University Press.

Fuller, L. (1969). *The morality of law.* New Haven, CT: Yale University Press.

Hart, H. L. A. (1961). *The concept of law.* Oxford, UK: Oxford University Press.

Hayek, F. A. (1973–1979). *Law legislation and liberty* (Vols. 1–3). Chicago: University of Chicago Press.

Raz, J. (1979). The rule of law and its virtue. In J. Raz (Ed.), *The authority of law.* Oxford, UK: Clarendon Press.

Selznick, P. (1999). Legal cultures and the rule of law. In M. Krygier & A. Czarnota (Eds.), *The rule of law after communism.* Aldershot, UK: Dartmouth.

Shapiro, I. (Ed.). (1994). *The rule of law.* New York: New York University Press.

Shklar, J. (1998). Political theory and the rule of law. In J. Shklar (Ed.), *Political thought and political thinkers.* Chicago: University of Chicago Press.

Unger, R. M. (1976). *Law in modern society.* New York: Free Press.

RULES OF ORIGIN

Rules of origin are used to make more precise any aspect of trade law or trade policy that treats goods differently depending upon their country of origin. For example, quotas, countervailing duties, and antidumping actions restrict import goods from specific producing nations. The export products of World Trade Organization (WTO) member states generally face lower import barriers than the exports of nations that do not qualify for most-favored nation status. Many bilateral and regional trade agreements exempt the products of member countries from various requirements.

In each of these cases, rules of origin are needed because the identity of the producing country cannot be reliably inferred from the point of entry. Consider the case of the North American Free Trade Agreement (NAFTA), under which many goods produced in Mexico enter the United States duty free, while imports produced in other countries face U.S. tariff barriers. Because NAFTA was designed primarily to benefit firms and workers in North America, it is clear that goods manufactured elsewhere cannot be allowed to circumvent U.S. tariffs simply by being transshipped through Mexico on the way to the United States. Nor should it be possible for free riders to claim those foreign goods as "Mexican" that have received perfunctory labeling, repackaging, or processing in Mexico solely for the purpose of qualifying for preferential treatment under NAFTA. However, in the era of global manufacturing, final products are frequently assembled from components originating in many different countries. At what point should foreign inputs that do not qualify for favorable treatment be deemed to have been transformed into a new product that does qualify? Precise legal standards—specific rules of origin—vary widely across nations, but most use the criterion of an *ad valorem* percentage of value added, anywhere between thirty-five and sixty percent, computed in a prescribed manner.

Rules of origin have become increasingly controversial as the preferential tariff regions and antidumping arrangements that require them have mushroomed. As a result, most international agreements now contain provisions for nations to negotiate over specific criteria for specific products. For example, NAFTA has recently adopted the rule that any tea that is fermented or packaged in a NAFTA country should be deemed to have satisfied the rule of origin, regardless of where it was originally grown.

The WTO is also expanding its perspective on rules of origin. General Agreement on Tariffs and Trade (GATT) recognized the danger that the misuse of rules of origin could transform their role from that of an administrative support for trade policy into an autonomous policy instrument. Thus, it required that rules of origin be transparent and administered in a consistent, uniform, impartial, and reasonable manner. The WTO is now seeking to render these restrictions more precise and to harmonize rules across nations by building on the Agreement on Rules of Origin adopted in 1994. Rules of origin can also be used to interpret statutes governing labeling requirements, such as "Made in . . ." stickers, and to assist in compiling bilateral trade statistics.

—*Bruce E. Moon*

See also North American Free Trade Agreement; World Trade Organization

Further Readings and References

Moon, B. E. (2005). Free trade vs. protectionism. In M. Snarr & D. N. Snarr (Eds.), *Introducing global issues* (3rd ed.). Boulder, CO: Lynne Reinner.

Reyna, J. V. (1995). *Passport to North American Trade: Rules of origin and customs procedures under NAFTA*. New York: McGraw-Hill.

Sanctions

In relation to governance, sanctions involve the actual or threatened imposition of costs to achieve political goals. Sanctions are usually associated with legitimate political authority, so that, for example, those who break the law risk costs such as fines or imprisonment. They are also inherently implicit in the provision or offer of positive incentives, as there is always the possibility that those incentives will be withdrawn. Hence sanctions are ubiquitous in governance—in the film *The Eiger Sanction,* Clint Eastwood's character is meant to assassinate (sanction) a secret agent while climbing a mountain—and include measures such as international travel restrictions imposed upon members of target governments.

Types of Sanctions

Most commonly, the term *sanctions* is used to mean economic sanctions—the actual or threatened use of monetary means by states or international organizations to impose costs in order to achieve goals in international politics. For example, the European Union (EU) threatened to impose tariffs on U.S. goods entering the EU to try to force the U.S. government to reduce subsidies to U.S. steel producers, which were giving them an advantage against EU steel producers. Changes in economic sanctions reflect changes in global governance. First, economic sanctions are increasingly imposed by international organizations such as the World Trade Organization. This can and does impose financial penalties on states for violating international trade rules. Second, global neoliberalism is reducing the scope states have for the use of economic sanctions. Global neoliberalism is theoretically aimed at eliminating barriers to the free movement of goods, capital, and labor. Some see it in practice as tending to prioritize the advantages of powerful, tax-subsidized corporations: Others maintain that it is promoting the spread of prosperity. Either way, it can run counter to the desire of states to pursue political goals through sanctions, as these by definition involve restrictions on the corporate pursuit of profit.

Inflicting economic costs—such as sinking a ship full of commercial goods—is not normally defined as an economic sanction. Sanctions take many forms, such as tariffs (that is, taxes on imports from the target), boycotts (refusal to buy or accept a particular category or amount of item), embargoes (refusal to sell or provide something), freezing of assets, fines, exclusion from bidding for contracts, or cuts in aid. Sometimes the line between sanctions and other policy instruments can be blurred, as in the phrase economic warfare, which is usually associated with comprehensive economic sanctions. These involve the use of monetary means to impose extremely high levels of economic cost, sometimes with the aim of undermining the target state's military capabilities or bringing about the collapse or overthrow of the government ruling it. This is akin to medieval siege warfare. It is the exception to the general perception that sanctions fall between diplomatic persuasion and military force. The economic sanctions imposed on Iraq by the United Nations between 1990 and 2003 combined with the effects of war and the Iraqi government's prioritization of its own elite produced devastating effects. The United Nations Children's Fund (UNICEF) calculated that there were 500,000 excess deaths among children under five between 1991 and 1998 alone. This case contributed to a debate over smart sanctions, that is, sanctions that target political leaders to provide maximum political effectiveness and minimum costs for the population of a state. For some, the phrase "smart sanctions" was a means of producing political cover for the continuation of the highly damaging sanctions on Iraq with only minor modifications. For others, the phrase signified a real search for more humane and more effective instruments of foreign policy.

The Disputed Effectiveness of Sanctions

In the view of some, economic sanctions rarely achieve major foreign policy goals despite being frequently used by states. The first analytical task is then to work out why they rarely work on major issues. One possibility is that the states imposing them do not pursue them with much rigor and the target states have a strong incentive to resist them. This suggests the importance of ensuring that the effects of economic sanctions are severe and that the demands made of the target are clear and reasonable in relation to the gains to be made by the target in having the sanctions lifted. The second analytical task for those with this perspective is to analyze why they are used so often if they work so rarely. Part of the answer could be that the use of force can be even less attractive politically. For others, this focus on failure to achieve goals in difficult cases misses the point. They argue that they can be used successfully on lesser issues and have to be combined with other policy instruments, including the use of force, to produce success in difficult cases. The

central problem for any debate about the effectiveness is disagreement on the objectives being pursued. For example, if the U.S. grain embargo imposed on the Soviet Union was aimed at reversing the Soviet intervention in Afghanistan in 1979, it failed. If it was aimed at symbolizing U.S. disapproval and imposing costs on U.S. grain producers to show the extent of that disapproval, it was a success.

—*Eric Herring*

See also Functionalism; Humanitarian Intervention; United Nations Security Council; World Trade Organization

Further Readings and References

Baldwin, D. A. (1985). *Economic statecraft.* Princeton, NJ: Princeton University Press.

Cortright, D., & Lopez, G. A. (2000). *The sanctions decade: Assessing UN strategies in the 1990s.* Boulder, CO: Lynne Rienner.

Cortright, D., & Lopez, G. A. (Eds.). (2002). *Smart sanctions: Targeting economic statecraft.* Lanham, MD: Rowman & Littlefield.

Doxey, M. (1996). *International sanctions in comparative perspective.* London: Palgrave Macmillan.

Drezner, D. (1999). *The sanctions paradox: Economic statecraft and international relations.* Cambridge, UK: Cambridge University Press.

Hufbauer, G. C., Schott, J. J., & Kimberley, A. E. (1993). *Economic sanctions reconsidered* (Vols. 1–2). Washington, DC: Institute for International Economics.

Weiss, T. G., Cortright, D., Lopez, G. A., & Minear, L. (Eds.). (1997). *Political gain and civilian pain: Humanitarian impacts of economic sanctions.* Lanham, MD: Rowman & Littlefield.

SATISFACTION

The term *satisfaction* is usually used in reference to citizens' evaluations of the functioning of political or economic institutions. Satisfaction is distinct from support for or normative commitment to these institutions or their principles. For example, "satisfaction with democracy and market economy" is a different phenomenon than "support for democracy and market economy." This can be illustrated best by the discrepancies in the levels of positive evaluations and support for democracy and market economy in the democratizing countries of East Central Europe in the 1990s. Here citizens strongly supported democracy and the market economy as institutional models, but they tended to be dissatisfied with how they operated in practice in their respective countries. Satisfaction is thus an indicator of perceptions of institutional performance and not of principles prevailing among the general public. However, high levels of satisfaction with democracy or economic performance may positively influence citizens' adherence to the normative principles.

Satisfaction with political or economic performance is usually studied in the context of democratic or democratizing states, as this is where citizens' evaluations are relevant for a regime's legitimacy and survival. Low levels of satisfaction with institutional performance may threaten a regime's democratic legitimacy as it fails to fulfill its citizens' expectations and significantly diverges from the benchmark of the ideal political and economic models. Dissatisfaction with political and economic performance in established democracies may mean loss of credibility by the current government, while in democratizing states it may hamper the process of democratic consolidation.

Political and economic satisfaction reflects the evaluations of institutional performance; however, it is also influenced by a number of other factors. For example, evaluations of the quality of political and economic institutions in a given country are influenced by the citizen's political winner/loser status, where citizens who voted for the current government (winners) are more positively predisposed in their evaluations. Levels of satisfaction are also influenced by the normative ideals held by citizens, as their ideological position will affect their approval or rejection of certain policies. Political and economic satisfaction also depends on an individual's sociotropic well-being assessment, where disadvantaged individuals will tend to be less satisfied with the overall institutional performance. Finally, satisfaction is context sensitive. For example, citizens of a rapidly democratizing country are likely to be more satisfied with how democracy works in their country than citizens of an established democracy, despite the fact that objective

indicators rate the quality of democracy in the latter much higher than in the former.

—*Natalia Letki*

See also Effectiveness; Institutional Performance; Legitimacy

Further Readings and References

Anderson, C. J., & Guillory, C. A. (1997). Political institutions and satisfaction with democracy: A cross-national analysis of consensus and majoritarian systems. *American Political Science Review, 91,* 66–81.

Evans, G., & Whitefield, S. (1995). The politics and economics of democratic commitment: Support for democracy in transition societies. *British Journal of Political Science, 25,* 485–514.

Pharr, S. J., & Putnam, R. D. (Eds.). (2000). *Disaffected democracies: What's troubling the trilateral countries.* Princeton, NJ: Princeton University Press.

SATISFICING BEHAVIOR

A decisionmaker is said to exhibit satisficing behavior when he or she chooses an alternative that meets one or more specified criteria, but that need not be optimal with respect to any particular set of preferences or objectives. For example, a chief executive officer might hope to achieve an acceptable performance on the dimensions of revenue growth, cost stability, customer and employee satisfaction, and risk management without seeking to attain the highest possible level of expected after-tax profits.

Satisficing was the term selected by Herbert A. Simon to refer to a mode of decision making that he viewed as more realistic than the maximizing mode that is ordinarily postulated in economic theory and related areas of social science. (Contrary to what is often assumed, he did not invent this term himself by redundantly melding "satisfy" and "suffice," but rather rescued from oblivion an archaic word that he claimed was of Scottish origin.) Simon's strong and iconoclastic convictions about the nature of human decision-making processes were influenced by his anthropological field study, conducted in 1934 and

1935, of the behavior of public works administrators in Milwaukee, Wisconsin. Like managers everywhere, the municipal officials responsible for this city's recreation program—and in particular its public playgrounds—had limited resources available for a variety of commendable uses, such as routine maintenance of equipment, safety inspections and upgrades, landscaping and general beautification, and supervision of children at play. In this situation, an idealized rational agent would endeavor to equate the marginal value of spending on each such use, but Simon found that the administrators he met failed to behave in a way that could plausibly be described in these terms. The obvious reason for this failure was that they had no sensible basis for quantitative measurement of the value function that a marginal analysis would have required, and that even in general terms, the several divisional managers tended not to agree on which expenditures should be given priority. In environments of this sort, Simon argued, the successful decisionmaker would be the one who resisted becoming preoccupied with a particular subgoal (e.g., improving the visual appeal of Milwaukee playgrounds), who thereby managed to achieve an acceptable result on all important dimensions of performance, and who did not waste time attempting to lend his or her tradeoffs between various objectives a spurious exactitude.

While Simon's writings on this topic have undeniably been influential, opinions remain divided as to the importance of his critique and the usefulness of the notion of satisficing for modeling purposes. It has also been suggested that behavior with the appearance of satisficing could result from optimal decision making with the costs of deliberation and information gathering taken into account, although Simon himself explicitly rejected such proposals.

—*Christopher J. Tyson*

See also Bounded Rationality; Decision Making; Optimal Decision Making; Rational Choice Theory

Further Readings and References

Simon, H. A. (1947). *Administrative behavior.* New York: Macmillan.

Simon, H. A. (1957). *Models of man.* New York: Wiley.

Simon, H. A. (1959). Theories of decision-making in economics and behavioral science. *American Economic Review, 49,* 253–283.

SCIENCE

Science is commonly understood as a body of knowledge about the physical world that accumulates by following systematic empirical observation and inductive principles. It is also an influential institution, characterized as an open society of scientists with expertise in various fields that communicate their findings to each other and provide specialist advice to the state and the public. Science may also be viewed in more abstract ways: as a political concept (for example, as a vehicle of global governance) and as a powerful positivistic ideological force whose reach extends beyond the scientific domain. These varied conceptions of science relate differently to notions of governance and the study of governance.

Science as the Open Society

The interrelationships of science and governance are largely opaque. For Steve Fuller, this is because debates center on the utopian promise or dystopic menace of science and technology, so little attention is given to how scientific knowledge is constituted or to the people that produce scientific knowledge. The institution of science is portrayed as an open society, which, in its pursuit of universal knowledge, assumes the authority to speak for all of society. But when science is seen as an institution that governs, this raises a series of questions that unravel the relationship between this open society and democracy. Is science anything more than an institutionalized assertion of faith that commands blind loyalty from the public? How can science be universal when not everyone can simultaneously participate, and a handful of unelected practitioners speaks for all? And who, precisely, is selected to give scientific advice?

Fuller studies science's internal organization, and instead of an open society finds a hierarchically driven institution, ruled from within by a small, self-selecting elite group of white, middle-class, middle-aged males, whose interests are distilled as expertise to the state and society. They speak for the whole scientific community and for all of humanity, although they regularly pronounce on areas divorced from their own scientific expertise and personal experience. Fuller questions how these scientists can speak for all when multiculturalism is ignored and when science's application may affect different people in different ways.

This is far removed from the promise of science as the open society, although Fuller believes this ideal can be realized. This entails a transition from government to governance through democratizing the organization of, and participation in, science and science policy. The first step is to deconsecrate the state funding of science through developing alternative programs of research to challenge the worldview of elite science. The second step is to encourage public participation in a republic of science. Rather than science literacy initiatives aimed at remedying the public's cognitive deficits, this should involve epistemic challenges to the authority of science and deliberative engagement in science planning and policy. The aim is to secularize or decenter this unelected governing institution by loosening its ties to state power and weakening its dominion over knowledge claims.

Science as a Political Concept

The ability of science to assume the authority to speak on behalf of all people in a manner that transcends all cultural and economic barriers entails that science may conceptually be understood as a vehicle of global governance. Echoing Francis Fukuyama, Fuller notes that an unchecked universal science can put an end to history: When one society fully harnesses the natural trajectory of science to its future, the course of history (and politics) will be the rest of the world replicating the same steps to catch up with that society. Politics will be the story of global liberation through modernization. The standardization of the public provision of education and health care throughout the world is taken as evidence of science being the force that steers policy.

While science may be understood as a vehicle of global governance, we may observe a concurrent and supposedly contradictory global trend toward the governance of science within national science and technology policies. Realizing research cannot be directly governed, governments attempt to use policy levers and financial incentives to direct research toward national technological advances and enhanced international competitiveness. While recognizing that outcomes cannot be guaranteed, it is hoped they will be partially predictable.

Science as an Ideological Force

The experimental science paradigm guides national research policies in and beyond the scientific domain and that science has become a powerful positivistic ideological force that is employed in political language to delineate what is and is not a legitimate knowledge claim or a valid enterprise for public funding. Science policy in the United Kingdom defines social science as a positivistic enterprise belonging to and working for science and so dismisses the potential utility of interpretative approaches. Economics is taken to exemplify the empirical neutrality, refinement, and policy application to which the social sciences may aspire; while sociology is held to represent all that is lacking—interpretivism is pathologized and the discipline is accused of propagating the spurious orthodoxies of Marxism and radical socialism.

The governance of social science is guided by research policy networks dominated by natural scientists that do not understand what social science is. The consequences are that (1) the "everyday epistemology" of social science is regulated by non–social scientists so that governments fund social science that makes sense to natural scientists; (2) this produces a "slave social science" devoted to social aspects of technology focused initiatives; and (3) perpetuates the "science wars" by promoting user-oriented, fact-finding "positivistic" approaches using (preferably quantitative) empirical methods and by marking interpretivism as "deviant" social science.

Prolonging the science wars affects how the concept and process of governance itself is legitimately theorized and investigated: At its extreme, a positivist approach will focus on rationalism, determinism, and mathematical modeling, while an interpretative approach that decenters governance will be deemed unacceptable.

—Claire Donovan

See also Research and Development; Technology; World Health Organization

Further Readings and References

Donovan, C. (2005). The governance of social science and everyday epistemology. *Public Administration, 83*(3), 597–615.

Finlayson, A., Bevir, M., Rhodes, R. A. W., Dowding, K., & Hay, C. (2004). The interpretive approach in political science: A symposium. *British Journal of Politics and International Relations, 6,* 129–64.

Flyvbjerg, B. (2001). *Making social science matter: Why social enquiry fails and how it can succeed again.* New York: Cambridge University Press.

Fuller, S. (2000). *The governance of science: Ideology and the future of the open society.* Buckingham, UK: Open University Press.

SECOND-TRACK DIPLOMACY

Second-track—or multitrack and unofficial—diplomacy encompasses all informal efforts at peace building and sustainable development to prevent war or restore society after war through the building of culture and institutions that sustain peace, as well as conciliation—talking across division during conflict. Second-track diplomacy stands in contrast to first-track diplomacy, or traditional and formal international diplomacy, where officially designated representatives, such as heads of state and ambassadors, come together for political reasons. High-profile nongovernmental organizations and citizen activists are often publicized with unofficial diplomacy. A wide range of less-visible stakeholders, however, can be quite influential in nonrepresentative activities and forums. In many conflicts, the stakeholders are not publicized. Those interested in scrutinizing multitrack diplomacy must ask: Who is

acting to prevent conflict? Who is acting to mediate, or assist with negotiating, difference?

The growing emergence of second-track diplomacy parallels changing issues, as well as transfer of powers, rights, and functions to organizations within civil society. For example, in some parts of the world, security—in its traditional sense—has not been a concern for years. Instead, challenges that require regional cooperation, like resource disputes, have priority. Actors concerned with environmental and other complex international tension, like ethnic conflict, are pioneering a multistakeholder process that includes many of the actors listed in the following paragraph.

Our most powerful international actors are no longer necessarily the heads of state but include transnational corporations, churches, and nongovernmental organizations like Amnesty International. General Electric is credited with promoting peaceful conflict resolution between India and Pakistan. Joseph Elder's conciliation work in Sri Lanka as a Quaker has been publicly noted. Susan Collin Marks is another publicized example, describing her citizen involvement in mediating South Africa's transition. Philanthropy, finance institutions, professional and labor groups, academia, and media also play roles as opinion leaders or other exercisers of influence.

Naturally, involvement of these stakeholders alone does not guarantee diplomacy. Transnational corporations and churches have been instrumental to violent and corrupt dynamics, including notorious war crimes. In such circumstances, developing civic society strong enough to weaken, or at least check and publicize, authoritarian abuse of power reflects second-track diplomacy. Strong citizens are less likely to be manipulated by governments committing genocide, for example. Empowering communities in the face of self-interested political leadership can be their best, perhaps only, option for building peace.

Private stakeholders are often best situated to respond to particular needs. They may have practical insight and information not readily available to government. Civil society groups are often more flexible than government bureaucracies, allowing them to act swiftly and more creatively to newly arising issues and concerns. Civil society is most often acknowledged for closeness to people. Visionary initiative can create unexpected opportunities. Those who can operate flexibly, with access to people and networks that can be mobilized quickly, have rare potential to take this lead. The Oslo Accords, as one example, were preceded by months of informal communication preparing the ground for formal negotiation. Relationships between sides were built; common ground was identified.

Increasingly, formal and informal diplomacy merge. The negotiation of South Africa's transitional constitution also brought official and second-track diplomacy together, opening and soliciting meetings to the public through a media campaign, making materials accessible on the Internet, and widely circulating a draft Constitution for review, comment, and objection.

Government and business need independent watchdogs to oversee and stimulate their activity. Nongovernmental organizations often serve as these watchdogs.

At its best, informal community diplomacy fills critical gaps in international capacity. Intranational and cross-ethnic disputes often fall outside international authority. Without second-track alternatives, minority ethnic groups may see a violent effort for independence as their only option, attempting to form their own nation-states for formal legitimacy.

Second-track diplomacy gives those involved opportunities to gain understanding, transform costly destructive attitudes, build bridges, balance between rights and responsibilities, and create lasting resolution. Concrete ways for citizens to develop democratic capacities are common.

Restorative justice's instrumental role in emerging international systems emulates second-track diplomacy. Truth and reconciliation commissions deliberately engage interested community, including victims of crime and nongovernmental organizations, in negotiating the repair of harm, with offenders admitting culpability.

Likewise, emerging international law and mechanisms explain growth in unofficial diplomacy. Traditionally, international law was literally interpreted as between two nation-states. Now, however, citizens are free to bring grievances, such as human rights violations, outside their state of citizenship. Business can craft arbitration of disputes and circumvent national forums. The international community and its organizations can call issues to the forefront and create truth and reconciliation to investigate the culpability of a nation's citizens and leaders.

Second-track diplomacy raises serious questions about the impact of independent, uncoordinated efforts, which can be potentially problematic if at odds with formal efforts. Yet given the seemingly intractable challenges traditional diplomacy faces, the optimal situation is for unofficial diplomacy to enhance and support formal diplomacy, perhaps even creating the conditions necessary for official efforts to succeed, as the Oslo Accords did. If second-track diplomacy can relieve some of the formal pressure and rectify a few failings and limits, institutional systems are freed to strengthen capacity and realize ideals. Some officials are recognizing this potential and initiating multitrack partnering. The multistakeholder process involving United Nations Economic Commission for Europe (UNECE) Aarhus Convention on Access to Information, Public Participation in Decision-Making and Justice in Environmental Matters, as one instance, is heralded as a model for multilateral policy making, emulating the democratization of global institutions.

—*Nancy Erbe*

See also Dialogic Public Policy; Peace Process

Further Readings and References

Davies, J., & Kaufman, E. (2002). *Second track/citizens' diplomacy.* Lanham, MD: Rowman & Littlefield.

Diamond L., & McDonald, J. (1996). *Multi-track diplomacy: A systems approach to peace.* Bloomfield, CT: Kumarian Press.

Erbe, N. (2004). The global popularity and promise of facilitative ADR. *Temple International & Comparative Law Journal, 18,* 343–389.

Erbe, N. (2005). Communications theory and restorative justice: Approaches to proactive conflict resolution. *Business Research Yearbook, 12,* 696–700.

Erbe, N. (2006, Spring). Appreciating mediation's global role in promoting good governance. *Harvard Negotiation Law Review, 11,* 355–419.

SECURITY

Our perceptions of what constitutes security and any potential threats to it have changed greatly since the end of the Cold War both in theory and in practice. The Cold War was a time of intense nuclear confrontation, but in essence the conflict was contained through deterrence; threats were clearly defined and international relations were predictable, as many states organized themselves into opposing military and ideological blocs. In comparison, current threats are multiple, diffuse, and unpredictable. Fears of rogue states, international terrorism, religious fundamentalism, and the proliferation of weapons of mass destruction preoccupy the developed world as it tries to come to terms with asymmetric warfare. Established solutions such as increasing military superiority through advances in military technology offer little comfort, as even its unquestioned military supremacy was not enough to prevent the September 11, 2001, terrorist attacks on the United States. Additionally, weak states in the developing world are unable to guarantee security to their citizens, leading many to challenge their authority, and in Africa in particular, internal wars have been a major cause of instability. The evident disparities between the world's rich and poor states, coupled with the effects of global environmental degradation, are leading many to question the current division of global wealth and resources. In short, it is not clear how security can be guaranteed anymore.

Security is also a contested concept in international relations theory. For many years, Arnold Wolfers's 1962 definition of security was a standard. He defined national security in an objective sense as the lack of threat to acquired values and the fear that those values will be attacked.

Since the end of the Cold War, though, many of his assumptions have been questioned, as people asked questions about what sort of values were to be protected, who had the responsibility or right to provide such protection, and whose values were to be secured. Theoretically speaking, in recent years we have seen a development in the use of the concept of security from the original, narrow, predominantly state-centric, military definition to a much wider concept, which has both broadened the concept to include the consideration of nonmilitary security threats, such as environmental or economic threats, and also deepened it to suggest the state is not the only referent of security, but also that societal groups and individuals can be at risk. Equally important, growing international interdependence makes it increasingly difficult not to think in terms of international or global security rather than purely national security. This approach again attempts to dislodge the state as the primary referent of security, placing greater emphasis on the interdependency and transnationalization of nonstate actors. This development has not gone unchallenged by people like Stephen Walt, who continue to restrict the application of security to threats in the military realm to the nation-state, but this change has made security more relevant to the global governance debate.

Changing Understandings of Security

So why has this change in both theory and practice taken place? It is necessary to understand how and why our understandings of security have evolved. Before the Cold War, states were primarily concerned with ensuring their own territorial security, sometimes in temporary alliance with other friendly states. In short, policymakers followed the traditional realist/ neorealist theories of security, which assume that the international system is anarchic. This does not mean it is chaotic but that there is no central authority capable of controlling state behavior. Consequently, sovereign states will inevitably develop offensive military capabilities to defend themselves and extend their power and so are potentially dangerous to each other. State survival will be the predominant motive governing behavior: This is known as the security dilemma. War is a constant historical feature of international politics that is unlikely to disappear, and the attempts of states to look after their own security needs leads to rising insecurity for others.

This state-centric view of security had a long historical pedigree. The creation of the modern state system in the 1648 Treaty of Westphalia established the national state as possessing a monopoly of legitimate use of force and thus fostered an organized and disciplined use of military power. The French Revolution's 1789 *levée en masse* further developed this by introducing the concept that the whole of a nation's human and economic resources can be utilized in the pursuit of security for the state. Then came the Industrial Revolution, which provided the technology and financial resources for modern armed conflict and the development of the state-centric form of warfare that was culminated in the military revolution of World War I, which introduced much of the military technology (excepting nuclear weapons) that is still in use today.

During the Cold War, security was understood in collective terms as two ideologically opposed blocs of states (the North Atlantic Treaty Organization and the Warsaw Pact) led respectively by the two superpowers, the United States and the USSR, each of which came to view the other as its only true security threat. Within bloc security, communities emerged—that is, groups of states where cooperation is so instinctive that going to war with one another becomes unthinkable. Escalating mistrust, though, between the blocs led to a vast amount of resources being spent on nuclear and conventional weapons to try to gain military superiority. This struggle for supremacy became an arms race, and the conflict became a military stalemate, where behind the nuclear deterrent—the factor that prevented actual war taking place (although many so-called proxy wars supported by the two blocs did take place)—there lay mutually assured destruction. In other words, there was a permanent military threat.

At the end of the Cold War, brief hopes for a new phase of global peace were shattered by numerous brutal internal wars in the former Yugoslavia, Rwanda, and Sierra Leone to name a few. Some scholars have characterized these conflicts as "new wars," arguing that they marked a distinct break with traditional warfare. These new wars include the following differences:

- Wars today are increasingly intrastate rather than interstate.
- Wars are characterized by state failure and a social transformation driven by globalization leading non-state groups, often led by warlords with private armies, to compete violently over the control of natural resources and the shadow or illegal economy rather than states defending or seeking to expand their interests.
- Combatants often view their identity in ethnic or religious terms rather than national ones.
- Civilian casualties and the forced displacement of people form a much greater proportion of all casualties, and civilians are often deliberately targeted in a brutal fashion.

To summarize, it is argued that a breakdown in state authority, which renders weak states unable to provide security for their citizens (and, consequently, in some cases becomes a security threat to its own citizens), blurs the distinction between public and private and between combatants and civilians.

The need to deal with these new wars led to a new humanitarianism. This has brought new actors into the security discourse; most notably transnational actors such as humanitarian aid agencies, given that most of these wars take place in underdeveloped regions. Development concerns have become increasingly important to how security is understood. It has also reinvigorated ideas about common security or international security. In other words, noninvolved states came to accept that instability anywhere in the world has the potential, in today's interdependent world, to also affect them through migration, economic, social, or environmental consequences. This, coupled with a growing belief in the universality of key human rights and the consequent limits to state sovereignty that this belief entails, led in the 1990s to rising levels of international peacekeeping and peace enforcement and interest in the conceptualization of security in human security terms. In contrast to national security, human security focuses on the threats to personal and community safety—rather than the defense of borders. The role of the United Nations, and in particular the UN Security Council, is prominent in contrast to traditional realist views of great powers maintaining global order. Typical human security policy initiatives have included: the ban on antipersonnel landmines through the Ottawa Treaty; the establishment of the International Criminal Court (ICC) to prosecute genocide and crimes against humanity; the protection of refugees, women, and children in conflict zones; small arms control; and a halt to human trafficking. As a prescription for action, human security has been explained as encompassing humanitarian intervention (the responsibility to protect), peacekeeping, postconflict peace building, and conflict prevention, management, and resolution. This view of security is supported by UN institutions.

This move toward thinking of security more in terms of human or international security has parallels in another security debate that took place in the 1990s, and which was sparked by globalization. As globalization has gradually moved politics, policy, and regulation onto a more transnational footing, states have considered the associated nonmilitary threats in relation to their core values. Concerns about states' abilities to provide their citizens with economic, environmental, social, and cultural security led many to think in terms of nonmilitary solutions to these nontraditional security threats. It is frequently said, for example, that climate change represents the biggest threat to the continuation of the world as we know it, but it is hard to see the armed forces playing any role to counter it. These discussions on the changing nature of security threats took place within both scholarly and practitioner circles.

However, since the turn of the century, new security trends and thinking have emerged that both confirm and contradict the changes in understanding of security that took place in the 1990s. The terrorist attacks by Al-Qaeda on September 11, 2001, against the United States can be understood in two different ways. First, it can be understood as a new type of asymmetric military attack on a nation-state's territorial integrity. A combination of rising levels of weapons of mass destruction (WMD) proliferation and the conviction that international terrorists, who draw their perceived legitimacy from fundamentalist religious or civilizational clashes, know no bounds and would use WMDs has led some states to refocus again on ensuring their own defenses. They are doing this by increasing defense and homeland security resources and also by recognizing that territorial defense might include rigorous intervention, in both those weak states thought to harbor terrorists and in rogue states thought to encourage WMD proliferation

and terrorism. This latter facet has been dubbed the war on terrorism.

The terrorist attacks can also be understood as proof that the global economic, environmental, social, and security disparities that globalization has revealed so starkly must be tackled if those currently left with no hope of progress are not to find religious or cultural fundamentalism and even potentially terrorism as the only possible way to get their voices heard. Such an understanding would suggest that now, even more than in the 1990s, security must be understood in human and international terms, and that limits to state sovereignty must be accepted. This would suggest higher levels of both military and nonmilitary intervention into the areas and societies who have lost rather than gained from the globalization process. This perspective again links security strongly to questions of equitable international governance.

What Next?

Kaldor has argued that there are three possible patterns of security governance for the future: a clash of civilizations, coming anarchy, or cosmopolitan governance. A clash of civilizations would see the formation of civilizational blocs calling on cultural identity for legitimacy, aiming to defend their civilization at home and abroad. Those who prophesy anarchy point to collapsing states in many places but no compensatory emerging global governance, which will lead to islands of civil order in the midst of anarchy. Kaldor's alternative to these undesirable possibilities is cosmopolitan governance based on some form of transnational governance backed by national and local governments, calling on a humanist legitimacy, which would mean that cosmopolitan law enforcement would end modern war.

Others agree that a shift to thinking in terms of global security is vital. Paul Rogers has argued that the factors most likely to influence patterns of conflict in the future are the socioeconomic divide, environmental constraints, and the spread of military technologies. These factors, he contends, are likely to lead to antielite action, increasing migratory pressures, and environmental conflicts, especially over resources and climate change. Finally, he suggests the vulnerabilities of wealthy states to paramilitary actions and asymmetric warfare mean that the status quo is not a viable option. His alternative is for states to work together for a common global security through cooperation on arms control and demilitarization, embracing sustainable economic development, and reversing socioeconomic polarization.

However, those who believe that military and economic strength can indeed enforce control over this unstable world to maintain the status quo oppose this shift to an internationalist perspective. Spending more on national defense, investing in counterterrorism and counterproliferation measures, and coupling these defensive strategies with an aggressive expansion of the Western orthodoxies of free markets and democratization to the rest of the world are viewed as sufficient to pacify dissent. Views on what constitutes security and how best to obtain it remain as contested as ever.

—*Jocelyn Mawdsley*

See also Confidence-Building Measure; Crisis Management; Global Governance; North Atlantic Treaty Organization; Private Military Companies; Realism and Neorealism; Security Community; United Nations; War on Terrorism

Further Readings and References

Buzan, B., Wæver, O., & de Wilde, J. (1998). *Security: A new framework for analysis.* Boulder, CO: Lynne Rienner.
Duffield, M. (2001). *Global governance and the new wars: The merging of development and security.* London: Zed Books.
Kaldor, M. (1999). *New and old wars: Organised violence in a global era.* Cambridge, UK: Polity Press.
Rogers, P. (2002). *Losing control: Global security in the twenty-first century.* London: Pluto Press.
Walt, S. (1991). The renaissance of security studies. *International Studies Quarterly, 35*(2), 211–239.
Wolfers, A. (1962). *Discord and collaboration: Essays on international politics.* Baltimore: Johns Hopkins Press.

SECURITY COMMUNITY

A security community is made up of states that rule out war as an instrument of resolving their conflicts.

Historically speaking, there have been two kinds of security communities: pluralistic and amalgamated. While both have developed based on expectations of peaceful change, the latter emerged when states decided to merge (as in the case of United States), whereas in the case of the former, members retain their independence (as in the Nordic security community). Some kind of integration (defined as the creation of a sense of community and the construction of institutions and practices to sustain that "we feeling") has taken place in both cases, but it is in the case of the former that states have decided to forego their independence and merge under a unitary or federal government. Viewed as such, a security community is an inward-oriented setup. As opposed to seeking to defend members against outside threats (as in the case of collective defense organizations such as NATO), a security community seeks to create a zone of peace within its geographical confines (as with the European Union). It is envisaged that the creation of expectations of peaceful change among members would also render the community more secure against external threats, for this would minimize the grounds for external intervention.

Karl W. Deutsch and the Idea of Security Community

It was Karl W. Deutsch who coined the term and developed the idea of security community during the 1950s when the Cold War was at a high point and the prospects for peace seemed dim. At the time, Deutsch's main concern was the cessation of interstate violence and the creation of dependable expectations of peaceful change by way of strengthening relationships among a group of states. In a project entitled *Political Community and the North Atlantic Area,* Deutsch set out to map the road to the creation of security communities. His conviction was that once the conditions and processes that give rise to security communities were identified, it would be possible to replicate them in other parts of the world so that (the preparation for and the idea of) war would not enter into the calculations of those states.

In order to understand the processes and conditions that foster the creation of security communities,

Deutsch studied the frequency and intensity of interstate transactions. He maintained that transactions generate responsiveness, reciprocity, and mutual predictability of behavior and lead to the discovery of new areas of interest and identifications, thereby resulting in the creation of security communities.

However, as Emanuel Adler and Michael Barnett argued, in the absence of an account as to how actors' willingness to enter into transactions with each other could be molded by transnational forces, interactions, and structures that emerge and evolve due to the actions of the very same (state and nonstate) actors, the potential for the creation of security communities worldwide could not be fulfilled. They have maintained that Deutsch's emphasis on quantitative methods when analyzing the relationship between transactions and the shaping of states' interests and identities, although constituting a major contribution, did not enable him to develop a better understanding of the social relations that generate, and are in turn generated by, those transactions or the dynamic way in which actors' identities and interests are shaped and reshaped to enable, further, or forestall future transactions. Instead, Adler and Barnett proposed a constructivist framework that promised a better understanding of the mutually constitutive relationship between structure and actors' interactions.

Deutsch's own research focused on the potential for the creation of a security community in the North Atlantic area (defined as all countries geographically situated on the North Atlantic Ocean or the North Sea). Although he was positive regarding the potential for the idea of the security community to travel to different parts of the world, his ideas remained largely on paper for four decades until they were revived by Adler and Barnett in an edited volume where the contributors considered the potential for the creation of security communities in different world regions. Thus, Adler and Barnett not only updated the study of security communities by giving Deutsch's framework a constructivist twist, but also broadened the geographical horizons of research into security communities, thereby boosting the prospects for the creation of security communities in a non-European locale. After all, imagining the formation

of a security community would constitute a first step taken toward its creation.

Security Communities in World Politics

Deutsch envisaged the creation of a security community as a top-down process whereby governments that seek to minimize wars would come together and seek ways through which conflicts could be resolved through nonviolent means. From such a perspective, the European Union could be considered a security community par excellence due to the centrality to the project of European integration of the prevention of another European war. The European project has indeed been successful in ruling out war as an instrument of conflict resolution among member states. The expansion of the European Union has meant the export of this security community building method to the new members, thereby expanding the security community to Southern and Eastern Europe.

However, there are two implications of such a top-down approach to security communities for world politics. First, as the Nordic experience has shown, security communities could also be created by the bottom-up approach. In the Nordic case, the initiative came from nonstate actors, who, through increasing interactions, integration, and creation of a "we feeling," rendered it difficult, if not impossible, for their governments to use war as an instrument of statecraft. It is not only the absence of war but regional actors' achievements in finding nonviolent solutions to otherwise complex conflicts that has characterized the Nordic area as a security community. The Deutschian framework, by way of its top-down approach, fails to explain the emergence of the Nordic area as a security community in the absence of a security project on the part of governmental actors. The second implication of this top-down framework is that it makes it difficult to envision the case of imagining security communities in those parts of the world (such as the Middle East) where there is little, if any, governmental interest in the creation of a security community. The bottom-up understanding of security communities, in turn, not only accounts for the Nordic case more completely but also constitutes a model to be emulated by those community-minded actors who seek to create zones of peace in their own geographical locale. After all, it is through the agency of community-minded actors who present the governments with an alternative reading of their situation—a reading informed by an alternative conception of security that shows them as victims of regional insecurity rather than as victims of each other—that concrete steps toward the creation of security communities could be taken.

—Pinar Bilgin

See also Association of Southeast Asian Nations; European Union; North Atlantic Treaty Organization; Peace Process; Security; Top-Down Approach

Further Readings and References

Adler, E., & Barnett, M. (Eds.). (1998). *Security communities.* Cambridge, UK: Cambridge University Press.

Deutsch, K. W., Burrell, S. A., Kann, R. A., Lee, M., Jr., Lichterman, M., Lindgren, R. E., et al. (1957). *Political community and the North Atlantic area: International organization in the light of historical experience.* Princeton, NJ: Princeton University Press.

SEGREGATION

Segregation in the simplest terms means separation. It is usually, however, associated with the separation of groups of people with differing characteristics (for example, race and sex) and is often taken to connote a condition of inequality. Segregation can reflect many states of affairs, ranging from deliberate and systematic persecution through more subtle types of discrimination to self-imposed segregation. Yet it can also be an outcome of circumstances that we might not find morally troubling.

Examples of extreme segregationist policies include the treatment of Jews in Nazi Germany following the passing of the Nuremberg Laws in 1935 and the treatment of Blacks during the South African Apartheid regime. In both cases segregation was fully institutionalized in the legal system. Such segregation denies civil and political rights to the oppressed group and drastically affects their living conditions. Oppression of this sort has been experienced throughout history by women, members of castes, homosexuals, and assorted religious groups, among others, and it has frequently ignited ferocious struggles for equality, such as the Suffragette movement in Great Britain in the early twentieth century and the Civil Rights movement in the United States during the 1960s. Even after such battles have been formally won, however, deep-rooted prejudices often remain intact and hinder substantive integration and equality. Such prejudices are habitually manifested, for example, in the denial of equal opportunities across educational and labor market settings.

Segregation can also be voluntary or self-imposed. The Latino Separatist movement in the United States in the 1960s, rejecting the idea that they would be able to equally flourish within the dominant White culture, demanded racial segregation and campaigned for an independent state. Other groups (for example the Amish in the Eastern United States or certain immigrant groups across host societies), believing that their particular cultural practices are better preserved by remaining separate from mainstream society, tend to cluster geographically and residentially.

Conceptually, we should be careful not to equate segregation and inequality, a common misunderstanding. Segregation is made up of two dimensions, namely vertical and horizontal segregation. Using occupational sex segregation as an example, pay differentials between men and women across occupations within a given labor force characterize vertical segregation. Horizontal segregation, by contrast, merely illustrates the separation of various individuals in terms of the concentration of the sexes in different types of occupations and does not necessarily indicate discrimination or inequality. Theoretically, then, it is possible for individuals to be completely segregated horizontally without any vertical dimension, or vice versa. Yet more usually, a given labor market will be segregated to different extents along both vertical and horizontal lines. Segregation, in and of itself, therefore is not a normative concept, like injustice. Instead, it is a condition that, in order to ascribe causation, requires an investigation of both of its dimensions.

—Jude Browne

See also Civil Rights; Equity; Gender Equality

Further Readings and References

Blackburn, R., Brooks, B., & Jarman, J. (2001). Occupational stratification: The vertical dimension of occupational segregation. *Work, Employment and Society, 15*(3), 511–538.

Branch, T. (1999). *Pillar of fire: America in the King years.* New York: Simon & Schuster.

Browne, J. (2005). *Gender inequality and social change: Sex segregation in the modern labour market.* Bristol, UK: Policy Press.

SELF-GOVERNMENT

To be self-governing is to be subject to no rule other than your own. Both individuals and groups aspire to self-government. One is self-governing when one obeys only those laws, rules, or norms of which one is the author, or can reasonably endorse in some way. A city, state, or group is self-governing when it is free from external domination, and thus free to pursue its own chosen ends of its own will. Although related, these two conceptions of self-government are distinct. One can live in a self-governing community and yet also live nonautonomously in various ways, driven mainly by appetite and desire. Still, with Jean-Jacques Rousseau and Immanuel Kant the two are brought more closely together. Self-government is valuable because of its close connection to rational autonomy and freedom, and the notion that human beings are owed a special kind of respect that is inconsistent with their being dominated or used by others, including tyrannical or arbitrary government.

The problems arise with defining the extent and scope of self-rule. How can a citizen simultaneously rule and yet also be ruled? The strongest claim would be that all those subject to the power of the state must have an equal say and share in how that power is to be exercised—as well as the capacities to do so. Although it is possible that a benign prince or class of elites could frame laws that reflect the true general will of the body politic, this can't be relied upon. Thus, Rousseau, who offers the most ambitious (and notorious) solution to the problem of reconciling political membership with autonomy, insists that citizens are only genuinely self-governing when they form a new political association in which they are subject only to those laws they prescribe for themselves from the standpoint of the general will, which expresses the common good of the community of which they are a member. One of the deep challenges faced by Rousseau's solution is that it presupposes there is indeed a common good that can be ascertained from this common viewpoint and that it is authoritative for each of us. In response, one can loosen the exact sense in which people are said to have equal responsibility in how power is to be exercised over them, and one can thin out the content of the common good or identity Rousseau presupposes to be shared between members of a political community. But then one is also loosening the sense in which there is indeed a self that is self-governing and the extent of control over the power being exercised over it. Genuine self-government thus remains elusive given the complexity of the relations within which the selves asserting their autonomy are always situated.

—Duncan Ivison

See also Civic Capacity; Democratic Theory; Dilemma; Nationalism; Neighborhood Association; Representation; Tribal Governance

Further Readings and References

Machiavelli, N. (1965). Discourses. In A. Gilbert (Trans.), *Machiavelli: The chief works and others* (Vol. 1). Durham, NC: Duke University Press.

Rousseau, J.-J. (1968). *The social contract* (M. Cranston, Ed. & Trans.). Harmondsworth, UK: Penguin.

Skinner, Q. (2002). *Visions of politics II: Renaissance virtues.* Cambridge, UK: Cambridge University Press.

SELF-ORGANIZING SYSTEM

Self-organization is a process where a system reproduces itself with the help of its own logic and components (i.e., the system produces itself based on an internal logic). Self-organizing systems are their own reason and cause; they produce themselves (*causa sui*). In a self-organizing system, new order emerges from the old system. This new order can't be reduced to single elements, it is due to the interactions of the system's elements. Hence, a system is more than the sum of its parts. The process of the appearance of order in a self-organizing system is termed *emergence*. The logic underlying self-organizing systems resembles the dialectical principles of the transition from quantity to quality, negation, and negation of the negation.

Characteristics of Self-Organizing Systems

Self-organizing systems have a multitude of characteristics, including the following:

Systemness—Self-organization takes place in a system, in a coherent whole that has parts, interactions, structural relationships, behavior, state, and a border that delimits it from its environment.

Complexity—Self-organizing systems are complex systems. The term *complexity* has three levels of meaning: (1) There is self-organization and emergence in complex systems. (2) Complex systems are not organized centrally, but in a distributed manner; there are many connections between the system's parts. (3) It is difficult to model complex systems and to predict their behavior, even if one knows, to a large extent, the parts of such systems and the connections between the parts. The complexity of a system depends on the number of its elements and the connections between the elements (the system's structure).

Control parameters—A set of parameters influences the state and behavior of the system.

Critical values—If certain critical values of the control parameters are reached, structural change takes place and the system enters a phase of instability and criticality.

Fluctuation and intensification—Small disturbances from inside the system intensify themselves and initiate the formation of order.

Feedback loops, circular causality—Feedback loops occur within a self-organizing system; circular causality involves a number of processes: $p_1, p_2, \ldots, p_n$ ($n \geq 1$), and p_1 results in p_2, p_2 in p_3, $\ldots$, p_{n-1} in p_n and p_n in p_1.

Nonlinearity—In a critical phase of a self-organizing system, causes and effects cannot be mapped linearly: Similar causes can have different effects and different causes similar effects; small changes of causes can have large effects, whereas large changes can also result in only small effects (but nonetheless it can also be the case that small causes have small effects and large causes have large effects).

Bifurcation points—Once a fluctuation intensifies itself, the system enters a critical phase where its development is relatively open, certain possible paths of development emerge, and the system has to make a choice. This means a dialectic of necessity and chance. Bifurcation means a phase transition from stability to instability.

Selection—In a critical phase that can also be called the point of bifurcation, a selection is made between one of several alternative paths of development.

Emergence of order—In a critical phase, new qualities of a self-organizing system emerge; this principle is also called order from chaos or order through fluctuation. A self-organizing system is more than the sum of its parts. The qualities that result from temporal and spatial differentiation of a system are not reducible to the properties of the components of the systems; interactions between the components result in new properties of the system that cannot be fully predicted and cannot be found in the qualities of the components. Microscopic interactions result in new qualities on the macroscopic level of the system. The emergence of order includes both (a) bottom-up emergence (a perturbation that causes the system's parts to interact synergetically in such a way that at least one new quality on a higher level emerges) and (b) downward causation (once new qualities of a system have emerged, they, along with the other structural macroaspects of the system, influence—that is, enable and constrain—the behavior of the system's parts). This process can be described as a top-down emergence if new qualities of certain parts (seen as wholes or systems themselves) show up.

Information production—Self-organizing systems are information-producing systems.

Fault tolerance—Outside a critical phase, the structure of the system is relatively stable concerning local disturbances and a change of boundary conditions.

Openness—Self-organization can only take place if the system imports entropy that is transformed; as a result, energy is exported or dissipated.

Symmetry breaking—The emerging structures have less symmetry than the foundational laws of the system.

Inner conditionality—Self-organizing systems are influenced by their inner conditions and the boundary conditions from their environment.

Relative chance—There is a dialectic of chance and necessity in self-organizing systems; certain aspects are determined, whereas others are relatively open and subject to chance.

Hierarchy—The self-organization of complex systems produces a hierarchy in two distinctive senses: (1) The level of emergence is a hierarchically higher level—that is, it has additional, new emergent qualities that cannot be found on the lower level that contains the components. The upper level is a sublation (*Aufhebung* in the Hegelian sense of the term) of the lower level. (2) Self-organization results in an evolutionary hierarchy of different system types; these types are hierarchically ordered in the sense that upper levels are more complex and have additional emergent qualities.

Globalization and localization—Bottom-up emergence means the globalizing sublation of local entities; downward causation means the localization of more global qualities.

Unity in plurality (generality and specificity)—A self-organizing system is characterized by a number of distinctive qualities that distinguish it from other self-organizing systems. Each type of self-organizing system also shares general principles and qualities with all other types of self-organizing systems. Both generality/unity and specificity/plurality are characteristic of self-organizing systems.

The concept of emergence is the central notion of self-organization concepts. Important aspects of emergence are synergism, novelty, irreducibility, unpredictability, coherence/correlation, and historicity. New qualities of a system are due to synergies from the interacting elements of the system. Emergent qualities are qualities that have not been previously observed and have not previously existed in a complex system ("a whole is more than the sum of its parts"). The newly produced qualities are not reducible to, or derivable from, the level of the producing, interacting entities.

Niklas Luhmann introduced the concept of self-referentiality as a sociological application of self-organization theory. In his view, the elements of a social system are self-producing communications, (i.e., a communication produces further communications and hence a social system can reproduce itself as long as there is dynamic communication). For Luhmann, human beings are only sensors in the environment of the system. Luhmann puts forward a functional theory of society that is based on a dualism of system and human actors.

Another type of self-referentiality in social systems has been introduced by considering interpreting the relationship of social structures and social practices and actions as dialectical. Social structures enable and constrain social actions and are produced and reproduced by social actions. This process can be interpreted as a dynamic self-organization process. Social systems are re-creative; they permanently produce and reproduce actions and structures.

—Christian Fuchs

See also Anarchy; Autopoiesis; Complexity; Cooperation; Sociocybernetics; Space; Systems Theory

Further Readings and References

Fuchs, C. (2003). Dialectical philosophy and self-organisation. In V. Arshinov & C. Fuchs (Eds.), *Causality, emergence, self-organisation* (pp. 195–244). Moscow: NIA-Priroda.

Fuchs, C. (2003). The self-organization of matter. *Nature, Society, and Thought, 16*(3), 281–313.

Fuchs, C. (2003). Some implications of Pierre Bourdieu's works for a theory of social self-organization. *European Journal of Social Theory, 6*(4), 387–408.

Fuchs, C. (2003). Structuration theory and social self-organization. *Systemic Practice and Action Research, 16*(2), 133–167.

Luhmann, N. (1984). *Soziale systeme.* Frankfurt, Germany: Suhrkamp.

SELF-REGULATION

Regulation is an element of everyday life. Regulation, as is governing in general, is one of the main activities of governments in welfare states. However, regulation seems to become increasingly problematic. Societies (the general public, distinct groups, private enterprises) seem to resist public administrators' regulatory attempts. The causes for this resistance vary. At least three regulation problems can be formulated. All three lead to inefficacy.

Regulation Problems

First of all, problems exist in the context of regulation. Internal as well as external complications in policy programs' implementation are recognized: bureaucratic politics, historical and international developments, doubts on the legitimacy of politics, and problems that are specific for certain policy areas. Second, there are problems of closure. Closure of actors or policy networks constitutes a second set of complications for regulation. Third, a learning capacity of society should be mentioned. People have the ability to reflect on regulations and to even anticipate them. Consequently, they may avoid regulation or use them for their own benefit, regardless of the intentions of government.

Beyond State-Centered Government

Regulation once had only one source, which is legislation made up by an elected government. One might say that regulation was the main example of state-centered and monopolistic government. But policy making, hence regulation as a specific kind of policy making and policy instrumentation, has long ceased to be a prerogative of elected governments. Policy sciences and public administration have provided insights that teach us that other sources of regulation exist beyond formal political decisions. Multilevel governance leads to local adaptation of national policies, among others. Street-level bureaucracy has, to some extent, the same affect; it results in standard procedures and adaptation to what suits street-level bureaucrats. Insights in the

network society have shown that governments depend on the cooperation of other societal actors; regulation is the result of public-private negotiations. System theories, not least theories on autopoiesis, tell us society has differentiated in subsystems that are self-constituting, self-steering, and closed to governmental steering. Finally, society has gained social capital, resulting in a society able to govern itself.

Self-Regulation as Solution

In such a situation in which government does not have a superior position over other parts of society, how can it produce binding decisions and how can it regulate societal developments? Some scholars and policymakers, therefore, promote self-regulation by societal actors as a solution to regulation problems, with ideological as well as more pragmatic arguments. Self-regulation means that those who are subordinated to regulation and are obliged to comply are the same people that are responsible for drawing the regulations, executing monitoring, and maintaining the regulations. People, groups, and parts of society bind themselves to their own rules.

Self-regulation is assumed as having advantages over government regulation. It is supposed to be a solution to the overloaded agenda of government and the courts. Another supposed advantage is that self-regulation can be more flexible than governmental regulation because interested parties will do their best, and in due time, to make the necessary alterations. Last but not least, maintenance reputedly is more effective, because the ones who have to comply are the ones who made up the regulations. People have to live up to their own rules.

The Ambiguity of Self-Regulation

Despite the obvious benefits of self-regulation, it nevertheless is not without problems. In a strict form, self-regulation may cause all kinds of undesirable side effects.

First, it has to be safeguarded that all relevant interests have a share in the self-regulatory processes. The government may need to guard the access of weak or poorly articulated societal interests. The costs of the regulation might otherwise be spread in an unequal and unjust way.

Second, in many countries there is a difference between the kinds of legal protection of individual citizens. In some countries, legal protection against the implementation of government regulation tends to be better than against private law regulations. Self-regulation arrangements, then, will lead to decreasing legal possibilities for individual citizens.

Third, self-regulation may not be as flexible as expected. Especially in those cases in which highly incompatible interests are supposed to coordinate and draw shared regulations, it may take quite some time before the regulations are set or changed.

Fourth, self-regulation will not necessarily be as powerful as was hoped. The maintenance of some regulations may still need penal law, a type of law that only governments are allowed to make.

It may, therefore, be advisable for governments to intervene in the self-regulatory processes. However, this is a hazardous obligation. A government may destroy the readiness and ability to self-regulate.

Intervention in Self-Regulation

Even though government lacks the power to intervene, there are reasons to pay extra attention to it with regard to possibilities for regulation. Most important, government is supposed to be responsive to societal needs; moreover, it is held responsible for solving societal problems.

However, there are some preconditions. The government has to take into account that governmental regulations are not self-executing. The addressees need to accept the regulations. Negative perceptions of government, disregard, and disrespect will have almost prohibiting effects on regulation. The government, therefore, should constantly make an analysis of its environment. If the environment is a friendly and accepting one, old-fashioned regulation may be possible. In a hostile environment, regulation may have all kinds of effects, even reversed ones.

What is necessary is a model of what may be called inciting governance, which has the following characteristics. Intervention takes into account a nonhierarchical position of government. Government intervention and regulation aim at coupling autonomous self-regulating actors and applying diverse steering instruments. Regulation no longer aspires to regulate society at large, but instead offers policy options; the effectiveness of those options increases if a choice between a limited set of options is mandatory. Varying ways and means of intervention is important to prevent domination of one kind (e.g., juridical instruments).

—*Linze Schaap*

See also Corporate Codes of Conduct; Governability; Government; Internet Governance; Regime Theory; Regulation; Sensemaking

Further Readings and References

Dunsire, A. (1996). Tipping the balance: Autopoiesis and governance. *Administration & Society, 28*(3), 299–334.

Luhmann, N. (2000). *Law as a social system.* London: Oxford University Press.

Papaefthymiou, S. (1990). *On a 'Constructivist epistemology of law'* (EUI Working Paper Law No. 1990/3). San Domenico di Fiesole, Italy: European University Institute.

Teubner, G. C. M. (Ed.). (1988). *Autopoietic law: A new approach to law and society,* Berlin, Germany: Walter de Gruyter.

Veld, R. J., Schaap, L., Termeer, C. J. A. M., & van Twist, M. J. W. (1991). *Autopoiesis and configuration theory: New approaches to societal steering,* Dordrecht, Netherlands: Kluwer Academic.

Sensemaking

Sensemaking is an approach to designing and implementing systems and activities. Sensemaking has been under development since 1972. It consists of a set of philosophical assumptions, substantive propositions, methodological framings, and methods. Sensemaking literally means the making of sense of social actors that need to construct the situations they experience in a meaningful way. Some perspectives emphasized sensemaking as an individual activity, while others focus on the social nature of this process. Sensemaking is the process through which people make sense of their situations. Sensemaking is described as placing stimuli into frameworks, comprehending, dealing with surprise, constructing meaning, interacting to produce mutual understanding, and the patterning of experience.

Karl Weick systematically explored, explained, and organized the properties of sensemaking in seven elements: (1) grounded in the construction of individual and organizational identity; (2) retrospective in nature; (3) based on enacting sensible environments to deal with; (4) fundamentally a social, not an individual process; (5) an ongoing and dynamic process in that changes occur as events occur; (6) focused on cues in the environment and focused by cues in the environment; (7) driven by the plausibility of possible interpretations.

Sensemaking requires enactive and sensible environments. In organizational life, members of the organization often contribute to production of the environment or at least part of the environment they live in. Action is also required for sensemaking. Sensemaking cannot occur without an action in the environment. The environment cannot produce an action without individual members' conscious effort. Organization and the environment are factors that influence each other.

Sensemaking is also a social process. Human thinking and social functioning in an environment are essential aspects of sensemaking. Sensemaking is an ongoing (learning and action) process. It is not easy to determine a starting or an ending point for sensemaking. Sensemaking is focused on and by extracted cues (signs). In life, people are confronted with a lot of cues. Sometimes cues are too much to notice. A sensemaker will only notice a few cues based on sensemaker's filter and interest. A sensemaker's interests and unconsciousness depend on what cues a sensemaker focuses on. Sensemaking is driven by plausibility. Most of the time, people are cognitively lazy. When we find an answer to the question, we stop searching.

Weick's example of, "How can I know what I think until I see what I say?" explains how these seven elements are used in sensemaking:

Identity: The recipe is a question about who I am as indicated by discovery of how and what I think.

Retrospect: To learn what I think, I look back over what I said earlier.

Enactment: I create the object to be seen and inspected when I say or do something.

Social: What I say and single out and conclude are determined by who socialized me and how I was socialized, as well as by the audience I anticipate will audit the conclusions I reach.

Ongoing: My talking is spread across time, competes for attention with other ongoing projects, and is reflected on after it is finished, which means my interests may already have changed.

Extracted cues: The "what" that I single out and embellish as the content of the thought is only a small portion of the utterance that becomes salient because of context and personal dispositions.

Plausibility: I need to know enough about what I think to get on with my projects, but no more, which means sufficiency and plausibility take precedence over accuracy.

Sensemaking in Organizations

Weick stated that information is the common raw material that all organizations and individuals process. Weick said the goal of organizing is to make sense out of equivocal information. This means that any message can have a number of meanings. Through communication, participants collectively interpret and make sense of information in their environment. In dealing with organizational issues, sensemaking requires us to look for explanations and answers in terms of how people see things rather than structures or systems. Sensemaking suggests that organizational issues—mission, strategies, change, goals, strategic plans, tasks, teams, and so on—are not things that one can find out in the world or that exist in the organization. Rather, their source is people's way of thinking and understanding.

Weick presented a model of organizational sensemaking that is based on a conceptualization of organizations as loosely coupled systems in which individual participants have great latitude in interpreting and implementing directions. The purpose of organizational information processing is to reduce the equivocality of information about the environment.

Weick summarizes a sensemaking-organizing model as follows: The central argument is that any organization is characterized by the way it runs through the processes of organizing. This means that we must define organization in terms of organizing. Organizing consists of the resolving of equivocality in an enacted environment by means of interlocked behaviors embedded in conditionally related processes. Organizing is directed toward information processing in general and, more specifically, toward removing equivocality from informational inputs.

Weick described how people enact or actively construct the environment that they attend to by bracketing experience and by creating new features in the environment. Sensemaking is induced by changes in the environment that create discontinuity in the flow of experience, engaging the people and activities of an organization. These discontinuities constitute the raw data that have to be made sense of. The sensemaking recipe is to interpret the environment through connected sequences of enactment, selection, and retention. In enactment, people actively construct the environments that they attend to by bracketing, rearranging, and labeling portions of the experience, thereby converting raw data from the environment into equivocal data to be interpreted. In selection, people choose meanings that can be imposed on the equivocal data by overlaying past interpretations as templates to the current experience. Selection produces an enacted environment that provides cause-effect explanations of what is going on. In retention, the organization stores the products of successful sensemaking (enacted or meaningful interpretations) so that they may be retrieved and reflected in the future.

—*Naim Kapucu*

See also Communicative Action; Communicative Rationality; Interpretive Policy Analysis; Interpretive Theory; Organizational Learning; Self-Regulation

Further Readings and References

Brown, A. D. (2000). Making sense of inquiry sensemaking. *Journal of Management Studies, 37*(1), 45–75.

Savolainen, R. (1993). The sensemaking theory: Reviewing the interests of a user-centered approach to information seeking and use. *Information Processing & Management, 29*(1), 13–28.

Weick, K. E. (1993). Collapse of sensemaking in organizations: The Mann Gulch Disaster. *Administrative Science Quarterly, 38,* 628–652.

Weick, K. E. (1995). *Sensemaking in organizations.* Thousand Oaks, CA: Sage.

Weick, K. E. (2001). *Making sense of the organization.* Oxford, UK: Basil Blackwell.

SERVICE DELIVERY

Service delivery can be defined as a process whereby governments deliver publicly identified goods and services to citizens or the community through various mechanisms, instruments, and relationships. Service delivery is a term that has gained prominence in the governance literature over the past half century, particularly under the pressures and promises of an expanding welfare state. Classical notions of service delivery have focused on the role of government in authorizing and delivering basic goods and services to select individuals or the broader community. But over time, interpretations of service delivery have been expanded to include the entire policy process (specifically, policy design, policy implementation, operational management or contractual arrangements, public resources—both financial and human—and monitoring and feedback). The development of service delivery has been influenced by changing ideas over public provision and alternative ways of providing goods and services in the context of economic and budgetary pressures.

There are three main modes through which goods and services can be provided. First, services can be delivered through direct governmental action. Often considered the traditional responsibility of public administration, delivery through this mode occurs when services are directly distributed by the administrative or bureaucratic apparatuses of government (i.e., ministries and departments of state) to individuals or communities. No intermediaries are necessary for service delivery to occur and, hence, the state is considered to hold a direct relationship with the recipients of services.

Second, service delivery can occur through the interactions and transactions between different orders of government. In federated systems, where constitutions or intergovernmental agreements define the parameters of public action, grants or transfers to subnational governments often provide the resources necessary to deliver services that could not be provided by one area of government alone. Patterns of service delivery may originate with the highest order of government (national or federal) and cascade to the lower orders of government for implementation; the pattern rarely flows in the opposite direction. Intergovernmental service delivery involves multiple public agencies collaborating in the provision of services to the community. However, with multiple government agencies collaborating to achieve service delivery outcomes, the problems of intent, priority, implementation, and quality assurance can emerge.

Third, service delivery can take place through specialist, nongovernmental providers contractually employed to implement programs. These third-party providers can include large publicly listed companies, privately incorporated firms, nonprofit ideological or faith-based organizations, the voluntary sector, and community-based welfare groups. Governments use third-party providers for various philosophical and financial reasons, namely cost, quality of service, specialization, access to clients, debureaucratization, and to remove government agencies from delivery responsibilities.

The services delivered through these modes are expansive in nature (ranging from income support for individuals to services that benefit the entire community) and vary enormously across jurisdictions. However, services common to most jurisdictions can be said to consist of: core state services (such as law and order, public safety, national defense, and monetary functions); business and economic services (such as regulation, industry support schemes, and tax expenditures and concessions); infrastructure and physical services (such as road, rail, ports, telecommunications, and technology services); social and welfare services (such as pensions, income support, medical services, and assistance to disadvantaged groups); environmental and quality-of-life services (such as public parks, urban renewal projects, sporting fields, cultural events, and museums).

Social and welfare services are, by far, the largest cluster of services provided by governments—especially in terms of the financial resources they consume. Their role in providing safety-net income or in maintaining the social and economic fabric of modern polities is often cited as major reasons for their aggregate growth over the past half century. Other forms of services, while also significant aspects of contemporary governance, will tend to vary in accordance with the changing political, economic, and social values of a given society. For example, the delivery of infrastructure and physical services (e.g., ports or railways) or business and economic services (e.g., industry-assistance programs or tax concessions) will differ according to notions of public versus private responsibility, stages of economic development, and state traditions.

Policy Instruments of Service Delivery

Governments employ a multiplicity of policy instruments to ensure that services are delivered to individuals and the community. The type of service-delivery instrument utilized can vary significantly between and within jurisdictions, but is usually dependent on the type of service delivered, the personal experiences and philosophies of decisionmakers, the political, social, economic and legal structures of a society, the internal capacities of service providers, and the expectations of the individuals and communities who are the recipients of the services. The commonly used instruments include: cash provisions, grants to other governments or individuals, contractual arrangements, regulation, client incentives and behavioral modification, education, and moral persuasion.

Over the past three decades, Western governments have turned to many nonbureaucratic or market-inspired instruments of delivery that fall beyond the traditional bounds of administrative activity, particularly in the area of social and welfare service provision. Governments have experimented with new and more flexible delivery instruments as a consequence of economic and budgetary constraints and community pressure for better services and a greater say in how they are delivered. Through such new instruments as contracting out, service purchasing, corporatization, sponsorship of private enterprise, government insurance, tax credits or tax expenditures, grants, vouchers, and loan guarantees, governments have incrementally extended the realm of service delivery and increased the number of agents involved with service provision.

Dominated by such new instruments and an increasing number of delivery agents, service delivery has evolved into a complex kaleidoscope of governmental and nongovernmental activity where it is as much a consequence of networks and relationships as it is direct political authority. However, it is important to note that many of these instruments have tended to complement, but not replace, the traditional bureaucratic forms of service delivery. As governments seek to respond to the changing demands and pressures of individuals and communities, service delivery will continue to be at the forefront of government's relationship with communities—whether it is provided by the state, on behalf of the state, or in addition to the state.

—*Alexander Gash and John Wanna*

See also Contracting Out; New Public Management; Public Sector; Service Provider; Service Quality

Further Readings and References

Doherty, T., & Horne, T. (2002). *Managing public services: Implementing changes.* London: Routledge.

Organisation for Economic Co-operation and Development. (1996). *Responsive government: Service quality initiatives.* Paris: Author.

Perry, J. (Ed.). (1989). *Handbook of public administration.* San Francisco: Jossey-Bass.

Peters, G., & Pierre, J. (Eds.). (2003). *Handbook of public administration.* Thousand Oaks, CA: Sage.

Salamon, L. (Ed.). (2002). *The tools of government: A guide to the new governance.* New York: Oxford University Press.

SERVICE PROVIDER

Service provider refers to all those organizational entities or individuals that are directly involved in the delivery of a vast range of services to clients, consumers, or citizens at private or public levels. The term refers to a variety of forms of ownership and structures; it is broad enough to encompass individual and organizational providers, governmental and nongovernmental organizations, for-profit and nonprofit entities, and professionals and nonprofessionals.

In many countries, the state remains the main service provider as it takes responsibility for the delivery of a sizable core of public services. However, the full picture of state service providers is characterized by a significant degree of diversity. At the two extremes, there are vertically integrated ministries and independent, state-owned enterprises. In between lies a diverse range of public bodies that differ in their organizational forms and their governance structures, among other ways. Analysts have distinguished between delegated service providers and devolved service providers. Delegated providers, while being direct subsidiaries of ministries, generally function under a quasi-contractual relationship with their reporting ministry. Devolved providers, on the other hand, are separate legal entities that enjoy a greater scope of autonomy and have their own governance structures. Both groups function under public law.

When the organizational provider is the public sector, the boundaries may be blurred between service provision and other key related functions, such as funding, purchasing, and regulatory responsibilities. Although all these functions may be assumed by a single entity, a clear distinction between them is one prerequisite for having clear lines of accountability and for providing for appropriate incentives for effective allocation and use of public resources.

Although public entities continue to offer a significant part of public services in most countries, recent changes in public administration have been marked by the efforts of states to reinforce their strategic, purchasing, and regulatory capacity while delegating the provision functions to private providers. Among the range of options available, public payers may contract with individual or collective private providers. In other cases, the service provision is completely in the realm of the private sphere and delivered by for-profit private providers funded through private insurance or out-of-pocket payments. With both options, the service provision is ensured by private entities that function under private law and have a fully separate legal identity from the state.

Alongside the public and for-profit private providers, there is also a third sector with a range of nonprofit organizations: faith-based organizations, associations, charities, and so on. In some countries, such as the Netherlands, a large part of education and medical services are delivered by these providers.

As has already been pointed out, service providers cannot be restricted merely to organizational entities. Nearly all services require individual providers that come into direct contact with clients (teachers, nurses, doctors, lawyers, etc.). Yet the attention paid to these frontline service providers should not cause us to overlook the contribution of a range of other groups largely playing a supporting role and making possible the delivery of services. Similarly, the primacy given to formal providers with extensive training and legal recognition conferred by licensure, registration, or certification should not divert attention from the range of informal providers, such as traditional healers, volunteers, or community workers, who also make a significant contribution, particularly to community-based support services.

—Carl-Ardy Dubois and Damien Contandriopoulos

See also Contracting Out; Purchaser-Provider Split; Quasi-Market; Service Delivery

Further Readings and References

Contandriopoulos, D., Denis, J.-L., & Langley, A. (2004). Defining the 'public' in a public healthcare system. *Human Relations, 57*(12), 1573–1596.

Dubois, C.-A., Nolte, E., & McKie, M. (2006). *Human resources for health in Europe.* Berkshire, UK: Open University Press.

SERVICE QUALITY

Service quality represents value judgments about results, impacts and outcomes of what organizations do or provide. These qualities might be intended by management in the form of a specification or standard, or they may be a subjective assessment by customers, clients, or other recipients of products or services. Subjective assessments are arrived at by comparing the service level expected from the organization with that which the organization is perceived to deliver.

Both definitions of service quality apply to various stages of organizational product or service production as well as the ultimate one(s). For example, a quality standard may have been determined by management, which specifies how welfare department clerks will relate to applicants for public assistance. However, there may be variance between behavior required by the standard and the client's perception of the clerk's behavior in this intermediate processing stage (rather than final service delivery). The client may also have a negative perception of an end result, such as one that denies public assistance. Service quality perceptions may be mixed, such as when a long wait for emergency room service results in a negative view of the service provider, although the actual service given by the physician, when it occurs, may be deemed excellent by the sick or injured person.

As previously mentioned, service quality is an element of organizational production functions. From an operational perspective, production functions include several elements of which quality is an important part. First, various inputs (e.g., money, human resources, materials) are applied to some conversion process (e.g., decision making, machinery, an entire program) to produce outputs (e.g., hour miles of police patrol, public policies, program services). Management-developed quality standards may be applied at all of these stages. However, of considerable importance are those at the output and outcome stages. For example, a program of after-school tutoring might require an output of a fixed number of hours per student as a service-quality standard. Outcome measures are indicators of accomplishments or results. In the previous example, not only did the students have the set period of time for tutoring (the output standard), but a results standard might require that a specified percentage of students achieve a given skill-level gain in reading.

Results can also include measures of public perceptions (e.g., timeliness, safety, and cleanliness of transit vehicles). Special studies might be conducted to help determine quality of results (e.g., public accessibility to transit measured as the size and distribution of populations being served).

Perceived positive or negative service quality can sometimes result in vigorous public reactions. For example, a major finding on the effect of citizen's service-quality perceptions was uncovered by a study in Eastern Europe, where survey research revealed that tax evasion is lowest among those who believe they are getting good quality government services for the taxes they pay.

—Gilbert B. Siegel

See also Effectiveness; Efficiency; New Public Management; Service Delivery

Further Readings and References

Governmental Accounting Standards Board of the Financial Accounting Foundation. (1993). *Service efforts and accomplishments reporting: Its time has come.* Norwalk, CT: Author.

SITUATED AGENCY

Situated agency has to do with the relationship between conduct and context involving meaningful human actions. Central to giving an explanatory account of human behavior and social practices, whether explicitly or implicitly, is a conception of the relationship between concepts and practices, meaning and action. When we view people as situated agents, we attribute to them the ability to reason and act in novel ways despite the background that they necessarily inherit, which provides a context for their creative innovations. Situated agents always set out against a background of some social discourse or tradition but because they are not wholly constructed by it, they can create traditions and practices through local reasoning and modify the very background that influences them. To attribute situated agency to people is thus to regard them as capable of using and modifying their social context (e.g., language, discourse, traditions) according to the meanings they hold. Regarding people as situated agents allows us to properly take into account how people's intentionality is the source of their conduct.

The idea of situated agency is most commonly discussed in relation to postfoundational debates about subjectivity, particularly on the issue of how we should understand meanings to be derived. As a reaction to the primacy of the subject in the modern era, postfoundationalism repudiates the autonomous view of the self according to which individuals would be able, at least in principle, to have experiences, adopt beliefs, exercise reason, and perform acts independent of any contexts. Postfoundationalists typically reject autonomy on acceptance of the fact that individuals necessarily experience the world in ways that reflect the influence upon them of traditions, ideologies, or discourses. The rejection of autonomy leads many postfoundationalists to focus exclusively on the construction of subject identities toward an oversocialized concept of humans as passive constructs of social forces when this need not be so. The suggestion that individuals are always situated within social contexts leaves open the possibility that they are situated agents who can innovate against the background of such context. Moreover, situated agency entails only the ability to creatively transform an inherited tradition, language, or discourse; it does not entail the ability to transcend social context.

Situated agency thus stands as a critique of both the traditional autonomous view of the self and contrary approaches that see subject identities as almost wholly constructed. The idea that people are shaped by circumstances and institutions has ceased to be controversial, but to say that everything we do can be explained by social forces, places, and functions is by no means obvious and no more compelling than the view of autonomous individuals prior to any social context. Individuals are never merely the passive supports of prescribed roles or social processes; nor can human actions be explained solely in causal, functional, or mechanical terms. Social actors must be understood, at least in part, as intentional subjects acting in response to an understood situation and whose actions must also be seen in terms of a symbolic or meaningful character for the agents themselves. The concept of situated agency is thus useful for analyzing or explaining a social practice, where we should want to elucidate the ways in which people respond to dilemmas creatively from within their existing beliefs.

—Naomi Choi

See also Decentered Theory; Dilemma; Embeddedness; Interpretive Theory; Local Reasoning; Narrative Theory; Tradition

Further Readings and References

Bevir, M. (2004). Governance and interpretation: What are the implications of postfoundationalism? *Public Administration, 82*(3), 605–626.

Bevir, M., & Rhodes, R. (2006). *Governance stories.* London: Routledge

Taylor, C. (1986). Foucault on freedom and truth. In D. Hoy (Ed.), *Foucault: A critical reader.* New York: Basil Blackwell.

SOCIAL CAPITAL

Social capital refers to aspects of social organization, including social networks and norms of reciprocity and trust, that facilitate cooperation and the accomplishment of goals. It is a resource created and accumulated through repeated everyday interactions among and between individuals. It includes not only the social networks and connections among individuals, but also the physical and political context that supports network development and the resources produced. The social aspect of social capital is the interactions between individuals to achieve goals. The capital aspect of social capital is the resources realized as a result of these interactions. Incorporated in this definition are two related, but disparate, notions of social capital. One notion relates to social capital as a structural resource and examines resources that individuals access as a result of their membership in a particular social structure. The other notion

refers to the nature and extent of one's involvement in relationships, regardless of context. Both conceptualizations share a focus on the productive potential of social capital; social capital makes possible the achievement of ends that might be impossible in its absence.

The first view of social capital takes a social structural approach, viewing social capital as something realized through interactions embedded in a particular social and political context. In this view, social capital is neither owned nor embodied by particular individuals or groups, but is a structural resource available to individuals for personal gain. Whereas economic and human capital are the property of individuals, social capital is an emergent property of relationships. Unlike other forms of capital, individuals both contribute to social capital and use it, but they cannot own it. This view of social capital includes work by Pierre Bourdieu, who in 1985 employed an instrumental economic approach, using the term to explain social class formation and power. Bourdieu's definition implies the deliberate investment of individuals in a network for later personal use or access with an unspecified obligation of reciprocity. Other work related to this view of social capital stems from James S. Coleman, who provided a similar functional definition in 1988, viewing social capital as the aspect of social structure that facilitates actions of individuals and institutions within social structure. Coleman believed that social capital had the potential to strengthen community social fabric because it builds bonds based on information, trust, and solidarity among people, most often as by-products of their activities.

The second view of social capital theory, popularized by Robert Putnam in 1993, focuses on the norms of trust and reciprocity that emerge from interactions among individuals, regardless of social structural context. Social capital is redefined in this school of thought as an attribute that individuals or groups either possess or do not possess. Here, social capital refers to the collective value of social connections and the inclinations that arise from these relationships to accomplish mutual goals. Individual gain might result, but social capital is more importantly related to the achievement of collective ends. Within this view, three dimensions of social capital are defined as bonding, bridging, and linking. The dimensions are not either-or categories, but differences in the ratio of the three may yield different outcomes. Bonding social capital refers to ties among like individuals who generally share similar sociodemographic characteristics. Bridging social capital refers to ties among dissimilar individuals, while linking social capital refers to one's ties to authority, such as public or private institutions. Bridging and linking social capital are thought to contribute to a productive and well-functioning civil society because both types increase opportunities for civic participation, broaden networks of exchange, and increase access to resources. Bonding social capital, on the other hand, has the potential to create strong in-group identities, boundaries, and intolerance of outsiders. Bonding social capital may also foster group norms that are so powerful that they restrict individual choice and freedom by disallowing exit from the group and creating strong demands for conformity.

Putnam introduced the idea that social capital carries with it social rewards, such as the better functioning of society. His view holds that when people share a sense of identity, possess similar views, trust each other, and act reciprocally for mutual benefit, social capital exists. The presence of social capital impacts on the social, political, and economic nature of society in which it exists. Thus, Putnam's conceptualization of social capital has gained prominence with those interested in society and governance. In fact, social capital has been referred to as "the raw material of civil society." Civic engagement and associational life become key attributes (and indicators) of social capital in this view.

Putnam's definition has come under attack as being conflated with neo-Tocquevillean notions of civil society and for discounting power and the role of political and institutional contexts, such as the state. Some favor Putnam's definition of social capital because it affirms the importance of trust, generosity, and collective action in social problem solving. Others see it as setting up an excuse for government to disinvest in community and social problems and to ask communities to solve problems themselves that might otherwise be in the purview of the state.

Social capital is a multifaceted and complex term, laden with definitional and measurement ambiguities. So many varieties of the social capital doctrine exist that using the term without clarification conveys little information.

—Dana Petersen

See also Brokerage; Civic Capacity; Civic Engagement, Civil Society; E-Democracy; Institutional Performance; Neighborhood Association; Physical Capital; Sociology of Governance; Trust

Further Readings and References

Bourdieu, P. (1985). The forms of capital. In J. Richardson (Ed.), *Handbook of theory and research for the sociology of education* (pp. 241–258). New York: Greenwood.

Coleman, J. S. (1988). Social capital in the creation of human capital. *American Journal of Sociology, 94*(4), S95–S120.

de Tocqueville, A. (1998). *Democracy in America.* (P. Ranshaw, Ed., & H. Reeve, Trans.). Garden City, NY: Doubleday. (Original work published 1835)

Portes, A. (1998). Social capital: Its origins and applications in modern sociology. *American Review of Sociology, 24,* 1–24.

Putnam, R. (1993). *Making democracy work: Civic traditions in modern Italy.* Princeton, NJ: Princeton University Press.

SOCIAL CHOICE

The first text in social choice theory was Kenneth J. Arrow's 1951 *Social Choice and Individual Values.* Arrow's approach, which was consistent with rational choice, and his result, stated in the impossibility theorem, served to end the social welfare economics tradition and to construct the new field of social choice. In the 1930s and 1940s, social welfare economics was embroiled in a worldwide debate over whether either a capitalist free market pricing system or a socialist planned economy represented the superior means to organize a society. Given both the Great Depression and the successes of economic planning during World War II, especially evident in the Manhattan project, debate was rampant. The difficulty of formulating a social welfare function, which could be used as a public policy tool for understanding the economic effects of redistribution, had already been established by social welfare economists. However, the impossibility theorem definitively proved that it is impossible to achieve any collective statement of social welfare from individuals' preferences in a complex society. Arrow's impossibility theorem, which gave rise to social choice research, demonstrated the unfeasibility of the social welfare economic structure widely presupposed prior to the theorem.

Social choice differs from the prior social welfare economics tradition by substituting the rational choice framework of studying individual choice for the prior calculus-based diminishing marginal utility method. The rational choice framework quickly led to the development of a social choice approach to studying questions of collective welfare. The new approach relies on an axiomatized system that states basic conditions that should be met by any collective choice procedure. In addition to assuming that individuals may have any rational preferences over alternatives, and that no dictator imposes a single decision on the group of individuals, two conditions receive much scrutiny for their role in undermining the possibility of reaching rational collective outcomes. One is the acceptance of the idea that comparing the intensity of individuals' preferences among alternatives can play no role in the group decision. The other is that the collectively rational expression of individual interest must yield a total ranking of all alternatives that remains unchanged, even in the case that one of the alternatives is removed from consideration. If either of these latter two conditions is relaxed, then it is possible to derive a statement of collectively rational preference over alternatives from individuals' preferences.

Even though social choice has, to a large extent, worked to ameliorate the negative result stated in the impossibility theorem, the theorem remains the basic entry point into all research in this field. For researchers adopting the public choice approach, social choice is suspect for continuing to attempt to make positive statements about collective welfare or collectively rational choices. However, by closely analyzing the formal conditions of collective choices, social choice has contributed means by which to make progress in supporting the public policy objective of addressing citizens' interests. For example, social choice demonstrates that it is possible that a strict adherence to individuals' rights over personal choices may, surprisingly, violate the criterion of Pareto optimality generally assumed to characterize market transactions.

—*S. M. Amadae*

See also Impossibility Theorem; Pareto Optimality; Positive Political Theory; Public Choice Theory; Rational Choice Theory

Further Readings and References

Amadae, S. M. (2003). *Rationalizing capitalist democracy: The Cold War origins of rational choice liberalism.* Chicago: University of Chicago Press.

Arrow, K. J. (1963). *Social choice and individual values* (2nd ed.). New Haven, CT: Yale University Press.

Sen, A. K. (1985). Social choice and justice: A review article. *Journal of Economic Literature, 23,* 1764–1776.

SOCIAL CONSTRUCTIVISM

Constructivists argue that social reality is constructed out of human knowledge, beliefs, or meanings. Typically they add that human knowledge is also constructed. Such constructivism stands in stark contrast to accounts of our knowledge as resting directly on the facts of the matter. It denies that our knowledge can derive from pure experiences of an independent reality. To the contrary, it emphasizes the positive role played by social traditions and cultural conventions in determining the content of our experiences. Hence, constructivism often acts as a form of critique. It suggests that ideas that might appear to be inherently rational or natural are in fact the artifacts of particular traditions or cultures. Likewise, it implies that our social and political practices are not the result of natural or social laws; they are the product of choices informed by contingent meanings and beliefs.

Social constructivism has been applied to a range of concepts. Perhaps the most controversial, in philosophical terms, are concepts such as truth and reality. The most controversial in social terms have perhaps been race, sexuality, and gender, all of which might be thought to have a basis in given facts about our bodies. Constructivism has also been applied to social and political institutions, including nations, corporations, agencies, and governments. This constructivist view of institutions challenges many of the leading approaches to social science and also related approaches to public policy. Constructivist theories of governance stress the role of tradition, discourse, and culture in constructing contemporary patterns of rule. They thereby highlight the contingency and contestability of governance in contrast to those who see it as inevitable, rational, or explicable by reference to natural or social processes. They suggest that contemporary governance is a social construction. It arose out of particular traditions or particular regimes of knowledge.

Varieties of Constructivism

All forms of social constructivism emphasize the constructed nature of the social world. However, there are different ways of unpacking constructivism, and we should distinguish between them. Although it is tempting to think of each type of constructivism as an account of society as a whole, each of them might apply to some (but not all) of our concepts.

A general version of constructivism insists that we make parts of the social world by our intentional actions. People act for reasons that they adopt in the light of beliefs and tacit knowledge that they acquire in part through processes of socialization. For example, when shopkeepers price goods, they make an aspect of the social world in accord with their beliefs about how to make a profit and their perhaps tacit concepts of market economics and fair exchange. Other aspects of the social world then arise as the unintended consequences of such intentional actions. For example, if a shopkeeper prices her goods higher than her competitors, and if potential customers buy goods at the lower prices available elsewhere, she will go bankrupt irrespective of whether or not anybody intended or foresaw that outcome.

All kinds of social scientists allow that we make the world through our intentional actions. Often they seek to explain actions in terms of allegedly social or natural facts about institutions, social class, gender, or a universal human rationality. In contrast, constructivists usually argue that the intentions of actors derive in part from traditions, discourses, or systems of knowledge that are also social constructs. This linguistic social constructivism implies not only that we make the social world by acting on certain beliefs and meanings, but also that we make the very beliefs and meanings upon which we act. In this view, our concepts are contingent products of particular discourses and practices; they are not natural or inevitable ways of conceiving and classifying objects. Again, our concepts are the artificial inventions of a particular language, culture, and society; they are not a universal vocabulary that picks out natural kinds in the world. Constructivism thus implies that varied traditions or cultures can categorize objects differently. For example, it is a commonplace that Eskimos have many words for the different types of snow or that the people of the Kalahari Desert have words that pick out various shades of red. Therefore, linguistic social constructivism consists of what is called antiessentialism. It asserts that our concepts do not refer to essences: Our concepts do not pick out core, intrinsic properties that are common to all the things to which we might apply them and that also explain the other facets and behavior of those things. It is certainly possible that none of our social concepts refer to essences, especially if we define a social concept as one that cannot be unpacked solely in terms of our bodies, their movements, and their reactions. However, to say that our social concepts do not refer to essences is not to say that they do not refer to anything at all. We should distinguish between pragmatic, critical, and antirealist forms of constructivism.

Linguistic social constructivism implies an antiessentialism according to which concepts do not have objective boundaries but rather are determined by social factors. Sometimes this antiessentialism inspires a pragmatic account of social concepts. In this view, social concepts are vague; they capture family resemblances and they are conventional ways of dividing up continuums, rather than terms for discrete chunks of experience. But although pragmatic concepts do not refer to essences, they do refer to groups of objects, properties, or events—often groups that have vague boundaries. Social factors determine pragmatic concepts because there are innumerable ways in which we can classify things and because it is our purposes and our histories that lead us to adopt some classifications and not others. Nonetheless, the role of social factors in determining pragmatic concepts does not mean that these concepts have no basis in the world. To the contrary, we might justify adopting the particular pragmatic concepts we do by arguing that they best serve our purposes, whether these purposes are descriptive, explanatory, or normative. We might justify a pragmatic concept, such as new public management, on the grounds that its content derives from family resemblances between recent public sector reforms. We also might defend ascribing particular content to concepts, such as neoliberalism, on the grounds that doing so best explains the resemblances between public-sector reforms. And we might adopt a particular concept of democratic accountability on the grounds that it best captures those patterns of rule that we should regard as legitimate given our normative commitments.

Critical constructivism arises when we want to suggest a concept is invalid. In such cases, we might argue that the concept is determined by social factors and that it fails to capture even a group. For example, we might reject the concept of new public management as unfounded, especially if it is meant to refer to a global trend. We might argue that different states introduced very different reforms with widely varying results. And we might add that the reforms drew upon, and resembled, each state's traditions of administration far more than they did a common neoliberal blueprint. In such cases, we dismiss concepts as unfounded by arguing that there is no fact of the matter—neither an essence nor a group—that they can accurately pick out.

Some antirealists have adopted a kind of global critical constructivism, applying it to all of our concepts. Typically these antirealists argue that the role of prior theories and traditions in constructing our experiences precludes our taking these experiences to be accurate of a world independent of us. They argue that we only have access to our world (things as we experience them) rather than some world independent of us (things in themselves). And they then conclude that this means that we have no basis on which to treat our concepts as true to the world. In their view, there is no outside the text and thus no world outside our linguistic constructions.

Constructivist Approaches to Governance

Different types of social constructivism might inspire different approaches to governance. Whatever the merits of antirealism as a global theory, it is important to say—especially perhaps in the *Encyclopedia of Governance*—that there is nothing incoherent about an antirealist or critical account of the new governance. The new governance is often defined in terms of the hollowing out of the state: The state is said to have lost the ability to impose its will and to have come to rely instead on negotiations with other organizations with which it forms networks and partnerships. In contrast, we might suggest that the state never had the ability to impose its will. The state always had to operate with and through organizations in civil society; it always has been plural and dispersed. Hence we might conclude that there is no fact of the matter that can be accurately picked out by the concept of the new governance.

Even if we took an antirealist stance toward the new governance, we still might be interested in abstract questions about governance conceived as an account of features of all patterns of rule. The general and pragmatic versions of social constructivism are most relevant to these abstract questions. Because constructivists argue that we make the social world by acting on contingent sets of meanings, they generally analyze changing patterns of governance in terms of competing traditions and bodies of knowledge. They favor the interpretive approaches to governance that concentrate on elucidating the meanings that make possible any particular pattern of rule. Similarly, because constructivists emphasize the contingency of traditions, they sometimes highlight the diversity of traditions at play within a pattern of rule and the contests between these traditions. They favor bottom-up approaches to governance that explore how meanings are created, sustained, contested, and transformed by human activity within practices saturated with relations of power. Finally, when constructivists emphasize the contingent and diverse nature of traditions, they offer critical genealogies of alternative accounts of governance. They reject any suggestion that a natural or social logic determines the content or the development of any given pattern of rule. They argue that political scientists efface the contingency of social life when they attempt to ground their theories in apparently given facts about human rationality, the path-dependence of institutions, or the inexorability of social developments.

Although constructivists typically favor interpretive, bottom-up, and critical approaches to governance, they disagree among themselves about the details of such approaches. The main disagreements seem to distinguish governmentality and decentered theory. These two forms of constructivism appear to embody different views of meaning. Governmentality theorists often imply that meanings exist as quasi structures in that their content derives from their relationship to one another within discourses: Individuals are just the passive supports or constructs of such discourses. In contrast, decentered theorists take meanings to arise from the use individuals make of language to express their beliefs; discourses are just clusters of intersubjective beliefs adopted against the background of similar traditions.

Constructivists adopt different views of meaning largely because they hold different views of the individual. Governmentality and decentered theory alike reject the idea of an autonomous individual. They insist that individuals are inherently located within social contexts that influence them. Governmentality theorists appear to also want to reject the idea of human agency. Many of these theorists concentrate exclusively on the ways in which social contexts or discourses give individuals their intentions and beliefs—their identities. Decentered theorists want to defend the idea of situated agency, even as they reject that of autonomy. They argue that individuals can

reason and act in novel ways, albeit that they can do so only against the background of inherited traditions that influence them. Although people always set out against the background of a discourse or tradition, they are agents that can act and reason in novel ways to modify this background. Hence they conclude that although a linguistic context forms the background to people's statements and a social context forms the background to their actions and practices, the content of statements and actions does not come directly from these contexts, but rather from the ways in which people replicate, use, or respond to these contexts in accord with their intentions.

—*Mark Bevir*

See also Communicative Action; Communicative Rationality; Decentered Theory; Discourse; Governmentality; Interpretive Theory; Neotraditionalism; Norms; Regime Theory; Tradition

Further Readings and References

Barry, A., Osborne, T., & Rose, N. (1996). *Foucault and political reason: Liberalism, neo-liberalism and rationalities of government.* London: University College London Press.

Berger, P., & Luckmann, T. (1966). *The social construction of reality: A treatise in the sociology of knowledge.* Garden City, NY: Doubleday.

Bevir, M., & Rhodes, R. (2003). *Interpreting British governance.* London: Routledge.

Bevir, M., & Rhodes, R. (2006). *Governance stories.* London: Routledge.

Bevir, M., Rhodes, R., & Weller, P. (Eds.). (2003). *Traditions of governance: History and diversity* [Special issue]. *Public Administration, 81*(1), 1–17.

SOCIAL DEMOCRACY

Social democracy is a governance system that integrates the equity goals of socialism within a democratic framework. Social democracy is a political-economic response to capitalism, arguing that, although it has certain economic strengths, capitalism fails to realize social equity and often fails to achieve the economic ends of full employment.

The term *social democracy* is more an ideological declaration than a technical description. Rather than a list of structural characteristics, it represents a general advocacy of the social welfare responsibilities of government within a democratic structure that is more group than individual oriented. Social democracy is a reaction against the perceived shortcomings of socialism, communism, capitalism, and democracy.

Socialism

Socialism describes an economic organization of society with collective ownership of resources and institutions. In practice, socialism is less an absolute concept and more a continuum of possible configurations. To the extent that nations have more collective ownership of resources and institutions, they are more socialist. Both socialism and communism advocate collective ownership of the means of production. However, socialism tends to refer to ownership by the government (sometimes called state socialism), while communism refers to direct ownership by the people.

Direct ownership of resources by the people is more an ideal than a reality. While under the final development of communism, the state (and state ownership of resources) withers away. The reality is that most self-identified communist governments maintain totalitarian, top-down governance structures where resources are controlled by the state. However, both communism and socialism advocate collective ownership of resources.

Socialism is sometimes portrayed as a balance between capitalism and communism. Where capitalism leaves most economic decisions to individuals, under socialism those economic decisions are made by the collective. While capitalism relies on free enterprise to facilitate the most efficient allocation of resources, socialists argue that capitalism results in inequality, suffering, and the loss of human dignity. A truly equitable society can only be achieved through a collective ownership and administration of resources. As described in the following sections, social democrats advocate a policy mix of the two perspectives.

Finally, a common differentiation between socialism and communism involves the use of violence to achieve power. Communism advocates the revolutionary overthrow of current structures, asserting that only through force will capitalistic institutions surrender power. Most socialists and all social democrats call for a more evolutionary and peaceful transition to collective ownership and believe economic structures can be changed through democratic institutions. In addition to its advocacy of peaceful transition, social democracy does not completely reject liberalism and a market economy.

Democracy

While democracy means rule by the people or *demos,* it does not address resource ownership. All policy issues are arrived at through the democratic process, leading to the possibility of inequitable social and economic policies chosen through a democratic political process.

For large aggregations of people (such as states), democracy normally means representative democracy, which can be pursued through a variety of electoral systems. A political approach to democracy focuses on the formal decision-making structure rather than the content of policies or how they are implemented. While representational democracy specifies rule by the people, it does not limit the decisions people will make. While liberal democracy may preserve some individual rights and civil liberties, social democracy presupposes egalitarian economic and social welfare policies within a liberal democratic structure.

Social democracy may be juxtaposed to liberal democracy, as socialism is to capitalism. Liberal democracy locates the democratic process within a classical, liberal economic framework of individual rights and a market economy, while social democracy locates democratic institutions within a framework of collective ownership, group rights, and a self-declared valuation of human dignity.

Liberalism understands individual success and failure that results from differences in skills and abilities to be legitimate and morally justified. Individuals deserve what they achieve. Inequality based on such differences is fair, equitable, and even necessary for social development. The capitalist economic framework requires inequality as incentive for individual effort. The collection of individual efforts, in turn, is asserted to lead to an increase in overall benefits for everyone. Inequality, under classical liberalism, ultimately leads to the greater good of all.

Social Democracy

The social democratic construct does not separate economic inequality from political inequality. It argues that concentration of economic wealth prevents true democracy, which is dependent on the equitable distribution of resources and the preservation of human dignity. Equality and freedom are shaped not only by the availability of political rights, but also by individual human capacity and access to resources. Without equal access to resources and the capacity to use them, inequities lead to concentrations of power in the hands of those with greater personal, social, and economic resources. It is the concentration of power that blocks effective and equitable democracy. Where capitalism argues that the good life is achieved through an aggregate increase in goods and services, socialism and social democracy argue that the good life can only be achieved when there is equitable distribution of those resources.

Social democracy attempts to resolve social and economic inequalities within a specifically democratic framework. State control of resources enables it to equalize power and resources among citizens through redistributive and regulatory balancing coupled with social welfare policies. Social democrats argue that without equalization of resources, democracy is hollow because those with greater resources are able to unequally influence the collective decision-making system. It is equality of power, not simply individual rights, that preserves democracy.

The combination of Keynesian macroeconomic policies and social welfare programs within a democratic political structure forms the foundation of social democracy. Social democrats tend to embrace the economic theory developed by John Maynard Keynes, which argues that unbridled capitalism will lead to a less-than-full-employment economy. Capitalist principles depend on keeping labor costs low, in part

through unemployment. An increased labor supply leads to lower labor costs. The success of the economy, therefore, is borne by those least able to bear it. Social democrats specifically advocate central government intervention through macroeconomic policies to maintain full employment.

Social Democratic Corporatism

Social democracies in Europe often include the concept of corporatism, which envisions a government partnership with labor and business interest groups to ensure social equity. The adjective "democratic" is often applied to corporatism (as it is to socialism) to envision a pluralist structure that is not elitist. Democracy, or rule by the people, can be pursued either by political structures that aggregate individual preferences, or by peak interest groups that represent various perspectives. Corporatism (or neocorporatism to distinguish from authoritarian structures) argues that structured interest group governance can better represent labor and other lower socioeconomic groups than capitalism.

Inequities in Democratic Systems and the Balance of Power

Both liberal democracy and social democracy question the ability of pure democracy to be truly equitable. Liberal democracy fears the threat of governmental power wielded by the majority to the individual and seeks to balance that threat through limits on government and by guaranteeing individual freedoms. Social democracy fears the inequitable results of a capitalistic economic system and seeks to balance that threat through state-based macroeconomic and social welfare policies.

Both social democracy and liberal democracy profess to pursue the well-being of citizens. Both are concerned that unbridled democracy will lead to inequities and possibly tyranny. Social democracy affirms the framework of a capitalistic economy and liberal democratic protections but seeks to also balance economic power among citizens.

Social democrats believe the capitalist economy can be effectively steered by political means to produce desirable outcomes. They put their faith in Keynesian-type economic management, a certain degree of planning, and a positive sum relationship between equality and efficiency.

Conclusion

Social democracy is an ideological declaration that allocation of resources matters, and only the government can facilitate equitable distribution. It is a response to the political shortcomings of socialism and the equity shortcomings of capitalism. In a social democracy, economic equality is combined with political equality to create the foundation for democratic participation. Equitable economic outcomes are important both normatively for equality and to promote a more balanced and equitable democratic system.

A Globalization Postscript

The evolution of economic globalization is argued by some to threaten the effectiveness of social democratic systems. In the global marketplace, national economies are subject to international influences and are affected by multinational and cross-national organizations. While states control their political structures, they have less sovereignty over economies that do not end at political borders. While social democracy strives to balance economic allocation of resources, achievement of economic equality in a globalized world may be beyond the control of states, instead requiring cross-national and multinational partnerships and relations. The challenge for social democracy in a globalized world is to promote and protect the social and economic capacities of its citizens in a world where economic and political structures are increasingly enmeshed in relationships beyond individual state control.

—*Jonathan F. Anderson*

See also Capitalism; Communism; Corporatism; Democratic Theory; Global Governance; Globalization; Keynesianism; Liberalism; Political Economy; Representative Democracy; Third Way

Further Readings and References

Esping-Andersen, G., & van Kersbergen, K. (1992). Contemporary research on social democracy. *Annual Review of Sociology, 18,* 187–208.

Giddens, A. (1999). *The third way: The renewal of social democracy.* Malden, MA: Polity Press.

Hay, C. (2000). Globalization, social democracy and the persistence of partisan politics: A commentary on Garrett. *Review of International Political Economy, 7*(1), 138–152.

Huber, E., Ragin, C., & Stephens, J. (1993). Social democracy, Christian democracy, constitutional structure and the welfare state. *The American Journal of Sociology, 99*(3), 711–749.

Mishra, R. (1999). *Globalization and the welfare state.* Northampton, MA: Edward Elgar.

Przeworski, A. (1985). *Capitalism and social democracy.* New York: Cambridge University Press.

SOCIAL EXCLUSION

See SOCIAL INCLUSION

SOCIAL INCLUSION

The concept of social inclusion has increasingly been seen as a new paradigm informing public policy. Responding to the changing nature and role of the state, in particular, the constraints imposed upon it by the actions of international and transnational actors, social inclusion promotes the involvement of a broader range of actors, including civil society organizations as well as governments, in addressing the multifaceted nature of disadvantage. Extending the understanding of disadvantage beyond the simple redistribution of material resources, the concept of social inclusion focuses attention on the civil, political, and social spheres.

Although employed by a range of actors from civil society groups, organizations such as the European Union, and transnational bodies such as the World Bank, no single definition for the term exists, and the concept itself is highly contested. Social inclusion is often presented in opposition to social exclusion, with the relationship between the two being seen as a dialectical one. Furthermore, the concept of inclusion and its other, exclusion, is based upon a mechanistic understanding of human relations where people satisfying certain criteria are bounded as included and those who do not are considered outside this boundary and thus excluded.

Understanding what constitutes inclusion varies widely among users and in the academic literature. Inclusion is generally regarded as common membership, governed by a particular vision of the political good, thus producing cohesion. Several paradigms conceptualizing inclusion have been identified, each espousing a particular conception of what it is to be included. This has implications for the analytical methods each paradigm relies upon and the moral discourses associated with them. These paradigms are employed variously across actors, and often individual actors utilize multiple discourses emanating from several different paradigms. For example, in the case of the New Labour government in Great Britain, there is evidence that several different discourses about inclusion are employed at different times. For example, on one level inclusion is defined solely in terms of paid employment: Individuals can only be included in society if they participate in paid employment, and they are excluded from it if they do not participate. However, on another level, New Labour employs a multidimensional conception of inclusion whereby inclusion is achieved through participation in a variety of activities, not just employment.

Despite its portrayal as a concept able to consider both processes and outcomes and thus agency and structure, critics of the term contend that the concept obscures structural inequalities by focusing only on horizontal relationships between in and out rather than vertical delineations between up and down. Moreover, by portraying the relationship between inclusion and exclusion as binary, the concept is used to isolate the excluded and to ignore those doing the excluding. This consequence is particularly acute when analyzing the examples previously given—where inclusion is conceptualized only in terms of paid employment. In the discourses of both the European Union and New Labour, exclusion is conceived as a condition,

not a process, and therefore not something that can be inflicted onto people. Thus, when such actors talk about inclusion it is not used to address the structural economic processes or agents that inhibit inclusion and so resorts to an agent-focused notion of exclusion, where it is individuals themselves that are responsible for their own exclusion.

Furthermore, critics argue that the term *inclusion* implies conformity to already existing social conventions or to a particular vision of the political good. By arguing against exclusion and so for the inclusion of those outside society, social thinkers are weakening the possibility of change. Rather than employing the discourse of inclusion and exclusion, discourse critics argue that it is inherently conservative thinkers that should be seeking to challenge the dominant culture and norms of society and so redefining what is meant by inclusion in the first place.

—Caroline Kenny

See also Communitarianism; Good Governance; Multiculturalism; Social Democracy; Unemployment

Further Readings and References

Askonas, P., & Stewart, A. (Eds.). (2000). *Social inclusion: Possibilities and tensions.* London: Palgrave Macmillan.
Bowring, F. (2000). Social exclusion: Limitations of the debate. *Critical Social Policy, 20*(3), 307–330.
Judge, A. (1995, February). *Social exclusion: A metaphoric trap? Moving beyond false dialogue.* Paper presented at the European Continental Forum on Citizenship and Ways out of Social Apartheid, Paris.
Levitas, R. (1998). *The inclusive society? Social exclusion and New Labour.* Hampshire, UK: Palgrave Macmillan.
O'Reilly, D. (2005). Social inclusion: A philosophical anthropology. *Politics, 25*(2), 80–88.

SOCIAL JUSTICE

While activists may argue that achieving social justice is the most significant social justice challenge, scholars may argue that defining social justice is more of a challenge. Over the ages, many books and articles have been written about social justice without ever defining it. This may be partly due to a reticence to define a term that often changes, depending upon the times (and this is a major critique of social justice movements; that the term itself is an umbrella term to encompass virtually any movement). The reticence to define the term may also be partly due to the attachment of the term to at least two major arenas: ideological and pragmatic. For ideologues, social justice may mean one thing. For those working in practical and everyday ways to address social justice issues, it may mean something else entirely. Definitions also change depending upon what brings one to social justice work: morals, politics, or social or economic concerns?

Social justice is often referred to (or designated) as a moral virtue: It is linked with religious or other similar movements or orders (for example, some orders of Catholics, specifically the Jesuits and the Benedictine orders, are particularly concerned with social justice). Social justice is also often referred to (or designated) as part of certain political movements: It is associated with socialism, Marxism, and other radical or progressive political parties. Finally, social justice is often referred to (or designated) as a social or economic movement; it is associated with national and international movements for peace, equity, economic justice, racial justice, human rights, women's and children's issues, living wages, and social and physical safety and security.

The term *social justice* appears first to have been used in the 1840s by Italian priests. John Stuart Mill, in his 1863 text *Utilitarianism,* defined social and distributive justice as a standard of equality toward which all institutions and virtuous citizens should treat people. The term came to prominence as an appeal to the ruling classes to attend to the needs of those displaced in a shift from rural to urban economies. Social justice is social in that it involves working with and organizing socially to work together toward some goal of justice and in that it involves works of justice that benefit the common.

Justice is defined as the quality of being just or fair. Most definitions of justice contain references to moral rightness. Social justice, as previously indicated, is typically linked to distributive justice, or the just (right) distribution of limited resources relative to demand. Distributive justice is often closely linked to the concepts of human dignity, the common good, and human rights. Distributive justice refers to what society owes individual members in proportion to: the individual's needs, contribution, and responsibility; the resources available; and society's responsibility to the common good. Implied here is that society and virtuous citizens have a duty to individuals in serious need. Also implicit is that all individuals are entitled to equal access to the basics necessary for living humanely. Distributive justice is not the same as legal justice, which is defined as the rights and responsibilities (social contract) to honor and obey laws and regulations deemed necessary to protect peace and social order.

Social justice can be restricted to an ideological or ethical concern or it can be a pragmatic force, leading to programs and activities developed to redistribute resources and alleviate human suffering. For many religious and social groups, social justice is encompassed in the everyday acts they do to promote peace, justice, equity, and to ameliorate problems related to poverty, violence, discrimination, and oppression. As such, any analysis or action of social justice requires that our habits and practices around power and powerlessness be interrogated. In addition, most social justice movements also require that our assumptions around dominant political economies also be interrogated. In addition to working to ameliorate the problems leading to human suffering, social justice practitioners also work to change the political and economic structures that lead to these problems. While some may argue that issues requiring social justice have been with us since the beginning of civilization, it also can be argued that many contemporary social justice issues have their direct roots in economic and political systems that favor the haves over the have-nots. In contemporary times, the gulf between these two groups is growing, leading to even more social justice issues. In addition, a decentering of expertise and of power have brought both more social justice issues to the attention of those seeking social change and also made access to resources (knowledge, power, and influence) more available to people and groups suffering from social justice problems. Social justice, then, is pursued not only by religious (moral) or social and political (ideological) groups, but also by those directly affected by social and economic inequities.

All said, whether or not we can define social justice may be irrelevant. The definition is linked to working toward equity and fairness in the ways in which resources are distributed in human society. Furthermore, work that redistributes resources in fair and equitable ways can also be deemed social justice activities.

—Cheryl Simrell King

See also Civil Rights; Gender Equality; Good Governance; Multiculturalism; Social Democracy; Social Inclusion

Further Readings and References

Mill, J. S. (1998). *Utilitarianism* (R. Crisp, Ed.). New York: Oxford University Press.

Novak, M. (2000, December). Defining social justice. *First Things, 108,* 11–13.

Social Learning

Social learning is an approach to policy analysis that originated in the work of Albert Bandura. His examination of how behavior is acquired and regulated through a cognitively oriented theory was explained in terms of the processing of both direct and symbolic sources of information. In the context of governance, social learning generically refers to a process through which policymakers adjust their ideas and practices to changes in their environment and how these changes become manifestations in the revisions of policy that ensue as a result. It is perhaps most associated with the work of Hugh Heclo and Peter Hall.

Heclo's work in the 1970s focused on the processes through which learning took place among social policymakers in Great Britain and Sweden, concerned especially with the processes of puzzling used to resolve policy problems, with policy making being a

form of collective puzzlement on society's behalf. Heclo suggested that learning takes place in two particular forms, termed *classic conditioning,* which is effectively routine, conditioned policy responses, and instrumental conditioning, which is where policy learning takes place in situations of major policy change. In periods of relative stability, both in terms of the continuity of those making policy as well as the policy environment, Heclo suggested that classical conditioning is likely to be prevalent, a mode of policy making where policymakers effectively muddle through, making small adaptations to policies as necessary, but without much need for thought. For instrumental conditioning, however, something more radical must take place in which policymakers come to question their underlying ideas. For this to happen, Heclo suggested, it is likely that we will need a change in government, even though the learning takes place from elites, whose views become attached to a popularly organized group. Heclo was fairly clear about the processes involved in classic conditioning in his work, but instrumental conditioning appeared to be somewhat less developed.

Heclo's work was hugely influential, but not placed in a coherent theoretical framework until the 1990s, when Peter Hall's examination of UK macroeconomic policy change led him to construct a model of social learning that he suggests state policymakers engage in. Hall defined social learning in the policy context as a deliberate attempt to adjust the goals or techniques of policy in response to past experience or new information. Learning is indicated, Hall suggested, when policy changes as a result of these deliberate attempts at change. Hall suggested there are three central features in the prevailing model of social learning utilized by contemporary theorists of the state.

The first central feature suggested by Hall is that policymakers' goals are influenced by policy legacies, and that the influence of the past is more significant than prevailing economic and social conditions. The major locations of these policy legacies are in the people and practices of the civil service bureaucracy and the state. This clearly follows Heclo's suggestion that the major sources of learning are not politicians, but civil servants and other elites. This feature is significant because it suggests that policy is subject to considerable inertia—it is theoretically possible for policy to change quickly, but is unlikely to do so because of the difficulty of changing practices inside a government bureaucracy. Second, Hall suggests that those promoting policies are likely to be experts in the relevant field, including elected officials and civil servants. Again, this follows Heclo, that is, a technocratic model of policy with a large role to play for experts. Finally, Hall's third feature is that the social learning model is concerned with the capacity of states to operate without pluralistic considerations—to be able to operate with autonomy from societal pressures in the formulation of policy goals. This last feature allows the state to be insulated, to some extent, from societal change and so, again, creating a tendency toward inertia.

Logically following from these three features of policy, Hall suggested there are three types of policy change with particular modes of learning attached to each. First-order change is where policymakers adjust the settings of the policy instruments they use. This is routine, day-to-day policy change of little relative significance. This is the type of behavior associated perhaps most with incrementalism—policymakers muddle though, engaging in routinized behavior, delegating control to government officials who, through their expert knowledge, hold privileged positions. An example of first-order learning is where a routine, small adjustment to the interest rate takes place. The decision is probably highly programmable and ultimately noncontentious. This is Heclo's classic conditioning, albeit in a clearer form.

Second-order change is where policymakers abandon the policy instruments they have so far being using in favor of others, but within the same overarching hierarchy of policy goals. In other words, they are finding new ways of achieving the same ends. We have a change in policy, but not a change in the goals policymakers are pursuing. Hall used the examples of competition and credit control (CCC) in the United Kingdom in the 1970s and the abandonment of strict monetary growth controls by the Thatcher government. In each case, the policy changes represented a change of emphasis by the government in power, but

not the abandonment of its underlying policy goals. This stage is new in Hall's framework—it does not appear in Heclo's work. Second-order change, then, arguably represents a degree of learning from policymakers—they are showing a willingness to experiment beyond the limits of the rather automatic policy making represented by first-order change.

Third-order change is where policymakers abandon the policy goals they have been pursuing in favor of others—strictly speaking they adopt a new hierarchy of goals that is significantly different from what went before. Third-order learning is associated with a paradigm shift in policy. The example that Hall used is the shift from Keynesian (from John Maynard Keynes) macroeconomic management to monetarism in the United Kingdom at the end of the 1970s. This is Heclo's instrumental conditioning, but in a far more explicit framework. Hall suggested that third-order change, which is the most obvious example of policy learning, is most likely to occur as a result of policy failure. This is because failure is most likely to lead policymakers to try both first- and second-order changes without success and thus become forced to reconsider the underlying principles upon which they base their policy decisions. Only in the face of an incommensurable gap between the expected outcomes of policy decisions and the resulting outcomes are policymakers prepared to abandon a policy paradigm and adopt another.

Because policy paradigm shifts are so radical, they appear most likely to occur after a change in government, rather than as a result of an existing government changing direction completely—such a reversal in policy would result in a considerable loss of credibility. As such, the movement from one policy paradigm to another is likely to be preceded by a period of significant experimentation, perhaps taking place in the relative security of opposition. As paradigmatic anomalies accumulate (differences between the paradigm's view of the world and what appears to be happening), it will attempt to patch up the paradigm and make it consistent with the anomalies it is facing. But modification of paradigms leads to a loss of their internal coherence and explanatory power until they become fatally undermined. Under these circumstances, competing paradigms will be in a position to offer alternative, possibly untried solutions to the problems that policymakers are facing and so potentially provide an attractive alternative to the continued failures they are facing. It is notable, however, that paradigms are unlikely to be ideologically neutral; in macroeconomic policy, for example, we would expect governments of the Left and Center to be inclined toward Keynesian-derived paradigms because of their redistributive potential, and governments of the Right to be more inclined to monetarist views of the world that favor minimal government intervention and liberalized marketplaces.

To institutionalize a policy paradigm shift, a new team of advisors will be required as a consequence of the previous advisors' ideas being discredited. Therefore there is also the likelihood of both a significant change in political personnel and a likely change in government. Accompanying such a change will be a reliance on alternative sources of knowledge associated with the new policy paradigm as the "locus of authority" changes. The example of this, again, is the sea change that resulted from the shift in economic policy paradigm from Keynesianism to monetarism in Hall's work, with a change in government (from Labour to Conservative), a reliance upon new policy advisors by the Thatcher government (utilizing the Centre for Policy Studies extensively), and a politicization of the civil service to attempt to ensure that the new monetarist ideas were worked through and applied. All of this increases the chance of the institutionalization of the new policy paradigm being successful, in turn, leaving a legacy that policymakers of the future will have to face up to. Once third-order policy change has taken place, it will be difficult to reverse, suggesting that policy paradigm shifts are relatively infrequent. Therefore there is a considerable amount in common between studies of social learning and studies based on the concept of path dependence.

Hall's framework has been considerably utilized by scholars who study policy change in a number of areas, from further studies in macroeconomic policy to the policy areas of alcohol and health. Extensions to the framework are less common. Michael Oliver extended a footnote from Hall's paper that suggested a possible fourth order of change, or "learning to learn," to examine how policymakers might become more reflective in their approach to learning and of possible links to the notion of policy transfer. Oliver extends Hall's work in two directions, helping to provide a more detailed view of what a policy paradigm might comprise of, as well as linking Hall's work with the possibility of learning from abroad. Fourth-order change, Oliver suggests, can be a framework within which we can better understand the need for first-, second-, and third-order learning. By focusing more specifically on how policymakers come to learn, we can come to understand their capacity to do so.

Ian Greener examined the difficulty of isolating a policy paradigm shift and focused on how second-order learning can be the symptom of policy malaise, and so perhaps more significant than when it first appeared in Hall's model. Greener also suggested that policy paradigms are more ideologically biased than Hall's work implied, and he began to outline the wider significance of a policy paradigm shift in terms of political credibility.

Critics of the social learning approach suggest that it is too heavily based on the historical institutionalist approach to political science, focusing on the role of institutions in constraining action and relying upon external (exogenous) events to instigate policy change rather than the actions of policymakers themselves, who can appear in some accounts to be puppets reacting to the events going on around them in a turbulent political environment rather than being particularly proactive in their approach to policymaking. This criticism is largely justified—the social learning model appears to rely extensively on the external policy environment to provide impetus for change. But this in itself is a problem because the policy environment does not come to us in an ideological vacuum; instead we must interpret it discursively, and so the policy environment will tend to be interpreted by policymakers according to the policy paradigm that is in place. Also, the notion of policy crisis, which will most likely lead to a policy paradigm shift, is not as unproblematic as it first appears. Crises are the result not only of policy anomalies, but also the response of significant societal stakeholders, especially the media, to their discovery. As such, politically sensitive areas such as health care and education may be more likely to "throw up" crises than less-regarded areas, such as social security, resulting in the former areas having an increased tendency toward policy crisis coming from their increased media coverage.

Equally important, there can appear to be remarkably little role for learning in social learning—policymakers appear to spend much of their time being fairly instrumental in adjusting existing means of attaining policy goals and only abandoning those where they cease to work. Oliver's work addressed this, but it is still noticeable that learning only really takes place in the face of policy failure—there appears to be little capacity for a reformulation of ideas when they are already working. This may be a comment on the limited ability of policymakers to deal with the complexities before them or perhaps a shortcoming of a model based around a concept (learning) that is notoriously difficult to conceptualize.

Finally, there is little idea from Hall what the dimensions of a policy paradigm might look like—how for example, does a policy paradigm differ from the social science concepts of ideology or discourse? Are paradigms underpinned by an ideology or are they the policy expressions of a particular discursive approach? Policy paradigms are clearly not ideologically neutral, but instead have whole rafts of assumptions underlying them. Only by unpacking those assumptions can we come to understand the logical assumptions upon which policy paradigms rest and thus the extent of their coherence (or incoherence) and their ideological presuppositions.

—*Ian Greener*

See also New Institutionalism; Path Dependence; Policy Learning

Further Readings and References

Bandura, A. (1977). *Social learning theory*. Englewood Cliffs, NJ: Prentice Hall.

Blyth, M. (1997). "Any more bright ideas?" The ideational turn of comparative political economy. *Comparative Politics, 29,* 229–250.

Greener, I. (2001). Social learning and macroeconomic policy in Britain. *Journal of Public Policy, 21,* 133–152.

Hall, P. (1993). Policy paradigms, social learning and the state. *Comparative Politics, 25,* 275–296.

Heclo, H. (1974). *Modern social politics in Britain and Sweden.* New Haven, CT: Yale University Press.

Oliver, M. (1997). *Whatever happened to monetarism? Economic planning and social learning in the United Kingdom since 1979.* Aldershot, UK: Ashgate.

SOCIAL MARKET

The concept of the social market is rooted in the perspective of economic sociology, which understands the capitalist market as a system of exchange based on social as well as economic foundations. It consists of economic transactions embedded in a complex network of formal and informal social interactions and organizations. Rejecting both the liberal, free market economy and the socialist, centrally planned economy, it seeks to achieve a third way by linking social safeguards to market processes. With the understanding that economic exchange is a collective reality shaped by social norms and values, the social market underscores the potential for cooperation, challenging classic liberal economists' assumption that the governance of capitalist markets is determined by individualized, rational decision making. Instead, it perceives symbolic and dynamic interpersonal and interinstitutional interaction as important in generating multiple meanings in exchange relationships.

The idea of the market as a set of social customs and organizational rules is part of a broader social market theory developed in Germany in the 1930s. In an attempt to transition away from a planned economy, while avoiding the undesirable effects of free markets (e.g., monopolization, excessive economic inequity, and social exclusion), it underscored two key elements: (1) managed markets as a means of striking a balance between personal freedom and societal equity on the one hand and economic efficiency and social justice on the other and (2) a clear legal and political regulatory framework to support and protect these markets. Implemented after World War II by market regulators, this model came to be known as the social market economy.

What mechanisms contribute to developing and preserving social markets? Key elements such as private property and competition are drawn from classic economic theory. However, the social market deemphasizes utility maximization and profit as the primary motives for economic action. Additionally, it rejects the price system as the central means of economic coordination, as well as the notion that markets work best absent state interference. Instead, it relies on a strong but limited state to uphold the competitive economic order, mediate between competing societal interests, and protect citizens from social risk.

By counteracting market failures and undesirable developments in the labor supply, the state serves a corrective function in the economy. However, it does so through institutional forms of coordination involving vertical and horizontal power sharing. The former occurs through the inclusion of the third sector in the exercise of public functions, and the latter involves the unification of labor and capital in the formulation and implementation of public policy. Constituting a network of rules and norms that restrain the exercise of power and facilitate participation and solidarity, these public-private partnerships provide the foundation for effective governance.

—*Vanna Gonzales*

See also Economic Sociology; Embeddedness; Market; Third Sector; Third Way

Further Readings and References

Barry, N. (1993). The social market economy. *Social Philosophy and Policy, 10*(2), 1–25.
Bruyn, S. (1991). *A future for the American economy: The social market.* Palo Alto, CA: Stanford University Press.
Peacock, A., & Willgerodt, H. (Eds.). (1989). *Germany's social market economy: Origins and evolution.* London: Macmillan.

SOCIAL MOVEMENT THEORY

Social movement theory addresses the nature and dynamics of sustained, collective challenges to national and international systems of governance. It seeks to characterize the factors that compel individuals to join movements; the conditions under which movements emerge, flourish, and dissolve; the mobilization and utilization of material, organizational, symbolic, and tactical resources; and the impact of movements on participants, public policies, and society at large. Variants of social movement theory differ in their emphasis of explanatory variables and levels of analysis. Structure-oriented perspectives explain movement emergence and outcomes as a result of macrochanges in the political, economic, and sociocultural organization of society. Agency-oriented perspectives emphasize microcontexts, including resource mobilization, organization, and strategy. In addition, different cultural dimensions of meaning construction have played an increasingly important role. Social movement theory has traditionally focused on national movements in Western Europe and North America; however, the last ten years have witnessed a rapidly growing scholarship of movements in developing and transition countries, as well as transnational social movements.

A social movement is the persistent convergence of disputatious action by formally and informally linked groups and individuals with a common set of beliefs and a commitment to change political or cultural forms (or both) of order sustained by powerful social entities such as the state. While social movement theorists in the 1970s and 1980s focused on frequently hostile protest in support of civil rights, free speech, peace, or the environment, more recent writing acknowledges that social movement activity is not confined to unconventional forms but includes the use of institutionalized political tools, such as lobbying, voter mobilization, and education. Moreover, Charles Tilly, Sidney Tarrow, and others have urged students of social movements to view them as only one of many forms of "contentious action" characterized by a similar array of causal mechanisms.

The relevance of social movement theory to contemporary governance has multiple dimensions. Social movements have historically shaped and been shaped by the evolution of the nation state. As evidenced by movements for abolition, civil rights, peace, women's rights, the environment, and other causes, social movement organizations have successfully challenged public policies and the role of the state itself; in the former Soviet Union and Eastern Europe, movements played a key role in dismantling communist regimes. Governments, in turn, have influenced the dynamics of contention through various instruments of control. Hence, the gradual transfer of state powers, rights, and functions to civil society, the private sector, and international bodies witnessed during the last quarter century has created new opportunities and led to the professionalization and transnational expansion of social movements. In many cases, social movement organizations alone or in cooperation with others have created new forms of governance above and beyond the state. At the same time, social movement challenges to systems of governance have continuously forced contemporary societies to reflect on the meaning of their trajectories.

Origins of Social Movement Theory

The student, peace, and civil rights movements of the 1960s and 1970s marked a critical turning point in social movement theory. A new generation of scholars, many with first-hand movement experience, contended that prevailing theories failed to capture the collective phenomena they observed. These theories centered on crowds, mass society, and relative deprivation; emphasized microlevel over macrolevel processes; viewed movement dynamics as the aggregation of individual attributes; neglected political and organizational contexts; and lacked empirical grounding. Although these views have since been discredited in scholarship, they continue to influence media coverage of recent protest events.

Early theorists looked at eighteenth-century national social movements; focused their analyses on extremism, deprivation, and violence; and characterized the French Revolution, urban street riots, and other manifestations of collective enthusiasm as irregular and irrational. Gustave Le Bon argued that crowd participants share a collective mind characterized by traits an individual person would not exhibit, especially an inherent tendency toward violence. The

driving force of collective behavior was argued to be of a psychological nature, consisting primarily of pent-up frustration and aggression. Although collective behavior approaches retained an emphasis on the emergent character of collective behavior, later scholars in this tradition gradually moved away from the extreme positions of crowd theorists and began to reject the notion that collective behavior was pathological or irrational. Later scholars moved the field toward a structural-functional conception of movements as a normal response to social strain. The idea that social transformations precipitate social movements was also advanced in the mass society perspective. Its emphasis was on the atomized individual whose social ties were increasingly fragmented and whose feeling of alienation and anxiety created by social isolation, especially in authoritarian and totalitarian regimes, leads to action. In a final variant of early social movement theory, other scholars began to explore collective protests as products of relative deprivation resulting from economic downturns, inflated expectations, or status inconsistency mechanisms, rather than as products of absolute deprivation. It remained rare, however, for scholars to link individual attributes and joint action.

Resource Mobilization

Microsociological and micropsychological approaches unraveled in the 1960s, partly as a result of the rise of microeconomics and its application to collective action. The portrayal of individuals as rational actors with fixed interests and a benefit-maximizing approach to movement participation became the foundation of the resource-mobilization perspective in social movement theory. Although it successfully countered the earlier characterization of social movements as aberrations, critics have argued it exaggerates rationality and continues to ignore the larger political context and cultural embeddedness of movements.

Mancur Olson, Jr. argued in his influential *The Logic of Collective Action* (1965) that rational individuals only participate in collective action if provided with incentives that do not apply to nonparticipants; else they prefer to free ride. John McCarthy, Mayer

Zald, and Anthony Oberschall adopted Olson's ideas and proposed that the main challenge faced by social movements consists in mobilizing the resources necessary to sustain collective action. Discontent is now assumed a constant feature of society, and variability in the distribution of resources is the explanation for movement emergence. The task of social movement organizers is to build effective organizations, raise money, mobilize participants, and provide them with appropriate incentives. Formal organizations are as critical to movement emergence as to movement maintenance. The resource mobilization perspective constructed an entirely new, economically inspired vocabulary of movement entrepreneurs, movement industries and sectors, and movement product differentiation. Yet, some have argued that resource mobilization looks beyond rational choice and acknowledges strategic behavior on the part of organizations, including cultural persuasion, particularly in variants that emphasize alliance systems as sources of material and nontangible resources.

Resource mobilization has met a variety of criticisms. Most of all, the assumptions underlying rational choice are seen as untenable. Weaker forms of the model acknowledge a limited role for cultural dimensions, including social norms, and admit that individuals generally settle on the first satisfactory option. Critics also argue that individual interests, rationality, and cost-benefit calculations vary over time and across cultures, rather than being exogenous to the actors. Finally, they have argued that resources are necessary but not sufficient, and that dimensions of the political environment need greater emphasis. Resource mobilization theorists have responded by expanding the definition of resources, including moral support, public opinion, psychological predispositions, and favorable symbolism, but running the risk of becoming tautologous.

Political Process and Political Opportunities

Dissatisfaction with exaggerated assumptions of rationality and the lack of emphasis on the historical and political dimensions of governance led a number of scholars to expand on resource mobilization. The resulting political process perspective, promoted by Charles Tilly, Sidney Tarrow, and Doug McAdam, also built on earlier European traditions in social thought that explain the roots of collective action in broad social, demographic, economic, and political processes, such as industrialization, urbanization, and bureaucratization.

The continuity with the resource mobilization perspective is apparent in McAdam's analysis of the U.S. civil rights movement, which argues that organizational capacities in the aggrieved community and a positive assessment of the chances for success are necessary for the emergence of social movements. Transitioning to a more structural approach, however, McAdam found that people participate not because of individual characteristics, but because they are compelled by their structural location in the world, such as prior contact with movement members, membership in organizations, or history of prior activism.

However, most political process approaches to social movements focus on resources external to the movement, especially political opportunities, which are commonly defined as dimensions of the political environment that create incentives for collective action. Broad definitions include access to decision making, political realignment among key actors, appearance of influential allies, emerging splits among the elite, and decline in state repression. Many of these can be situational and temporally limited. Narrower definitions exclude strategic interaction and focus on structural, more permanent variables, preferring the term *political opportunity structure*. The dimensions of political opportunities are also historically specific. Accordingly, changes in political opportunities during the last quarter of the twentieth century are explained on the basis of spreading affluence and postmaterial values or the emergence of new domains of public interest created by the expansion of the welfare state. The study of new social movements, which looks at women's, environmental, peace, and gay and lesbian movements, is generally associated with European scholars and has emerged from the notion that the same expansion has also gradually politicized private space.

Critiques of the political process perspective focus on the overextension of the concept of political opportunities, which has led to the conflation of structural, strategic, and cultural factors. Critics also assert that the clear distinction between outsiders who are forced to use unconventional tactics and insiders who can use institutional tactics works well for movements struggling for civil and other rights, but not for postcitizenship movements that foster collective identities and lifestyles, rather than political change. Finally, as early as the 1980s, theorists such as Bert Klandermans argued that the field of social movements was becoming dominated by a macrobias and sought to return to more social psychological explanations.

Culture

Culture has proven to be no easier to delineate than resources or political opportunities. Unlike resource mobilization and political process models, culture does not constitute a separate perspective. Rather, scholars focusing on ideology, meaning, identity, emotions, and other cultural variables argue that they permeate the foundation of any model. Culture is commonly defined as learned and shared patterns of thought, action, and material objects. Accordingly, notions of grievance, rationality, interests, resources, and opportunities can be understood as context-specific cultural constructs, rather than objective truths.

Early social movement theorists associated culture with the presumed irrational behavior of crowds. Rationalists that substituted exogenous materialist for psychopathological motivations were equally unprepared to find systematic explanatory strength in cultural variation. As a consequence, scholars who revived meaning construction in the 1980s tended to extend predominant approaches. Grafting Erving Goffman's notion of framing onto resource mobilization, David Snow and Robert Benford developed a series of hypotheses proposing how social movement organizers strategically create and utilize collective action frames as schematized interpretations of grievances, solutions, and reasons for action in order to mobilize and retain movement participants. The concept of framing has engendered a wealth of research

that looks at specific kinds of frames, frame alignment processes, the role of the media, and the relationship between framing, resources, opportunities, and identity. The notion that social movement participants cultivate a strong sense of insiders and outsiders has led theorists to studying collective identity, which can be defined as the shared cognitive, moral, and emotional connection with a broader community. The concept seeks to provide additional clues to why collective actors come into existence, why they are propelled into action, what determines their strategic choices, and what impacts movements have beyond policy changes.

Framing and collective identity have raised a number of questions. Critics argue, for instance, that framing approaches have focused on how organizers construct frames and neglected how participants perceive them. Furthermore, the relationship between frames and emotions remains underspecified, as frames only lead to action if they evoke the right feelings. Collective identity approaches, on the other hand, fail to clarify whether identities emerge as a result of mobilization and movement participation or precede them, whether they are created for or by the movements, and whether they have the same meaning for outsiders and participants.

Social Movement Theory and Governance

Social movement theory responds to important questions of contemporary governance, not least because the state has historically been the primary target of social movements. In analyzing the circumstances under which social movements wax and wane, theorists therefore invariably point to such key dimensions of the prevailing system of governance as are previously outlined. Moreover, social movement theorists posit a coevolving relationship between movement tactics and state response. As the nature of the state changes and an increasing number of key powers, rights, and functions are transferred down, up, and out, social movements adjust their repertoires accordingly. States, in turn, modify their strategies for dealing with movement challenges.

Although scholars frequently address social movements as if they constituted unified empirical phenomena, in reality they consist of a large variety of different social actors. The task of mobilization and movement maintenance usually falls to professional social movement organizations, which are mostly nongovernmental organizations and other types of voluntary associations. Because many of them pursue policy advocacy through channels of institutionalized politics, the boundary between theories on social movements and interest group politics is blurred. Moreover, some of these organizations' programs, for instance in welfare service provision and education, are funded by the state. Hence, social movements are increasingly embedded in contemporary systems of governance, rather than separate and in opposition to them. Because social movement theory has generally focused more on movement emergence than movement outcomes, the outlines of the impact of this increasing embeddedness largely remain to be examined.

In contemporary governance, state power is also increasingly transferred to regional and international settings. Social movement theory posits that this shift leads to organizational and tactical adaptation by social movement organizations. In fact, transnational movements and their protests, as well as interstate cooperation in policing and intelligence, have assumed an important role in international politics and theoretical writing. Political scientists, international relations scholars, and sociologists have argued that the main outcomes are the creation, implementation, and monitoring of international norms in the area of human rights and environmental protection. International advocacy, which some argue is the prerogative of more professionalized and institutionalized transnational advocacy networks and international nongovernmental organizations, has in many cases led to the creation of new systems of governance involving an emerging global civil society.

—*Jörg Balsiger*

See also Advocacy Networks; Civil Rights; Sociology of Governance; Transnational Social Movement

Further Readings and References

della Porta, D., & Diani, M. (1999). *Social movements: An introduction.* Oxford, UK: Basil Blackwell.

Giugni, M., McAdam, D., & Tilly, C. (1999). *How social movements matter.* Minneapolis: University of Minnesota Press.

Jasper, J. M. (1997). *The art of moral protest: Culture, biography, and creativity in social movements.* Chicago: University of Chicago Press.

Klandermans, B. (1997). *The social psychology of protest.* Oxford, UK: Basil Blackwell.

McAdam, D. (1982). *Political process and the development of Black insurgency, 1930–1970.* Chicago: University of Chicago Press.

McAdam, D., Tarrow, S., & Tilly, C. (2001). *Dynamics of contention.* Cambridge, UK: Cambridge University Press.

McCarthy, J. D., & Zald, M. N. (1977). Resource mobilization and social movements: A partial theory. *American Journal of Sociology, 82,* 1212–1241.

Olson, M., Jr. (1965). *The logic of collective action: Public goods and the theory of groups.* Cambridge, MA: Harvard University Press.

Snow, D. A., & Benford, R. D. (1988). Ideology, frame resonance and participant mobilization. *International Social Movement Research, 1,* 197–219.

Tarrow, S. (1998). *Power in movement: Social movements and contentious politics.* Cambridge, UK: Cambridge University Press.

Tilly, C. (1978). *From mobilization to revolution.* Reading, MA: Addison-Wesley.

SOCIAL NETWORK THEORY

Social network theory is based on the assumption that social relations are the key to explaining both individual action and collective outcomes. Networks may be defined as bounded sets of actors, be they organizations, institutions, or individuals that are connected by specific relationships. Network theory refers to the study of the structural forms—or patterning—of the ties that link these units. Attention to social networks has a long tradition, specifically in social anthropology, social psychology and sociometrics, as well as economic sociology and organizational theory. Lately, real-world phenomena, such as changes in the organization of capitalism, experiments in new forms of decentralized governance as well as advances in the computer-based analytical tools associated with network theory, have increased interest in network approaches in other parts of the social sciences as well.

Most work on social networks has tended to emphasize the importance of informal structures in interaction and the way in which formal organizations are embedded within other, less-visible institutional structures. Here an influential strand of research has revived the notion of the "embeddedness" of economic exchanges within social relations.

Network analysis criticizes approaches that focus primarily on the specific characteristics or attributes of a given unit, be it an individual, organization, social class, or a nation-state, to explain its behavior or specific outcomes. Instead, it is argued that such characteristics or attributes only acquire meaning when set in relation to others. Ultimately, it is relationships that form the resources that pattern constraints and opportunities of actors. Whether it is cognition, practices, trust, or resource flows, exchange is understood as always already structurally biased through the shape of a given network. This type of view contrasts with analysis of structure in terms of fixed categories, such as class or race, formal institutional frameworks or strands of individual behavioralism. In this sense, network theory refers to a type of structural analysis that locates structure, including cognitive or behavioral patterns within—and originating from—the observable form and content of relationships among a set of relevant actors or units, providing both resources and limits for action.

Analysts subscribing to this approach are united by a number of common sensitivities and core concepts, yet the use of common terms often masks widely different approaches.

Whereas all network analysts agree on the fundamental importance of relational interdependence for describing and explaining social phenomena, opinions differ as to what extent network theory constitutes a proper theory. Some see it as primarily referring to a specific mode of analysis applicable to a wide range of phenomena, a practical toolbox for more precisely describing and measuring relational configurations and their structural characteristics. Others see it moving toward a more or less consistent body of theoretical propositions and explorations that speak to long-standing debates in anthropology and social psychology about the contextual nature and evolution of social life. Indeed, for its most ambitious adherents, network theory holds out the promise of bridging micro- and macrolevels of social analysis by pointing to ways in which large-scale social patterns may be created and sustained by distinct individual or organizational network dynamics.

Researchers differ in their reliance on real or cognitive data in building up networks for analysis as well as in the way a given network should be bounded. Similarly, quantitative and qualitative approaches to networks may assign different explanatory significance to the dynamics within or the stable architectural features of a given network.

More fundamentally, even the basic role and definition of social structure can vary across network theorists. For adherents of a strong network program, ideas and roles that actors take on are categories and attributes that emerge from relationships. Yet others hold these relationships to be merely the most proximate and observable form of structure, themselves influenced by deeper cognitive or material structures, thus pointing back to often underresearched origins of relational networks themselves.

Network Theory's Toolkit

Network characteristics are used to more precisely describe existing groupings or configurations of specific units as well as to specify hypotheses regarding emergent socializing effects of various natures.

The relations or ties that link actors within a network can be differentiated according to their different content, intensity, or direction. These can then be used to explain the diffusion of institutional forms, ideas and information, influence flows, the nature of resource exchanges, or the way access to information and resources is structured.

Core attributes of whole networks refer to their density or looseness, measured by the number of linkages among actors within a given network, and its centrality, a measure that can refer to the level of connections of a specific actor within a network structure or to the overall connectedness (centralization) of a network. Network measures also help identify the role of more closely connected clusters or subgroups, such as cliques, within a broader network, and much analysis has explored the significance of notions of cohesion—units who hold similar relationships to each other—as well as the role of structurally equivalent actors—units connected in similar ways to third actors.

Networks as Analytical Approach and Substantive Phenomenon

In studies of governance, network analysis often provides a way to explain unexpected policy results and specify organizational relationships that are difficult to define or categorize by hierarchy. New international production systems, rapidly expanding communication capacities, attempts to decentralize governance, attempts to reinvent government or outsourcing, the multilevel governance structures emerging in the European Union, and the demise of the vertically integrated firm are all seen as leading to increasingly networked forms of governance.

In this context, network analysis refers to alternative models of governance distinct from those based on formal hierarchies or market exchange. Working though coordination, as opposed to command and control, network forms of governance are seen to create stable, but adaptive, relationships often based on mutual trust or common principles or both.

From this real-world starting point, network analysis has expanded as researchers have used it to investigate an ever broader range of issues, spanning from relationships among individuals, organizations, linkages across state and civil society to those among nation-states or broader societal forces as well as ideologies or concepts.

In such studies, the content of ties that connect a network has ranged from affective ties, advice networks, common attendance at social events, institutional relationships, kinship ties to material exchange-relationship, contractual links, geographical closeness, shared norms, or information flows. Each of these ties may be analyzed as separate networks or be superimposed upon each other. In multidimensional networks,

analysis can then show a single action to have different effects in each dimensional realm. Whereas network theory emphasizes the particular nature of relational configurations and their impact, it has formulated strong general arguments about diffusion and homogenizing pressures within networks.

Networks and Change

Two questions emerge from the relationships of network theory to the study of change. One relates to the origin or decline of networks or both, the other to the applicability of network analysis to periods of rapid social change.

There is no clear consensus about the origins of networks, yet different factors have been highlighted: Among them are age—networks develop over time. Robert Putnam's study of civic networks in Italy might prove an example where organizations that worked together over years developed ties of trust and legitimacy. Here, direct conclusions about the success and failure of societal development are drawn from the patterning of these structures. In other realms, work on epistemic communities has focused on professional groups working on similar issues, ultimately shaping common goals that in turn promote cooperative relations. Other factors may relate to territory, where within a certain location people tend to collaborate, or relations based on resource dependence and primarily material relationships.

Network theory has been criticized for a bias toward nonconflictual relations and for diffusing or neglecting questions of responsibility or value conflict within networks. Further, its emphasis on stable relationships has been criticized for offering few tools to analyze dynamic or rapid change. However, others have argued that informal networks in particular increase in importance in situations of change or flux, when formal institutional frameworks are put in question.

—*Anna Schmidt*

See also Advocacy Networks; Collaborative Governance; Embeddedness; Epistemic Community; Informal Organization; Interorganizational Coordination; Network; Network Society; Policy Network; Production Network; Sociology of Governance

Further Readings and References

Emirbayer, M. (1997). Manifesto for a relational sociology. *American Journal of Sociology, 103*(2), 281–317.

Granovetter, M. (1985). Economic action and social structure: The problem of embeddedness. *American Journal of Sociology, 91*(3), 481–510.

Padgett, J., & Ansell, K. (1993). Robust action and the rise of the Medici: 1400–1434. *American Journal of Sociology, 98*(6), 1259–1319.

Putnam, R. (1993). *Making democracy work: Civic traditions in modern Italy.* Princeton, NJ: Princeton University Press.

Wasserman, S., & Faust, K. (1994). *Social network analysis: Methods and applications.* Cambridge, UK: Cambridge University Press.

Watts, D. (2003). *Six degrees: The science of a connected age.* New York: W. W. Norton.

Wellman, B., & Berkowitz, S. D. (Eds.). *Social structures: A network approach.* Cambridge, UK: Cambridge University Press.

SOCIAL PRACTICE

So far, only few researchers have systematically dealt with the relationship between governance and social practices. On the one hand, the development of the fairly large and rapidly growing literature on governance has almost exclusively been undertaken by political science (including public administration). On the other hand, the theoretization and analysis of social practices have almost exclusively been undertaken by anthropology and sociology.

Perhaps the two most important exceptions to the above-mentioned tendency are Pierre Bourdieu's reflexive sociology and Michel Foucault's genealogy. Admittedly, neither applies the term *governance,* but rather the notion of power. Nevertheless, this entry deals with these two analytical frameworks anyway, because for them governance would simply be another term for practices and institutions of governing and thereby ultimately exercises of power. A third and final framework included in this entry is Ludwig Wittgenstein's later writings on language games. While Wittgenstein studied neither governance nor power, his ideas have recently inspired works on governance, policy processes, and politics in general.

Bourdieu's Reflexive Sociology

In the attempt to develop a theory of practice (alternatively named reflexive sociology or praxeology), French sociologist Pierre Bourdieu has dealt extensively with the relationship between modern forms of power and social practices. Thus, one of the overarching ambitions of his reflexive sociology was to reveal how, in modern societies, power tends to work through symbolic and often-unnoticed mechanisms.

Bourdieu suggested that we understand social practices in terms of the embodiment of social structures, which includes economic, cultural, and political relations. The individual embodiment of these social structures is neither an absolutely voluntary act nor an absolutely determined act. Instead, each and every person is disposed to incorporate (objective) social structures in a particular fashion according to his or her so-called habitus. The latter is at once the product of the person's previous experiences and socialization and the producer of the person's actions. It is, above all, through these dispositions incorporated into the body of each and every individual that modern power comes into effect. Thus, in modern societies, power works above all through indirect, symbolic means rather than through direct, coercive devices. It is through symbolic capital (authorized understandings and classifications), which acts as a kind of translation mechanism, that other forms of capital (economic, cultural, or social) are translated into effective power. Without this translation, the other forms of capital may be useless.

In any social field where power is put into play, it is linked to and depends upon a particular symbolic capital or authorized understandings and classification. This entails that certain understandings are taken for granted or go undisputed; they constitute the *doxa.* While no single individual or group in modern societies are able to control *doxa* at their will, *doxa* is produced and reproduced in a manner that tends to favor those positively endowed with economic, cultural, or social capital. For example, academics and others, rich and poor, spontaneously tend to support the idea that entry to a university should depend solely on academic merit, not on wealth. While this may be regarded as a reasonable and nonbiased standard, educational policies based on this *doxa* nonetheless systematically favors students of academic parents and, to some extent, students with rich parents who are able to pay for their children's enrollment in expensive, elite schools.

Of course, it may happen that a *doxa* is made explicit and perhaps even called into question by competing understandings. However, even in this case, where *doxa* is momentarily transformed into *heterodoxa,* the outcome of such a political conflict will tend to suit the interests of those favorably endowed with one or more forms of capital, essentially because they often share these with those dominant in the political field. Because the elite of the political field (key politicians and top civil servants) are often socialized in a way that endow them with forms of (particularly cultural and social) capital that correspond to those in other social fields, state policies will systematically, though not unanimously, tend to favor elites in other social fields. Bourdieu's reflexive sociology has subsequently inspired a range of studies on the politics and policies of education and media.

Foucault's Genealogy

The understanding of governance as a set of social and political practices has perhaps been most explicitly developed by French historian and philosopher Michel Foucault. He argued that government should be addressed as "regime practices." These consist of two axes: (1) problematizations, calculations, and forms of knowledge on the problems and objects of governing activities and (2) concrete schemes, procedures, and techniques seeking to regulate the conduct of individuals, groups, and populations.

By focusing on the historical formation and transformation of one or more regimes of practices, Foucault tried to make contemporary ways of thinking and acting less given. The present to Foucault was an event like any other, not a necessary outcome of some given historical process. For him then, genealogy was an instrument of disturbing the present. Like Bourdieu's reflexive sociology, Foucault's genealogy is an apparatus for critical conception and analysis of

power as a particular social practice that is linked intrinsically to other social practices. However, unlike Bourdieu's reflexive sociology, Foucault's genealogy has no scientific pretensions. It explicitly abstains from formulating a theory of practice in Bourdieu's sense of claiming to produce a superior kind of knowledge of the world. Likewise, the critical potential of genealogies of truth-production, power relations, and forms of subjectivity rests not with their ability to tell us what to do, but with their capacity to irritate present ways of thinking and acting.

Once understood as a regime of practices, genealogy may address a wide range of governing practices. The literature on governmentality examines in different ways the rationalities and technologies that have developed as part and parcel of the neoliberal (or advanced liberal) approach to governance. These studies essentially argue that while liberal and social problematizations of government still play an important role for contemporary forms of governing, they have been supplemented and perhaps even displaced by the problem of how best to stimulate and activate the self-steering capacities of individuals and organizations. Outsourcing of public services, public-private partnerships, benchmarking, self-evaluation, and social contracts between public authorities and various groups in need of public assistance are all measures that, in one way or another, seek to make use of or facilitate the capacities of individuals and organizations to solve problems (whether their own or those of others) by themselves.

A Foucauldian-inspired analysis of government would pay attention to how this problematization enables distinctions between those who are able and willing to be active and participate in the proper way and those who are unable or unwilling to do so.

Wittgenstein's Language Games

In his 1968 book *Philosophical Investigations,* Ludwig Wittgenstein rejected theories and explanations of language as a formal system of representation and began to view it as a multiplicity of activities, of "language-games." Even if he is fundamentally concerned with social practices—and the role language plays in this—the late Wittgenstein, like Foucault but unlike Bourdieu, refuses to posit a theory of practice. Rather than providing an undisputable explanation, he seeks to provide us with a different and thought-provoking understanding of social practices.

Wittgenstein's analysis of social practice is essentially launched as a critique of what he sees as mistakes in human and social sciences. In particular, the tendencies to explain social practices as caused or governed by rules that somehow stand outside these practices is flawed. For Wittgenstein, rules exist only in and through their use (i.e., in concrete language games or, more generally, in social practices). Therefore, the question is not how rules govern social practices, but rather how rules themselves are formed through social practices.

Only a few studies of governance are strictly based on Wittgenstein's notion of language games. Existing studies of governance, policy making, and public organizations inspired by the notion of language games tend to add to this a blend of subjectivist approaches, including ethnographic, ethnomethodological, and action-oriented approaches. Thus, unlike Bourdieu's reflexive sociology, which seeks to unravel the *doxa* sustaining popular misrecognition of objective social structures, these subjectivist appropriations of Wittgenstein's language games seek to unravel the lived experiences of civil servants and other individuals engaged in policy processes, as Wagenaar noted in 2004. An important exception to this rule is James Tully's conception of freedom as an agonistic game played by citizens. Here, Wittgenstein's notion of language game is not reduced to subjective, lived experiences, but rather is seen as actions systematically linked to and dependent upon practices of governance.

—*Peter Triantafillou*

See also Governance; Governmentality; Institution; Interpretive Theory; Reflexivity; Situated Agency

Further Readings and References

Barry, A., Osborne, T., & Rose, N. (Eds.). (1996). *Foucault and political reason.* London: University College London Press.

Bourdieu, P. (1977). *Outline of a theory of practice.* Cambridge, UK: Cambridge University Press.

Bourdieu, P. (1988). *Homo academicus.* Cambridge, UK: Polity Press.

Foucault, M. (1977). *Discipline and punish: The birth of the prison.* London: Penguin.

Harrison, P. (2002). The Caesura: Remarks on Wittgenstein's interruption of theory, or, why practices elude explanation. *Geoforum, 33*(4), 487–503.

Wagenaar, H. (2004). "Knowing" the rules: Administrative work as practice. *Public Administration Review, 64*(6), 643–655.

Wittgenstein, L. (1997). *Philosophical investigations* (G. E. M. Anscombe, Trans.). Oxford, UK: Basil Blackwell.

SOCIOCYBERNETICS

The traditional concern of sociocybernetics has been societal steering and social control. The approach can be quite difficult to trace because of its interdisciplinary roots, although it is closely related to a particular form of systems theory. In order to address this often-disparate topic, it is necessary to briefly trace the origins of the approach, its major variants, and some of the implications for problems of governance.

The Origins of Sociocybernetics

There are close associations between sociocybernetics and older forms of social systems theory such as those of Herbert Spencer and Edward Alsworth Ross. Norbert Wiener, often attributed the title of "the father of cybernetics," was one of the first to point out the possibility for a theory transfer of cybernetics to the study of society. It is for this reason that the origins of sociocybernetics are often located in engineering. At the outset of the theory transfer, the cybernetics of society very quickly became entangled with more-established notions of the social system.

Cybernetic models of control are often mistakenly believed to have been established in sociology through the work of Talcott Parsons. Although Parsons alluded to cybernetics, his structural functionalism has been deemed largely unsuitable for the task of integrating the principles of cybernetics into sociology. The most significant figure to effectuate the transfer was Walter Buckley, who is now widely regarded as the father of sociocybernetics.

Given the roots of sociocybernetics in mathematical and computational science, it is not surprising to discover an underlying attitude of scientific unity in its application. As a result, some of the tone of explanation that the theory transfer involves was initially met with a degree of suspicion in mainstream sociology. Yet sociocybernetics is not a simple theory transfer from the physical sciences to the social sciences. Social systems require different treatment than physical systems, and the approach that is sociocybernetics would eventually reflect that difference. Social systems are not mechanistic systems but are related to complex adaptive and thinking people, they cannot therefore be likened to the steering mechanism of an antiaircraft battery or an equilibrium-seeking thermostat. With this in mind, one of the most significant theoretical developments in the emergence of sociocybernetics was the development of the second-order cybernetics.

Second-order cybernetics involved a shift in thinking from observed to observing systems. Knowledge became based on the difference between the observer and the observed and both were intricately linked. The researcher would become observed as part of the system, which was in turn continually and actively constructed. The central implication of this was that all observations in society were essentially self-observations. What made it more complicated was that systems themselves often change through the process of observation. The dual problems of self-reference and self-organization therefore became one of the defining problems of sociocybernetics. These issues also have significant implications for the problem of governance, for example, how is it possible to govern or steer a society full of complex, self-referring, and adaptive systems?

Sociocybernetic Variants

Sociocybernetics also reflects the well-established division between actor and communication-centered theory in social science. For some, the unit of analysis is the actor, where this refers to the actor or organization, and society as a whole is formed on the basis of interacting actors. For others, the unit of analysis is communications and how these are organized: The work of Niklas Luhmann stands in direct contrast to an action-centered frame of reference, for example, because it focuses on communications and their organization.

Sociocybernetics and Governance

The problem of governance was central within the actor-centered approach of sociocybernetics, although it was formulated differently as the problem of societal steering. From the perspective of action-centered sociocybernetics, social systems are composed of people that group and organize themselves in different ways, what is extra complicated is that they can all have different views of the system and can act on it differently. They might desire power and control or they might react against power and control. The fact is that because they have their own views of the system, this limits any attempt to steer the system. The scientist interested in the sociocybernetic problem of steering must also place himself or herself into this equation. They must ask themselves to what extent they ought to be steering social systems? It might well be the case that too much control of social systems would make the same systems less humane. This is the paradox of planning. While it might be desirable to be able to control social systems from the top down, by so doing we might reduce the ability of people to self-steer. Perfect planning would imply perfect knowledge of the system, and the use of such knowledge would result in the system becoming deterministic. In short, people in such systems would lose their freedom to conduct their own steering.

The implications of a hierarchical management for government are quite clear. Governments, which have complex and multiple goals and who operate with top-down accountability and steering mechanisms, often become constrained and less responsive. Crucially, such governments are often viewed as less accountable and more out of control. Perhaps this is why the government is often referred to as often appearing aloof and inaccessible. The reasons for this are because top-down management can only be undertaken through an imperfect model of the state of various social systems or societies. This is why sociocybernetics is critical of oversimplified approaches to the study of social systems. Sociocybernetics is highly critical of economic models that claim to be able to accurately model aspects of society but singularly fail to include all of the essential variables. In many economic models, people are reduced to rational, calculating actors or are excluded altogether. Such models invariably fail because they cannot account for actors who will respond to governance by resisting or avoiding the negative consequences of control where possible. A consequence of this line of reasoning is that a theoretical choice has to be made between either a top-down or bottom-up approach to governance.

As we have suggested, top-down approaches fail because they are based on imperfect models generated from an imperfect understanding of the situation being modeled. It might also be because action-centered approaches define steering as the action of steering that, in turn, requires one to state a subject, object, and goal for the steering act. A consequence of this is that the whole effort to steer becomes split and external factors impact on the act of steering. As a result, one can have unexpected side effects, faults of implementation, and self-fulfilling and self-defeating prophecies. It is not unusual, for example, to spend lots of energy on improving the working conditions of women only to discover that, once implemented, many of the policies can result in negative consequences for women in the labor market. The argument is that putting one's purpose through steering into the world can result in one being against the world, and the inevitable consequence of this is failure.

An alternative approach might be to consider improving the self-steering potential of actors so that they can determine their own control of the systems that they are involved with. Within such an approach, society could become self-steered and the need for control could be reduced. This approach is characterized by encouraging actors to become involved in producing social change rather than attempting to remodel society toward a final perfect state. It is here that we find approaches that utilize the terms synreferentiality and autopoiesis.

Synreferentiality was developed in the work of Peter Hejl, who saw people as central to the problem of governance. Put simply, synreferentiality refers to systems that are based on the shared realities, shared behavioral programs, and shared norms and values. Therefore, a social system is composed of individuals that participate in a synreferential domain and that interact on the basis of the assumption that other autonomized (note not autonomous) systems are present.

This theoretical program suggests that social systems can be regulated and influenced, but this can only occur within the possibilities accorded to them through their synreferential domain. Systems can be influenced, but only through the use of an accurate model of the system that accords an understanding of its key dynamics. Within this approach, in order to effectively regulate social systems' governments, it is necessary to be aware first that these systems are composed of humans that are closed and coevolve with the system and second that the synreferentiality of the social system implies that there will be limits on possible alternative states for the system. The implication is that systems are best regulated and governed through the individuals that are part of the system and also through a focus on the internal structure and dynamics of the system.

The actor-centered approach of Hejl contrasts with Luhmann's autopoietic systems theory. For Luhmann, social systems are communication systems and nothing else; examples include the economy, law, and the political system, among others. The political system is composed of three further subsystems: the "public," "politics," and "government," each of which is operationally closed but nonetheless coupled to each other. They interact, albeit with each other in unpredictable ways through the exchange of energy. The public finds government unresponsive and this takes the form of popular opinion for the political system, which in turn sees this as a demand for more responsiveness in government, even though politics cannot directly impact on government; all it can do is perturb or irritate it. Government might, in turn, respond to these irritations by increasing the size of its bureaucracy in order to try to improve accountability, and paradoxically this can subsequently reduce its ability to be responsive. So the public perturbs politics, which in turn affects government. And what this leads to is the increasing loss of responsiveness, which only serves to further alienate the public.

The point that Luhmann is making is that a society that is composed of functionally differentiated subsystems cannot be steered from the center. Rather, it is the systems themselves that do the steering. Each system operates according to their internal program and can only react to their specifically defined environment. Action theory fails because it hides the system that is attempting to steer itself. In turn, a functionally differentiated society cannot be steered, not only because the subsystems of society are self-steering entities, but also because there can be no overall unrivalled representation of society. There can be myriad representations of society from the perspective of politics, the law, and economics, among other things. Given these multiple representations, it would seem particularly difficult to develop a plan for the future of society that is not, for the most part, located within one or the other system. In addition, it is a particular insight of Luhmann's approach that the reduction of planning to one subsystem perspective on society actually reduces and limits the possibilities that are available for steering. In this respect, for Luhmann, steering is always self-steering, and self-steering of systems rather than actions. It is the underlying idea of a polycentric society that has influenced more recent writers like Lars Qvortrup to suggest that we are living in the era of the hypercomplex society.

It is with Qvortrup that an adequate characterization of society is secured that fits with the sociocybernetic perspective. There have been numerous attempts in sociology to characterize society from a single point of reference, for example the network society or even the risk society. Qvortrup's suggestion is that if we were to seek a single word to guide our view of society, that hypercomplexity would fit. Society is evolving according to the principle that external complexity can only be matched by increasing internal complexity. Paradoxically, the only consistent aspect of society is the distinct absence of a guiding principle. Society is not moving toward a final utopian state of perfect communication or utopian communism. Rather, society is differentiating into separate spheres of specialized communication designed to manage specific areas of complexity. The problem for governance is that society is not developing through the skilled manipulation of rationalistic overseers, but that it has an imperfect view of its environment and is, in turn, evolving according to this imperfect perspective.

Conclusion

Sociocybernetics is a broad school of thinking in sociology that unsurprisingly reflects many of the existing differences within sociology as a whole. Its central concern with the issue of societal steering makes it of central importance to governance. The theory transfer of cybernetics to sociology would quickly intersect with the older and established tradition of systems theory to produce a specific blend of sociology. In this blend, the distinction between action- and communication-centered theory emerged. Action-centered theories of sociocybernetics have focused on people as members of groups, but who have self-reflecting properties that make the task of governance difficult. This difficulty is further compounded when the person attempting to observe has to be included as part of the system of observation.

The complexity of the task of studying self-regulating and self-reflexive actors led to a focus on steering from the bottom up and the development of concepts such as synreferentiality and autopoiesis. With the emergence of autopoiesis, the final challenge for governance is that we are now living in a decentralized and polycontextural society. The complexity of this society paradoxically means that steering has real limits but is open to possibilities as long as the guiding condition of complexity is understood within an adequate theoretical framework.

—Barry Gibson

See also Autopoiesis; Network Society; Systems Theory

Further Readings and References

Buckley, W. (1998). *Society—A complex adaptive system.* Amsterdam: Overseas Publishers Association.

Burns, T. R., Baumgartner, T., & DeVille, P. (1985). *Man, decision, society: The theory of actor-system dynamics for social scientists.* New York: Gordon and Breach.

Hejl, P. M. (1997). Communication and social systems: Evolutionary and developmental aspects. In P. Sweigart (Ed.), *Human by nature: Between biology and the social sciences.* Mahwah, NJ: Lawrence Erlbaum.

Luhmann, N. (2002). Limits of steering. In C. Calhoun, J. Gerteis, J. Moody, S. Pfaff, & I. Virk (Eds.), *Contemporary sociological theory.* Oxford, UK: Basil Blackwell.

Qvortrup, L. (1998). *The hypercomplex society.* New York: Peter Lang.

Ross, E. A. (1901). *Social control: A survey of the foundations of order.* New York: Macmillan.

Spencer, H. (1897). *Principles of sociology.* New York: D. Appleton.

Wiener, N. (1950). *The human use of human beings: Cybernetics and society.* Boston: Houghton Mifflin.

SOCIOLOGICAL INSTITUTIONALISM

See NEW INSTITUTIONALISM

SOCIOLOGY OF GOVERNANCE

If sociology is the study of society, and governance is the activity of managing or ruling human affairs, then the sociology of governance is the study of the societal dimensions of managing human affairs. No established subfield named the "sociology of governance" exists within the discipline of sociology, as does for example the "sociology of religion." Nevertheless, this entry argues that classical and contemporary sociology has much to say about the theory and practice of governance.

Sociology has three classical concerns directly relevant to the study of governance. One concern is domination—the capacity or opportunity for some people to exercise power over others. Sociologists seek to understand the sources of power in society and how it is wielded to produce both desirable and undesirable outcomes. They have been fundamentally concerned about the legitimacy of this power and about the capacity of individuals and groups to resist domination. A second concern is social order—how is it that society coheres? Why doesn't society break down into what the English philosopher Thomas Hobbes referred to as a war of everyone against everyone? Sociology tries to understand the bases of human solidarity—how does society exist in the first place? The third concern is for what is distinctively social, as opposed to biological or cognitive, in human behavior. What aspects of behavior arise as the result of domination and social order? Although sociology would grant that meaning, morality, and social norms have some basis in biology, it focuses on how these achievements arise from human interaction.

It is perhaps obvious that these core concerns are deeply interconnected. The work of one of the founding figures of sociology, Émile Durkheim, for instance, was a response to the view that social order could only be achieved by relinquishing power to a leviathan, a powerful state that would achieve social control through domination. He was also reacting against the classical economists' view that self-interested exchange is the basis of social order. Durkheim argued, by contrast, that it was the distinctly social bases of human life—morality and social norms—that made social order possible. Morality comes prior to social control or market exchange.

At least three different perspectives on the relationship between society and governance are possible. First, a societal perspective treats the social dimension of human collectivities as an all-encompassing system and thus explains outcomes based on the archetypal characteristics of those systems. This perspective is typically civilizational or cultural. A societal approach to the governance of new enterprises in Shanghai, for example, might appeal to fundamental characteristics of Chinese civilization or culture—say, the tendency to use personal connections—*guanxi*—to influence the behavior of others. Second, a differentiation perspective, typically associated with modernization theories, assumes that the state and the economy have become differentiated from society. Such an approach typically singles out society as a distinctive arena of governance. Contemporary discussions about civil society or the public sphere provide a good example. Third, an embeddedness perspective sees the social as one dimension of all spheres of activity, but does not interpret society as an all-encompassing system. Instead, this perspective suggests that even the most instrumental activities—like economic exchange or political lobbying—have a social dimension. The state or the economy are hence embedded in society.

Several subfields in sociology are particularly relevant for understanding basic mechanisms of governance. Organization theory studies formal organizations as patterns of human coordination and cooperation. We live in an organizational society, and this is nowhere as true as where governance is concerned. Schools, armies, and hospitals are the agencies of modern governance. Economic sociology studies occupations, firms, and markets as modes of allocation of values and resources that shape social stratification and societal power. Political sociology studies the development of the state as a mode of political power and social movements and other forms of contentious action as forms of collective action and social protest.

It is perhaps true that sociology and its subfields are more interested in the unintended consequences of organizations, markets, and states than they are in the ostensible purpose of governing. Thus, sociology tends to view organizations as agents of social control (domination), as a form of social structure (social order), or as communities (social organisms) rather than as mechanisms of effective human coordination. Likewise, markets are more likely to be seen as producers of social inequality than as efficient producers of consumer products. Yet if the aims of inquiry are often different for sociology than they are for public policy or public administration or management theory, it is important to acknowledge that governance may be a benign expression for domination or social control.

In the following sections, this entry briefly traces some of the broad connections between sociology and governance.

Classical Sociology and Modernity

The founders of classical sociology—Karl Marx, Émile Durkheim, and Max Weber, among many others—were concerned about understanding what today we might broadly describe as modernity. Marx, of course, analyzed the development of modern capitalism and predicted the emergence of increasingly polarized class conflict. As previously described, Durkheim focused on society itself and analyzed the changing bases of solidarity and social control. Arguably, however, the founding sociologist with the greatest influence on contemporary discussions of governance was the German sociologist Max Weber. More than Marx and Durkheim, Weber's analysis led him to focus his attention on the development of the modern state and the rise of modern forms of organization.

Weber's intellectual project has been variously described. His work has been described as "sociology of domination" or a project to uncover the history of rationality. And it has been described as an attempt to understand why modernity first emerged in the West—out of European civilization. All these descriptions are apt. We might sum them up by saying that his intellectual project was to understand why a new, modern form of domination—rational-legal authority—developed first in Europe.

Weber's sociology of domination is most immediately apparent in his description of three forms of authority: traditional, charismatic, and rational-legal. Weber famously defined authority as "legitimate power" and he argued that to be stable, social orders must be legitimate. Authority and legitimacy were thus central concepts around which he built his conception of institution, and his ideas continue to be influential in current discussions of governance. Historically, Weber argued that the customary authority of traditional orders and the visionary authority of charismatic leaders gave way, in modern institutions, to an impersonal form of authority that Weber called rational-legal. Science and law, as exemplars of rational-legal authority, were thus the basis for the legitimate use of power in modern institutions. As Weber pointed out, the emergence of modern bureaucracies—both in states and in business enterprises—was a reflection of the growing importance of rational-legal authority, a development he regarded with some cynicism.

Weber's analysis of the development of rational-legal authority was linked to his analysis of rationalization on a much longer time scale. He viewed rationalization as a phenomenon that developed over millennia and as rooted in the Judeo-Christian religious traditions of the West. This historical analysis is beyond the scope of this entry. However, with regard to governance, it is worth pointing out that rational-legal authority was only one dimension of his broader conception of rationalization. For Weber, rationalization was a process whereby "ends" and "means" were progressively clarified and then related systematically to one another. One important consequence of rationalization was the differentiation of institutional spheres—the economy, the political system, society, and religion. And rational-legal institutions such as state bureaucracies became "means" to achieve the ends of state, with state officials developing "neutral competence" to serve these ends.

The major themes developed by Weber—rationalization, bureaucracy, legitimacy, and authority—remain foundational concepts in many discussions of contemporary governance. Moreover, these themes were refined and elaborated by sociologists that followed him.

Elite and Pluralist Views of Governance

Weber ushered in a new age of modern organization and managerialism. Building on Weber, sociologists recognized that organization had important consequences for social stratification and domination. A protégé of Weber's, Roberto Michels, who was also influenced by the elite theory developed by fellow Italians Gaetano Mosca and Vilfredo Pareto, argued in a now-classic study of political parties that organization inevitably leads to oligarchy—control by the few. Centralized bureaucratic structures, he argued, create a managerial elite that controls the levers of organizational power. Bureaucratization leads to what was later called goal displacement—with the organization coming primarily to serve needs of the elite that controlled it rather than those of its intended constituency. Thus, we can say that the Weberian tradition (and indeed, Weber himself) was ambivalent about the neutral competence of managers.

The generation of scholars following Michels was alive to possibilities for goal displacement and also

to the "iron law of oligarchy." Philip Selznick, for instance, applied Michels's goal-displacement model to a now-classic study of the institutional evolution of the Tennessee Valley Authority. Perhaps even more widely influential, C. Wright Mills extended the Michels analysis to interorganizational relations, arguing in *The Power Elite* that bureaucratization led to the creation of elite networks that organized across societal sectors. Along with work studying local communities, Mills's work led to a genre of sociological work called "community power studies." The conclusions of this work, however, was challenged by pluralist theorists, mostly from political science, that argued that elites rarely achieve the kind of collusive unity suggested by elite theorists. By contrast, the pluralists shifted attention from the state to society. Influenced by Alexis de Tocqueville, they emphasized the importance of intermediary institutions—voluntary associations and interest groups—as key organizers of politics. Political sociology of a pluralist bent also developed Tocqueville's emphasis on the civic quality of societies. Although the debates between elite theorists and pluralists were not always fruitful, they did help both political scientists and sociologists to clarify conceptions of political power.

Poststructuralist Perspectives

In the late 1960s and early 1970s, a new wave of social theory arose that challenged some of the basic assumptions of the classical sociological tradition. This new social theory was particularly critical of the strongly structuralist bias of classical sociological theory, meaning its emphasis on the explanatory importance of mental, social, or economic structures and the corresponding lack of attention to possibilities for individual choice. The two dominant sociological theorists at that time were Talcott Parsons, who had developed a structural-functionalist theory on the back of Durkheim and Weber, and the French anthropologist Claude Levi-Strauss, who had elaborated a highly structuralist interpretation of the Durkheimian tradition. Although less represented among scholars, the Marxism of this era also emphasized structure over agency, with the influential French Marxist Louis Althusser offering a highly structuralist interpretation of Marx's theory of classic conflict. Influenced by (and influencing) the new social movements of the 1960s and 1970s, a new generation of sociological theorists attacked the reigning structuralism.

Three of these new theorists—Anthony Giddens, Pierre Bourdieu, and Michel Foucault—provided particularly influential visions of a revised poststructuralist interpretation of the classical sociological tradition. Of the three, it was perhaps Giddens who was most concerned about regrounding classical sociology itself in new poststructuralist assumptions. Therefore, his collected work reads like a poststructuralist reinterpretation of Marx, Weber, and Durkheim, among others, with the goal of refounding the classical tradition. He did not reject the idea of "structure," which he saw as central to the sociological tradition, but rather sought to reemphasize the importance of "agency"—the importance of individual action and choice. His central concept—structuration—argued that there is a duality of structure and agency: Agency is necessary to create structure, and structure in turn both constrains and enables agency. While structure is static, structuration was dynamic.

Bourdieu's work can be read as challenging two fundamental structuralist tenets. First, challenging the widely held Marxian view that the reproduction of social class was a product of economic structure, Bourdieu emphasized the social and cultural dimensions of class distinctions. Second, in opposition to the Levi-Straussian view that society was organized around elemental mental structures that were prior to activity, Bourdieu focused on activity itself—or practice—as the source of social structure. Like Giddens, Bourdieu did not so much reject the idea of structure as reinterpret it as a more active concept. Bourdieu argued that social structure developed out of the habitual and often taken-for-granted understandings of individuals. This "habitus"—as Bourdieu called it—was as much a cultural as an economic product and, as with Giddens, both enabling and constraining. Thus, Bourdieu has been an important contributor to the contemporary idea of social capital.

Perhaps the basic thrust of Foucault's work was to historicize what appeared to be universal categories or practices. His work falls in many respects in both a Weberian tradition that seeks to understand the history of different forms of domination and a Durkheimian tradition that explores different logics of punishment. His work is notable, however, in extending beyond descriptions of broad social and political structures—the state, bureaucracy, and professions—to explore how knowledge and power are concretely instantiated in conceptions of the self. A central theme in Foucault's historical essays is the development of disciplinary technologies that produce social control through a disciplining of the body. Foucault's attention to the active organizing quality of these disciplinary technologies is perhaps an analogy to Giddens's concept of structuration and Bourdieu's emphasis on practice.

Although the work of the poststructuralists sometimes speaks directly to work in the field of governance—particularly Foucault's—it has more often provided scholars with basic theoretical lenses through which to approach questions of governance. Governance, for example, might be interpreted as a process of structuration, a social practice, or a disciplinary technology.

The Sociology of the State

One of the consequences of the social movements of the 1960s and 1970s was an invigorated interest in history. Historical sociology emerged as a particularly lively subfield in sociology, and one of its central themes was renewed attention to the state and its historical development. Drawing on both Marxist and Weberian traditions, historical sociologists focused on understanding the development of the modern European state in broad political, economic, and social terms. The work of Charles Tilly was particularly influential in promoting a range of work on state building. Tilly argued that the expanding administrative and coercive capacity of European states resulted from geopolitical competition and the imperative of mobilizing societal resources for war.

The renewed attention to the state in historical sociology was memorably captured in a 1985 volume edited by Peter Evans, Dietrich Rueschemeyer, and Theda Skocpol entitled *Bringing the State Back In*. To understand the relevance of their argument—after all, where had the state gone?—it is necessary to situate the volume in sociological debates of the time. In part, the volume was an argument with the society-centric views of pluralists. The volume argued that pluralists focused too much on the power of interest groups and too little on the power of the state. Pluralism was regarded as having been overly influenced by the weak state tradition of the United States, which failed to acknowledge the much more powerful European state. A related debate was influenced by a renewed neo-Marxism. Classical Marxism regarded the state as in the service of the capitalist class, but neo-Marxists began to pose the question of when the state might achieve autonomy. The Evans, Rueschemeyer, and Skocpol volume took the position that the state was a critical political actor with its own interests distinct from those of powerful economic actors or of society.

This attention to the role of the state, in turn, led to greater interest in the relationships between the state and society and the state and the economy. Joel Migdal, for instance, argued that a weak state that confronts a strong society will be penetrated by societal groups and unable to effectively govern society. The state-building literature framework thus became a lens through which to understand the development of states in developing countries, which were often being implicitly compared to the development of strong European states.

New Sociological Institutionalism

This renewed attention on states coincided with a revived interest in institutions. As an institution, the state was, of course, *primus inter pares*. Although there were many versions of what came to be called new institutionalism, this section will describe the sociological version of the new institutionalism, which grew out of organizational sociology. Deeply influenced by Peter Berger and Thomas Luckmann's phenomenological interpretation of institutions in *The Social Construction of Society* and influenced by post-structuralism and developments in organization theory (described in the following paragraphs), the new sociological institutionalists sought to break with the old structural-functional view of institutions. Yet in many respects, and notably in their emphasis on the importance of legitimacy, they remained closely tied to the Weberian tradition.

A leading figure in this new sociological institutionalism was John Meyer. He and his collaborators argued that rationality was a dominant myth and that organizations achieved legitimacy by adopting the outward forms of rationality. This legitimacy was particularly important in ensuring their survival in institutional environments where organizations were evaluated as much by their symbolic compliance with dominant myths as by any more specific performance standard.

Many of the basic ideas of the new sociological institutionalism were collected in a volume edited by Walter Powell and Paul DiMaggio, *The New Institutionalism in Organizational Analysis.* Powell and DiMaggio traced the sources of new sociological institutionalism back to the work of Philip Selznick, but they distinguished their version from his in terms of their more cognitive and less normative attitude toward institutions (among other differences). The old institutionalism, they argued, emphasized the importance of socialization through the internalization of values as the key mechanism of institutionalization. The new sociological institutionalists, by contrast, viewed cognitive mechanisms—in keeping with both Giddens's concept of structuration and Bourdieu's theory of practice—as more important. Thus, they interpreted institutions as taken-for-granted ways of thinking and acting rather as than internalized values.

Organizations

New sociological institutionalism can also be located in a broader set of developments in organizational sociology that began in the 1970s. Earlier developments in organizational studies had already emphasized that organizations need to be understood as open systems shaped by their environments. However, in the 1970s, new approaches to organization emerged that pushed this open-systems perspective much further, shifting attention from what was happening inside organizations to what was happening between organizations. Three new schools of thought developed around this shift in perspective in the 1970s: resource-dependency theory, new sociological institutionalism, and population ecology. Resource-dependency theory viewed organizations as dependent on resources secured from their environments and viewed other organizations as the critical controllers of these resources. New sociological institutionalism emphasized that institutions arose in the environment at the level of what it called the organizational field—sets of interacting organizations. Population ecology developed a model of interorganizational competition to explain the types of organizations that dominated a particular organizational population (defined, essentially, as industries).

One question that united new sociological institutionalism and population ecology, in particular, was why organizations in a field or population often came to adopt such similar forms. These two schools of thought, however, pointed to different mechanisms to explain why organizations converged on a dominant form. New sociological institutionalism argued that organizations in a particular organizational field would adopt forms that had achieved legitimacy in their environments. Population ecology, by contrast, argued that the mechanism was competition for scarce resources. More effective or efficient forms would compete more successfully and therefore become the dominant mode of organization. This debate was fairly fruitful, and although significant differences in emphasis remain, both the institutionalists and the population ecologists revised their models to incorporate elements of the competing theory.

This focus on explaining how organizations converged on a particular form—isomorphism—has also led to interesting work on social and institutional mechanisms. An influential article by DiMaggio and Powell, for instance, argued that there were three institutional mechanisms producing isomorphism: coercive, normative, and mimetic. The state is the main agent of coercive isomorphism. For instance, the state might require schools or firms to adopt particular procedures or programs. The professions are the main agent of normative isomorphism. Their training in systematic bodies of knowledge makes them carriers of similar norms into different organizations. Finally, DiMaggio and Powell argued that mimetic isomorphism—or copying—is particularly important under conditions of high uncertainty. When recipes for success are uncertain, it is rational to copy those organizations that appear successful.

Economic Sociology and Social Networks

Much of contemporary economic sociology might trace its roots back to Marx or Weber, to the American institutional economists John Commons and Thorstein Veblen, or the Austrian anthropologist and historian Karl Polanyi. In an extremely influential study of the historical development of the modern British economy, Polanyi argued, in essence, that markets are embedded in both social and political institutions, by which he meant that these institutions were necessary precursors for the creation of markets. An influential statement of contemporary economic sociology was made in the mid-1980s by Mark Granovetter when he argued, extending Polanyi's study, that modern markets were embedded in social networks. In doing so, Granovetter emphasized that market exchange requires trust and that trust often depends on the prior existence of personal relationships of obligation and reciprocity. Much like Durkheim's critique of classical economics, Granovetter argued that exchange is often social. Many studies in this tradition have demonstrated that even archetypical markets—the stock market or banking—are embedded in social networks.

The study of social networks is an important subfield in its own right in sociology. Social networks can be thought of as important to governance because they are channels of influence; the informal bases of political mobilization and power; and the conduits for the diffusion of information, norms, and innovations. In addition, the concept of network is often conceived as a way to represent the complexity of social or political processes. The sociological approach to networks, social network analysis, is distinguished by a formal mathematical approach to representing and analyzing networks. It is now a commonly used technique to understand complex patterns of alliance and exchange in firms and markets.

Because much of modern governance is the governance of markets, such insights have important implications. Economic sociology is often, in fact, often closely aligned with the sociology of the state, social network analysis, new sociological institutionalism, and organization theory. One of the intellectual threads that often links them together is a social constructivist perspective: a desire to demonstrate that institutions—including states, markets, and organizations—are the embodiments of ideas, symbols, categories, or narratives rather than part of the natural order. For example, Neil Fligstein's *The Transformation of Corporate Control* develops the idea of "conceptions of control" as a basic institutionalist idea for understanding historical shifts in the governance of business firms. Another example is Frank Dobbin's *Forging Industrial Policy,* which argues that different political cultures have produced different conceptions of rationality in the development of industrial policy in the United States, Great Britain, and France.

The Intersections of Sociology and Governance

Up to this point, this entry has sought to provide an overview of sociology itself as a discipline, focusing on both the classical traditions of sociology and its contemporary interpretations. This section reverses the logic. Instead of asking how sociology as a discipline speaks to governance, the entry now considers how current trends in governance call for sociological analysis.

The term *governance* has, of course, varied connotations. However, a common argument is that the term *governance* is being contrasted with the term *government.* Whereas government emphasizes the role of the state to rule or govern society, governance expands the focus to include nonstate institutions and society itself as essential components of the governing process.

This sense of the changing relationship between state and society and between public and private sectors creates both opportunities and demands for a more important role for sociology. For example, new kinds of organizations are receiving increased attention as critical in contemporary governance. Nonprofit organizations are now seen as critical providers of social services and dubbed collectively the third sector. Nongovernmental organizations (NGOs), and their variant, international nongovernmental organizations (INGOs), are increasingly seen as important interlocutors in policy formation and implementation. There is also a renewed interest in voluntary organizations as important intermediaries in collective political action and dispute resolution. Sociological work in organization theory, social network analysis, and social movement theory is often particularly relevant for understanding these organizations.

The study of governance, as opposed to government, also renews interest in communities and community building. Although the era of increasing state centralization often overlooked the role of local communities, new decentralization trends have renewed interest in the character of communities and their capacity to engage in governance. A new (or renewed) communitarianism has emerged in the social sciences, as exemplified by sociologists like Robert Bellah and Philip Selznick and political scientists like Robert Putnam. The concept of social capital, as developed by sociologists like Bourdieu and James Coleman, has become a central concept in the governance arsenal. Social capital is seen as being rooted in local communities.

Another area where a sociological perspective has become increasingly valuable is in studies of professionals and professional knowledge. Although the role of experts in government has long been a topic of concern, governance is often seen as a highly technical, hence professionalized, sphere of activity. In contemporary discussions of governance, professionals are increasingly viewed as semiautonomous actors in policy making and implementation. Networks of professionals, and the professional knowledge they mobilize, are seen as key factors shaping governance. Sociology has a distinguished tradition of studying professions and processes of professionalization. Part of the importance of the professions arises because of the increasing prevalence of science as a form of regulatory and administrative decision making. The sociology of knowledge has been one perspective from which to analyze (and often to criticize) the knowledge claims of experts.

Conclusion

This entry has suggested that sociology's basic concerns about domination, social order, and society have many implications for contemporary discussions about governance. Communities, organizations, professions, social movements, states, markets, and social networks are among the most basic elements of governance, and sociology provides critical intellectual resources for understanding them. Many subfields within sociology are relevant to governance, but this entry has focused on organization theory, economic sociology, and political sociology as particularly relevant. These subfields provide fundamental insights into the most critical institutions of contemporary governance—organizations, states, markets, and social movements.

—*Chris Ansell*

See also Communitarianism; Economic Sociology; Institutionalism; Interpretive Theory; Nongovernmental Organization; Nonprofit Organization; Organization Theory; Patrimonialism; Professionalism; Rule of Law; Social Capital; Social Constructivism; Social Movement Theory; Social Network Theory; State Building

Further Readings and References

Berger, P. L., & Luckmann, T. (1966). *The social construction of reality: A treatise in the sociology of knowledge.* Garden City, NY: Doubleday.

Bourdieu, P. (1993). *Outline of a theory of practice.* Cambridge, UK: Cambridge University Press.

DiMaggio, P. J., & Powell, W. (1983). The iron cage revisited: Institutional isomorphism and collective rationality in organizational fields. *American Sociological Review, 48,* 147-160.

Dobbin, F. (1994). *Forging industrial policy: The United States, Britain, and France in the railway age.* New York and Cambridge, UK: Cambridge University Press.

Evans, P., Rueschemeyer, D., & Skocpol, T. (1985). *Bringing the state back in.* Cambridge, UK: Cambridge University Press.

Fligstein, N. (1990). *The transformation of corporate control.* Cambridge, MA: Harvard University Press.

Foucault, M. (1984). *The Foucault reader* (P. Rabinow, Ed.). New York: Pantheon Books.

Giddens, A. (1986). *Central problems in social theory: Action, structure, and contradiction in social analysis.* Berkeley: University of California Press.

Granovetter, M. (1985). Economic action and social structure: The problem of embeddedness. *American Journal of Sociology, 91,* 481–510.

Michels, R. (1959). *Political parties.* New York: Dover Books.

Migdal, J. (1988). *Strong societies and weak states.* Princeton, NJ: Princeton University Press.

Mills, C. W. (1956). *The power elite.* New York: Oxford University Press.

Powell, W. W., & DiMaggio, P. J. (1991). *The new institutionalism in organizational analysis.* Chicago: University of Chicago Press.

Selznick, P. (1984). *TVA and the grassroots: A study of politics and organization.* Berkeley: University of California Press.

Tilly, C. (1992). *Coercion, capital, and European states: AD 990–1992.* Cambridge, MA: Basil Blackwell.

Weber, M. (1947). *The theory of social and economic organization.* New York: Free Press.

SOUTH EAST ASIA TREATY ORGANIZATION

During the Cold War, the United States developed a number of military alliances, which included the South East Asia Treaty Organization (SEATO). In the early Cold War years, the United States had not played an especially active role in the Southeast Asian region. This changed in 1950s following the French withdrawal from Indochina. Initially, the United States focused its attention on the formation of the Australia, New Zealand, and United States (ANZUS) Treaty of 1951, which tied the treaty members to a U.S. anti-communist containment policy in Southeast Asia. Direct U.S. involvement in the region came in September 1954 when the United States, Great Britain, France, Australia, New Zealand, Thailand, the Philippines, and Pakistan met in Manila and signed the South East Asia Collective Defense Treaty, which became SEATO, in 1955.

SEATO should be viewed as part of a complex network of anti-communist military alliances championed by the United States. At the core of this system was the North Atlantic Treaty Organization (NATO), and attempts were made to develop SEATO into a NATO-style institutionalized alliance system. This failed for a number of reasons. First, there was no real consensus among members as to what the purpose of SEATO was; the Southeast Asian states sought to safeguard their own national security, the United States saw SEATO as a psychological weapon in the struggle to contain communism, and Great Britain, France, New Zealand, and Australia were never especially committed to SEATO. Second, none of the allies sought to establish a unified command structure, and attempts to designate national forces for SEATO purposes were limited. Third, competing interests within SEATO meant that the organization remained inactive in the face of two regional security crises—a military coup in Laos in the 1960s and the crisis in Cambodia in 1970. During the 1970s, as the United States normalized relations with communist China, SEATO entered a dissolution phase—it was disbanded in 1977.

It should also be noted that SEATO emerged at a time when decolonization had given rise to a growing sense of third-world identity. It was the Association of Southeast Asian Nations (ASEAN), formed in 1967 and made up entirely of (pro-capitalist) Southeast Asian states, that was ultimately much more successful in securing the region. ASEAN differed from SEATO in that it was concerned with a wider range of issues than simply containing communism—most notably its commitment to regional economic cooperation. The United States endorsed the creation of ASEAN, viewing it as a regional organization that was better able to counter nontraditional security threats (poverty in particular).

—*Juanita Elias*

See also Asian Governance; Association of Southeast Asian Nations

Further Readings and References

Dreisbach, K. (2003). Between SEATO and ASEAN: The United States and the regional organization of Southeast Asia. In M. Frey, R. W. Pruessen, & T. T. Yong (Eds.), *The transformation of Southeast Asia: International perspectives on decolonization* (pp. 241–256). Armonk, NY: M. E. Sharpe.

Rafferty, K. (2003). An institutionalist reinterpretation of Cold War alliance systems: Insights for alliance theory. *Canadian Journal of Political Science, 36*(2), 341–362.

SOUTHERN AFRICAN DEVELOPMENT COMMUNITY

The Southern African Development Community (SADC) is the successor to the Southern African Development Coordination Conference (SADCC). It is necessary to have a brief understanding of the SADCC in order to introduce the SADC. The SADCC was created in 1980 as a result of an agreement among Angola, Botswana, Malawi, Mozambique, Tanzania, Zambia, and Zimbabwe, which had undergone a process of regionalization for over a century. The SADCC created a political regionalism based on two key concerns that united the member states. First, these economically weak states wished to assert a collective strength in contrast to the Apartheid regime in South Africa. Second, the SADCC aimed to facilitate the disbursement of aid from Western donors, the more progressive of which understood support for the SADCC as part of an anti-Apartheid development policy.

The SADCC was formally replaced by the SADC in 1992. This was a result of the abolishment of Apartheid in South Africa, and indeed South Africa joined the SADC in 1994, the year in which Nelson Mandela won the presidency of that country. The SADC now includes Angola, Botswana, the Democratic Republic of Congo, Lesotho, Madagascar, Malawi, Mauritius, Mozambique, Namibia, South Africa, Swaziland, United Republic of Tanzania, Zambia, and Zimbabwe. Institutionally, the SADC is constituted by regional summits, a complex regional bureaucracy mainly based in Botswana, interministerial groups, and an SADC interparliamentary forum.

With the entry of a democratic South Africa, both of the founding *raisons d'être* for the SADCC melted away; the SADC is an attempt to maintain a southern African regional project in light of these historic changes. But, the entry of South Africa—which has an economy that is larger than the sum of all the other members—has been far from straightforward, and in fact the SADC has at best instituted a halting and tentative regionalism. The key issues underpinning the SADC's limited progress are listed in the following paragraphs.

The SADC's regional economic strategy has undergone a substantial change. The assumptions about state planning and inwardly focused regional economic development have been replaced by a more market-driven development strategy that aims to make southern Africa a more competitive region within a global economy reflecting a broader global shift toward neoliberalism. This form of regionalism—often called open regionalism—can only work if the member states have adequate levels of economic integration and complementarity. Southern African states are not highly integrated or complementary in this sense.

South Africa has established itself as the hub of the region. Where there is regional integration, it is not multilateral but rather "hub-and-spoke" in its spatial patterning: Mozambique, Botswana, and others all maintain strong linkages with South Africa but have far less interaction with other neighbors. The economic inequalities of the region have not been significantly mollified; South Africa remains a core in a region of peripheries. And Western aid strategies have been refocused on South Africa.

The SADC is now one form of regionalism in a complex of overlapping regional organizations. The East African Community and the Community of Eastern and Southern African States have also incorporated SADC members into their own institutions. It is unclear how this multiregionalism will affect the SADC.

—*Graham Harrison*

See also African Governance; Neoliberalism

Further Readings and References

Tsie, B. (1996). States and markets in the Southern African Development Community (SADC): Beyond the neoliberal paradigm. *Journal of Southern African Studies, 22*(1), 75–98.

SOVEREIGNTY

Sovereignty is a key concept in modern political thought. It is both a complex institution and an artificial political arrangement. As such, it must be understood in the context of its historical development and its various political applications. Nonetheless, its core features are relatively stable and allow a general framework to be drawn to clarify what is at stake when speaking about sovereignty.

Sovereignty regulates relations between the rulers and the ruled, as well as relations between sovereign entities in the international arena. In both domestic and international spheres, sovereignty encompasses three aspects. The first is institutional: Sovereignty is tightly linked to the emergence of the modern state and the peculiarities of the powers it exercises. The second aspect refers to its doctrinal underpinnings: Sovereignty operates as a legitimizing concept depending on who is deemed to be the holder of sovereignty (the monarch, the nation, the people, the state). Finally, the legal dimension of sovereignty refers to the limits of power exercised by the holders of sovereignty.

The meaning of sovereignty can be explained by reference to the emergence of the modern state at a time when medieval lawyers, in particular in France and Great Britain, sought to legitimate the rights of kings and princes to assert centralized authority over the numerous entities and communities (such as feudal lords, guilds, monasteries) that had until that time enjoyed virtual autonomy within their jurisdictions. They also explicitly, and successfully, challenged the constraints imposed by the nominally supreme authority of the Pope and Holy Roman Emperor. Indeed, the first doctrinal texts dealing with sovereignty mainly focused on the necessity to preserve the state from outside pressures and internal disorder. This primacy principle must be viewed in conjunction with the principle of exclusivity: A sovereign state is mainly a territorial institution because its exercise of exclusive authority is limited to the geographic perimeter of its territory. Sovereignty encapsulates the idea that there exists a final and absolute authority in the political community, and that no final and absolute authority exists elsewhere.

To the extent that sovereignty is tied to the territorialization of power, it is also illustrative of the secularization trend. In this context, absolute authority also means that state sovereignty is indivisible, that is to say it cannot exist in degrees: A state is either sovereign or is not. Sovereignty also implies a unitary condition because the sovereign state is considered as a whole. As a result, all of the competences exercised by the sovereign state are ultimately attributable to and embodied by a single legal personality. Sovereign authority is mainly characterized by the monopoly on the legitimate use of physical force, along with an exclusive capacity to make and enforce legal norms. The making of rules and enforcement of authority are therefore the most important means to measure state sovereignty. This does not rule out the fact that some competences might be delegated to subentities (in the case of a federal state, for example) or supraentities (such as the European Union), but these political entities are still not considered to be sovereign and are not deemed to exercise a form of power characterized by the same traits.

Alongside this qualitative aspect of sovereignty is a more substantial aspect relating to the range of prerogatives exercised by the state (justice, diplomacy, defense, minting currency, regulating markets, levying taxes, etc.). The number and the nature of functions performed by the state have varied over time and according to regions. The mere fact that competences may be transferred to other entities (for example the European Union or private actors) does not necessarily mean that sovereignty is divisible or jeopardized. This is because, in most cases, these processes are themselves ultimately decided by the sovereign state itself.

Following from the first essays on state sovereignty, scholars, lawyers, and philosophers developed different and sometimes antagonistic views about who constitutes the sovereign. Those who challenged the concept of absolute state sovereignty argued that if the king exercises sovereign power, he is only empowered to do so in the name of the people (as the *corpus politicum*) and not just in the name of God. This idea led to a revolutionary conception of political power, which asserted that political society is a voluntary association of people, and that they are the genuine holders of sovereignty. This redefinition of political power gradually upset the traditional top-down approach. The people—mainly conceived as a group of citizens falling under the authority of a single government—became vested with new individual and collective rights, in particular the right to self-determination that would later trigger the development of the democratic state model.

Henceforth, the legitimization of obedience and coercion had to be adapted in order to fit these new ideals. According to the social contract model, obedience can be justified by the fact that citizens are themselves the source of the law. Legal norms are thus deemed to express the general will, and the government is expected to behave as the true representative of its people.

This revolutionary perspective had an enormous impact on the legitimacy of the political authority but did not really alter the main features of sovereignty. To this day, the terms *national sovereignty*—which is consistent with the idea of representation developed as a condition to ensure the implementation of the sovereign right of the people—and *state sovereignty* are usually used interchangeably and function according to the same logic.

Popular and national sovereignty essentially amounts to a limitation of the power of the state and puts an end to absolutist conceptions. But the issue of the limits of sovereign power must be framed within a broader picture in order to take into account the legal aspect of the concept of sovereignty. Since the seventeenth century, sovereignty has, at times, been criticized for providing the justification for the wielding of unlimited powers, whether on behalf of the king (according to divine law), the state (i.e., the *raison d'etat*), or the people (through the general will). This kind of argument has been used in particular by proponents of liberal doctrines, who are more inclined to defend the rights of individuals against the state. Before analyzing the changes brought about by liberalism in this field, it is important to underline that originally absolute power did not mean unlimited power. In fact, the evolution in the nature of limits, which are generally conceived in legal terms, varied according to the ideologies dominant in a given place and time. First, natural or divine laws were considered normative constraints on the sovereign. On a larger scale, a metajuridical order that combined references to God, to the laws of nature, and to the main customs (*us et coutumes*) of the country served this purpose. Of course, the effectiveness of these limits did not depend on external authorities (such as the Pope or the emperor) from which modern political authorities broke away, but rather on the way the sovereign chose to interpret them, rendering them arbitrary and potentially hazardous. Furthermore, the very nature of the social contract, as defined by Thomas Hobbes, serves to limit sovereign power: The sovereign state is instituted to guarantee the safety and security of the people, which is the ultimate reason why individuals choose to relinquish the freedom they enjoy in the state of nature. As a consequence, a state that is incapable of fulfilling its basic duties cannot legitimately demand obedience from its subjects.

The idea of sovereignty gradually began to fit into a general pattern inspired by rationalism and humanism, which were to become the principal factors explaining the development of constitutionalism and the advent of the rule of law. This development encountered serious resistance but finally became the dominant ideology in support of sustaining state authority (particularly in Western countries).

It is clear that early liberal doctrines, in avoiding the use of the word sovereignty, demonstrate their reluctance with regard to the concept. But the political system they pledged for implicitly relies on the national sovereignty model. As a matter of fact, the way in which state power is exercised and legitimized cannot be understood without reference to the main features of sovereignty previously described (supreme authority and unitary condition). On the one hand, the elaboration of mechanisms like the separation of legislative, executive, and judicial powers; the necessity to ensure a balance of powers; and the reference to reason and justice as supraconstitutional values aimed at neutralizing excessive governments served to guarantee the rights and freedoms of individuals against the state (as the sovereign authority). On the other hand, these innovations did not actually challenge the principle of the sovereign as wielding supreme authority over a defined territory. Indeed, law and especially the supreme law of the state enshrined in

the constitution mainly appeared as a useful tool for civilizing and legitimizing the exercise of sovereignty, even if the idea of imposing legal constraints on political authorities had been hotly debated.

Briefly said, the rule of law principle is based on a structural link between a state and its legal system similar to the one that brings the state and the nation together under the sovereignty principle. The three dimensions of sovereignty (state sovereignty, popular sovereignty, legal sovereignty) are intertwined in the contemporary discourse on sovereignty and operate according to the logics of its main features. However, this is not to say that tensions or contradictions between these three levels have never occurred in practice. One can point to many cases of secessionist claims or popular upheavals in which the government is no longer considered to be the genuine representative of the nation. Moreover, at the theoretical level, several authors have pinpointed discrepancies between political and academic discourses and the realities to which they purport to refer. They have raised important questions concerning the relevance of sovereignty for consolidating democratic regimes and enhancing civic participation. Nonetheless, sovereignty continues to pervade the discourses of the main political actors and represents an enduring principle for organizing and legitimizing the relationship between rulers and ruled.

As previously noted, sovereignty is also an institution structuring the international arena. The spread of the sovereignty model concurrent with the multiplication of states having exclusive jurisdiction over their domestic affairs has logically lead to the emergence of an international order (the so-called Westphalian system) characterized by the absence of a paramount political authority. On one hand, anarchy in international relations stems from the recognition of the political independence (also referred to as external autonomy) of states as a governing principle. But anarchy does not necessarily amount to disorder or chaos. As indicated by some authors, sovereignty implies a set of constitutive rules (equality of states before the law, self-determination, reciprocity, nonintervention, membership and participation in the society of states, notably in international organizations) that are considered foundational because they lay the groundwork for certain activities. On the other hand, the regulative rules of sovereignty pertain to the day-to-day interactions between sovereign entities.

If sovereignty follows a specific path in the international sphere, the meaning of external sovereignty can also be illustrated by reference to the three previously mentioned aspects.

State sovereignty implies external autonomy, which refers to the right of each state not to be subject to another political authority. This is the negative side of the concept that expresses the formal and juridical aspect of sovereign statehood and takes the form of a legal entitlement conferred by the international society upon an entity by recognizing it as such. Negative sovereignty is therefore an absolute condition. Conversely, positive sovereignty (defined as the capacity of the state to act in international relations, that is to say its ability to project power) and operational sovereignty (whereby states choose to limit their legal freedom of action in a process of bargaining with other states when establishing principles or rules of international governance) are variable by nature. Due to its unitary condition, however, the sovereign state acts as the sole interface between the domestic and international spheres through its officials. Some other actors (for example, federal entities and NGOs) may participate in international affairs, but the ultimate authority to endorse legally binding agreements rests with the state.

The popular or national dimension of external sovereignty can also be viewed through the same lens. According to the principle of self-determination, external political authorities are not entitled to interfere in the political, social, and economic choices made by the citizens of a country (negative sovereignty). Foreign policies and diplomatic activities are supposed to serve the interests of the nation (positive sovereignty), and national interests are also deemed to determine the conditions under which a state will participate in international organizations or activities (operational sovereignty).

And finally, in the domestic sphere, limits have been set with a view to restraining the exercise of crude power politics in international affairs. Some limits are considered as inherent features of sovereignty (such as the nonintervention principle), while others relate to the natural law of nations, the common law of mankind (the metajuridical order). That which is actually considered to be the legal international system is mainly grounded in the positivist tradition. This views sovereignty as providing the means by which people can express consent to the application of international legal norms and to the competences exercised by international organizations. As a consequence, activities performed by international organizations, even if they relate to issues that are traditionally viewed as pertaining to domestic affairs, are not in contradiction with the sovereignty principle per se. If the state has previously accepted to abide by conventional or customary norms and to participate in international organizations, its sovereignty is not infringed on by the intervention of third parties willing to ensure the effectiveness of its legal commitments, as long as the ways and means of the intervention are consistent with international law (for instance, unilateral military intervention is ruled out by the United Nations Charter).

Given the absence of a superseding political authority, the international legal system appears to be less effective than domestic law. Moreover, there is an enduring difficulty in disentangling the meaning of sovereignty from the ideological controversies that surround it. Some still consider it to be an anachronistic concept that permits barbarism within and across state boundaries, whereas others continue to view sovereignty as an arrangement that is particularly conducive to upholding certain values that are considered to be of fundamental importance to individual and collective security (such as international order among states, membership and participation in international organizations, political freedom of states, and pluralism or respect for the diversity of ways of life of different groups of people, to name a few).

—*Barbara Delcourt*

See also Authority; Border Theory; Commonwealth of Independent States; Failed State; Governance; Humanitarian Intervention; Nation; Pooled Sovereignty; Realism and Neorealism; Rule of Law; Self-Government; State; United Nations Security Council

Further Readings and References

Bartelson, J. (1995). *A genealogy of sovereignty.* Cambridge, UK: Cambridge University Press.

Biersteker, T. J., & Weber, C. (Eds.). (1996). *State sovereignty as social construct.* Cambridge, UK: Cambridge University Press.

Hinsley, F. H. (1986). *Sovereignty.* Cambridge, UK: Cambridge University Press.

Spruyt, H. (1994). *The sovereign state and its competitors.* Princeton, NJ: Princeton University Press.

Thomson, J. E. (1995). State sovereignty in international relations: Bridging the gap between theory and empirical research. *International Studies Quarterly, 39,* 215–217.

Weber, C. (1997). *Simulating sovereignty: Intervention, the state and the symbolic exchange.* Cambridge, UK: Cambridge University Press.

SPACE

From a governance perspective, space is far from a natural, pregiven, purely external condition of social action. It comprises socially produced grids and horizons of social action that divide the material, social, and imaginary worlds into different places, areas, territories, and scales and also orient actions in terms of such divisions. Even the space-time coordinates of a given physical space can intersect with many spaces, places, and scales that have different identities, spatiotemporal boundaries, and social import. Cyberspace also poses complex governance issues. Such issues may even arise and have real-world consequences with regard to purely imaginary spaces and places, such as utopias, dystopias, heavens, and hells. In all cases, the material and symbolic delimitation of spaces, places, and scales and their social meanings is inherently contestable.

Overall, as a product of social practices that appropriate and transform physical and social phenomena and invest them with social significance, space can function as a site, object, and means of governance. Inherited spatial configurations and their opportunity structures are sites where governance may be established, contested, and modified. Space is an object of governance insofar as it results from the fixing, manipulating, and lifting of material, social and symbolic borders, boundaries, and frontiers. Space can be a means of governance when it defines horizons of action in terms of inside and outside and configures possible connections among actors, actions, and events inside and outside. Because boundaries contain and connect, they frame interactions selectively, privileging some identities and interests over others and they structure possible connections to other places and spaces across different scales. While such spatial divisions may generate fundamental antagonisms and more or less unrestrained conflict, they may also facilitate and require coordination across spaces, places, and scales through solidarity, hierarchy, networks, markets, or other governance mechanisms. Which mechanisms, if any, dominate and their relative success or failure vary with the primary forms of sociospatial organization, ranging from simple nomadic bands and segmentary societies through center-periphery relations to world society with its multiscalar functional differentiation and multiple bases of social fragmentation.

Space is constructed and governed at many scales, ranging from the corporeal to outer space. Individuals create their own personal space materially and socially, with intimacy and distance varying by locale, type of social relation, and capacities for surveillance-intrusion. External efforts also occur to govern bodies (including hearts and minds) and their interrelations in many ways. Thus, Michel Foucault analyzed the anatomo-political (individual) and bio-political (population-focused) practices of modern states and other disciplinary apparatuses. Other sites of spatial governance, involving enormous heterogeneity in objects, stakes, mechanisms, actors, and potential lines of conflict, include residential areas, markets, workplaces, schools, prisons, places of worship, (de-)militarized zones, public spaces, private and common land, the built environment, airspace and outer space, areas of outstanding natural beauty or special scientific interest, and so on. Even this incomplete list suggests that there is no "one best way" to govern time and space and that no actors are inherently privileged or powerful in this regard.

This said, modern states do claim special responsibilities for control over political territory as a crucial site, object, and means of governance. Statehood involves authoritative power that is collectively binding on those present in a given territory. The classic case is the modern Westphalian state system based on mutually exclusive, hierarchically organized, sovereign national states that coconstitute an essentially anarchic interstate system that is governed, if at all, quite differently from domestic relations within states. Besides the classic Westphalian international balance of power system, we find relations of dependency, suzerainty, and colonial domination. Earlier forms of the state include city-states, classic agrarian empires with complex center-periphery relations, the patchwork medieval state system, and absolutism. A recent innovation is the European Union, with its variable geometry and evolving multiscalar system of government, governance, and metagovernance. Many other novel forms of spatial governance, such as those concerned with cross-border regions, free ports and free enterprise zones, or international trade, investment, and service regimes, are also emerging in the postnational era, leading some to suggest the arrival of a neomedieval polity. This raises interesting questions about the relations among different spatial scales of governance.

Scale concerns the articulation of bounded spaces of differing size (e.g., local, regional, national, continental, and global). A crucial governance issue here is the relative dominance of different scales and their possible disjunction across social spheres. Scale dominance derives from the exercise of power by forces at certain spatial scales over other forces at the same, higher, or lower scales. It can rest on the articulation of scales *qua* strategically selective terrains of power and domination or the capacities and activities of individuals, networks, and organizations at different scales. A particular scale may gain special sociopolitical significance by playing the dominant role in the scalar division of labor within and across different fields of social practice. For example, in Western Europe, the national scale became dominant during the postwar economic boom due to a socially constructed coincidence of national economies, national states, and national citizenship regimes. Nodal scales lack such dominance but have key roles in delivering certain activities in a spatiotemporal order. Local states, to continue the example, were nodal in postwar Europe. More marginal or peripheral scales may become sites of resistance. Creating new scales of action, reordering them, and jumping scale (selecting the scale on which effective power is exercised) are important features of power relations and the reordering of governance.

Debate continues whether the current global era has (or could have) a dominant scale of organization comparable to the national scale in postwar Europe and elsewhere or, on the contrary, it will remain characterized by a complex, tangled, disjointed, and inherently multiscalar set of social relations with no primary scale of governance.

Spatial grids and horizons of action are complexly interwoven with their temporal equivalents. Key questions of governance arise here from space-time distantiation and compression. Space-time distantiation stretches social relations over space and time so that they can be controlled or coordinated over longer distances, greater areas, or more scales and over longer periods of time (including into ever-more-distant futures). It results from the growing spatial reach of practices and is enabled by new material and social technologies of communication, transportation, command, control, and intelligence. Space-time compression involves the intensification of discrete events in real time or the increased velocity of material and immaterial flows over a given distance. It is linked to material and social technologies that enable the conquest of space by time and permit more precise control over ever-shorter periods of action. Differential abilities to stretch or compress space-time help to shape power and resistance in the emerging global (dis)order and are important for governance success and failure. For example, hypermobile, superfast, financial capital in a deregulated world market is destabilizing and has provoked countervailing efforts to redesign global economic governance.

Governing the spatial and scalar division of economic labor on a local, regional, national, or global scale poses different issues from governing social relations in a multicultural, multiethnic neighborhood. To multiply examples and complications, consider governing interfaith access to Jerusalem's holy sites, regulating flows of asylum seekers and economic migrants, monitoring extraordinary rendition, dealing with uneven economic development, controlling offshore tax havens, regulating multinational companies, defining norms of extraterritoriality in diplomacy, organizing cyberspace, and controlling military and commercial uses of outer space. This multiplicity is reflected in the variable coincidence (and noncoincidence) of boundaries, borders, or frontiers of economic, political, and other types of activity or process in diverse contexts, in the changing primacy of different spatial or temporal horizons of action, and in the wide range of spatial governance objects, mechanisms, and subjects. Rather than convergence on one best way to govern space-time in all its heterogeneity, we find different types of spatiotemporal fix, linked to different ways of marking spatiotemporal boundaries and governing relations inside, outside, and across them. While each fix distinguishes inside from outside, the outside has a key role in facilitating effective governance inside. Spatiotemporal fixes also differentiate winners and losers internally and externally, facilitate institutionalized compromises, and enable those engaged in governance to claim success if the effects of governance failure are largely externalized. In short, space as site, object, and means of governance is intrinsically linked to temporal questions as well as to place, space, and scale and, equally importantly, to what lies outside given frontiers, borders, and boundaries as well as what lies inside.

—Bob Jessop

See also Glocalization; Governance Failure; Self-Organizing System; State

Further Readings and References

Anderson, M. (1996). *Frontiers: Territory and state formation in the modern world.* Cambridge, UK: Polity Press.
Collinge, C. (1999). Self-organization of society by scale. *Society and Space, 17*(5), 557–574.
Foucault, M. (1980). *The history of sexuality, vol. 1: An introduction.* Harmondsworth, UK: Penguin.
Jessop, B. (2002). *The future of the capitalist state.* Cambridge, UK: Polity Press.
Tuan, Y.-F. (1977). *Space and place: The perspective of experience.* London: Edward Arnold.

SPECIAL DISTRICT

One of the least understood institutions of local government is the special district. Special districts are service providers that operate within specifically defined areas and in response to public demand, though they are created by state legislation. As originally authorized, and still to a large extent, they provide a single service such as education, cemeteries, transportation, and fire protection, to name a few.

California and other Western states pioneered the special district instrument for water and agricultural needs in the nineteenth century. As of 2002, there were 35,052 special districts nationally and about another 15,000 when independent school districts were included. The Western and Midwestern states, including Texas, led in the use of this form of government.

One classification of types of special districts covers three sets of contrasting features: single-function versus multifunction, enterprise versus nonenterprise, and independent versus dependent.

Single-Function Versus Multifunction Districts

Most special districts perform one service or function. The following are single-function special districts listed by the U.S. Census Bureau: school building authorities, libraries, hospitals, health, highways, air transportation, fire protection, drainage/flood control, irrigation, sewerage, solid waste management, water supply, cemeteries, and mosquito abatement. Multifunction districts are: parks and recreation, housing and community development, industrial development and mortgage credit, natural resources and water supply, and sewerage and water supply. Not commonly found, but nevertheless extant, are single- and multifunction special districts, such as bridge authorities and, again in California, community service districts, which can offer up to sixteen different services.

Enterprise Versus Nonenterprise Districts

Special districts possess many of the same governing powers as cities and counties. They can enter into contracts, employ workers, and acquire real property through purchase or eminent domain. They can also issue debt, impose taxes, levy assessments, and charge fees for their services. Special districts, like other governments, can sue and be sued. They can also adopt a seal and alter it at will.

Because of the nature of some services and products provided, it is difficult to finance the work of certain special districts by taxing all recipients. For example, gas, water, and electricity utilities usually charge customers by quantity consumed. Services commonly provided by nonenterprise districts include fire protection, libraries, and police protection. Sometimes nonenterprise districts charge use or service fees, which are minor sources of revenue, such as from rental of facilities and swimming pool admission charges. However, nonenterprise districts basically rely on property taxation or other taxes, such as sales tax.

Independent Versus Dependent Districts

Independent districts have their own separate boards of directors elected by the district's voters for fixed terms. Governing boards vary in membership with the size and nature of the district. One extreme example is the Metropolitan Water District of Southern California, which has thirty-seven board members. The number of members in this case is a reflection of public jurisdictions and other interests serviced by the district.

Dependent districts are governed by the elected bodies of general-purpose governments. Larger independent districts usually have a professional manager similar to a city manager to assist board members. Small dependent districts in large cities or counties, such as street or lighting maintenance or mosquito abatement districts, are often clustered together for administrative purposes in public works or engineering departments.

An incipient application of special districts, yet to be extensively tried, is use as service providers under the emerging emphasis on governance. The definition of governance is: The sum of the many ways that individuals and institutions, public and private, manage their common affairs.

In municipal governments, an aspect of governance has been requirements for public consultation and interaction with constituents on policy issues. Public hearings, referenda, petitions, polling, and the like

are traditional devices of communication with constituents. More and more, however, the need to communicate even closer to citizen grass roots has been recognized. One emerging means used, especially in large urban governments, is formation and empowerment of neighborhood councils. The City of Los Angeles's experience has been most informative, with neighborhood councils serving both as channels of articulation of political demands as well as supports in relations with city councils, commissions, and departments. Although channels and agendas have traditionally been controlled by the government (except in anomic demonstrations), neighborhood councils often have their own issues. Also, the Los Angeles experience appears to demonstrate that as citizen perception of the importance of an issue increases, so does the tendency for neighborhood councils to coalesce, presenting a more formidable political force.

While neighborhood councils may, at times, be able to influence budgetary allocations to favor perceived needs of constituents, usually in a revenue shortfall situation this is difficult to do. If the need is important enough, however, there are the self-financing alternatives of special assessments and special districts. Usually, special assessments are selected for one-time projects, such as sidewalks and curbing, and special districts are used for ongoing service provision, such as street lighting, park maintenance, and storm-drainage management.

—*Gilbert B. Siegel*

See also American Governance; Local Governance; Urban Governance

Further Readings and References

Chandler, R. C., & Plano, J. C. (1982). *The public administration dictionary*. New York: Wiley.

STAKEHOLDER

Stakeholding has been articulated as a foundation for both corporate and societal governance toward economic democracy. A stakeholder can be defined as any individual, social group, or actor who possesses a stake (e.g., interest, legal obligation, moral right) in the decisions or outcomes of an organization (typically firms, corporations, or governments). Thus, stakeholders are characterized by either being affected by or affecting the achievement of an organization's objectives. The stakeholder approach is based on the assumption that governance is more advantageous when it is guided by a principle of inclusiveness. However, the viability of a multistakeholder process is not only determined by its inclusiveness, but also by its capacity to deliver its objectives, that is, its effectiveness.

The first formulation of the term is credited to the Stanford Research Institute (SRI) in the 1960s as a generalization of stockholder or shareholder. SRI's work was focused on firms, and the stakeholder concept was focused on the firm's most closely related actors. In the mid-1980s, a stakeholder approach emerged from the work of Ian Mitroff, Richard Mason, James Emshoff, and, specially, Edward Freeman. In 1984, Freeman broadened the definition of stakeholder as including any person or group affecting or affected by the achieving of organizational objectives. The meaning of the concept has been subsequently stretched through the development of its social and political dimensions and is now a key concept for governance in general.

Stakeholder Theory and Analysis

Freeman's work was seminal in the development of stakeholder theory and in advancing academic debate. Since 1984, academic interest in a stakeholder approach has both grown and broadened. Indeed the number of citations using the word stakeholder has increased enormously. The stakeholder concept is being embraced by many as an inclusive philosophy, which can be justified by the organizations' increasing need of dealing with complex contexts. The term is widely used by academicians, politicians, managers, and consultants. However, the academic validity of the concept is disputed by those that argue that stakeholding is too vague and imprecise and the term can mean almost anything the author desires. The stakeholder approach has also been contested because of its

marginal treatment of critical concepts such as equity, power, and resistance.

Stakeholder theory proposes that stakeholding has a dual instrumental-normative quality. On one hand, incorporating stakeholders' participation enhances the organization's management capabilities in a globalized context characterized by increasing socioeconomic interconnectivity. On the other hand, promoting plurality and inclusivity and recognizing the intrinsic value of stakeholders' interests makes it morally superior (e.g., in terms of democracy and social justice) to traditional managerial approaches based on the mere optimization of shareholders' gains.

In more practical terms, stakeholder theory seeks to describe and examine the connections between stakeholder legitimate interests, stakeholder management practices, and the achievement of the goals of an organization. This examination should lead to: (1) a better understanding of needs of stakeholders in order to set the bounds of operation and (2) the formulation of recommendations for increasing governance efficiency.

Stakeholder analysis typically consists of the systematic identification and characterization of the most relevant stakeholders for an organization or initiative: that is, those stakeholders exerting, or trying to exert, influence on the company's decisions and activities. Stakeholders with similar interests, claims, or rights can be classified into different categories according to their roles (e.g., employees, shareholders, customers, suppliers, regulators, nongovernmental organizations). In corporate governance, stakeholders are often classified into primary and secondary groups. Primary stakeholders are fundamental for the firm's operation and survival. Such stakeholders include owners, investors, employees, suppliers, customers, and competitors, as well as nature (physical resources and carrying capacity). Secondary stakeholders are those influenced by the firm's operations, but not directly engaged in transactions with the firm, and consequently not essential for its survival. Examples of secondary stakeholders are local communities and local business support groups. Secondary stakeholders can be of high strategic importance for the success of particular operations and activities of a company. A second methodological step consists of determining the stake of stakeholder. Stakes and groups can be categorized as threats and opportunities that build a stakeholder strategy matrix.

Business literature has focused heavily on assessing the differential threats caused by primary and secondary stakeholders. A major purpose of these developments is to help corporate managers understand their stakeholder environments and manage their relationships with external actors more effectively (e.g., by reducing unnecessary conflict). Through stakeholder analysis, corporate managers can improve the social value of the outcomes of their actions and minimize the disservice to, and from, stakeholders. Thus, stakeholder theory would provide tools for equipping managers to develop more effective relationships with the company's environment (e.g., by reducing the firm's vulnerability to stakeholder opposition).

Stakeholder analysis is also used for policy analysis, project management, and the generation of multistakeholder processes for participatory public decision making. Public institutions can be interested in generating multistakeholder initiatives in order to avoid conflict, gain legitimacy, and deepen democracy. However, in the context of public policy, the objectives of stakeholder analysis and management are not only related with the instrumental interests of public institutions, but also with the common good and the reaching of fair decisions (e.g., by giving marginalized stakeholders a significant voice). Multistakeholder processes are associated with new styles of governance for promoting higher transparency, openness, and extended participation in public policy.

Finally, stakeholder participation has been proposed in the context of decisions characterized by high risks, uncertainty, and complexity. In these contexts, purely technocratic approaches present fundamental limitations and may lead to misguided decisions. Stakeholders' values can orient the type of scientific information (e.g., among several disciplines) that is more relevant for each decision. The identification of these values can provide the weighting of the criteria for reaching more representative decisions. Therefore, the identification of relevant stakeholders and their values is a preliminary step for taking complex decisions marked by high stakes and uncertainty. For instance, key decisions affecting water quality issues would require the identification of everyone that has influence upon the quality of the water (e.g., polluting industries, municipalities, farmers) and anyone who is impacted by the quality of the water (e.g., fisherman, consumers, waterfront owners). According to a stakeholder approach, these people are said to have a stake in any decision affecting water quality, and their involvement is considered crucial for water governance.

Stakeholder Management and Corporate Governance

Stakeholder management contributes to corporate governance by helping to handle the multiple and often conflicting stakes held by the complex networks of groups that surround any company. The interactions, coalitions, behaviors, roles, resources, and preferences within and across the various groups composing these networks are highly dynamic. Individual stakeholders have various means of exerting influence, such as rhetoric, ethics, ruling, pressure, coercion, and market mechanisms. In practice, it is often difficult and costly, if not impossible, to identify and meet all the demands of a company's stakeholders. Consequently, it is crucial for governance to identify, analyze, and assess the meaning and significance of each individual group of generic stakeholders and to determine their respective power in order to be prepared for the conflict that may follow from the prioritizing of competing groups of stakeholders.

Stakeholder management for corporate governance provides a useful framework for managers that are forced to operate in environments characterized by unprecedented levels of turbulence and change. Traditional strategy frameworks were rendered inadequate for dealing with the quantity and kinds of change that started to occur in the business environment of the 1980s. Stakeholding proposes that corporate governance must acknowledge that stakeholders place limits on the action of the firm. However, investors that are only interested in financial returns might penalize firms that spend resources in stakeholder management. In any case, the stakeholder approach broadens the concept of strategic management beyond its traditional economic roots and situates firms in a wider governance arena by emphasizing their interrelations with their environments.

Two main stakeholder approaches have been formulated for corporate governance. The least-inclusive approach seeks for strategies that, while considering the limitations posed by stakeholders, still lead to orienting management toward the maximization of the benefits of shareholders. In contrast, the most-inclusive approach is often formulated in terms of a new, enlightening corporate philosophy or ethos in which integrating the stakes of all stakeholders is seen as both a moral duty and a requirement for the success of the corporation. Thus, successful strategies are those that integrate the interest of all stakeholders, rather than maximize the position of one group within limitations provided by the others.

The implementation of stakeholding within a firm implies pluralistic governance structures with more than one center of authority (e.g., management board, supervisory board, social council). Multistakeholder structures tend to increase organizations' complexity. Initially, companies considered their key stakeholders to be employees, legislators, and consumers. However, as the action span of corporations broadens, a wider group of players perceives the opportunity of being regarded by companies as legitimate stakeholders. Obviously, the inclusion of an increasing number of stakeholders renders the decision-making process more costly and complicated, which is at odds with efficiency claims. A counterargument to this premise is that the stakeholders' challenging and eventual ratification (or rectification) of the board's decisions can prevent the emergence of social conflict and avoid eventual mistakes that sometimes cannot easily be reversed.

The stakeholder approach to corporate governance is closely related to the presently popular notion of corporate social responsibility. This notion highlights the increasing pressure exerted on firms by all kinds of stakeholders (e.g., consumers, governments, non-governmental organizations, competitors) to formulate voluntary commitments to behave ethically and contribute to economic development while improving the quality of life of its stakeholders and society at large.

Stakeholding and Societal Governance

The notion of stakeholder processes is not only considered a crucial element of corporate governance but also of policy making in the broadest sense, including for instance economic policy, welfare, and sustainable development. In some cases, it has even been proposed as a platform for widespread economic and political reform to restore the state's legitimacy through major participation in the decisions of public institutions. Authority within a public system conventionally comes from the state. However, democracy is founded on citizens' representation and participation, which for efficiency reasons is traditionally limited to elections of representatives to a people's government. Multistakeholder decision making, with the direct involvement of citizens in the process of decision making, could therefore be seen as an evolution toward a more participative, and even deliberative, democracy.

Stakeholding in policy making provides a framework for dealing with the crisis of legitimacy that the modern state is experiencing due to globalization, the complexities derived from the so-called knowledge economy, and the challenges of global environmental change. On one hand, a growing number of stakeholder groups (e.g., private sector, nongovernmental organizations, civil society) are entering both the national and international political arenas. Stakeholder groups are defined here as more or less organized groups of people that could be affected by the implications of a decision and that can directly or indirectly influence the decision and its consequences. These new players are constantly challenging the state's authority and the legitimacy of its power. By seeking consensus between different social actors, the state can restore its legitimacy and defend its weakened role more effectively. On the other hand, the emergence of increasingly complex issues on the political agenda is constantly challenging the limits, structure, and modus operandi of the state. In contrast to traditional policy making, which takes place within ministries and governments, these new issues demand multiscale and interdepartmental responses requiring the involvement of diverse actors beyond institutional and traditional political arenas. This relevance of stakeholding for policy making has been formalized through the explicit reference made to stakeholder processes in the Rio Declaration (1992), the Millennium Development Goals (2000), and the World Summit on Sustainable Development Plan of Implementation (2002). All these international policy instruments acknowledge the importance of stakeholders' involvement for sustainable development. Stakeholding is said to provide the state with an opportunity to show its capacity to deal with increasingly higher expectations and maintain its legitimacy and position as the most relevant actor within the public system. Stakeholder processes create an appearance of deliberative democracy, which is increasingly critical to liberal democratic states.

The articulation of multistakeholder processes implies a certain reconstruction of public policy frameworks toward a more participative democracy with significant implications for societal governance. In contrast to rational and centralized explanations of decision making, this reconstruction implies incremental decision-making methods. Incremental decision making is based on the hypothesis that decisions result from pressures, compromise, coalitions, and negotiations among a plurality of interdependent actors. The method of analysis implies successive comparisons among the consequences for each group of available alternatives. The objective is to reach an agreement that allows reconciling the diversity of interests as an outcome of the adjustments among the involved parts. Depending on the subject, representatives from different fields of society are not only consulted but also directly integrated in deliberative decision-making processes. Therefore, stakeholders are given the opportunity of shaping the policies that affect them.

Nonetheless, stakeholding for societal governance faces significant oppositions grounded on methodological, theoretical, and ethical questionings. From a methodological perspective there exists a critical difficulty in the definition of what really constitutes a legitimate stakeholder. There is not an objective method for distinguishing those individuals and groups that should be counted as stakeholders from those that should not. In addition, even if there were an accepted method for their identification, there is still the issue of how much relative and absolute importance is to be assigned to stakeholders. Identifying and assigning relative importance is a crucial factor for both the fairness and efficiency of any multistakeholder process. Furthermore, this factor will also determine the ability of an initiative to engage the different stakeholders after having identified them. From a theoretical perspective, stakeholding can be criticized for imposing a too-simplified view of society in which people and groups are only concerned about defending their own interests. From an ethical perspective, stakeholding for societal governance is mostly justified for its contribution to participation and democracy. However, participation can be limited by how representation is defined, the type of processes designed, and the benefits in relation to the effort required. Decisionmakers, who are the stakeholder group charged with analyzing and justifying the final decision, are usually responsible for these choices about the stakeholding process itself. In this sense, it has been argued that governmental bodies can be tempted to set up fake stakeholding processes and use them as a means for increasing the legitimacy of already-made decisions. Regardless of these important questions, there is little doubt that stakeholding is going to be a powerful concept for understanding the increasing dependency of the state on organizations in civil society.

*—David Manuel-Navarrete and
Cecilie Modvar*

See also Corporate Governance; Economic Governance; Interdependence; Public-Private Partnership; Third Way

Further Readings and References

Donaldson, T. (1995). The stakeholder theory of the corporation: Concepts, evidence, and implications. *Academy of Management Review, 20,* 65–91.

Freeman, R. E. (1984). *Strategic management—A stakeholder approach.* Boston: Pitman.

Freeman R. E., & McVea, J. (2002). *A stakeholder approach to strategic management* (Working Paper No. 01-02). Darden Graduate School of Business Administration, University of Virginia.

Stoney, C., & Winstanley, D. (2001) Stakeholding: Confusion or utopia? Mapping the conceptual terrain. *Journal of Management Studies, 38,* 603–626.

Vallejo, N., & Hauselmann, P. (2004). *Governance and multi-stakeholder processes.* Winnipeg, MB, Canada: International Institute for Sustainable Development.

STATE

The idea of the state has been associated with the notion of managing an area by legal order. The concept of the state has tended to be qualified by prefixes such as "welfare," "warfare," and "developmental," denoting the particular organization and functions of the state's institutions.

The state combines two key elements. The first element is a historical institutional reality that is linked to the specific society, political culture, and economy within which it operates and with which it interacts. The three institutional elements of the democratic state are the executive branch, the legislative branch, and the judicial branch. The second element is a philosophical idea, wherein the various theories of the state have assumed a particular relationship between the state, society, and the individual.

The significance of the state for the process of human development has remained essentially contested by the principal ideologies of liberalism, conservatism, socialism, and Marxism. The liberal democratic notion of the state, whose central underlying assumption is that the state represents the general or the public interest, has been countered by Marxist conceptions of the state that have defined state power as an instrument of political action and societal control exercised on behalf of the private interests of the dominant capitalist class.

During the 1970s, the postwar social democratic and Keynesian consensus about an expanded role for the state into the fields of macroeconomic policy, full employment welfare provision, nationalized industries, and public services was challenged ideologically by the agenda of the New Right. Contending that the state had become overloaded, sclerotic, and a source of welfare dependency, the Reagan Administration in the United States and the Thatcher Government in the United Kingdom sought to roll back the frontiers of the state through policies of privatization, deregulation, and liberalization, and to roll forward the frontiers of the market, competition, and entrepreneurship. These neoliberal policies have subsequently become the orthodoxy shaping the institutional governance of global markets. The ubiquity of the so-called Washington Consensus has been reflected by the World Bank's narrow definition of the role of the state as the construction of institutions for the market.

In the modern era of globalization and governance, the sovereignty of the state, as the highest power in its particular territory, has been challenged by the role of new public and private actors. In the public domain, the state has seen its policy choices constrained by the pattern of multilevel governance that has arisen from the constantly changing network of regional, international, and supranational institutions that constitute contemporary global governance. In the private domain of nonstate actors, both the power of the transnational corporation operating in liberalized markets for finance, trade, and investment, and also the capacity of terrorist networks (such as Al-Qaeda) to penetrate the architecture of national security to a devastating effect have presented dramatic new threats.

As a consequence, during the 1990s, the central debate in political studies focused upon the nature and impact of globalization upon the sovereignty of the state. On the one hand, proponents of the power of globalization have claimed that nation-states have now been replaced by region-states, which provide ports of entry for entrepreneurs and corporations to global markets. On the other hand, skeptics of this thesis of the powerless state have asserted that the nation-state continues to retain a significant role in both national and international governance, not least because the nature and impact of globalization have been greatly exaggerated.

The idea of the state, both as an institutional reality and a philosophical idea, remains in constant flux in debates about contemporary governance. For example, following the collapse of communism, Francis

Fukuyama had asserted the convergence of former totalitarian states toward the end point of mankind's ideological evolution. However, Fukuyama has subsequently twice modified his "end of history" theory of the state. First, he has acknowledged the importance of culture and society in determining whether the role of the state in different national models of capitalism has been shaped by the presence or absence of shared values of trust, that is, solidarity and social cooperation. Second, Fukuyama has distanced himself from his former neoconservative allies' support for the invasion of Iraq. Here he has claimed that the New Right's agenda of rolling back the frontiers of the state and rolling forward the frontiers of the market has neglected state building. Fukuyama has argued that state building depends on effective organizational design and management, the political design of state institutions and their possession of legitimacy, and the development of democratic norms, values, and culture. Because much of this latter development can only be manipulated by public policy at the margins, the transition of many weak states from their former authoritarianism toward a more liberal democratic future may be far from certain.

—*Simon Lee*

See also Civil Society; Globalization; Governance; Government; Hierarchy; HIV/AIDS; Hollow State; Marxism; Nation; Political Business Cycle; Postcolonialism; Sovereignty; Space; State Building; Territoriality; World Health Organization

Further Readings and References

Fukuyama, F. (1989, Summer). The end of history. *The National Interest, 16,* 3–18.

Fukuyama, F. (2004). *State building: Governance and world order in the twenty-first century.* London: Profile Books.

Hirst, P., & Thompson, G. (1996). *Globalization in question: The international economy and the possibilities of governance.* Oxford, UK: Polity Press.

Ohmae, K. (1995). *The end of the nation state: The rise of regional economies.* London: HarperCollins.

Weiss, L. (1998). *The myth of the powerless state: Governing the economy in a global era.* Cambridge, UK: Polity Press.

World Bank. (1997). *The state in a changing world: The 1997 World Development Report.* Washington, DC: Author.

STATE BUILDING

In its most generic form, the term *state building* refers to the construction of an apparatus of governance defined by its monopoly of the legitimate use of violence in a given territory. Defining the modern state is a contentious project, but most scholars would recognize a core set of features, including a standing army; a diplomatic corps; a centralized bureaucracy (especially for tax collection); the replacement of ad hoc, patrimonial legal procedures with standardized, legal-rational ones; the demarcation of national economies; and the incorporation of populations as citizens rather than status groups.

This constellation of features first developed in Western Europe in the sixteenth century through the mutually reinforcing, though analytically separate, processes of making war, raising taxes, and constructing a centralized officialdom to oversee and maximize success in both war and taxation. In Western Europe, these changes were marked by the transition from feudalism to absolutism to the nation-state. State-building theory tends not to dwell on the differences of political regime that may accompany the state-building process; both democracy and authoritarianism are possible complements to modernization, but each requires a state to defend its borders, govern its citizens, and extract resources from them. An important exception to this last point is more recent scholarship on the link between democratization and state building. One influential argument is that the development of professional and effective state bureaucracies is more difficult in areas where democratization precedes the consolidation of core state institutions.

Decolonization after World War II and, later, the collapse of the Soviet Union greatly added to the number of states in the international system. The success of these state-building efforts, however, has been highly variable, ranging from failed states such as Afghanistan to neopatrimonial states such as Nigeria to developmental states such as South Korea. Changes in the international system have altered the basic dynamics of state building: The harsh selection mechanism of interstate military competition that characterized the emergence of Western Europe's nation-states no longer prevails.

Thus, the drive for rationalization is no longer an imperative of state survival, and from the state-builders' perspective, it is no longer as crucial that growth in state size be matched by increase in state capacity—especially its capacity to stimulate economic development. Instead, a host of other factors may drive state expansion. A commonly cited factor is the need to maintain a domestic governing coalition, especially in societies with divided political elites. This may lead to rapid state expansion fueled by political patronage or targeted pork-barrel spending; it may also take the more passive form of surrendering state capacity through insider privatization and the toleration of official corruption. Some have argued that international aid to less-developed countries has also had the unintended effect of diverting resources from state-building capacity.

Given these differences between early- and late-developing states, state building is perhaps best understood not in generic terms but as the result of political dynamics bearing the indelible imprint of their historical moment.

—*Conor O'Dwyer*

See also Capacity Building; Coercion; Contracting Out; Failed State; Sociology of Governance; State

Further Readings and References

Fukuyama, F. (2004). *State-building: Governance and world order in the 21st century.* Ithaca, NY: Cornell University Press.
Shefter, M. (1993). *Political parties and the state: The American historical experience.* Princeton, NJ: Princeton University Press.
Skocpol, T. (1979). *States and social revolutions.* New York: Cambridge University Press.

STATE CAPTURE

The concept of state capture has been used in political science literature as referring to the way in which private, often corporate, power has dominated public policy making. Thus, the phenomenon of state capture was described in the early critique of pluralist scholars. Pluralism's claim was that a multiplicity of interest groups prevented any particular group from being dominant. However, the counterargument is that interest groups are not equally endowed with resources. Many commentators argue that business represents a very strong power system—far stronger than any other social group or institution—that challenges and threatens to dominate public power. The term "capture" describes how public bureaucracies have become dominated by strong and powerful interest groups. In a context characterized by a complex multitude of interest groups, the bureaucrats tend to deal with the best-organized groups as a way of reducing complexity. State capture has been used in the critique of corporatism as well. Corporatism refers to the permanent representation of well-organized hierarchical interest groups in the state apparatus, a phenomenon that may be seen as a way of the state giving in to specific interests. Both the critics of pluralism and of corporatism argue that private corporate power must be controlled by democratic institutions.

In the literature on postcolonial societies, the concept of state capture refers to the fact that neopatrimonial rulers tend to favor their own ethnic or regional group rather than the nation as such; the state is thereby captured by a specific group. A weak state may be the most prone to be captured by interest groups or even by strong individuals. A relatively strong, institutionalized state may therefore be necessary in order to avoid state capture. An institutionalized party system also may be important, for where parties are weak, traditional forms of elite interaction tend to prevail, enabling elites to capture the state apparatus.

State capture has recently been related to the postcommunist region where it describes the way the policy process, for example of privatization, has been dominated by powerful oligarchs that belonged to the old *nomenklatura* elite. Joel Hellman and colleagues thus defined state capture as a situation in which decisions are made to appease specific interests, maybe even through illicit and nontransparent private payments to public officials, rather than to the national interest aggregated and mediated through a democratic process. State capture takes place when the basic rules of the game are shaped by particularistic interests rather than by the aggregated national interest.

The literature on governance focuses on how authority migrates away from the central state both upward to supranational organs, downward to subnational units, and outward to civil society interest groups. The notion of state capture is conspicuous for its absence in this literature that mainly emphasizes the win-win potential of state-society networks. However, societal actors in the networks may well take over, and hence capture, decision making and implementation. In the World Bank, state capture is seen to be closely related to governance, particularly corruption, because giving in to particular interests often involves the use of public means for private purposes, which is the essence of corruption.

—Anne Mette Kjær

See also Corporatism; Corruption; Governance; Interest Group; Pluralism; Policy Network; Political Exchange; Rent Seeking

Further References and Readings

Hellman, J., Jones, G., & Kaufman, D. (2000). *Seize the state, seize the day—State capture, corruption, and influence in transition* (Policy Research Paper 2444). Washington, DC: World Bank Institute.

McConnel, G. (1966). *Private power and American democracy.* New York: Knopf.

STATE-SOCIETY RELATIONS

Understanding relations among centralized political organizations (states) and the social collectivities (societies) they govern remains a perennial theme of social scientific, historical, and philosophical inquiry. With almost all the world's territories and peoples formally under state authority—or some form of pooled sovereignty—any discussion of governance builds on an understanding of these associations. Their centrality, however, belies their essential indescribability: Defining state and society continually tests scholars, to say nothing of efforts to characterize the wide diversity of state-society relations across time and space. Rather than presenting a single, comprehensive definition, this discussion points to a series of critical considerations for evaluating these configurations' historical emergence and contemporary manifestations.

Two primary concerns serve as the locus around which approaches to state-society relations typically diverge or overlap: the demarcation of states from their societies and the character of their engagement. The degree to which one can (or should) differentiate states from societies is critical to any conceptualization of domestic politics and governance. Moreover, there are compelling reasons for viewing the two in tandem or as inexorably coupled. After all, few societies of contemporary interest exist, or have ever existed, without some form of institutionalized political leadership or governing bodies. Similarly, it is difficult to imagine a set of formal political institutions disconnected from both a constituent population and territory. (Governments in exile may be one exception, although even they make claims to both a society and a territory.) Analyzing or comparing states alienated from their social context consequently risks undue formalism (i.e., focusing on empty institutions) or reifying (i.e., speaking of the state as a unified actor) what is in fact a conglomeration of potentially competing and overlapping institutions, officials, laws, and socioeconomic interests.

Recognizing the complexity of state forms, some scholars understand states as expressions of their social and historical contexts. However, such an approach is not without its hazards. Assuming that state behaviors and forms reflect broader social trends may mean ignoring the often-decisive role states play in shaping societies' preferences and interests, and those critical instances in which states act more or less independently. This is most evidently important in international relations (e.g., war, diplomacy, trade negotiations), where national government representatives occasionally make decisions or commitments with relatively limited reference to domestic political opinion or social interests.

The autonomy of socially embedded states is also visible in the domestic sphere. Although Karl Marx famously once defined the modern state as little more than a tool for the bourgeoisie, his more sophisticated writings describe a semiautonomous state that balances competing interests within the ruling classes.

Even the pluralists, who see government priorities and actions primarily as an expression of social interests, grant states a certain level of autonomy as they mediate conflict in pursuit of collective goals. In almost all cases, states are at once captured by (or responsive to) social interests while retaining some capacity to act independently against powerful social actors. Such discussions appear again in Joel Migdal's influential work, especially his dialogue of strong and weak states and, later, in his state-in-society approach. While useful, the question of where the boundaries lie between states and societies remains a matter of debate.

However problematic, the willingness to analytically grant the state autonomous status points to a second area of differentiation in approaching state-society relations: the qualities of links between the two. Echoing Thomas Hobbes's *Leviathan,* authors influenced by the German sociologist Max Weber typically focus on the state's ability to monopolize and systematically apply physical power (i.e., violence) over a society contained by geographic boundaries. Such expressions may take benevolent forms, with states using their coercive mandate to pursue the common good by preventing social conflict, enforcing contracts, and protecting the rights of individuals and groups. There are also conspicuous occasions when the state's coercive apparatus is used in more malevolent (and autonomous) ways: to alienate or persecute subnational populations, to conduct military operations outside its borders, or in the kind of aggressive transformative agendas undertaken (most extremely) by Adolph Hitler, Joseph Stalin, and Pol Pot.

Marxists and other structuralists accept the importance of physical power in governance, but privilege material exchanges between state and social actors in the form of taxes, pensions, wages, and other forms of spending on social and economic programs. A focus on material relations also draws attention to forms of clientelism (where states are tied to populations through payoffs), kleptocracy (where states maintain power by stealing), or the peculiar forms of governance (rentier states) that occur when state leaders' access to internationally marketable raw materials (e.g., oil or gemstones) allows them to retain power outside of any contact with the majority of their citizens.

A focus on nonmaterial ties between states and societies similarly reveals signs of both autonomy and capture, albeit through different mechanisms. Antonio Gramsci's work, for example, balances classical Marxism's materialism by drawing attention to the role of discourse, education, and language in shaping relations between political and social actors. This is visible in the ways social and political elites (who need not be state officials) consciously use state influence over the mass media, education, and the arts to promote values and behavioral norms that serve their interests. A similar focus on the power expressed through symbolic and ethical relations among residents and political leadership appears again in anthropological treatments of the state and in sociological institutionalism (new and old). These perspectives reveal that while values, norms, and symbols sustain state legitimacy and serve as powerful resources for some, they also constrain and bind the state by defining state responsibilities while limiting the scope of acceptable political action.

In almost all instances, states and societies relate in all of the ways previously described. The relative importance of these connections depends in part on one's specific area of inquiry and on historical circumstances. Indeed, comparison of political practice over time and space draws critical attention to the development of various social and political interests, the varied means of domination and resistance, and the diverse political formations these produce. Importantly, recent scholarship underscores the value of disaggregating states and societies by identifying the frequent internal contradictions and conflicts that occur within each as a source of dynamism and change. It should be recognized, however, that while such a perspective provides a holistic framework for understanding the emergence of particular political configurations, the need for historical specificity often frustrates those seeking to make broader, comparative generalizations.

Reconsidering the State-Society Framework

The previous section outlines a number of critical points for understanding the relationships between domestic states (or state actors) and their societies.

Adding to the already acute challenges of grappling with state autonomy and the nature of state-society relations, contemporary studies of governance must consider these relations in light of new processes and political trends: decentralization, globalization, and state collapse. All three are generating new political configurations that question the validity and utility of a perspective privileging dyadic relations between states and societies. Throughout much of the world, a dual process is taking place in which the authority and responsibility once vested in central states is (1) being shifted to subnational political or administrative units (e.g., provinces, regions, and municipalities), and (2) being voluntarily or involuntarily ceded to supranational, regional, and global bodies.

Driven by quests to improve government response and administrative efficiency—or to manage demands for local autonomy—decentralization and devolution are leading subnational administrative authorities to take on many of the state's primary functions, including service provision, economic policy, and elements of international relations. Due to design or the weakness of central states' regulatory capacities, such devolution generates opportunities for considerable variations in governance across a single national territory. This is sometimes formalized in federal arrangements, but often appears in less institutionalized configurations, some of which may contradict official policy. Under such conditions, speaking about state-society relations *in toto* becomes almost impossible or beside the point. One must instead make sense of the growing number of semiautonomous governing institutions, each with their own dynamic relations to each other and subnational populations.

Often accompanying devolution and decentralization, domestic state responsibilities are being transferred—through plan and practice—to regional or global bodies. This is most apparent in formal programs of economic and political integration, such as the European Union and similar (if less comprehensive) initiatives in North America, Latin America, Asia, and Africa. There are parallels in efforts to create regional or global bodies responsible for regulating areas as diverse as international trade, environmental protection, and even immigration, an issue over which

domestic authority has long been considered almost absolute.

Multinational corporations—private businesses simultaneously operating in multiple national territories—are also redefining patterns of decision making, restructuring labor markets, and affecting citizens' relations to domestic authorities (i.e., the state). These actors' material resources, frequently overshadowing those controlled by domestic authorities, mean that their investment decisions can fundamentally reshape patterns of human settlement (e.g., urbanization, household structure), infrastructure development, and social mobilization. Moreover, the relative ease with which such corporations shift investments and production—and their ability to negotiate favorable tax regimes—challenges the national government's ability to exact taxes, enforce progressive labor laws, or maintain the social democratic regimes common to past generations.

In many of the world's poorer countries, humanitarian and development aid is having similar effects on state-society relations. In certain instances, aid has enhanced ties between governments and societies by providing poor or largely irrelevant states with the resources needed to regulate or assist their citizens. Elsewhere, international assistance has encouraged (or required) officials to implement policies developed without popular consent or involvement. Even where development assistance programs demand public participation, input may be structured in ways that avoid contestation by limiting the scope of debate or excluding critical parties. Humanitarian and developmental aid's visible effects may also lead citizens to see the international community as responsible for providing services that would otherwise be deemed state responsibilities. In many instances, state actors have themselves promoted these shifting logics of political responsibility by using international actors as scapegoats: a means of absolving themselves and their administration for shortcomings or inaction.

The long-term effects of these processes on state society-relations are not yet fully realized. What is all but certain is that they will not be uniform. When supranational bodies exercise a narrow range of responsibilities or compete with relatively well-resourced and organized domestic states, relations between those states and their societies are unlikely to undergo significant change. When the autonomy of these superordinate bodies is greater and domestic capacity is limited, logics of responsibility and political action are likely to shift in ways that may fundamentally reshape governance by circumventing national or local leadership. The last decade has seen growth in forms of political mobilization that are transnational in either their organization or in the targets of their activities. The 1999 protests against the World Trade Organization's meeting in Seattle are a conspicuous example, while appeals to global/international human rights standards by domestic and international advocacy organizations (e.g., Amnesty International) or separatist groups (e.g., the Mexican Zapatistas) further suggest a need to question the value of focusing exclusively on domestic state-society relations. The increased prevalence of such actions—many taking place outside of formal means of interest articulation—indicates a renegotiation of the social contract and a more general change in state-society relations as international actors are insinuated into domestic politics.

State Formation and Failure

Throughout much of the world, the legacies of Soviet communism and European colonialism have created patterns of state-society relations that significantly differ from those envisioned by classical theorists of citizenship, the social contract, and the nation-state. In many countries, state formation remains incomplete, with subpopulations (and their social, economic, and political processes) all but living beyond the influence of central states. Although decreasing numbers of people live in these nonstate spaces, the retreat of state influence through much of the world—a consequence of financial and political crises and reforms oriented to generating a minimalist state—has extended the number of societies (or subnational societies) that exist in near stateless environments. Such configurations are visible in poor countries' rural peripheries, although they are also appearing in the burgeoning urban slums of Africa, Latin America, and Asia. In both cases, social life is characterized by economies that are largely unregulated by the state, that have few

publicly provided social services, and also have forms of political organization that do not focus on the state or, more critically, explicitly work to escape state influence. As with other processes of engagement or disengagement, these disconnections are often driven by a combination of resource scarcity, politicians' attempts to avoid responsibilities, and efforts by residents to circumvent states that they see as predatory, unjust, or simply useless.

Conclusion

The often-disparate perspectives on state-society relations previously described stem from a diversity of normative perspectives (what we believe the state should do), the focus of our inquiries (what links between state and societies we believe are most significant), and the multiple forms in which state-society relations are realized. The growing diversity of these configurations due to decentralization, globalization, and state failure only heightens the challenge of developing a unified framework for analysis or descriptive generalization. Increasingly, the study of governance will need to rely on an approach that understands the historical origins and the contemporary dynamics influencing state-society relations in individual countries, regions, or globally. Although the state must remain a central component of critical analysis, there is also now a need to make analytical space for transnational actors and forms of political organization that exist outside a state-society framework but have direct influence on state-society relations. The administrative frailty of states throughout much of the world also demands a consideration of nonstate spaces and variations in state-society relations across a single, national territory. This may undermine the state as the fundamental unit for comparative study, but promises to improve the accuracy—and utility—of future analyses.

—*Loren B. Landau*

See also Association; Center-Local Relations; Citizenship; Clientelism; Constitutionalization; Decentralization; Embeddedness; Globalization; Governance Failure; Humanitarian Intervention; Marxism; Multilevel Governance; Network; Network Society; Political Business Cycle; Postmodernism; Power; Rule of Law

Further Readings and References

Agnew, J. (1999). Mapping political power beyond state boundaries: Territory, identity, and movement in world politics. *Millennium, 28,* 499–522.

Bratton, M. (1994). Peasant-state relations in postcolonial Africa: Patterns of engagement and disengagement. In J. S. Migdal, A. Kohli, & V. Shue (Eds.), *State power and social forces* (pp. 231–250). Cambridge, UK: Cambridge University Press.

Castells, M. (2000). *The rise of the network society* (2nd ed.). Oxford, UK: Basil Blackwell.

Foucault, M. (1991). Governmentality. In G. Burchell, C. Gordon, & P. Miller (Eds.), *The Foucault effect: Studies in governmentality* (pp. 87–104). Chicago: University of Chicago Press.

Friedland, R., & Alford, R. (1991). Bringing society back in: Symbols, practices, and institutional contradictions. In W. W. Powell & P. J. DiMaggio (Eds.), *The new institutionalism in organizational analysis* (pp. 232–266). Chicago: University of Chicago Press.

Hansen, T. B., & Stepputat, F. (Eds.). (2001). *States of imagination: Ethnographic explorations of the post-colonial state.* Durham, NC: Duke University Press.

Migdal, J. (1994). The state in society: An approach to struggles for domination. In. J. Migdal, A. Kohli, & V. Shue (Eds.), *State power and social forces: Domination and transformation in the third world* (pp. 7–36). Cambridge, UK: Cambridge University Press.

Rhodes, M. (1995). Subversive liberalism: Market integration, globalization and the European welfare state. *Journal of European Public Policy, 2,* 384–406.

STATE STRUCTURE

In almost all of the literature on governance, the state is appealed to as a structural variable—a context in which actors are situated rather than an actor in his or her own terms. This structural emphasis upon the state is reflected in the centrality of the term *state structure* to the analysis of processes of governance. State structure refers to the institutional form that the state takes in a particular location at a particular point in time—from the responsibilities it takes on, to the functional differentiation of tasks between the institutions and organizations that together comprise it, and to its (often regulatory) relationship to both the market and the realm of civil society.

Somewhat more specifically, state structure might usefully be seen as one of a family of related terms, operating at different levels of abstraction or generality. At the highest level of abstraction, theorists of the state refer to the concept of state form—the most general type of state to which a particular state might be seen to belong. Thus, we might speak of the capitalist, feudal, or patriarchal form of the state. At an intermediary level of abstraction, state theorists refer to the concept of state regime. In so doing, they appeal to the existence of more or less stable stages in the development or evolution of a particular state form. Therefore, having identified a particular state as a capitalist form of the state, we might further categorize it as, say, a (Keynesian) welfare state or as a competition state. Thus, we are identifying the state regime to which it might be said to correspond. Finally, and at a somewhat lower level of abstraction, theorists of the state refer to state structure. Consequently, they focus on the specific institutional and organizational configuration of the state in a particular context at a particular point in time. Therefore, having identified the state in Sweden in 1970, for instance, as a capitalist state (its state form) and as a Keynesian welfare state (its state regime), we might focus in on the distinctive institutional and organizational features of this particular Keynesian welfare state at this particular point in time. Hence, we would be describing its state structure.

The appeal to the concept of state structure reminds us of the extent to which the autonomy and agency of political actors are both shaped and conditioned by the contexts within which they are exercised. As such, it sharpens the political analyst's purchase on the opportunities and constraints that political actors must negotiate in exercising power. Political analysts sensitive to the state as a structured domain of political action are less likely to see political actors in voluntarist terms—as free-willed subjects in almost complete control of their destiny and able to shape political realities in the image of their preferences and volitions. In contrast, state theorists tend to see the ability of actors to realize their intentions as conditional upon often-complex strategic choices made in densely structured institutional contexts that facilitate certain strategies while militating against others.

As this suggests, the parameters of political possibility are, to a significant extent, delimited by state structure.

—Colin Hay

See also Marxism; Regulation Theory; State

Further Readings and References

Hay, C. (1996). *Re-stating social and political change.* Buckingham, UK: Open University Press.

Hay, C., & Lister, M. (2005). Theories of the state. In C. Hay, M. Lister, & D. Marsh (Eds.), *The state: Theories and issues.* Basingstoke, UK: Palgrave.

Jessop, B. (1990). *State theory: Putting capitalist states in their place.* Cambridge, UK: Polity Press.

STEERING

Steering is one of the metaphors commonly associated with governance. Scholars have discussed governing in terms of the role of the coxswain and have noted that there may be several helmsmen involved in the steering process, with politicians and bureaucrats often competing for control over policy. The familiar metaphor of the "ship of state" implies that there is a need to provide direction to the economy and society, and that the public sector is charged with a principal role in providing that direction.

Although the steering metaphor is a useful one, and is one that is commonly employed to describe governance, if it is to be any more than just a metaphor then various dimensions of steering need to be considered and developed. Therefore, the process of steering in government is from the perspective of (a) Who steers? (b) How do they steer? (c) What are they steering toward, and who gets to decide on the goals? (d) How accurate does steering have to be? and (e) How do governments respond to their own decisions about steering and what enhances the steering capacity of governments (and their partners)? To some extent these questions represent a general set of questions concerning governance, but this entry will attempt to focus attention on the process of steering itself.

Who Steers?

As indicated at the beginning of this article, there has been a good deal of debate about who is, and who should be, responsible for steering contemporary societies. This debate occurs at two levels. At the more general level, scholars have been engaged in a debate over the relative roles of official and unofficial actors in governing. Within the public sector there has been a discussion over the relative importance of elected officials and bureaucrats in governing. These two levels of debate have both empirical and normative dimensions, questioning the actual practice of governing, as well as the pattern of governance that would be most desirable, given the particular set of premises that any one analyst may bring to the debate.

The discussion about the role of nongovernmental actors in governing reflects the power of social actors and networks in some societies and the more general movement of governments to involve societal actors in making and delivering public policy. It is difficult to deny that nongovernmental actors play a significant role in the overall process of steering, although it may be too easy for some enthusiasts of this approach to forget that the influence of these social actors is exerted within a framework that depends heavily on public authority and law. Likewise, it is also easy to forget that the involvement of social actors is not exactly novel but has been in existence for decades.

The second debate centers on the relative capacity of politicians and civil servants to steer and to govern effectively. Elected politicians are often characterized as less knowledgeable than their civil servants about the policy areas for which they are responsible; elected politicians often are under significant time pressures that leave them virtually incapable of providing direction to their ministries. On the other hand, civil servants may be too closely tied to their individual departments and programs and hence incapable of guiding the society in other than a very narrow manner. The normative arguments in this debate are perhaps more compelling than the empirical ones, given the importance of maintaining democratic control over policy and public organizations.

How to Steer?

Steering is not easy, given that governments (and their partners) are attempting to alter the behavior of large numbers of actors and influence complex social and economic processes that have their own internal logics. Governments may appear powerful but society is too, and society is often resistant to change. In attempting to steer in these treacherous waters, governments have a number of instruments at their disposal. Any number of classification schemes have been advanced for the instruments available to government, with all of these schemes (including law, money, and information) as central assets for the public sector when it attempts to exert its influence. Therefore, the choice of instruments to match both the characteristics of the situation and the resources available to the actors responsible for governing is a crucial aspect of public governance.

The involvement of social partners in governance is also relevant for this dimension of steering. Lester Salamon argued in 2000 that steering is moving toward new governance, involving consultation rather than command and control, and depending heavily on the social partners. The new governance therefore implies that steering may be done at a distance, and governments will be able to exert their influence through less direct, but perhaps in the end more effective, mechanisms. These instruments for implementing governance will also have to be matched with the particulars of policy and social settings and may not be feasible in all settings. For example, when there are sharply conflicting policy views in a domain, or if the fundamental rights of citizens are in question, governments may have to undertake more of the steering function themselves, rather than depend upon cooperative solutions to the problems.

Toward What Goals Is Society Being Steered?

The governance literature often ignores the crucial question of goal selection when it discusses steering. The selection of goals, and especially collective goals that can encompass and integrate a range of individual policies, is crucial to governance, just as having a

destination is crucial for steering a ship. It is important for each program and organization delivering public policies to develop its own goals, but steering implies a more strategic vision of where the society should be going, and what instruments are required to get it there. Such a strategic conception of steering involves a means of identifying those collective goals and of coordinating and linking the actions of individual programs.

Goal selection as an aspect of the steering process may be less amenable to the involvement of the social partners in governance than are the other dimensions. Social groups may know what their members want and need, but by definition may not be particularly interested in broader visions of a societal future that always gives each group what it wants. While these groups and organizations should certainly be involved in determining goals for society, a more authoritative process, and one that has clearer decision rules, may be needed for goal selection. Also, goal setting as a precondition for steering therefore requires decision-making processes that can reconcile competing values and competing conceptions of appropriate goals. Given the existence of constitutional rules, and the legitimacy derived from direct connections with the electorate, this aspect of steering may be the particular province of the formal institutions of government. Social actors should not be denigrated too much, however, given that political actors will also continue to press for their own views of the desirable goals for the society despite apparent losses at different stages of the process.

Even for government institutions, developing goals that cut across existing boundaries of programs and policies is not easy. The only actors that have any strong incentive to develop such goals are the executives at the apex of government—presidents and prime ministers—and the central agencies, such as ministries of finance charged with both serving those top executives as well as deciding on priorities among competing programs. Thus, steering in a manner that does more than simply validate the preferences of individual departments, and their allies in the society, can be centralizing and drives decisions upward in the public sector. Much of the political and managerial ideology of the past several decades has stressed decentralization, but as governance becomes a focus for the public sector, there may have to be greater emphasis on the possible virtues of more centralized solutions to public problems.

How Accurate Does Steering Need to Be?

Striving to reach social goals is obviously important for governance, but societies need to think about how close to those goals is sufficient to say that governance is effective. Again, the answer to that question could depend in part on the particular policies in question and perhaps on the individual political system. For example, reaching economic targets within a few percentage points may be acceptable in affluent countries, while the same level of success or failure might be less acceptable in poor countries striving to provide a minimal standard of living for its people. Likewise, achieving targets on protecting fundamental civil and political rights may be more important than targets on even economic problems.

The importance of the accuracy of steering in governance may be a function of the political culture of countries as well. In liberal societies such as the United States that tend to depend less on the public sector than do many others, the accuracy of steering may be relatively unimportant. Likewise, strong societies provide some redundancy for the public sector so accurate public steering may be less crucial for success. On the other hand, in newly industrializing countries that have adopted a state-led model of economic development, the accuracy of steering may be much more central to the overall success of the social and economic systems than in more affluent and less étatiste (state) systems. Certainly the failure of centrally planned economies to be able to steer accurately was one of the causes for the demise of most of these systems.

How Do Steerers React to Their Previous Actions?

It is worth considering steering as a continuing process rather than as a single decision. When steering an automobile, steerers react to their own previous actions to keep the car on the road and going where they want it to go. This is especially true if driving on slippery roads where a slight bit of oversteering may cause a skid and lead to an accident. Systems of governance also need to identify the results of their own actions and continue to adjust interventions in order to reach their goals, and to do so as efficiently as possible.

In 1964, Karl Deutsch wrote about a cybernetic model of government. Deutsch argued that one could conceptualize governing as a cybernetic system, analogous to a thermostat and its relationship to temperature in a house. The thermostat registered the temperature of the house and when there was a need for more heat, it turned on the furnace. When "governance" was successful in implementing a policy, then the "thermostat" turned the "furnace" off. Likewise, attempts to steer on the part of government would involve assessing the success or failure of efforts at policy making and adjusting subsequent steering attempts. Thus, the assessment would require a predetermined set of goals (analogous to the desired temperature) as well as a mechanism to implement changes in the existing conditions.

Actors involved in governance would like to have as simple a task as that of the thermostat. In most instances, there are no clear indicators of success, failure, or the desirable state for the economy or society. Likewise, those desirable outcomes of governance are rarely agreed on by all segments of society, so the political battles over the types of interventions by public action will be as continual as the need to respond to changes in the environment. Even when there are relatively clear measures of goals available to decisionmakers, as in economic policy, there may be a number of important goals—high growth, low inflation, high employment—that need to be balanced, and finding and implementing that balance can be a difficult political process.

A society in which the actors are involved in public governance plays a significant role in the capacity to respond to previous attempts at governance. Governance theorists have stressed the importance of social actors for governing, and these actors may be especially important for providing feedback to official actors about the effectiveness of efforts at governing. The effectiveness of the official actors in registering such feedback will depend, of course, on their receptivity to that information. Paradoxically, a strong society may also make governance more difficult if the social actors are unwilling to cooperate and are unwilling to deviate from their inertial patterns of coping with issues.

While society tends to preserve its own patterns of behavior, governments may also. Therefore, even if the evidence coming from previous public interventions is less than positive, governments may not alter their steering patterns, but rather may simply continue to do what they have been doing, but do it better or more intensely. Governments as a whole, and especially the individual departments and programs in government, have their own ideologies and routines that will reduce their responsiveness to their own actions or indeed any other feedback. These tendencies are exaggerated in political systems with a tradition of étatiste dominance over society.

Conclusion

Steering is not easy. Although governments, whether alone or in league with social actors, may appear powerful, they often confront equally powerful social forces. Societies that governance actors confront are often highly inertial and tend to persist in established patterns unless there is a good reason to change. Likewise, the governance actors themselves tend to find change difficult, and may not want to abandon failing programs even in the face of largely negative feedback from their actions. All of these rigidities tend to reduce the capacity of public action to respond effectively to needs and opportunities in society and to match interventions with the continuing change in society. However, a well-developed society may also be an asset for would-be steerers, providing that the society contains social actors that are capable of cooperating with the public sector.

One clear conclusion from the previous discussion is that not all steering devices are suitable for all instances, whether policy areas or political systems. The assumption of much of the analysis of governance is that the public sector should attempt to adopt a single model of governance that can be suitable, and

effective, in almost any case. It can be argued that instead of that uniformity steering, including at least the types of instruments utilized, the involvement of social actors, and the necessary accuracy of the resultant steering, it should instead be considered contingent on the nature of the state and society involved in the process. Further, the contemporary governing ideology favoring decentralization may have to be reconsidered in light of needs to provide central direction and steering.

—*B. Guy Peters*

See also Complexity; Culture Governance; Governance; New Public Management; Policy Network; Political Exchange

Further Readings and References

Deutsch, K. W. (1964). *The nerves of government.* New York: Free Press.

Hood, C. (1976). *The tools of government.* Chatham, NJ: Chatham House.

Peters, B. G. (1987). Bureaucrats and politicians in the process of governing. In J.-E. Lane (Ed.), *Bureaucracy and public choice.* London: Sage Ltd.

Rhodes, R. A. W. (1997). *Understanding governance.* Buckingham, UK: Open University Press.

Rose, R. (1978). *What is governing?* Englewood Cliffs, NJ: Prentice Hall.

Salamon, L. M. (2000). Introduction. In L. M. Salamon (Ed.), *Handbook of policy instruments.* New York: Oxford University Press.

Sbragia, A. M. (1999). European Union as coxswain: Governance by steering. In J. Pierre (Ed.), *Debating governance.* Oxford, UK: Oxford University Press.

STRATEGIC PLANNING

Strategic planning is an unavoidable part of organizational management and decision making in public, private, or nonprofit organizations. It is a means of establishing major directions for organizations and a structured approach to anticipating the future and exploiting the inevitable. Through strategic planning, resources are concentrated in a limited number of major directions in order to improve effectiveness and performance of an organization. Strategic planning is a tool for finding the best future for the organizations and the best path to reach that destination. As with any management tool, it is used to help an organization do a better job—to focus its energy, to ensure that members of the organization are working toward the same goals, and to assess and adjust the organization's direction in response to a changing environment. In short, strategic planning is a disciplined effort to produce fundamental decisions and actions that shape and guide what an organization is, what it does, and why it does it, with a focus on the future.

The strategic planning process is strategic because it involves preparing the best way to respond to the circumstances of the organization and its environment. The process is disciplined in that it calls for a certain order and pattern to keep it focused and productive. The process raises a sequence of questions that helps organizational leadership examine experience, test assumptions, gather and incorporate information about the present, and anticipate the environment in which the organization will be working in the future. Strategic planning is ultimately a set of decisions about what to do, why to do it, and how to do it. Strategic planning sets priorities for organizations. Because it is impossible to do everything that needs to be done, strategic planning implies that some organizational decisions and actions are more important than others. Much of the strategy lies in making the tough decisions about what is most important to achieving organizational effectiveness.

Strategic Thinking and Strategic Planning

Strategic planning is only useful if it supports strategic thinking and leads to strategic management. Strategic thinking means asking, "Are we doing the right thing?" Strategic management entails attention to the big picture and the willingness to adapt to changing environments. There are a variety of perspectives, models, and approaches used in strategic planning. The way that a strategic plan is developed depends on the nature of the organization's leadership, the culture of the organization, the complexity of the organization and its environment, and the size of the organization.

Strategic planning can provide a long-term map on how to get from where the organizations are and where they want to be. Because it encompasses activity over several years, a strategic plan will need to be twisted over the course of time; various assumptions made in creating the plan ultimately will not hold true.

Why Is Strategic Planning Essential?

Formalized strategic planning grew out of budget exercises of the 1950s in the United States and spread rapidly. By the mid-1960s and throughout the 1970s, strategic planning was occurring in most large corporations. Even the federal government used a Planning-Programming-Budgeting System (PPBS) during this time. Public and nonprofit organizations recognized the usefulness of strategy formulation during the 1980s, when the notion of marketing for public and nonprofit organizations gained prominence. Most well-known models of public and nonprofit strategic planning have their roots in the Harvard policy model developed at the Harvard Business School. The systematic analysis of strengths, weaknesses, opportunities, and threats (SWOT) is a primary strength of the Harvard model and is a step in the strategic planning model.

Benefits of Strategic Planning

Strategic planning clearly defines the purpose of the organization and establishes realistic goals and objectives consistent with that mission in a defined time frame within the organization's capacity for implementation. It communicates those goals and objectives to the organization's constituents. Strategic planning develops a sense of ownership of the plan. Strategic planning ensures the most effective use is made of the organization's resources by focusing the resources on the key priorities. It provides a base from which progress can be measured and establishes a mechanism for informed change when needed. Strategic planning brings together everyone's best and most reasoned efforts that have important value in building a consensus about where an organization is going.

The indicators to be used in assessing organizational effectiveness must be chosen from several possible areas and data gathered from several possible sampling frames. The pattern of strategy in an organization is determined not only by the plans and actions of its leaders but also by forces in its external environment. Because both organizations and environments can change over time, and because different agencies operate under different conditions, no single strategy is universally viable.

Organizations cannot be effective unless they know where they are headed. Effectiveness is not random—it begins with a clear vision, mission, and goals. Formal strategic planning approaches establish missions, goals, and visions. Strategic management offers a means of systematically thinking about and reviewing an organization's direction, environment, and strategies. Strategic planning is essential and continues the process for public organizations that wish to determine their own vision and mission. But strategic planning and continuous change requires committed leadership, a supportive organizational culture, an established structure for coordinating and managing the implementation process, and the ability on the part of organizational members to participate in the planning process. Participation can be a powerful device for directing the energy of participants in the public organization.

Recently, we recognize the world of public and nonprofit organizations to be unstable, filled with fluctuation and change. In this rapidly changing environment, complexity limits management control and continuous learning is essential. To cope with this environment, public and nonprofit managers should develop a comprehensive strategy for effective organizations. The result of this recognition is an understanding that public and nonprofit managers must develop comprehensive strategic planning and management. The effective public organization is one that maintains a state of continuous learning and renewal.

—*Naim Kapucu*

See also Collaborative Planning; Communicative Rationality; Dirigisme; Leadership; Planning; Policy Development; Urban and Regional Planning

Further Readings and References

Bryson, J. (2004). *Strategic planning for nonprofit organizations: A guide to strengthening and sustaining organizational achievement.* San Francisco: Jossey-Bass.

Mintzberg, H. (1994). *The rise and fall of strategic planning.* New York: Macmillan.
Moore, M. (1995). *Creating public value: Strategic management in government.* Cambridge, MA: Harvard University Press.
Steiss, A. W. (2003). *Strategic management for public and nonprofit organizations.* New York: Marcel Dekker.

STREET-LEVEL BUREAUCRAT

Used for the first time in 1980 by Michael Lipsky, the expression street-level bureaucracy indicates the public services whose agents, called street-level bureaucrats, are in direct relation with the public (teachers, police officers, legal aid lawyers, social workers, agents of institutions managing social payments). The interest of such an approach is to analyze public action, not from the point of view of institutions but by bottom-up observation of the interaction between agents and clients. It is generally at this level that the citizens' representations of the institutions and state are built. The way in which administrations individualize the treatment of social problems through face-to-face relations between their workers and the public is not a residual dimension of public action but, on the contrary, a structural characteristic of bureaucratic work.

The relations between street-level bureaucrats and clients are generally seen as ones of domination. This domination is not abstract but very concrete. The agents that categorize individuals using social, racial, and behavioral stereotypes construct them in a bureaucratic identity. But in fact, these relations are more complex than it appears. The good ordering of interactions depends upon the implementation of routines by the agents and on the acceptance by the client of his or her bureaucratic identity. But this order changes when the latter rejects the way in which agents construct them as a problem. The personal characteristics (gender, body, reasoning, and affects) of the agent and client then become important and make the exchange much more subjective. Thus, the client becomes a genuine actor developing strategies (violence, tricks, seduction, claims, or suffering) in order to transform their identity and at the same time those of the agents. This process reveals human resources that are normally invisible during a routine activity.

The crisis of traditional social regulation has increasingly transformed the public services into places for the expression of dissatisfactions and misfortunes. This development explains why many institutions have created ombudsmen to manage a process of institutional adaptation to this new reality. In this context, the role of street-level bureaucrats is to make permanent adjustments between the obligation to observe abstract bureaucratic rules and the necessity of adapting them to singular situations. Their autonomy and their capacity of interpretation confer on them the role of policymakers. Of course the content of public policies depends on broader political and socioeconomic elements; nevertheless, their implementation by street-level bureaucrats can transform their meaning.

—Jacques Faget

See also Bottom-Up Approach; Bureaucracy

Further Readings and References

Dubois, V. (1999). *La vie au guichet. Relation administrative et traitement de la misère* [Life with the counter: Administrative relation and starvation wage]. Paris: Economica.

Lipsky, M. (1980). *Street level bureaucracy: Dilemmas of the individual in public services.* New York: Russell Sage.

Structural Contingency Theory

Structural contingency theory is a paradigmatic framework for understanding how organizational factors of size and strategy and environmental factors, such as changes in technology and markets, shape the internal structure of organizations. Its three chief claims are (1) no one organizational structure is effective for all organizations, (2) some ways of organizing are better than others, and (3) organizations whose characteristics best match environmental requisites will do better than those whose features do not. The underlying premise is that organizations are not merely autonomous, self-directed entities oriented toward their individual ends but instead are components of larger social systems. As such, they are subject to external and internal pressures that must be taken into account when organizing tasks and lines of authority. Organizational size and strategy and environmental uncertainty generated by technological innovation and market change determine organizational hierarchies of authority, power and control, rules and norms governing decision making, communication and information flows, and patterns of both formal and informal behavior.

The goal of contingency theory is to identify and explain differences between organizations in terms of the relationships between structure and the contingencies shaping it. To achieve successful performance, an organization aligns its structure with these contingencies. In contrast to classical management theories of organizations that posit an all-purpose, best way to organize an enterprise, contingency theory turns toward identifying the appropriate (rather than maximal) degree of authority and specialization. Because organizations whose characteristics best match environmental requisites will do better than those whose features do not, some ways of organizing are better than others.

Contingency theory addresses a fundamental fact of organizational life: Changes in the size of an organization alter its structure. Growth increases the need for multidivisional structures to accommodate specialization. But it also determines the degree to which the activities of the enterprise follow a formal set of rules that govern authority relationships. As organizations increase their scale, they create rules and norms governing decision making, communication flows, and information processing. The design of organizations in the classical framework is based on the expectation that the optimal structure for any enterprise consists of a set of relationships in which planning and decision making emanate from the top and penetrate lower levels as tasks become increasingly routinized. In this framework, organizational effectiveness (success or failure) rests on the extent to which formal authority relationships regulate behavior as a firm grows. However, after a certain point, centralized decision making is inefficient. Bureaucracies are good examples of the threshold effects of growth on the internal arrangement of organizations. As the number of organizational members increases, a well-coordinated centralized structure is superseded by a decentralized one. Delegation of authority is the hallmark of large enterprises with complex structures, while smaller firms can maintain simpler command structures because management can personally make effective decisions.

Contingency theory also addresses the effects of strategic choice on organizational design. In order to achieve a high level of effectiveness, organizations adapt their structures to changes in strategies. Like size, strategy affects functional and divisional ways of assembling organizations. A divisional structure (i.e., differentiated by multiple product or services lines) best fits a diversified strategy because it has numerous product or service markets and these must be organized into their own divisions. In contrast, a strategy that issues in a single product line or a simple set of tasks fits best with a functional structure (i.e., differentiated by functions such as marketing, sales, and production) because its focus on a limited market or service requires specialization. Creating an increasingly differentiated structure introduces difficulty in the coordination of organizational processes, creates conflict, and increases the need for resources devoted to coordination and control. Increasing structural complexity includes the advantages of predictability and routinization but is often accompanied by the disadvantages of rigidity and organizational dysfunction.

Because no organization can generate all its own resources, organizations must engage in exchange relationships with other organizations in their environments and these relationships create interdependencies. Different environments create different kinds of dependencies, and organizational structure reflects differential environmental influences. Environmental uncertainty entails changes in market conditions and technologies. Environmental uncertainty enters an organization by way of the tasks and work performed. Innovation increases task uncertainty because new technologies for doing previously routine organizational activities may now predominate. The more uncertain the task, the more information that must be processed, and the less likely tasks can be routinized. With increasing innovation, diverse (nonroutine) organizational subunits may become important players in carrying out tasks. This alters coordination and control of activities. Research shows that centralized structures and hierarchical relationships are most effective only when tasks are certain and environments stable. A hierarchical structure matches a stable environment because this type of structure is most efficient when activities can be planned and coordinated in advance. Centralized control is efficient for routine operations, although a less hierarchical, decentralized, more participatory structure is better for nonroutine decision making. Tasks with relatively low uncertainty are more effectively performed in the context of centralized hierarchical authority, because, in addition to ease of planning, it is cost effective. As task uncertainty increases, hierarchical coordination and control must give way to more flexible relationships. These include greater participation and team-based networks that can quickly adapt to changing conditions. Organizations that do not modify their structures when these contingencies prevail are likely to experience diminished performance.

—*Matthew E. Archibald*

See also Organizational Structure; Organization Theory; Resource Dependency Theory

Further Readings and References

Donaldson, L. (1996). The normal science of structural contingency theory. In R. S. Clegg, C. Hardy, & W. R. Nord (Eds.), *The handbook of organization studies* (pp. 57–77). Thousand Oaks, CA: Sage.

Donaldson, L. (2001). *The contingency theory of organizations.* Thousand Oaks, CA: Sage.

Lawrence, P. R. (1993). The contingency approach to organizational design. In R. T. Golembieski (Ed.), *The handbook of organizational behavior* (pp. 9–18). New York: Marcel Dekker.

Lawrence, P. R., & Lorsch, J. W. (1967). *Organization and environment: Managing differentiation and integration.* Boston: Harvard University.

Thompson, J. D. (1967). *Organizations in action: Social science bases of administrative theory.* New York: McGraw-Hill.

SUBSIDIARITY

The principle of subsidiarity involves a method of governance implying a distribution of competences for public action between various levels of power. In recent years, subsidiarity has become an important concept in a number of fields: philosophical, legal, and political.

It is difficult to give a precise definition of this term, which is characterized by strong fluidity and a polysemous nature. To do so, it is necessary to take into account the formal dimension of the principle by examining its use and instrumental dimensions. The application of the principle of subsidiarity varies widely according to cognitive, institutional, and political configurations.

Subsidiarity: A Time-Honored and Polysemous Principle

Applied to a large number of fields of analysis, the principle of subsidiarity is multifaceted and flexible. Historically, ancient medieval thought did not take into account the aspect of efficient public action presently denoted by this term. The principle of subsidiarity is mentioned in the works of philosophers such as Aristotle and Saint Thomas Aquinas. The objective of the principle was to determine the link between the community (cities, village, family) and the individual. The central idea was that whenever an individual is capable of meeting one's needs, the community should not interfere. The principle was applied by the Roman Catholic Church in a similar manner in an encyclical of 1931, which defined a doctrine of organizing social relationships.

From these philosophical and religious approaches, the concept of subsidiarity gradually came to be used as a legal and political principle for the distribution of competences between various levels of public action. As it became a legal and political norm, the principle of subsidiarity became a method of governance that was seen as an effective and democratic form of direct government close to citizens. Therefore, the aim of subsidiarity was to determine a fair balance of competences while taking into account the skills and resources of different levels of power. In this way, the principle represents a good and just rule of governance.

The Principle of Subsidiarity: A Method of Governance

The principle of subsidiarity is a method of legitimate recourse to a certain kind of action. Given the fact that subsidiarity is perceived as being not only a principle of organization, but also one of efficiency (subsidiarity management enables better implementation thanks to proximity, competence, and autonomy) as well as a political doctrine, its application varies according to the levels of intervention and the institutional and political configurations of the actors.

The principle is used most often as a standard of legitimacy and thus as an element of what some people call good governance. Under such circumstances, the lack of precision of the concept partly explains the success of the principle. At the present time, the subsidiarity method is observed more and more on the national, community, and even international levels (such as the Rio de Janeiro Declaration on the Environment and Development in 1992).

On the national level, the principle of subsidiarity has served as the basis of the constitutional and legal architecture of both the Federal State of Germany and the Swiss Union, each with a relatively different formal dimension due to their historical and political logics.

However, it is unquestionably at the level of European integration that the principle of subsidiarity has been the most successful. More than a simple legal principle within the community framework, it is a resource that can justify either the change or the maintenance of a system of public action, whether it is at the European, national, or regional level. The European institutions, as well as the states, have accepted this principle, expecting it to serve their perspective interests.

As far as the Treaties of the Union are concerned, the principle of subsidiarity appeared for the first time in the Treaty of Maastricht, adopted in 1993. The application of this principle at the community level indicates its ambivalence. Subsidiarity is not synonymous with decentralization. On one hand, the subsidiant principle can allow community institutions to intervene in certain fields and, on the other hand, place restrictions on the competences of the European Union. For example, in 1990, the principle was used during the Intergovernmental Conference on Political Union and on Economic and Monetary Union in order to limit the increase of community competences. In the field of social affairs, justice, freedom, and security, European states remain attached to the implementation of the subsidiarity system because it is often in the name of this principle that it is possible to prevent certain questions from appearing on the European Community's agenda. The use of this method also has an impact on the process of the construction of the European Union.

In the name of subsidiarity, an action can be refused or accepted depending upon institutional and political conditions and configurations. By virtue of the aspect of polysemous inherent in subsidiarity, this method of governance is destined for success given by strength of internationalization and Europeanization. More and more, the concept is referred to as a political norm allowing better regulation at both the EU (for example, Project of the European Constitution, Title III Article 9 on Union competences) and international levels. The understanding of the principle thereby constitutes a highly pertinent heuristic prospect as a legitimate act.

—*Antoine Mégie*

See also Center-Local Relations; Decentralization; European Governance; European Union; Interregional Relations

Further Readings and References

Blichner, L., & Sangolt, L. (1994). The concept of subsidiarity and the debate on European cooperation: Pitfalls and possibilities. *Governance, 7*(3), 284–306.

Faure, A. (Ed.). (1995). *Territoires et subsidiarité: L'action publique locale à la lumière d'un principe controversé* [Territories and subsidiarity: The local public action in the light of a principle discusses]. Paris: Harmattan.

Höffe, O. (1996). Subsidiarity as a principle in the philosophy of government. *Regional Politics and Policy, 6,* 56–73.

Schilling, T. (1994). A new dimension of subsidiarity: Subsidiarity as a rule and a principle. *Yearbook of European Law, 14,* 203–256.

SUBSTATE REGIONALISM

Regionalism is an ideology and political movement that seeks to advance the cause of regions. But it is necessary to distinguish two quite different meanings of the term *region*. In international relations theory, it refers to a group of countries, such as Western Europe, the Western Balkans, or Southeast Asia, that are linked by geography, history, or economic features. Used in this sense, regional integration refers to attempts to reinforce the links between these countries. Today, the foremost example of such an attempt is the European Union (EU). In the second meaning of the term, region refers to a territory that is located within, or sometimes across the borders of, a nation-state. In this sense, different kinds of regions may be distinguished: political regions, which usually possess some form of elected regional government; administrative regions, which are geographical entities created for the purpose of administering a service such as a health region or an electricity region; geographical regions, which refer to a geographical feature, such as mountain regions, island regions, coastal or maritime regions; and, finally, economic regions, such as agricultural, industrial, or declining industrial regions. As a general rule, the political or administrative regions refer to levels of government or administration immediately below the national level. But, in some cases, as in the Netherlands, it refers to a level located between the *provincie* (county) and the *gemeente* (municipality). In Sweden and Finland, what are sometimes translated as regions—the *län*—are what would be called counties in the United Kingdom. Furthermore, the two experimental regions in Sweden, *Västra Götaland* and *Skåne,* which were established by amalgamating existing counties, are, constitutionally, simply counties. In some countries, as in Spain and Italy, there is a hierarchical relationship between the region, or autonomous community, and local authorities, while in others, such as France and Sweden, there is no hierarchical relationship. The difficulty of comparing across states is illustrated by the EU's classification of subnational levels of government and administration for statistical purposes, called N.U.T.S. (*nomenclature des unités territoriales statistiques*). N.U.T.S. 1 is the level below the central state. In some countries, such as Belgium, the regions below the central state are N.U.T.S. 1 level, while in Finland, the regions are N.U.T.S. 2.

A final distinction may be made between regionalization and regionalism. Regionalization is a top-down process emanating from central governments or the EU to either set up political or administrative regions within a state or to implement regional policies. It is a policy or administrative process aimed at a territory, the formulation and implementation of which does not necessarily involve the inhabitants of that territory. Regionalism, on the other hand, is both an ideology advocating the setting up of political regions within nation-states and a political movement through which the population of a territory seeks to achieve this end. Regionalist demands may be based on the affirmation of linguistic or cultural identity or both, on perceptions of oppression by the nation-state, on the demand for political or economic equality, or on a combination of all these elements. These two distinctions are sometimes called top-down regionalism and bottom-up regionalism, but the distinction used previously is clearer in that it uses a different word for what is, in reality, quite a different phenomenon.

Regionalism has its roots in nineteenth century Europe and was a reaction to the emergence of the unitary nation-state as the dominant form of political organization. As a political ideology, it was developed by individual thinkers and groups opposed to the emergence of the nation-state and the liberal democratic political system associated with it. It was found especially among the Bretons in France, the Flemings in Belgium, the Catalans and Basques in Spain, and the Sardinians in Italy. In the United Kingdom, the movement for Home Rule in Ireland and similar movements in Scotland and Wales could be regarded as forms of regionalism. Sometimes, regionalism took the form of minority nationalism, as in the Basque Country, Brittany, Corsica, and Ireland, and there was some overlapping between adherents of the two movements. The difference between regionalism and minority nationalism was that regionalists limited their demands to a greater degree of political autonomy within the nation-state, while minority nationalists sought complete independence and the setting up of their own nation-state. In the nineteenth and first half of the twentieth centuries, regionalists were usually found on the Right of the political spectrum, and they sought to defend traditionalist and corporatist models of society for their regions. A minority of regionalists was on the Left. In the period between the two world wars and during World War II, some regionalists and minority nationalists identified with the extreme Right and, in France and Belgium, collaborated with the Nazi occupants or, in Corsica, with the Italian occupants.

Although collaboration involved only a minority of regionalists, it discredited political regionalism in France after World War II. As a result, regionalists in Brittany, Corsica, and the French Basque Country concentrated first on demands to improve the economic condition of their regions (economic regionalism) and then on cultural issues such as language (cultural regionalism). The economic regionalism of the Bretons was especially successful in the 1950s through the activities of the *Comité d'Etudes et de Liaison des Intérêts Bretons* (CELIB) and led to the regionalization of the French national plan. Other regions, such as Corsica and the French Basque Country, attempted to imitate this success. During the 1950s and early 1960s, regionalist demands became increasingly political and some regionalist groups began to demand greater political autonomy (political regionalism). These regionalist movements were in reality coalitions of different political tendencies from moderate Jacobins to extreme nationalists and, when the demands on the central state were not met, they tended to disintegrate, thus leaving the way open to the reemergence of minority nationalism. Regionalist groups appeared in other European countries and followed a similar pattern from economic to political regionalism and minority nationalism. In Northern Ireland, the Civil Rights Association, a widely based movement seeking simple equality of treatment for Catholics, ultimately gave way to the armed struggle of the Irish Republican Army. In Scotland and Wales, minority nationalism was dominant. In Spain, the ETA (Euskadi Ta Askatasuna) was active in the Basque Country.

The political evolution of these regionalist and minority nationalist movements can be understood in the context of the creation and development of welfare states in developed capitalist states during the period of the *Trente Glorieuses* (1945–1975). These were the thirty glorious years of the postwar economic boom, of expanding social services to meet increasing social rights of citizens, but also of centralized and bureaucratic states. Regional policy during this period took the form of regionalization and usually paid scant regard to political regionalism and particularly minority nationalism. The aim of regional policy and regionalization was not to respond to the demands of these movements but to build up the national polity by bringing regions into production that were backward both economically and socially. Groups within disadvantaged regions responded to this in three ways. First, they demanded a greater share of the national pie on the basis of their status as citizens of the state (this was the original basis of Breton and Corsican demands in France and of the early Northern Ireland Civil Rights Association). This was economic regionalism. Second, when the central state did not always respond to this demand, or responded in an inadequate and piecemeal way, at least some of the regionalists began to make stronger political demands to modify the political institutions of the state in order to give them greater control over their own affairs. This was political regionalism, or the demand for greater political autonomy. Finally, a minority within some groups became disillusioned with the state itself and sought separation from it to set up their own ministates. This was minority nationalism or separatism. The political model of the minority nationalists was the nation-state itself. Minorities within this group resorted to violence to achieve their ends (in Brittany, Corsica, the Basque Country, and, to a limited extent, in Wales, although Northern Irish violence was of a different nature and magnitude compared to these other cases).

During the 1960s, there was an ideological shift within regionalism, with some regionalist groups moving to the Left and even embracing Marxist ideology. The latter used theories of unequal exchange that had been applied to international affairs to formulate the theory of internal colonialism, that is, they argued that their regions had been colonized by the central state. Their political strategy, therefore, should be one of national liberation, like the movements in the third world. In Corsica, the main violent separatist groups, the Front de Libération Nationale de la Corse (FLNC) took its name directly from the Algerian Front de Libération Nationale (FLN). At the same time, some mainstream Left-wing parties, such as the French Socialists, which were traditionally strongly Jacobin, began to adopt more regionalist positions. The British Labour Party was in its majority centralist but, in Scotland and Wales, had some members sympathetic to regionalism and minority nationalism. The French Socialist Party, which had been constituted by François Mitterrand in 1971, launched extensive decentralization and regionalization reforms in 1982, following their election to power in 1981. Tony Blair's New Labour Party adopted a program of devolution following their election in 1997. On the other hand, many regionalists remained politically conservative, or at least anti-Marxist, and some adopted the ideology of European federalism.

The period of the *Trente Glorieuses* and the creation of the welfare state marked the culmination of the process of nation-state building in Europe that had begun with the French Revolution. The process of European integration began in the late 1940s and early 1950s at the same time as the first steps in building the welfare state. Regionalists were divided in their attitudes to European integration. Some of them were federalists that espoused both a federal Europe and the federalization of their national states, which would give them greater political autonomy. Some European federalists, such as Denis De Rougement, who advocated a "Europe of the Regions," or Guy Héraud, who advocated "L'Europe des Ethnies," promoted a model of a federal Europe in which the units of the federation were not the nation-states but the "natural" regions and ethnic communities. The more radical Marxist regionalists and the minority nationalists opposed the process, either on the grounds that it was a capitalist ploy to incorporate their regions in a great European division of labor that would see them relegated to simple tourist havens or agricultural regions feeding the richer regions or because European integration threatened the principle of national sovereignty. In the United Kingdom, Sinn Féin, Plaid Cymru, and the

Scottish Nationalist Party all opposed the UK's entry into the then-European Economic Community (EEC) in 1973.

The crisis of the welfare state, of Keynesian economic policies in the 1970s, and the hegemony of the neoliberal paradigm in the 1980s radically changed the context of regionalism. First, national governments, to greater or lesser degrees and in different ways, initiated a series of administrative and policy reforms that reduced governmental intervention in the economy and particularly within the regions. Regions were sometimes left to fend for themselves, and this developed into a new theory of endogenous regional development or innovative regionalism, which was mostly making a virtue out of necessity. But, simultaneous with these changes at the level of the nation-state and closely related to them was the "relaunch of Europe," beginning with the Franco-German partnership in 1975, the Declaration on European Union by the European Parliament in 1984, and the arrival to the presidency of the European Commission of Jacques Delors in 1985. The driving force behind greater European integration was the Single Market programme of Delors, which led to the revisions of the Treaties at Maastricht, Amsterdam, and Nice.

As part of the deal for supporting the Single European Act of 1986, some of the member states with serious problems of regional underdevelopment, such as Spain and Italy, demanded some form of compensation and protection against the possible harmful effects of a Europe-wide market. This took the form of upgraded regional funds and eventually the creation of the Structural and Cohesion Funds. The decline of national sovereignty because of accelerated European integration and the financial inducements found in the new funds had an important impact on Europe's regions. First, the regions themselves were encouraged to look outside their national borders and not simply to their national governments for funding. Second, a vast regional mobilization took place across Europe that involved both collaboration and competition among regions. Collaboration took the form of the creation of pan-European regional associations of which the Assembly of European Regions is the main representative of the regional interest in Europe. Some

associations represent specific geographical or economic interests, such as the Association of Cross-Border Regions or the Conference of Peripheral and Maritime Regions. But, at the same time, regions began to compete with each other for scarce resources available both from the EU and from international investors. This led to competitive regionalism.

But the availability of EU funding could also disempower regions. In Germany, the Länder have competence for regional policy. But, because the EU can only negotiate with national governments and not other levels of government, EU regional funds were being channeled to the federal government, thus threatening the Länder's prerogatives. In reaction, the Länder launched a "Europe of the Regions" movement and, for a time in the 1990s, this was very much on the political agenda. The concept, though, was rather different from the original formulation by Denis De Rougement and was not really an attempt to create a regionalized federal Europe but to force the EU and the German federal government to respect the competences of subnational levels of government. The culmination of these developments was the creation of a Committee of the Regions by the Treaty of Maastricht, which began to function in 1994. However, the Committee of the Regions has proved to be a disappointment to those that wished to see a stronger regional representation in the EU, because it has a simply consultative function that is limited to emitting opinions on a range of issues, rather than the European equivalent of the German *Bundesrat,* as some of the most ardent European regionalists had hoped. At the same time, the Committee, originally modeled on the Economic and Social Committee, has slowly strengthened its functions and role with each successive revision of the Treaties. But disappointment with the initial settlement meant there was a period of regional demobilization, and the regional question was scarcely mentioned either at Amsterdam or Nice and only with great difficulty during the Convention on the Future of Europe, which drew up the new European Constitution.

Despite these setbacks, the regional issue is still very much alive in Europe, although the political, economic, and social context today has quite dramatically changed since the 1970s. The two key changes have been the transformation of the nation-state itself and accelerated European integration. Today, all the large countries in which regionalist movements demanded greater autonomy have both regionalized and decentralized their states. Decentralization in the form of setting up autonomous communities, as well as entry in the EU, in Spain was closely associated with the transition to democracy. Although the Catalans and Basques are still not fully happy with the settlement, nevertheless, the transition has been quite successful. The Zapatero Socialist government in 2004, in collaboration with the socialist-led coalition government in Catalonia, began negotiations with regard to strengthening the Autonomous Communities yet further and even toward recognizing Catalonia as a nation rather than simply a nationality. France launched decentralization reforms in 1982, which included the establishment of elected regional assemblies that began to function in 1986. Although the Corsican problem remains and the majority of Bretons would like to have greater regional powers, the establishment of political regions was a significant change in the French political system. In Italy, the crisis of the party state led to important constitutional reforms in the 1990s, one element of which was the enhancement of the regions through the federalization of the Italian state. Finally, among the large states, the United Kingdom was the last to adopt a regional form of organization with the devolution reforms, which began in 1998 and have seen the establishment of a Scottish Parliament, a National Assembly for Wales, a Northern Ireland power-sharing assembly (which functions sporadically), and a Greater London Authority. Among the smaller countries, such as Ireland, Greece, Portugal, and the Scandinavian countries, the tendency has been to set up administrative rather than political regions for purposes of receiving EU funding. Finally, there has been a regionalization of the countries of East and Central Europe, even though central governments in those countries have been reluctant to cede decision-making power to lower levels of government. This is exacerbated by the fact that these countries contain ethnic and religious minorities, and it has proved difficult to draw the boundaries between them because they often overlap geographically and even spread across into neighboring states. The importance

of political decentralization and regionalization for democratic practice may be seen from the Council of Europe's Charter on Local Self-Government and its many declarations recommending regional self-government. However, the Council has had great difficulty in producing a Charter on Regional Self-Government because of the resistance of a number of its members.

Two other contemporary developments, directly related to the European dimension, may be noted by way of conclusion. First, the old anti-European, separatist regionalism and nationalism that was found in a number of states in the 1960s has given way to a new formulation of the aims of minority nationalism. The slogan today is "Independence within Europe," and many minority nationalists are sympathetic to the idea of a "Europe of the Regions," which they see as weakening the position of their nation-states or at least of their national governments. Second, the nature of regionalist mobilization has changed after the disappointment caused by the Committee of the Regions. Today, there is a division between the stronger regions, the regions with legislative powers, such as Scotland, Flanders, or Catalonia, and those without these powers, such as Rhône-Alpes or Lombardy. The former group now has its own groupings and are strongly lobbying for a greater role with the EU decision-making machinery. The latter continue to be mainly represented by the Assembly of European Regions, which seeks a more diffuse recognition of the regional interest in Europe.

—John Loughlin

See also City-Region; Interregional Relations; Mesoregionalism; Monetary Union; New Regionalism; North-South Regionalism; Open and Closed Regionalism; Urban and Regional Planning

Further Readings and References

Keating, M., & Loughlin, J. (Eds.). (1997). *The political economy of regionalism.* London: Frank Cass.

Keating, M., Loughlin, J., & Deschouwer, K. (2003). *Culture, institutions and economic development: A study of eight European regions.* Cheltenham, UK: Edward Elgar.

Loughlin, J., Aja, E., Bullmann, U., Hendriks, F., Lidström, A., & Seiler, D.-L. (2004). *Subnational democracy in the European Union.* Oxford, UK: Oxford University Press.

SUSTAINABILITY

Sustainability refers to the long-term viability of a community, set of social institutions, or societal practice. The idea rose to prominence with the modern environmental movement, which rebuked the unsustainable character of contemporary societies where patterns of resource use, growth, and consumption threaten the integrity of ecosystems and the well-being of future generations. Sustainability is presented as an alternative to short-term, myopic, and wasteful behavior. It serves as a standard against which existing institutions are to be judged and as an objective toward which society should move. With respect to governance, it implies an interrogation of existing modes of social organization to determine the extent to which they encourage destructive practices as well as a conscious effort to transform the status quo to promote the development of more sustainable patterns of activity.

Sustainability resonates with cognate concepts such as sustainable yield, sustainable society, and sustainable development. Sustainable yield relates to the harvest of a specific (self-renewing) natural resource—say timber or fish. Such a yield is one that can in principle be maintained indefinitely because it can be supported by the regenerative capacities of the underlying natural system. A sustainable society is one that has learned to live within the boundaries established by ecological limits. It can be maintained as a collective and ongoing entity because practices that imposed excessive burdens upon the environment have been reformed or abolished. And sustainable development denotes a process of social advance that accommodates the needs of the current generation and of futurity, and which successfully integrates economic, social, and environmental considerations in decision making.

In contemporary debate, sustainability often serves as a synonym for sustainable development. On other occasions, it is associated more exclusively with environmental constraints or environmental performance, and the expression environmental sustainability is used to emphasize this point. Parallel references can be found to social sustainability, economic sustainability, and cultural sustainability, which allude to threats to long-term well-being in each of these domains. Local sustainability emphasizes the importance of place. Corporate sustainability is another common usage, which relates both to the survivability of the individual corporation and to the contribution that corporations can make to the broader sustainability agenda. Central here is the notion of the triple bottom line—that businesses should pay attention to social and environmental performance as well as to financial returns. And there are connections to debates about reforming corporate governance, encouraging corporate responsibility, and designing alternative (sustainable, green, or ethical) investment vehicles.

While all sorts of practices are cited as threats to sustainability (political corruption, social inequality, the arms race, and profligate government expenditure), environmental issues remain at the heart of the discussion. Of course, what is conducive to environmental sustainability remains a matter of intense debate. Approaches range from a moderate "greening" of current social institutions to a radical transformation of the global political and economic order. A gradual adjustment toward sustainability relies on governmental initiatives to orient production and consumption into less environmentally destructive channels. This implies a reengineering of industrial and agricultural processes, a transformation of land use practices, and a shift in household consumption. Potentially renewable resources should be managed to conserve their long-term viability; nonrenewable resources should be extracted at rates that allow an ordered transition to alternatives; emission of waste and toxic substances must remain within the assimilative capacities of natural systems; and more vigorous measures must be taken to preserve species, habitats, and ecosystems. Managing long-term environmental issues such as climate change and the loss of biodiversity are of critical importance.

Governments can deploy an array of policy tools to affect such changes, including regulation, fiscal instruments, negotiated agreements, informational tools, and normative injunction. Yet many problems are resistant to solution because the offending (unsustainable) practices are linked to deeply embedded structural constraints and supported by established definitions of values and interests.

But there are also more radical takes on sustainability. For some "greens," true sustainability is only possible in small-scale communities, where human beings can live in close contact with natural processes and rhythms. The catastrophic practices of industrial civilization must give way to a different mode of living where humans "walk lightly" on the planet, harmonizing their activities with natural cycles. While other radical greens may accept a high-tech, postindustrial civilization, here, too, there must be a clear break with existing economic practices and power structures. And the globalizing project of twenty-first century industrial elites must be subverted if society is to adopt a more sustainable orientation.

With respect to academic discussion, sustainability has been approached from various perspectives. Economic analysts have sometimes defined the concept in terms of nondeclining per capita income flows over time and debated how to maintain the capital endowments needed to sustain those income flows. Controversy over the substitutability of natural and man-made capital has divided proponents of weak and strong sustainability—with the former arguing that the two types of capital are largely interchangeable, while the latter insist that natural capital is increasingly the scarcest factor of production. Ecologists and systems theorists have tended to approach sustainability in terms of physical interdependencies, energy flows, and population dynamics. They have emphasized the design features that suit social systems for long-term survival, including robustness, resiliency, redundancy, and adaptability. For their part, political analysts have focused on the ideological and normative implications of sustainability, on the character of green political projects, and on the public policy implications.

—James Meadowcroft

See also Climate Change; Endangered Species Protection; Environmental Governance; Global Governance; Globalization; Natural Resource Management; Sustainable Development

Further Readings and References

Costanza, R. (1992). *Ecological economics: The science and management of sustainability.* New York: Columbia University Press.

Meadowcroft, J. (1999). Planning for sustainable development: What can be learned from the critics? In M. Kenny & J. Meadowcroft (Eds.), *Planning sustainability* (pp. 12–38). New York: Routledge.

Paelke, R. (2004). Sustainability. In R. Durant, D. Fiorino, & R. O'Leary (Eds.), *Environmental governance reconsidered: Challenges, choices and opportunities.* Cambridge: MIT Press.

Spangenberg, J. (2002). Environmental space and the prism of sustainability. *Ecological Indicators, 2,* 295–309.

SUSTAINABLE DEVELOPMENT

Sustainable development refers to a process of societal advance embodying a more equitable and environmentally aware pattern of development that requires a careful integration of economic, social, and environmental objectives. Since the 1990s, the concept has increasingly been endorsed by governments and official bodies, and it has gradually emerged as a new international norm qualifying the sort of change that is to be regarded as authentic development. In governance terms, sustainable development raises the challenge of how human societies are to address urgent environment and development problems and how existing systems of governance (at the international, national, regional, and local levels) can be reformed to ensure a more desirable pattern of societal advance.

Initially popularized by the Report of the World Commission on Environment and Development (WCED) in 1987 and formally endorsed by world leaders at the United Nations Conference on Environment and Development in Rio de Janeiro in 1992, the idea of sustainable development is now routinely cited by governments as a fundamental policy objective. The WCED defined the concept as development for the present that does not compromise the future, emphasizing both the moral imperative of responding to the urgent development needs of the world's poor and the threat to continued progress represented by the failure to respect environmental limits.

As further elaborated in international political debate, sustainable development has come to be associated with a series of normative ideas including: protection of the environment, particularly the essential life support functions of the global ecosphere; promotion of human welfare, especially the urgent development needs of the poor; concern for the well-being of future generations; and public participation in environment and development decision making. It is often spoken about in terms of ensuring an appropriate balance between three pillars—environment, economy, and society.

Sustainable development is a complex and contested concept, and despite the pages of "consensus documents" adopted by international agencies and conferences, there remain many different perspectives on what it entails and on the scale of political and social reform required to give it force. One often hears complaints about its fluidity and about the difficulty of translating the idea into specific policy prescriptions. Some environmentalists argue it has been co-opted by governments and corporations, while some enthusiasts of unfettered economic growth claim it is a creation of the environmental lobby. Nevertheless, the term remains at the heart of contemporary discourses of environment and development. Like other normative political concepts (such as liberty or democracy), it helps to frame and focus debate while being open to constant interrogation and reinterpretation.

Within industrially advanced countries, reconciling continued economic and social improvement with a radically reduced environmental burden stands at the crux of sustainable development. Although developed states have proven relatively successful in promoting economic growth and social welfare, much of the progress over the past half-century has been purchased at the expense of the global environment. Moreover, evidence suggests that the extension of prevailing patterns of "Northern" consumption across the globe would result in catastrophic damage to the biosphere. Yet there can be no ethical justification for denying people of developing countries access to living standards currently enjoyed in affluent states. Thus, it is incumbent upon developed countries to free up environmental space—dramatically reducing resource consumption and pollutant release—to make room for further growth in the developing world. This requires a decoupling of economic activity from environmental loading. In global terms, the significance of this decoupling is particularly evident with respect to climate change, where stabilization of the climate system will

eventually require a decline in global carbon dioxide emissions to a small fraction of current levels. But threats to long-term ecological integrity are manifest in many other areas, including water use, the management of forests and fisheries, patterns of land utilization, soil degradation, biodiversity loss, chemical releases, and the disposal of wastes.

Significant reductions in the burdens developed societies place on the global environment will require dramatic changes to established patterns of production and consumption and a fundamental transformation of key economic sectors including energy, transport, construction, manufacturing, and agriculture. Some analysts have spoken of the need for a fourfold or even tenfold increase in resource efficiency in coming decades. But even change on such a scale will not ensure sustainable development unless attention is explicitly paid to maintaining environmental pressures within the assimilative capacity of natural systems and to enhancing the integrity of ecosystems. Of course, the real challenge is to dramatically improve environmental performance while also meeting other social aspirations.

Developing countries face a somewhat different set of circumstances, and in this context sustainable development emphasizes the importance of meeting the basic needs of the population—including requirements for clean water, food, housing, fuel supplies, employment, health care, and education. There is a clear recognition that less-affluent countries will necessarily place greater relative weight on achieving economic growth and meeting social priorities. But environmental considerations are not to be neglected. Public health, local livelihoods, and economic prospects can be damaged by environmentally unsustainable practices (for example, uncontrolled deforestation). And developing countries also have responsibilities for protecting the global environmental commons. Sustainable development implies that developing countries should ultimately seek a path of economic advance that avoids many of the destructive practices that were historically employed by today's affluent states. And, in seeking to leapfrog environmentally damaging technologies, developing countries have a legitimate claim on the industrialized world to provide them with assistance.

This brings to the fore a critical element of the idea of sustainable development—its international and internationalist foundations. At the core of the notion lie ideas about global interdependence and international solidarity. It is not just that human societies are increasingly interconnected, but also that there are moral obligations that bind people across continents. In particular, the developed states have an obligation to take the lead in transforming environmentally destructive patterns of production and consumption and to assist developing countries in meeting their developmental and environmental objectives. For their part, developing countries should pay particular attention to poverty alleviation and strive to avoid the environmentally destructive development path adopted by the North.

Governance Challenges

At heart, sustainable development can be understood as a governance problem. If contemporary societies have adopted unsustainable development paths—which threaten the integrity of global ecosystems and fail to meet the basic needs of large sections of the world population—then this represents a failure of existing institutional arrangements. And conscious action to reform established patterns of societal governance will be required to reorient development onto more sustainable lines. Thus, sustainable development embodies a specific "steering" logic. It does not imply an ambitious exercise in pattern matching—attempting to ensure that progress fits the profile of a preplanned development trajectory. But it does involve the more modest task of displacing the direction of social movement so that current (authentic) developmental priorities are attained, while the preconditions for subsequent social advance are not eroded. Value choices—about the kind of a society in which humans want to live and about the kind of a world they want to leave to posterity—are central to sustainable development. For while the concept indicates issues that should be of concern, its practical bearing cannot be established independent of the concrete life circumstances of a particular society and the needs, interests, values, and aspirations of its members. At base, it is not a technical project—although technical expertise is essential—but a political project. It involves problem solving in conditions of great uncertainty and the collective discovery of preferred social development pathways.

Turning from theoretical considerations to the practical world, it is evident that to date the scale of change associated with engagement of sustainable development has been modest. There has been some progress in the elaboration of international environmental agreements: International bodies have begun to take environmental assessments more seriously in their decision-making processes and a "basic needs" orientation has become more significant within development organizations. And yet international gatherings, such as the 2002 World Summit on Sustainable Development held in Johannesburg, have issued increasingly somber assessments of the failure of the international community to come to grips on the scale of the environment and development problems the world now faces.

Within the industrialized countries, sustainable development has been associated with a series of adjustments in the environmental policy field, including a greater emphasis on pollution prevention (rather than "end of pipe" solutions), a shift toward a more diverse portfolio of policy instruments (rather than almost exclusive reliance on regulation), involvement of a broader range of ministries and agencies (rather than only a specialized environment ministry), and an internationalization of policy approaches. Institutional innovations have included the preparation of national strategies and plans, which assess environmental burdens in a more comprehensive and long-term manner. Attention has been paid to measuring the state of the environment and to developing indicator sets that evaluate different dimensions of sustainable development. There has also been a trend to involve stakeholders from business and environmental nongovernmental organizations in environment and sustainable development processes. Increasingly, regions and urban centers have been seen as key loci for sustainability planning.

In this context, the most consistent theme to emerge from contemporary efforts to come to terms with sustainable development is the idea of integrating economic, social, and environmental considerations in decision making across society. In the broadest sense, integration refers to all three pillars, to decisions made by individuals and by collectivities of all types and across all fields of societal endeavor. To the extent that governance for sustainable development relies on decentered networks and extensive practices of self- and cogovernance, such societal integration is essential. But the foundation for such extensive societal integration must be established in the more specific realm of policy integration—integration within the sphere of government itself. And this is not just because governments are themselves important social actors, but also because they possess policy levers that can encourage other actors to alter their behaviors. Policy integration involves a deliberate search for win/win options—policies that simultaneously promote economic, social, and environmental goods. But it also involves balancing goals that can be only partially reconciled, accepting trade-offs, and making hard choices. And if it is to mean anything more than business as usual, it also implies that in some circumstances environmental policy priorities will trump established economic and social objectives.

In the longer term, it is clear that more consistent efforts by national governments to confront the challenge of sustainable development will involve a series of tasks including the following:

- Encouraging scientific and technological innovation directed to reducing environmental loadings in the major spheres of production and consumption (energy, transportation, construction, manufacturing, agriculture, and so on)
- Improving the integration of different kinds of knowledge in decision making, including knowledge from the natural and social sciences, lay and traditional knowledge, and knowledge representing different societal vantage points
- Developing multinodal patterns of governance with expansive stakeholder involvement, which will include not just multilevel governance (local, regional, national, international) but also governance nodes organized on functional lines defined by themes, ecosystems, and environmental problems
- Ensuring continued public discussion and social reflection about existing practices, desired goals, and alternative futures

- Developing improved systems of measurement and monitoring to track changes in environmental state and the health and environmental impacts of societal activities
- Deepening the understanding of ecological and social systems, of the reach and limits of current knowledge, and of the potential (but also the limits) of attempts to consciously adjust social and ecological processes
- Perfecting a more elaborate array of policy instruments, including performance agreements, comanagement regimes, ecological fiscal reform, and changes to liability regimes to encourage actors to internalize environmental values
- Encouraging a public ethic of concern for the environment and the integration of sustainable development issues into the educational and cultural spheres

As this list suggests, while sustainable development is in some sense a new concept (particularly in the way it links together ideas about human progress, preservation of the global ecosphere, and intergenerational and intragenerational equity), it also relates to many issues that have long preoccupied political leaders and analysts. These include the place of normative ideas and moral argument in politics and policy making; the extent to which the state can or should seek to orient societal development; the appropriate linkages among decision making in international, national, regional, and local spheres; the roles of citizens, politicians, bureaucrats, and experts in democratic decision making; and the management of technological change.

Governance for Sustainable Development by William M. Lafferty points to a set of problems that appear destined to become more important as the twenty-first century advances and as the ecological strains related to the still-growing global population and the widening impacts of industrialization continue to increase. In this respect, climate change appears as a quintessential sustainable development problem. It is an issue of global reach, involving generational time frames and great uncertainty. It threatens serious environmental disruption and has the potential to aggravate many existing problems. Mitigation will entail significant economic costs and a disruption to established ways of doing things. And on the political front there are enormous obstacles to developing the international cooperation required to address this issue seriously. On the other hand, the problem presents societies with an opportunity to move away from environmentally destructive and inequitable patterns of production and consumption, to improve environment and development decision making, to harness new technologies that provide welfare and environmental gains, and to reform international institutions to encourage collective solutions to global problems. And this is the pattern of societal development toward which this emergent international norm of sustainable development is intended to point.

—*James Meadowcroft*

See also Climate Change; Commission on Global Governance; Common but Differentiated Responsibilities; Development Theory; Ecosystemic Approach; Endangered Species Protection; Environmental Governance; Functionalism; Global Governance; Kyoto Protocol; Millennium Development Goals; Multilevel Governance; Natural Resource Management; Poverty Reduction; Precautionary Principle; Sustainability; United Nations Educational, Scientific and Cultural Organization; World Development Indicators

Further Readings and References

Lafferty, W. (Ed.). (2004). *Governance for sustainable development: The challenge of adapting form to function.* Cheltenham, UK: Edward Elgar.

Lafferty, W., & Meadowcroft, J. (Eds.). (2000). *Implementing sustainable development: Strategies and initiatives in high consumption societies.* Oxford, UK: Oxford University Press.

Meadowcroft, J. (1997). Planning for sustainable development: Insights from the literatures of political science. *European Journal of Political Research, 31,* 427–454.

Organisation for Economic Co-operation and Development. (2001). *Sustainable development: Critical issues.* Paris: Author.

United Nations. (2002). *Report of the world summit on sustainable development.* New York: Author.

World Commission on Environment and Development. (1987). *Our common future.* Oxford, UK: Oxford University Press.

SYSTEMS THEORY

A system is a complex arrangement of elements related to a whole. The body, for example, is a whole that is comprised of a complex of interacting cells, organs, limbs, and so on. The study of society as a social system has a long history in the social sciences. The conceptual origins of the approach are generally traced to the work of Herbert Spencer and Émile Durkheim in particular.

Herbert Spencer, influenced by Charles Darwin's theory of evolution, argued for a unitary form of the social system. In his approach, the system of society was constantly evolving into an even more complex state of perfection. However, alternative forms of social systems theory argue for a very different view of social evolution. In these perspectives, society is not evolving toward some perfect state; rather, it is reaching a state of increasing complexity. This was called structural differentiation.

Structural differentiation refers to the adaptation of the organism or society to its environment through changes in its internal complexity. An important aspect of social differentiation is deciding just how adaptation occurs. Put simply, the question is, How do changes in the structure of the system relate to the processes of the system?

There are several solutions to this problem. On the one hand, society can be viewed as a total organism that is sustained by the various processes that comprise it. An alternative view argues that stabilizations in social systems occur not because of any rational plan of overall survival, but simply because they happen to work. These differing views of society have been labeled structural functionalist and functional structuralist, respectively. Other forms of systems theory include the actor systems approach and the sociocybernetic perspective.

Systems theory is relevant to governance because it is involved in analyzing how society adapts to its environment through adjustments in its structure. The problem of governance from this perspective becomes the problem of reaching an adequate understanding of the complex processes of social evolution. If social systems theory were followed, governance would become preoccupied with eliminating inadequate social control and reducing deviance. The problem of steering becomes the problem of recognizing that society is multicentered and formed on the basis of a multiplicity of coevolving systems. Systems theory carefully outlines that there are very real limits to our ability to steer society. On the other hand, because society is so complex, the social scientist can, nonetheless, have an appreciation of the large range of adaptive possibilities for social systems.

—Barry Gibson

See also Autopoiesis; Self-Regulating System; Sociocybernetics; Sociology of Governance

Further Readings and References

Buckley, W. (1998). *Society—A complex adaptive system: Essays in social theory.* Amsterdam: Overseas Publishers Association.

Burns, T. R., Baumgartner, T., & DeVille, P. (1985). *Man, decision, society: The theory of actor-system dynamics for social scientists.* New York: Gordon and Breach.

Durkheim, É. (1933). *The division of labour in society* (G. Simpson, Trans.). Glencoe, IL: Free Press.

Luhmann, N. (1995) *Social systems.* Palo Alto, CA: Stanford University Press.

Parsons, T. (1971). *The system of modern societies.* Englewood Cliffs, NJ: Prentice Hall.

Taoist Governance

Taoism (or Daoism) refers to a philosophical and religious tradition that has played a prominent role in the history of East Asia. Core Taoist texts present the vision of a universe that is ruled by the principle of the "Tao" or "Way." The Tao may be characterized as moral principle, as "Nature," or as limitless, metaphysical reality. Because many Taoist teachings reject social and political institutions as interfering with the natural development of human character, some scholars have concluded that Taoist governance, if it exists at all, is anarchic. However, most Taoist texts do make explicit reference to governance, arguing that the role of the ruler is not to direct people's actions or to strengthen the state but rather to facilitate the emergence of the Tao in every member of society.

The primary principle of Taoist governance is that of *wu-wei*, or "nonaction." The Taoist worldview posits a universe in which all things resonate to a cosmic principle, or Tao, and suggests that human potential is best realized when allowed to follow natural patterns of behavior. In political Taoism, the ruler is seen as a reflection of this cosmic principle, which has become obscured over time by overarticulated social norms. To practice "nonaction" means to give up attempts to direct the moral development of others through the assertion of political control. Although leadership through nonaction may sound paradoxical, it rests on the notion that rulers with a true understanding of their own cosmic nature will gain such great moral authority that their subjects will recognize this virtue and, modeling themselves on it, act in the best interests of themselves and their society with no direct action on the part of the ruler.

This political vision was originally articulated as a response to the structured, hierarchical relationships advocated by Confucian governance and other Chinese schools of thought: Where Confucianism sets up a potentially authoritarian relationship between ruler and ruled and suggests that institutions are the foundation of a moral society, Taoist governance neither advocates hierarchies nor makes recommendations about ideal institutional forms. Indeed, Taoist texts argue that it is the institutionalization of sociopolitical norms that leads to the distortion of human nature and the development of conflict.

Since the 1980s, Taoist principles of nonaction and naturalism have been increasingly employed in Western writings on management, government, self-help, personal relationships, and many other areas. Such writings argue for a "looser" management style in which work is viewed as a means to self-fulfillment and in which leaders' primary goals are conflict resolution, community building, and "going with the flow."

—Alison Adcock Kaufman

See also Confucian Governance; Religion

Further Readings and References

Ames, R. T. (1983). *The art of rulership: A study in ancient Chinese political thought.* Honolulu: University of Hawaii Press.

Clark, J. J. (2000). *The Tao of the West: Western transformations of Taoist thought.* London and New York: Routledge.

Political Taoism and Anarchist Theory [Special issue]. (1983). *Journal of Chinese Philosophy, 10*(1).

TECHNICAL-RATIONAL EXPERTISE

Technical-rational expertise refers to the role that scientific knowledge, and experts in general, have in political processes. From the point of view of democracy, this is a complex matter because it is centrally focused on the organization of politics and the role that such expertise should have in a democratic political system.

From a historical point of view, expert knowledge has been related to politics, both in practical as well as in theoretical terms. In practical terms, monarchs and rulers have always had advisors and counselors of all kinds. Likewise, the monarchs' interest in advancing technical knowledge has traditionally served specific political strategies (i.e., new military technology for territorial domination). In more theoretical terms, though, political philosophers throughout time have assigned different but central roles to scientists and scientific knowledge in the task of governing a society. This is the case of Plato, in ancient Greece, when he argued in his work *The Republic* for philosophers to rule. In relation to the consolidation of the modern state in the mid-nineteenth century, Max Weber argued that the best possible mode of political organization was based on a rational bureaucracy, as opposed to those based on personal charisma or religious dogma. His argumentation was largely based on the Enlightenment notion of state action as neutral, equal to all, and logically consistent.

With the advent of the democratic welfare state in the aftermath of World War II, the tension between democratic principles and technical-rational expertise becomes obvious. On the one hand, the functional expansion of state involvement to highly technical and complex areas (like medical care, environmental protection, consumer safety) requires adequate knowledge resources to make appropriate decisions, decisions that typically involve risk assessment (i.e., should a specific medicine or genetically modified organism be released onto the market?). On the other hand, there is a growing acknowledgment that these decisions have a political character because they affect the entire society. And why should obscure technocrats and experts take such important decisions outside governmental procedures?

This tension has been obvious since the 1970s with the legitimacy crises of technical matters most typically related to environmental protection and decisions concerning risk and safety. Society has become a risk society, with a clear risk-aversion attitude of the public and growing political contestation. But the nature of scientific knowledge has changed as well. The traditional unanimous style of scientific authority is giving way to a growing number of disputes among scientists and the emergence of alternative sources of valid knowledge outside authorized academia, which are changing the nature and dynamics of knowledge production. Both these trends are questioning the single rationality of the traditional scientific method along new lines in the philosophy of science and the hitherto technocratic form of experts' involvement in democratic political processes. However, the specific way in which this technical-rational expertise will be democratized is highly debated among political theorists.

—*Susana Borrás*

See also Bureaucracy; Rationality; Research and Development; Science; Technology

Further Readings and References

Beck, U. (1992). *Risk society: Towards a new modernity.* London: Sage Ltd.

Nowotny, H., Scott, P., & Gibbons, M. (2001). *Re-thinking science: Knowledge and the public in an age of uncertainty.* Oxford, UK: Polity Press.

Turner, S. P. (2003). *Liberal democracy 3.0: Civil society in an age of experts.* London: Sage Ltd.

TECHNOLOGY

Technology can be understood in the simplest terms as techniques for making and doing things. Originally derived from the Greek *technos* for art or craft and *logos* for speech or word, technology referred to the discourse on all arts. It was not until the seventeenth and eighteenth centuries in Europe that technology came to be understood as the techniques by which humans strive to change or control their environment. A key differentiation to highlight is that between technology and science. Technology has its origins in the earliest efforts of humans to develop tools that were used systematically in daily practice. These efforts were not always pursued based on a clear knowledge of physical or chemical properties and expected outcomes, thus technology must be seen as separate from, and primary to, the rationalistic practices of modern science. Technology analysts argue that many techniques in the past lasted much longer than would be justified by rationalism, such as the practice of alchemy, but technologies can become incorporated into social practices in ways that are difficult to change. Today, as a result, technology is often closely associated with the progress of scientific research; however, technology itself and technological inquiry long predate current scientific practice.

The history of technology thus involves discussions of thousands of years of innovations from the periods prior to the invention of the wheel to the development of tools utilized for almost instantaneous communication across vast distances and the mapping of the human genome. For these purposes, however, the discussion will highlight some key technologies in history, with a focus on those technologies that have had substantial effects on social and political organization. This will provide the context for a discussion of more recent advances in technology to emphasize current innovations that have important implications for governance.

Selected Technological Advances

Technological advances can be considered in all industries, but the innovations that have generally had the most significant effects on society at large are those with applications across many fields. One significant technology that fits this condition is the printing press.

The Printing Press

During the fifteenth century, individuals began to print documents using moveable metal type. Of particular importance was Johannes Gutenberg's establishment of a large printing shop, which was able to produce book-length texts. This shop incorporated the use of a printing press to produce regular and even text. Within fifty years, books were being printed in at least fourteen countries, and the total number of editions was nearly 40,000. This invention had wide-ranging implications.

One initial result of new printing methods was increased pressures on the paper industry, which resulted in driving reforms in the industry's structure. More significantly, increased access to printed texts created the opportunity for broad-based literacy. While the Catholic Church initially considered requiring licenses for printing presses, in the end they resisted this strategy and presses spread quickly through Europe. Ironically, one key subsequent result of increased access to printed materials was the creation of a wide audience for the writings of Martin Luther, thus precipitating the Protestant Reformation. More generally, this implied greater opportunities for the general public to access knowledge and establish an environment for debate.

A final implication of the printing press for governance was the increased importance of authorship. Consistency across copies of a text made it possible to cite the particular edition and give reference to the author. The ability to easily copy a text created important concerns for appropriate citation, and this eventually led to the establishment of copyright laws. Innovations in manufacturing and engineering during the industrial revolution led to additional print-related changes, such as the ability to produce newspapers and books for a mass audience.

The Industrial Revolution

The Industrial Revolution is a broad term that encompasses a range of social, economic, and technological changes occurring in Great Britain during the eighteenth and nineteenth centuries and then spreading to continental Europe and North America. The major drivers of initial stages in this period are the introduction of steam power and automated machinery in manufacturing. The first true commercial steam engine was developed by Thomas Newcomen in 1712. Important for the ultimate success of steam engines is that there was a specific industrial role for which they were properly suited at the time of their emergence. In the British coalfields there was a need to keep the mines empty of water, and Newcomen's steam engine was highly appropriate for achieving this goal. Steam power subsequently became the main source of power for industries during this period, thus contributing to the major shifts in industrial production of the time.

The late nineteenth century is considered the "Second Industrial Revolution," and this period was characterized by the ability to mass-produce steel cheaply, particularly for the needs of the railroads, in addition to more automation in other industries. This effort was facilitated by the availability of steam engines and contributed to major changes in transportation in Great Britain and many other countries.

The Industrial Revolution is seen by many as having driven a major shift in social organization. The emergence of more automated technologies was seen by some as a threat to the jobs of skilled workers. The Luddite movement in Great Britain destroyed many wool and cotton mills in the early 1800s until being suppressed by the national government. Analysts such as E. P. Thompson and Karl Polanyi argue that the introduction of new pricing mechanisms and free market policies during this period was the real threat to workers. Thompson posits that the actual source of the Luddites' antagonism was a shift from prices determined by custom to a fluctuation of prices based on free market principles. Polanyi had previously argued that economic reforms in Great Britain created a situation in which individual laborers were unprotected from the forces of the market. As a result, the government was forced to enact additional reforms to support the general welfare.

Nuclear Technology

The twentieth-century discoveries in atomic physics led to potentially unmatched changes in the character of warfare. While advances in nuclear fission and fusion were the important scientific foundations of nuclear weapons, the success of these weapons depended on major technological advances involving the building of large nuclear reactors and developing technology to protect humans during the handling of radioactive materials. Further advances in the technology of bombs in the postwar period contributed to continued build up and proliferation of weapons.

The use of nuclear weapons to date has been limited to attacks during World War II. However, the long-term implication of access to these weapons has been significant in terms of global governance. In the postwar period of global dominance by the United States and the Soviet Union, the development of more advanced nuclear weapons was a key factor in national defense strategies. After the Soviet Union achieved effective nuclear parity with the United States, the countries entered a situation of mutual assured destruction (MAD). MAD entailed that the full-scale use of nuclear weapons by one side would result in a similar response by the defender, thereby resulting in the destruction of both countries. Thus, an ongoing strategy of deterrence resulted in which it was perceived as necessary to maintain a large deployment of weapons in order to create the threat of retaliation for the enemy. In the post-Soviet period, a major concern of governments has been the proliferation of nuclear weapons to more countries in addition to the potential for nonstate actors to access weapons. Although the Cold War provided an inherently threatening environment, the logic of deterrence created what seemed to many to be a generally stable situation. More recently, without a clear strategic logic to guide government action under the threat of continued proliferation, national governments are faced with what may be a much less predictable nuclear situation.

The dominance of nuclear weapons also had important effects on a broader aspect of society. The growth of weapon-related industries played an important economic role in each country, while the fact of potential nuclear war also influenced the character of society in both countries for multiple generations. References to nuclear war entered into popular art and literature in addition to regular attention in the news media. Thus, the development of a new military technology by the government contributed not only to a new era of military strategy, but also to changes in economic structures and the character of society.

Recent Technological Advances

At the beginning of the twenty-first century, discussions about technology are often linked to recent innovations, such as biotechnology, information and communication technology, and nanotechnology. The implications of these technologies from a governance perspective are extensive and still emerging.

Biotechnology

Biotechnology refers to the application of discoveries made in the biological sciences to other fields. Biotechnological advances have played an important role in many areas, particularly medicine and agriculture, with genetic engineering playing a key role. In medicine, genetic engineering led to the production of human interferon, human growth hormone, and human insulin, as well as new techniques for use in diagnosis and oncology. The most controversial uses of biotechnology have been in the cloning of organisms, particularly large mammals such as sheep, and the genetic engineering of plants and animals.

Genetic engineering of plants has played an important, and again controversial, part in the agricultural sector. Because the long-term health effects of eating genetically modified foods and growing genetically modified crops are still undetermined, many people, particularly in Europe, have resisted the use of these products. At the same time, genetically modified crops have played an important role in increasing agricultural productivity in many other parts of the world and are often seen as more environmentally friendly than traditional crops.

Information and Communication Technology

Information and communication technology (ICT) refers to all of the technologies used to process and share information. ICTs became important tools in government, business, and people's personal lives as computers became smaller and less expensive, thereby making it easier for individuals to purchase personal computers for their homes and for businesses to purchase computers for their staff. The development of the Internet in the late twentieth century created the technological means to link computers and share information between them. In the 1990s, the widespread access to the Internet increased opportunities for individuals and groups to communicate with each other through their computers or other digital communication devices.

The potential for information and communication technologies is seen as incredibly broad because of the potential for their use across all industries, in the public sector, and by individuals. At the same time, access to these technologies is still limited for the majority of the world's population. Efforts to provide access are a key part of the agenda of most multilateral development organizations, such as the World Bank and the United Nations Development Program, in addition to many smaller nongovernmental organizations.

Nanotechnology

Nanotechnology is a general term used to refer to technological research and developments on the nanometer scale, with one nanometer equal to one millionth of a millimeter. An important aspect of nanotechnology is the belief that as tools get smaller, the physical forces acting on them will produce differing effects than what we currently observe. It is expected that gravity would play a lesser role in the interaction of nanotools and that surface tension and van der Waals forces would play greater roles.

The development of nanotechnology is still in its early stages at the beginning of the twenty-first century. Analysts expect that nanotechnology could be used in a wide range of fields and industries, from computers to ceramics, as applications are developed. One difficulty for progress is that researchers are still developing techniques for incorporating atoms and molecules into particular devices for specific purposes. Advances in chemistry and biology are seen as providing potential techniques for achieving these goals. Also important to consider are the potential detrimental effects of new technologies. Science fiction–style perspectives highlight the risks of nanorobots that could replicate and destroy the Earth's ecosystem through a process of global ecophagy. Less extreme threats come from the potential problems of human interaction with products such as nanodust, which could be dangerous if inhaled or ingested. As with all technologies, the potential side effects of use must be considered as a part of the development process in order to avoid such counterproductive outcomes.

All of these advances in technology create new issues for governance. As previously noted, genetic engineering has become a topic of intense international debate, particularly between the United States and the European Union. The growth in information and communication technologies has also led to a variety of new issues for governments. At one level, governments now have the ability to interact with their citizens through technology by providing government services online and thus reducing the costs of accessing these services for many individuals. Although online voting may provide an opportunity to improve vote counts, experiences in the United States also show that there are risks of vote rigging, even with electronic systems. On another level, Internet commerce and increased access to the Internet presents additional tasks for government. National governments must determine how they will tax domestic and international online purchases to ensure both growth of e-commerce and adequate national income from taxes. Issues of personal information privacy and data security on the Internet are also key issues that governments must consider in response to these new technologies.

This review of technology highlights a small portion of the thousands of technological innovations that have had an impact on social and political life. The twentieth century in particular is seen as the most

significant period of technological innovations in human history and it is expected that the twenty-first century will easily surpass this achievement. With each new technological innovation, new issues potentially arise with respect to governance that must be analyzed and reconciled with the values and goals of the polity. Governments play an important role in subsidizing research that contributes to technological innovations, while at the same time offering the most important source of regulation on the limits and bounds of technological endeavor in consideration of the benefits and threats to society.

—*Jennifer Bussell*

See also E-Democracy; E-Government; High-Reliability Organization; Science; Technology Transfer

Further Readings and References

Biotechnology. (2004). *Encyclopædia Britannica.* Retrieved from http://www.britannica.com/eb/article?tocId=9079278

Polanyi, K. (2001). *The great transformation* (4th ed.). Boston: Beacon Press

Technology, history of. (2004). *Encyclopædia Britannica.* Retrieved from http://www.britannica.com/eb/article?tocId=9108659

Thompson, E. P. (1966). *The making of the English working class.* New York: Vintage Books.

TECHNOLOGY TRANSFER

The term *technology transfer* has been used in two important ways during the latter half of the twentieth century and into the twenty-first century. In the first case, technology transfer is used to refer to the process by which research organizations and the research and development arm of public and private enterprises attempt to develop commercial uses for new technological innovations. The second use of the term refers to the transfer of technologies developed in one environment to a new environment and most often refers to the use by developing countries of technologies designed in developed countries. Each of these uses will be discussed in turn, for each process plays an important role in the availability of new and innovative technologies to various groups.

Applications for Research

Developing practical applications and commercial uses for research innovations is a fundamental aspect of business development. Both the development of initial applications for research results and the design of new applications for currently available technologies are important parts of business innovation. As a result, many government, university, and private-sector research organizations have dedicated offices for evaluating research and recognizing the commercial potential of particular results. In addition, many independent organizations and business concerns have emerged to offer support to research organizations for developing new applications. Academic research on the processes of technology transfer itself has also become an important source for analysis.

An important example of the perhaps only partially realized potential of research organizations is that of Xerox Palo Alto Research Center (PARC). PARC has produced many significant innovations that have been highly commercially viable, such as the laser printer and Ethernet. At the same time, the organization has been critiqued for failing to recognize the commercial potential of many of the organization's innovations. This highlights the importance of the technology transfer process itself and the difficulties entailed even in research organizations closely linked to commercial enterprises.

The status of research organizations as a part of commercial businesses has been a concern for government regulators in some technology industries. In the telecommunications industry, the Bell Labs component of AT&T was instrumental in the development of the theoretical foundation and technological components of telecommunications networks in the United States. Inventions such as the transistor, first developed at Bell Labs, were also subsequently used across a range of industries. After the antitrust case against AT&T in 1982, the company reduced its efforts to derive proprietary commercial benefits from the research of Bell Labs. For the most part, transfer functions continue to play an important role in companies with significant research and development capacities. Opportunities for technology transfer in this form also create significant incentives for links between major research universities and the private sector.

Technology Use in New Environments

The second important usage of technology transfer is with regard to the process by which technologies developed in one country are introduced in another country. The practice of borrowing technological tools has existed for as long as people from different areas have encountered each other, particularly through long-distance trade. More recently, opportunities for technology transfer have been highlighted as a key factor in economic development. The analysis of opportunities for "borrowing" technologies developed in other places has been an important aspect of economic historians' evaluation of the processes of the Industrial Revolution. Thorstein Veblen argued that Germany was able to industrialize quickly because it was using technologies developed in Great Britain, thereby reducing the size of investment in terms of time and capital in Germany and offering opportunities for more efficient use of these tools. Alexander Gerschenkron drew on this argument to highlight the ways in which late developers can take advantage of previously developed technologies, while also arguing that the processes of industrialization can lead to significant social and political strife. For the former colonies in the postwar period, development economists such as Albert Hirschman argued that industrialization, often using technologies designed in the already industrialized countries, could reduce the economic dependence of these countries on developed countries and utilize the underemployed populations. These efforts produced mixed results in terms of economic growth and employment, particularly in Latin America, and often led to political repression.

Therefore, an important rejoinder to the technology transfer discussion is the argument that the introduction of technologies developed for a different environment can produce unexpected outcomes when they are "borrowed." Thus, the social, political, and economic context in which a technology is introduced should be considered prior to any transfer initiative. In the 1970s, a movement began to consider what are called "appropriate technologies," or the most simple and benign technologies available to achieve a particular goal, thus minimizing potential negative consequences. This movement has emphasized sustainable technological practices and technologies that are designed for the particular context and purpose for which they will be used. Proponents of technology transfer are thus encouraged to consider the ways in which borrowed technologies will affect the environment in which they are implemented and the suitability of these technologies for particular new tasks and applications.

The opportunities for technology transfer are seen to expand well beyond industrial technologies, and this concept has been applied in recent decades to agricultural technologies, as in the green revolution, information and communication technologies, and biotechnology. The potential of all these initiatives depends at least in part on the relevance and fit of the technologies themselves with the needs and abilities present in the environment in which they are introduced.

In both cases discussed here, technology transfer involves a process by which the ideas developed in a research environment are adapted for practical use, either for the first time or for a later application in another environment. With the requisite attention to the context in which these technologies are applied, technology transfer serves as a fundamental piece of technological innovation.

—*Jennifer Bussell*

See also Communication; Science; Technology; Transnationalism

Further Readings and References

Gerschenkron, A. (1962). *Economic backwardness in historical perspective: A book of essays.* Cambridge, MA: Belknap Press of Harvard University Press.
Hirschman, A. O. (1981). The rise and decline of development economics. In A. O. Hirschman (Ed.), *Essays in trespassing.* New York: Cambridge University Press.
Veblen, T. (1954). *Imperial Germany and the Industrial Revolution.* New York: Viking Press.

TERRITORIALITY

Territoriality is the development and exercise of power through control or influence over a bounded space and its contents, including both population and resources. The closely related term *territorialization* can be defined as processes that foster territoriality in particular circumstances, usually through the assertion or material creation of linkages between particular social identities or activities and specific places. Typically, territoriality requires the division of space into areas with clear boundaries that are widely recognized both by those within them and those outside of them. Also, it is often accompanied by the creation of organizational structures dividing the claimed and controlled territory into an internal hierarchy of spatial units (e.g., states, counties, and townships).

Many theories of territoriality center on the territorialization of state power; they focus on control over a given territory as a critical component of sovereignty. However, it is vital to recognize that territoriality is also a feature of many nonstate actors, from multinational corporations to churches and from transnational social movements to informal cliques. All these actors territorialize their power, claiming bounded spaces and seeking to control or influence activities within those spaces as a way to secure and consolidate their power and then using these organized spaces to enable future activities. Moreover, it is important to note that territorialization is done not just by various actors, but to them: People can be territorialized against their will. For instance, the geographer Derek Gregory wrote a powerful account in 2004 of how the U.S. government insisted on territorializing the mobile, nonstate opponent Al-Qaeda, identifying it first with the territory of Afghanistan and then with that of Iraq, with the effect that the entire populations of those countries were then subject to U.S. efforts of territoriality.

It is not surprising that theories of territoriality have focused on the nation-state. The modern era, particularly the twentieth century, has been defined in large part by the dual territorializing processes of (a) dividing the world up into contiguous and nonoverlapping areas, each identified with a sovereign state, and (b) developing increasingly intensive territorializations of state power within those areas. So successful and pervasive were these forms of territoriality that even within the social sciences it seemed almost natural that geopolitics, social movements and change, economic growth and competition, and eventually even culture and society themselves were conceived of predominantly at the scale of nation-states. Even theories that saw capitalism as the primary shaper of the modern world accepted that for the most part, capital was territorialized into, and worked through, distinctive nation-states.

Thus, it came as a tremendous shock when states, the primary organizing "containers" of social activity, began to leak. In the last quarter of the twentieth century, linked processes often referred to collectively (if imprecisely) as "globalization" put growing pressure on dominant state-centered territorializations. Economic aspects, often referred to collectively as the decline of Fordism and the rise of a new international division of labor, included the end of the Bretton Woods agreement and the introduction of floating currency exchange rates, tremendous internationalizations of productive and finance capital, the development of major new markets, and the creation of ever-more comprehensive free trade areas and agreements. Political aspects included the breakup of the Soviet Union and end of the Cold War, the proliferation of multilateral agreements and institutions, and explosive growth in the numbers and influence of nongovernmental organizations (NGOs) and transnational social movements. Citizenship and its relationship to state territoriality were called into question by growing numbers of migrants and refugees, as well as both resurgent nationalisms and new, Diasporic nationalisms. Finally, increased awareness of the global or transboundary nature of many environmental problems and the increased ease of electronic communications of many sorts both added to the forces calling into question the relevance and utility of state-centered territoriality. States seemed to have less and less control over who and what crossed their borders and what happened within their territories.

Work on territoriality and territorialization in recent decades has focused on debates over deterritorialization and reterritorialization in the context of globalization. To many analysts, the previously described trends all revolved around increased mobility of various sorts and hence signaled an era of deterritorialization. Capital and commodities, people and political allegiances, toxins and information all appeared to move easily across national borders in new flows and networks while lacking clear national identities themselves. Many observers concluded that places, distances, and borders no longer mattered, and that these trends thus heralded the end not only of the nation-state but also of geography itself. These profound analytical mistakes flowed from the deep and largely unrecognized naturalization of state-centered territorialities in the social sciences. Challenges to, or even departures from, state-centered territorialities are only deterritorialization if the state is the natural or only scale of territoriality. Rather, the processes previously discussed are all instances of reterritorialization. Forms of territoriality—claims to and forms of control over bounded spaces—remain vital to each of the previously described developments. The comparative advantages of regionally specific production complexes are arguably more important when capital is freer to move. Diasporic nationalisms still typically draw upon or seek specific territorializations of identity. In practice, movements that call for "global" commons for environmental reasons seek new forms of control over bounded areas (e.g., the oceans), while relying upon highly territorialized clusters of participants and forms of influence for their support. Moreover, as many observers have noted, nation-states remain central and essential to many of the processes above—for example, as parties to multilateral agreements and providers of the legal and physical conditions of production for multinational firms.

—*James McCarthy*

See also Border Theory; Glocalization; Nation; State

Further Readings and References

Agnew, J. (2005). Sovereignty regimes: Territoriality and state authority in contemporary world politics. *Annals of the Association of American Geographers, 95,* 437–461.

Amin, A., & Thrift, N. (1997). Globalization, socio-economics, territoriality. In R. Lee & J. Wills (Eds.), *Geographies of economies* (pp. 147–157). London: Arnold.

Brenner, N. (1999). Beyond state-centrism? Space, territoriality, and geographical scale in globalization studies. *Theory and Society, 28,* 39–78.

Gregory, D. (2004). *The colonial present: Afghanistan, Palestine, Iraq.* Malden, MA: Basil Blackwell.

Johnston, R. (2001). Out of the 'moribund backwater': Territory and territoriality in political geography. *Political Geography, 20*(6), 677–693.

Sack, R. (1986). *Human territoriality: Its theory and history.* Cambridge, UK: Cambridge University Press.

Taylor, P. J. (1994). The state as container: Territoriality in the modern world-system. *Progress in Human Geography, 18,* 151–162.

TERRORISM

The use of terror as a method of political influence has a long history. From the Assassins and the Ku Klux Klan to Al-Qaeda and the dictators of the nineteenth and twentieth centuries, political entrepreneurs have recognized the value of employing atrocity and exemplary violence to achieve their aims; liberal democratic states have also employed terrorism on many occasions. The era of modern terrorism is generally agreed to have begun in the late 1960s. It emerged as a significant international security issue in the 1970s when a series of spectacular bombings, kidnappings, and airline hijackings were transmitted to a worldwide audience via the global media. The multifaceted challenges posed by terrorism and counterterrorism have taken on even greater salience since the devastating attacks of September 11, 2001, and the subsequent war on terrorism.

A Contested Concept

Terrorism is a highly contested concept and no agreement can be found for its definition; in both scholarly literature and official policy documents there exist hundreds of competing definitions and approaches. It is a highly pejorative term that no person or group voluntarily adopts, and with its culturally shaped connotations of savagery, criminality, and illegitimacy, the act of labeling particular instances of violence as terrorism is almost always a political judgment rather than an analytical or definitional exercise. The popular adage, "one person's terrorist is another's freedom fighter" expresses this reality. Arguably, the central problem in defining terrorism revolves around the legitimacy of violence. Although states take the view that violence by any actor other than appointed authorities is both illegitimate and illegal, there is a political tradition that maintains that violent resistance to brutal and unjust state repression is legitimate, even if it is strictly illegal. For example, the resistance to Nazi rule during World War II, anticolonial struggles in Africa and Asia, and the anti-Apartheid campaign in South Africa were all perceived as legitimate forms of non-state violence against a recognized state. Similarly, the violent resistance by the Palestinians to what is perceived by them to be an illegal and unjust military occupation by Israel is to many observers a legitimate form of struggle.

Despite these controversies, it is possible to identify some key characteristics of terrorist violence that distinguish it from other forms of violent action. First, terrorism is a form of politically motivated violence. This characteristic distinguishes it from criminal violence, although there are intense definitional contests over what constitutes a political motive. There can be many political motivations for employing terrorist violence: publicizing a cause or grievance, intimidating a population to enforce compliance, forcing a change in government policy, instigating popular revolution or social disorder, providing an additional strategy to revolutionary or guerrilla struggle, eliminating rivals or opponents, or illustrating the weakness of the state as a keeper of law and order—among many others.

A second feature of terrorist violence is that it is a form of political communication—what the early anarchists called, "propaganda of the deed." It is an act of exemplary violence designed to send messages to a range of audiences: the wider society, the authorities, external observers, potential and actual supporters, and members of the terrorist group. For this reason, the vast majority of terrorist attacks are directed at symbolic targets that serve to amplify the various messages. Thus, it is misleading to describe terrorism as random and aimed at mass casualties. Some scholars have suggested that terrorists want a lot of people watching, rather than a lot of people dead. Terrorist violence is also instrumental; it is a means to an end, rather than an end in itself. Unlike military violence, terrorists do not aim to capture strategic territory, degrade the enemy's capabilities, or physically dominate their opponent. Whether the victims of terrorist violence are chosen deliberately or incidentally, they are treated as means to objectives other than murder or destruction. These features highlight the important role of the media in the calculations of terrorist violence; in one sense, media exposure functions as the amplifier of terrorist violence.

For critical scholars, the promiscuous overuse of the term by the media and the authorities, its pejorative and judgmental connotations, and the political uses to which the language of terrorism is frequently put have robbed it of any precise or analytical value. Terrorism also functions as a modern cultural and political taboo, which paradoxically prevents terrorism scholars from contact with their primary subjects: terrorists themselves. The fear of moral contamination means that most terrorism experts have never met a terrorist and would never attempt to do so; they rely solely on secondary and usually official sources. To critical scholars, most of what passes for terrorism studies is an extension of state security discourses.

Types of Terrorism

As a generic term, terrorism encompasses a vast and heterogeneous collection of groups, tactics, and motivations for political violence. At the broadest level, a distinction is frequently drawn between state terrorism and nonstate terrorism (or terrorism from above and terrorism from below). State terrorism includes the use of terrorist violence to discipline domestic opponents, as well as the direct or indirect involvement in acts of terrorism against foreign or external enemies. Nonstate terrorism refers to groups or individuals acting outside of the authority of the state, usually directed at a particular government and in pursuit of nationalist or ideological aims. Within this basic typology, the problem of state terrorism appears far more serious than that of nonstate terrorism; terrorism from above has killed tens of millions in the previous century, while terrorism from below has resulted in tens of thousands of deaths. Reflecting its institutional bias, the field of terrorism studies remains almost solely focused on the subject of nonstate terrorism.

Within the category of nonstate terrorism, a distinction is sometimes drawn between professional and amateur terrorism. In the former category are those groups with sophisticated networks and support structures that are fighting for clearly articulated nationalist or ideological causes and who have accumulated tactical experience over a long period of sustained struggle. The Northern Ireland paramilitaries, such as the Irish Republican Army (IRA) and the Ulster Volunteer Force (UVF), the Euskadi Ta Askatasuna (ETA) in Spain, Palestinian military groups, the Tamil Tigers, Al-Qaeda, and a great many other nationalist and ideologically driven groups fall into this category. On the other hand, amateur terrorism refers to lone individual terrorists, such as the Unabomber (Ted Kaczynski) or Timothy McVeigh, or to millennial groups like the Aum Shinrikyo cult in Japan. These groups lack the tactical experience and support networks of professional terrorists and frequently have only rudimentary political programs.

Within the professional terrorism category, it is common to distinguish between nationalist, ideological, and more controversially, religious groups. Nationalist terrorism typically emerges from an ongoing struggle for self-determination or regional autonomy: Palestinian, Northern Irish, Kurdish, Basque, Tamil, Chechen, Armenian, Iraqi, and Kashmiri terrorism are all examples. Ideological terrorism reached its zenith in the 1970s, although there are still plenty of contemporary examples. Motivated by extreme Right-wing or Left-wing ideologies, these groups typically hope to provoke social revolution through violent acts: the Red Brigades in Italy, the Weathermen in America, the Japanese Red Army, the Tupamaros in Uruguay, Shining Path in Peru, and Action Directe in France are examples. The notion of religious terrorism is a recent addition to existing typologies and refers to groups with primarily religious motives for their violence. The term is usually applied to Islamic fundamentalist groups like Al-Qaeda, although it is also used to describe Right-wing antiabortion groups and cults like Bhagwan Shree Rajneesh in Oregon and the Lord's Resistance Army in Uganda. Controversy surrounds whether religion acts as a primary motive or whether it is simply a mobilizing tool for what are essentially political goals. For this reason, some scholars feel that the term *religious terrorism* is employed primarily as a political tool to paint certain groups as fanatics who lack genuine political grievances.

There are many other typologies and subcategories applied to terrorist groups, including revolutionary terrorism, dissident terrorism, nihilist terrorism, communal terrorism, criminal terrorism, narcoterrorism, ecoterrorism, cyberterrorism, and international terrorism. What they illustrate, apart from the highly contested domain of the field, is that terrorism covers an incredibly diverse array of actors, contexts, motivations, strategies, and tactics. In an important sense, each terrorist group emerges from a unique combination of historical and political contexts. From this perspective, the indiscriminate and imprecise use of the term by both the authorities and scholars serves to obscure rather than illuminate the nature and causes of specific acts of political violence.

The Threat of Terrorism

By any measure, terrorism by nonstate groups is a minor form of criminal activity and a miniscule risk to personal safety and state security. On average, nonstate terrorism is responsible for between 1,000 and 7,000 deaths per year globally—compared to the millions who have been murdered by repressive regimes. The vast majority of terrorist attacks take place in a relatively small number of countries beset by intense political conflict: Israel-Palestine, Russia-Chechnya, Kashmir, Colombia, Algeria, Iraq, Pakistan, and Spain—among others. The vast majority of countries

in the world experience no terrorism at all. Contrary to popular perceptions, the number of terrorist attacks around the world has remained steady or even declined in recent decades (depending upon the data source), the great majority of terrorist attacks are against property rather than people, and mass casualty terrorism is extremely rare; out of more than 10,000 recorded terrorist attacks since 1968, only around a dozen have caused more than 100 fatalities.

The deaths caused by nonstate terrorist violence are dwarfed by the 40,000 people who die each day from hunger, the effects of small arms in civil conflicts (500,000 deaths globally per year), and deaths caused by diseases like influenza (3.9 million annual deaths) and HIV and AIDS (2.9 million annual deaths). Statistically, the risk of being killed in a terrorist attack ranks somewhere near the risk of being killed by home repair accidents, bee stings, or getting struck by lightning. No country has ever been seriously threatened by terrorism, although a number of states have experienced severe instability when violent counterterrorist campaigns have undermined social and political order—such as Germany's disproportionate reaction to the Red Army Faction (RAF) in the early 1970s.

However, the sheer visceral horror of the September 11, 2001, attacks heightened social fear and raised the issue of mass casualty terrorism and the threat posed by so-called "super-terrorism" or "catastrophic terrorism." While the raw number of terrorist attacks has remained steady in recent years, terrorist attacks are steadily increasing in lethality. Some terrorism scholars have suggested that there is a real risk of terrorist groups using weapons of mass destruction (WMDs), such as dirty bombs or chemical attacks. They point to the Tokyo underground sarin attack and the attacks against New York and Washington, DC as evidence of increasing terrorist ruthlessness. Other scholars argue that terrorists are unlikely to use WMDs because the risks and costs are too great: they are sometimes difficult to obtain and deploy effectively compared to conventional weaponry, the risk of massive retaliation by the target state is very high, and the use of WMDs may undermine support and sympathy for the group. It is suggested that the authorities (and terrorism experts) deliberately exaggerate the threat posed by terrorism in order to expand state powers, increase military spending, discipline opponents, and create a more docile society.

The Causes of Terrorism

There is little agreement about the causes of terrorism. In large part, scholarly efforts to discover the origins of terrorist violence have been hampered by the taboo nature of the subject; the moral and political dangers of developing sympathy for their cause militate against in-depth interviews with known terrorists, for example. While the authorities encourage the popular perception that terrorists are psychopathic or mentally unbalanced individuals, every serious psychological study on the terrorist personality has concluded that terrorists are most often normal, well-adjusted individuals with no discernible psychopathology. There is no single terrorist personality; individuals join terrorist groups for an infinite number of personal and political reasons, from the desire for excitement and to be part of a tight-knit group to idealistic notions of changing the world for the better or revenge for humiliation experienced by their community. In contrast to the psychological profile of recidivist criminals for example, most terrorists are educated, emotionally stable, and economically well-off.

Other approaches suggest that terrorism arises out of a complex set of background and immediate causes that are intimately connected to local issues and historical and sociological factors, such as relative deprivation or historical injustice. From this perspective, searching for generic causes is fruitless because each terrorist group emerges from a historically specific context. Nonetheless, there is some agreement that for nationalist terrorism at least, its origins lie in the lack of effective institutions for articulating political grievances and the lack of progress in political negotiations. As levels of frustration grow across society, extremists gain support and violent struggle is seen as a legitimate form of resistance. A wide range of background and immediate factors can influence whether an oppressed society produces terrorist groups, including cultural attitudes toward violence; the level of social cohesion; the type of leaders, opportunity, and means; and historical relations between groups.

A final approach to the causes of terrorism suggests that it is the result of rational calculation based on situational exigencies and ideological considerations. From this perspective, terrorist violence is seen as the optimal strategy for achieving a group's political goals—given the nature of the enemy, the constraints the group has to operate under, and the lack of success of alternative strategies. In many cases, such as the adoption of terrorism by the African National Congress (ANC) in South Africa, it is the outcome of an evolutionary political progression in which other nonviolent strategies were first tried but then abandoned because they failed to achieve any concrete gains. Usually, terrorism appears as an effective strategy of resistance when direct military confrontation is unfeasible. Importantly, this perspective suggests that genuine political dialogue and social reform can encourage terrorist groups to abandon their violent struggle.

Responding to Terrorism

There are a great many ways of responding to terrorism. Most governments respond using force-based and coercive strategies, including suppression campaigns, punitive and preemptive military strikes, and covert operations, such as targeted assassinations, sabotage, hostage rescue missions, and rendition programs. The authorities may also attempt to enhance security around potential terrorist targets, improve emergency response procedures, and apply economic sanctions against states they suspect of supporting terrorism. Legalistic responses, by contrast, focus on enhancing law enforcement and criminal investigation and include measures such as the passing of new laws, the creation of special task forces within domestic law enforcement agencies, and improving surveillance and investigation of targeted communities. International law can provide the context for law enforcement cooperation between states, such as extradition treaties and intelligence sharing, as well as special tribunals for prosecuting terrorists. Political and conciliatory responses to terrorism involve attempts to deal with the underlying grievances and issues driving the violence. In such cases, states may engage in diplomatic negotiations with terrorist groups or their representatives or make specific political concessions in exchange for an end to the violence. Alternatively, a broad program of social and political reform may be necessary to rehabilitate the environment that caused the terrorism to emerge in the first place.

While small terrorist movements can sometimes be suppressed through force, serious terrorist campaigns have most frequently been ended through a mixture of intelligence-based and law enforcement measures, combined with substantial political progress on the central issues articulated by the terrorist groups and their constituencies. By contrast, the record of force-based terrorism or repressive counterterrorism has been very poor; in most of these cases, including Israel, Sri Lanka, Northern Ireland, Algeria, and Chechnya, the application of massive counterterrorism violence by the state has resulted in ever-greater levels of terrorist violence. So-called wars against terrorism are not only impossible to win, but they are often counterproductive; frequently, they are damaging to human rights and the functioning of democracy. In dealing with terrorism, global governance can play an important role in facilitating the political resolution of the world's intractable conflicts where most terrorism is currently taking place and providing the institutional context for enhanced international law enforcement cooperation.

—*Richard Jackson*

See also Emergency Powers; Peace Process; Post-9/11; Security; War on Terrorism

Further Readings and References

Barker, J. (2003). *The no-nonsense guide to terrorism.* Oxford, UK: Verso Books.

Crenshaw, M. (1981). The causes of terrorism. *Comparative Politics, 13,* 379–399.

Herman, E., & O'Sullivan, G. (1989). *The terrorism industry: The experts and institutions that shape our view of terror.* New York: Pantheon Books.

Kegley, C. (Ed.). (1990). *International terrorism: Characteristics, causes, controls.* New York: St. Martin's.

Martin, G. (2003). *Understanding terrorism: Challenges, perspectives, and issues.* London: Sage Ltd.

Sederberg, P. (1989). *Terrorist myths: Illusion, rhetoric, and reality.* Englewood Cliffs, NJ: Prentice Hall.

Townshend, C. (2002). *Terrorism: A very short introduction.* Oxford, UK: Oxford University Press.

Whittaker, D. (Ed.). (2001). *The terrorism reader.* London and New York: Routledge.

Zulaika, J., & Douglass, W. (1996). *Terror and taboo: The follies, fables, and faces of terrorism.* London: Routledge.

THIRD SECTOR

The third sector is an intermediary realm between the private business sector, the public sector, and the personal sector comprising family and friends. As the sum total of not-for-profit enterprises and voluntary associations within a society, the concept of the third sector is often used interchangeably with two better-known terms: the voluntary sector and the nonprofit sector.

A confluence of recent historical processes has increased the scope and depth of third-sector activity, making it an important arena of contemporary governance. The collapse of socialism and the crisis of the welfare state have diminished confidence in the capacity of the public sector to deal with contemporary economic pressures. At the same time, rapid advances in technology and communication and the growth of social movements have spawned greater public awareness of the rising social and environmental costs of expanding capitalist economies. Under these conditions, third-sector organizations provide a means of responding to the increasingly complex challenges facing modern societies.

The identification of third-sector organizations varies across disciplines. Sociologists tend to include all institutions joining individuals in voluntary association. Public administrators and economists tend to be more discriminating. The former generally equate the third sector with voluntary-based, government-directed service organizations, and the latter focus on cooperatives and nonprofit enterprises operating within the market economy. Despite the absence of a definitive, broadly accepted typology of third-sector organizations, they are generally understood as having some degree of institutionalization, formal autonomy from both the public and private sectors, and a nondistribution requirement that prevents profits from being passed on to members or owners.

There are two distinctive frameworks for understanding third-sector governance. The first situates the third sector within the context of welfare state development. Focusing on the fields of welfare, education, and health, this perspective examines the dynamics and effectiveness of service provision. In so doing, it explores issues of self-governance, such as organizational design and management, as well as issues involving public-private relations, such as regulation, financing, and accountability. The second framework emphasizes the third sector's relationship to the development of civil society. Emerging from a more sociopolitical perspective, it explores institutionalized patterns of cooperation and solidarity, the factors that affect these patterns, and their implications for democratic participation and social involvement.

While awareness of the third sector has broadened over the last decade, it continues to be underutilized as a research subject within the social sciences. As a result, key areas of interest, such as its role in policy making and its capacity and efficacy in pursuing public purposes, require further analysis.

—*Vanna Gonzales*

See also Association; Civil Society; Nonprofit Organization; Social Market

Further Readings and References

Anheir, H., & Seibel, W. (Eds.). (1990). *The third sector: Comparative studies of nonprofit organizations*. Berlin, Germany: Walter de Gruyter.

Evers, A., & Laville, J.-L. (Eds.). (2004). *The third sector in Europe*. Northampton, MA: Edward Elgar.

Gidron, B. Kramer, R., & Salamon, L. (Eds.). (1992). *Government and the third sector: Emerging relationships in welfare states*. San Francisco: Jossey-Bass.

THIRD WAY

Historically, the term *third way* has been used in a multitude of ways to refer to a variety of forms of governance—from Nordic social democracy to fascism.

In its most recent incarnation, it was deployed first by then Director of the London School of Economics, Anthony Giddens, in a string of influential publications from 1998 to 2002 to refer to an alternative to both neoliberalism and social democracy in an era of globalization. It has been associated most clearly with the New Labour administration of Tony Blair in Great Britain, but also, if less directly, with a number of Center-Left administrations, notably those of Bill Clinton's New Democrats in the United States and Gerhard Schröder's Social Democratic Party (SPD) in Germany. The term is taken to variously refer to a new and distinctive policy program, to a new political economy, to a new conception of social justice, and, by many of its critics, to a Center-Left capitulation to neoliberal globalization.

Anthony Giddens is relatively specific as to the policy content of the third way, distinguishing it unequivocally from both neoliberalism to the Right and a "traditional" conception of social democracy to the Left. But herein lies the first potential confusion. Though clearly framed in the first instance to chime with the mood of modernization associated with the birth of New Labour in Great Britain, the aspirations for the third way have grown over time. So too has its intended audience. It is now presented as a guide to good governance, appropriate to conditions of globalization and complex economic and social interdependence for developed and developing economies alike, as Giddens noted in 2002. Yet arguably it continues to betray its origins in domestic British political discourse. For instance, the conception of social democracy, from which it distances itself, is scarcely recognizable to students of the latter's distinctive (and arguably defining) Nordic/Scandinavian form. Indeed, the conception of social democracy to which Giddens's third way is a response in fact owes far more to Great Britain's peculiar experiments with corporatism in the 1960s and 1970s than it does to the continental European tradition of social democracy— a tradition to which the British Labour party and movement never really belonged. Indeed, the rather ambiguous nature of the relationship between the third way and social democracy is merely compounded by periodic references to the third way as a "modernized" social democracy fit for the new prevailing social, political, and economic landscape of contemporary capitalism. This sits uneasily alongside the idea of the third way as "beyond Left and Right," that is, beyond social democracy and neoliberalism.

Yet whether conceived as an alternative to, or an updating of, the social democratic tradition, the central and defining features of the third way are set out very clearly by Giddens:

1. A commitment to the seemingly paradoxical notion of the radical center and, with it, to the idea that a modernizing Center-Left administration can draw radical zeal from Left and Right simultaneously

2. An emphasis on the "new democratic state" and with it a commitment to a more open and dialogic conception of international politics (and, rather naively, as it was to turn out, to "states without enemies"), to raising environmental consciousness and, domestically, to a far more transparent, direct, and open form of participatory government that empowers the citizen

3. An associated emphasis upon a more active and engaged civil society that has taken greater responsibility for its own governance through a proliferation of more community-based initiatives and an expanded role for the third sector

4. A commitment to the sustenance by public policy of the "democratic family" and with it an associated emphasis upon support for coparenting, gender equality, and life-long parental contracts

5. An emphasis upon the "new mixed economy" and an acceptance (from neoliberal variants of public choice theory) of the need for public-private partnerships, private finance initiatives, and the incentivization of consumer-friendly public service provision

6. A commitment to "equality as inclusion" and with it a far greater emphasis upon providing appropriate opportunities for citizens to improve themselves (for instance, investing in their own human capital) rather than the pursuit of equality of outcome

7. An associated commitment to the notion of "positive welfare" and of "no rights without responsibilities"

8. A commitment to the development of the "social investment state" and to the use of public resources to build the national stock of human capital, thereby contributing to competitiveness and good economic performance

9. An emphasis upon the development of a genuinely "cosmopolitan nation" celebrating cultural diversity and pluralism

10. A commitment to extending such cosmopolitan values into the international areas through a democratization of the institutions of global governance

This is undoubtedly an original and distinctive combination of programmatic commitments and one that clearly draws inspiration from both Left and Right. However, what is perhaps odd is that having set out to chastise traditional social democracy, the third way seems to embrace a series of policy goals that arguably have been most successfully pursued in social democratic regimes. Notable here is the third way's commitment to raising environmental consciousness (and standards), to the democratic family, to coparenting, to greater gender equality, and to a social investment state. These have been mainstays of continental European social democracy throughout much of the postwar period; arguably traditional social democratic regimes continue to enjoy far greater success in fulfilling their commitment to these goals than those states whose leaders have come to embrace the third way.

A second interesting point is that the political economy of the third way is seemingly rather underdeveloped. Indeed, if much of the social and ecological policy innovation of the third way can—or at least could—trace a direct lineage from traditional social democracy, the economic policy content seems decidedly neoliberal in tone. Notable here is the enthusiastic endorsement of market and quasi-market mechanisms in the delivery of public services and in the incentivization of public-sector performance. This is particularly significant because, it seems, much of the third way is about scaling back social democratic expectations and ambitions so they do not challenge economic competitiveness in an era of globalization.

Although it is rarely presented in such terms, this may suggest the third way is underpinned centrally by an understanding of the constraints imposed on Center-Left administrations by globalization. Indeed, the third way is perhaps best seen less as a self-contained ethos and conception of social justice informing policy rather than as a more pragmatic downscaling of social democratic aspirations to an age of diminished policy-making autonomy. Again, this reveals a certain ambiguity at the heart of the third way. Its pragmatism and realism in the face of insurmountable, external, and (largely) economic constraints is prominent. Yet, simultaneously, it is invariably held by its advocates to provide a guiding ethic and a universal conception of social justice to inform policy choices in a programmatic way. As such, we might expect it to provide an exacting ethical standard against which, for instance, contending economic and social policy choices might be gauged. Yet the third way tends not to hold economic and social policy accountable to an ethical standard so much as to construct a standard of perceived political economic viability against which any ethical considerations must first be assessed. Indeed, it seems, particular perceptions of political economic constraints—associated in particular with globalization—impose a recalibration of a more traditional social democratic ethos. It is in this sense that the third way is an updating of traditional social democracy. It seeks to retain those elements of a social democratic ethos that are still held to be compatible with economic growth in an era of presumed globalization.

As this suggests, despite impressions to the contrary, third way political economy comes prior to its ethics. Indeed, it is assumed to both correspond to, and arise naturally out of, an economic reality that has rendered social democracy redundant. As this makes clear, the third way rests upon a set of economic assumptions—about the extent and nature of globalization and the degree to which it is incompatible with social democracy. Yet those economic assumptions are far from unquestioned and, as a growing body of scholarship now shows, are in fact increasingly difficult to reconcile with the empirical evidence.

Despite the third way's reliance upon a particular, and now contested, conception of economic constraint associated with globalization, in economic policy terms at least, what it sanctions or embraces is far from clear; it is far clearer about what it rejects than what it sanctions or embraces. The third way rejects Keynesianism, the economic theory of John Maynard Keynes. Moreover, if taken to imply an unconditional right of access of all citizens to a comprehensive welfare state, a belief in democratic economic governance (as distinct

from the governance by the economy of the realm of political choice), and a commitment to egalitarian social outcomes (as distinct from opportunities), it is post–social democratic. More substantively, it rejects nationalization, interventionism, active industrial policy (which it characterizes as "backing losers"), what it sees as regulation for its own sake, deficit financing, corporatism, and the appeasement of labor more generally.

This excepted, there is no sustained discussion of the economy in Giddens's 1998 work, *The Third Way.* That discussion came in 2000, in *The Third Way and Its Critics.* Here, having acknowledged the criticism that there is no economic policy content to the third way, Giddens retrospectively linked the ethical vision outlined in *The Third Way* to a new Keynesianism, with which he can hardly be said to be fluent. This is never fleshed out in any detail. Giddens makes a passing reference to the importance of policy for the supply side of the economy. Similarly, the importance in the new knowledge economy of investment in human and, indeed, social capital is included. Together, these underdeveloped remarks exhaust the substantive content of third way political economy. Given that the third way presents the economic aspect as circumscribing the parameters of policy autonomy in a quite fundamental way, this comparative silence is all the more remarkable. The need for an alternative to the first and second ways (neoliberalism and social democracy respectively) is presented in economic terms. Yet the case is never made. Consequently, the third way, unlike other political philosophies or conceptions of social justice, demands an economic analysis that it does not provide.

This has serious implications for the conception of social justice that it is capable of articulating. Any consistent conception of social justice is compromised by the perceived need to scale one's ethical aspirations in accordance with assumed (economic) constraints and imperatives. In other words, rather than defend, in its own terms and from first principles, a particular conception of social justice, the third way must choose its conception of social justice pragmatically, having first eliminated all those deemed incompatible with the harsh economic realities of a global era. Where issues of equity and economic efficiency are seen to clash, the overriding imperative is economic growth. Social solidarity and, one must presume, social justice are viewed as something of a luxury: desirable, certainly, but only where the imperatives of the former allow. What this in turn suggests is that if a distinctive third way ethic emerges, it is more by chance than by design or conviction.

This makes the status of the third way as a guiding political ethos somewhat unclear. In strictly ethical terms, is it normatively superior to the social democratic ethos it seeks to replace? Or is it merely the best one can aspire to when the (presumed) incompatibility between social democracy and globalization is acknowledged? Is the third way the best in this best of all possible worlds, to paraphrase *Candide*'s Doctor Pangloss? Or is it the best conceivable ethos in a world of diminished expectations and radically circumscribed political autonomy? One thing is clear—it is disingenuous to present it as both.

This brings us to a final observation. The third way does not provide an ethic that can inform future policy choices so much as a language that legitimates choices that have already been made. Presented with a particular policy challenge, it would be difficult to argue that a quick read of Giddens's *Third Way* might allow one to derive the "correct" policy response, as distinct from the language that defends policy choice. There is no single third way answer to the question, Should an economy have a minimum wage? The third way supplies an ethical lexicon with respect to which either choice might be legitimated; it does not provide discriminating ethical standards that might inform the choice itself. Herein lies its much-vaunted pragmatism. New Labour policy is legitimated not by appeal to ethical standards and principles but with respect to the presumed truth of certain social (and economic) facts. This is nowhere more clear than in the economic sphere. The third way rests on a set of presumed truths about the economic context in which Center-Left economic governance is played out. Such "truths" rest on strong claims about globalization, whose validity is now seriously challenged.

—*Colin Hay*

See also Globalization; Political Economy; Public-Private Partnership; Social Democracy; Social Market; Workfare

Further Readings and References

Bevir, M. (2005). *New Labour: A critique.* London: Routledge.

Finlayson, A. (1999). Third way theory. *Political Quarterly, 70*(3), 271–279.

Giddens, A. (1998). *The third way: The renewal of social democracy.* Cambridge, UK: Polity Press.

Giddens, A. (2000). *The third way and its critics.* Cambridge, UK: Polity Press.

Giddens, A. (2002). *The global third way debate.* Cambridge, UK: Polity Press.

Hay, C. (2004). Credibility, competitiveness and the business cycle in third way political economy. *New Political Economy, 9*(1), 39–56.

Hay, C. (2005). The impact of globalization on states. In J. Ravenhill (Ed.), *Global political economy.* New York: Oxford University Press.

Hirst, P., & Thompson, G. (1999). *Globalisation in question* (2nd ed.). Cambridge, UK: Polity Press.

THIRD-WORLD DEBT

The rapid growth in the external debt of third-world states has been a key issue since the early 1980s. Debt itself is not something that is unique to the third world. The United States also has a huge public debt, but at present it has the means to manage it. Debt only becomes a potential problem when the borrower is unable to generate sufficient funds to meet the repayments. Many countries in the third world have encountered such difficulties, and often commentators have used the term *debt crisis* to describe the situation. The issue became public knowledge in August 1982 when Mexico declared that it could no longer meet the repayments on its external debt. Since then many of the poorest countries in the world have had to make sacrifices in key areas of public spending in order to service their debt.

During this period the World Bank and International Monetary Fund (IMF) have become key players by offering conditional loans and advice to try to help manage third-world debt. Nevertheless, debt remains a major issue for many countries in the third world. For 2002, the total stock of external debt for all developing countries stood at approximately

US$2.3 trillion. This represents thirty-nine percent of the gross national income (GNI) of these countries. For sub-Saharan Africa, where the majority of the world's most heavily indebted countries are to be found, external debt rises to seventy percent of the GNI.

Historical Origins

The origins of the debt crisis in the third world can be traced back to the oil price shock of 1973–1974. At the time, the member states of the Organization of Petroleum Exporting Countries (OPEC) limited the supply of oil, which resulted in a huge increase in the price. This had a significant impact on all importers of oil, including many newly independent countries in the third world. The excess profits that OPEC members received were then invested in the Western commercial banking sector. The banks then sought to find new borrowers to lend this money to. Countries in the third world, which were in need of development assistance to soften the impact of increased oil prices, were considered a sensible and safe option by the banks. This meant that during the second half of the 1970s, a significant proportion of the flows of capital to the third world came from commercial banks. This flow of funds from OPEC-member states to commercial banks and then on to countries in the third world is often described as petrodollar recycling.

Three key factors led to the emergence of a crisis in third-world debt in the early 1980s. First, there was a second oil price shock in 1979. This led to economic recession in Western economies and also put a further strain on the balance of payments of oil-importing countries in the third world. The banks offered further loans to third-world countries at this point so they could satisfy these pressures. Second, a shift in economic policy making took place in the West (in particular the United States and the United Kingdom), and this resulted in the use of interest rates to control inflation. With inflation set to rise sharply as a result of the increase in oil prices, interest rates were significantly increased in an effort to contain inflation. This rise in global interest rates dramatically increased the costs of debt servicing for third-world countries. Third, the recession in the West multiplied the

problems for the third world. Faced with the need to raise additional foreign exchange to meet their debt repayments, one option would have been to increase their exports. However, the market for what were mostly primary commodities had declined as a result of the economic downturn in the West, and this depressed prices for the majority of third-world commodity exports.

What Kind of Crisis?

Two different interpretations of the nature of the third-world debt crisis have dominated the debate since the early 1980s. The majority view in the West has been that the crisis poses a threat to the stability of the international financial system as a whole. This stance is often associated with the view that most of the responsibility for the crisis rests with the borrowing countries. It is suggested that they must take responsibility for the loans they took out. Many liberal theorists would argue that by ignoring the underlying problems of their economies, and by using private banks to fund serious balance of payments problems, governments in the third world were avoiding the issue of economic adjustment. An alternative reading of events, mostly to be found in the third world itself, argues that while the collapse of the international financial system appears to have been avoided, the issue of third-world debt remains a crisis of development. Here more responsibility is assigned to the commercial banks that, with the support of governments in the West, engaged in a reckless lending strategy.

Management of the Debt

The initial response to the third-world debt crisis was an approach centered on short-term measures to prevent debt defaults. The IMF and World Bank provided loans that were conditional on borrowing countries following a series of structural adjustment measures. These were designed to increase the productivity of their economies in the hope that this would enable them to resolve their problems. By the mid-1990s it had become clear that the debt crisis was a long-term phenomenon. Despite most third-world countries following the adjustment policies of the IMF and World Bank, the debt problem remained. This resulted in the launch of the heavily indebted poor countries (HIPC) initiative in 1996. For the first time, limited relief of debts owed to the World Bank and IMF became part of the approach. However, critics of the HIPC have argued that this relief was still linked to structural adjustment conditions that were similar to those attached to earlier loans. In contrast to all these measures, over recent years the Jubilee Debt Campaign and other global civil society organizations have called for wholesale debt cancellation.

—*Stephen R. Hurt*

See also International Monetary Fund; Neocolonialism; Oil Crisis; Organization of the Petroleum Exporting Countries; Washington Consensus; World Bank

Further Readings and References

Cline, W. R. (1995). *International debt reexamined.* Washington, DC: Institute for International Economics.
George, S. (1988). *A fate worse than debt.* London: Penguin.
Hertz, N. (2004). *IOU: The debt threat and why we must defuse it.* London: Fourth Estate.
World Bank. (2004). *Global development finance 2004: Harnessing cyclical gains for development.* Washington, DC: Author.

TOBIN TAX

The Tobin tax is a proposed tax on short-term currency transactions. The tax is designed to deter only speculative flows of hot money—money that moves regularly between financial markets in search of high short-term interest rates. It is not meant to impact long-term investments. The effective rate of tax will be higher the shorter the investment cycle (i.e., the time between buying and selling a currency), thus providing market-based incentives for lengthening the term structure of investments. Such taxes tend to be named after James Tobin, the Nobel laureate in Economics who first popularized the idea of a levy on

currency transactions in the early 1970s. In one of his final interviews for the German newspaper *Der Spiegel,* Tobin subsequently distanced himself from the campaign that now typically bears his name, arguing that campaigners were right to support a currency transactions tax, but they were doing so for the wrong reasons. Three reasons are usually cited for introducing such a tax and, while Tobin concentrated on the economic justifications for taxing speculative flows of hot money, others have recently focused instead on the positive global causes that could be financed from the revenue from the tax.

This is perhaps understandable because the daily turnover on foreign exchange markets is now so out of proportion compared with all other forms of economic activity that even the tiniest currency transactions tax would raise huge sums of money. It would provide a means of global redistribution, enabling poverty to be tackled at the source. Despite concerns about the viability of enforcing the tax, its revenue would allow any number of development goals to be met. In addition, a Tobin tax would also act as a defense mechanism against destabilizing speculation within the foreign exchange market. As the Asian financial crisis proved so conclusively, whole economic systems can fall prey to the effects of momentum trading, whereby the loss of confidence in a currency can lead to wholesale economic collapse.

However, neither of these were Tobin's reason for supporting the imposition of a currency transactions tax. Tobin's concern was that policymakers should be able to determine policy in a context that was undisturbed by flows of hot money destabilizing the domestic currency. The tax therefore represents a means of reactivating a sphere of autonomous policy making. Tobin tailored his argument primarily to the position encountered by developing countries. He wished to see developing countries integrated more fully into the dynamics of international trade, and using public policy to reduce speculation against their currencies assisted this goal. At the time that Tobin was writing, speculative pressures against the currencies of developing countries proved particularly difficult to resist, which added a considerable degree of exchange rate risk into, and hence undermined, their trading relationships with other countries.

—*Matthew Watson*

See also Derivative; Foreign Exchange Market

Further Readings and References

Eichengreen, B., Tobin, J., & Wyplosz, C. (1995). Two cases for sand in the wheels of international finance. *Economic Journal, 105,* 162–172.

Tobin, J. (1978). A proposal for international monetary reform. *Eastern Economic Journal, 4,* 153–159.

Weaver, J., Dodd, R., & Baker, J. (Eds.). (2003). *Debating the Tobin tax: New rules for global finance.* Washington, DC: New Rules for Global Finance Coalition.

TOP-DOWN APPROACH

The top-down approach, described as an "iron fist" or "velvet glove" mode of governance, is characterized by a powerful, hierarchical state where a political elite devises policy that is then implemented through a strict, sequential, and stable chain of command via bureaucrats and service providers. It emphasizes national planning, rationality, command, control, obedience, and constraints, and evokes notions of red tape and bureaucracy.

A top-down approach to governance presents a clear divide between top-level policy formulation and the subsequent implementation of these preset goals by administrators and service providers. The process of enacting policy is viewed as an implementation chain where links must be forged between various agencies. However, the more links there are in a chain, the less the likelihood of successful implementation.

Several "ideal types" of this approach have been formulated, where, against a backdrop of perfect communication and no time constraints, the state uses regimented, clear lines of authority to control a series of causal stages to enforce its norms and objectives and to minimize any conflict or deviation from its aims. The quality of intragovernmental relations is vital; these relations must encompass clear and recognized goals, close cooperation, and adequate resources. Implementation failure occurs due to incorrect strategy, weak operationalization, the wrong use of policy instruments, or poor programming of the bureaucracy. In other words, if the correct sequence of events is pursued, the policy will succeed. Hence, the practical role of political science is to provide rational analysis (and mathematical modeling) to provide steps for the policy elite to control or improve the implementation process.

With the advent of alternative bottom-up approaches, these "ideal types" drew heavy criticism. Empirical work found such prescriptive rational models to be flawed in theory and practice, and the top-down approach to governance was viewed as a myth that collapsed when compared with everyday political life. With bottom-up approaches, the traditional focus of political scientists on how those at the top exercise their political will neglected the impact of bureaucrats and "street-level" service providers on whether a policy is successfully implemented and overlooked the dynamism these groups bring to the policy process.

The top-down approach came to be seen as a theory devoid of human interaction that grossly oversimplified the complexity of implementation and assumed what counts as successful public policy outcomes was uncontentious. It depoliticized the relationship between policy and action, and underplayed notions of power and dependence between agencies. It overlooked complex patterns of human motivations, behavior, and interests. Conflict, bargaining, and compromise were seen as dysfunctional, whereas these are essential features of bottom-up approaches.

More recent criticisms are that top-down notions are more about government than governance and disempower public servants and citizens; and the emphasis on centralized command and control is anachronistic and does not square with the decline or "hollowing out" of state power.

—*Claire Donovan*

See also Bottom-Up Approach; Bureaucracy; Hierarchy; Hollow State; Policy Implementation; Security Community; State

Further Readings and References

Hood, C. (1976). *The limits of administration.* London: Wiley.

Parsons, W. (1995). Delivery analysis. In *Public policy: An introduction to the theory and practice of policy analysis.* Aldershot, UK: Edward Elgar.

Pressman, J., & Wildavsky, A. (1973). *Implementation.* Berkeley: University of California Press.

TRADE AGREEMENTS

The underlying framework for trade agreements resides in one of the multilateral institutions created under U.S. leadership after World War II. Those institutions include the International Monetary Fund (IMF), to help countries with temporary balance of payments problems; the World Bank, to provide support for reconstruction and economic development; and the General Agreement on Tariffs and Trade (GATT), to provide a framework for international trade-policy negotiations and a mechanism for settling trade disputes. A more comprehensive international trade organization was planned to facilitate liberalized trade among nations but was not ratified by the U.S. Congress for fear of yielding control over trade policy to an international entity. Much of the rationale for GATT was to harness mercantilist motives in the interest of trade liberalization.

Thus, GATT's articles of agreement codified behavioral principles for participating nations' trade in goods from 1947 to 1995, when the World Trade Organization (WTO) was founded. These behavioral principles included first and foremost a commitment to negotiating reduced tariffs, which, as tariff levels have been reduced over successive rounds of negotiations, has expanded to include a host of nontariff barriers to trade. A second principle is nondiscrimination in imports and exports, expressed in the form of most-favored nation (MFN) treatment, now replaced by the term *normal trade relations* (NTR). This principle ensures that a tariff reduction made to one nation is extended to all nations to whom a country has extended MFN status, typically all GATT (now WTO) member nations. An exception to the MFN rule is established in GATT Article XXIV, which allows for the creation of preferential trade agreements (PTA) outside of the GATT framework, if they increase the domain of liberalized trade. Examples of this type of agreement would include a free trade area (FTA) and a customs union (CU). (In an FTA, there is free movement of goods originating from within the member countries, whereas in a customs union, internal free trade is accompanied by a common external tariff—on goods from outside the member nations.) Among the successful regional agreements that have been negotiated are the European Union (EU), North American Free Trade Agreement (NAFTA), Mercosur, the Andean Community (the latter two now merged to form the South American Community of Nations), the East African Community, and the Association of Southeast Asian Nations (ASEAN) Free Trade Area.

A second exception to MFN was envisioned for the developing countries and expressed in GATT Article XVIII, which gave them additional leeway in using tariffs and quantitative restrictions to achieve development objectives. These provisions came to be seen as inadequate, and in 1964 the first United Nations Conference on Trade and Development (UNCTAD), held in Geneva, put developing countries' demands for aid and preferential access to rich nations' markets on the multilateral negotiating menu. After initial reluctance, rich nations eventually implemented a preferential arrangement, the generalized system of preferences (GSP) for developing countries' manufactures, though the program was circumscribed by safeguard measures to limit market disruption.

A third principle is the prohibition of quantitative restrictions on trade, but GATT Article XI articulates that the principle had a long list of exceptions, such that one could say it began as a principle in principle. In GATT framework, no agreement governing trade in agriculture was put in place, and rules have only slowly been agreed to over the years. In the meantime, quantitative restrictions (quotas) were widely used to protect domestic agriculture. However, in the Uruguay Round of multilateral GATT negotiations that concluded in 1994, GATT member countries agreed to transform quantitative restrictions into tariff form, at least in part to provide a basis for comparison across countries and to facilitate negotiations to lower levels of protection. Despite that progress, the goal of reducing protection for domestic agriculture remains exceptionally challenging.

Similarly, provisions under GATT Article XIX for temporary import restrictions to alleviate serious injury from imports were frequently sidestepped as countries employed safeguards and escape clauses once intended for temporary relief to engineer enduring restrictions on trade. Orderly marketing agreements (OMA) and voluntary export restraints (VER) came into wider and wider use, notably in textiles, and arrangements between the United States and Japan to limit Japan's cotton textile exports in the late 1950s grew into the Multifiber Agreement (MFA) of 1974. Under the MFA, the industrialized countries negotiated quotas on textiles and clothing imports from developing countries. The Uruguay Round secured agreement to terminate the MFA beginning in 2005.

The Uruguay Round, which also put in place the machinery of the World Trade Organization (WTO), launched in 1995, followed a number of earlier successful multilateral negotiating rounds to reduce tariffs under the auspices of the GATT, most notably the Kennedy and Tokyo Rounds. These rounds successfully lowered the average level of tariffs in developed countries and fostered a massive expansion of global trade that continues into the present. Currently, multilateral negotiations are under way in what is known as the Doha Round, with agriculture, abuse of antidumping measures, services, and Trade-Related Aspects of Intellectual Property Rights (TRIPS) among the agenda items.

While multilateral negotiating rounds under the GATT/WTO generate tariff and trade barrier reductions for all member countries, PTAs discriminate between member countries and the rest of the world. For a customs union, such as the EU, this raises the question of whether the formation of the PTA expands trade among member nations (trade creation) more than it reduces prior trade with low-cost producers in the rest of the world (trade diversion because of the common external tariff). Such considerations must be balanced against the potential efficiency gains from economies of scale in a larger market as well as the potential for increased competition. Finally, although multilateral nondiscriminatory liberalization has characterized much of the trajectory of trade agreements since World War II, bilateral and regional trade agreements have proliferated in recent years, and progress on difficult issues may be made first within trading blocs and only eventually multilaterally. These agreements may also introduce new challenges to trading relations. NAFTA's inclusion of labor and environmental issues in the agreement brought those two contentious issues to the forefront of multilateral negotiations as well. And some of Singapore's newly concluded bilateral agreements go beyond trade to include factor flows such as foreign direct investment, which over time can alter the country's underlying endowments and change the basis for trade.

—*Thomas Willet and James A. Lehman*

See also Asia-Pacific Economic Cooperation; World Trade Organization

Further Readings and References

Destler, I. M. (2005). *American trade politics* (4th ed.). Washington, DC: Institute for International Economics.
Jackson, J. H. (1997). *The world trading system: Law and policy of international economic relations* (2nd ed.). Cambridge: MIT Press.

TRADE UNION

Trade unions are groups of workers who combine together in order to defend and enhance their political, legal, and civil rights, and to maintain and improve their terms and conditions of employment through collective bargaining with the representatives of employers and government. The principal bargaining tool of the trade union has been the capacity for its members to threaten the withdrawal of their labor, through either official or unofficial strikes.

Trade unions were formed initially in Great Britain, the world's first industrial nation. Following the mass migration of agricultural laborers into squalid living and working conditions in England's polluted and overcrowded industrial cities, groups of workers began to combine in an attempt to improve their quality of life in general and pay and conditions of employment in particular. Until 1824 it remained illegal for workers to organize themselves into trade combinations, and it was not until February 1867 that the formation of a Royal Commission of Inquiry into Trade Unions finally established their legal status in Britain. The following year, the Trade Union Congress (TUC) was founded to provide the world's first national body for the representation of workers' interests.

The peak of trade union activity was during the first half of the twentieth century. For example, in Britain during 1926, a record 160 million working days were lost to strike activity. Eventually, the prevalence of labor disputes became a source of national shame and ridicule. The disruption of production by strike action became known as the "British disease." In 1969, the government under Harold Wilson attempted to reduce strike activity through its "In Place of Strife" legislation, but the legislation was defeated by divisions within the Cabinet over the issue. A decade of industrial unrest followed, which culminated in the Winter of Discontent, the loss of 29 million days lost to strike action during 1979, and the election of Prime Minister Margaret Thatcher.

Labeling the trade unions as "the enemy within," the Thatcher government's reforms of labor markets, including the removal of the trade unions' legal immunity from prosecution for the costs arising from strikes, ushered in the era of deregulated labor markets and declining union membership and strike activity. By 1994, the number of working days lost to labor disputes in the United Kingdom had fallen to only 0.3 million.

Although in autumn 2003, 7.4 million British workers remained trade union members, this amounted to only twenty-seven percent of those in employment, compared with twenty-nine percent in 1995.

The wider role played by trade unions in national governance has been most evident in the overthrow of authoritarian regimes in Apartheid South Africa and communist Eastern Europe. In South Africa, the formation of the Congress of South African Trade Unions (COSATU) in December 1985 provided a major landmark on the road to the abolition of Apartheid. Members of COSATU were also in the vanguard of the African National Congress as it evolved from a campaigning group against Apartheid to a party of government following the release of Nelson Mandela from prison. However, it was in Eastern Europe during the 1980s that the role of trade union power in transforming the pattern of governance was most prominent.

In Poland, Solidarity, a federation of thirty-six regional trade unions, was founded on September 22, 1980, following a series of strikes at the Gdansk shipyards. Under the leadership of Lech Walesa, Solidarity soon attracted a membership of more than ten million Polish workers and began to press for wholesale political and economic reforms to the communist system, including the introduction of free elections. Following a series of major strikes during 1981, martial law was imposed on December 13, 1981, and the union officially was disbanded by the Polish Parliament on October 8, 1982. Although the trade union movement was driven underground, it reappeared in 1988 when workers pressed for the official recognition of Solidarity. Two months after its official legalization in April 1989, Solidarity won 99 of 100 seats in the newly established upper house of the Polish Parliament. It also won all 161 seats that could be contested by opposition political parties in the lower house. The transformation of Solidarity from an underground political movement to an official party of government was completed, first, in August 1989 when it formed a coalition government and, second, in December 1990 when Lech Walesa was elected as the President of Poland.

The decline in the political significance of trade unions in many major industrialized economies may be attributed to a number of factors, including the deregulation of labor markets, the privatization of state industries, the liberalization of the markets for goods and services, and the increasing salience of female, part-time employment in service industries. Nevertheless, trade unions continue to play a significant role in global governance. Trade unions are represented internationally by the International Confederation of Free Trade Unions (ICFTU), which was established in 1949 and now possesses 233 affiliated organizations in 154 countries. The total membership of ICFTU's affiliates is 145 million, forty percent of whom are women. In the governance of labor markets, the ICFTU has played a prominent role in campaigning for international labor standards, trade union rights, gender and racial equality, and the eradication of forced and child labor.

Since the creation of the World Trade Organization (WTO), the ICFTU has provided a series of important reports for the WTO's General Council Review, including analyses of the extent to which the United States and the member states of the European Union have ratified the eight core International Labour Organization (ILO) conventions on core labor standards. While most of the EU's twenty-five member states have ratified all eight conventions, the United States has ratified only two so far. Thus, the degree of trade union rights for workers continues to vary considerably between major markets.

—*Simon Lee*

See also Collective Wage Bargaining; Corporatism; Social Democracy

Further Readings and References

Van Roozendaal, G. (2002). *Trade unions and global governance*. London: Continuum.

TRADITION

Traditions are webs of related practices comprised of inherited patterns of thought and actions. They are constituted by beliefs and practices that are handed down from the past. A tradition is a temporal chain that exhibits the historical continuity of the individual beliefs and practices that make it up, each of which expresses some formative influence on subsequent incarnations. In addition to the temporal connections that result from providing the starting point for its later exemplars, the instances properly thought to make a tradition embody conceptual connections with one another. The beliefs and practices of a tradition that are transmitted over time exhibit at least a minimal level of conceptual coherence and consistency, forming an intelligible whole that evinces why they go together. Thus, we call tradition the chain of variant interpretations that people make, as in the Kantian tradition or the liberal tradition. As a sequence or chain of interpretive variations that people receive and transmit over time, traditions are connected by the development of common themes, not limited to the contiguity of presentation and departure or descent from a common origin.

Many things affect human behavior and that which can be socially transmitted through time is a broad category, including ritual practices, habits, images of people and events, and beliefs of all kinds—be they secular or sacred, transmitted orally or through writing, formed through experience or arrived at by ratiocination and logical deduction. Material objects may well be thought to comprise traditions—a particular monument, building, machine, painting, or novel is sometimes invoked as a particular tradition. But it is the cluster of qualities and ideas they embody in representation that are properly thought to make a tradition. No concrete practice, institution, or object itself endures through time, since an action ceases to exist once it is performed and objects are undergoing continuous morphosis due to their inherent molecular activity and by dint of their changing environment. The transmissible parts of human life that can endure as traditions, however, are the mental images, memories, patterns of actions, and clusters of related ideas about them.

Traditions are normative as they constitute conditions for subsequent actions and in most cases also precedents for what future actions should be like. The patterns that guide action have to do with not only the ends sought but the conceptions of appropriate and effective means to attain those ends, along with the relationships that result from and are maintained by those actions. Traditions are thus normative in the sense that they incorporate beliefs for requiring, permitting, recommending, or otherwise regulating its reenactment. For this reason, traditions perform the role of socialization and the inculcation of particular beliefs, value systems, and specific conventions of behavior. Because traditions rely on group membership—in the form of communities that are either real or artificial—they not only symbolize but also legitimize social cohesion. Traditions are further normative in the sense that they establish or endorse particular social institutions and relations of power and authority.

Despite the many normative aspects of traditions, being handed down does not itself logically entail any explicit expectation that it should be accepted, appreciated, or otherwise assimilated. Traditions do not independently establish or reproduce themselves; no tradition can elaborate or promulgate itself. Only living, knowing, and desiring human beings can enact and reenact a tradition. No tradition exists apart from those who propound, subscribe to, and otherwise recognize various conceptions as such. Above all, the characteristic feature of a tradition is that the pattern of thought and action in question is created and recreated by people through their interactions with each other, relayed through several generations of remaking by interpersonal means. When we speak of any tradition, thus, we speak of that which has exemplars and custodians.

Because a tradition's constellations of symbols and meanings are only received and modified through interpretations by people, traditions remain contingent, open to change both while in the possession of their recipients as well as in the process of transmission. No tradition can be fully closed, if for no other reason than that its practitioners must face constantly changing circumstances. In the course of events over time, a tradition will evolve, shift, and change as the constitutive people respond to challenges from the outside or otherwise discover that aspects of their beliefs conflict with other, higher order, beliefs. In facing changed circumstances and responding to dilemmas that arise as a result, adherents of a tradition may adopt new beliefs or reject certain portions of their shared ideas. Particular traditions can develop because a desire to create something truer, better, or more convenient motivates those who acquire and possess them. Traditions can also deteriorate, in the sense of losing their adherents, because possessors cease to present them, or those who once received and reenacted them come to prefer other lines of thinking and conduct, or

because new generations to which they were presented find other traditions of belief more acceptable according to the standards they accept.

The continuity through discontinuity present in any tradition is best understood as the emergent, (i.e., generative) interplay between inherited ideas and rational reflection against the wider social circumstances in which people are situated. Thus, it is reasonable to expect that what exactly is handed down, how long it has been so, and the degree of rational deliberation that entered into a tradition's creation, presentation, and reception are all likely to be contested to the extent that they are interpreted differently. Even if we had sufficient records for named institutions and could presume their dates of foundation precisely, it is much more difficult to assert the point of origin of ideas, the webs of beliefs and patterns of meaning that comprise traditions. Moreover, although traditions shift and change as people are compelled to reinterpret and rearticulate their beliefs, they require sustained assault from many sources before giving way to significant change because traditions also encompass tacit beliefs and habitual relations between practitioners and their objects. Despite their essential flexibility, traditions are generally enduring webs of beliefs and modes of conduct.

The concept of tradition is useful for explaining governance where governance is broadly understood as ways in which the state exercises power as well as the various ways in which power operates in and through nonstate actors and practices. More specifically, governance refers to a pattern of rule and public administration through networks of various kinds. Insofar as studies of governance attempt to give accounts of why certain forms of life, power, and utterances have the content that they do, the concept of tradition allows us to explain governance processes, modes, and trends by helping us to elucidate the relationship between conduct and contexts for action. As agents that are always embedded within some social context, people exercise the capacity to adopt new beliefs and actions for reasons of their own against a background or social context that already exists as a common heritage, which provides them with the situation for doing so. We can understand the concept of tradition as that which provides this social background for agents to come to hold the meanings they do, which in turn informs their beliefs, actions, and practices. Thus, we can understand people as always situated against the background of some social tradition, or overlapping traditions, which at least initially provides them with a set of theories and ideas and thus a context for adopting new beliefs and acting in novel ways to modify, develop, or even reject their inheritance.

Even as a tradition forms the background to people's utterances and actions, the content of their utterances and actions does not come directly from these contexts but rather from the ways in which they replicate or develop these traditions in accord with their intentions. Thus, traditions constitute a necessary background to the beliefs people adopt and the actions they perform, but they do not determine their beliefs and desires, nor do they fix or limit the actions they can perform successfully. Tradition is an initial influence on people. Its content will appear in their later actions only as far as their situated agency has not led them to change it. Because tradition is unavoidable only as a starting point, traditions do not possess a fixed context to which we can ascribe variations. There may be occasions when we can point to the persistence of some core idea within a tradition over time. In other cases, however, we might identify a tradition with a group of ideas that were widely shared by a number of people, although no one idea was held by all of them. Alternatively, we might equate a tradition with a group of ideas that passed from generation to generation, changing incrementally each time, so that no single idea persisted throughout. A particularly long-lasting tradition, such as Roman Catholicism, incorporates so many developments and changes of emphasis that many of its historical aspects may be unrecognizable to some of its contemporary adherents.

As an explanatory concept, the concept of tradition provides a means of analyzing social change because it allows for situated agency. Change arises as a result of people's ability to adopt beliefs and perform actions for reasons of their own when they creatively respond to dilemmas from within their existing beliefs. A dilemma arises for individuals whenever they adopt a new belief that stands in opposition to their existing

beliefs and so forces a reconsideration of the latter. In accepting a new belief, people pose to their existing beliefs the question of how they will accommodate it. They respond to the dilemma, whether explicitly or not, by changing their beliefs to accommodate the newcomer. Traditions change over time and we cannot explain these changes unless we accept that individuals are capable of altering the traditions they inherit.

We should not understand traditions as having a given or necessarily rational path of development because the way in which people respond to a dilemma is open ended in that there are always many plausible ways in which they might modify their existing beliefs. It is entirely possible for a tradition to include, or be largely composed of, beliefs that are accepted without intense reflection or explicit articulation as such. In fact, to the extent that they provide a background context for action, traditions will often remain abstract and largely unarticulated. Neither of these conditions, however, cancels out the fact of beliefs being held and transmitted by people through time. Whether there is acceptable evidence for the truth of the tradition or whether the tradition is accepted without its validity having been established in no way discounts a tradition's ontological status as providing contexts for action or the explanatory usefulness of the concept of tradition for understanding social and political phenomena.

The concept of tradition, together with that of dilemma, provides us with a means of giving accounts of governance that embody recognition of the particularity and contingency of social life. The concept of tradition suggests that a social inheritance comes to each individual who, through his or her agency, can then modify and transform this inheritance, even as he or she passes it on to others. Because the concept represents an abstraction, it can do explanatory work only insofar as we can unpack it, at least in principle, in terms of contingent, intersubjective beliefs, desires, and actions—these typically incorporate specific ideas about human nature, right conduct, social inquiry, and the good that may be taken for granted to some degree by the participants in the relevant mode of governance. Because traditions provide the framework in which problems are conceived and addressed, we can reveal the historical contingency and contestability of these shared beliefs by showing how they arose against the background of a particular tradition. Thus we can unpack the composition of governance in terms of the beliefs of individuals, where these beliefs are necessarily influenced by a social inheritance. We can explain the rise of new patterns of governance by reference to the intersubjective traditions and dilemmas that inform the changing activities of various clusters of situated actors—be they officials, politicians, or citizens—who all participate in governance processes.

A special 2003 issue of *Public Administration* on recent public-sector reforms across seven advanced, industrial democracies serves to demonstrate the usefulness of the concept of tradition both for explaining the particular trajectories of public-sector reform in the several countries and for lending a comparative perspective on the changes cross-nationally. In it, scholars identify the multiple and competing governmental traditions in Australia, Great Britain, France, Germany, the Netherlands, Norway, and the United States and explore how particular state traditions have informed the beliefs and practices of national political and administrative elites. The authors identify the variously constructed dilemmas, problems, and issues that promoted the search for new practices and thus explain how national governmental traditions helped to shape reform. To explain why elites and officials held the beliefs they did and sustained the particular practices of governance they did, the authors use the actors' own words or texts drawn from primary sources, such as parliamentary debates, committee hearings, government papers and statistics, media reports, memoirs, diaries, and biographies, and interviews with officials past and present.

Each of the studies documents elite constructions of dilemmas using historical narratives that provide distinctive interpretations of state transformations from American antistatism, Norwegian pragmatism, British gradualism, Dutch consensual corporatism, French statism, and the German classical tradition to Australian antipodean exceptionalism. The comparative perspective that emerges shows the contrast between European parliamentary systems and Westminster systems. The editors show how the latter share a tradition of strong executive government such that reform in response to economic pressures could be pushed through. In the Netherlands, despite ostensibly similar economic pressures, reforms hinged on coalition governments operating in a tradition of consensual corporatism, while in France, the combination of departmental fragmentation at the center, coupled with the *grand corps* tradition and its beliefs about a strong state, meant that public-sector reform rested on the consent of those about to be reformed. Antipodean exceptionalism is also accounted for by the way elite actors in New Zealand and Australia saw their country as acutely vulnerable to the pressures of globalization. The editors also show how the concept of tradition and dilemma are useful for explaining variations in the speed of reform across states, so for instance, Westminster systems with executives subjected to few constraints have been able to legislate with relatively few obstructions.

The concept of tradition thus enables scholars to explore the changes in the governance of the state and notably serves to compare stories that inform the actions of national elites across states. The elucidation of particular traditions and dilemmas shows how reform is a continuous, contingent political process in which the meaning of change itself is also contested. More broadly, the concept of tradition helps to show how governance is constructed differently and continuously reconstructed according to the intersubjective understandings of political actors.

—*Naomi Choi*

See also Decentered Theory; Dilemma; Interpretive Policy Analysis; Interpretive Theory; Neotraditionalism; Situated Agency; Social Constructivism; Social Learning; Social Practice

Further Readings and References

Acton, H. B. (1952). Tradition and some other forms of action. *Proceedings of the Aristotelian Society, 53,* 1–28.

Bevir, M. (1999). *The logic of the history of ideas.* Cambridge, UK: Cambridge University Press.

Bevir, M., Rhodes, R. A. W., & Weller, P. (Eds.). (2003). *Traditions of governance: History and diversity* [Special Issue]. *Public Administration, 8,* 1.

Hobsbawm, E., & Ranger, T. (Eds.). (1983). *The invention of tradition.* Cambridge, UK: Cambridge University Press.

Oakeshott, M. (1991). *Rationalism in politics and other essays.* Indianapolis, IN: Liberty Fund.

Shils, E. (1981). *Tradition.* Chicago: University of Chicago Press.

TRAGEDY OF THE COMMONS

The tragedy of the commons highlights the conflict between individual and collective rationality. The idea was made popular by Garret Hardin, who used the analogy of ranchers grazing their animals on a common field. When the field is not over capacity, ranchers may graze their animals with few limitations. However, the rational rancher will seek to add additional livestock, thereby increasing profits. Thinking logically but not collectively, the benefits of adding additional animals adhere to the rancher alone, while the costs are shared. The tragedy is that ultimately no rancher will be able to graze the field due to overconsumption. This scenario is played out on a daily basis in numerous instances, having grave consequences for the world's resources.

It is commonly recognized that one of the primary roles of government at the local, state, national, and international levels is to define and manage shared resources. However, there are a number of practical problems associated with this. Management inside clear political boundaries is a relatively straightforward task, even more problematic are resources shared across jurisdictions. For example, neighboring cities may seek to maximize their benefits by competing for industry, but minimize their costs by pushing residents outside their jurisdictions. Another dimension is added at the international level when nation-states are not bound by a common authority and may view restrictions on resource extraction as a threat to sovereignty. Additional difficulties arise when resources cannot be divided or are interrelated, such as in whale hunting treaties when the farming of their food source (plankton) is separately regulated.

The mechanisms to resolve these tragedies are part of a larger set of theories dealing with social dilemmas in fields such as mathematics, economics, sociology, planning, public affairs, and environmental sciences. In these arenas, scholars have identified and structured a number of tentative solutions, such as enclosing the commons by establishing property rights, regulating through government intervention, or developing strategies to trigger collective behavior. Eleanor Ostrom argued that these strategies generally deal with problems of commitment and problems of mutual monitoring.

As the world's population rises and demands more access to resources, the issues associated with the commons become more severe. Ultimately, this may test the role and practicality of nation-states, leading to a redefinition of international governance. Among other important questions to consider is the proper role of supranational governments, such as the United Nations or the World Trade Organization. As resources become more limited, some argue that managing the commons may have neither a technical nor a political solution. This, indeed, may be the ultimate tragedy.

—*Margaret E. Banyan*

See also Climate Change; Common-Pool Resource; Endangered Species Protection; Free Riding; Natural Resource Management; Political Economy; United Nations; World Trade Organization

Further Readings and References

Hardin, G. (1968). The tragedy of the commons. *Science, 162*(3859), 1243–1248.

Ostrom, E. (1999). Coping with tragedies of the commons. *Annual Review of Political Science, 2*(1), 493–535.

TRANSACTION COST

Transaction costs represent the economic losses that can result from arranging market relationships on a contractual basis. While most economists studied frictionless models of perfect competition, John Commons and Ronald Coase were early students of contractual relationships and highlighted the various costs that could arise. In recent decades, transaction costs have come to the fore in scholarship on for-profit organizations and public bureaucracies, and this progress has had great significance for the field of governance.

The study of transaction costs originates from economics' aggregative social modeling arising from individuals operating under competitive self-interest. At the highest level of abstraction, there are only markets and everyone is free to enter into contractual relations with everyone else. Under this view, the firm is seen famously as a nexus of contracts. But proponents of the approach expect that contracts will be violated not occasionally, but whenever the parties to them find it possible. One theoretical line that emerges from this approach is agency theory, which sees firms in terms of contractual relations. But a different tactic has been transaction cost economics (TCE), which focuses on the limitations of contractual relationships.

The TCE approach seeks to explain why there are some markets with many organizations in them and why there are some industries dominated by just a few large organizations—called hierarchies. Oliver Williamson, the approach's leading innovator and architect, sketches a historical argument that explains the transformation of an economy based on many small transactions to one based on large hierarchies that transact among themselves and into which individuals are absorbed. The organizational developments that characterize our current economy, dominated as it is by such hierarchies, are seen as a more efficient way to organize economic relationships.

TCE consists of four main elements:

1. The world is uncertain and therefore unpredictable.

2. Small numbers bargaining and asset specificity make it costly for parties who enter into economic relationships to leave them.

3. Bounded rationality limits individuals' opportunities to scan the environment for all possible options.

4. The inherent opportunism of individuals in economic relationships makes contractual enforcement over a long-term period difficult.

Together, these four factors make it difficult to contract at low costs and create frictions (i.e., transaction costs) in the marketplace. The capitalist solution is to integrate up and down the production chain by buying out suppliers and the people one sells to. Variations in the way the four factors affect different economic relationships determine the degree to which an industry is concentrated or not.

TCE argues that the modern large firm represents a substitution of contractual relationships with an authority relationship. Entrepreneurs who create large hierarchies no longer have to write complicated contracts, but can instead use organizational tools such as incentives, coercion, and monitoring to maintain behavioral control. Hence, transaction costs represent a central idea for governance scholarship because governance structures form the rules by which parties interact in different organizational and political contexts. Governance structures in the firm award monitors power to oversee and discipline.

In the realm of political science, transaction cost ideas have been pushed most by the work of Terry Moe. He argues that we can understand the organization of public bureaucracies and the behavior of bureaucrats by thinking about the incentives and constraints that the political process and political structure (i.e., governance) impose on interest groups, politicians, and bureaucrats. Uncertainty and shifting fortunes distinguish the political realm, so these actors must design bureaucracies to attain long-run objectives within the constraints of the political process. They must make concessions to opposing groups while at the same time they lock in their gains by setting bureaucratic rules so the organization becomes inflexible and difficult to change. Moe stresses that Americans should not be surprised by the behavior of their bureaucrats because their behavior has often intentionally been designed to fit the context of American governance.

—*Gabriel E. Kaplan*

See also Contract Enforcement; Coordination; New Institutionalism; Political Economy; Sociology of Governance

Further Readings and References

Coase, R. (1937). The nature of the firm. *Economica, 4,* 386–405.

Moe, T. M. (1994). Integrating politics and organizations: Positive theory and public administration. *Journal of Public Administration Research and Theory, 4*(1), 17–25.

Williamson, O. (1985). *Economic institutions of capitalism.* New York: Free Press.

TRANSGOVERNMENTALISM

The notion of transgovernmentalism refers to the process of internationalization of policy making through the interaction of government agencies or government officials. The concept challenges state-centric approaches to international relations and, in particular, the assumption of states as unitary actors. Transgovernmentalism also places emphasis on the interaction between international and domestic policy making and the blurring of boundaries between the two levels.

While the concept is linked to debates on transnational relations and actors, its starting point is the direct interaction among single units and agencies or governmental officials (e.g., members of the higher civil service and political leaders, rather than the interaction with or among nongovernmental actors). Transgovernmentalism has been informed by analysis of intergovernmental policy coordination in the context of international regimes as well as in the context of the European Union (EU). The notion is also discussed in the context of world politics more widely and the question of a new world order.

The debate on transgovernmentalism has been shaped by the writings of Robert Keohane and Joseph Nye from the 1970s. They define transgovernmental relations as direct interactions among different governments' subunits and point out that these subunits are not directly controlled by the center of government. The differentiation between two modes of transgovernmentalism, transnational policy coordination and transnational coalition building, is still reflected in more recent writing in that context. While functional interdependence makes transnational policy coordination necessary, this policy coordination establishes channels of communication and facilitates frequent interaction among governmental units from different countries. These interactions, in turn, cause changes in the attitudes and beliefs of governmental officials and thereby lead eventually to the emergence of transnational networks. Common worldviews and interests, as well as professional orientations, sustain the relationship between individuals across national boundaries. In that context, international organizations and their bureaucratic backbones (like secretariats) play an important role in providing access points toward transnational channels of communication.

Transnational networks could also be the outcome of strategic behavior of individuals rather than emerging from continuous interaction. This is captured in the notion of "transnational coalition building," which refers to the strategy of governmental units that use actors from other governments as allies against opposition within the domestic arena. More recently, that argument has been expanded to the strategic choice of an institutional arena that is possibly more open than others for a specific policy initiative (venue shopping).

While the interests of Keohane and Nye were mainly directed toward the influence of transgovernmentalism on the development of interstate cooperation, Anne-Marie Slaughter placed the notion of transgovernmental networks at the center of her concept of a new world order in the late 1990s. She argues that most reasoning about the international order was unrealistic in that it required centralized rule making and hierarchic institutions spanning the whole world. She also denies that nonstate actors could develop a transnational world order and substitute state power. However, the web between functionally distinct parts of the state (including not only administrative agencies, but also courts and even parliaments) could constitute a new transgovernmental order.

Transgovernmental interaction feeds back into national regulatory decisions in as diverse domains as international trade, banking, and environmental regulation, creating a web of increasingly transnational regulations. Because these transnational regulations are based on mutual recognition and adaptation, they are not imposed on national regulators. Slaughter also develops a more normative scenario that includes the incremental adaptation of domestic democratic mechanisms (within the nation-state) toward transnational networks of regulation.

While the existence of transgovernmental and transnational networks is accepted as a fact of global governance today, how far these networks transform world politics remains in debate. It is also widely accepted that these transgovernmental interactions and networks shape international law and policy making and that they feed back into domestic regulation.

However, it remains contested whether a diversity of domain-based transgovernmental networks could transform the basic international order.

In the context of the EU, the concept of transgovernmentalism has been reflected in two major ways. First, the idea of routine interaction leading to shared beliefs across national boundaries (within policy domains) is a recurring theme in research exploring the transformation of EU policy making from intergovernmentalism toward supranationalism. While some have argued that the "membership" of top civil servants and politicians in different constituencies facilitates the development of a supranational worldview, the transgovernmental perspective suggests that role orientations of officials in specialized departments are neither intrinsically national nor supranational, but are rather shaped by the key role of knowledge and professional norms in domain-based policy making. Second, Helen Wallace has introduced the notion of intensive transgovernmentalism as one mode of governing in the EU. Intensive transgovernmentalism refers to direct policy coordination at the European level in areas of "high politics" that used to be at the core of the national realm (foreign policy, finance policy).

The concept of transgovernmentalism played an important role in the context of governance. In particular, the shift from the image of unitary and rational states toward the view of a functionally differentiated state, which is engaged in an increasingly dense web of regional and transnational networks of regulations, accords with the core of the wider governance debate. How deep transgovernmental mechanisms have changed international and domestic policy making remains a contested issue. In some areas of high international policies (arms proliferation) as well as domestic policies (welfare state), peer-to-peer transgovernmental networks may be less relevant. Other transnationalization is not only driven by transgovernmental interaction but also by developing supranational institutions (e.g., EU) or the activities of transnational nongovernmental actors (international nongovernmental organizations, multinational corporations). Understanding interaction between these various driving forces remains a key challenge in research on transnational and transgovernmental governance.

—*Kai Wegrich*

See also Capital Market Integration; Global Civil Society; Global Governance; Multilateralism; Transnational Governance; Transnationalism

Further Readings and References

Keohane, R. O., & Nye, J. S. (1974). Transgovernmental relations and international organizations. *World Politics, 1*(1), 39–62.
Keohane, R. O., & Nye, J. S. (1977). *Power and interdependence: World politics in transition.* Boston: Little, Brown.
Slaughter, A. M. (1997). The real new world order. *Foreign Affairs, 76*(5), 184–186.
Wallace, H. (2005). An institutional anatomy and five policy modes. In H. Wallace, W. Wallace, & M. A. Pollack (Eds.), *Policy-making in the European Union* (5th ed., pp. 49–89). Oxford, UK: Oxford University Press.

TRANSLATION

Translation is a process whereby a body of meaning expressed in one semiotic medium (namely a book, a speech, a ritual, and so on) is conveyed through another semiotic medium. Translation is a ubiquitous mode of communication that is to be found within as well as between languages or cultures. It is accordingly an important element in understanding the communicative and interpretive aspects of governance.

Translation is a complex interpretive endeavor. First, it involves an understanding of the source text; in turn, this understanding requires sensitivity to the specific circumstances and to the general linguistic and cultural conventions involved in the formulation of the text. Then, once understood, the original meaning is reconstructed and given a new semiotic form. This reconstructive process requires the same sensitivity to circumstances and conventions, only this time with respect to the target audience and language (or culture). In other words, a fine translation is that which not only transfers a body of meaning but also displays understanding and recognition of the mutual distinctness of the source and target languages or cultures.

Translation is an important aspect of governance that is understood as social and political communication, given the developments in the practice and study of governance that have exploded the classical, Weberian (from Max Weber) model of government. According to this model, political authority is exercised by a monolithic bureaucracy, characterized by a uniform administrative culture and standardized procedures of political communication. Furthermore, the state is conceived in the classical model as exercising authority over a clearly demarcated, relatively homogeneous national entity. Such a model implies a conception of political communication that, in its ideal form, is fully transparent and purged of any need for translation.

Conversely, the contemporary concept of governance involves an inherently pluralistic understanding of political activity. Governance is viewed and practiced as taking place across networks comprising state institutions, nonprofit organizations, private firms, and transnational actors. Such political diversity necessarily entails, in turn, a plurality of cultural identities and organizational languages and practices. Under such circumstances, the challenge of exercising political authority across these semiotic boundaries becomes, in some of its most fundamental aspects, a problem of translation. Moreover, translation is not only involved at the macrolevel of political life, it also constitutes part of the stuff which everyday, microlevel organizational practices are made of.

Finally, issues of translation have started to attract the attention of theorists of deliberative democracy as well as of governance. Future theoretical reflections situated at the intersection of those two fields might consequently find the conceptual framework provided by translation theory to be of value.

—Asaf Kedar

See also Communication; Interpretive Theory; Political Communication

Further Readings and References

Buck, T., & Shahrim, A. (2005). The translation of corporate governance changes across national cultures: The case of Germany. *Journal of International Business Studies, 36,* 42–61.

Yanow, D. (2004). Translating local knowledge at organizational peripheries [Special Issue]. *British Journal of Management, 15,* S9–S25.

TRANSNATIONAL GOVERNANCE

Transnational governance is the coordination of policy decision making or enforcement in a given issue area across national borders. Transnational governance typically involves nonstate actors as principals, as nongovernmental organizations (NGOs), multinational firms, or international organizations respond to problems that cross national jurisdictions—often in the absence of meaningful involvement by national governments.

Transnational governance can be distinguished from three forms of interstate cooperation—supranationalism, multilateralism, and transgovernmentalism. Supranational governance involves the operation of formal, superordinate institutions that subsume existing national institutions, such as the International Criminal Court. Multilateral governance establishes norms and rules that constrain countries' policy-making prerogatives in given issue areas, such as the Kyoto Protocol on global warming, but which tend not to apply to nonstate actors (at least directly). Transgovernmentalism, for its part, involves coordination among specialized national officials and agencies tasked with enforcing policy in their respective jurisdictions to combat global problems, such as drug trafficking or terrorist financing. Although transnational governance shares the cooperative and cross-border attributes of each of these models, it is distinct in its less formal, networked form and greater role for nonstate actors.

Transnational governance typically emerges when formal international coordination mechanisms designed by and for sovereign states prove incapable of responding to specific transnational problems. International NGOs are often initiators of transnational governance, as they promote their vision of "good" behavior from governments or firms in contexts of insufficient formal regulation, whether at the international, national, or local level. These networks typically promote stakeholder participation in defining and monitoring relevant issue-area standards, presenting a form of global civil society self-government that simultaneously rivals and complements traditional national and international forms of regulative authority.

Transnational governance does not impose formal international institutional authority on states, but rather uses "softer" mechanisms of nongovernmental monitoring and certification of specific principals' performance in meeting a relevant set of broadly consensual standards. For example, a system of forest management certification of logging firms conducted by the Forest Stewardship Council (FSC) and its partners monitors and reports on these firms' practices, typically with voluntary participation of the firms themselves. Governance networks such as the forest management certification system bring together global and local stakeholders to deliberate shared goals and solutions and to enforce these solutions through the use of informal (especially reputational) inducements and costs rather than more formal command-and-control regulation.

Although transnational governance networks may be more flexible and possibly more efficient than traditional forms of top-down governance, they also face their own difficulties. They rely on the voluntary participation of principals, they lack internally generated material resources, they have indeterminate legal status, and they lack clear mechanisms of democratic accountability. However, unlike traditional multilateral governance in particular, their focus on nonstate actor participation may be particularly appropriate to issue areas and contexts in which these principals are the primary drivers of global processes.

—*Edward A. Fogarty*

See also Coalition; Global Governance; Kyoto Protocol; Transgovernmentalism; Transnationalism; Transnational Social Movement

Further Readings and References

Hall, R. B., & Bierstaker, T. J. (Eds.). (2002). *The emergence of private authority in global governance.* Cambridge, UK: Cambridge University Press.

Rosenau, J., & Czempiel, E.-O. (1992). *Governance without government: Order and change in world politics.* Cambridge, UK: Cambridge University Press.

Slaughter, A.-M. (2004). *A new world order.* Princeton, NJ: Princeton University Press.

TRANSNATIONALISM

Transnationalism refers to those economic, political, and cultural processes extending beyond the boundaries of nation-states. It suggests a weakening of the control a nation-state has over its borders, inhabitants, and territory. Increased immigration in developed countries in response to global economic development has resulted in multicultural societies where immigrants are more likely to maintain contact with their culture of origin and less likely to assimilate. Therefore, loyalty to the state may compete equally with allegiance to a culture or religion. With increased global mobility and access to instantaneous worldwide communication technology, boundaries dissolve and the territorial controls imposed by the traditional nation-state become less relevant. However, state definitions of citizenship and nationality and the rules for political participation may become more relevant for transnational groups.

Globalization is a related concept that represents the intensification of economic, cultural, and political practices accelerating across the globe. Although many large corporations have been operating globally for decades, the Internet now enables small organizations and individuals access to an instantaneous worldwide communication network. Global processes are closely related to transnationalism, yet tend to be separate from specific national boundaries. Transnational processes, on the other hand, are anchored in and transcend one or more nation-states. The impacts of the transnational migration of groups, although different, need to be understood within the context of globalization. The changes created by each are mutually reinforcing.

Processes of Transnationalism

Processes contributing to transnationalism include the economic influences of corporations operating globally, often referred to as transnational corporations, and cooperative agreements between governments. These arrangements offer new trade and industrial opportunities for private business and government alike. New prospects for employment in developed nations tend to draw migrant groups from less-developed nations. New advances in transportation and communication technologies, such as the Internet, provide potential avenues of virtual connectivity among these individuals and groups moving across national borders. The political-economic processes in the European Union have resulted in reexamining long-term relationships with transnational groups (such as the Turkish and Kurdish populations).

Another major process influencing transnationalism is the growing economic dependence among developed nations on migrant group labor. The relationship between these groups and their nation of residence has become one of interdependence. Beyond economic considerations, this implies that host countries reciprocate by providing avenues for civic participation and in some cases the rights of citizenship for transnational groups.

Transnationalism and Nationalism

Transnationalism is commonly contrasted with nationalism. Here, nationalism is characterized as a strong belief among people that share a common language, history, and culture that the interests of the nation-state are paramount. This requires a strong sense of belonging, identity, and loyalty where the benefits of membership are acquired through citizenship. Historically, migrant groups moving from one nation to another were expected to prove their belonging and loyalty by adopting the prescribed moral and political values of their nation of immigration. Permanent residence carried an expectation of acquired citizenship and nationality in those countries based on notions of "national assimilation" (United States and France) as opposed to ancestry (Germany). After a generation, many of these groups were fully assimilated into the dominant culture of the nation of immigration. For many, the connection with their country of emigration took the form of Diaspora—a reification of homelands, traditions, collective memories, and longings—and the formation of tightly

bounded communities on the basis of common cultural and ethnic references between places of origin and arrival. This dynamic gave rise to large numbers of ethnic communities within nation-states, retaining elements of culture in terms of identity, yet remaining subservient to national loyalty. Today, the loyalties of migrant groups may transcend this critical feature of the nation-state with primary allegiance and identity given to religion or their culture of origin. Dual loyalties are now causing some nations to liberalize their laws regarding dual citizenship or provide rights and privileges to noncitizen groups who permanently reside within their borders (Turkish guest workers in Germany). In some cases, as with the Mexican immigrant population in the United States, the trend is in the opposite direction.

Transnational Communities and Pressure for Change

Transnational community refers to those groups who migrate and reside in a receiving nation for a considerable time, yet maintain strong transnational ties. These ties may be reinforced formally by the rules and regulations of the state (immigration laws, definitions of citizenship), by links with political parties or religious groups, or informally through connections among families and households in the sending and receiving nations. As developed nations have become more economically dependent on immigrant workers, there is more political pressure for the state to enter reciprocal relationships with these groups, particularly those of long-term residence. For example, until 2000 the rules and regulations for defining and obtaining German citizenship excluded the substantial, long-residing Turkish population in the country. Many Turkish citizens have lived in Germany for over 30 years and desire dual citizenship. They define citizenship in terms of political representation and nationality as an ethnic identity conflicting with the German definition of citizenship, which combines citizenship with nationality. The Turkish minority is rooted in a Turkish national identity and a Muslim religious identity, both foreign to the German collective identity, yet

Germany is in many ways economically dependent on this minority. Pressure for change resulted in the reform of Germany's citizenship and nationality law in 2000. While still not allowing for dual citizenship, the regulations governing naturalization of foreign nationals have been liberalized, and it is now possible to acquire German citizenship as a result of being born in Germany.

The economic interdependence between nation-states and their transnational communities, engendered by forces of globalization, are forcing state action to redefine concepts such as citizenship and nationality, which are deeply embedded in a nation's culture, history, and traditions.

Transnationalism raises a number of concerns for contemporary governance. While the nation-state, in its traditional sense, appears to run counter to the emergence of transnational communities, it may be that its political structure needs to be redefined. Such a redefinition may need to adapt to the changes presented by the global structures placing demands on it and an inclusive approach to the multiple identities represented by transnational communities.

—*Richard F. Huff*

See also European Union; Global Civil Society; Globalization; Immigration; Transnational Social Movement; Transnational Urbanism

Further Readings and References

Benhabib, S. (2002). Citizens, residents, and aliens in a changing world: Political membership in the global era. In U. Hedetoft & M. Hjort (Eds.), *The postnational self: Belonging and identity* (pp. 85–119). Minneapolis: University of Minnesota Press.

Kastoryano, R. (2002). Citizenship and belonging: Beyond blood and soil. In U. Hedetoft & M. Hjort (Eds.), *The postnational self: Belonging and identity* (pp. 120–136). Minneapolis: University of Minnesota Press.

Soysal, Y. N. (2002). Citizenship and identity: Living in Diasporas in postwar Europe? In U. Hedetoft & M. Hjort (Eds.), *The postnational self: Belonging and identity* (pp. 137–151). Minneapolis: University of Minnesota Press.

Tambiah, S. J. (2000). Transnational movements, Diaspora, and multiple modernities. *Daedalus, 129,* 163–176.

TRANSNATIONAL SOCIAL MOVEMENT

The term *transnational social movement* refers to a collectivity of groups with adherents in more than one country that is committed to sustained contentious action against governments, international institutions, or private firms. Prominent examples include the anti-globalization movement and the movement against genetically modified organisms (GMOs). A narrow definition of the concept emphasizes its differences with international nongovernmental organizations and transnational advocacy networks, which are generally more institutionalized, professionalized, and frequently funded or promoted by particular states or international organizations. A broader conception includes or focuses on other types of transnational actors and posits a causal relationship between globalization and the development of transnational activism. Accordingly, this broader view affords them a greater role and influence in national and international systems of governance, where their primary achievements are the creation, strengthening, implementation, and monitoring of international norms.

Although conceptual approaches to the study of transnational social movements are in many ways similar to the analysis of national social movements, the automatic extension of national social movement definitions and perspectives to the international arena is contested. Some claim that the transfer of state powers, rights, and functions to international bodies implies that challengers redirect their efforts accordingly. Others argue that this transfer does not automatically lead to the emergence of transnational social movement activity and that true mass-based transnational social movements are difficult to mobilize and hard to maintain. In this view, the international women's, labor, and antiglobalization movements may be the only true transnational social movements. Hence, transnational contention is usually undertaken by members of transnational networks that are linked to national movements.

The efforts of transnational social movements, international nongovernmental organizations, and transnational advocacy networks raise a number of issues for contemporary governance. First, because international organizations have little coercive power at their disposal, they must rely on soft enforcement mechanisms involving information, persuasion, and moral pressure. In turn, these empower and favor transnational social movement actors who have traditionally demonstrated great skill in the strategic use of information. Second, because political opportunities— political dimensions that advance or constrain collective action—differ at the national and an international level, the dynamic interactions between these levels becomes a critical factor in the analysis of transnational social movement activity. Third, as national social movement organizations extend their patterns of cooperation and influence across borders in response to the transfer of decision-making power from states to international bodies, interstate cooperation evolves or intensifies in reaction to movement transnationalization, for instance in the area of protest policing. States may therefore reassert certain powers as a consequence of transnational activism.

—*Jörg Balsiger*

See also Advocacy Network; Antiglobalization; Globalization; Social Movement Theory; Transnationalism; Transnational Urbanism

Further Readings and References

Guidry, J. A., Kennedy, M. D., & Zald, M. N. (2001). *Globalizations and social movements: Culture, power, and the transnational public sphere.* Ann Arbor: University of Michigan Press.

Khagram, S., Riker, J. V., & Sikkink, K. (2002). *Restructuring world politics: Transnational social movements, networks, and norms.* Minneapolis: University of Minnesota Press.

O'Brien, R., Goetz, A. M., Aart, J., & Williams, M. (2000). *Contesting global governance: Multilateral economic institutions and global social movements.* London and New York: Cambridge University Press.

TRANSNATIONAL URBANISM

The concept of transnational urbanism refers to the sociocultural and political processes by which social actors forge connections between localities across national borders that increasingly sustain new modes of politics, economics, and culture.

Transnational urbanism is an optic for envisioning the emergent transnational practices through which social actors are materially linked to socio-economic opportunities, political structures, and cultural practices found in urban settings. Cities are thus one key locus of communication circuits and organizational networks that span national borders. Conceptually, transnational urbanism captures a sense of social relations under globalizing conditions that are locally situated yet operate across geographic distance and are also embedded in processes of state power and governance.

The concept was first developed in the 2001 book, *Transnational Urbanism: Locating Globalization.* This book offered an agency-oriented approach to globalization. It used the metaphor transnational urbanism to underline four contested dimensions of the international regulatory framework now known as global governance. These include attention to (1) the transnational networks responsible for the ideological production of the neoliberal variant of globalization; (2) the local and cross-border cultural networks that mediate global economic restructuring and reprocess global consumerism; (3) the emergence of transnational countermovements against neoliberalism; and (4) the continuing significance of the nation-state as a repository of language, national cultures, and state-centered projects in the face of the emergence of transnational networks.

The agency of transnational migrant networks has been another key area studied through the lens of transnational urbanism. Transnational cities are key loci of cross-border migrant networks in part because cities are concentrated sources of employment for transnational migrants; they offer the means for migrants to deploy remittances to families that remain behind in their communities of origin. The migrants also maintain close ties to the localities from which they came. Sometimes this takes the form of efforts by migrants to promote and finance community development projects in their localities of origin. In so doing, the migrants forge enduring ties between a receiving city in one country and their sending locality in another country. This newly constituted cross-border social space has come to be termed a translocality.

Transnational cities are also sites for concentrating the social, physical, and human capital used to forge other types of socio-economic and political projects across borders. The complex interconnectivity of transnational urbanism thus encompasses a wide variety of social and political fields. These range from the social practices of transnational migrant networks to the politics of transnational social movements, the cross-border proselytizing activities of organized religions, the economic connections of commodity chains and criminal syndicates, and the machinations of transnational terrorist networks. The complex interconnectivity of transnational urbanism is thus multidimensional by virtue of encompassing social, economic, and political relations as well as cultural and interpersonal networks and technological linkages. Transnational urbanism foregrounds the continuing significance of cities as the human foundation of contemporary transnationalism.

—*Michael Peter Smith*

See also Global Governance; Globalization; Glocalization; Migration; Neoliberalism; Network; Situated Agency; Transnationalism; Transnational Social Movement

Further Readings and References

Smith, M. P. (2001). *Transnational urbanism: Locating globalization.* Malden, MA, and Oxford, UK: Basil Blackwell.

Smith, M. P., & Guarnizo, L. E. (Eds.). (1998). *Transnationalism from below.* New Brunswick, NJ: Transaction.

TRANSPARENCY

Transparency allows outsiders to obtain valid and timely information about the activities of government or private organizations. While related to governance ideas such as accountability, openness, and responsiveness, the concept of transparency originated in the financial world, referring to a corporation's duty to provide accounts of its activities to shareholders, oversight bodies, and the public.

The United States' 1966 Freedom of Information Act, providing limited guarantees of citizen access to government information, was a transparency milestone. It has been emulated, and in many cases exceeded in scope, by legislation in other countries. Democratic and market reform, and a growing anticorruption movement, did the most to make transparency a key governance concept. Transparent political processes are seen as more accountable and democratic, while transparency in the economy facilitates free-market processes. In both spheres, rights of access to information and the parallel obligations of institutions to uphold those rights are proposed as safeguards against abuses and as good governance activities in their own right.

Thus, transparency is portrayed as integral to a variety of political goals, including corruption control, fair financing of election campaigns, enhancing democracy in existing institutions such as the European Union, consolidating democracy in transitional societies, and limiting international conflict. An international anticorruption coalition founded in 1993 calls itself Transparency International. Transparency in business is advocated as a safeguard against corporate fraud, infiltration by organized crime or political interests, and crises such as the Asian economic meltdown of the late 1990s, which was made worse by shady banking and lending practices.

In practice, however, transparency raises questions. Someone must be looking in: Where civil society is weak, or citizens and the press are intimidated, opportunities to obtain information will go unused and may be risky. Information on technical issues may be difficult to understand; officials may release disinformation, create expensive and complex transparency procedures, or disseminate material in obfuscatory forms. Institutions and procedures for implementing transparency and genuine commitment to the principle itself need continuing attention.

Equally problematic are the limits of transparency: Few would require a government to reveal strategic decisions in wartime or a business to give legitimate trade secrets to all comers. But how should exceptions be defined and invoked? Officials need a sphere of autonomy within which they can freely debate options and from which they can implement policies authoritatively. Excessive transparency may undermine autonomy, drive decision making into undocumented back channels, and create more corruption. Transparency in private dealings may expose citizens to official or personal reprisals. Strong governments can enforce business transparency, but other states are weak, and international businesses can be so decentralized that no country's transparency policy will be effective. Sovereign governments may break their own laws with impunity, and international organizations may be so remote that civil society has little influence upon them.

Finally, transparency can have unintended consequences. Disclosing political contributions may expose donors to pressure from incumbent officials, thus discouraging donations to challengers. Sunshine laws mandating open meetings and requests for documentary evidence are useful to public officials who seek to intervene in other agencies' doings. Transparency could check international conflict by clarifying actions and intentions or produce disinformation and "noise" that increase risks. At best, transparency is subject to limitations applying to all public policies; at worst, it places the burden of checking authority upon those most vulnerable to abuses.

—Michael Johnston

See also Accountability; Audit; Corporate Governance; Corruption; Corruption Perceptions Index; Democratic Deficit; Due Process; Good Governance; Government Performance and Results Act; Performance Measurement; Public Information

Further Readings and References

Finel, B. I., & Lord, K. M. (1999). The surprising logic of transparency. *International Studies Quarterly, 43,* 315–339.

Frost, A. (2003). Restoring faith in government: Transparency reform in the United States and the European Union. *European Public Law, 9,* 87–104.

Grigorescu, A. (2003). International organizations and government transparency: Linking the international and domestic realms. *International Studies Quarterly, 47,* 643–667.

Hanson, M. (2003). The global promotion of transparency in emerging markets. *Global Governance, 9,* 63–79.

Héritier, A. (2003). Composite democracy in Europe: The role of transparency and access to information. *Journal of European Public Policy, 10,* 814–833.

Stirton, L., & Lodge, M. (2001). Transparency mechanisms: Building publicness into public services. *Journal of Law and Society, 28,* 471–489.

TRIADIZATION

The concept of the Triad has its roots in the trilateral relationship between the United States, the European Union, and Japan, the three leading powers of the world economy. The concept underwent an expansion to embrace the Triad regions (North America, Western Europe, and East Asia) as a consequence of several factors: the end of the Cold War, the appearance of "new regionalism," and the emergence of East Asia as the third center of the world economy. It was further strengthened by the establishment of interregional relations among the Triad regions in the 1990s. By the mid-1990s, the new Triad concept had become a major feature in the discourse about the emerging international order.

The three core regions or the Triad are not only economically advanced but also politically stable. Together, they make a large part of the world economy. The Triad accounts for two-thirds to three-quarters of the world economic activity, with shifting patterns of resources across each region. Thus, they also exercise global power. Each of the three regions has been competing to make inroads to the world outside its own region through exercising ideological hegemony.

Reflecting their different traditions, the core countries of the Triad have generally practiced three forms of capitalism: the unregulated capitalism of North America, the administered capitalism of East Asia, and the social capitalism of Europe. Some have speculated that the latter two are better prepared to deal with the growing social and political demands, which may require state intervention and redistributive policies.

Skeptics of globalization have argued that the concepts of triadization, internationalization, or regionalization provide a more valid description of the process mistakenly identified as globalization. Supporters have countered that the causal factors of interregionalism, and of regionalism alike, are the ongoing processes of globalization and regionalization. Thus, interregionalism appears to have become a lasting feature of the international system. A wide array of forms and types of interregionalism are likely to continue to coexist, thereby further enriching (and complicating) the emerging multilayered system of global governance.

Far from an integrated global economy, skeptics say they see an increasing concentration of world economic activity within the triadized blocs, each with its own center and periphery. This triadization of the world economy is associated with a growing tendency toward economic and financial interdependence within each of these zones at the expense of integration between them. The current triadization is different from the *belle époque* of globalization (1890–1914). Triadization is a posthegemonic order because no single center can dictate the rules of global trade and commerce.

It reflects the macrofacet of the development of regional trade and investment blocs, and that trade, investment, and financial flows are concentrated within these blocs.

To get some order in this emerging web of transregional relations, one can distinguish between relations within the Triad, on the one hand, and relations between the core regions of the Triad and their various regional partners outside, on the other hand. Unsurprisingly, the relations within the Triad are rather tense, due to power balance concerns as well as the somewhat different economic ideologies that were previously referred to. Transregional links within the Triad are constituted by various transatlantic (U.S.-EU) agreements; the Asia Pacific Economic Cooperation (APEC) forum, where the United States is the driver; and the Asia-Europe Meeting (ASEM) process, involving the EU and selected Asian countries. The institutionalized transatlantic links are weak, not to speak of interregional arrangements between the EU and the North American Free Trade Agreement (NAFTA), which, as a matter of fact, are nonexistent. The reason for this is that the United States prefers bilateralism, which prevents the building of institutions of interregionalism.

Research clearly indicates that the modern world economy comprises three competing center clusters, each of which has a dependent hinterland of periphery clusters. The relative power of the three center clusters is unequal. Among them, there is a hegemon cluster led by a global state that has more power in the world system than any other. The relative power of the global states within the center clusters, as well as those within the periphery clusters, is also unequal. If one were to presume that the global information and communication flow follows the pattern of this triadized center-hinterland structure, this reformulated world system perspective offers a rich theoretical framework for conducting global communication research.

A 2002 study by Sheldon Gunaratne found strong support for the following propositions:

1. The pattern of world exports supports the existence of three world center clusters, each of which has at least one dependent periphery cluster.

2. The distribution of computing power and exports of high-technology manufactures (constituting the Information Society Power Index) confirms the triadization structure and helps identify the hegemon cluster of the triad (i.e., the United States).

—*Shelton A. Gunaratne*

See also Global Governance; Global Market; Globalization; Regional Governance; Varieties of Capitalism

Further Readings and References

Amin, S. (1996). *Capitalism in the age of globalization.* London: Zed Books.

Gunaratne, S. A. (2002). An evolving triadic world: A theoretical framework for global communication research. *Journal of World-Systems Research, 8*(3), 329–365.

Hänggi, H. (1999). ASEM and the construction of the new Triad. *Journal of the Asia Pacific Economy, 4*(1), 56–80.

Held, D., & McGrew, A. (2003). The great globalization debate: An introduction. In D. Held & A. McGrew (Eds.), *The global transformation reader: An introduction to the globalization debate* (2nd ed., pp. 1–50). Cambridge, UK: Polity Press.

Hettne, B. (2003, March). *Regionalism, interregionalism, and world order: The European challenge to pax Americana.* Lecture sponsored by Council on Comparative Studies at American University.

Hirst, P., & Thompson, G. (1999). *Globalization in question* (2nd ed.). Cambridge, UK: Polity Press.

Lloyd, P. J. (1992, Spring). Regionalization and world trade. *OECD Economic Studies, 18,* 7–44.

Tribal Governance

Indigenous peoples are the original inhabitants of a geographic space that was subsequently taken from them by outside peoples either by conquest, occupation, settlement, or some combination of all three. The social and political organizational structure of some indigenous peoples has historically been referred to as "tribal," a problematic term not only for its inconsistent usage but also for the negative connotation often associated with it. The term *tribe* is linked to outdated anthropological assumptions (particularly of the nineteenth century) about the inferiority and political simplicity of non-European peoples. It has historically had a pejorative connotation and has been used to refer to political communities of indigenous peoples throughout the world, which are presumably smaller, less-technologically developed, more "natural," and more static, with less-formal governing structures and with more emphasis on common ancestral heritage than European-style states. In more recent times, however, tribal organization has also been recognized as more dynamic, more heterogeneous, and less parochial than previously characterized by colonizing Europeans. Tribal governance is the myriad of ways in which these communities of indigenous peoples have been, and continue to be, governed, autonomously and via external management.

The extent and basic nature of tribal governance varies from place to place. Despite the vast diversity of tribes in the world, tribal governance typically includes the defining and implementing of the following elements: (a) jurisdictional divisions between tribes and other political entities, such as colonial states; (b) citizenship internal to the tribe, as well as within the colonial state, which can and often are practiced simultaneously; (c) policy decisions over particular fields of tribal jurisdiction, such as policing and land zoning; (d) services delivered to tribal members; (e) financing of the tribe, including taxation; (f) intergovernmental relations between tribes and other governments, such as provincial, state, federal, and municipal governments; (g) legal and constitutional relations within the tribe and in relation to other recognized legal entities, such as state governments, courts, and electoral commissions; (h) the historical and cultural context that informs governance practices.

In almost all cases, tribal governance is still subject to the limits and management placed upon it by the political and legal apparatus of a colonial state. In some cases, however, tribal governance is also a legally recognized part of the colonial state governance system, as is the case in India, the United States, and many African countries.

Representatives of tribal governing bodies participate in many international forums, such as the World Council of Indigenous Peoples and the United Nations (UN) Permanent Forum on Indigenous Populations. However, the recognition of tribal governance in international law remains uncertain. Although the inherent rights of self-determination and self-government, as well as historical rights found within particular treaties and agreements, have been affirmed by the UN Draft Declaration on the Rights of Indigenous Peoples, the power to interpret and implement remains largely within the framework of the traditional sovereign-state system. The draft declaration has not been ratified and, as such, little international law remains that recognizes tribal governance.

—*Robert Lee-Nichols*

See also Indigenous Governance; Postcolonialism; Self-Government

Further Readings and References

Anaya, S. J. (2004). *Indigenous peoples in international law* (2nd ed.). Oxford, UK: Oxford University Press.

Deloria, V. (2002). *The Indian Reorganization Act: Congresses and bills.* Norman: University of Oklahoma Press.

Ray, D., & Reddy, P. S. (Eds.). (2003). *Grass-roots governance? Chiefs in Africa and the Afro-Caribbean.* Calgary, AB, Canada: University of Calgary Press.

TRUST

Trust entails reliance upon the actions and intentions of others and the recognition that people are interdependent in a variety of ways. Trust is the anticipation of the actions of others as favorable and as the basis of one's own actions on this positive prediction. Trust is one mode by which the actions of others affect our own actions. Distrust is the anticipation of the actions of others as negative and adjusting one's own actions accordingly. Acting on the basis of trust requires acting without full knowledge and entails risk. In situations of trust, disappointment is always a possibility. Trust is such a broad concept that it can have many definitions. Trust can be seen as an irrational passion or as a rational choice. The notion of trust is treated by the fields of ethics, political theory, psychology, sociology, and economics. Many theorists consider trust in some form to be necessary for cooperative action and to be a precondition for the possibility for acting in concert with others.

Trust and Governance

In contrast to trust in interpersonal relationships, trust in political contexts is often impersonal and characterized by conflicting interests. Trust can be divided into two levels: the microlevel, as seen in personal and immediate relationships, or the macrolevel, where trust exists between distant strangers or between people and institutions. Trust in governance exists on the macrolevel in relationships between citizens and governmental representatives, institutions, and systems. Many theorists suggest that citizens must have a certain level of trust in government in order for that government to be legitimate and reliably continue to function. Trust, rather than first-hand contact and monitoring, tends to connect citizens to many public, private, and civil institutions. Trust requires faith in the operating of just institutional processes and in the ethical personal action on the part of representatives and administrators. Trust can also be invested in citizens by their government, by allowing citizens the maximum amount of freedom possible.

Trust and Power Relationships

Many theorists hold that asymmetrical power relationships tend to breed mistrust. Histories of past abuse in relationships, whether interpersonal or institutional, can reduce the level of future trust. Cultural differences also influence how much trust citizens have in political institutions. Distrust in political systems is not always unfounded or a negative phenomenon. Differences in power make trust more risky for less-powerful parties in a society. The source of political trust on the part of elites may be based on the privilege that they gain from the political system, and the distrust on the part of the others can be the result of being disadvantaged by the same system. Distrust in this case can form the basis for political resistance by excluded people and groups.

One example of how trust and distrust can be exemplified is in the prisoner's dilemma. This dilemma illustrates the difficulty of trust, and therefore cooperation, between two self-interested actors. Each actor will gain advantage if the two cooperate, but the worst-case scenario is to act on trust but be disappointed by the action of the other party. Unless each actor is assured of mutual benefit, or is assured of sanction for the other party's lack of cooperation, trust is impossible. There are some possible problems with the prisoner's dilemma as a model of trust. First, it assumes that the ideal relationship of trust is a relationship where parties are equal in power; however, this ideal excludes relationships of necessary dependence, such as between a parent and child or between a patient and a doctor. Second, some theorists would hold that trust is not a rational choice based on self-interest, but is a moral principle that we should act on regardless of what we get in return.

The Importance of Trust in Modern Societies

In modern societies, social complexity and technological sophistication require members to trust each other and to trust institutions; otherwise acting in concert for the purpose of reaching common goals becomes virtually impossible. This is due to the broad levels of expertise and specialized knowledge that are distributed among different members of society. Not all members of society are in positions to evaluate the information from varied fields, such as medicine, public policy, and nuclear energy. Because an analysis of the information that experts act on is not possible for the vast majority of their trustees to evaluate, there is a question of how trust in experts can be established. In trustworthy governmental institutions, experts are generally trusted not to act according to their own agendas, but according to the public good. Some social scientists emphasize the prevalence of network forms of organization in modern society. These networks are nonhierarchical in structure and share knowledge across organizations and institutions. Such networks can generate trust because the power of the actors is equal and information is shared for mutual benefit.

Diversity of both perspectives and social positions among society members makes trust between citizens as political coactors difficult, but likely necessary. In modern democracies, for example, citizens of vastly different backgrounds and interests often work to trust each other in order to cogovern their society. The potential for the loss of trust between members of society has many perceived causes, including the loss of hierarchical control, the increased stratification of wealth and power, and the ability of others to opt out of social interaction and cogovernance.

Many theorists claim that an increased level of trust in a society enhances the amount of social capital in a society. They argue that greater cooperation yields greater productivity in all areas of human endeavor. Trust can allow for smoother social, political, and economic processes due to the fact that oversight and management of those processes is not as necessary. For example, in a society with a high level of interpersonal trust, there is less need for surveillance, security, and the policing of people's behavior. This allows for the expenditure of social capital in other areas.

—*Jennifer L. Eagan*

See also Capitalism; Game Theory; Network; Prisoner's Dilemma; Risk; Social Capital

Further Readings and References

Baier, A. (1986). Trust and antitrust. *Ethics, 96*(2), 231–260.

Fukuyama, F. (1995). *Trust: The social virtues and the creation of prosperity.* New York: Free Press.

Gambetta, D. (Ed.). (1988). *Trust: Making and breaking cooperative relations.* New York: Basil Blackwell.

Luhmann, N. (1979). *Trust and power.* Chichester, UK: Wiley.

Warren, M. E. (Ed.). (1999). *Democracy and trust.* Cambridge, UK: Cambridge University Press.

UNEMPLOYMENT

Unemployment signifies that part of the population (mostly people between 15 and 64 years of age) that is eligible for and registered as wanting work. The "problem" of unemployment has attracted attention from economists, politicians, and the population at large. In particular, the volatile levels of unemployment are a salient topic in liberal democracies with responsible government and universal suffrage. The first question to be answered is: What exactly is unemployment and how should it be measured? Measurement, here, is not only an academic question regarding methodological rigor (i.e., validity and reliability), but also an indicator for how societal resources are distributed across the population (e.g., for men and women) and by economic sector. Both the level and the distribution effects of unemployment have social and political consequences. Economists, policy analysts, and political scientists have developed explanations of unemployment that will be discussed. The lesson that can be learned from this overview is that economic explanations tend to focus on the levels of unemployment, whereas sociopolitical explanations tend to focus on the effects of unemployment.

Concept, Definition, and Measurement

Statistically, unemployment is the numerical difference between supply and demand for work within a given territory. From this definition, one can observe that advanced democracies use a rather narrow concept of unemployment. It does not consider those who are laid off, disabled, or work as homemakers. Nor does it involve those who study, who do not register, or have disappeared from the labor market. In short, in addition to the official definition of unemployment, there exists another type that could be called "broad" and hidden unemployment (and which is, by definition, hard to measure). It is argued that this exact gap between the official level and the level of broad unemployment is a more adequate indicator of whether the level is politically and socially disturbing or not.

Explaining Developments in Unemployment

There are three types of factors that are considered to be explanatory in political economy literature. The first category considers economic developments as the primary mechanism in regards to variations in unemployment. The second category focuses on the influences of economic and electoral cycles as a result of changing levels of unemployment. The third category concerns the role of public policy in relation to the effects of unemployment.

Economic Factors

In political economy literature, one can find a bedazzling number of variables that are relevant.

Among these variables is, for example, the Phillips curve. This theory claims that high levels of unemployment are the opposite of low levels of inflation and vice versa. Hence, a rise in unemployment is the result of inflationary pressures. Another important economic factor is productivity growth per unit of labor time: the absence of such productivity has a negative impact on comparative competitiveness on the world market. Likewise, it is argued that the exposure to international trade and the global economy will be negative for the national levels of unemployment. In fact, one observes a change in the working of labor markets: The locus of production is shifting across the world and has led to the deindustrialization of many national economies among the advanced economies.

Political Factors

John Keynes and Michal Kalecki, two economists from the 1930s and 1940s, pointed to the role of politics to cope with (high) levels of unemployment. The former became famous for his ideas of counter-cyclical monetary policy making; the latter focused mainly on what he called the Political-Business Cycle. The idea behind this phenomenon is that the business cycle allows the organized interests of labor to press for higher wages during a *hausse* (market analysis) and, conversely, force business organizations together with the state to allow for higher levels of unemployment. This idea has led to many studies in which Kalecki's thesis was translated into electoral politics: Low growth rates together with higher levels of inflation and unemployment would be conducive to electoral losses for government. In fact, the economic cycle is often considered a predictor of electoral outcomes.

Public Policy Factors

There are two schools of thought regarding the impact of governmental policymaking in advanced democracies: the mixed economy and the role of big government. Whereas the adherents to the idea of the mixed economy see the state as a guardian that facilitates and directs the market economy for the sake of public welfare, critics of big government argue that the

state is a last resort to organize social and economic relations in society, and therefore its role ought to be minimal.

Many argue that the mixed economy has a bearing on unemployment. On the one hand, it ameliorates the individual effects of being unemployed through welfare systems, on the other hand and more importantly, social security benefits may well impair reemployment. According to the Organisation for Economic Co-operation and Development, high replacement ratios and long duration of unemployment benefits increase the level of unemployment. Hence the mechanisms of a labor market are structurally in disequilibrium. However, there appears little or no comparative evidence over time to sustain the hypothesis that extended welfare states are more vulnerable to higher levels of unemployment than others.

Supporters of big government argue that high taxation and public spending (e.g., on Social Security) impede the market economy and a nation's competitiveness in the world economy. As it turns out, one can determine that from a macroeconomic perspective, critics of big government have a point: The postwar growth of taxation and spending has certainly changed the social construction of contemporary society and thus also the behavior of individuals. Yet, recent policies of welfare retrenchment or of reducing labor market policies have not brought about a remarkable difference in terms of levels of unemployment.

—*Hans Keman*

See also Capitalism; Economic Governance; Keynesianism; Market Failure; New Poverty Research; Political Business Cycle; Social Inclusion; Welfare State

Further Readings and References

Castles, F. G. (1998). *Comparative public policy: Patterns of post-war transformation.* Cheltenham, UK: Edward Elgar.

Keynes, J. M. (1936). *The general theory of employment, interest, and money.* London: Macmillan.

Layard, R., Nickell, S., & Jackman, R. (1991). *Unemployment: Macroeconomic performance and the labor market.* New York: Oxford University Press.

Tufte, E. R. (1978). *Political control of the economy.* Princeton, NJ: Princeton University Press.

UNITED NATIONS

The United Nations (UN) was founded in 1945 as an international, universal membership organization to replace the earlier League of Nations of 1919. Its membership now stands at 191. Only Taiwan and the Vatican City are not members. The UN is headquartered in New York City, with major programs based at Geneva, Vienna, and Nairobi, and a global spread of offices in many capital cities. The UN was created by the allied powers during World War II. The charter was negotiated in 1944 at Dumbarton Oaks, Washington, DC, by four of the five permanent powers: China, Great Britain, the USSR, and the United States (the excluded allied power being France). The charter was adopted by fifty-one member countries at San Francisco in July 1945. The charter came into force on October 24, 1945. The charter that still governs the UN is therefore a prenuclear, pre–Cold War vision of the post–1945 world order that was created on the assumption of continued allied cooperation. In Article 27, the five great powers gave themselves permanent seats on the Security Council and power of veto over its resolutions. They also created a veto over the reform of these arrangements as set out in Article 108.

The founding purpose of the UN is defined in its charter as a fourfold mission. The first is the maintenance of international peace and security. Member states pledge not to threaten or use force against each other in Article 2 and agree to seek peaceful settlement of their disputes by negotiation in Article 33. If war does occur, the members further agree to take collective measures to suppress threats to the peace and acts of aggression. The second purpose of the UN is to develop friendly relations among states based on respect for equal rights and self-determination of peoples. Thirdly, the members agree to address international problems of economic, social, and humanitarian needs, including the promotion of human rights. Finally, the UN exists to provide a center for harmonizing the actions of its members. In pursuit of these objectives, the UN is not only a global center for the conduct of multilateral diplomacy, but also through its recognition of several thousand international nongovernmental organizations (INGOs), it is a major focus of global civil-society efforts to lobby and influence the multilateral system.

Principal Organs

The General Assembly is the locus of all political, economic, and social debate and decision in the UN. The General Assembly is one place in the international political system where the legal principle of sovereign equality of all member states is respected. All members may table agenda items, debate them, and have one vote on resolutions adopted by simple majority in the General Assembly. Since its foundation, international norms and standards on issues such as decolonization, economic development, and human rights have evolved in the annual debates of the General Assembly. The General Assembly also elects ten of its total number to serve on the fifteen-member Security Council. The Security Council was created to exercise primary responsibility for the maintenance of international peace and security. Its membership comprises five permanent members, China, France, Russia, the United Kingdom, and the United States, and ten members elected by a regional formula for a two-year term, five from Asia and Africa, two from Latin America and the Caribbean, two from Western Europe, and one from Eastern Europe. Resolutions brought to the Security Council require nine affirmative votes to be adopted. Each of the five permanent members can exercise a veto to prevent the adoption of a resolution. The Security Council can apply economic sanctions and ultimately endorse military action against any state that, in its view, represents a threat to international peace and security. The other members accept that the Security Council acts on their behalf.

The Economic and Social Council (ECOSOC) is a fifty-four-member subsidiary of the General Assembly. ECOSOC was created to provide supervision of economic and social programs accountable to the General Assembly. For example, the United Nations Children's Fund (UNICEF), the United Nations Development Program (UNDP), and the United Nations Environment Programme (UNEP) are accountable to the council through annual reports to ECOSOC. More tenuously, the charter also provides for ECOSOC to coordinate the work of the otherwise independent specialized agencies, such as the World Health Organization (WHO) and the United Nations Educational, Scientific and Cultural Organization (UNESCO).

The Trusteeship Council was created to administer the non-self-governing territories inherited from the League of Nations in 1946, themselves former colonial possessions of the defeated powers in 1918, such as Namibia and Palestine. The council suspended its activities in 1994, following the independence of its last responsibility in Palau. Rather than being disbanded, some reform proposals have suggested that the council could either inherit an enlarged role for sustainable development, or, more controversially, it might provide a standing mechanism for the administration of long-term, postconflict administration and reconstruction in territories that require a semipermanent UN presence.

The UN Secretariat of 8,900 staff administers the programs adopted by the members and performs the headquarter's central services. This includes internal services, such as translation between the UN's six official languages, and fieldwork in development programs across the world. A Secretary-General who is elected by the Security Council heads the Secretariat. He or she serves a five-year term. This may be renewed once. Following convention both during the Cold War period and since, the Secretary-General has been elected from a traditionally neutral country. Previous incumbents were elected from Norway, Sweden, Burma, Austria, Peru, and Egypt. The current holder, Kofi Annan of Ghana, will hold office from 1997 to 2006. All members of the UN are also party to the Statute of the International Court of Justice. The court exists to apply judicial settlements to conflicts between member states. The UN operates on a two-year budget cycle; currently it is $3.160 billion for the period of 2004–2005. This budget comprises the fixed costs distributed between the members in assessed contributions. Assessed contributions are levied on the members by a complex formula that approximates their share of world product with very substantial reductions for the majority of less-developed countries. The scale of contributions ranges from 22 percent

for the United States to 0.001 percent for the poorest and least populous members. Japan contributes 19.4 percent and Germany 8.6 percent. The G8 (Group of Eight) countries are responsible for more than sixty-seven percent of the assessed contributions. Separate assessments are levied for peacekeeping missions undertaken to maintain international peace and security. This scale of contributions is weighted toward a larger share for the permanent members as an additional responsibility to balance their additional powers of veto over the creation of peacekeeping missions. Further resources are donated by the member states and individuals for particular programs. In practice, the developmental and humanitarian programs, such as UNDP and UNEP, rely heavily on these extrabudgetary or voluntary donations.

Effectiveness

The UN is judged primarily on its security role. Bringing the resort to force under the control of an international authority has formed an explicit goal of liberal-internationalism from Woodrow Wilson's Fourteen Points that was used to justify U.S. intervention in World War I in 1917. It was enshrined in both the League Covenant of 1919 and in the United Nations Charter of 1945. The end of the Cold War revived the possibility that the international control of the use of force might be established in a veto-free Security Council. However, the model case of economic sanctions and then military force being authorized to restore the sovereignty of Kuwait after Iraq's invasion in 1990 and 1991 has not been repeated. The conditions necessary for the full-scale application of collective security doctrine as described in the charter in Articles 39 through 42 have not become established. The scheme has not deterred the occasional use of force by determined aggressors, nor does the UN Charter adequately address cases of civil war, which have created most conflicts and casualties since 1945. Although permitted under Article 39 to define any situation as a breach of the peace or act of aggression, the Security Council has historically been reluctant to extend armed intervention into its member's internal conflicts. The presumption in favor of national sovereignty almost always overrides occasional attempts to extend the application of international human rights standards. Peacekeeping was developed to fill the legal and operational gap created by the nonapplication of collective security after 1953. The original rationale of peacekeeping was to deploy UN forces, volunteered by willing members to supervise and police cease-fires with the consent of host parties. Lightly armed forces would maintain a physical separation between hostile parties and so reduce the risks of malicious or accidental breaches of the cease-fire. Operations of this sort have become long established in the Golan Heights, Cyprus, and Kashmir. The expansion of UN peacekeeping activities after 1990 involved not only substantial numerical growth in the number and size of missions mandated, but also expanded the tasks associated with peacekeeping to include election supervision, as in El Salvador, Namibia, and Cambodia. More complex missions, such as extending protection to NGOs' (nongovernmental organizations) humanitarian relief efforts in Somalia and Bosnia and the declaration of safe havens for civilian populations, also in Bosnia, were widely judged to have failed in the 1990s and have not been repeated without explicit invitation and consent of host countries, especially after the civil conflict in Liberia, where cease-fires were finally established in 2003. The UN has also attempted preventive deployment of missions in anticipation and deterrence of future hostilities, as in Macedonia and Burundi.

The founding members originally sought to address global economic security, convinced of its connection to military security and international stability. Chapter IX of the charter seeks to create conditions of stability and well-being, which are necessary for peaceful and friendly relations among nations. As the charter's military-security worldview was shaped by the experiences of appeasing dictators in the period from 1931 to 1939, the depth and duration of the Great Depression after 1931 was regarded as a contributory factor to the causes of the World War II, and the charter was drafted to prevent its recurrence. In particular, the UN Charter planned to create a liberal, international economic order favoring free trade and expanded economic interdependence. The charter also makes commitments to seeking higher standards of living, full employment, and the solutions to economic, health, and social problems. These include respect for and observance of human rights and fundamental freedoms. Under the impact of decolonization and the majority of new membership coming from third-world countries after 1970, the focus of these economic and social activities of the UN shifted toward economic development, restyled as sustainable development in the 1990s and poverty reduction among the world's poorest two billion people.

Future

The UN has passed through numerous phases in its existence since 1945. The period since 1970 has been particularly problematic. The institution was founded as an expression and reflection of post–1945 U.S. dominance of the international system and passed into a phase of third-world, majority-led hostility to Western leadership after 1970. For more than twenty years, the UN General Assembly, in particular, was more often associated with profound division rather than harmonization of the members' interests. The end of the Cold War did not entirely remove these disputes. Many other multilateral organizations, including the G8, the European Union, NATO (North Atlantic Treaty Organization), NAFTA (North American Free Trade Agreement), ASEAN (Association of the Southeast Asian Nations), and APEC (Asia-Pacific Economic Cooperation), have experienced more substantial growth in membership, functions, and funding in the period since 1990 than has the UN. However, the coincidental experience of globalization and democratization has transformed the views of the majority of members on human rights, transparent governance, and the adoption of neoliberal economic policies. The aftermath of the September 11, 2001, attacks on New York and the Pentagon also had the effect of unifying the membership in response to terrorism.

Proposals for the reform of the UN have been an almost continuous feature of its history, with limited results to date. Track 1, or administrative reform, initiated by the Secretary-General and which does not require charter amendment, contrasts with Track 2 reform, which must be initiated by the member states.

No reform of the charter has actually been achieved since 1965. Recent administrative reforms initiated by Kofi Annan have concentrated upon staff reductions, greater budgetary and accounting transparency, and the reorganization of Secretariat departments to achieve greater focus on peacekeeping, sustainable development, and humanitarian relief. The most widely debated example of Track 2 is the reform of the composition and powers of the Security Council. Since 1998, consensus has been established on the need for expansion. Disputes remain as to the exact composition of an enlarged Security Council and on whether the new members would acquire veto powers. Japan, Germany, Brazil, and India are the most widely canvassed candidates for permanent member status. The most recent report of the Secretary-General's High Level Panel on Threats, Challenges and Change, published in December 2004, emphasized the need for the UN to enlarge its conceptualization of threats to international security and to add large-scale human rights abuses within states, the proliferation of weapons of mass destruction, terrorism, and organized crime to the conventional preoccupation with wars between states and sustainable economic development. Security Council reform is not just a question of enlargement. More controversial and problematic than size are disputes concerning the voting powers, especially the Article 27 veto powers of certain members. For some, enlargement should not include the extension of the veto to new permanent members. Meanwhile, critics of the existing veto powers of the five members argue for voluntary restraint in veto use, for instance, by only using the veto in relation to Chapter VII and the use of force. Radical critics of the current UN structure have argued variously for an enlarged role for NGOs and independent financial resources for the UN derived from taxing the global commons, such as international aviation, arms sales, seabed mining charges, or currency trading. Under the present charter, reform proposals require a two-thirds majority vote in the General Assembly, and a resolution of the Security Council, and also ratification by the domestic legislatures of the permanent five members. In practice, the consensus required to effect any charter reform would appear to be receding rather than advancing.

—*Mark F. Imber*

See also Commission on Global Governance; Functionalism; Global Governance; Global Warming; Group of 77; Human Security; International Courts; International Labor Organization; Internet Governance; Millennium Development Goals; Peace Process; United Nations Conference on Trade and Development; Security; Tragedy of the Commons; United Nations Educational, Scientific and Cultural Organization; United Nations Security Council; World Bank; World Health Organization; World Trade Organization

Further Readings and References

Berdal, M. (2004). The UN after Iraq. *Survival, 46*, 83–102.

McKnight, A. (2000). *The changing united.* New York: Palgrave.

Mingst, K. A., & Karns, M. P. (2000). *The United Nations in the post–Cold War era.* Boulder, CO: Westview.

Price, R. M., & Zacher, M. (Eds.). (2004). *The United Nations and global security.* New York: Palgrave.

Schechter, M. G. (Ed.). (1997). *Future multilateralism.* Tokyo: UNU Press.

Taylor, P., & Groom, A. J. (Eds.). (2000). *The United Nations at the millennium.* New York: Continuum.

United Nations. (2004). *A more secure world: Our shared responsibility.* New York: Author.

UNITED NATIONS CONFERENCE ON TRADE AND DEVELOPMENT

The United Nations Conference on Trade and Development (UNCTAD) was formed in 1964 as a forum for intergovernmental deliberations relating to the integrated treatment of trade and development. UNCTAD is often thought of as a pressure group that exerts influence on the international trade and development policy process. There are a number of interrelated features of the post–World War II political and economic climate that contributed to its creation.

There was an explosion of developing country membership in the UN system following the process of decolonization. The subsequent emergence of a third-world coalition is one of the most striking features of the period. These countries were unified by the shared belief that the liberal international trading regime was not furthering their development.

The coalition was heavily influenced by the work of Raul Prebisch, an economist associated with dependency theory, who became the first Secretary-General of UNCTAD. He posited that the fundamental structure of the liberal trading regime tended to reproduce disparities between the developed core and the developing periphery, increase developing countries' dependence on the developed countries, and thus hamper development. Prebisch's analysis opposed Smithian (Adam Smith) or Ricardian (David Ricardo) free-trade ideologies; while he acknowledged that free trade could improve total global welfare, he maintained that it could not ensure that the gains from trade are distributed equally.

Developing countries thus called for a restructured and development-centered trade governance regime, where developing countries would be able to pursue national regulation and trade protectionism to facilitate industrialization, further development, and reduce dependency. They also believed that the extant mechanisms of global governance, namely international institutions such as the International Monetary Fund (IMF) and the General Agreement on Tariffs and Trade (GATT), merely reflected developed countries' interests and thus were ill-equipped to serve their needs.

These factors all fuelled demands for the establishment of a new organization to coordinate trade and development policy on developing countries' terms. This eventually led the UN General Assembly to establish UNCTAD. It is under the auspices of UNCTAD that the developing world coalition was formalized and became known as the Group of 77 (G77).

UNCTAD's Organizational Structure and Role

UNCTAD is an institutionalized set of intergovernmental conferences. It also consists of a trade and development board and a permanent Secretariat, which carries out its administrative functions. It is intergovernmental insofar as its membership is made up of different national governments; it currently has 132 members. Conferences take place on a four-year basis, and each conference tackles a different set of policy issues. To date, there have been eleven conferences, and the next will be UNCTAD XII in 2008.

UNCTAD does not only provide a forum for state actors. Its conferences are attended by organizations of the UN system, other intergovernmental institutions, nongovernmental organizations, the private sector (including trade and industry associations), and members of research institutes and universities. Reflecting contemporary ideas of governance, it consists of and works with sub- and supranational groups and associations. It operates as part of a complex network of trade- and development-related governance.

States have devolved certain functions to UNCTAD. First, UNCTAD provides a formal and informal forum for negotiations aimed at building consensus around issues of domestic and international trade and development policy. Second, it undertakes research and policy analysis to provide ideas on the policy process. Third, it provides technical assistance tailored to the requirements of developing countries.

Although UNCTAD performs these tasks, some question the extent to which it can constrain state behavior. Its influence is severely curtailed by the fact that it cannot set and enforce rules on trade and development, and it has no negotiating authority. Some might counter that UNCTAD remains a participative arena for debate and knowledge generation. While it has no formal power to implement and enforce state policy, it propels beliefs, concerns, and ideas onto the global stage that shape and influence policy, albeit in less measurable or tangible ways. This foregrounds certain questions. How influential a role does UNCTAD play in concrete policy making? Can UNCTAD steer trade and development norms?

Contemporary Challenges Facing UNCTAD

UNCTAD's focus on developing states reflects a global awareness of the interrelated problems of development, economic interdependence, and representation. First, some states and regions are considerably more economically developed than others. In terms of trade, for example, Africa, with fifteen percent of the world's population, accounts for around two percent of world trade, whereas the United States, with five percent of the world's population, accounts for around thirteen percent of world trade. UNCTAD endeavors to generate ideas about how we might work to resolve such global imbalances in economic capabilities. For instance, UNCTAD has led the campaign for special or differential treatment of developing countries in regimes of trade governance. But, given that states' development and thus interests can differ markedly, how can global governance consistently and justly accommodate diverging interests?

Second, ever-increasing economic interdependence means that a state's domestic policies can have a direct impact on overseas development. In the European Union, for example, agricultural subsidies can lower the price of produce and lead to overproduction; this cheap produce then floods developing countries' markets, crowds out local producers, and negatively affects development. These international economic linkages require state managers, particularly in developed countries, to elaborate techniques of governance that balance domestic obligations with international development objectives. UNCTAD carries out policy analyses with the aim of furthering knowledge of such linkages and thus enhancing this balance; development can no longer be perceived as a distant and self-contained problem.

Third, it has been argued that UNCTAD's role is vital because it represents the poorer, weaker countries. Global governance is understood, by some, to overly represent those developed states that have the resources, capabilities, and knowledge to create and regulate its complex and expensive networks. In this way, UNCTAD's existence partially rectifies representational asymmetries.

These three problems require states to develop global governance systems that respond representatively to the differentiated needs of states and that give primacy to techniques of governing that help those that need it most.

UNCTAD's Critics

Historically, UNCTAD has made limited headway in qualitatively reshaping the norms of the liberal trading regime; for instance, its attempts to establish a New International Economic Order in the 1970s and 1980s did not succeed. The reason for this failure is hotly debated; it could be attributed to developed countries' opposition as easily as it could be to the nature of UNCTAD as an institution.

UNCTAD has also drawn the criticism that it has progressively become less representative of poor countries' interests. In particular, its ideological shift to the support of "freer trade" or more "market friendly" policies is thought to conform more to the developed world's agenda than to the developing world's agenda. Other observers might rejoin that UNCTAD has merely adapted to the changing nature of the global order; globalization and the ideological ascendancy of neoliberalism in the 1980s has oriented the policy agenda toward trade liberalization and away from global economic regulation. This opens the floor for some important questions about UNCTAD and contemporary governance. How can government mechanisms respond to changes in the global order without obstructing development goals? Has UNCTAD retained its mandate to represent and protect developing countries' interests? Or is it now beholden to the very countries it was designed to lobby?

—*Simon Carl O'Meally*

See also Development Assistance Committee; Development Theory; Group of 77; United Nations

Further Readings and References

Dadzie, K. (1993). The UN and the problem of economic development. In B. Kingsbury & A. Roberts (Eds.), *United Nations, divided world: The UN's roles in international relations.* New York: Oxford University Press.
Nye, J. S. (1973). UNCTAD: Poor nations' pressure group. In R. Cox & H. Jacobson (Eds.), *The anatomy of influence.* London: Yale University Press.
Taylor, I. (2003). The United Nations conference on trade and development. *New Political Economy, 8*(3), 409–418.
Williams, M. (1991). *Third world cooperation: The Group of 77 in UNCTAD.* London: Pinter.
Williams, M. (1994). *International economic organisations and the third world.* Hassocks, Sussex, UK: Harvester.

UNITED NATIONS EDUCATIONAL, SCIENTIFIC AND CULTURAL ORGANIZATION

The United Nations Educational, Scientific and Cultural Organization (UNESCO) is a specialized agency of the United Nations system founded in 1945 and is headquartered in Paris. UNESCO's mandate is the widest of all of the specialized agencies, a mission that extends far beyond the functionally specific responsibilities usually associated with the technical, humanitarian, and economic agencies of the United Nations. UNESCO was founded with the constitutional objective to contribute peace and security by promoting collaboration among the nations through education, science, and culture. The explicit commitment to liberal and democratic values is further embedded in the constitutional goal to further universal respect for justice, the rule of law, human rights, and fundamental freedoms.

UNESCO Traces Its Origins to the Conference of Allied Ministers of Education

The Conference of Allied Ministers of Education (CAME) was organized among the exiled governments of occupied Europe during World War II. Current membership stands at 190 governments, which sit in a General Conference. The General Conference, in turn, elects an executive board of fifty-eight members. In addition to government representation, UNESCO maintains a National Commission in each member state for direct liaison with civil society and non-governmental organization (NGO) groups.

Major programs are organized in five divisions: education, natural sciences, social sciences, culture, and communications and information. Among the landmark achievements of the organization are literacy programs in areas of conflict and reconstruction and the preservation of cultural heritage, which includes both tangible artifacts (such as architectural monuments designated as World Heritage sites) and intangible cultural heritage (a concept embracing oral history, performance art, and ritual, especially those endangered by the decline of traditional societies). UNESCO's most widely cited science program is the Man and the Biosphere Program, which pioneered an awareness of sustainable development concepts within the UN system after 1968.

The breadth and academic nature of UNESCO's activities has also created problems for the organization. The great majority of its programs are not unique—they are also performed by numerous other national, transnational, and intergovernmental organizations. These characteristics left UNESCO vulnerable to charges of duplication and overlap. During the 1980s, UNESCO was also exposed to intense ideological disputes.

At various times in its history, UNESCO has been challenged by withdrawals of some leading member states. The Soviet Union, wary of the organization's explicitly liberal commitments, did not join until 1954. South Africa withdrew during the apartheid era of 1956 to 1994. The United States withdrew between 1984 and 2003, followed by the United Kingdom from 1985 to 1997. The U.S. dissatisfaction centered upon proposals for a new world communications order. Proposals for the licensing of journalists were interpreted by the United States as an attempted censorship of Western news media freedoms. Additional U.S. criticisms centered on alleged budgetary and Secretariat quality deficiencies. Singapore also withdrew in 1985 and has not since rejoined.

—*Mark F. Imber*

See also Functionalism; Human Rights; International Organization; Sustainable Development; United Nations; World Health Organization

Further Readings and References

Coate, R. (1988). *Unilateralism, ideology, and US foreign policy: The United States, in and out of UNESCO.* Boulder, CO: Lynne Rienner.

Wells, C. (1987). *The UN, UNESCO, and the politics of knowledge.* Basingstoke, UK: Macmillan.

UNITED NATIONS SECURITY COUNCIL

The Security Council is a principal organ of the United Nations (UN). Under the UN Charter, the Security Council is charged with the primary responsibility of the maintenance of international peace and security. The charter also gives the Security Council wide powers under Chapter VI to use diplomatic means to assist the parties of a dispute to resolve their conflict by peaceful means. In the event that no peaceful reconciliation is possible, Chapter VII of the charter also confers on the Security Council the right to define a breach of the peace, that is to name an aggressor, and thereafter mobilize economic sanctions and, ultimately, military force against any member state that the Security Council judges to be a threat to international peace and security. The wider UN membership of 192 countries agrees to accept and carry out the resolutions adopted by the Security Council. In this way, the Security Council is credited with a unique moral and legal authority in the post-1945 construction of international order.

The Security Council comprises fifteen member states. Five are permanent members, which have occupied their positions since the founding of the UN in 1945. The permanent members are: China, France, Russia, the United Kingdom, and the United States. Ten additional nonpermanent members are elected by a regional formula and serve a two-year term. The ten regional members are elected from five groups: five from the African and Asian regions combined, two from Latin America and the Caribbean, two from Western Europe, and one from Eastern Europe.

The Security Council operates under a rotating presidency. This advances monthly by the English-language name of each member. The presidency is responsible for calling and chairing all meetings of the Security Council during that month. The UN Secretary-General can also bring matters to the attention of the Security Council. Resolutions adopted by the Security Council are binding in international law. Although the charter forbids the UN to interfere in matters of domestic jurisdiction, this protection does not extend to conduct that the Security Council, acting under Article 39, judges to be a threat to international peace and security.

The adoption of a resolution by the Security Council requires a majority of at least nine of the fifteen members. However, each of the five permanent members has veto power over the adoption of any substantive resolution by the Security Council. The original logic of this provision was to limit the adoption of resolutions and the potential military commitments entailed to those that had the consensual support of the five victorious powers of the 1945 settlement. It was also intended to prevent any one of them from using the mechanism of the UN to legitimate a war on each other. The five permanent members also have veto power over the reform of these entrenched powers. Any reform of the UN Charter requires a resolution to be adopted by the Security Council and ratification by the five powers' constitutional processes. In the case of the United States, this would require a vote of the Senate.

The aggregate use of the veto from 1945 to 2004 is: USSR/Russia 120, United States 76, United Kingdom 32, France 18, and China 5. Since 1990, veto use has declined drastically.

Conventional wisdom acknowledges that the veto culture of the Cold War period prevented the Security Council from employing the collective security doctrine as defined in the charter. The Security Council was instrumental in organizing the defense of South Korea (1950–1953) due to the temporary absence of the USSR from the council. Unable to agree on large-scale military interventions, the Security Council did, however, pioneer the technique of UN peacekeeping that evolved as a modest, consensual technique of containing regional conflicts that great powers agreed to limit. Peacekeeping forces were typically dispatched to supervise cease-fires in the aftermath of successive wars in the Middle East and Central and South Asia. In some cases, the presence of UN peacekeeping forces became institutionalized over decades, such as their presence in Jerusalem, Kashmir, and Cyprus. Since 1990, and with wider support from the Security Council members, many more ambitious peacekeeping missions have undertaken expanded tasks in civil policing, election supervision, transitional government, and long-term reconstruction.

The possibility of UN-endorsed military actions was revived in 1990. A sequence of resolutions was adopted between August and November 1990, which gave clear warning to Iraq of the forthcoming military campaign to restore the sovereignty of Kuwait in the Gulf War of 1991. After 1994, this brief period of consensus faded.

The genocide in Rwanda, in 1994, was an example of the member's selective concerns and unwillingness to confront domestically driven human rights abuse. Differences between the permanent members over Bosnia also limited the effectiveness of the Security Council's role. Both China and Russia were opposed to the extension of UN competence into civil wars. Thereafter, the threat of a Russian veto led the United States and the United Kingdom to use NATO authority to conduct its campaign in Kosovo in 1999. In 2003, the United States, the United Kingdom, and their allies were unable to secure explicit renewed endorsement from the Security Council for their actions in Iraq.

The Security Council has only been reformed once, by enlargement from twelve members to its current fifteen members in 1965. Enlargement has been widely discussed since 1990, usually in terms of reestablishing the representational balance to reflect the enlarged third-world membership of the UN. However, Japan and Germany have been widely promoted as additional candidates for permanent membership in view of their financial contributions to the UN. Leading third-world claimants include India and Brazil. Other members have advanced claims on grounds of population and regional status. Enlargement is therefore controversial and problematic. The issue has also been linked to the reform of the veto power. None of the established permanent members is willing to relinquish or dilute this particular status. Enlargement might create three categories of membership, with the new permanent members not having veto powers.

—Mark F. Imber

See also Humanitarian Intervention; Peace Process; Sanctions; Sovereignty; United Nations

Further Readings and References

Dedring, J. (2000). The security council. In P. Taylor & A. J. R. Groom (Eds.), *The United Nations at the millennium* (pp. 61–99). London: Continuum.

Russett, B., O'Neill, B., & Sutterlin, J. (1995). Breaking the Security Council restructuring logjam. *Global Governance, 2*(1) 65–80.

Urban and Regional Planning

Urban and regional planning is a notion that encompasses the whole set of social activities aimed at anticipating, representing, and regulating the development of an urban or a regional area. It thus articulates intellectual activities of the study of social and economic forecasting with more concrete activities, such as infrastructure programming, land reservation, and land-use regulation. Planning operates at different scales: neighborhood, city, or region. Generally speaking, the smaller the area addressed, the more precise and coercive planning regulations are.

Under the postwar Keynesian-Fordist compromise, a relatively static capital required the intervention of the state and its public policies to stabilize the workforce and to constitute homogeneous national economic spaces where standardized products could be sold. During this postwar period and until the late 1970s, urban and regional planning policies were an element of these demand-side policies. They were aimed at stabilizing the workforce by providing cheaper access to housing and enlarging the access to urban collective consumption goods to a larger part of the urban population. The principal tools of this Keynesian-Fordist version of planning were the mass production of social housing, the provision of collective infrastructures, the public acquisition of land, and the regulation of estate speculation. From this perspective, elected officials and public planners were the dominant figures of planning, and the comprehensive land-use regulation plan was the most common tool used to enforce these redistributive objectives.

The concept of governance has subsequently been used to describe the devices through which urban and regional plans were elaborated and implemented following the end of the Keynesian-Fordist consensus and the new objectives set for these devices. According to neo-Marxist and regulationist scholars, the 1970s economic crisis is the sign of the entrance of Western economies into a new era, where competition between firms is no longer based on their proximity to raw material sources or their ability to build masses of standardized products but instead on their ability to diversify their production and to incessantly innovate. Thus, firms are less dependent on public demand-side policies. On the contrary, the fiscal burden of these policies hinders the profitability of their business within international competition. The same rupture occurred at the urban and regional level. In a new context where growth has been slowing, where state transfers have rarified, and where firms have become increasingly mobile, the objectives of urban and regional planning have been changing. Shifts from demand-side policies to supply-side policies and from a redistributive stance to a competitive and marketing stance have taken place. The central aim of plans is not to regulate economic growth and its effects on urban and regional territories but rather to activate it.

As a consequence, planning practices and the very forms of plans have been changing. Rather than comprehensive land-use regulation plans, plans are taking the shape of marketing weapons. The vogue of strategic plans launched in the mid-1980s is the most obvious example of this. These plans do not intend to regulate growth and redistribute it throughout the territory through land-use regulations. Instead, they identify the strengths and the weaknesses of the city or the region, the opportunities that it can take advantage of, and the threats it could face, and, on this basis, try to define strategies in terms of economic development or urban renewal. In a context of governance, on the one hand, plans are less precise in that they do not intend to set up regulations for each space of the city. On the other hand, they are more precise in that they focus on strategic areas that can be valorized and on which specific policies should be implemented. The inspiration of these plans is more

neoliberal than reformist in that redistributive objectives are relegated to the background, whereas issues like competitiveness and economic attractiveness are prioritized because the plan is not principally aimed at setting up obstacles to market dynamics. In terms of planning practices, these new plans give a much more important place to economic actors and social elites. The plan is not conceived as the mere outcome of the public planner's expertise, but as the result of bargains between public and private actors and between different levels of public authorities. The political effectiveness of the plan is no longer expected to stem from its regulatory status, but rather from the consensus that the elaboration process of the plan has enabled the build up between a plurality of stakeholders.

This interpretation of the recent story of urban regional planning as a clear-cut example of the invasion of neoliberal recipes and the giving up of any public ambition to control territorial dynamics has been challenged by several scholars. Some of them doubt whether new forms of planning, such as strategic plans, can be interpreted as simply giving up of public ambitions on the evolution of cities and regions. The new forms of planning practices using networks and interactive, iterative, and incremental decision-making processes are also aimed at producing institutional capital, that is, a set of cognitive, relational, and identity resources that will enable the creation of a common rationale for the interventions of different actors on the territory. The rise of strategic plans is the sign of a communicative turn in planning. Planning is not only about elaborating the graphic representation of a substantive vision of the territorial common interest whose definition is set only by officials and public planners. Instead, it is about managing processes of political mediation and enabling mutual comprehension between different social interests, the outcome of which will be the sharing of a common vision of the future of a territory. Strategic planning may be a sign of a new form of territorial governance, where public expertise and actors are not omnipotent but do not inevitably promote a neoliberal agenda.

If neo-Marxists and regulationists defend a substantive definition of governance as a policy content, other scholars propose a definition of governance as a research agenda that can help understand the recent evolution of urban and regional planning. If recent evolutions like globalization, construction of regional ensembles like the European Union, or devolution trends have modified the way urban and regional development is steered, this does not necessarily mean that planning systems are promoting neoliberal agendas. Rather these evolutions have modified the way social and territorial change is organized and, in particular, the division of labor between political/bureaucratic and market and civil society regulations in the governance of territorial development. However, in this approach, the term *governance* does not presume the neoliberal policy content deriving from these new arrangements. Rather, governance is presented as a new research agenda for the understanding of collective actions aimed at controlling and promoting urban and regional development.

—*Gilles Pinson*

See also Center-Local Relations; City-Region; Local Governance; Planning; Regime; Substate Regionalism

Further Readings and References

Campbell, S., & Fainstein, S. (Eds.). (1996). *Readings in planning theory.* Oxford, UK: Basil Blackwell.

Healey, P., Khakee, A., Motte, A., & Needham, B. (Eds.). (1997). *Making strategic spatial plans: Innovations in Europe.* London: University College London.

Le Galès, P. (2002). *European cities, social conflicts, and governance.* New York: Oxford University Press.

Pinson, G. (2002). Political government and governance: Strategic planning and reshaping of political capacity in Turin. *International Journal of Urban and Regional Research, 26*(3), 477–493.

URBAN GOVERNANCE

See LOCAL GOVERNANCE

Varieties of Capitalism

Capitalism is a profit-oriented, market-mediated system of economic organization that has developed at different times and places. Moreover, although increasingly organized on a global scale, it remains quite variegated in form, dynamics, and overall performance. There is no single best way to organize and govern capitalism, and, notwithstanding claims about long-term convergence, several varieties of capitalism persist due to the heterogeneity of the commodities produced for sale and the inevitable embedding of capitalist production and markets in broader sets of social relations. Such variation is evident in the wide range of capitalist firms, industries and sectors, complexes and clusters, localities, regions, national economies, plurinational systems, transnational networks, and trading blocs. Unsurprisingly, then, prompted by interest in competitiveness, best practice, and the social costs of capitalism, the rich variety of capitalism has long fascinated capitalists, workers, social movements, policymakers, social critics, and social scientists. In the social sciences, interest in varieties of capitalism has been strongest in institutional and evolutionary economics, comparative political economy, and economic sociology. It is weakest in orthodox economics, with its penchant for abstract modeling and its expectations that market forces should eventually lead to a single, maximally efficient model of economic organization.

Thus, observers have distinguished national paths to capitalist development (e.g., Dutch, English, French, Prussian, American, Japanese, East Asian), typical stages in capitalist development (e.g., mercantilism, liberalism, imperialism, state monopoly capitalism, transnational networked capitalism), varieties of consolidated capitalism (e.g., liberal market economies, bank-coordinated economies, state-guided market economies), regional patterns (e.g., Rhenish, Scandinavian, Mediterranean, East Asian), and forms of transnational economic domination (e.g., military conquest, free trade, integrated economic blocs). Most of the literature on varieties of capitalism focuses on national systems or "families" of capitalism differentiated in terms of technological, organizational, institutional, or sociocultural factors. Thus, we find typologies based on criteria such as social innovation systems, relations between industry and finance, industrial relations, education and training, the nature and role of the state, modes of growth, modes of competition, modes of governance, high or low trust, and alternative "spirits of capitalism."

The centuries-old interest in varieties of capitalism is linked to questions of economic development, defense of national economic and political interests, social welfare, and global competitiveness. The key role of national states in facilitating or hindering capitalist development has biased work on varieties of capitalism, which are usually identified with different national capitalisms, as if these were not just analytically distinct but also really operated in isolation from each other, rather than in complex cross-border, plurinational, or global systems. The Cold War prompted interest, often heavily ideological, in communism and capitalism as competing systems, rather than in their specific varieties. The collapse of the Soviet Bloc, the rise of Japan and other East Asian economies as serious competitors to Western economies, and, most recently, intensified globalization have all renewed interest in varieties of capitalism, their persistence, and the scope for their eventual convergence, whether through market competition or explicit global policy initiatives.

Many of the typologies capitalism developed during the postwar boom in North America and Western Europe and its subsequent crisis in the 1980s and 1990s have focused on four key variables: the dominant forms of production, forms of economic specialization, and forms of labor process; the relative primacy of industry, banks, and the state in allocating capital to different uses and in governing the economy; industrial relations patterns; and forms of education, vocational training, and security of employment. Almost all typologies identify a distinctive liberal market (or Anglo-Saxon) model, with a strong market-friendly complementarity among its different components, and a model based on a key coordinating role for the state in promoting a coherent, modernized core in its national economy as a basis for economic development. This variety often includes one or more East Asian models, characterized by a strong developmental state oriented to catch up with the advanced capitalist economies. Disagreement emerges beyond this all-too-predictable market versus state dichotomy. Two varieties often mentioned are: first, a distinctive social democratic or Scandinavian model, with strong roles for highly organized labor and a well-developed universal welfare state in a small, open economy; and, second, a Rhenish model, typical of the Western European heartland along the Rhine, from Austria and Switzerland through Germany to Belgium and the Netherlands, where more balanced or decentralized forms of corporatism and Christian democracy have proved important factors. Less-often noted is a southern European or Mediterranean model, with a weak, fragmented labor force, a weak state incapable of a

strong guiding role, and underdeveloped welfare regimes. Interesting work has also examined the distinctive features of rentier economies (income is derived mainly from assets rather than labor; especially those blessed—or cursed—with oil reserves), import substitution in Latin American economies, the distinctive problems and trajectories of postsocialist economies, and the importance of informal economies in failed states.

Four main criticisms are leveled against the varieties of capitalism literature. First, it fetishizes national models or distinctions, treating them as rivals or competitors, ignoring potential complementarities within a wider international or global division of labor. A focus on the latter is associated with interest in a single variegated capitalism rather than distinct varieties of national capitalism. Second, there is often wide variation within any individual national economy across its different sectors or regions, calling into question the idea of the national economy as a unit of analysis. In response, reference is frequently made to the role of national states in shaping institutional and regulatory frameworks for all economic players in a national economy. Third, a focus on national economies fails to do justice to emerging supranational blocs, global city networks, global commodity chains, and so on. And, fourth, concern with varieties of capitalism may lead to neglect of the competitive pressures and political initiatives that encourage convergence, whether in the form of European integration and harmonization or U.S.-sponsored expansion of international economic regimes to promote a more neoliberal, market-friendly pattern of world economic organization. Despite these criticisms, research continues to demonstrate significant differences in economic performance, economic specialization, welfare regimes, crisis tendencies, crisis-management capacities, and so on. This indicates the continued importance of studying varieties of capitalism and their place within globally variegated capitalism.

—Bob Jessop

See also Capitalism; Convergence and Divergence; Corporatism; Economic Sociology; Governance Failure; Liberal Market Economy; Market; Marxism; New Institutionalism; Regulation Theory

Further Readings and References

Amable, B. (2004). *The diversity of modern capitalism.* Oxford, UK: Oxford University Press.

Coates, D. (Ed.). (2003). *Varieties of capitalism* (3 vols.). Cheltenham, UK: Edward Elgar.

Hall, P. A., & Soskice, D. (Eds.). (2001). *Varieties of capitalism: The institutional foundations of comparative advantage.* Oxford, UK: Oxford University Press.

Whitley, R. (1999). *Divergent capitalisms: The social structuring and change of business systems.* Oxford, UK: Oxford University Press.

VIRTUAL AGENCY

A virtual agency is called as such because it has no physical or simple jurisdictional existence. It is essentially a Web portal that integrates a thematically organized range of information and online public services drawn from various "real" departments and agencies. It presents these to citizens in an easily navigable format. Virtual agencies are a key component of most e-government programs. Some analyses suggest that they can go beyond their virtual status and spur lasting organizational change.

Beyond the simple presentation of information on the Web by a single agency, virtual agencies are characterized by the sharing of information held in databases and work patterns based on networks of problem-solving "teams," often involving public- and private-sector actors. The implementation of such projects across government, especially in the United States, expanded under the George W. Bush administrations of the 2000s, with the creation of www.grants.gov, www.kids.gov, www.students.gov, and www.export.gov, to name a few.

Virtual agencies mark a significant departure from previous approaches to service delivery. They promise greater coordination across government. They also signal recognition that the identities of users of public services are rarely monolithic and that a detailed knowledge of the structures of public bureaucracies should not be a prerequisite for access to services. By conceiving of the user base as highly segmented, in much the same way as private-sector firms, proponents argue that improved customer service can be delivered to those who are perceived to be most in need. In time, so the argument runs, decisive organizational change will occur, as the virtual agency cannibalizes the "real" agencies from which it first grew.

Yet despite the promise of increased coordination, some scholars have argued that virtual agencies have sometimes proved difficult to implement, not least because they may involve job losses, or, for those who are fortunate enough to retain their job, because a new agency might take the power of decision away from previously important managers. There are also long-standing problems with counteracting the "silo" culture of departmentalism in government. As a result of the new public management, public bureaucracies in many countries are not the relatively monolithic entities that they were twenty years ago. The situation is compounded by the differing technological demands of individual departments and agencies, as well as the fact that some, in effect, "go it alone" with their own technologically inspired projects. The latter has largely been the case with the implementation of e-government in British local government—developments led by the Office of the Deputy Prime Minister, rather than the body responsible for the rest of the program, the Cabinet Office E-Government Unit. E-government may thus increase competition within and between organizations, increasing fragmentation rather than reducing it. Thus, there are significant obstacles to the vision of increasing coordination through virtual agencies.

—*Andrew Chadwick*

See also Citizen-Centric Government; Coordination; Disintermediation; E-Democracy; E-Government; New Public Management

Further Readings and References

Bellamy, C., & Taylor, J. A. (1998). *Governing in the information age.* Buckingham, UK: Open University Press.

Borins, S. (2004). A holistic view of public sector information technology. *Journal of E-Government, 1*(2), 3–29.

Fountain, J. E. (2001). *Building the virtual state: Information technology and institutional change.* New York: Brookings Institution.

VIRTUAL COMMUNITY

A virtual community is a group of individuals who are connected through the use of information technologies, such as computers, mobile telephones, and the Internet. Attributed to Howard Rheingold and his book, *The Virtual Community: Homesteading on the Electronic Frontier,* the term is now associated with a broad range of online interactions among groups of people. Although virtual communities are now most often associated with the World Wide Web, electronic interactions began with earlier technologies, such as electronic bulletin boards, Usenet groups, chat rooms, and e-mail. Thus, virtual communities are seen to exist in cyberspace, the realm of activity created by computer networks. Members of these communities may also meet and know each other in the offline world. It is not necessary that members of a virtual community have strong links to each other, and a given person may participate in a community regularly, irregularly, or only for a period of time. There will also be variation in levels of participation and the range of topics discussed, from pure entertainment communities to those engaged in serious political discussions. The term *community* is then used in relation to virtual communities to refer more to communities of interest than to a group of individuals living and acting in close contact with each other.

Virtual communities are also seen as holding the potential for broad social movements unbounded by national borders. Rheingold argues that the technology enabling these communities can provide substantial intellectual, social, commercial, and political leverage for ordinary citizens, but this depends on their ability to learn about how to utilize these technologies. One of the most well-known political movements supported by use of the Internet is that of the Zapatistas in Chiapas, Mexico. Information on the uprising of the Zapatista National Liberation Army against the Mexican government was circulated on the Internet and Usenet lists, and various interested organizations collected news and made it available online. This led to international awareness and an increase in support for the movement both inside and outside of Mexico. Margaret Keck and Kathryn Sikkink have highlighted the ways in which actors in one country can gain the attention of actors outside their country to support a domestic cause. This kind of activity is facilitated by access to the Internet and the creation of virtual communities to share information about, and build support for, a cause. The Zapatista movement is also linked to a broader anti-neoliberalism movement that gained force in many parts of the world in the late 1990s. One major event that marked the potential of this movement was the protests against the meeting of the World Trade Organization in Seattle in 1999. This protest involved significant organization through online discussions.

Analysts of the use of virtual networks more generally have argued that the virtual interaction of individuals can enable new modes of operation that are more effective than organizational structures of the past. The work of John Arquilla and David Ronfeldt emphasizes the ability of people networked together through technology to act in a nonhierarchical manner to achieve significant goals. In particular, they emphasize the use of networks by armies to perform maneuvers more efficiently and by terrorists to mobilize and conduct attacks. Business analysts have similarly argued that networked teams working together across long distances can be as productive as teams working together in an office environment. Web-enabled software programs such as Groove have been developed for the express purpose of facilitating virtual team project work. In this manner, technology-enabled communities can be used to facilitate group processes, whether they are for the public or private sector.

Virtual communities were also seen as playing an important role in the emergence of new grassroots mobilization techniques in the 2004 U.S. presidential election. The Howard Dean campaign was recognized early in the Democratic primaries for utilizing online community building techniques to mobilize volunteers and voters. Similar techniques were subsequently utilized by both the Democratic and Republican nominees to organize campaign events across the country and facilitate the fund-raising process. Although online organizing has not supplanted traditional campaign techniques, the virtual communities developed during the 2004 campaign and similar communities are expected to play a continuing and evolving role in campaigns of the future.

In the early years of virtual communities, some commentators and observers worried that participation in online activities would draw some individuals away from participation in the real world. Recent debates have focused more on the risks associated with the content of discussions conducted online. Thus, children's participation in online games, as well as the availability of communities for sharing and discussing pornography, have been highlighted as potentially problematic outcomes of the proliferation of tools for building and accessing virtual communities. In this way, virtual communities can be utilized for a broad range of activities, and the social and political contribution of technologies facilitating virtual interactions is dependent on the way in which they are utilized by society at large.

—*Jennifer Bussell*

See also Civil Society; Disintermediation; E-Democracy; E-Government; Social Movement Theory

Further Readings and References

Arquilla, J., & Ronfeldt, D. (2001). *Networks and netwars: The future of terror, crime, and militancy.* Santa Monica, CA: RAND.

Cleaver, H. (1994). *The Chiapas uprising and the future of class struggle in the new world order.* Retrieved from http://www.eco.utexas.edu/facstaff/Cleaver/chiapas uprising.html

Keck, M., & Sikkink, K. (1998). *Activists beyond borders: Advocacy networks in international politics.* Ithaca, NY: Cornell University Press.

Rheingold, H. (2000). *The virtual community: Homesteading on the electronic frontier.* Cambridge: MIT Press.

WAR ON TERRORISM

The war on terrorism is the term used to describe the American-led global counterterrorism campaign launched in response to the terrorist attacks of September 11, 2001. In its scope, expenditure, and impact on international relations, the war on terrorism is comparable to the Cold War; it represents the beginning of a new phase in global political relations and has important consequences for security, human rights, international law, cooperation, and governance.

The war on terrorism is a multidimensional campaign of almost limitless scope. Its military dimension has thus far involved major wars against Afghanistan and Iraq; covert operations in Yemen, the Philippines, and elsewhere; large-scale military assistance programs to cooperative regimes; and major increases in military spending. Its intelligence dimension has comprised institutional reorganization and considerable increases in the funding of America's intelligence-gathering capabilities, a global program of capturing terrorist suspects and interning them at Guantanamo Bay, expanded cooperation with foreign intelligence agencies, and the tracking and interception of terrorist financing. Its diplomatic dimension includes continuing efforts to construct and maintain a global coalition of partner states and organizations and an extensive public diplomacy campaign to counter anti-Americanism in the Middle East. The domestic dimension of America's war

on terrorism has entailed new anti-terrorism legislation, such as the USA Patriot Act; new security institutions like the Department of Homeland Security; the preventive detainment of thousands of suspects; surveillance and intelligence-gathering programs by the FBI and local authorities; the strengthening of emergency response procedures; and increased security measures for airports, borders, and public events.

The successes of the first three years of the war on terrorism include the arrest of hundreds of terrorist suspects around the world, the prevention of further large-scale terrorist attacks on the American mainland, the toppling of the Taliban regime and subsequent closure of terrorist training camps in Afghanistan, the capture or elimination of many of Al-Qaeda's senior members, and increased levels of international cooperation in global counterterrorism efforts.

However, critics argue that the failures of America's counterterrorism campaign outweigh its successes. They contend that the war in Afghanistan not only failed in its primary goal of capturing Osama bin Laden, but effectively scattered the Al-Qaeda network, thereby making it even harder to counteract. The attacks on Afghanistan and Iraq increased anti-Americanism among the world's Muslims, amplifying the message of militant Islam and uniting disparate groups in a common cause. The pattern of terrorist attacks since the fall of the Taliban suggests that Islamic militants are now acting autonomously of Al-Qaeda's leadership; at the same time, the ongoing violence in occupied Iraq is providing a focus for militant struggle. These developments have arguably increased the risk of terrorism. Other critics allege that the war on terrorism is a contrived smokescreen for the pursuit of an American neoconservative geopolitics that includes controlling global oil reserves, increasing defense spending, expanding international military presence, and countering the strategic challenge posed by various regional powers.

The long-term effects of the war on terrorism are not yet clear but may include: widespread rearmament and a new global arms race; the erosion of civil liberties and human rights across the globe; the corrosion of the international legal order through the rewriting of the laws of war; increased regional instability in the Middle East, the Caucasus, and parts of Asia; political damage to the institutions of global governance; and the distraction of the international community from dealing with issues such as poverty, disease, and environmental change.

—*Richard Jackson*

See also Arms Control; Post-9/11; Security; Terrorism

Further Readings and References

Booth, K., & Dunne, T. (Eds.). (2002). *Worlds in collision: Terror and the future of global order.* New York: Palgrave Macmillan.

Cole, D. (2003). *Enemy aliens: Double standards and constitutional freedoms in the war on terrorism.* New York: New Press.

Halliday, F. (2002). *Two hours that shook the world: September 11, 2001: Causes and consequences.* London: Saqi Books.

Hiro, D. (2002). *War without end: The rise of Islamist terrorism and global response.* London: Routledge.

Jackson, R. (2005). *Writing the war on terrorism: Language, politics, and counter-terrorism.* Manchester, UK: Manchester University Press.

Mahajan, R. (2002). *The new crusade: America's war on terrorism.* New York: Monthly Review Press.

WASHINGTON CONSENSUS

The term *Washington Consensus* is commonly used to describe the neoliberal policy recommendations to developing countries, and Latin America in particular, that became popular during the 1980s. The Washington Consensus usually refers to the level of agreement between the International Monetary Fund (IMF), World Bank, and U.S. Treasury. All shared the view that the operation of the free market and the reduction of state involvement were crucial to development in the Global South.

With the onset of the third-world debt crisis in the early 1980s, the major Western powers, the United States in particular, decided that both the World Bank and the IMF should play a significant role in the management of this debt and in global development policy more broadly. When John Williamson, who later worked for the World Bank, first used the term Washington Consensus in 1989, he claimed he was actually referring to a list of reforms that he felt key players in Washington could all agree were needed in Latin America. However, much to his dismay, the term has become widely used in a pejorative way to describe the increasing harmonization of the policies recommended by these institutions. It often refers to a dogmatic belief that developing countries should adopt market-led development strategies that will result in economic growth that will "trickle-down" to the benefit of all.

The World Bank and IMF were able to promote this view throughout the developing world by attaching policy conditions, known as stabilization and structural adjustment programs, to the loans they made. In very broad terms, the Washington Consensus reflects the set of policies that became their standard package of advice attached to loans. The first element was a set of policies designed to create economic stability by controlling inflation and reducing government budget deficits. Many developing countries, especially in Latin America, had suffered hyperinflation during the 1980s. Therefore, a monetarist approach was recommended, whereby government spending is reduced and interest rates are raised to reduce the money supply. The second stage was the reform of trade and exchange rate policies so the country could be integrated into the global economy. This involved the lifting of state restrictions on imports and exports and often included the devaluation of the currency. The final stage was to allow market forces to operate freely by removing subsidies and state controls and engaging in a program of privatization.

By the late 1990s, it was becoming clear that the results of the Washington Consensus were far from optimal. Increasing criticism led to a change in approach that shifted the focus away from a view of development as simply economic growth and toward poverty reduction and the need for participation of both developing country governments and civil society. This change of direction led to the term *post–Washington Consensus*.

—*Stephen R. Hurt*

See also Development Theory; Globalization; International Monetary Fund; International Organization; Neoliberalism; Political Business Cycle; Post–Washington Consensus; Privatization; Regional Development Bank; Third-World Debt; World Bank

Further Readings and References

Gore, C. (2000). The rise and fall of the Washington Consensus as a paradigm for developing countries. *World Development, 28,* 789–804.

Naím, M. (2000). Washington Consensus or Washington confusion? *Foreign Policy, 118,* 86–103.

Williamson, J. (1993). Democracy and the Washington Consensus. *World Development, 21,* 1329–1336.

WEAK INSTITUTION

A weak institution is an institution in decline. An institution is commonly defined as a stable, durable, and valued arrangement that prescribes and prohibits specific behavior for specific situations. An institution can take various forms (think of a respected custom, a long-standing law, or a widely admired organization). When its influence wanes, and it is no longer taken for granted but formally still persists, we speak of a weak institution.

A good example is the declining importance of marriage in many Western countries. The church, which in many countries has lost its once-dominant position in state and society, provides another instructive example. Some types of organizations—think of unions and newspapers—have seen their influence in society gradually diminish. In the public sector, defining organizations can lose their mythical status without being terminated; the National Aeronautics and Space Administration and the Federal Bureau of Investigation are clear examples.

Institutions have a built-in tendency to weaken in time: The same mechanisms that drive institutionalization account for the reverse process of deinstitutionalization. Institutions typically evolve as adaptive responses to critical problems; effective responses are repeated and embedded in rules, routines, customs, and organizational cultures and structures. As the responses prove their worth over time, people begin to value and reproduce them.

However, the embedding of certain behavioral repertoires for specific situations undermines their flexibility. As the context changes, once-effective courses of action lose their relevance or may even become counterproductive. Institutions persist until it becomes clear to all that the prescribed behavior no longer works. This constitutes an institutional crisis.

An institutional crisis marks the moment when once-valued responses become widely recognized as dysfunctional. The institution becomes delegitimized as it loses societal and political support. Its deep roots in society and its valued history of effectiveness—a hallmark of institutionalization—usually save an institution from immediate termination. But if nothing is done to revive an institution, it will eventually flounder and disappear.

The effects of weakening institutions tend to be significant. Public institutions, by definition, exert an ordering effect on (substantial parts of) the public sector; processes of deinstitutionalization tend to cause confusion, fragmentation, and stress. The weakening of an institution invites restorative efforts or may give rise, in time, to a new institution.

Deinstitutionalization is not an irreversible process. After an institutional crisis occurs, a realignment of the institution with societal and political expectations can lead to institutional restoration. A key factor in the rise and fall of institutions is the capacity to adapt without sacrificing the valued core of the institution. This capacity does not automatically evolve; it has to be built into an institution.

—*Arjen Boin*

See also Failed State; Institution; Institutionalism; Institutional Performance

Further Readings and References

Baumgartner, F., & Jones, B. D. (1993). *Agenda and instability in American politics.* Chicago: University of Chicago Press.

Berger, P. L., & Luckmann, T. (1966). *The social construction of reality: A treatise in the sociology of knowledge.* Garden City, NJ: Doubleday.

Goodin, R. E. (Ed.). (1996). *The theory of institutional design.* Cambridge, UK: Cambridge University Press.

Meyer, M. W., & Zucker, L. G. (1989). *Permanently failing organizations.* Thousand Oaks, CA: Sage.

WELFARE REFORM

Welfare reform broadly refers to the changes made to the funding and delivery of welfare services. Today, it usually refers to the reform of the welfare state. After World War II, the state became the dominant funder and provider of welfare services in places such as Britain. The experience of national collectivism during the war helped lay the foundation for an expansion of state intervention within welfare. State funding and provision was thought to be the best way of guaranteeing universal access to health and education, and this was embodied in institutions such as the National Health Service. Welfare reform is important because changes in the way that welfare is governed impact on individual well-being.

Today, many observers believe that the welfare state is in need of reform. This arises for a variety of reasons. There are those who believe the welfare state is no longer feasible. For example, some argue that globalization has hollowed out the capacity of the state to intervene within welfare affairs. Consequently, any viable system of welfare has to go beyond the state. Others point to the problems posed by the rise of a consumer-driven society. According to this argument, users are increasingly unhappy with the standard level of service delivered by the state. This dissatisfaction over provision creates difficulties because it undermines the public's commitment to the collective funding of welfare services through taxation. There are also those who think that even if the welfare state is feasible, it is not desirable. For example, public choice theorists argue that the architects of the welfare state assumed that public servants were motivated by an ethic of service. Public choice theorists argue that rather than being "knights," public servants are in fact "knaves" motivated by self-interest. Public servants use the welfare state to advance their private ends (job security, career ladders, and so on), rather than the public interest. From this standpoint, the welfare state ought to be reformed so that welfare services are based on the assumption that public servants are knaves.

Third Way

During the 1980s, public choice thinkers and the rest of the New Right dominated ideas and policies toward reform. The new public management contracting out the internal market and purchaser-provider splits are shaped largely by New Right concerns. Today, debates about reform are framed largely with reference to the third way. Advocates of the third way say that there is a need to rethink a commitment to the welfare state for a combination of the reasons previously mentioned. However, these individuals also reject the prescriptions advanced by the New Right. Advocates of the third way say that while the architects of the welfare state made a faulty assumption that public servants were always knights, public choice thinkers make the equally flawed assumption that public servants are always knaves. A public service ethic is an essential feature of welfare services, and there is a need to refashion services on the assumption that public servants are knaves and knights.

Supporters of the third way seek to steer a course beyond the governance arrangements of traditional social democrats and the New Right. If this denotes what the third way is against, it does not map out what it is in favor of. The third way is a large space that is compatible with a range of distinct, and sometimes contradictory, projects. Some individuals try to fashion a third way in funding by looking at ways that the public and private sectors may combine to build new hospitals, schools, and prisons. Public-private partnerships and the private finance initiative are examples of attempts to develop models of funding that do not rely only on the public purse (as in traditional social democracy) or private finance (as with free market liberals). Innovations also occur in provision. The "new localism" is a recent attempt to recast the relationship between central and local institutions so that local autonomy plays a much more important role in the delivery of services. The new localism allows central institutions to play a role in the regulation of basic standards but permits local bodies to have considerable freedom over the setting and implementation of policy at a local level. Proponents of the new localism argue that in place of the one-size-fits-all model of state provision, there will be local variations to reflect local circumstances. "Public interest companies" are one way these services may be delivered. Public interest companies are organizations independent of the state charged with delivering welfare services in the public interest. Foundation hospitals are an example of the public interest company model. These hospitals are funded mainly from national taxes, although they can raise limited funds from capital markets for the purposes of investment. They have a stakeholder system of governance that provides patients, the broader public, staff, and partner organizations with representation within the governance of these hospitals. Foundation hospitals can be shaped in a variety of ways. Choice can be introduced by providing hospitals with overlapping jurisdictions and allowing patients to choose among different hospitals. Voice can be enhanced by providing stakeholders with greater opportunities to shape and make decisions.

Third-way welfare reform has not gone unchallenged. Some believe that foundation hospitals are a fig leaf for privatization. They argue that while foundation hospitals are not allowed to make dividend payments, the fact that they can raise money from capital markets means that private companies can make a claim on health service resources and thus constitutes privatization. Others are concerned about the adverse impact that the new localism may have on equality. According to this viewpoint, the state is the only agent capable of carrying out the redistribution that is

essential for equality. The devolution of policy implied by the new localism weakens central intervention and so undermines equality. Empirical evidence is important for resolving these matters. Although the third way is intended to overcome the defects of both the welfare state and the free market, the presence of these criticisms underlines that within public policy, the introduction of potential solutions to existing problems can themselves raise new questions and controversies.

—*Rajiv Prabhakar*

See also Clinical Governance; Communitarianism; Corporate Governance; Gender Equality; Market Failure; New Poverty Research; New Public Management; Third Way; Welfare State

Further Readings and References

Bevir, M. (2005). *New Labour: A critique*. London: Routledge.
Crouch, C. (2003). *Commercialisation or citizenship: Education policy and the future of public services*. London: The Fabian Society.
Le Grand, J. (2003). *Motivation, agency, and public policy: Of knights and knaves, pawns and queens*. Oxford, UK: Oxford University Press.
Prabhakar, R. (2004). Do public interest companies form a third way in public services? *British Journal of Politics and International Relations, 6*(3), 353–369.

WELFARE STATE

The concept of a welfare state is difficult to define. In the simplest terms, it refers to a state that has assumed some responsibility for individual welfare through the provision of both income transfers and social services. Government provision of social programs includes pensions, unemployment insurance, invalidity and sick pay, social assistance, family assistance, parental leave, health care, care for the elderly and people with disabilities, employment services, specialized services (e.g., alcohol and drug treatment and foster care), and housing. The earliest welfare state developed in Germany in the late nineteenth century, when the Chancellor Otto von Bismarck extended health and social insurance benefits to workers. Today, most advanced industrial countries would be classified as welfare states, with social expenditure in 2001 accounting for an average of over twenty percent of Gross Domestic Product in Organisation for Economic Co-operation and Development (OECD) countries, according to OECD figures.

However, many scholars have argued that this definition is radically incomplete. First, government involvement in individual welfare is affected by far more than social policy, with regulation of private provision of services and transfers, support for family provision, and a broader set of state policies in the labor market, education, and overall macroeconomy all playing an important role. Second, social policy generally aims at doing more than narrowly producing individual welfare, and indeed, is often linked to a broader set of economic (and occasionally religious or military) policies. Gøsta Esping-Andersen argued in 1990 that we should look at welfare state regimes or forms of welfare capitalism rather than at the welfare state narrowly, examining the links between social welfare policies and differential state and capitalist structures. This argument presents the governance of the welfare state as part of the broader governance of the modern capitalist economy.

Esping-Andersen argues that the fundamental goals of different welfare states diverge and therefore produce different distributional and social outcomes. Building on Richard Titmuss's early typology of welfare states, Esping-Andersen identifies three types of welfare regimes: Social Democratic, Conservative, and Liberal. For Esping-Andersen, the concept of decommodification is central to this divergence, and he argues that strong unions and social democratic parties were able to use the welfare state to change the character of advanced capitalism. This outcome is best achieved in the Social Democratic regime, which provides high-quality universal services that crowd out private (and family) provision, emphasizes full employment, and thereby produces high levels of decommodification. The Conservative regime also entails high levels of social spending, but this spending occurs primarily through status-maintaining income transfers and policies that support traditional notions of the family and church. These policies reproduce market disparities through welfare transfers, meaning decommodification is less extensive. Finally, the Liberal regime is characterized by meager, means-tested benefits that cater to a mainly poor clientele and entail social stigma, low quality, basic services, all of which force individuals to rely on the market and thereby entail minimal decommodification. For Esping-Andersen, the Scandinavian countries are examples of the Social Democratic model, the Continental European countries represent the Conservative model, and the English-speaking countries generally fall into the Liberal model.

A number of scholars have challenged not only Esping-Andersen's historical account of the rise of the welfare state, but also his understanding of the welfare state as a form of governance that alters capitalist organization in particular ways. For instance, scholars examining the formative role of business interests and the middle class in the development of the welfare state contest the view of the welfare state as decommodifying. This perspective stresses the constructive relationship between markets and the welfare state, arguing that far from decommodifying workers, advanced welfare states have played a key role in sustaining the interests of capitalists or the middle classes. Marxist scholars of the welfare state also stress its role in buttressing advanced capitalism, arguing the welfare state does not roll back the frontiers of advanced capitalism but is something akin to "riot insurance" that buys off working class discontent, as noted by Frances Piven and Richard Cloward in 1971. In a different vein, feminist scholars argue that by narrowly focusing on the welfare state as a nexus between politics and markets, this view obscures the role of the family as a producer of welfare and social stratification, as noted by Ann Orloff in 1993. Finally, scholars of political institutions argue that the preferences of key actors alone do not explain the character or extent of modern welfare states, and that preexisting institutional structures and bureaucratic capacity mediated early reformers' efforts in particular ways. The question of what the welfare state is, where it comes from, and what it means for modern political and economic governance is highly contested.

Modern welfare states have matured far beyond these origins. In many countries, the question of contemporary governance of the welfare state is not how to build and expand it, but instead how to manage it in an era of permanent fiscal austerity. This challenge involves balancing growing social demands with the rising costs and more limited fiscal leeway associated with an aging population, greater labor market volatility, and globalization. Pierson argued in 1996 that these challenges have created a scenario where the patterns of cutbacks to social welfare programs follow a different logic from that of expansion. Pierson remarks that relatively little retrenchment has occurred, and the governance of the welfare state is increasingly characterized by the politics of avoiding blame. For Pierson, policymakers attempt to square the circle of fiscal pressures that push for cutbacks and electoral incentives to avoid cutback by governing through low-visibility, incremental reform. While most welfare states are experiencing these common challenges, they have manifested themselves differently across advanced countries, with some experiencing more severe problems of unemployment, inequality, and budgetary stress than others. As a result, the question of how to balance competing goals of securing individual welfare, economic growth, and fiscal discipline in modern welfare states may be resolved in highly differentiated ways.

—Jane Gingrich

See also Health Care; Social Democracy; Social Justice; Unemployment; Varieties of Capitalism; Welfare Reform

Further Readings and References

Baldwin, P. (1990). *The politics of social solidarity: Class bases in the European welfare state, 1875–1975.* Cambridge, UK: Cambridge University Press.

Esping-Andersen, G. (1990). *The three worlds of welfare capitalism.* Princeton, NJ: Princeton University Press.

Iversen, T., & Wren, A. (1998). Equality, employment, and budgetary restraint: The trilemma of the service economy. *World Politics, 50*(4), 507–546.

Mares, I. (2003). *The politics of social risk: Business and welfare state development.* Cambridge, UK: Cambridge University Press.

Organisation for Economic Co-operation and Development. (2004). *Social expenditure database 1980–2001.* Paris: Author.

Orloff, A. S. (1993). Gender and the social rights of citizenship: The comparative analysis of gender relations and welfare states. *American Sociological Review, 58,* 303–328.

Pierson, P. (1996). The new politics of the welfare state. *World Politics, 48,* 143–179.

Piven, F. F., & Cloward, R. A. (1971). *Regulating the poor: The functions of public welfare.* New York: Pantheon Books.

WORKFARE

Workfare is a policy of making the receipt of unemployment benefits conditional upon the requirement to look for work or actively engage in other prescribed activities. For example, in 1998, the Labour government in Britain introduced a New Deal program for young people. Funded by a windfall tax on the profits of the privatized utilities, this policy meant that all 18- to 24-year-olds receiving unemployment benefits had an obligation to accept a job with a private-sector employer that is paid a wage subsidy, work with a nonprofit voluntary organization, work for the government's own environmental service task force, or study on a full-time approved course. A green paper noted that there would be no fifth option of simply remaining on unemployment. Over time, the Labour government has extended the New Deal program to cover other groups, such as the over-50s and single parents. Workfare is important because it suggests that individual duty or responsibility is integral to any legitimate or well-functioning set of governance arrangements.

Workfare is an example of conditional benefits, that is, the receipt of benefits is tied to the exercise of various conditions. Workfare is not the only way that conditional benefits may be manifested. For example, the entitlement to make full use of public health services might be linked to a duty not to smoke. However, workfare is the most prominent recent example of this approach.

Workfare has arisen because of dissatisfaction with benefit payments in the post-1945 social democratic welfare state. Although conditions were not entirely absent in the welfare state, much greater emphasis was placed on the unconditional nature of social benefits, such as health and education. On the Right, neoconservatives voiced concerns during the 1980s that the welfare state perpetuated rather than resolved problems as people came to depend on the state rather than to take measures to help themselves escape their problems. Unconditional unemployment benefits meant that either people did not have an incentive to look for work or they were irrational and needed formal instruction to get a job. On the Left, reformists argued during the 1990s that unconditional benefits violated a principle of reciprocity. The view is that the provision of benefits to an individual imposes a reciprocal obligation on the recipient to use these benefits in a proper manner. This stance is found within writings on the third way and is captured in the doctrine that there should be no rights without responsibilities. Although parts of the Left and Right both endorse workfare, the nature of their justifications is different. For the Right, this is linked to concerns about a dependency culture. For the Left, reciprocity is emphasized as a way of preventing people from free riding on the contributions of others.

Workfare is not accepted uncritically. Some reject all conditional benefits, arguing that they are illiberal and license authoritarian state interventions. Others in Britain have criticized the New Deal by saying that this is not the most cost effective way of reducing unemployment. These disagreements highlight that debates within public policy are rarely settled. Conflicts exist within the framework of the same values (a debate between reciprocity versus illiberalism points to different ethical judgments of workfare), as well as between different values (the ethical case for the New Deal versus the costs of running this program).

—*Rajiv Prabhakar*

See also Communitarianism; Neoliberalism; Third Way; Welfare Reform

Further Readings and References

Prabhakar, R. (2003). *Stakeholding and New Labour.* Basingstoke, UK: Palgrave.

White, S. (2000). Social rights and the social contract–political theory and the new welfare politics. *British Journal of Political Science, 30,* 507–532.

WORLD BANK

The World Bank is actually a group of five intergovernmental organizations that together seek to promote development in the Global South. It is a specialized agency of the United Nations (UN) and its headquarters are in Washington, DC. In recent years, its focus has been on the reduction of poverty. It pursues this agenda through a combination of loans, grants, policy advice, and technical assistance. It is a highly significant actor in the field of development and is involved in projects in almost every developing country in the world. Moreover, its influence is enhanced by the fact that loans made by the World Bank act as a "seal of approval" for other potential lenders and investors in the developing world. The governments of the nation-states that constitute the membership own all five institutions that together are known as the World Bank Group. However, the majority of its finances are raised on international financial markets through the selling of bonds. Voting power of member countries is weighted according to the financial contributions made.

The World Bank is the popular shorthand for the International Bank for Reconstruction and Development (IBRD), which was created at the UN Monetary and Financial Conference held in 1944 at Bretton Woods, New Hampshire. Originally, its mandate was to assist in the rebuilding of those countries that had been devastated by World War II. Actually, this role was mainly performed by the United States through the Marshall Plan because it was decided that in the context of the Cold War, such matters should not be left to a multilateral organization. Then, during the period of decolonization, the attention of the World Bank was diverted toward the developing world. The International Development Association (IDA) was created in 1960 to provide assistance to the world's poorest countries, and, unlike the IBRD, a substantial portion of its resources comes from donations made by member countries. There are three other arms of the World Bank Group. First, the International Finance Corporation (IFC) provides support for projects in the developing world undertaken by the private sector. Second, the Multilateral Investment Guarantee Agency (MIGA) encourages foreign investment in the developing world by providing risk insurance. Third, the International Centre for Settlement of Investment Disputes (ICSID) also supports the promotion of privately funded foreign investment in the developing world by offering host governments and investors mediation and dispute settlement assistance.

Changes in Development Policy

During its existence, the approach adopted by the World Bank to the promotion of development has been regularly reassessed and altered. In the early years, it tended to focus on the financial and technical support of large-scale capital investments in infrastructure. During the 1970s, under the presidency of Robert McNamara, the World Bank adopted an approach known as basic needs. This approach aimed at targeting the poorest sections of society, which critics had argued were not enjoying the benefits of its project lending. Attention was switched to the development of human capital, through programs supporting health, education, rural farming, and family planning.

A significant change of direction occurred again in 1980 when the World Bank introduced structural adjustment programs (SAPs). The emergence of the debt crisis in the third world has led to the World Bank, along with the International Monetary Fund (IMF), becoming involved in providing loans to help developing countries with serious balance of payment difficulties. These loans were conditional on the borrowing country following a series of policy measures, which the World Bank believed would enable them to avoid such problems in the future. A typical SAP involved policies designed to reduce the role of the state and increase the role of the market in the economy in an attempt to help the developing world adopt a development strategy centered on export-led growth. During this period, the widespread implementation of SAPs put tight constraints on the ability of developing countries to adopt any alternative development strategies.

Although attention has always been paid to the operations of the World Bank, the development of SAPs generated a significant increase in the amount of scrutiny and numerous criticisms. The SAPs' primary focus on economic growth was questioned. Critics, in particular social movements, argued that their impact was detrimental to the poorest sections of society, including women, and for some they also posed a threat to the environment. The World Bank was also subject to the charge that it was an undemocratic organization that did not listen to either the wishes of the citizens of the countries that had been subject to its policies or the range of opinions within global civil society.

Recent Reforms

The World Bank responded to these criticisms by undergoing a period of reform that resulted in the prioritization of poverty reduction over economic growth. This period of reform was given momentum by the appointment of James Wolfensohn as president in 1995 and Joseph Stiglitz as chief economist in 1997. The World Bank has also sought to incorporate issues of gender and sustainable development into its recent strategy. In terms of democratic input, it has developed an approach based on partnership and consultation. These reforms are reflected in the Comprehensive Development Framework (CDF), launched in 1999, which seeks to develop a more holistic approach to development. The CDF also suggests that developing countries should own their development strategy, rather than have it imposed through conditionality. These reforms have failed to satisfy some commentators, who argue that there is still a large measure of continuity in the approach to development adopted by the World Bank.

—Stephen R. Hurt

See also Bretton Woods; Globalization; International Monetary Fund; Liberal Market Economy; Neocolonialism; Poverty Reduction; Third-World Debt; Washington Consensus, World Development Indicators

Further Readings and References

Gilbert, C. L., & Vines, D. (Eds.). (2000). *The World Bank: Structure and policies.* Cambridge, UK: Cambridge University Press.

Mosley, P., Harrigan, J., & Toye, J. (1991). *Aid and power: The World Bank and policy-based lending* (Vols. 1 & 2). London: Routledge.

Pender, J. (2001). From 'structural adjustment' to 'comprehensive development framework': Conditionality transformed? *Third World Quarterly, 22*(3), 397–411.

Pincus, J. R., & Winters, J. A. (Eds.). (2002). *Reinventing the World Bank.* Ithaca, NY: Cornell University Press.

WORLD DEVELOPMENT INDICATORS

The World Bank publishes the World Development Indicators (WDI) annually. They represent a comprehensive set of data and statistics that allow the evaluation of the development of most countries in the world. In 2004, the World Bank published about 800 different WDI. To be able to assess development strategies, it is useful to have quantitative measures available. The availability of the WDI allows for more informed public and private policy making. In 2000, the Millennium Development Goals (MDG) were agreed upon, and eight major goals in particular were set for the year 2015. The WDI provide data that allow for measurement of progress toward all of these goals. Since these were adopted, the World Bank's publication of the WDI has highlighted the levels of progress made toward these specific targets. Critics might question both the reliability of some of the data and also whether it is possible to quantify all the related concepts, many of which are subjective.

In fact, the term *development* itself is a contested concept. What we mean by the term is open to debate and interpretation. A rather limited view of development that has dominated the view of many key actors in the past is simply gross national income (GNI) per capita. This can be converted using purchasing power parity to allow simple comparison between countries. However, the growing consensus today appears to be that development should also be about poverty reduction. This consensus was reflected in both the adoption of the MDG and the subsequent United Nations Conference on Financing for Development held in Mexico in March 2002.

The WDI include a broad group of statistics that measure economic development. These include wealth, equality, the levels of external debt, and the degree of integration a country has within the world economy (both in relation to trade and financial flow). They also provide data related to good governance, where good governance is interpreted as creating the right conditions for a market economy to flourish. Here one can compare the availability of basic infrastructure, the suitability of tax policies for attracting investment, and political transparency. The WDI also focus on measures of human development. These include demographic indicators, poverty, education, the status of women, and health. Over recent decades, governments, intergovernmental organizations, and the business sector have also become aware of the direct relationship between development and the limited availability of natural resources. The World Summits on Sustainable Development are evidence of an awareness of this issue. Therefore, the WDI also include measures related to the environment, such as pollution, urbanization levels, and the sustainable use of energy resources.

—*Stephen R. Hurt*

See also Development Theory; Millennium Development Goals; Poverty Reduction; Sustainable Development; World Bank

Further Readings and References

World Bank. (2004). *World development indicators.* Washington, DC: Author.

WORLD ECONOMIC FORUM

The World Economic Forum (WEF) is an annual gathering of leading figures from the corporate, political, academic, and media worlds. The forum meets in the exclusive Swiss Alpine resort of Davos (with the exception of 2002, when it met in New York City) at the height of the ski season (usually in January). Its self-stated aim is to provide an environment conducive to the sharing and dissemination of information and policy, as well as the development of ideas among the delegates with a view to improving "the state of the world." Delegates attend the WEF only by the invitation of the managing board. The handpicking of delegates is said to add to the forum's clublike atmosphere. The importance of those gathered and the WEF machinery that brings them together gives the forum a formidable say in shaping global political and economic policy.

Business professor, entrepreneur, and current Executive Chairperson Klaus Schwab has been the driving force behind the WEF since its creation. The WEF counts 1,000 large corporations and 200 small businesses among its members. Though membership is said to be drawn from in excess of 100 countries, there is a heavy bias toward European and U.S. corporations. A small group of forty "strategic partners" play a leading role in steering the WEF's agenda and activities. Accenture, Coca-Cola, Microsoft, Deutsche Bank, IBM, Nestlé, Time Warner, PriceWaterhouseCoopers, and Nike figure among this group.

The WEF first met in 1970 as the European Management Forum (EMF); though it did not become a regular feature of the Alpine ski season until January 1971. In 1987, the EMF was renamed the World Economic Forum. The new name reflected the changed purpose of the gatherings. While the WEF retained a core focus on international business strategy, it added an explicitly political dimension. The WEF publicity credits the EMF with helping to kick-start the Uruguay Round of General Agreement on Tariffs and Trade (GATT) negotiations, nudging along German reunification, facilitating the Middle East peace process, and accelerating South African reconciliation.

Since becoming the WEF, the forum has held a series of continental and special summits focusing on regional or specific issues. For instance, the WEF held a "peace and reconciliation" meeting in Jordan in the wake of the formal end to the Gulf War. The influence of the WEF and its elitist nature has attracted much interest and opposition from civil society organizations. The most visible response was in 2001 with the establishment of a World Social Summit (held first in Porto Alegre, Brazil, then in Mumbai, India); but it has also been subject to mass public demonstrations. The WEF's attempts to placate its critics have so far failed, and the growing size of the gatherings is increasingly seen as undermining the WEF's uniqueness.

—*Rorden Wilkinson*

See also Antiglobalization; Corporate Governance; Global Governance; Globalization; Washington Consensus

Further Readings and References

Graz, J. C. (2003, November). How powerful are transnational elite clubs? The social myth of the World Economic Forum. *New Political Economy, 8*(3), 321–340.

Pigman, G. A. (2002, August). A multifunctional case study for teaching International Political Economy: The World Economic Forum as Shar-pei or wolf in sheep's clothing? *International Studies Perspectives, 3*(3), 291–309.

WORLD HEALTH ORGANIZATION

The World Health Organization (WHO) is an agency of the United Nations (UN) that funds and organizes programs to promote human health worldwide. WHO's primary roles concern eradicating disease (especially infectious diseases and epidemics), using nutrition and medicine to increase health, and aiding developing nations to improve the physical welfare of their citizens. The main goal of WHO is to ensure that all human beings have access to quality health care of every variety, whether it is provided by WHO itself or by other health organizations and practitioners, and where health includes social and mental as well as physical well-being. WHO was established in 1948 largely on the model of the Health Organization, an agency of the League of Nations.

Organizational Structure

The chief decision-making body of WHO is the World Health Assembly which meets once a year. The assembly is made up of delegates from most participating nations: The exceptions are those nations that do not belong to the UN and so are allowed to register only as associate members of WHO. Although the assembly decides the goals and general policies of WHO, an executive board defines its agenda, reviews its decisions, and gives effect to its policies. The executive board consists of thirty-two members, each of whom is deemed knowledgeable in the fields of medicine, nutrition, and disease, and each of whom serves a three-year term. The Director-General of WHO is nominated by this executive board and appointed by the assembly for a five-year period. The Director General reviews and approves the program presented by the Assembly. The day-to-day running of WHO is undertaken by a Secretariat consisting of eight thousand technical, administrative, and support staff.

WHO is based in Geneva, Switzerland. Its member states are divided into six regions with considerable autonomy. Each region has a regional office headed by a regional director who is confirmed by the executive board after having been elected by the local regional committee. The local regional committees consist of the heads of the health departments of all member states within that region. They are responsible for putting into effect in their region the programs designed by the assembly.

Although the institutional organization of WHO derives largely from its member states, it has established a Civil Society Initiative to formulate arrangements between WHO and nongovernmental agencies such as charity foundations and the pharmaceutical industry. Such arrangements are meant to lead to collaborative networks in the financing and provision of health programs.

Activities and Programs

One important activity of WHO is to lead campaigns based on information, finances, and health care against specific diseases. Its first campaign, the eradication of smallpox, was declared successful in 1979—the first time in history that a disease had been eradicated entirely by human action. WHO has also devised campaigns to counter plague, yellow fever, polio, measles, malaria, and also malnutrition and the consumption of tobacco. Recently WHO has begun campaigning against whooping cough and Acquired Immunodeficiency Syndrome (AIDS).

WHO also seeks to spread scientific information about health related issues. Of special note is the *International Pharmacopoeia,* which provides procedure recommendations, dosage information, and item quality know-how on legalized medical drugs. WHO first published *International Pharmacopoeia* in 1979. It is used by many member states when they compose drug-related laws and legislations.

Some of WHO's recommendations in the area of health have sparked controversy, often because of their potential effect on private commercial interests. One example was the hypothesis that the electromagnetic field around cellular phones is hazardous. Another was the claim that sugars should provide only ten percent of one's daily diet.

—*Mark Bevir*

See also HIV/AIDS; Regional Authority; Regional Governance; Regionalism; Science; State; United Nations Educational, Scientific and Cultural Organization

Further Readings and References

Burci, G. L., & Vignes, C. H. (2004). *The World Health Organization.* The Hague, Netherlands: Kluwer Academic.
Siddiqi, J. (1995). *World health and world politics: The World Health Organization and the UN system.* Columbia: University of South Carolina Press.

WORLD TRADE ORGANIZATION

The World Trade Organization (WTO) was established on January 1, 1995. Membership had increased from 128 original signatories to 148 countries by February 16, 2005. Its major aim is to ensure that trade between nations is as free as possible. The creation of the WTO was one of the key outcomes of the Uruguay Round of the General Agreement on Tariffs and Trade (GATT). This represented the eventual realization of the intentions of the architects of the Bretton Woods System, which was to have an international trade organization working alongside the International Monetary Fund (IMF) and World Bank. It was argued that the WTO would strengthen the multilateral trading system by remedying some of the weaknesses of the GATT. In particular, the WTO has improved the surveillance of trade policies, intensified the levels of consultation between member states, and resolved disputes in a more effective fashion.

The WTO implements trade liberalization by adhering to two key doctrines that were the foundations of the GATT. The first doctrine is the rule of reciprocity, whereby all of the member states agree to adhere to the most-favored nation principle. The second doctrine is the idea of nondiscrimination, which requires that a member country must treat imports in the same way as domestically produced goods and services in such areas as taxation, regulation, transportation, and distribution. While the GATT was mostly concerned with the liberalization of trade in goods, the rules of the WTO have been extended to cover an increasing number of areas. These include trade in services and intellectual property rights—for example, patents and copyrights. One of the perceived disadvantages of the GATT was the lack of an effective mechanism for ensuring adherence to its rules. In contrast, the WTO has created its Dispute Settlement Understanding that is considerably stronger. Member states are free to raise an objection, and initially they are encouraged to resolve such disputes through negotiation. However, if this fails, a panel is created, and the WTO's dispute settlement mechanism is employed, which can ultimately result in the authorization of retaliatory measures. There have been fears that this multilateral approach to resolving disputes is still open to distortion by the most powerful members via threats of unilateral action.

The WTO is likely to face a number of challenges in the future. First, there is concern over the impact of the organization on developing countries. One of the Ministerial Conferences, held in Doha, Qatar, in November 2001, set out a process of negotiations focused on a number of issues of concern to developing countries, in particular the continued subsidization of agricultural production in the advanced industrialized countries. Second is the question of the democratic accountability of the WTO, with critics arguing that civil society organizations have insufficient input into the policy-making process. Third is the contentious issue of whether further trade liberalization will have a negative impact on the environment through its impact on both overall economic growth and production and, in particular, the extension of distribution networks.

—*Stephen R. Hurt*

See also Arab Integration; Bretton Woods; Cairns Group; Confidence-Building Measure; Global Compact; Globalization; Group of 77; International Division of Labor; International Organization; Internet Governance; Liberalization; Most-Favored Nation Principle; Neocolonialism; Organisation for Economic Co-operation and Development; Protectionism; Reciprocity; Rules of Origin; Sanctions; Trade Agreements; Tragedy of the Commons

Further Readings and References

Das, B. L. (2004). *The WTO and the multilateral trading system: Past, present, and future.* London: Zed Books.
Hoekman, B. M., & Kostecki, M. M. (2001). *The political economy of the world trading system: The WTO and beyond.* Oxford, UK: Oxford University Press.
Wallach, L., & Woodall, P. (2003). *Whose trade organization?* New York: New Press.

Index

Entry titles are in **bold**.

compliance, **1:**37
comprehensive, **1:**37
contract versus in-house, **1:**36–37
educative aspect of, **1:**38
efficiency, **1:**38
external, **1:**36, 37
history of, **1:**37–38
internal, **1:**36, 37
issues concerning, **1:**38
legislatures and, **1:**38
offices for performing, **1:**36
performance/effectiveness, **1:**38
private firms performing, **1:**36–37
timing of, **1:**37
Augustine, Saint, **2:**796
Aum Shinrikyo, **2:**961
Australasian governance, **1:**39–40
Australia
  APEC membership, **1:**30, **2:**812
  Cairns Group membership, **1:**65
  clinical governance in, **1:**100
  collaborative planning in, **1:**107
  DAC membership, **1:**219
  environmental issues and, **1:**357, **2:**511
  freedom of information in, **1:**323
  governance of, **1:**39
  health care in, **1:**406
  liberal market economy in, **2:**529
  new public management in, **1:**368
  NPM and, **2:**612
  OECD membership, **2:**639
  Pacific Islands Forum membership, **2:**657
  privacy legislation in, **1:**193
  SEATO membership, **2:**908–909
  tradition in, **2:**978
  See also **Australasian governance**
Australia, New Zealand, and United States
    (ANZUS) Treaty, **2:**908
Australian Labor Party, **1:**39
Austria
  consociationalism in, **1:**143
  coordinated market economy in, **1:**157
  DAC membership, **1:**219
  EFTA membership, **1:**288
  EU membership, **1:**288
  nationalism in, **2:**589
  neocorporatism in, **1:**171, 465
Austrian Freedom Party (FPÖ), **1:**22
Austrian school of economics, **2:**546, 598
Austro-Hungarian Empire, **2:**589
Austro-Marxism, **2:**598
Authoritarianism, **1:**40–41
  bureaucratic, **1:**40
  competitive, **1:**40
  dictatorships, **1:**386
  patrimonialism versus, **2:**670
  personality trait of, **1:**40–41
  ruling style of, **1:**40
  totalitarianism, **1:**386

Authority, **1:**41–42
  bureaucracy and, **1:**56–57
  charismatic, **1:**57, 450
  coordination and, **1:**159
  decline of, **1:**41–42
  definition of, **1:**41
  effectiveness of, **1:**41
  extra-state, **1:**42
  hierarchy and, **1:**412
  line-staff organization and, **2:**530–531
  models of organizational, **1:**486
  network management and, **1:**461
  organizational structure and, **2:**644–645
  patrimonialism, **2:**668–670
  political, **1:**363
  power versus, **2:**736
  regional, **2:**805–806
  traditional, **1:**56–57
Authorship, **2:**953
Autonomisation, **2:**759
Autonomous Communities (ACs), **1:**196, **2:**943
Autonomy
  budgetary, **1:**54–55
  center-local relations and, **1:**75–76
  rejection of, by postfoundationalists, **2:**872
  self-government and, **2:**862
  state and, **2:**925–926
Autopoiesis, **1:**42–43, **2:**865, 899–900
  See also **Self-organizing systems**
Axelrod, Robert, **2:**594
Axworthy, Lloyd, **1:**430
Azerbaijan, **1:**120

Bache, Ian, **1:**236
Bachrach, Peter, **2:**738, 739
Bahamas, **1:**71, 327
Baiyaa, **1:**501–502
Bakunin, Mikhail, **1:**18
Balance of powers, **1:**140, 505
  See also Separation of powers
Balassa, Bela, **2:**811
Baltic Air Surveillance Network (BALTNET), **1:**46
Baltic Assembly (BA), **1:**45–46
Baltic Battalion (BALTBAT), **1:**46
Baltic Council of Ministers (BCM), **1:**45–46
Baltic Defence College (BALTDEFCOL), **1:**46
Baltic Naval Squadron (BALTRON), **1:**46
Baltic state cooperation, **1:**45–46
Bandura, Albert, **2:**884
Bang, Henrik, **1:**121, 195, 298
Bangladesh, **1:**422
Bank of Credit & Commerce (BCCI), **1:**174
Bank of International Settlements (BIS), **1:**318
Banks
  central, **2:**572–573, 707–708
  regional development, **1:**384, **2:**806–807
  See also specific banks
Baratz, Morton, **2:**738, 739
Barbados, **1:**71, 327

intersubjectivity and, **1:**491–492

local knowledge and, **2:**536

local reasoning and, **2:**538

narrative in, **1:**491

narrative theory and, **2:**585–587

policy analysis and, **1:**489–490

principles of, **1:**490–491

relativism and, **1:**492

science and, **2:**853–854

INTERREG, **2:**562

Interregionalism, **1:**494, **2:**990

Interregional relations, 1:494–496

defining, **1:**494

globalization and, **1:**495

multilevel governance and, **1:**495

Intersubjectivity, interpretive theory and, **1:**491–492

Interventionism

capitalism and, **1:**68–69, 242

economic governance and, **1:**242

Keynesianism and, **2:**508

market failure and, **2:**544, 545–546

New Right criticism of, **1:**81–82

policies of, **1:**15

self-regulation and, **2:**866

skepticism about, **2:**693–694

Thatcherism and, **2:**704

trade integration and, **2:**714

See also **Public investment**

Interviews, **2:**586, 686–687, 772

Inventions

commercial effects of, **2:**957

societal effects of, **2:**953–956

Investment, 1:496–497

categories of, **1:**496

government policies affecting, **1:**497

incentives for, **1:**498

private, **1:**497

regulation of, **1:**497

See also **Foreign direct investment; Public investment**

Investment incentives, 1:498

Invisible hand theory, **1:**280, **2:**544, 597

Iran

Internet governance and, **1:**485

Islamic governance in, **1:**502

oil crisis and, **2:**632

OPEC membership, **2:**648

Iran-Iraq War (1980–1988), **2:**648

Iraq

neotraditionalism and, **2:**600–601

OPEC membership, **2:**648

pan-Arabism and, **1:**24

regime change in, **2:**800

sanctions against, **2:**850

terrorism in, **2:**961

UN Security Council and, **2:**1005

war on terrorism and, **2:**1015–1016

weapons inspection in, **1:**329

See also Iraq War (2003)

Iraq war (2003), **1:**3, 102, 401, 422, **2:**568, 628, 648, 923, 958

Ireland

DAC membership, **1:**219

decentralization in, **1:**196

EEC membership, **1:**288

free trade zone in, **1:**304

liberal market economy in, **2:**529

regionalism in, **2:**940, 943

Irish Republican Army (IRA), **1:**88, **2:**940, 961

Iron law of oligarchy, 1:499, 2:903

Iron triangle relationships, **1:**486, **2:**698

Irrational exuberance, 1:500

ISI. *See* **Import substitution industrialization**

Islamic Development Bank, **2:**806, 807

Islamic fundamentalism, **2:**725, 962

Islamic governance, 1:501–502

concept of, **1:**501

contemporary, **1:**502

foundations of, **1:**501

history of, **1:**501–502

See also Muslims

Isomorphism, in organizations, **2:**906

Israel

negotiations involving, **1:**334

oil crisis and, **2:**632

post-9/11, **2:**726

terrorism in, **2:**960, 964

U.S. support of, **1:**330

Issue networks, **2:**603, 697

Istanbul Cooperation Initiative, **2:**627

Istikhlaf, **1:**502

Italy

DAC membership, **1:**219

decentralization in, **1:**198

devolution in, **1:**197

ECSC membership, **1:**287

forecasting in, **1:**316

G7 membership, **1:**399

health care in, **1:**406

ILO membership, **1:**476

intergovernmental relations in, **1:**471

nationalism in, **2:**589

public-private partnerships in, **2:**774

purchaser-provider split in, **2:**779

regionalism in, **2:**940, 943

regions in, **2:**939

Iversen, Torben, **1:**150

Jackson, Robert, **1:**330

Jacobs, Francis, **1:**425

Jacobs, Norman, **2:**669

Jamaica, **1:**71, 327

James, C. L. R., **2:**727

James, William, **2:**683, 741, 742

Janis, Irving, **1:**401

Japan

APEC membership, **1:**30, **2:**812

Chiang Mai Agreement and, **1:**78

cooperation in, **1:**156

coordinated market economy in, **1:**158

DAC membership, **1:**219

Mitroff, Ian, **2:**918
Mitterrand, François, **2:**514, 941
Mittleton-Kelly, Eve, **1:**133
Mixed motives, **1:**334
Mobutu Sese Soku, **1:**386, **2:**600
Model Cities program, **1:**486
Modernity
    borders and, **1:**48
    characteristics of, **2:**730
    coordination necessary in, **1:**160–161
    crises and, **1:**182–183
    deinstitutionalization and, **1:**204
    Fordism and, **1:**314
    nationalism and, **2:**589
    nation concept and, **2:**588
    postcolonialism and, **2:**726, 730
    postmodern critique of, **2:**730–731
    reflexivity and, **2:**799–800
    risk society and, **2:**840–842
    sociology and, **2:**902–903
    trust and, **2:**993
Modernization
    bureaucracy and, **1:**59
    theory of, **1:**220–221
Moe, Terry, **2:**980
Mohamed, Mahathir bin, **1:**27, 239
Moldova, **1:**120, **2:**646
Monarchy, **1:**386
Monetarism, 2:570–572
    application of, **2:**571–572
    business cycles and, **1:**63–64
    Keynesianism and, **2:**571
    Keynesianism replaced by, **2:**508
    principles of, **2:**571
    theory of, **2:**571
Monetary policy, 2:572–573, 707–708
Monetary unions, 1:246, **2:574**, 637–638
Money. *See* Currency; **Monetarism; Monetary policy;**
    Monetary unions
Money laundering, **1:**174–175
Mongolia, **1:**180
Monnet, Jean, **1:**287
Monopolies, 2:574–575
    benefits of, **2:**575
    competition policy and, **1:**127
    definition of, **2:**574
    economies of scale and, **2:**544
    firm size and, **2:**575
    natural, **2:**768–769
    public investment to counter,
        2:768–769
Montesquieu, Baron de la Brède et de
    civic republicanism, **1:**86
    liberalism, **2:**526
    rule of law, **2:**844
    separation of powers, **1:**208,
        302, 386
Montreal Protocols, **1:**116, 274, 331
Montserrat, **1:**71
Moore, Mike, **1:**137
Moral individualism, **1:**443–444

Morality
    constitutionalization of, **1:**144–145
    norms and, **2:**623
    social justice and, **2:**883
More, Thomas, **2:**756
Morgenstern, Oskar, **2:**724
Morgenthau, Hans, **1:**153, **2:**796
Mosca, Gaetano, **1:**499, **2:**903
Mossberger, Karen, **2:**804
Most-favored nation principle, 1:497, **2:575–576,**
    578–579, 972, 1027
    See also Normal trade relations
Mozambique, **2:**909–910
Muckrakers, **1:**90–91
Muhammad (prophet), **1:**501
Multiculturalism, 2:576–578
    concept of, **2:**576
    cultural pluralism, **2:**680–681
    educational impact of, **2:**577
    ethnic groups, **1:**285–286
    governance and, **2:**577–578
    human rights and, **1:**427
    immigration and, **1:**435
    liberalism and, **2:**576–577
    objections to, **2:**577
    postcolonial critique of, **2:**729
Multifiber Agreement (1974), **2:**973
Multilateral Agreement on Investment (MAI), **1:**497, **2:**639
Multilateral economic institutions, **1:**348, 350, 384
    See also International financial institutions (IFIs)
Multilateral Investment Guarantee Agency, **1:**139, **2:**1023
Multilateralism, 2:578–579
    bilateralism versus, **2:**578–579
    characteristics of, **2:**578
    diffuse reciprocity and, **2:**579
    dispute settlement and, **2:**579
    global governance and, **1:**346
    indivisibility of interests and, **2:**578–579
    regionalism and, **2:**635
    security and, **2:**578–579
    stability of, **2:**579
    transnational governance versus, **2:**983
Multilevel governance, 2:580–583
    analytical application of, **2:**582
    characteristics of, **1:**235–236
    concept of, **2:**580
    EU and, **1:**235–236, 290, 371–372, 471, **2:**580–581
    federalism and, **2:**581
    glocalization and, **1:**358–359
    intergovernmental relations and, **1:**471
    interregional relations and, **1:**495
    normative application of, **2:**582
    scholarship on, **2:**580
    types of, **1:**236, **2:**581
    See also **Center-local relations; Intergovernmental relations**
Multinational corporations. *See* Transnational corporations
Multitrack diplomacy, **2:**854–855
Multitude, antiglobalization movement as, **1:**23
Mundell, Robert, **2:**637
Mundell-Fleming model, **1:**319
Murphy, Craig, **1:**348